1976

Grant P. Weber

Lake of the Woods

L. Superior

L. Michigan

L. Huron

L. Ontario

L. Erie

St. Lawrence

MOUNTAINS

Connecticut R.

Hudson R.

Delaware R.

Susquehanna R.

Potomac R.

James R.

Ohio R.

APPALACHIAN

PIEDMONT

COAST

Mississippi R.

Missouri R.

Kansas R.

Wabash R.

Ohio R.

Tennessee R.

Savannah R.

Arkansas R.

Red R.

Tombigbee R.

Alabama R.

...zos R.

...o R.

CENTRAL

PLAINS

ATLANTIC OCEAN

GULF OF MEXICO

BAHAMA ISLANDS

CUBA

The American Story

VOLUME ONE: YOUTH

McGRAW-HILL SERIES IN HISTORY

Albjerg & Albjerg	Europe from 1914 to the Present
Bannon	History of the Americas
	VOLUME I: The Colonial Americas
	VOLUME II: The American Nations
Blake	A Short History of American Life
Eckles & Hale	Britain, Her Peoples and the Commonwealth
Gustavson	A Preface to History
Lucas	A Short History of Civilization
Rae & Mahoney	The United States in World History
Riegel & Long	The American Story
	VOLUME I: Youth
	VOLUME II: Maturity
Schapiro	The World in Crisis
Turner	The Great Cultural Traditions
	VOLUME I: The Ancient Cities
	VOLUME II: The Classical Empires
Yanaga	Japan since Perry

THE AMERICAN STORY

VOLUME ONE: YOUTH

Robert E. Riegel

DARTMOUTH COLLEGE

David F. Long

UNIVERSITY OF NEW HAMPSHIRE

McGRAW-HILL BOOK COMPANY, INC.   NEW YORK TORONTO LONDON

1955

THE AMERICAN STORY
VOLUME ONE: YOUTH

Preface

History is essential for the understanding of the present world. Human institutions can be thoroughly comprehended only through an understanding of how they have risen, fallen, and interacted in the past. But human institutions are modified by the accidents of individual personality, and of geography and resources. Hence, while the present text is built around institutional developments, as of state, church, and school, it also gives recognition to important individuals, and is prolific with maps, which contain almost all the places mentioned in the narrative. In addition, the relations of the United States with the rest of the world are given special emphasis.

History should also be fun. Since a depressing avalanche of names and dates is not only tiresome but obscures the main points of the narrative, such material has been reduced to a minimum. All phases of life, including marriage, family life, and amusements, have been considered in the hope that they will be both interesting and informative. A real effort has been exerted to encourage understanding by making the narrative readable, in so far as that can be done without sacrificing essential accuracy.

The first volume carries the American story through the political reconstruction following the Civil War, on the assumption that ending the account short of that point is like stopping a hurdle race when a man has jumped the last bar but before he has breasted the tape. The colonial period is given relatively brief treatment as a background for later developments. The entire volume is an attempt at a balanced narrative, showing the development of a distinctive American culture, with its various complex interrelationships.

Any general history must be based heavily on the work of others, but unfortunately space does not permit specific credit in most cases—any more than to the thousands of students who have cheerfully served the authors as guinea pigs. The authors would, however, like to express their particular appreciation to Professors Oscar Zeichner of the College of the City of New York and Henry B. Parkes of New York University who read the entire manuscript, and to Professors Robert Gilmore, Philip Marston, Allan Partridge, and William Yale, all of the University of New Hampshire, who read particular sections. Their suggestions have been uniformly helpful, and they of course should not be blamed for any existing slips or omissions. Finally, the authors hope that they have succeeded in some degree in conveying their belief in the interest and importance of American history.

Robert E. Riegel
David F. Long

Contents

Preface   v

List of Maps   ix

CHAPTER 1. New Worlds for the Taking   (1000–1607)   1

2. Colonization and Imperial Conflict   (1607–1763)   16

3. Empire Cleavage   (1763–1776)   37

4. The American Revolution   (1776–1783)   51

5. Toward a National Government   (1783–1787)   65

6. The Constitution   (1787–1789)   76

7. Continuing Economic Colonialism   (1789–1815)   87

8. Producing an American Culture   (1789–1815)   99

9. Beyond the Appalachians   (1789–1815)   115

10. The Federalist Ship of State   (1789–1800)   129

11. "The Revolution of 1800"   (1800–1812)   139

12. Federalist Foreign Policy   (1789–1800)   146

13. Jefferson's Foreign Policy   (1800–1809)   154

14. "Mr. Madison's War"   (1809–1815)   164

15. The American Farm   (1815–1860)   177

16. Infant Manufactures   (1815–1860)   187

17. A Shrinking United States   (1815–1860)   201

18. Training the New Generation   (1815–1860)   219

19. Attaining Culture   (1815–1860)   234

20. Seeking Perfection   (1815–1860)   244

21. Westward Expansion   (1815–1860)   254

22. Nationalistic Politics   (1815–1828)   268

23. The Jacksonian Era   (1828–1840)   278

24. Whig versus Democrat   (1840–1850)   292

25. A More Nationalistic Diplomacy   (1815–1842)   304

26. Manifest Destiny   (1842–1846)   318

27. The Mexican War   (1846–1848)   328

28. The Diplomacy of Sectionalism   (1848–1860)   336

29. The Clouds Gather   (1850–1854)   346

30. Approaching Dissolution   (1854–1860)   356

31. The Union Cracks   (1860–1861)   365

32. Blue versus Gray   (1861–1865)   374

33. On the Seas and Across the Seas   (1861–1865)   390

34. Behind the Gray Lines   (1861–1865)   398

35. Behind the Blue Lines   (1861–1865)   407

36. Reconstruction Diplomacy   (1865–1877)   420

37. Executive Reconstruction   (1865–1866)   427

38. The Radical Juggernaut   (1866–1869)   436

39. The Age of Grant   (1869–1877)   443

Readings   455

APPENDIX I. The Declaration of Independence   479

II. Constitution of the United States of America   482

III. States—Dates of Admission, Area, Population   493

IV. Presidential Elections   495

Index   499

List of Maps

FRONT END PAPER. The United States:
Physical Features.

MAP

1. Early Explorations, 1492–1522.   5
2. Spanish Explorations in the Americas, 1500–1600.   7
3. The Southern Colonies.   17
4. The New England Colonies   21
5. The Middle Colonies.   26
6. The Caribbean during Later Colonial Times.   29
7. The Wars between British and French, 1689–1763.   32
8. The Struggle for a Continent, 1689–1763.   34
9. Europe in 1763.   35
10. British North America, 1775.   45
11. New England and Canadian Action, 1775–1776.   55
12. Military Action in the Middle States, 1776–1778. (New York and Environs, 1776).   57
13. The West during the American Revolution.   60
14. Military Action in the South, 1779–1781 (Yorktown, 1781).   61
15. The United States after Treaty of Paris, 1783.   63
16. State Cessions of Western Lands, 1784–1802.   71
17. The American Township.   72
18. The Northwest Territory, Established by Northwest Ordinance of 1787.   73

19. The United States about 1790.   88
20. The West during the 1790s.   116
21. Louisiana Purchase, 1803.   157
22. Lewis and Clark Expedition, 1803–1806.   158
23. The War against the Barbary States, 1803–1815.   159
24. Europe during Height of Napoleon's Power (1812).   167
25. Northern and Western War of 1812 Action.   169
26. Economic America, 1815–1860.   203
27. Transportation in the Far West, 1858–1869.   215
28. Removal of Eastern Indians, 1830–1840.   258
29. The Pre–Civil War West.   261
30. The United States after the Compromise of 1820.   275
31. The United States after the Compromise of 1850.   302
32. Europe after Congress of Vienna (1815).   306
33. The Acquisition of Florida (1818–1819).   308
34. Latin American States during the 1820s.   309
35. The Russian Ukase of 1821.   311
36. Maine Boundary Dispute, Settled by Webster-Ashburton Treaty, 1842.   315
37. Oregon Settlement, 1846.   322
38. Texas Annexation, 1845.   326
39. The Mexican War, 1846–1848.   331

40. Central America during the 1850s. 339
41. The Far East during the 1850s. 343
42. Western United States after Passage of Kansas-Nebraska Act, 1854. 352
43. Missouri-Kansas Area, 1854–1855. 357
44. The Election of 1860. 366
45. Confederate States of America, April, 1861. 368
46. Union Civil War Strategy. 375
47. The Civil War in the East, 1861. 376
48. The Civil War in the West, 1861–1863. 377
49. Trans-Mississippi Department. 380
50. The Civil War in the East, 1862. 381
51. The Civil War in the East, 1863. 384
52. The Civil War in the West, 1863–1865. 386
53. The Civil War in the East, 1864–1865. 388
54. Some Major Southern Railroads, 1861. 404
55. Abolition of Slavery, 1861–1865. 417
56. Purchase of Alaska, 1867. 423
57. Post–Civil War Caribbean. 424
58. Reconstruction, 1865–1877. 431
59. Election of 1876. 452
BACK END PAPER. Territorial Growth of the United States, 1783–1853.

New Worlds for the Taking

(1000-1607)

PROLOGUE

On a chill day late in December, 1606, a young man named John Laydon threaded his way down the narrow London streets, elbowed through the crowds, and approached a group of men waiting near a wharf that jutted into the Thames. A short distance offshore three small vessels rode at anchor. As Laydon scrutinized the ships that were to furnish his transportation to the land called Virginia, his mind filled with mingled emotions. Ahead lay adventure, a fresh start, a role in the new Britain overseas, perhaps a fortune in precious metals. Yet there was foreboding in the thought of the unknown, the fear of privations and dangers to be experienced—a gnawing ache at leaving all that was familiar and dear. The time for delay, however, had passed. Laydon had signed as a "laborer" with the London Joint-Stock Company to sail to the New World.

He studied the men standing by the wharf. There was assurance in the person of Christopher Newport, who would head the expedition. Laydon knew the captain by reputation as an able and fearless mariner. There was Bartholomew Gosnold, the second in command, who had sailed along the mysterious American coast some five years before. The elongated face of George Percy, brother of the great Earl of Northumberland, next caught Laydon's eye. He hoped that the typically mournful expression on Percy's face did not portend evil. The fine, martial figure of Captain John Smith, the famed soldier of fortune against the Turks, gave him renewed confidence.

The other men seemed to be a heterogeneous lot. One looked like a decayed fop fleeing, perhaps, a gambling debt. Another appeared to have been a farmer, if credence could be given to the evidence of his work-gnarled hands and stooped shoulders. A third had the pinched, sallow look that comes from long hours indoors. A refugee from Newgate Gaol? An unemployed artisan? Laydon ceased his musings; he would know each individual in the weary weeks to follow. He turned to stare again at the three ships in the river: the *Sarah Constance*, the *Goodspeed*, and the *Discovery*, the latter weighing only 20 tons. He hoped that he would not be assigned to the *Discovery*.

John Laydon was a product of the world in which he lived. As an Englishman he was also a European, molded by the historical currents

1

and forces that had formed the cultural pattern of sixteenth- and seventeenth-century Europe. Yet he was to be a transatlantic voyager; and if he survived the arduous crossing and the bitter first years in the Jamestown settlement,[1] he would become that new man, the transplanted European—in a word, the American. What forces in his society had made John Laydon willing to undergo the perils of thousands of watery miles in a ship weighing under 100 tons? What conditions could he expect to find in the American environment?

MEDIEVAL BACKGROUNDS

Tremendous changes had rocked Europe since the time when the unity of the Mediterranean world had been riven by the great Germanic folk migrations of the early Christian era. Although Roman language, religion, and modified land-holding systems were able to continue for centuries, Roman security, law, political stability, and peace had been shattered. European population remained static or actually declined, particularly after the North African coast fell to the Moslems. Cities dwindled in size, roads fell into disrepair, and local marauders joined invaders in looting and rapine. Slowly during the troubled years from 500 to 1000, the makeshift economic manorial system and its concomitant political feudalism developed, their roots deep in the Roman and Germanic past. By no means all of Europe was blighted during these so-called "Dark Ages." Ireland enjoyed cultural vigor during the seventh and eighth centuries; Charlemagne instilled new life into France and much of Germany for a few years; the Byzantine Empire continued both as the defender of the

Balkans against the Moslems and as the chief repository for the glories of classical civilization; and the Christian Church, the one great centralized organization remaining in the West, existed as a lonely spiritual and intellectual beacon. Despite these isolated bright spots, the Dark Ages were named with considerable accuracy.

Europe shuddered under constant attack. The Moslems threatened the whole Mediterranean periphery as they erupted from the deserts of Arabia to conquer an empire that stretched from the edge of India to the borders of France. From the arid steppes of Russia and Siberia, Avars, Bulgars, Magyars, and other Asiatic invaders swept into Central Europe. Terror and havoc attended the Scandinavian Norsemen, whose shallow craft were able to penetrate hundreds of miles up rivers to sack cities thought inviolate from sea raiders. For many years a common prayer intoned in European churches was "From the fury of the Norsemen, deliver us." [2]

Life in Europe during the Dark Ages was characterized chiefly by localism. With the decay of trade and commerce, each tiny area had to become as nearly self-sufficient as possible. Land became almost completely the only socially acceptable form of wealth, and the landless European masses scratched out their precarious existence as serfs bound to the nobles' estates. Even the latter's way of life was unbelievably barren according to modern standards. General intellectual activity, education, and the cultural niceties ebbed or remained stagnant.

Shortly after 1000, Europe began to stir with new forces. Contributing factors were the Crusades, those strange blends of religious piety and fanaticism, economic cupidity, wan-

---

[1] John Laydon was actually on the expedition to Jamestown. In fact, he survived the starvation and disease of the first year and in 1608 married Anne Burrows, the maid of a "Mistress Forrest." This was the first English marriage on the American mainland, so perhaps it is fitting that we start with John Laydon. The attempt to reconstruct his thoughts on the eve of departure is, of course, historical imagination.

[2] Norsemen made the first voyages to America. In the year 1000 Eric the Red sailed to "Vinland," located on either the Canadian or the New England coast. But the Norsemen left little record of their exploits and hence had no effect upon the later Age of Discovery. Evidence suggests that French Breton fishermen cast their nets in American waters long before Columbus, but their travels remained unknown to the outside world. Historical events must have cognizance before they can have significance.

derlust, and simple boredom with home conditions. The Crusades were technically failures in that they did not accomplish their stated aim—the permanent reconquest of the Holy Land (Palestine) from the Turks. Yet their importance can hardly be overestimated. Thousands of crusaders journeyed to the East, and many returned home to dazzle their envious neighbors with lurid accounts (some of them true) about the wonders of the superior civilizations that they had seen. An awareness of a better way of life spread through Europe and eventually led to burning intellectual curiosity. New products made their way into the West and created a demand that could not be denied. Luxurious fabrics, perfumes, superior arms and armaments, gold and silver *objets d'art*, and precious stones became almost necessities for the upper classes. Especially desirable were Oriental spices such as cloves, cinnamon, and pepper to season the dull, coarse, and often putrefied diet of those times before adequate refrigeration. Because of such voracious demands in Europe, new supply routes flourished between East and West.

Conditions in Europe improved during and after the Crusades. That civilization, rich, varied, but unlike our own, which we call "medieval" reached its climax during the thirteenth and fourteenth centuries. Feudalism and the manorial system improved to some degree. Cities began to wax as many a small settlement huddled outside a castle wall or at the ford of a river became an independent "commune," sometimes receiving a feudal grant and sometimes achieving independence by force. New intellectual strength was furnished by Oxford, Paris, Bologna, Salamanca, Heidelberg, and other universities. Yet the mental climate of Europe was otherworldly during medieval times. The Church was the most potent political as well as moral force in the West, and its teachings permeated all life. The belief that this world was at best an abode of sin, weakness, and unhappiness caused many to look to the hereafter. Truth was known to the medieval mind; it was to be found in the writings of the Church fathers and in certain classical authors. Unrestrained inquiry was looked upon askance.

THE DAWN OF THE MODERN AGE

The mighty intellectual upheaval called the Renaissance acted as a battering-ram against medieval unity. This transition period between medieval and modern times stressed a search for truths other than the supernatural and soon proliferated into many channels. New questions were asked; new answers received. Science began to make sensational advances, especially in the inventions that were to prove so useful for overseas expansion. The astrolabe and the compass made oceanic voyages more feasible, gunpowder assured advantage over primitive peoples, and the movable-type printing press disseminated information about the latest discoveries to an increasingly literate population.

During the fourteenth and fifteenth centuries, the Renaissance was centered in Italy; and from that peninsula came a titanic production of literary masterpieces and exalted works of art. Furthermore, the Italy of Lorenzo the Magnificent and his contemporaries went far beyond the intellectual and artistic wealth to a solid and substantial economic prosperity as well. The great mercantile city-states of Venice and Genoa had captured the lucrative trade between Europe and Asia, thereby siphoning off disproportionately large profits which in turn spread throughout Italy. Yet fabrics and spices from the East Indies, China, and India were priced at alpine levels. Many factors were responsible—the vast distances, the slow transportation, the danger from shipwreck, the exorbitant tariffs and harbor duties (sometimes amounting to sheer blackmail) demanded by local rulers along the main commercial routes, and the assessments of Venetian merchants and other middlemen all through northern and western Europe. Excluded from the profits of this carrying trade, the Atlantic states of Portugal, Spain, the Netherlands, France, and England sought means to break the iron monopoly of the Italians. A direct sea voyage to the Far East might be the solution.[3]

Western Europe contained some vigorous national states toward the end of the Renaissance. Although characterized by dynastic loyalty rather than "nationalism" in the modern sense of a common language, people, and cultural tradition, these states had made some progress toward those ends under the leadership of clever and aggressive monarchs. In medieval times the king was often only one of many nobles, ruling a small area contiguous to his capital city. Eventually the monarch began to receive assistance from the middle class (the *bourgeoisie*), which was being chafed by the economic and social restrictions imposed by a parasitic nobility. The rising urban class merged its interests with those of the national monarch, looking to the king for aid against the barons and in return lending him money he could use for hiring a standing army or for erecting strong fortifications. Under a unified national state, the middle class might hope that the myriad local taxes and tariffs, the duties and excises which so plagued commerce, would be superseded by centralized free trade within the royal domains. Again, the grateful monarch might reward his financial benefactors with bounties, subsidies, and monopolistic grants. Finally, the irritating local wars between nobles might be sternly repressed by the monarch. A potent alliance was formed between the king and the middle class; it served each well. The fifteenth century saw the steady increase of both royal power and bourgeois influence.

Another factor influencing overseas exploration was the desire of the king for recognition. As one of the newly rich, the national monarch was eager to flaunt his prestige before all. He tended to gather a brilliant court to do him homage; he often financed literary and scientific works and posed as a patron of the arts.

[3] The theory held for so many years that the Age of Discovery was detonated by the fall of Constantinople to the Ottoman Turks in 1453 has been somewhat discredited. The evidence seems to show that the Turks were eager for trade with Europe and had no desire to disrupt the existing commercial system.

Overseas exploration under the royal aegis would bring glory and might even return considerable revenues to the treasury, especially since the king need offer little direct monetary aid to the cost of any expedition.

The actual financing of exploration and settlement came in the main from the middle class. Nobles occasionally assisted, but since they were landowners most of their assets were tied to agriculture. The bourgeois amassing of cash was assisted by new banking and commercial-credit techniques that originated in Italy and were soon found in the Netherlands and Germany. The Italian Medicis and the German Fuggers managed to bring a new respectability to lending money at interest, a practice condemned by the medieval Church as usury. Double-entry bookkeeping and the use of letters of credit assured some degree of commercial continuity. The middle class in the Atlantic states often shared in banking and commercial profits. Early capitalistic enterprises called joint-stock companies were able to tap the monetary resources of many individuals to furnish backing for transatlantic adventure. Usually chartered by an obliging monarch and sometimes granted a geographical monopoly, joint-stock companies directed numerous explorations in the New World. With each successful venture, both individual and corporate financial reserves could be amassed and future voyages subsidized.

THE ATLANTIC STATES

❬ *Portugal.* While Italy and to a lesser degree Germany[4] drowsed content with the commercial *status quo* of the late fifteenth century, the Atlantic states were readying themselves for the challenge. The Portuguese monarchy took the first steps. Originally con-

[4] Commerce in the Baltic was controlled during medieval times by an association of free cities, German for the most part, called the Hanseatic League. In northern waters the Hanse was almost as influential as Venice in the Mediterranean. The prosperity of both ebbed when trade shifted to the Atlantic from the inland seas.

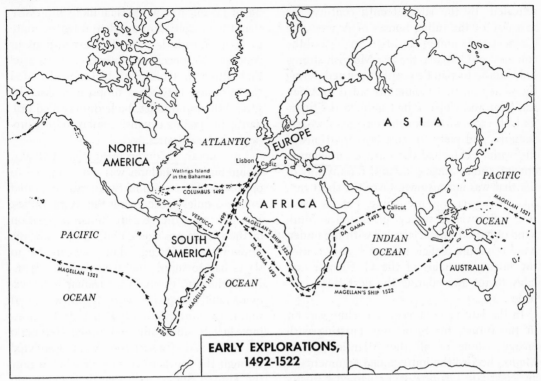

EARLY EXPLORATIONS, 1492-1522

quered by the Moslem Moors from Africa, Portugal slowly won back its independence during the long reconquest when Christian fought Moslem on the Iberian Peninsula. By 1460, intrepid Portuguese mariners, encouraged by Prince Henry and his famous school for navigators, had discovered (or rediscovered) the Azores and the Cape Verde Islands in the Atlantic. Simultaneously they were probing down the humid West African coast in search of a water route to the wealth of the East that could avoid the charges of rapacious Venetians. Following the accomplishment of Dias, who sailed about halfway in 1480, final success was achieved when Vasco da Gama triumphantly returned to Lisbon from Calicut and other ports in India with a cargo valued at *sixty* times the cost of his entire expedition (1498).

During the next half century, exploration and conquest brought Portugal an empire sprawling from the Spice Islands of the East Indies to South American Brazil. Condiments of all varieties, silks, gems, and works of art

from the East, as well as gold, slaves, and ivory from Africa, poured into Portugal, making that tiny kingdom the envy of the world.[5] Portugal, however, was simply too small to retain its possessions, and almost half of the men who left for its overseas possessions never returned. By 1580, Portuguese power had fallen so low that Spain temporarily annexed it.

(*Spain.* The story of Spain's meteoric rise to empire almost rivals fiction. Compared to Britain and France, Spain had outstanding weaknesses. The Spanish soil was infertile, its people oppressed, and its middle class had been almost wiped out after religious fanaticism had expelled both Jew and Moor from the national domains. But the Spanish character had been forged in the crucible of 700 years' intermittent war against the Moslems. Gradually territory was regained by the small Christian states in the north; grudgingly the Moor

[5] In a gesture of magnificence, Pope Alexander VI in his Papal Line of Demarcation (1494) divided the world between Spain and Portugal. Of course, the other nations ignored his decree.

retreated. By the late fifteenth century, the marriage of the ruling houses of Aragon and Castile largely united Christian Spain; and the conquest of Granada, the last Moorish stronghold on the Iberian Peninsula, occurred during the same year that Columbus sailed to America. War and violence had imbued the Spaniard of 1500 with enough courage, strength, stamina, and piety to seize large portions of the world. Yet he had also learned intolerance, cruelty, and a savage contempt for any way of life that was not his own. Over the short run, Spanish power was irresistible, but its harsh rule and enviable success instigated a whirlwind of hatred which, coupled with the underlying economic deficiencies at home, caused the mighty domains of the Castilian inexorably to rot away during the next three centuries.

In the late 1400s, however, decline was far in the future, for Spain was bursting with energy. Alone of all the Atlantic powers, Madrid heeded the impassioned arguments of an expatriate Genoese sailor named Christopher Columbus who maintained that the Asiatic mainland lay only some 2,500 miles due west of Europe. The belief that the world was round was not original with Columbus. European scholars, learned in the classics, had studied ancient Greek scientists and believed the latters' contention that the world was a sphere. But the masses did not know this, and Columbus' determination, drive, and courage were necessary before hypothesis became fact. With the aid of the Spanish crown, an expedition under the Genoese sailed on a fortunately calm voyage to the West Indies, where a landing was made on Watlings Island in the Bahamas (12 October 1492). Columbus was showered with accolades upon his return to the Spanish court, but his three subsequent expeditions to the New World were disappointingly scanty in their gold and silver return. Poverty-stricken and disgraced, Columbus died in 1506, finding his only solace in the erroneous conclusion that he had discovered the direct water route to Asia.

His actual accomplishment, of course, exceeded the explorer's wildest dream. The opening of a whole new world is far more impressive than the utilization of another, if better, route to lands already known. The expeditions of Amerigo Vespucci and others soon proved that although Columbus had miscalculated the distance between Europe and Asia by several thousand miles, he had succeeded brilliantly in opening expansive vistas to his European contemporaries.

The initial discouragement that followed Columbus' later failures was soon changed to optimism. Thousands of Spaniards emigrated overseas, quickly occupying the West Indies. In a few years, the delicate Indian population of the islands was liquidated through disease, brutality, and forced labor; African Negro slaves had to supply manpower for the Spanish Caribbean. From West Indian bases, explorers and conquerors went north, west, and south. In North America Ponce de León established Spanish rule in Florida; Hernando de Soto and Cabeza de Vaca wandered through the southern section of what is now the United States; and Francisco Coronado searched for the semimythical Seven Cities of Cibola through future New Mexico, Colorado, Kansas, Oklahoma, and Texas. In Central America, Vasco Núñez de Balboa waded into the Pacific to claim the limitless expanses of that mighty ocean for Castile. Any lingering doubt that the world was round evaporated when Ferdinand Magellan, a Portuguese sailing under Spanish auspices, circumnavigated the globe (1519 to 1522). Although Magellan himself was killed by Filipino natives, one of his three ships managed to creep back to Lisbon with only a handful of men still alive after a voyage of incredible privation and hardship.

It was in Mexico and Peru that the Spaniard proved himself a true conquistador. Hernando Cortes, a combination of courage, resolution, treachery, and cruelty, seized the sacred person of the Aztec emperor Montezuma in Mexico; finally, after crushing a savage revolt, he forced the Aztecs into abject surrender. Soon gold and silver from Mexico piled high in the Spanish treasury. Against even greater odds than Cortes faced, the illiterate ex-swineherd Francisco Pizarro aped his predecessor's tactics and

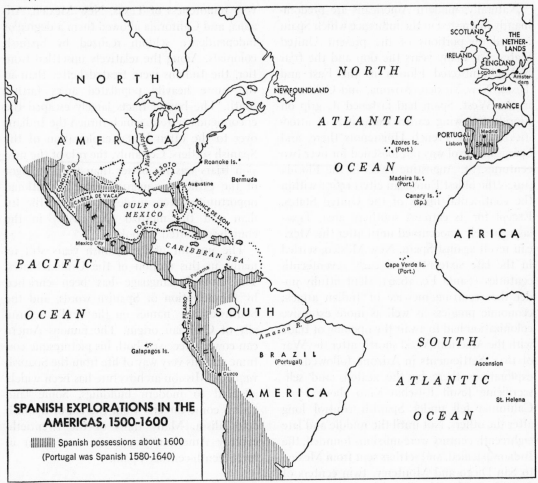

SPANISH EXPLORATIONS IN THE AMERICAS, 1500-1600

|||||||||| Spanish possessions about 1600
(Portugal was Spanish 1580-1640)

snatched for himself and the Spanish crown the extensive Inca Empire in western South America. More millions for Castilian power and glory rolled across the Atlantic to the great port of Cadiz. In both Mexico and Peru, the Spaniards were able to superimpose their control over large numbers of relatively civilized, sedentary, and docile Indians. Unlike Englishmen, Spaniards intermarried with the Indians, thus creating the mixed population that typifies modern Latin America.

❡ *Spain's American Empire.* At one time or another between 1500 and 1800, Spanish dominions in the New World blanketed most of the two Americas, extending from the pampas of Argentina to the pine woods of Georgia; from the Chilean Andes to the rainy forests of Oregon. Portuguese Brazil was the only major intrusion into the Castilian Empire. Spain proceeded to organize its American colonies. A system close to slavery was riveted upon the Indian, and actual bondage upon the Negro, despite the protests of certain humanitarian friars. A tightly controlled royal government ruled all aspects of life, and the resources of America were exploited for European advantage. Once a year, under heavy convoy, the plate fleet transported to Spanish coffers the yield of Mexican and Peruvian mines. This influx of bullion transformed Europe's economic system; prices soared, and old standards of value were drastically altered. In addition to gold and silver, other valued exports of Spanish America were furs, hides, and agricultural produce.

Naturally, modern Americans are predominantly interested in the influence which Spain exerted on portions of the present United States. For many years the don and the friar had administered Florida in the East and Texas, New Mexico, Arizona, and California in the West. Spain had fastened its grip on Florida following earlier exchanges of atrocities with the French Huguenots there, and Spanish control was not loosened for over two centuries. St. Augustine basks in the Florida sun as the oldest European city (1565) within the continental limits of the United States. Except for its extreme southern area, Texas lay relatively unoccupied until after the Mexican revolt against Spain. New Mexico, settled in the late sixteenth and early seventeenth centuries (Santa Fe, 1609), slept fitfully under the recurring menace of Indian attack; economic progress as well as more extensive colonization had to await the opening of trade with the American West shortly after the War of 1812. Settlements in Arizona followed the explorations there by the zealous and self-sacrificing Jesuit Eusebio Kino about 1700. California fell under Spanish control long after the others. Not until the middle and late eighteenth century were missions founded, the Indians pacified, and settlers sent from Mexico to San Diego and Monterey, twin centers of Spanish California, after the wearisome trek overland or the somewhat easier oceanic trip.

Certain patterns stand out in Spain's North American borderlands. In the territory which is now the Southwestern United States, Spanish control was now lax, now harsh. Brief periods of either expansion or contraction broke long years of relative inactivity. The distances concerned were too vast to allow steady colonization, and the labor problem remained pressing, since the Indians would usually fight and even die rather than toil in field or mine. The narrow mercantilism that typified Spanish colonial administration was not conducive to much individual economic exertion. Yet there were compensating factors. If the number of toilsome miles from Mexico City to the borderlands made problems of settlement and defense almost insuperable, the very remoteness of Texas, New Mexico, Arizona, and California allowed them a degree of independence seldom realized by Spanish colonials. Along the relatively unsettled frontier, the Indians were treated better than in the more heavily populated areas farther south. The border tracts largely escaped the encomienda system, which turned the Indians over to the often brutal exploitation of the Spanish settlers. Certainly, the rule of the mission friars was far better than the iron rigor of the earlier conquerors. Some educational opportunities were made available to the Indian and the mestizo (half-caste) in the church-supported schools.

The imprint of its Spanish years still remains in this section of the United States. The English language has been enriched by the adoption of Spanish words, and the Southwestern "names on the land" are usually of Castilian origin. The famous American cowboy received both his picturesque costume and his very way of life from the Spanish *vaquero*. Mission architecture has been widely adapted to modern buildings. Some land claims come directly from the era of Spanish colonialism. Many traits of the twentieth-century American Southwest were born in seventeenth-century Spain.

❬ The Netherlands. Naturally, the spectacular successes achieved by Spain in the Americas did not escape the envious notice of others. By the end of the sixteenth century, Spain sprawled across most of the hemisphere. From American mines came colossal mineral wealth to Madrid, and this subject was often broached in avid conversations in other Atlantic states. The Netherlands, France, and Great Britain were calculating the risks that would have to be taken in order to break the Spanish New World monopoly. The gamble was worth the hazard.

The Netherlands had made a rapid rise to international prominence. During medieval times it had hummed with economic activity, and such cities as Ghent, Liége, Bruges, and Antwerp rivaled any in Europe. Prosperous through its thriving textile industry, the

Netherlands had long been an object of contention among larger and more powerful neighbors. Passing under the rule of Charles the Bold, Duke of Burgundy, late in the fifteenth century, the Netherlands soon found itself a Hapsburg possession, thanks to the Hapsburg family's amazing propensity for fortunate marriages, which brought to it not only Austria, the Holy Roman Empire, and the Netherlands, but even Spain. When Philip II ascended the Spanish throne, complex social, religious, economic and political differences with his subjects in the Netherlands precipitated a civil war. The Netherlands divided, with the southern portion (modern Belgium) reverting to Spanish control, while the ten northern provinces became the United Netherlands, sometimes called Holland. By 1600 the Dutch had become a great seafaring people, respected rivals of the Spanish, the French, and the English. Backed by a stable home economy, the Netherlands spread throughout the world. In Asia, the Dutch East India Company attacked Portuguese possessions in the Spice Islands of the East Indies and seized them for the Netherlands. Almost simultaneously, the Dutch West India Company was preparing to establish a North American colony, which eventually would become New York.[6]

(France. France had made impressive strides toward political unity during the late 1400s, but early in the next century ambitious territorial aspirations in Europe proved too great a drain on French resources. In addition, religious troubles arising from the Protestant Reformation convulsed France for decades, and it was not until about 1600 that the reforms of the Bourbon Henry IV put the national house in order.[7] Once this had been

done, Frenchman joined Dutchman and Briton in founding North American colonies during the early 1600s. With a sturdy population of some twenty million, a flourishing middle class, and adequate financial backing, France was able to emulate its Atlantic rivals.

(Great Britain. A great deal of attention must obviously be directed to Great Britain,[8] for it was from this "jewelled isle" that the great majority of colonial American settlers came. England was in ferment during the century and a quarter before its permanent American colonization. Perhaps greater changes had taken place during these years than in the 500 years before. The civil struggles called the Wars of the Roses had eliminated most of the unruly and rebellious British nobility, and royal power became more firmly planted under the Tudor Henry VII. This penny-pinching monarch (he paid John Cabot £10 for his expedition to America in 1498) was able to bequeath a full treasury and a stabilized government to his flamboyant son, Henry VIII. Concurrently with his well-advertised matrimonial difficulties, Henry found time to lead Britain away from the Catholic Church into his own Church of England, which kept most of the Catholic sacraments but was under the control of the English Crown rather than the Papacy. Henry confiscated Catholic monastery properties and, through perspicacious use of these lands, created a new nobility, loyal to himself.

While these political and religious changes were occurring, a vast alteration in British agriculture was taking place. The process known as "enclosure" caused thousands of acres of cultivated farm land to revert to pasturage. Canny landlords had found that greater profits could be realized through sheep raising to supply the flourishing wool industry than could be gained from the sale of grains

---

[6] See p. 27.

[7] The important Edict of Nantes (1598) was among Henry's reforms. French Protestants (Huguenots) were granted complete political rights, freedom of individual worship, and somewhat limited rights of public worship. As a guarantee, the Huguenots were permitted to fortify some two hundred French cities. Most of the military and political power of the Huguenots was taken away by Cardinal Richelieu during the

next generation, and the edict itself was revoked by Louis XIV in 1685.

[8] Although technically Great Britain was not an entity until the Act of Union (1707) that combined England and Scotland, the term will be used interchangeably with England in the discussion of this earlier period.

and other foodstuffs. Yet pastures could support fewer persons than farms. One shepherd was sufficient to watch the flocks over an area that had easily supported four, five, six, or more farming families. The dispossessed farmers trooped to the cities—London in particular —where they found scant opportunity for work, and that at low pay. Despite the harsh penalties for such crimes, roguery, thievery, and highway robbery increased notably. Contemporaries were sure that Britain had a surplus population, and certainly thousands proved ready to abandon what they considered an intolerable existence at home for new opportunities overseas.

Religious controversy further roiled English currents. Roman Catholicism had not been eradicated when the Church of England [9] was established; Catholic rebellions occurred from time to time. Yet the deepest and most prevalent religious disorders came from the extreme Protestant wing. Since most points of Catholic dogma had been retained, a growing number of Englishmen became disgusted with the Anglican Church as "Papist" and turned to the Protestantism imported from the European mainland. The teachings of Martin Luther had little appeal to Englishmen of that time, but the middle class found a partial solution to its religious problems in Calvinism, which became the foundation of British Puritanism. Both Catholic and Calvinist were persecuted by the established Church, and religious reasons for migration mingled with the political and economic. Britain made a far wiser decision in regard to its religiously dissatisfied subjects than did either France or Spain. The royal government took the stand that religious dissenters should not infest the English landscape, but that if these "heretics" wished to establish themselves across the Atlantic, they could receive a charter for settlement there.

British industry boomed during the century before American colonization. Profits from wool production were sometimes utilized for

commercial enterprise. Joint-stock companies —such as the British East India Company for Asia; the Muscovy Company, granted a monopoly in the Russian and Baltic trade; and the Levant Company, formed to exploit the resources of the Mediterranean—became the models for the later London and Plymouth Companies, which founded the first permanent English colonies on the North American mainland.

In addition to this legitimate business activity, English mariners, who can be called either heroic adventurers or bloodthirsty pirates, depending upon one's frame of reference, attacked Spanish commerce in American waters. Relations between the two nations were worsened further by the machinations of King Philip II of Spain. Philip had been the husband of Queen Mary (Tudor), who had caused England to revert to Catholicism from 1553 to 1558. After Mary's death and the accession of Queen Elizabeth I, Philip continued to interfere in English matters by trying to place on the British throne the Catholic Mary Stuart. Elizabeth foiled his attempts, recognized the natural hostility between her nation and Spain, and adopted a devious and circuitous policy of publicly advocating peaceable relations between the two countries while secretly encouraging additional depredations against Spanish commerce. Such seamen as Hawkins, Frobisher, Gilbert, and Drake, operating with the Queen's tacit approval, plundered Philip's ships, raided his territories, and killed his subjects.

Wearying of Elizabeth's lame apologies, Philip decided to crush Britain. In 1588, he sent forth the famed "invincible Armada," which came to destruction first through British attacks in the English Channel and finally by a great storm that whistled out of the north to drive the remnants of the Spanish fleet, which was trying to escape around Scotland and Ireland, onto rocky Hibernian coasts. Spanish power was not broken by this catastrophe, but England was able to compete for overseas possessions on conditions approaching equality.

During the late sixteenth century, Britain

[9] The terms "Church of England," "Anglican Church," and "Episcopal Church" are all used for the same denomination.

made a few abortive attempts to found colonies in North America. Twice Sir Humphrey Gilbert tried to colonize Newfoundland between 1584 and 1591, but conditions on that bleak island discouraged the few settlers, who each time returned to England. At about the same time, Sir Walter Raleigh lost a fortune attempting to establish a colony at Roanoke Island between Virginia and North Carolina. Most of his colonists went home, and the few left behind mysteriously disappeared, possibly overwhelmed by Indian attacks. These failures seem to show that transplanting Englishmen to the New World was too weighty a task for the resources of any one man. Joint-stock companies finally accomplished what individual effort had not succeeded in doing.

By 1600, conditions in England were ripe for migration to America. A surplus population with economic, social, religious, and political drives; adequate financial support earned through successful investments; the desire of merchants to dispose of their wares in new markets; a favorable governmental climate; and a sense of national pride and destiny that had been whipped into activity by the writing of such men as Richard Hakluyt, who limned in glowing colors the glory and profits of colonial expansion, brought to seventeenth-century British colonial endeavor a success that had been denied to earlier generations.

THE AMERICAN LAND

The American land toward which the first English ships turned was of tremendous richness and variety. The broken Atlantic coastline was of great importance, stretching north and south for some 1,500 miles. East and west it ranged from the ocean back to the first rise in the land where the tidal waters ended, varying in depth from a narrow belt in New England to a broad sweep of over 150 miles in the South. A profusion of harbors assured protection from storms and afforded communication with Europe; many rivers offered easy access

to the interior. The climate was similar to that of Britain, although characterized by greater temperature extremes. Such British agricultural products as wheat, barley, and oats could easily be grown. The land ran a gamut from rich fertility to waste, although soil exhaustion rapidly took place in many localities once the forest humus was gone.

Everywhere in America were plants and animals unknown to the first English explorers. The wonders of America for the seventeenth-century Briton can be gleaned from an eyewitness observation of George Percy, a member of the Jamestown expedition in 1607:

Wheresoever wee landed upon this River [the James] wee saw the goodliest Woods as Beech, Oke, Cedar, Cypresse, Wal-nuts, Sassafras, and Vines in great abundance, which hang in great clusters on many trees unknowne; and all the grounds bespred with many sweet and delicate flowres of divers colours and kindes. There are also many fruites as Strawberries, Mulberries, Rasberries, and fruites unknowne. There are many branches of this River, which runne flowing through the Woods with great plentie of fish of all kindes; as for Sturgeon, all the World cannot be compared to it. In this Countrey I have seene many great and large Medowes having excellent good pasture for any Cattle. There are also great store of Deere, both Red and Fallow. There are Beares, Foxes, Otter, Bevers, Muskats, and wild beasts unknowne.

The character of the English settlements was largely determined by the environment in which colonization took place. In New England, the narrow apron of rock-filled land impelled many toward the sea or to other non-agricultural pursuits. The coastal strip widened toward the Middle colonies (New York–Pennsylvania area), the land was naturally rich, and soon this section's diversified agriculture became the breadbasket of colonial America. To the south, the wide plain encouraged the plantations of Virginia and the Carolinas. From north to south along the Atlantic coastal plain, the land was heavily wooded, and new agricultural techniques had to be learned, since the English forests had been long ago hewn down. In America, trees had to be felled, or at least ringed and left to die, before settlements could be supported. Wood, valued commodity in the Old World, was so abundant in the New as to constitute a nuisance. Farms carved out of the wooded area and situated close to rivers—the best available transportational routes—typified American agriculture for the next two centuries. Not until the development of dry-farming techniques, barbed wire, and irrigation systems made the Far West habitable did the American husbandman turn from forest farming. For many years after the United States became a nation, he tended to follow the heavily wooded river valleys.

Between the Atlantic coastal plain and the Appalachian Mountains lay the upland plateau called the Piedmont. Here diversified farming could flourish. The Piedmont was settled during the eighteenth century by Scots-Irish immigrants who spread throughout these western reaches of colonial America. Rising from the Piedmont was the Appalachian range, stretching from Maine to northern Georgia and Alabama. Colonial settlement lapped against this mountain barrier and remained relatively stationary while the disposition of lands beyond was determined by imperial struggle between France and Great Britain. This first hiatus in the march westward was probably fortunate for the English. Their colonists remained east of the Appalachians and were not dispersed as widely as the French, who spread over the great valley down the Mississippi to New Orleans. English energies turned to intensive development of the coastal strip and awaited transmontane expansion until victory over the French had been won by 1763.

As the land dropped from the Appalachian heights, the vast central plains of the North American continent started their 1,500-mile expanse from western Pennsylvania to the Rocky Mountains in Colorado and Wyoming. Drained by the mighty Mississippi-Missouri river system with its myriad tributaries, the great valley was divided beyond the Mississippi

at approximately the 98th meridian, running through the central Dakotas down to the Mexican border. East of this line, comparatively adequate rainfall contributed to the growth of wooded areas. Settlers could follow the forested riverbanks, where their prevailing agricultural methods could be utilized. West of the 98th meridian to the Rockies, the high, arid plains could not be farmed successfully until new means had been devised. As early as 1820, thousands of migrants were west of the Mississippi, but the dry plateaus had to wait for any considerable white settlement until after the Civil War.

Hurtling upward from the plains were the awesome Rocky Mountains, the Western cordillera. Range after range of the chain was interspersed with small valleys. On the western slopes the land dropped again, this time to the Great Basin, the "American desert," extending to the Sierra Nevada in California. With less rainfall than any other section of the nation, the plateau of Utah and Nevada lagged behind in development. For several decades, the arid plains, the mountains, and the Great Basin were used chiefly as avenues for passage from the East to California and Oregon. After the first rush to the Far West had partially spent itself, a backwash spread into the rugged mountains and formidable deserts. Yet the mountain West has had such difficult problems to solve (especially the lack of water) that even today it is the least populous section of the country.

The Pacific coastal area suffered from a dearth of natural harbors and faced Asia rather than the more important European markets. There were compensating advantages, however. Well watered and wooded, and with naturally fertile land occupying much of its total acreage, a large portion of the central valley stretching from California to Washington was an agricultural paradise. When these assets were combined with a wealth of mineral resources, scenic beauty, and a remarkably salubrious climate, it is little wonder that the Pacific slopes were in time occupied by a thriving population.

THE AMERICAN INDIAN

The character of the American topography was not the only important factor that caused the mutation of the European into the American. The Indian had occupied the continental land area of the United States for thousands of years before the coming of the white man. The precise origins of the American Indian are a matter of controversy; but most experts in the field, noting the Indian's physical and cultural similarities to the Asiatics, conclude that he arrived from Siberia by way of the Bering Sea islands and Alaska. Spreading south and east during remote antiquity, the red men developed their highest civilizations in Mexico and northern South America. Many of the agricultural practices of these natives who occupied the present area of the United States were probably acquired from Mexico.

When Columbus first sighted the New World, something less than a million Indians, in a bewildering complexity of groupings, lived between the boundaries of modern Canada and Mexico. In the matter of language, the American natives residing north of Mexico comprised some fifty-six separate families, and distinguishable dialects ran into the hundreds. So-called tribes were primarily ethnological groups rather than practical social organizations with clearly defined functions. General tribal councils might be held from time to time, but there was little real centralization, and the majority of personal controls were exercised on a local basis. Law was a matter of custom rather than of specific enactment, but nevertheless was enforced with vigor. The troublemaker, liar, thief, or murderer might expect to be punished by one of the soldier societies that enforced local customs, his property confiscated or destroyed, and he himself beaten and exiled into the wilderness without clothes or weapons. Since social groups were so small that misdemeanors were easily observed, the general good conduct of the Indian is understandable. Efficient though this localism might be to enforce compliance to tribal

mores, it was disastrous when real dangers existed. Indian separatism frustrated efforts to organize the tribes, despite the unstinting attempts of such individuals as "King" Philip, Pontiac, and Tecumseh, and permitted the white men to divide and conquer their adversaries.

Most Indians were agricultural peoples living in permanent towns, although hunting and fishing provided supplementary food. Villages, each with its corn, bean, and squash fields, were scattered throughout the country east of the Mississippi. In the Southwest, irrigation was practiced 350 years before white Americans adopted similar techniques. In the Northwest, fishing was a larger part of the Indian economy, with salmon the center of life. The open Great Plains proved less adequate for agriculture, and here Indian economy was based on the buffalo, which furnished food, clothes, housing, tools, arms, and fuel. The plains tribes had originally been farmers, but they had acquired new habits of life to adjust themselves to new conditions. Here and there the original economy was retained. The Mandans, part of the Sioux, were an interesting cultural relic as they continued to farm the plains after their kinsmen migrated from the Great Lakes region to the northern prairies in order to embrace buffalo hunting as a normal means of livelihood.

In regard to his tools and weapons, the Indian was in the stone-age pattern of human development. Earlier civilizations had used copper, but the art had been lost. The Indian had no written language, even though he could convey specific messages with pictographs. His only domesticated animal was the dog, commonly used to drag Indian possessions, for the principle of the wheel was unknown. Horses were acquired from the Spaniards, although not, as is commonly believed, by the escape of these animals from early exploring expeditions; probably the Indian was given horses by Juan de Oñate during the conquest of New Mexico around 1600. Although pitifully lacking in animal husbandry, the Indian had domesticated many plants and brought them to a high degree of perfection. For example, the corn that was viewed with envy by the first Europeans must have required generations of experimentation.

Indian life was quite complex, with an involved network of family, social, military, and religious groups. Religion was an integral part of all life, for the Indian was animistic and felt the need of propitiating the proper spirits in all his activities. Elaborate, religiously motivated ceremonials were believed necessary to make the corn grow, ensure a good hunt, produce victory in war, cure disease, or accompany any other important event. But the Indian was basically a realist. If his charms ("medicine") did not work, he threw them away and tried new ones. If the doctor's herbs and incantations were ineffective, the Indian took personal vengeance on the doctor, for the latter was a religious leader who had failed. Contrary to the opinion of most white men, the Indians were a home-loving people who thoroughly enjoyed storytelling and jokes and who were generally loquacious and fun-loving. Children were trained carefully and seldom given physical punishment, which was in vast contrast to the usual white attitude. Women were well-treated, even to the extent of being given a voice in tribal decisions. Ordinarily, they married with only their own consent and could divorce undesirable husbands. As was true in white society, work was divided on the basis of sex, and if the whites thought of Indian women as unrespected drudges, it was chiefly because certain of their occupations, such as farming, were not those of white women. Actually, there is considerable question as to whether the Indian squaw of 1500 was not better off than her white sister.

The first Europeans were treated by the Indians with respect almost akin to awe. The white faces seemed godlike, and the curious clothing, weapons, and implements miraculous. The white men were entertained hospitably, which was in the Indian tradition; unfortunately, this native generosity was frequently abused by its recipients. To the Indian, the least understandable trait of the white man was his urge to earn profits; the former gave freely to persons in need and otherwise traded merely for some article that he wanted. The idea of trading to produce a surplus of goods that were not immediately desired seemed unreasonable to the Indian. Many of the first Europeans in America saw the Indians as real children of nature, with no religion and no government, collecting their food without work—a handsome, healthy, and vigorous people, enjoying lives devoted to dancing and good fellowship. Here was the origin of the "noble savage"—idealized particularly by Rousseau—as an unspoiled, virtuous, generous child of nature. Yet the opposite viewpoint also prevailed: that the Indian was depraved, sensual, pagan, sly, untrustworthy, and cruelly brutish. Indian dances were described as previews of hell, and pious New England mothers attempted to frighten their children into good behavior by threatening to give them to the Indians. This ambivalent attitude was to continue throughout American history, producing alternately harsh and lenient policies, of which neither was based on real understanding of the Indian.

Individual reactions to the Indians were complicated by national backgrounds and policies. Spanish policy was extremely confusing. The Madrid government thought of the Indians as both souls to be saved and bodies to be worked. Unfortunately, neither idea could be applied very successfully, and to some extent they conflicted with each other. As souls to be saved, the Indians received priests among the vanguards of Spanish advance, but these men of God found that the great majority of Indians had no desire for salvation along Christian lines and even had to be forced to say the Pater Nosters and Ave Marias. As workingmen, the Indians were similarly uncooperative, showing no desire to toil in the fields and mines. Sometimes they starved themselves or killed their own children to avoid such fate. The Spanish government specified optimistically that the "Indians shall perform as free people," but the colonists found it necessary to introduce a system of forced labor. The natives were sold like cattle, forced to sleep in the fields, and sometimes beaten to death. European ways of life were imposed upon them even to the extent that "They shall not bathe as frequently as hitherto, as we are informed that it does them much harm." Such policies decreased the native population, until in some areas additional labor had to be imported.

The French got along better with the Indians because they did not wish extensive colonization or mineral exploitation. They were willing to improvise local administrative measures rather than to have them rigidly set by the home government. French traders and trappers lived happily with Indian wives over much of North America. The Dutch for a time tried to enslave the Indians, but ultimately were satisfied to best the natives economically through selling them guns and bad liquor. Apparently the Dutch also were not loath to have relations with the more attractive Indian women, and an Iroquois squaw was reported to bring somewhere between 1 and 3 shillings. The British were more interested in settlement; in a series of bloody and desultory wars, they steadily pushed the Indians westward. Often English ruthlessness was deplored by London, for the home government was concerned with preserving Indian lands for the fur trade. This policy culminated in the Proclamation of 1763, which was supposed to stop temporarily the white migration into the Indian country west of the Appalachians.

Europeans and their native American successors felt confident in their own minds that they had a superior civilization that Christian charity indicated they should bestow upon the benighted Indian, but the first four centuries of racial relations actually left the white man in debt to the redskin. The early European contributions were most notably horses, iron tools, petty trinkets, liquor, and disease. The trinkets may be dismissed as of little importance, but the liquor and disease were obviously bad, and such white afflictions as small-pox, measles, and venereal disease carried off the natives by the thousands. Even horses and such tools as guns were not unmixed blessings. They made possible the slaughtering of more game, which in turn led to the construction of larger houses to display the increased wealth. Therefore squaws' work became both more arduous and more necessary, leading to earlier marriages and increasingly frequent polygamous relationships. The availability of desirable commercial products enhanced Indian greed, which was further reinforced by white example. Indian morals declined, and disintegration of the whole social pattern soon followed. Certainly the Indian paid a high price in demoralization for the few implements and adornments that he received.

Considerably more impressive was the Indian contribution to white civilization, even disregarding the fact that the entire land and its resources were originally Indian, and also excluding as relatively unimportant the Indian names that have been retained for many American towns, rivers, lakes, and mountains. The Indians taught the white settler how to live in the wilderness, how to fight in the forest, how to trap and hunt, and how to use sign language and make smoke signals. They provided the hunting shirt, the legging, the moccasin, and the snowshoe; their canoe improved transportation. Above all, however, they furnished new plants and methods of cultivation. Among these Indian innovations were corn, potato (both white and sweet), tobacco, avocado, kidney bean, lima bean, artichoke, peanut, pineapple, squash, pumpkin, tomato, maple sugar, witch hazel, cascara, and American indigo. An estimate has been made that over half of the world's present agricultural produce consists of plants that originated in the Americas. Surely Americans should feel grateful for Indian contributions to modern civilization, even if they do not feel ashamed of despoiling a native culture by the force of superior arms.

CHAPTER 2

Colonization and Imperial Conflict

(1607-1763)

THE SOUTHERN COLONIES

⟦ *Virginia.* Virginia was the first permanent British colony to be established in North America. In 1605 two separate groups of "merchant adventurers" petitioned King James I for permission to establish "factories" [1] in the New World. The King combined the two in the Virginia Company under his royal supervision. One group, the London Company, was granted exclusive settlement rights from the 34th to the 38th parallels (roughly Virginia and North Carolina). The other, the Plymouth Company, received exclusive settlement rights from the 41st to the 45th parallels (roughly New England). The area between could be colonized by either. The London Company was to search for gold, export needed produce to supplement British economy (especially such naval stores as pitch, resins, and lumber for masts), convert the Indians to Christianity, and seek a northwest passage to the Pacific. Preparations for the expedition were completed in 1606; and after a weary

[1] The modern use of the term "factory" does not apply in this instance. "Trading post" would be a closer approximation to the seventeenth-century meaning.

four months' crossing, Jamestown, Virginia, was founded during the spring of the following year.

For almost twenty years the colony at Virginia hung on by its fingernails. It seems strange that starvation should afflict those living in a region where game of all kinds filled the forest, fish swarmed in every rivulet and creek, wild plants furnished an abundant fare, and Indian agriculture flourished. Starve, however, the Virginians did; counting those felled by disease, fewer than one-quarter of the 1,600 who migrated to the colony from England between 1606 and 1616 survived. The majority of the early migrants were from cities or from cleared farm land, unused to life in a rugged frontier environment. Malarial fevers killed many, fear of Indian attacks kept others close to their first settlements, and new techniques for forest survival developed slowly. The rule of the company was an irritating combination of harshness and laxity. In addition, the economic basis of early Virginia was faulty. The gold chimera consumed time that could have been better spent. The few exports, among them iron pyrites or "fool's gold," were insufficient to return a profit, and the food supply continued to depend upon imports from

England. But for the courage and determination of Captain John Smith and a few others, Virginia would have been abandoned altogether. Indeed, in 1610 the whole colony was en route home, but turned back when a relief expedition with food and new settlers arrived at the last moment.

A fortunate discovery helped put Virginia on a paying basis. John Rolfe, husband of the famed Indian princess Pocahontas, found a method for curing the native tobacco in 1616. Formerly the Virginia weed had proved too harsh and acrid for sensitive seventeenth-century palates accustomed to the milder Caribbean variety, but Rolfe's improvement made mainland tobacco a valued commodity. Exports of that plant boomed from almost nothing to 50,000 pounds by 1618. Tobacco became the staple crop of the colony, and Virginia's economic fortunes rode on its price in the London market. Tobacco was grown everywhere—even in the streets of Jamestown—and so complete was its domination that taxes to the local government and the salaries of Anglican clergymen were paid, not in coin, but in tobacco.

During the early years the colony's land-holding system was highly unpopular. All land belonged to the company, and individuals were slow to make improvements when rewards would accrue to overseas stockholders. In 1618, however, the company moved to attract immigrants by allowing individual ownership. A new settler was given 50 acres for each passage that he paid. Thus an English farmer with a wife and three children could start with a tidy 250 acres and proceed to plant the ubiquitous tobacco. Most Southern colonies followed Virginia's land-tenure system to acquire immigrants. Moreover, if a potential settler were unable to pay his passage fare, he could become an indentured servant—roughly akin to a temporary slave—who labored for a term of four to seven years on an average in return for his transportation costs and 50 acres once his indenture had been served. No particular shame was attached to this condition, and some men who eventually became prominent planters, justices of the peace, and colonels of local militia regiments gained their starts in America as indentured servants. Negro slavery existed in Virginia as well as in the other Atlantic seaboard colonies during the 1600s, but it did not become prominent until the next century.

THE SOUTHERN COLONIES

The rule of the company in Virginia was not popular in either America or Britain. A profit-sharing organization, the company was more interested in quick returns on its investment than in the permanent welfare of its colonists. Some of the early company governors—notably Sir Thomas Dale, who had men strapped to a wheel and their bones broken by repeated blows—were understandably not popular, despite the increased efficiency that terror might compel. Discontent in the colony finally forced the company to permit some local self-government. In 1619 the first elective legislature in America was convened when the House of Burgesses, composed of two representatives from each of the eleven "plantations" (boroughs), met at Jamestown.

Decisions reached in England finally ruined the company. King James I was dissatisfied with the management of his overseas possession, and when about 350 Virginians were slaughtered in the terrible Indian uprising of 1622, the King pushed a bill through a subservient Parliament which reorganized Virginia as a royal colony, despite the agonized wails of stockholders who received no recompense. Under Virginia's royal government, the King designated a governor who in turn appointed a council to assist him. The House of Burgesses was allowed to meet after a short lapse, thereby restoring some local self-government. This blueprint of King James' increasingly dominated colonial American administration at the expense of both the charter form of government, which typified New England, and the relatively feudalistic proprietorships that were granted to such aspiring individuals as Calvert and Penn.

Under its royal governors, Virginia recorded considerable progress. Economic prosperity was reasonably prevalent until the price of tobacco collapsed in the middle of the seventeenth century. Migrants poured into the colony, the Indians were pushed back, the tide of settlement spread to the west, and Virginia assumed its proud station as the largest and most populous British colony in the New World.

(*Maryland*. Maryland was the next Southern colony to be established, and both religious and economic motives influenced its origin. The Calverts, English Catholic nobility, desired to found an American colony for the good of Catholicism and the Calvert purse. A charter was received from King Charles I, and in 1634 the first settlement was made at St. Marys on Chesapeake Bay. Maryland was able to profit by the example of Virginia's bitter first years, and to avoid some of the same mistakes. The settlers were industrious, food could be borrowed from the Indians or from neighboring Virginia, and the first tobacco crop was soon planted. As early as 1640, Maryland was reasonably prosperous.

The Calverts tried to introduce feudalism to their proprietary colony. According to the original charter, the proprietor was permitted to make all laws, subject to the approval of a local assembly, which he could and did control for the first few years. The Calverts advertised for colonists who would bring feudal tenants with them to Maryland. This anach-

ronistic and unwieldy system failed—as did most feudalism in America—and well before the end of the seventeenth century, small farmers could easily acquire land in Maryland.

Religious squabbles continued to cause difficulties. While the Calverts were staunch Roman Catholics until 1715 (when the proprietor turned Protestant to regain his lands forfeited during the Glorious Revolution of 1689), they were intelligent enough to recognize the fanatical hatred that the typical Briton of that time felt toward the Roman Church. In order to protect Catholics from attacks by internal or external enemies, the Calverts promoted the Religious Toleration Act of 1649, in which freedom of worship was granted to all who believed in "Christ and the Holy Trinity." This act constituted a shield for the Catholics, a minority in Maryland throughout the colonial era. By the middle 1600s, Calvinist Puritans escaping persecution in Virginia swarmed into Maryland in sufficient numbers to become a temporary majority, although most later inhabitants were Anglicans.

Quarrels other than religious disturbed Maryland's tranquility. The local assembly complained eternally to the proprietor, the farmers assailed the quitrents [2] of the Calverts, and the colony often bickered with Virginia over boundary claims and conflicting rights on Chesapeake Bay. On the whole, however, Maryland's early years were relatively easy and prosperous. Its religious toleration, while by no means complete, was exceeded only by Rhode Island and Pennsylvania of all Britain's American mainland domains.

(*The Carolinas*. For almost three decades after the founding of Maryland, no new British colonies were established on the southern portion of the North American coast. Not until 1663 was a charter for the lands composing present North and South Carolina granted. During the interim between the

---

[2] A "quitrent" was not a "rental" as we would recognize the term today. It was a feudal due—a symbol of ownership—paid to the proprietor. While it was seldom large, colonists resisted its payment whenever possible, for they were opposed to almost all taxation.

founding of Maryland and of the Carolinas, epochal events had rocked British society to its core. Social, political, and religious drives had culminated in a civil war that erupted spasmodically between 1639 and 1649. In confused interchanges, King Charles and his Cavaliers fought the Parliamentary forces, Anglican warred on Puritan, Scotsmen vied with Englishmen, and the *bourgeoisie* opposed the nobles. The royal armies were finally defeated, and King Charles I was decapitated. The Stuart monarchy temporarily came to an end when Oliver Cromwell, commander of the crack Puritan army, became Lord Protector of the new English Commonwealth. Cromwell died in 1658; and most Britons, wearied of Puritan fanaticism and longing for more relaxed days, welcomed the Stuarts back to the throne in the person of the affable, amatory, intelligent, and treacherous Charles II (1660). Charles wished to reward some of his faithful followers; and when eight nobles appealed to him for services rendered, the King granted them the area between Spanish Florida and Virginia as a joint proprietorship.

The lucky eight made expansive plans for feudalism overseas in the future North and South Carolina. The eminent political philosopher John Locke (whose *Second Treatise on Government* formed most of the thoughts and some of the language in Jefferson's Declaration of Independence) was hired to plan the government. Locke tried to formulate an entirely new feudal system for the wilderness, complete with a special Carolina nobility, with partly Indian and partly European nomenclature. Such esoteric titles as "cacique" and "landgrave" were specified, but happily nothing came of this grandiose project, and the colony developed along more rational lines.

Originally the Carolinas were one, but relatively swiftly occurring events decreed that this unity be severed. Even before the proprietary grant had been received, an overflow from Virginia had infiltrated the shores of Albemarle Sound in what is now North Carolina. These settlers were not disposed to take seriously the claims of the proprietors and resisted attempts to enforce their obedience.

North Carolina had certain geographical characterics that hindered its development for generations. The reefs of Cape Hatteras extended for many miles along its coast, and good harbors were lacking. Thus the growth of trade and commerce was slow. The rivers were not particularly useful without well-protected ports at their mouths; and rather than uniting the colony through coastal trade, the river valleys tended to divide North Carolina into several distinct sections. Although tobacco and diversified crops were raised and stock breeding became important, some of the soil was infertile. North Carolina grew very slowly until the middle of the eighteenth century, when a considerable influx of settlers made the colony one of the most populous by the eve of the American Revolution.

The colony to the south forged ahead more rapidly. The year 1670 marks the date of the first settlements in South Carolina, although considerable numbers did not come until the founding of Charles Town (Charleston) a decade later. Some migrants sailed to the colony directly from England; hundreds of Huguenots expelled from France landed during the 1680s; and other groups, such as the Irish, the Scots-Irish, and the Swiss, gave to the streets of Charleston an early aspect of cosmopolitanism. Most settlers came from the British West Indies, and South Carolina maintained for years closer relations with Barbados, Bermuda, and the Bahamas than with its twin mainland colony to the north. A flourishing West Indian trade developed; Negro slaves labored in Carolina fields of rice and later indigo; and wealth poured into Charleston from the southern fur trade, which found its markets there. South Carolina shrugged off the cumbersome joint proprietorship to become a royal colony in 1719, and North Carolina followed its lead ten years later. The two Carolinas had grown apart, and their political separation was eminently sensible.

❮ *Georgia.* Three-quarters of a century was to elapse after the Stuart grant for Carolina before Georgia, the last British mainland colony, was founded. Georgia owed its existence to a strange combination of philanthropy and cold military logic. James Oglethorpe, a retired British general, became concerned about the bestial conditions in early-eighteenth-century English debtor jails. Determined to aid the unfortunate prisoners by furnishing new opportunity for them, Oglethorpe applied to his government for a colonial charter. He received a sympathetic reception from the Crown, which saw clearly that the thriving colony of South Carolina was in constant danger from Spanish Florida. A buffer state in Georgia would furnish needed protection. The first Georgia settlements were made at Savannah, but the colony grew very slowly. Fear of Spanish depredations, combined with unworkable reforms such as a ban on slavery and an early attempt to prohibit the consumption of alcoholic beverages, kept Georgia's population below 10,000 as late as 1775. Economically Georgia was an appendage of South Carolina, and its crops were similar.

THE NEW ENGLAND COLONIES

《 *Plymouth.* New England's origins illustrate considerable similarity to, as well as significant differences from, the development of the Southern colonies. Both New England and the South were predominantly farming in economics and English in population. Yet their farming techniques differed, and English migrants to the Northern mainland colonies formed somewhat dissimilar political and religious groups. Perhaps Plymouth Colony, the first colony in New England, can illustrate some of the differences. Actually Plymouth occupies a strange position in American history. Certainly it remained relatively insignificant during its years of independent existence (1620 to 1691), but such was the drama of its first years and so stalwart were its inhabitants that Plymouth has become part of our national folklore, and most Americans revere the "Pilgrims" to a greater extent than they do either

the early Virginians or the Puritans of Massachusetts Bay.

Granting that most migrants to any colony along the Atlantic Coast were primarily impelled by economic motives, religion appears to have played a more important part in New England generally and Plymouth in particular than elsewhere. Religious affairs in Great Britain during the 1600s were chaotic. The established Church of England attempted to follow a middle course between Catholic conservatism and Protestant reform. While allegiance to the Pope was discarded, marriage of the clergy was allowed, services were conducted in English rather than in Latin, and some subtle modifications of dogma had occurred, to thousands of seventeenth-century Englishmen their church remained steeped in "popery." They objected to the ritualized ceremonies, the incense, the ornate trappings, and the hierarchical organization that remained. Some of these dissenters resolved to reform the Church of England from within— to "purify" it—and so adopted the name "Puritan." A smaller and more radical group concluded that the Anglican Church was so permeated with sin and corruption that reform was impossible; salvation could be found only if the Church were abandoned altogether. The latter group was called "separatist," and the Pilgrims of Plymouth Colony belonged in this category.

Early in the seventeenth century King James promised to "harry out of the land" all separatists, and the small congregation in the town of Scrooby decided to migrate themselves. Leaving Britain, they settled in the Dutch city of Leyden during 1607–1608. While the refugees appear to have been cordially welcomed in this religiously tolerant city, they soon became uneasy there. The Pilgrims were farmers and artisans, lacking the technical skill to secure admittance to the guilds that dominated Leyden's economic life. They were forced to accept poorly paying jobs. Moreover, they objected to the "worldly pleasures" of urban life and feared that their children might be corrupted. The Pilgrims dreamed of a new country and decided to plant themselves in America on lands belonging to the Virginia Company. With company permission, as well as the assurances of King James that they would be unmolested if they caused no trouble, the Pilgrims turned to London merchants to borrow the funds necessary for survival until they could become self-sufficient.

Some of these dissenters sailed to America in 1620 on the famous *Mayflower*—which might seem to have had the capacity of the *Queen Mary* if credence can be granted to claims of the numerous descendants of the original coterie. Contrary winds and faulty navigation brought the *Mayflower* to the tip of Cape Cod in Massachusetts, well beyond the boundaries of the Virginia Company. These Pilgrims followed Cape Cod to the Massachusetts mainland, where they settled at "Plimouth," which had been named by Captain John Smith on an earlier expedition. The Pilgrims constituted a minority of the *Mayflower*'s passengers; most of them were ordinary Englishmen who came along for a variety of reasons, although economic considerations tended to predominate. The Pilgrim minority, fearful of internal dissension and realizing the need for governmental organization, persuaded the others to sign the Mayflower Compact, which called for general obedience to the laws of the government.

The first year at Plymouth was almost as difficult as the "starving time" in Virginia, and only Indian assistance managed to save about half of the original group. In the years that followed, the Pilgrims managed to achieve recognition of the validity of their dubious land claims and to pay off the heavy financial obligation owed to their London backers. Farming, the fur trade, and fishing furnished their economic lifeblood. Plymouth Colony was fortunate in having as its governor for some thirty years the intelligent, industrious, and pious William Bradford. Yet the colony remained minuscule, for most immigrants preferred to settle in larger and more prosperous Massachusetts Bay to the north. When the latter absorbed it in 1691, Plymouth's population was no more than 7,000.

《 *Massachusetts Bay: Calvinism and the British Civil Wars.* To understand colonial New England, its largest colony, Massachusetts Bay, must be comprehended. Since Massachusetts Bay was almost a theocracy—at least in its early days—the teachings of the famed French cleric John Calvin must be discussed, for from Calvinism emanated not only the religious, but much of the social, economic, intellectual, and political activities of that colony.

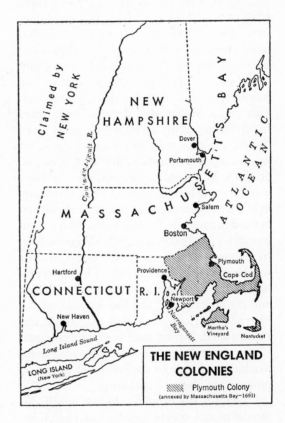

THE NEW ENGLAND COLONIES

░░░ Plymouth Colony
(annexed by Massachusetts Bay—1691)

In his influential work, *Institutes of the Christian Religion*, Calvin taught that men must live as God wished. The word of God was revealed in the Bible, hence men must conduct themselves according to Biblical tenets. Furthermore, humanity was so saturated in sin that it was ludicrous to assume that any puny "good works" could erase the tainted ledger. God had divided all men into two groups: a small number of the "elect" and the vast majority of the "damned." The elemental questions in life to the good Calvinist hinged on this: was he of the elect? If so, how could he know? It seems strange that such a grim emphasis on predestined salvation or damnation could have had any other effect upon its devotees than a dull, fatalistic acceptance of God's will. Yet the Calvinist proved to be surprisingly active in everyday affairs and deeply concerned with his own (and his neighbor's) behavior patterns.

Naturally, the devout Calvinist hoped desperately that he was of the elect, and there were two methods by which he might persuade himself that he was not damned eternally. One was to have a religious experience in which his mystical kinship to the Deity would suddenly and strikingly be evident. The second was to conduct his daily life on such high moral grounds that it would be obvious to all that so saintly an individual must be of the elect. To be sure, this would help in no way to achieve salvation, for that was predestined. Moral conduct was only a reflection; it could never be the source of light. Calvinists held that this concern with morals should go beyond the mere individual to the whole community. They believed that God needed help to improve society, and the good Calvinist would give doughty assistance. Thus the community was organized around both the Church and the government, and the activities of the two were so closely knit that they could not be separated. During most of the seventeenth century, a religious dissenter became automatically a traitor to the state and would be punished by the civil authority.

Calvinism was divided into two mildly disputant groups on the question of church organization. The more centralized first group held that individual churches should be somewhat controlled by a synod or "presbytery." The Presbyterian Church of Scotland, the Reformed Church of the Netherlands and Germany, and the French Huguenots maintained this position. The other wing, less centralized, assumed that each congregation could decide policy for itself, although actual practice often fell short of the philosophical ideal. The lat-

ter view was advocated by the Puritans of both old and New England, and the modern Congregational Church is their lineal descendant.

The effect of Calvinism on the political and economic structure of America has been profound. In another of the paradoxes that permeate this religion, Calvinism advanced democracy, even though it is difficult to imagine a more *undemocratic* concept than that which considers all mankind to be divided arbitrarily into a predestined elect and damned. Yet within the company of the elect, all were equal; and if the Calvinist were positive that he found himself in this fortunate category, he need bow to no man, but fear only God. In economics, Calvinism was also potent. Contrary to the medieval Catholic suspicion of business activity, Calvinism saw God's favor mirrored in prudence, diligence, and thrift. Efficiency in business became almost direct evidence of divine esteem, for certainly the Lord was not averse to honest profits. These egalitarian political credos and the philosophy of rugged individualism in economics were tailor-made for the pioneer; the pervasive stamp of Calvinism was carried into the wilderness by thousands of devout adherents. If its theology tended to become evasive and tepid with the passage of time, Calvinist doctrine remained throughout much of American history as a prime molder of the national character.

The early 1600s in England were a time of foreboding for Calvinists. While their numbers and influence tended to increase steadily, their growth was met by augmented resistance from the Crown and the Anglican Church. James I constantly threatened the Puritans, but took little direct action against them. When his son Charles I came to the throne in 1625, however, the skies darkened for English Calvinists. Charles announced his determination to enforce religious conformity, and indefatigable clerics zealously carried out their mentor's orders. In politics, Charles showed inclinations toward despotism when he answered Parliamentary defiance by dissolving that legislative body in 1629, thereby launching an eleven-year tenure of personal rule. Economic matters also troubled Britain's Calvinists. Southern and eastern England were Puritan strongholds, and the main industry of that area was the manufacture of woolen textiles. The onset of a severe depression caused much hardship, and many who were not particularly concerned with theological matters were vitally interested in the economic opportunities that might exist in a new world. Most Puritans doggedly battled for their complex beliefs at home through years of civil war, but thousands of others left England for New England before actual hostilities broke out. Massachusetts Bay was the destination of the majority.

(*Massachusetts Bay: Development.*   During the 1620s an English commercial company had managed to establish a few fishing and trading posts along the Massachusetts coast, but financial success had been conspicuously lacking. Astute Puritans saw a golden opportunity. Gaining control of the "Governor and Company for Massachusetts-Bay in New England," they received a charter from Charles I, who, presumably, was glad to rid himself of such troublesome subjects. The Puritans took the charter with them to America, for they feared that unsympathetic individuals might eventually become stockholders and nullify some of the charter's more advantageous provisions. Migration plans were carefully drawn, and in the spring of 1630 a seventeen-ship armada carried almost 1,000 migrants to the Boston and Salem environs. Although some difficulties were naturally encountered, in general Massachusetts Bay suffered far less acute natal pains than did either Virginia or Plymouth. Boston and its neighboring villages soon flourished. New settlers flooded into the colony from 1630 to 1640, resulting in a population of over 20,000 by the latter date. Immigration largely stopped during the British civil wars of the next two decades, for the Puritans were triumphant. Following the restoration of the Stuart dynasty in 1660, migration to Bos-

ton started again, but never attained the large proportions that characterized the first ten years of the Bay colony.

The transplanted Puritans had no desire to foster either democracy or religious toleration, and it is ridiculous for later generations to calumniate them for refusing to carry out policies that they openly and repeatedly assailed. Democratic leanings were viewed with abhorrence by Governor John Winthrop, the Reverend John Cotton, and other leaders of early Massachusetts Bay. They wished to establish the "Wilderness Zion," a holy state that would aid God to construct a more perfect society. With this end in mind, the Puritans erected an oligarchy—almost a theocracy—in which the Congregational Church was tied to the civil government so closely that opposition to one meant automatic opposition to the other.

Massachusetts Bay was rigidly controlled by this church-state alliance during its first years. Originally, the governor and his "assistants" ruled pretty much as they wished, but after a demand of the "freemen" to examine charter provisions, the ruling class grudgingly allowed some liberalization (1634). Yet throughout most of the seventeenth century, the franchise in Massachusetts Bay was allowed only to church members; and while attendance at divine worship was compulsory, membership was extremely difficult to achieve. In order to gain membership and a direct say in government, one had to experience a religious revelation of status as the elect, although this strict requirement was later somewhat relaxed. Late in the century, growing secularization of interests and increased prosperity toppled some of the old barriers. In spite of the impassioned protests of conservative divines, the theocratic power of the Puritan church was considerably weakened both by more democratic action from inside the colony and by the insistence of the British government that Massachusetts Bay's independence be limited. Under a new charter granted in 1691, Massachusetts became a royal colony, the Anglican Church was officially tolerated, and property ownership was to a certain degree substituted for religious belief as the basis for the franchise. Nevertheless, the Puritan ministry continued to wield great authority in New England until long after the American Revolution.

There is much about the inhabitants of the early Bay colony to arouse the derision and dislike of modern Americans. These "moral athletes" trained for their souls' salvation with the single-minded devotion of a high school sophomore determined to win his soccer letter. All the Puritan energies were thrown into this great struggle, and what we might consider the amenities of life—kindness, tolerance, humor, and affability—were not detested by him so much as overlooked. Perhaps the greatest blot on the Puritan record was the ugly intolerance that characterized the Bay's attitude toward dissenters. Those whom we would call harmless nonconformists were ruthlessly punished. Quakers seeking martyrdom were assured a warm welcome in Boston, where they were beaten, imprisoned, and mutilated, and four of their number were hanged. Emanating from a psychopathic dread of supernatural forces came the hysteria leading to the Salem witchcraft trials of 1692, during which nineteen unfortunate men and women were hanged and one pressed to death.

Yet we should be fair enough to judge the Puritan by the standards of his own day. When this is done, he comes off rather well. His narrow outlook and constant introspective analysis were typical of the whole period in history during which he lived. The strict codes of the New England settlements against sexual misbehavior, Sabbath-breaking, and dancing around the Maypole are also found in other supposedly more liberal colonies and in England itself. Quakers were persecuted all over the Western world, and more vigorously elsewhere than in the Puritan colonies. Witchcraft panics were characteristic of the sixteenth and seventeenth centuries. England, Scotland, and Germany executed literally thousands as witches rather than twenty.

Concerning the lighter side of life, the Puritans of Massachusetts Bay had more fun than is commonly imagined. When the local minister flayed his congregation for "lewd and lascivious" behavior, there must have been some fire behind all the smoke. When we consider the multiplicity of punishable acts in the Puritan legal system, we may well ask, "Are laws passed forbidding deeds that are not committed?" Even the modern stereotype of the Puritan is wrong. He is usually portrayed as a lank, cadaverous, somber-hued "bluenose," and he became the prototype of the prohibitionist during the 1920s. The record shows that he tended to array himself in all the colors of the spectrum, and as for being a prohibitionist —the amount of alcohol consumed by a seventeenth-century Massachusetts Bay congregation at the ordination of its pastor would make modern habitués of New York's Third Avenue blink with amazement.

(*Rhode Island, Connecticut, and New Hampshire.* Massachusetts Bay was the parent colony of New England; and from its confines divergently motivated groups fanned out to populate Rhode Island, the Hartford settlements in Connecticut, some New Hampshire towns, and the villages in the area that eventually became Maine. Religious dissent played a prominent part in the establishment of Rhode Island. Roger Williams, a minister surprisingly liberal for his day, defied the Bay-colony theocracy while preaching at Salem. Williams insisted that religious nonconformists should be granted a larger degree of toleration and that the civil authority should not be used to bolster the theocratic. Also, he attacked the governor himself and concluded by casting grave doubts on the legality of the land claims that the Puritans had received from the Indians. This was too much; Williams' deportation to England was ordered, but instead the intrepid rebel fled south to the shores of Narragansett Bay. Others who found conditions in Massachusetts intolerable joined him, among them the famed Anne Hutchinson, who not only criticized the Puritan ministry but claimed she had a right to preach herself. In 1643 the Narragansett settlements were unified under a grant from the Puritan "Long Parliament" as "Rhode Island and the

Providence Plantations." After the Stuarts returned to the throne, Williams managed to procure a permanent charter from Charles II.[3] The colony achieved some measure of prosperity through agriculture, fishing, commerce, and stock breeding ("Narrowhegansett" horses were prized possessions in colonial America). Rhode Island became an asylum for dissenters elsewhere, and many rugged individualists came to Newport and Providence. Rhode Islanders were distinctly unpopular with their more orthodox neighbors, and the colony was considered the *enfant terrible* of that time. It was not even invited to join the New England Confederation founded in 1644 for defense against the Indians, because of the objections of Massachusetts Bay, which feared that these "heretics" to the south might corrupt the pious folk of Boston.

Two colonies were established separately in what is now Connecticut. Thomas Hooker, pastor of the Newtown (Cambridge) congregation near Boston, learned of excellent land along the banks of the Connecticut River. Hooker led several hundred people to the present site of Hartford during 1636, a migration motivated more by the economic desire for fertile acres than by Hooker's relative liberalism in theological matters. The towns around Hartford were united under the Fundamental Orders of Connecticut, which has been called the first American constitution. Ample crops were soon harvested, additional inhabitants arrived, and the colony prospered. Close ties were maintained with the parent Massachusetts Bay.

The origins of the second Connecticut colony were quite different. The "Bible Commonwealth" of New Haven was founded by native rather than colonial Englishmen. John Davenport, a clergyman, and Theophilus Eaton, a London merchant, hoped to establish a "purer" "Wilderness Zion." Davenport and Eaton investigated Boston, but found even this Calvinist citadel too worldly for their palates and proceeded to the site of New Haven on Long Island Sound (1638). The legal code of New Haven was based solidly on the Biblical Mosaic law, and the ultra-Puritanical cast of that colony became widely known. New Haven's growth was slow, quarrels with the neighboring Dutch in New York caused difficulty, and the energies of the colony were somewhat dissipated by settling part of Long Island. Its independent existence lasted only a quarter century; the new Connecticut charter awarded by Charles II (1663) included the New Haven area within Connecticut's borders.

The land to the north of Massachusetts Bay had been granted as a proprietary colony to Sir Ferdinando Gorges and John Mason (1622); but their efforts to promote thriving settlements along the Maine coast failed, and their grant was forfeited. By 1640 an overflow from Massachusetts had spread into New Hampshire to found the villages of Portsmouth and Dover and into southern Maine. Other towns in New Hampshire were settled directly from England. The voracious appetite of Massachusetts Bay claimed both New Hampshire and Maine, but the desire of Charles II to embarrass the stiff-necked Bay Puritans was in part responsible for New Hampshire's separate charter as a royal colony (1679). Maine, however, continued to form the northern counties of Massachusetts until it became a state of the Union as a result of the sectional compromise in 1820.

Colonial New Englanders tilled their rocky and often unproductive soil, worshiped their God as they saw fit, martyrized their religious dissenters, started flourishing trade and commerce, fished the icy waters of the North Atlantic, established almost despite themselves a modified form of representative government, settled the wilderness to the west, persecuted the Indians with vengeful efficiency, founded the first real American school system, and debated the most abstruse points of Calvinist metaphysics with much the same intensity with which modern Brooklynites discuss the Dodgers. The varying facets of Puritan religious and political beliefs, and its intellectual and social creeds, were carried across the Ap-

---

[3] The charter of 1663 was still in effect in Rhode Island as late as 1840, being replaced then only after widespread disorders.

palachians into the great valley by its migrants. The stamp of New England's colonial experience is on us today.

THE MIDDLE COLONIES

⟨ *New York and New Jersey.* The Middle colonies formed the third major segment of Britain's colonial America. Although the Middle colonies were largely similar to New England and the South, there were significant differences in both population and topography from the other sections. North and south of

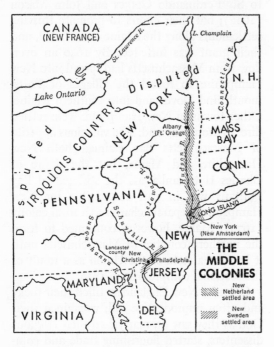

CANADA
(NEW FRANCE)

St. Lawrence R.

L. Champlain

Lake Ontario

Disputed

NEW YORK

N. H.

Connecticut R.

IROQUOIS COUNTRY

Albany
(Ft. Orange)

MASS
BAY

Hudson R.

CONN.

Disputed

PENNSYLVANIA

Delaware R.

Schuylkill R.

LONG ISLAND

Susquehanna R.

Lancaster
county

New
Christina

Philadelphia

NEW

New York
(New Amsterdam)

MARYLAND

JERSEY

THE
MIDDLE
COLONIES

New
Netherland
settled area

New
Sweden
settled area

VIRGINIA

DEL.

New York, New Jersey, Pennsylvania, and Delaware, the immense majority of settlers were of English descent. While that nationality predominated in the Middle colonies as well, a large influx of Germans, Scots-Irish, and Dutch resulted in a healthy mingling of peoples. Other sectional peculiarities derived from geographical factors. The area featured naturally fertile soil, relatively unvexed by the rocks that infested New England's fields. It had broad, navigable rivers, which emptied

into harbors unrivaled along the entire Atlantic Coast, and a climate that struck a pleasant balance between the semiequatorial heat of a Southern summer and the inflexible rigors of a New England winter. Contrast in scene and diversity in population gave to the Middle colonies a vigor and cosmopolitanism somewhat akin to modern America.

New York was the first site to be settled between Connecticut and Maryland. The Dutch explored New Netherlands (New York) [4] at about the same time the English were landing in Virginia and the French in Canada. A few years later (1626) the Dutch West India Company founded New Amsterdam on the southern tip of Manhattan Island as a permanent trading post to exploit the resources of the lower Hudson Valley. Pressing up the great river, a thin belt of Dutch territory soon hugged the banks of the Hudson from New York Harbor to Fort Orange (Albany). The lucrative fur trade poured wealth into Dutch coffers. Shrewd Netherlanders maintained amicable relations with the fierce Five (later Six) Nations of the Iroquois Confederation; Seneca and Mohawk middlemen transported the pelts caught by western tribes from the Great Lakes to the fur marts of Fort Orange.

Nevertheless, the Dutch committed some serious errors in New York. Their ill-advised attempt to impose feudalism in a raw country failed as resoundingly as similar British experiments in Virginia and the Carolinas. The New Netherlands government granted lavish tracts along the Hudson to feudal "patroons" who would promise to bring tenants with them.[5] These aristocrats preempted so much of the best land that the freeholder—the independent yeoman farmer who added so much vitality to those colonies which afforded easy

---

[4] Dutch claims to New York were based upon an expedition (1609) led by Henry Hudson, an Englishman employed by the Dutch East India Company. The latter was superseded by the Dutch West India Company (1621), which carried on the actual colonization.

[5] These patroon grants were surprisingly large. A choice was usually offered: 16 miles along one bank of the Hudson or 8 miles along both, extending indefinitely inland.

land tenure—tended to avoid New Netherlands. Hence New Netherlands grew very
slowly.

Furthermore, the Dutch proved to be rather
belligerent neighbors, and their overly aggressive attitude won them few friends. Sporadic
bickerings were carried on with the Connecticut Puritans, particularly for control of Long
Island, and under the last Dutch governor—
the choleric, one-legged Peter Stuyvesant—an
expedition marched south to conquer Sweden's American outpost at New Christina on
the Delaware River (1655).[6] New Netherlands' time was running short, however. The
Dutch fought three commercial wars with
England in the seventeenth century; and during the second conflict a British naval force
conquered New Amsterdam, despite Stuyvesant's frantic efforts to incite effective resistance. Later the Dutch recovered New York
for a short time, only to lose it permanently.

New York became a British colony under
the proprietorship of James, Duke of York;
when he assumed the throne, its status
changed to that of a royal colony. Yet the
Dutch influence on New York lasted for generations. The Dutch were allowed full rights,
their land claims were respected, and the
Dutch Reformed Church tolerated. The policy
of awarding vast lands to individuals continued, and the intermarriage of English Liv-
ingstons and Morrises with Dutch Van Rens-
selaers and Roosevelts formed a binational
New York aristocracy that dominated the colony and the state until long after the American
Revolution. As late as the nineteenth century,
Dutch was heard as often as English on the
streets of Albany. New York City rapidly became a great commercial port whose cosmopolitanism rivaled that of Charleston; but to
achieve national leadership, New York City
and New York State had to wait until after
1800.

In one of the many proprietary grants that

Charles II scattered as largess to his loyal followers, Lords Berkeley and Carteret received
New Jersey. Settlements there dated from the
middle 1600s, and many Puritans from New
England were attracted to the area by generous
land offers. New Jersey, however, remained one
of the least populous British American colonies. Some of the land was sandy or marshy,
and the coastline suffered from the same lack
of good harbors that plagued North Carolina.
Economically, New Jersey's northeastern section tended to gravitate toward New York,
while the southwest was dominated by Pennsylvania. Berkeley and Carteret could not
maintain their holdings very long, and proprietors changed with lightning rapidity until
New Jersey became a royal colony (1702).[7]

❮ *Pennsylvania and Delaware.* The greatest
success story of Colonial America was written
along the banks of the Delaware and Schuylkill Rivers. Pennsylvania was the lifework of
an attractive personality, the Quaker William
Penn. A scion of the aristocracy, Penn was impressed by the fortitude and heroism with
which Quakers courted martyrdom, and he became a convert. Penn's move took great courage, for the Quakers (Society of Friends) were
looked upon with suspicion and often hatred
by their contemporaries. This sect believed
that the "inner light" of God shone within all
men, making an organized ministry superfluous. Socially, their egalitarian creed caused
Quakers to ignore certain aspects of civil
authority. Their literal interpretation of the
Biblical commands against murder impelled
them toward ardent pacifism. All these tenets
were diametrically opposed to the usual seventeenth-century viewpoints, and the Quaker
was regarded in both Britain and America with
all the genial warmth and friendly sympathy
accorded to a carrier of the bubonic plague.

William Penn suffered both imprisonment
and temporary disinheritance because of his
Quaker affiliation; but eventually his distrait
father forgave him and bequeathed a consider-

---

[6] New Sweden had been founded in 1638 inside the
Dutch grant. Most authorities credit the Swedes with
introducing to America the famous log cabin, which
appears to have been unknown in England.

[7] For a short time New Jersey had twenty-four
proprietors.

able fortune to his son, part of which was an unpaid claim of £16,000 against the Stuart dynasty. The wily Charles II was, as always, in debt; and this affable monarch welcomed an opportunity to meet his obligation by chartering his creditor as the proprietor of lands along the Delaware River.

Penn planned his community intelligently. He decided to advertise for settlers throughout Europe and launched a vigorous promotional campaign, although no unduly wild assertions were made. In 1681, migrants attracted by accounts of a healthful climate, religious freedom, and good land either free or remarkably inexpensive sailed to take part in Penn's "holy experiment." English Quakers, French Huguenots, Germans from the Palatinate of the Rhine,[8] Scots-Irish,[9] and a host of others were soon pouring into Philadelphia. Although many stayed in the city, most Germans trekked to the fertile limestone region of Lancaster County, while the majority of Scots-Irish headed farther west. Pennsylvania's growth was unparalleled in America; inside of a few years it was one of the most populous and prosperous colonies in the world; and the rocketing population of Philadelphia made it, by the time of the American Revolution, larger than any other American or British city except, of course, London.

Reasons for the boom along the Delaware and the Schuylkill are not hard to find. Penn granted religious freedom to all who worshiped Jesus Christ, and the spiritually dissatisfied flocked to his colony. Pennsylvania was spared the horrors of Indian warfare for many years, because of the astute negotiations that were conducted with the Indians. Penn's subordinates paid the local tribes an honest price and lived up to their promises. With a river harbor offering unusual protection from wintry Atlantic gales, yet close enough to the

ocean for overseas vessels to dock in Philadelphia, a flourishing commerce whitened the oceans with Pennsylvania sails. The agricultural riches of the back country were copious enough to find eager buyers for Pennsylvania produce.

William Penn was also the proprietor of Delaware. He saw the strategic need to control the mouth of the Delaware River so that Philadelphia ships could not be denied egress to the sea. He received Delaware from Charles II and ruled it concurrently with Pennsylvania. Later he responded to appeals from the inhabitants of his smaller colony and granted them a separate legislature, but Delaware continued to share governors with its larger neighbor until the American Revolution.

Unlike many proprietors, Penn twice came to America, although these were visits rather than any permanent changes in address. He found his proprietorship difficult, despite the tremendous success of his venture. Since he refused to collect quitrents, he made little money. Penn suffered a temporary eclipse of his personal fortunes after the expulsion of James II in 1688 and lived long enough to understand the dissolute nature of his heirs, who were to squander their patrimony. Yet William Penn's services were far-reaching in implication. More than any other founder of an American colony, Penn during the seventeenth century foreshadowed the democracy and liberalism that came into fruition during the nineteenth and twentieth centuries.

THE BRITISH WEST INDIES

Because our national origins have derived from the thirteen colonies on the North American mainland, there has been a tendency to overlook some eighteenth-century facts that were never forgotten by contemporary directors of British colonial policy, namely, that the colonies along the Atlantic Coast were only a part, and economically a relatively unimportant part, of Britain's American empire. While some Englishmen were landing on the

---

[8] These Germans are the "Pennsylvania Dutch," who are not Dutch at all. The confusion was caused by the similarity between the German word *Deutsch* and the English word "dutch."

[9] The Scots-Irish were Scotsmen who had migrated to Ulster in northern Ireland during the 1500s. They are Scots, not Irish, and Presbyterians rather than Roman Catholics.

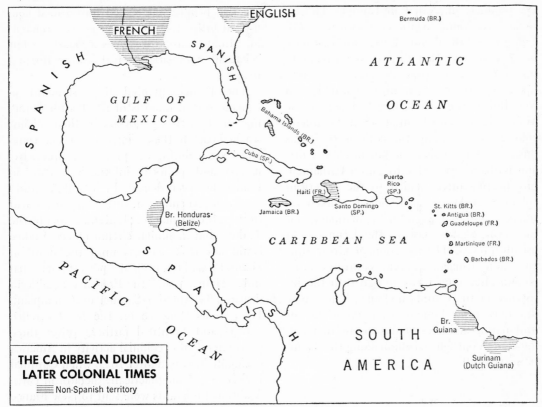

FRENCH

ENGLISH

Bermuda (BR.)

ATLANTIC

OCEAN

GULF OF MEXICO

SPANISH

SPANISH

Bahama Islands (BR.)

Cuba (SP.)

Puerto
Rico
(SP.)

Haiti (FR.)

Santo Domingo
(SP.)

St. Kitts (BR.)

Antigua (BR.)

Guadeloupe (FR.)

Martinique (FR.)

Barbados (BR.)

Br. Honduras·
(Belize)

Jamaica (BR.)

CARIBBEAN SEA

PACIFIC

SPANISH

OCEAN

Br.
Guiana

**SOUTH
AMERICA**

Surinam
(Dutch Guiana)

**THE CARIBBEAN DURING
LATER COLONIAL TIMES**
≡ Non-Spanish territory

mainland during the early 1600s, others were simultaneously planting the English flag on Atlantic and Caribbean islands.

Bermuda first attracted British attention in 1608, and settlements date from 1612. During the next few years rapid colonization of St. Kitts, Antigua, Barbados, and the Bahamas took place. Jamaica was wrested from Spain in 1655 and soon became the most important segment of the British West Indies. Slaves from the West Coast of Africa were brought by the thousands to the Caribbean islands, and their toil produced flourishing acres of tobacco and the even more important crops of cotton and sugar. It is difficult for the modern world to recognize the transcendent value of these sugar islands during the seventeenth and eighteenth centuries. A tiny dependency such as Barbados was considered (and rightly so) a brighter jewel in the imperial diadem than all New England.

Great Britain, as well as the other European powers of that time, was a wholehearted pro-

tagonist of the economic philosophy called "mercantilism," which advocated a planned economy, stressed the value of gold and silver bullion in royal treasuries, and promoted vigorous colonial activity to dovetail with the economy of the mother country. Tropical products such as sugar were at a premium and were vitally needed to supplement home commodities. Therefore the British mercantilists esteemed the sugar islands of the West Indies far above their colonies on the northern mainland, for the latter exported foodstuffs, lumber, fish, and manufactured articles that competed with home industries in Britain. French mercantilists were of one mind with their cross-Channel colleagues. In 1763 the former concluded that the Caribbean islands of Martinique and Guadeloupe were worth more than Canada and the Mississippi Valley combined.

The American colonies on the mainland had extremely close commercial ties to the West Indies, which were natural markets for northern products unwanted in Europe. The intimate economic relations between South Carolina and the islands to the southeast have been mentioned. In addition, New England's prosperity was in large measure dependent upon exports of fish, lumber, livestock, and foodstuffs to the Caribbean.[10] If, however, the West Indies were essential to the mainland colonies economically, the political story was different. The planters of Jamaica, St. Kitts, and Barbados were able to gain a Parliamentary hearing often denied to the American colonists. A West Indian lobby worked assiduously in London; and if the mainland and the sugar islands clashed, the latter would usually prevail. The adoption of Great Britain's more stringent economic controls over its empire after 1763 was due partly to the insistence of the Caribbean lobby. These new directives from London were important in formulating attitudes of discontent that culminated in outright rebellion along the Atlantic seaboard.[11]

FRENCH CANADA

While the British were spreading from Atlantic beaches to the foothills of the Appalachians, the French busied themselves in Canada to the north. Internal difficulties during the seventeenth century directed the energies of both French and English American colonials to the elemental problem of wilderness survival. Once some degree of stability in the New World had been achieved, friction between

the two peoples intensified into armed conflict, at first caused by power politics emanating from European dynastic clashes, but eventually motivated by real intracontinental rivalry.

The French planted their standard in Canada within months of the British founding of Jamestown, although their claims reached back to the explorations of Verrazano and Cartier during the previous century. Religious and political internecine strife in France, however, deflected national attention from colonial endeavor. British expansion had to await the restoration of internal order by the Tudors; and in similar circumstances, France could not look overseas until the Bourbon Henry IV had established a powerful national state. At that point, the French were able to dispatch to America Samuel de Champlain. He founded Quebec on the St. Lawrence (1608) and Montreal farther upriver three years later. Gallic colonial activity in America decidedly increased after 1624, when Cardinal Richelieu became practically dictator in Paris. Additional migrants were sent to New France (Canada), crops were planted, fur trade with the Indians inaugurated, and explorers dispatched to the interior.

New France remained a disappointment, however. The unfortunate religious fanaticism that denied to French Huguenots entry into Canada turned away thousands of potential settlers who might have infused new life into the territory along the St. Lawrence. Instead, these Protestants enriched British America and France's European rivals. Only French Catholics were welcome in Canada, and most Frenchmen of that persuasion were reasonably satisfied with home conditions, hence few wished to migrate. Another source of weakness in New France resulted from the imposition of feudalism in the northern wilds. Land was granted to seigneurs (nobles), who in turn sublet portions of their domains to tenants called habitants. The independent farmer so characteristic of British America was almost unknown in New France.

Inside Canada little personal liberty was per-

---

[10] The famous New England "triangular trade" flourished during the eighteenth century. Rum was shipped to Africa and traded for slaves. The slaves were transported to the West Indies and bartered for sugar's by-product, molasses, which was carried to New England to make rum—with a handsome profit realized on every point of the triangle.

[11] Struggling establishments at Honduras and Guiana were other British American colonies. Newfoundland, Nova Scotia, and the territory around Hudson Bay in northern Canada were taken from the French in the Treaty of Utrecht (1713). The rest of Canada was snatched in 1763.

mitted; the despotic government in Paris was mirrored in Quebec; and most aspects of social, economic, and intellectual life were meticulously controlled.[12] Finally, the development of New France was far too extensive; rather than restricting themselves to a relatively small area close to water communications with Europe, as had the British, the French dissipated their strength over an immense area reaching from Nova Scotia to the Great Lakes, and from north of the St. Lawrence down to New Orleans and Biloxi on the Gulf of Mexico.[13]

Naturally the Canadian picture had a brighter side. Excluding the powerful Iroquois Confederation, the French were able to command Indian support far more readily than could the English. Primarily traders and trappers rather than farmers, the French could utilize with the tribes the telling argument that their coming did not mean the end of the forests or the termination of the Indian way of life—the British could honestly make no such claim. Peripatetic French fur trappers called *voyageurs* or *coureurs de bois* roamed through the interior of the American continent, discarding European manners and customs to live with the Indians on terms of easy amiability. Courageous Jesuit missionaries defied the most horrible tortures from Iroquois braves and squaws to preach Christianity to the savages. New France's restrictive and closely knit administrative system, which proved so disastrous for the growth of internal development, was able to accomplish military miracles. It is amazing that the French, outnumbered thirty to one by the British Americans during the middle of the eighteenth century, could have fought so effectively. Certainly much was due to French leadership. Especially noteworthy were Count Frontenac, who ruled Canada intermittently during the

late 1600s, and the Marquis de Montcalm, commander of the French forces during the showdown battle for North America (1754 to 1763).

Despite New France's assets, its liabilities predominated. During its entire century and a half of colonial existence, French Canada was never self-sufficient in food supply; to avoid starvation, annual imports of foodstuffs from Europe remained necessary. By 1750 there were almost 1,500,000 inhabitants of Britain's mainland colonies, but only some 50,000 French lived in the extensive North American territories under the lily flag of the Bourbons.

CONTINENTAL CONFLICT

⟨ *First Phases.* The initial Anglo-French clash in the New World had its genesis in European rather than American difficulties.[14] An alliance, headed by King William III of Great Britain (successor to James II), opposed French aggression in the Rhineland and commenced hostilities against Louis XIV. After desultory European fighting, the indecisive Treaty of Ryswick was signed (1697). American colonials had been drawn into action. An English expedition successfully laid siege to Port Royal in Acadia (Nova Scotia); and from Canada Count Frontenac sent war parties, French-led and Indian-manned, which sacked

---

[12] No newspaper—not even a printing press—existed in all New France as late as 1763.

[13] Louisiana (which included all the Mississippi Valley) fell into French possession late in the seventeenth century through the explorations of the Sieur de La Salle, the Jesuit missionary Marquette, the trader Joliet, and others.

[14] Because the terminology used in these seventeenth- and eighteenth-century dynastic struggles is difficult, a brief outline may be helpful:

Dates	European name	American name
1689–1697	War of the League of Augsburg	King William's War
1701–1713	War of the Spanish Succession	Queen Anne's War
1744–1748	War of the Austrian Succession	King George's War
1756–1763	Seven Years' War *	French and Indian War * (1754–1763)

* Since both the European and American names for this decisive struggle are erroneous, the "Great War for the Empire" shall be used throughout this work to cover both European and American aspects.

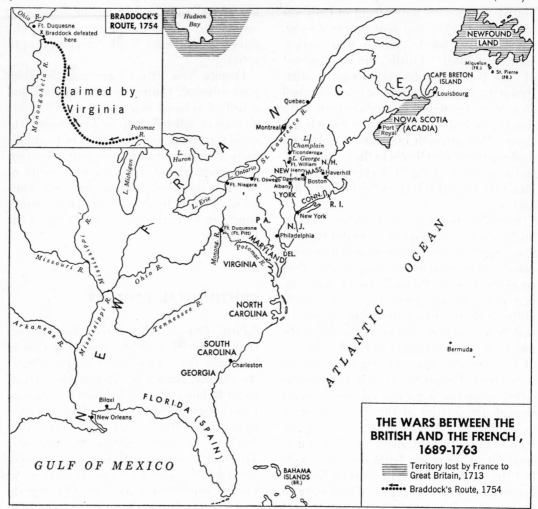

THE WARS BETWEEN THE
BRITISH AND THE FRENCH,
1689-1763

Territory lost by France to
Great Britain, 1713

Braddock's Route, 1754

some settlements along the New York and New England frontiers. It was all rather meaningless; any territory taken was returned at Ryswick.

Within a few years the great powers were at it again, this time over the determination of Louis XIV (the "Sun King") to seat his grandson on the throne of Spain. This War of the Spanish Succession lined up Britain and a few allies against France and Spain. Victory attended English arms in Europe and America. On the Continent, Winston Churchill's illustrious ancestor John Churchill, Duke of Marlborough, mauled the Sun King's troops at Blenheim and other battles. Britain wrested from Spain the strategic Balearic island of Minorca in the Mediterranean and, even more

important, the powerful bastion of Gibraltar between Europe and Africa. In America, French Acadia fell, there was considerable marching and countermarching, and the New England periphery trembled once more before the tomahawks and scalping knives of Canadian Indians who ravaged Deerfield and Haverhill, Massachusetts. Major territorial alterations in America were written into the Treaty of Utrecht (1713). Britain received Newfoundland, Nova Scotia (save for the immediately adjacent island of Cape Breton), and the potentially valuable fur regions around Hudson Bay.

Both English and French America were able to live in relative peace with one another for the next thirty years, despite an occasional Indian foray against New England outposts. While English population in America soared, the French increased very slowly, although Gallic penetration of the western interior continued apace. Again rivalry in Europe broke the tranquility, however, and for the third time blood flowed in America for overseas reasons. Hostilities erupted in 1744 [15] between France, Spain, and Prussia on one side; Great Britain and Austria on the other. Little of importance happened on the Continent. In America, an "army" under Sir William Pepperell startled everyone by capturing France's "impregnable" fortress of Louisbourg on Cape Breton Island. Military experts have since pondered to their total confusion how the ill-trained, semi-mutinous, and disease-racked Yankees were able to accomplish their victory. New England's greatest triumph was thrown away at the Treaty of Aix-la-Chapelle when Louisbourg was returned to France in exchange for the city of Madras in India. Boston's rage and frustration can be imagined. Some balm for Massachusetts' lacerated pride was forthcoming when the British government assumed all costs of the Cape Breton expedition.

(*The Great War for the Empire.* Unlike the first three engagements between Britain and France, the conclusive struggle began on this side of the Atlantic. The Great War for the Empire was truly a world war, fought in America, in Europe, in Asia, and wherever on the high seas belligerent vessels met. To be sure, it was not a modern total war in which the mass of citizens are called upon for great expenditures of manpower and money. Yet the Great War for the Empire must rank as one of the more momentous of modern times. Almost immediately after the end of King George's War, the French decided to check English penetration into the Ohio River Val-

ley by constructing a string of forts between the Great Lakes and the disputed river. A decade or two earlier this might have passed almost unnoticed, but by 1750 English Americans were eagerly calculating the economic possibilities that lay beyond the Appalachians. Prominent colonials—Virginians in the main —formed companies to speculate in French-claimed western lands. A preview to general conflict was shown when Virginia's Governor Dinwiddie sent the youthful George Washington to protest the construction of a French fort at Duquesne (Pittsburgh). Rebuffed, Washington returned the next year (1754) with a small detachment, but was forced to surrender. The British swiftly reacted against this defeat by sending into the forests of western Pennsylvania General Edward Braddock with an army composed of British regulars and colonial auxiliaries. While en route to Fort Duquesne, Braddock fell into an ambush; the general himself was killed, about a third of his army destroyed, and the survivors dispersed.

Braddock's defeat (1755) does not typify the efficacy of the British army under frontier conditions. A stereotype has grown up that shows blundering British professional soldiers wandering helplessly through the American forests, saved from the inevitable result of their incompetence only by hawk-eyed colonial scouts. The facts of the matter are quite different. Braddock's defeat was an exception; the British army was usually about as effective in the tangled wilds overseas as on the cleared battlefields of Europe. Trained British regulars, adept at close bayonet fighting, were more than a match for Frenchmen and Indians and, it must be admitted, for Americans too. Not until late in the American Revolution did our raw recruits become hardened by battle and by such harsh European drillmasters as Von Steuben and De Kalb. The frantic petitions with which colonial legislatures bombarded the British government for troops during the wars with the French bear witness to the worth of the red-coated infantry.

Neither British regular nor colonial militiaman enjoyed much success during the first three years of the Great War for the Empire.

[15] Actually, Britain and Spain had been at war since 1739 in the conflict known by the charming appellation, the "War of Jenkins' Ear." Jenkins, an English smuggler, reported his loss after the Spaniards had separated him from his ear. British public outcry against this atrocity forced the Walpole ministry into partial belligerency toward Spain, which merged with the general war in 1744.

THE STRUGGLE FOR A CONTINENT, 1689-1763

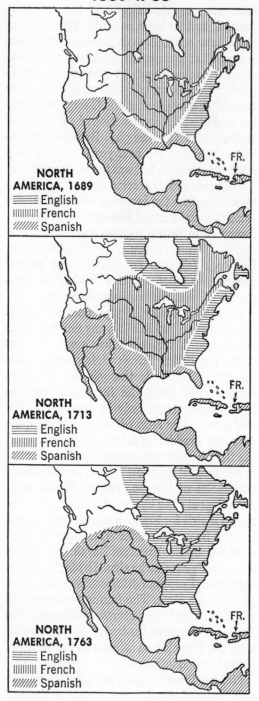

NORTH AMERICA, 1689
≡ English
||||||| French
/////// Spanish

FR.

NORTH AMERICA, 1713
≡ English
||||||| French
/////// Spanish

FR.

NORTH AMERICA, 1763
≡ English
||||||| French
/////// Spanish

FR.

Not only had the western frontier been largely abandoned to the enemy by Braddock's defeat, but flames from burning cabins reddened wintry New England skies in the wake of victorious Canadian war parties. The Marquis de Montcalm, after his capture of Fort Oswego in upstate New York, took Fort William Henry on Lake George and the next year defeated an English army under General Abercrombie, who was attempting to retake the stronghold. By 1757 these military setbacks in America, when combined with European defeats and naval disasters, appeared to forecast a great French victory.

At this dark hour the pendulum commenced to swing the other way. William Pitt the Elder was promoted to the prime minister's post, and new vitality promptly surged through the British war effort. Additional manpower was found, the navy was overhauled and strengthened, and younger, abler officers were promoted over the heads of their do-nothing superiors. A great offensive in America was undertaken. General John Forbes and Lord Jeffrey Amherst cleared the outnumbered French from the Great Lakes area and recaptured control of vital Lakes Champlain and George in northern New York, rolling the enemy back into the St. Lawrence Valley.

The year of British victory in North America was 1759. The skillful General James Wolfe moved against Quebec, but was temporarily foiled by the high cliffs upon which the French stronghold was located. In a daring midnight ascent to the Plains of Abraham on the outskirts of the city, Wolfe forced Montcalm to fight. Both commanders were mortally wounded in the brisk engagement, but victory attended British standards. The conquest of Canada was completed with the fall of Montreal during the next year.

For the first few years of the Great War for the Empire, Frederick the Great of Prussia, England's ally, was in desperate trouble. The powerful alliance of France, Austria, and Russia was too much for him. Yet here too the unfortunate French saw victory snatched away; the defection of Russia, switching from one

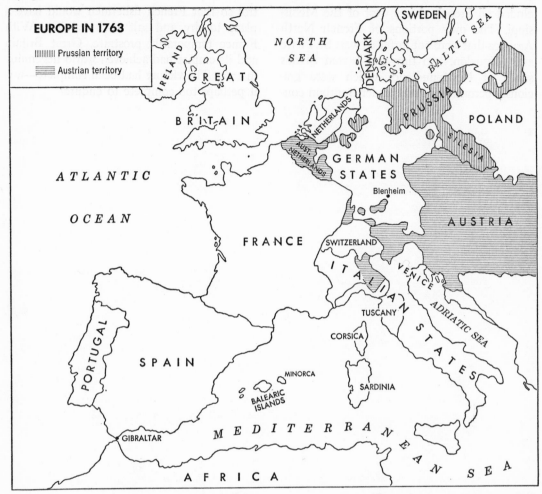

side to the other, enabled the crafty Prussian to defeat his other enemies piecemeal. The same story of French disaster was written in India. An unknown clerk of the British East India Company named Robert Clive proved himself a military genius and was able to destroy combined French and Hindu armies sometimes (as at Plassey in 1757) twenty times the size of his own. Bled white by military defeats all over the world, its navy hopelessly beaten, and its citizens groaning under a tax burden heavy enough to finance both martial endeavors and the riotous extravagances of the dissolute and stupid Louis XV, France was forced to sue for peace in 1763.

Few powers in modern history have suffered more humiliating reversals than did France across the council tables at the Treaty of Paris that ended the war. French territorial ambitions in Europe were thwarted, almost all its holdings in opulent India were lost, and especially in North America was the bitterness of utter disgrace tasted. France kept the valuable West Indian islands of Haiti, Martinique, and Guadeloupe, but lost to Great Britain Canada, the Great Lakes territory, and all lands east of the Mississippi. To compensate its Spanish ally for the loss of Florida,[16] Paris ceded to Madrid Louisiana territory that in-

[16] Spain had entered the war on the side of France in 1761, just in time to lose Cuba and the Philippines to Great Britain. To regain these lost territories, the Spaniards had to abandon Florida to Britain. Florida again reverted to Spain after the American Revolution (1783).

cluded all French claims west of the Mississippi. The only portions of French North America that were not forfeited were St. Pierre and Miquelon, two tiny and barren islands south of Newfoundland, which were graciously permitted to stay under Bourbon control so that French fishermen would have a place to dry and salt their catches. With France temporarily prostrate, Great Britain and its empire had achieved world hegemony in 1763. The victory had been complete—was it perhaps too complete to endure?

CHAPTER 3

Empire Cleavage

(1763-1776)

EARLY CONFLICTS

The successful conclusion of the world conflict against the French intensified problems that had existed in America since the first British colonies there were founded. Wranglings of over a century had failed to delineate precisely where British imperial authority ended and American authority began. Before the heightened crisis (1763 to 1775) can be comprehended, prior differences between the mother country and her colonial brood must be reviewed.

Basic to understanding is a fact so elemental that it is sometimes overlooked: the nature of *time* during the seventeenth and eighteenth centuries. *Distance* has remained constant, but time has been drastically slashed in recent years. Almost 3,000 miles stretch between Britain and America now as they did 200 years ago. But today their crossing is a matter of a few hours—six to eight weeks during the colonial era. This situation meant that it was impossible for the British government to supervise closely its overseas possessions when perhaps three months had to elapse while orders were sent from London across the Atlantic, acted upon there, and reported back to England. Considerable local autonomy burgeoned in America simply because there was no reasonable alternative.

Moreover, British internal conditions during the first half century of American colonization operated to the advantage of considerable self-government. The early Stuarts might have preferred to supervise pervasively their American dominions, but events ruled that royal energies had to be utilized at home preparing for and fighting the civil wars of the mid-seventeenth century. The Puritan Commonwealth, however, was able to increase empire controls—a policy followed by the restored Stuart, Charles II, and markedly accelerated under his successor, James II, during the four years before the latter's ouster in the Glorious Revolution of 1689.

The accession of William and Mary (1689), followed by Anne (1702) and the House of Hanover (1714), somewhat relaxed these British controls, although never after the turn of the new century did the colonials enjoy the freedom that had been theirs from 1607 to 1650. The conclusion of the Great War for the Empire inaugurated considerably stricter controls upon American economic and political activity than had ever been known before.

Controls had been present to some degree all through English colonization on the Atlantic Coast; but after 1763 their frequency and severity noticeably increased, even if British direction seems more remarkable for its relative absence than for exhibiting any grinding oppression.

BRITISH MERCANTILISM AND THE NAVIGATION ACTS

During much of the colonial period, Britain's oversea supervision was animated by the economic policy of mercantilism. The mercantilists maintained that a nation must be self-sufficient in time of war. Two imperatives were a strong merchant marine to transport colonial produce necessary to the home country's domestic economy and a navy powerful enough to protect this commerce. Acting with these ideas in mind, the Puritan Commonwealth, menaced by strong Dutch competition for the English carrying trade, passed the Navigation Act of 1651. Although enacted by a Puritan Parliament that was soon to be repudiated, the economic principles expressed in this first Navigation Act were retained and augmented by subsequent royal action. This initial legislation specified that all goods from Africa, Asia, and America could be transported to England, Ireland, and the British colonies *only* in English, Irish, or colonial ships. European commodities could be imported into England only by English, Irish, or colonial vessels, in addition to the ships of the European nation that produced or manufactured the goods. For example, French wines could be brought into British territory in English, Irish, colonial, or French ships, but not in Dutch, Spanish, Prussian, or any other vessels. It should be noted that American colonials possessed the same privileges in the carrying trade as did Englishmen.

The restoration of the Stuarts in 1660, rather than altering the Puritan Navigation Act of 1651, strengthened and extended it. Two important principles were embodied in the Navi-

gation Act of 1660: first, all trade to and from the colonies had to be carried by British-, Irish-, or colonial-built, owned, commanded, and manned ships; second, certain articles called "enumerated commodities," which were deemed essential for British prosperity and protection, could be exported only to the home islands; and a duty had to be paid before reexport. Among the first items "enumerated" were sugar, tobacco, indigo, dyewoods, and ginger. Rice, copper ore, furs, molasses, and naval stores were some important commodities added during the next century. By 1763 only fish and rum were major American colonial exports that still remained off the enumerated-commodity list.[1]

In 1663 Parliament passed the Act for the Encouragement of Trade, also known as the Staple Act. This legislation attempted to augment colonial purchases in the British market by requiring that most foreign goods en route to America must land in England so that a duty might be levied. This corresponded to a primitive protective tariff, and it was hoped that the duties imposed would be high enough to enable the British merchant to undersell his foreign competitor. The reasonable desire to obtain additional revenue for the royal treasury was another factor that motivated the Staple Act.

It was not long before shrewd American captains found a method to defeat the purposes of enumerated commodities and special duties. Tobacco, let us say, might be shipped from Virginia to Pennsylvania—a transaction which required that no duty be paid, hence that no record of the shipment be kept. When the Virginia tobacco was shipped from Pennsylvania, no duty could be collected. To plug this loophole, the Revenue Act (1673) was passed. The shipper was forced to pay a tax— the "plantation duty"—on the enumerated commodity in the colony where it was origin-

[1] Certain exceptions in the enumerated-commodity list were made in the case of sugar (1739) and rice (1735), which were permitted to be exported directly to that part of Europe south of Cape Finisterre in northern Spain. The best markets, however, were in northern rather than southern Europe.

ally produced. The duty was usually high enough to allow the British shipper to compete on equal terms with his colonial rival. Yet another Navigation Act was passed in 1696 that tightened up previously enacted restrictions and duties and stipulated that special vice-admiralty courts try cases under the Navigation Acts, rather than presumably more lenient juries of fellow-townsmen in the American colony.

The final trade regulation before 1763 was the Molasses Act (1733), which would have been ruinous to colonial prosperity if it had been enforced. Molasses is a by-product of sugar and a basic ingredient in the manufacture of rum. New England, the center of the thriving industry, usually bought molasses in the French West Indies, for the French preferred cognac to rum and were therefore willing to sell molasses far cheaper than could the planters of the British West Indies. The latter's potent lobby in Parliament worked diligently to interfere with this Franco-American trade, and the Molasses Act reflected its accomplishment. The heavy duty of sixpence per gallon on foreign molasses was patently unfair; the British West Indies could not possibly have met the American demand. Hence the Molasses Act was ignored with easy and affable uniformity.

It is difficult to assess how well the Navigation Acts were enforced. Certainly the Molasses Act was violated more commonly than the others. Obviously, however, all of them were broken repeatedly. Two thriving industries of the late seventeenth and early eighteenth centuries were in part spawned by these British trade restrictions. American colonials often sold goods to smugglers to avoid duty payments and bought commodities from pirates. The latter reached their point of greatest number and influence from about 1690 to 1720, when scores of ships flying the "Jolly Roger" infested the sea lanes between the West Indies and the American mainland. Once some honest and efficient colonial governors decided that the pirate menace must be eradicated, that flourishing maritime industry tumbled into a lasting depression.

INTERNAL ECONOMIC CONTROLS

Maritime economics were only a part of the entire British colonial economic picture. As time passed, Britain attempted to formulate some centralized pattern for its empire. Coordinated policy had been almost nonexistent under the early Stuarts, and the Puritan Commonwealth could accomplish little more. The later Stuarts, however, inaugurated a continuous program with the appointment of the Lords of Trades and Plantations, a standing committee of the Privy Council. In 1696, the Lords of Trade gave way to a new committee, the Board of Trade, which became permanent. The Board was given the tremendous responsibility of furnishing information about empire economics to the Crown and to Parliament, instructing the royal governors, and reading all colonial legislation to see that it was not contrary to British law. Even if the Board had little direct authority, its recommendations tended to be acted upon favorably by Parliament or the Cabinet.[2]

Advice from the Board of Trade was primarily founded upon mercantilist economic philosophy. The mercantilists held that the chief value of the colonies was to supply the mother country with the raw materials needed for home industry. Therefore, colonial attempts to manufacture finished products were viewed with hostility; from time to time Parliamentary legislation tried to curb such practice. In 1699 the Woolens Act forbade the export of American wool and woolen textiles to Britain. More serious was the Hat Act (1732). British hatters were dependent upon pelts from the colonies to make the popular beaver-fur hats. Instead of exports of the pelts alone, finished American hats began to appear in England. In response to domestic protests, limitations were placed upon the American hat industry; and exports of hats from one

[2] As Parliament's influence waxed during the early eighteenth century, the powers of the Privy Council declined, and a Cabinet, responsible to a parliamentary majority, acted on policy matters. The Cabinet minister overseeing American colonial affairs was "The Secretary of State for the Southern Department."

colony to another, as well as from America to Britain, were forbidden. Although its provisions were often disregarded, the flourishing American hat industry received a crippling blow from this legislation. Policy of a similar nature motivated the Iron Act (1750). Raw iron in the form of pig or bar ingots was encouraged by a bounty, but American forges were forbidden to produce finished iron products. Violations of this enactment were common, but again, some hardship was forthcoming.

Parliamentary restrictions upon American monetary activity were similarly resented. Almost inevitably, any colonial area tends to be short of specie unless it possesses gold or silver mines. Without mines, however, the unfavorable balance of trade resulting from the export of cheap raw materials and the necessity to purchase more expensive manufactured products from the mother country is apt to drain the colonial supply of hard money. Even though French, Spanish, Portuguese, and Dutch money circulated as freely as did English, the American settlements were perpetually short of coin. Attempts to mint their own currency, as did Massachusetts Bay with its pine-tree shilling, were debarred. Therefore the colonials turned to paper money, and a rash of paper, bills of credit, notes, and even tobacco receipts broke out along the seaboard from New Hampshire to Georgia. A parliamentary ban on colonial paper money (1751) was followed by considerable grumbling from American debtors who desired high prices and easy-to-get currency.

It must not be thought that British economic legislation operated only against colonial interests, for many favors were also bestowed. If the Navigation Acts removed certain goods from free export, the British government paid bounties for masts, naval stores, indigo, and other commodities that were urgently needed by Great Britain. In addition, as part of the British Empire, the western settlements enjoyed the right to trade in a rich market, access to which was denied other nations. Open to all colonial Americans were the tropical riches of the British West Indies

and the lucrative English domestic market. As later generations were to discover, the wrench of dislocation from empire economic privileges was probably the highest price paid for American independence.

INTRACOLONIAL SQUABBLES

American colonists were a rambunctious and contentious lot. They quarreled among themselves over boundary lines and land claims, debated vociferously their religious rights, fought Frenchman and Indian, and with monotonous regularity aired the intracolonial dislike of the western back country for the tidewater—a sentiment that was cordially returned. It is therefore not surprising to find conflicts between the royal governor of a colony, representing the Crown, and the local assembly, representing at least some of the people. On occasion these disputes erupted into open rebellion, especially if the governor appeared to exceed his authority. Nathaniel Bacon led Virginians against the highhanded and choleric Governor William Berkeley during 1675–1676, furious over the latter's refusal to control the Indians. After some success, the uprising collapsed following Bacon's untimely death from disease; and the vindictive Berkeley was able to crush the revolt with sufficient brutality to prompt a surprised observation from the easygoing Charles II: "The old fool has hanged more men in that naked country than I have for the murder of my father."

A decade later James II attempted to introduce a measure of Stuart absolutism into New England and New York. Annulling the Massachusetts Bay charter in 1684, James combined New Hampshire, Plymouth, Connecticut, Rhode Island, and Massachusetts Bay with New York and New Jersey under the title of "The Territory and Dominion of New England." Sir Edmund Andros was appointed governor, all colonial legislatures were abolished, the Anglican Church was established (to the horror of Puritan Bostonians), property holders were threatened with quitrents, and taxation without any form of representation was installed. Although diligent and scrupulously honest, Andros was tactless, humorless, and despotic. Hostility and unrest were growing throughout the Dominion of New England when the welcome news reached America that James II had been overthrown. With collective enthusiasm Bostonians escorted Andros to jail and subsequently deported him to Great Britain. There were other local revolts against Andros, particularly in New York, where the populace rose under Jacob Leisler, although Leisler's democratic leanings soon lost him the favor of more conservative New Yorkers, who were able to execute him after a farcical trial (1691). Everywhere the Dominion of New England quietly fell to pieces.

The instances cited above are only the more prominent and the more violent of the continuing struggles between the royal governor and his American subjects. Royal government had become increasingly dominant along the Atlantic Coast as the years passed, until the late eighteenth century saw only Connecticut and Rhode Island as self-governing, and Pennsylvania, Delaware, and Maryland as proprietary colonies. The government of Massachusetts Bay might be described as "quasi-royal." [3] In the royal colonies the governor found himself in a most unfortunate position, since much of his salary was usually dependent upon appropriations by the provincial assembly. Thus the governor was caught between the frying pan of colonial popular opinion and the fire of British imperial policy. If he refused to countenance colonial demands, he paid through the pocketbook; if he listened too closely to his constituents, he might be discharged by the king. Usually the governor tended to take his chances with royal displeasure on the understandable ground that he preferred to eat. Therefore many of the colonial governors were willing to side with the

[3] After the overthrow of Andros, Massachusetts Bay received a new charter (1691). Although the colony gained more local autonomy than it had been permitted under the Dominion of New England, Massachusetts Bay was never as free from royal control as it had been before the abrogation of the first charter.

colonials, and others earned some popularity through sheer ability alone. New York's Cadwallader Colden and Massachusetts Bay's Sir William Phips and William Shirley exemplified the better governors. There were also some unmitigated scoundrels whose presence tended to taint the over-all picture of British colonial government.

In the majority of England's American possessions, the governor's Council was appointed by the Crown or by the governor himself, save in Massachusetts Bay. The Assembly—the lower house—was popularly elected, yet nowhere in the American colonies was universal manhood suffrage permitted. If religious restrictions upon the franchise gradually lessened, property qualifications for voting became more common. The colonial legislatures, although representing only a fraction of the potential electorate, assumed for themselves many of the prerogatives of sovereign governments, particularly in the matter of taxation, as the Assemblies stepped in to fill the absence of direct control from England that distance created. After 1763 the British commenced to insist upon parliamentary superiority over all relatively autonomous colonial governments and brought on a situation pregnant with the likelihood of American resistance.

IMPERIAL TENSIONS

《 *The British Point of View* (1763). Despite bickerings and even rebellions during the century and a half of British settlement in America, most colonials were well satisfied with their status in 1763; and it would take decisive happenings to destroy their feeling of unity. Loyal subjects of His Britannic Majesty on both sides of the Atlantic exulted deeply and proudly over their recent triumph in the Great War for the Empire. A shameful defeat had been inflicted upon France; never before had the British Empire stood upon so lofty a world pinnacle. Yet in the very moment of greatest victory, forces were operating in both the dependencies and the mother country that would shatter imperial bonds.

If the success over the French had been un-precedented, so too were the martial costs. Englishmen feared that their country could not stand under a public debt of £136 million [4] —trifling in comparison to modern astro-nomical deficits, but shocking to a more con-servative eighteenth-century viewpoint. Who would pay off this debt? Many Englishmen in-sisted that the war had been fought primarily for colonial purposes, that Americans had profited exceedingly by the removal of the French menace, and that the colonials should manfully shoulder some of the financial lia-bilities which had been part of victory's cost. Particularly insistent on this point were the English landed gentry, who objected to their tax burden of 20 per cent on income. Unlike most other British classes of that time, the country squires were adequately represented by the contemporary electoral system, and they were in a position to force Parliament to heed their complaints.

The Parliament that echoed with land-owners' appeals for taxation relief was a most peculiar organization. The last reapportion-ment of English electoral districts had been accomplished in medieval times, and later population shifts resulted in some areas being overrepresented and others underrepresented. Many parliamentary districts, called "rotten boroughs" or "pocket boroughs," had been thriving communities during the fifteenth cen-tury, but by the eighteenth had declined. In-deed, Dunwich was completely underwater by 1750 because of erosion of the coastline, but still sent to Parliament two representatives ap-pointed by the individual who held title to the land. By this time the Industrial Revolution was already commencing to transform the English midlands; thousands of displaced farmers and city artisans were moving to the textile factories springing up at Manchester, Birmingham, Sheffield, and Leeds. These man-ufacturing districts, however, were almost

completely unrepresented.[5] Englishmen found it hard to take seriously the complaints of American colonials that taxation without rep-resentation was illegal when so many of their British compatriots found themselves in pre-cisely that situation.

Moreover, there was no clear-cut party di-vision in the Parliament of that day. The old-line tories of early Georgian times had been largely discredited through their participation in the Jacobite disorders of 1745; the trium-phant Whigs had split into quarreling personal factions that maintained uneasy and ephem-eral coalitions through the attraction of public graft. The parliamentary personnel was for the most part unfit to direct complicated prob-lems of domestic and foreign policy. Hard-drinking, hard-riding, provincially minded country squires vied for forensic honors with the henchmen of dissolute noblemen, and neither were impressive public servants. Po-litical offices were bought and sold, contracts awarded by bribery, and important positions showered upon unworthy relatives. There were able men in Westminster—students of govern-mental philosophy, hard-working and intelli-gent administrators, and those who were sensi-tive to popular opinion at home and abroad. The general level of parliamentary member-ship, however, was at its nadir during the late 1700s.

These unfortunate conditions were further complicated by the recently crowned mon-arch, George III. In 1714 Queen Anne had died without surviving children; and the throne passed to the next of kin, the German Elector of Hanover who became George I. This king and his son, George II, took little interest in British affairs, including the Eng-lish language. The growth of a Cabinet re-sponsible to Parliament was given some im-petus by the disinclination of the first two Georges to attend Cabinet sessions held in an incomprehensible tongue. George III, how-

[4] This was approximately $700 million. It should be recalled that the purchasing power of any monetary unit was far higher in the eighteenth century than it is today.

[5] While Parliamentary electoral reform was in the air late in the 1780s, reaction from the French revolu-tionary excesses intervened, and about a half century passed before the Reform Bill of 1832 led to reappor-tionment.

ever, had been brought up as an Englishman and resolved to rule his domains personally. He had intelligence enough to realize that the era of divine-right monarchs had passed forever in Britain. In order to rule he had to control Parliament; and this he did by carefully bribing some of the ubiquitous personal factions, who became known as "the King's friends." The King was unable to resist dabbling in matters of imperial policy for temporary political advantage. One would have to be the most fatuous of optimists to expect a government headed by such a monarch and such a Parliament to evince the delicate and responsible statesmanship necessary to handle the extremely thorny problems that remained to be solved after 1763.

(*The American Point of View* (1763). American vistas were as confused as the British. The vast majority of colonials had joined their English cousins in celebrating the victory over the French. Indeed, the writings of contemporary Americans showed unmistakably that the colonial sense of belonging in the British Empire was at an unprecedented apex. But the dual motivations that run in torrents through history were operating at this time. Concurrently with the height of empire solidarity came an increase in attitudes of American independence. Both pro- and anti-British sentiments were simultaneously in existence, and both were extremely important; now one and now the other was on top from 1763 to 1775. Finally certain forces were intensified that led to America's development as an independent nation rather than as a growing and finally a leading member of an earlier British Commonwealth of Nations—which might have evolved.

Perhaps the changed international-power status in North America was the leading cause for an increase in American restiveness inside the empire. Apprehension of French attack no longer kept the colonies huddled close to the mother country for protection. English soldiers, formerly welcomed in America for their military efficiency, were regarded after 1763 as expensive nuisances at best and as minions of a ruthless despotism at worst. Some perceptive individuals had recognized that crushing the French in America might result in losing an American empire for Great Britain. The sage French Foreign Minister, the Comte de Vergennes, was particularly sure that such would be the future.

America's hostility to Britain between 1763 and 1776 developed in spurts, sometimes afire, sometimes quiescent, dependent both on the particular policy of Parliament at any given time and on the existence of internal prosperity or depression in America. Without question, only a tiny handful of Americans looked to independence as a solution to colonial dilemmas before 1776. Except for such incipient rebels as Samuel Adams and a few others, most Americans were sincere when they endlessly reiterated that they strove only for their rights as Englishmen. It took armed conflict during 1775–1776, a culmination of economic grievances, the British decision to hire mercenary troops, and some inspired propaganda by articulate pamphleteers to swing many Americans to decide that the end of their rainbow was beyond the British Empire.

Generalizations applying to the thirteen-year period before American independence are difficult to form. The controversies raging between colonies and inside colonies were as intricate as the disputes disturbing British-American relations. Colonial social cleavages were deep, although not solidified and stratified to the European extent. Democratically inclined small farmers harassed the wealthier and more aristocratic classes for debtor relief. The back-country west clamored against the unjust representation accorded it in colonial legislatures. Rich and poor clashed in the cities. Those who held human rights to be the basis of liberty vied against others who were more interested in property rights. Many of these intracolonial quarrels merged with the aggravated relations between America and Britain, making solutions even more difficult to attain.

Most Americans agreed on one cardinal

point in their relations with Great Britain. This philosophy was best articulated by John Dickinson of Pennsylvania in his influential work, *Letters from a Farmer*. . . . Dickinson conceded that Parliament had certain *external* rights such as regulation of trade and commerce, but that it did not have the *internal* right to tax America, for the latter legislation belonged only to the assemblies in the several colonies. To the British this argument was simply verbiage; Parliament was the supreme lawmaking body of the empire, and its enactments applied anywhere in British territory. The relative ideological unity of Americans as expressed by Dickinson lasted until warfare with the mother country broke out in 1775. At that point American opinion split into the twin camps of "patriot" and "loyalist."

STRENGTHENED CONTROLS AND HEIGHTENED RESISTANCE

Once the Great War for the Empire was over and recognition of colonial problems had arisen, parliamentary legislation regarding America tended to fall into three categories: to settle outstanding military problems, to raise revenue for the royal exchequer, and to assert the principle of parliamentary supremacy over any component parts of the empire. After 1763 Britain found itself master not only of Canada but also of the vast territory west of the Appalachians, south of the Great Lakes, and east of the Mississippi. This area was menaced by a great Indian threat organized by the noted Ottawa chief Pontiac. The tribes were restive at continued white encroachment into their lands, and under this stimulus unified behind Pontiac. In 1765 the Indians erupted in widespread hostilities. All the frontier posts save Fort Pitt, Fort Niagara, and Detroit fell to the scalping knife, and the devastation spread from the mountains to the Mississippi. Not for over a year were the Indians finally defeated; and although Pontiac was pardoned, his prestige was shattered. Soon the Indians reverted to their usual state of tribal

animosity, but the danger of their unification remained.

Especially disappointing to British officialdom was that Pontiac's rebellion occurred while the Crown was attempting to placate the Indians. Hoping to ward off Indian warfare, Britain incurred the enmity of American frontiersmen. By 1763 the vanguard of Western migration was spilling over the Appalachians; if it were halted, the Indians might stay at peace. By the Royal Proclamation of 1763 the trans-Appalachian frontier was closed to settlement from the East, reserving the region for the Indians. Land-hungry colonials, especially those who were speculating in the Ohio country, were outraged at this arbitrary fiat; and, typically, they ignored its provisions and continued to move across the mountains. Obviously the royal proclamation failed to calm the Indians.

If the back country was dissatisfied with imperial western policy, the seaboard was filled with irate consternation at the news that Lord Grenville had pushed through Parliament sweeping legislation pertaining to America. The Navigation Acts were to be enforced, a new Molasses Act (the Sugar Act of 1764) would reduce the tax on that West Indian import but insist that it be paid, and 10,000 British troops would be sent to the colonies. Resistance to these enactments was increasing, when the announcement of a new tax to raise revenue in America brought the storm to a head.

This catalytic agent was Grenville's Stamp Act (1765), stipulating that a stamp would have to be affixed to all legal documents, books (collected sermons were best-selling items), newspapers, college diplomas, bills of lading, and letters of credit. Parliament had passed the bill almost without debate; after all, the rates were not excessive, and Americans would be appointed stamp-tax collectors. British authorities on both sides of the Atlantic were unprepared for the hurricane of opposition engendered by the Stamp Act; but if they had considered the measure more thoroughly, they might have avoided their folly. Hardest hit were colonial newspaper editors, clergymen,

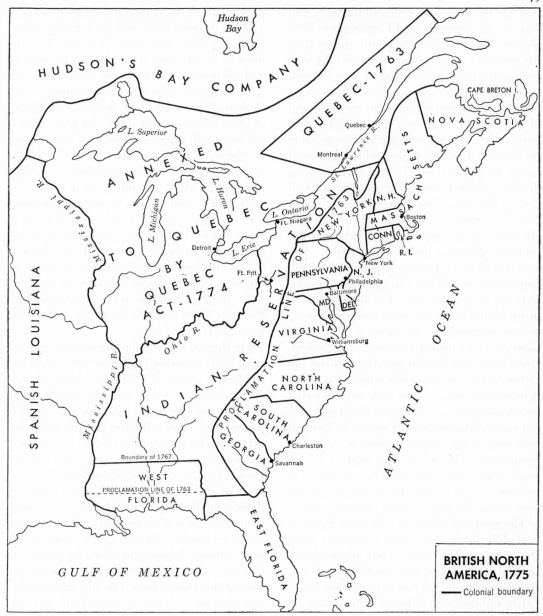

BRITISH NORTH AMERICA, 1775
—— Colonial boundary

teachers, lawyers, and merchants. All these have the common peculiarity of being both vocal and able to command an audience. Resistance to the Stamp Act was quickly brewed through sulfurous editorials, sermons drawing a close comparison between Grenville and Antichrist, commencement addresses rich with classical allusion to resistance against tyranny, and philippics hurled by merchant- or lawyer-politicians in colonial legislatures.

Patrick Henry openly defied King George. Those bemused Americans who saw a chance to make some easy money as stamp-tax collectors either abruptly resigned or became the guests of honor at local tar-and-feather parties.

While American opposition to the Stamp Act was at its height, a congress composed of delegates from nine colonies met in New York to protest "taxation without representation" and to threaten economic reprisals. The second was the more important; all the noise and fury of the congress could accomplish little until nonimportation agreements against British products were started. The ensuing protests of British merchants facing ruin through the loss of American markets forced both Grenville's resignation and the speedy repeal of the Stamp Act in 1766. On receipt of this cheery news, a wave of rejoicing swept along the Atlantic Coast, complete with testimonial banquets, parades, and iterated statements of devotion to the Crown. Few colonists noticed that, at the same time it repealed the Stamp Act, Parliament had quietly passed the Declaratory Act stating that Parliament was the supreme legislative body of the empire.

With the fall of the Grenville ministry, William Pitt became Prime Minister; but ill-health soon caused him to retire. The British government drifted leaderless until power was more or less assumed by the brilliant but erratic Charles ("Champagne Charlie") Townshend, Chancellor of the Exchequer. Townshend fell victim to the sophistry with which Americans deluded themselves: that colonials objected only to direct taxation such as the Stamp Act, but that they would tolerate special levies upon individual commodities as long as they were indirect taxes. He was 100 per cent wrong. As events during the American Revolution were to demonstrate, eighteenth-century Americans opposed taxation of any kind from any source.

The good will that had existed since the repeal of the Stamp Act vanished in a trice when the so-called Townshend Acts placed levies on lead, glass, paper, and tea (1767). Townshend soon died, but his policies were obstinately and doggedly followed by his successor, Lord North. Growling colonial resentment characterized the next three years, and by 1770 British exports to America had been halved because of resurrected nonimportation agreements.

Further tension was produced by the dispatch to Boston of British troops who had to be quartered in this "hot-bed of sedition" where colonial resentment was particularly strong. The British army of that time was poorly paid (and sometimes not paid at all), and its soldiers were subjected to the most ruthless punishment from their officers.[6] Armies of occupation are seldom very popular with civilians; as Kipling said, "Single men in barracks don't grow into plaster saints." Bostonians differed not a whit from other citizens of other times in their dislike for professional soldiery, and their contempt was augmented by the willingness of unpaid infantrymen to accept odd jobs in the cities so that they would not starve. Mobs of unruly men and boys whiled away winter hours stoning or iceballing sentries. On 5 March 1770, overt hostilities broke out in Boston when harassed British soldiers fired into a disorderly crowd. The efficacy of Revolutionary propaganda can be seen in the term used to describe this sordid episode. "The Boston Massacre" is the phrase that has thundered down the halls of time. Precisely five were killed.[7]

On the very day that bullets answered snowballs in Massachusetts, Parliament, cowed by the frantic appeals of British merchants to conciliate America so that nonimportation agreements would be canceled, repealed all the Townshend Acts, with the exception of the tax on tea. Once more Britain had surrendered to colonial pressure, and empire skies lightened with the dawn of approximately three years of good will. At about the same time a depression that had dogged the 1760s came to an end, and a more prosperous America was easier to handle. Disgusted at all this sweetness, Samuel Adams and other fire-eaters organized Committees of Correspondence among the radical groups in the several colonies and endeavored to keep high one another's spirits while awaiting new opportunities to stir up trouble. Their unrelenting vigilance was rewarded in 1773.

[6] The term "lobster-back" that was hurled by taunting crowds at British regulars was not, as is usually supposed, in reference to their bright scarlet uniforms, but rather to the effects of savage beatings which bloodied the backs of the unfortunate recipients.

[7] Furthermore, the soldiers responsible were tried for murder. John Adams, among others, defended the accused at the trial. Two were found guilty of manslaughter and branded on the thumb.

THE CRISIS DEEPENS

The event that precipitated the dramatic sequence leading toward open warfare between Britain and America concerned the British East India Company. This Asiatic giant had a huge oversupply of tea bulging its warehouses. The royal government listened sympathetically to the Company's cry for aid and decided to grant it a monopoly in the American market. To make it difficult for colonials to resist its blandishments, the Crown lowered the tea duty from twelvepence to threepence a pound. This meant that tea shipped from the Orient to England and transshipped to America sold at a cheaper price than tea in England and even undersold American smugglers. The radical Committees of Correspondence perceived that the Tea Act menaced their whole program of resistance to "illegal" taxing power. They combined with the alarmed smuggling interests to bar East India tea from America. In varying localities diverse action followed. In South Carolina the tea was landed but locked in warehouses. In New York and Philadelphia the tea ships were driven off. In Boston, however, resistance became open. Sam Adams and his confreres assembled in ludicrous Mohawk Indian disguises, complete with feathers, blankets, and war paint. Boarding the tea ships, they festooned the waters of Boston Harbor with £15,000 worth of East India Company's best.

This was the last straw for the outraged British government. Many irate Englishmen decided that if these "benighted colonials" would not accept the Tea Act's generous terms, the time for gentle consideration had passed, lest the whole empire be lost by default. To punish the New England insurgents, four "Intolerable Acts"—again we see that wonderful Revolutionary terminology—were whipped through Parliament. The port of Boston was closed except to foodstuffs until payment for the destroyed tea was forthcoming, the charter of 1691 was abrogated and self-government taken from Massachusetts, British officials charged with capital crimes in any colony could be taken to another province or to England for trial, and a Quartering Act gave power to commandeer buildings for soldiers' barracks. A fifth piece of legislation is usually included among the Intolerable Acts although it is dissimilar to the first four. The Quebec Act granted to Canada control of the trans-Appalachian West despite claims to these lands by Massachusetts, Connecticut, Pennsylvania, and Virginia. Furthermore, the Catholics of Quebec were given full political, legal, and religious rights. Although this might appear to be a commendable instance of religious toleration, Americans were quick to point out that Britain refused to follow the same course at home.[8]

The Massachusetts Committee of Correspondence quickly notified the other colonies about the British crackdown in the Bay region, advancing the argument that when one is in bondage, the liberties of all are threatened. Its appeal fell upon ready ears; both special conventions and colonial legislatures nominated delegates to a congress that met in Philadelphia during 1774. The First Continental Congress was split between radicals and conservatives. The former successfully promoted the Suffolk Resolutions from Massachusetts, calling for resistance to the Intolerable Acts and any other manifestations of British oppression. Conservative spokesman Joseph Galloway of Pennsylvania countered with a demand that representatives from all the colonies should convene in an American assembly that should have the power to control taxation, Indian affairs, and the common defense.[9] In addition, Galloway stated that legislation pertaining to America should have to pass both the American assembly and the British Parliament. The radicals won the narrowest possible victory

[8] The point was well taken. English Catholics were not allowed complete political rights until 1829.

[9] Galloway's plan was reminiscent of the one advocated by Benjamin Franklin at the Albany congress (1754). Franklin had hoped that an intercolonial assembly would control a provincial army, settle public-land questions, and levy taxes. Nothing came of this audacious attempt; opposition from both sides of the Atlantic was too intense.

when Galloway's motion lost by a single vote. The Continental Congress proceeded to pass widespread nonimportation, nonexportation, and nonconsumption agreements. Soon patriot-controlled "Continental Associations" were established to enforce compliance to these embargoes. The associations were powerful enough to intimidate American merchants who might have continued to trade with the mother country. The strain on the bonds of empire unity was becoming almost unbearable.

TO ARMS!

While Americans were discussing actions of the Congress in Philadelphia, an armed quasi-peace dragged on in Boston. General Thomas Gage, commander of the British garrison there, listened with growing apprehension to reports that local militia units (the "Minute Men") were training throughout the Massachusetts countryside and that military supplies were being amassed. By the spring of 1775 Gage decided that a show of British force was imperative. On the evening of 18 April some 800 English troops left Boston, heading toward Concord 20 miles to the west. Their orders were to arrest Samuel Adams and John Hancock, two of the more prominent New England radicals, at Lexington, and to seize the munitions stored at Concord. Patriot couriers from Boston managed to warn the countryside, and when the British arrived at Lexington Common early on the morning of the 19th, resistance was offered by about seventy Minute Men. In a brief skirmish, eight of the latter were killed.

The British marched on to Concord, where the farmers from miles around had swarmed to guard "the rude bridge which arched the flood" leading to the military depot. Outnumbered, the British were checked and were forced to retreat toward Boston, harassed all the way by snipers. The exhausted redcoats (they had marched about 30 miles by this time) were saved from complete annihilation by the arrival of a relief expedition at Lexington, and the reinforced army managed to fight its way back into Boston. Within a few days, organizations of Minute Men from all the surrounding area closed on Boston and besieged the city.

Spurred on by the news from Massachusetts, the Second Continental Congress met at Philadelphia on 10 May 1775, the radicals enjoying greater representation than they had in the first Congress. Conservatives were reassured by solemn avowals that the radicals' aim was not American independence, but the radical delegates acted differently from the way they spoke. Quickly they ordered an army to be raised and appointed George Washington as its commander in chief. During the fourteen months that intervened before 4 July 1776, Congress set up special committees to oversee the army; founded a navy; issued letters of marque and reprisal to privateers; [10] wrestled with the problem of financial solvency; and, most important of all, dispatched envoys to Europe to seek foreign aid. Almost despite itself, the Second Continental Congress found it necessary to act as an independent government. No other course was open; as the rebellion continued, the established regimes throughout the colonies began to collapse. Responding to a query from New Hampshire during January, 1776, about what should be done since its royal governor had fled, the Congress told it to go ahead and set up its own government. During the succeeding months other erstwhile colonies followed New Hampshire's example.

As late as the winter of 1775–1776 many Americans, even in Congress, continued to work for peace and a restored empire; but soon growing proindependence sentiments were discernible. By the spring of 1776, Forts Ticonderoga and Crown Point in the New York lake region had fallen to American standards, two

---

[10] These "letters" were commissions granted to merchant seamen to prey on enemy shipping in time of war. Without letters of marque and reprisal, captured crews were liable to prosecution as pirates. In both the Revolution and the War of 1812, privateers inflicted much greater damage to British sea power than could the minuscule American navy.

colonial expeditions had attempted to seize Canada, and the British had been forced to evacuate Boston.[11] As blood continued to flow and mutual atrocity stories circulated ever wider, the former colonies and the mother country drifted farther apart. Certainly the British government was not conciliatory during this period. By the end of 1775, London had proclaimed the colonies in rebellion, severed all trade relations with the dependencies, and hired foreign mercenary troops. The last action was particularly distasteful to Americans. British army recruitment had been so slow and so unenthusiastic that the Crown felt forced to turn abroad for assistance. Despicable German princes sold thousands of their subjects into the British army for several pounds a head and lavished their recompense on mistresses or to ape the French court. These unlucky "Hessians" (the majority were from Hesse in western Germany or from the Duchy of Brunswick) were simple peasants snatched from their farms and sent 3,000 miles to fight in a war utterly meaningless to them. Of course Americans were outraged that their king would hire foreigners to impose his despotism upon his own subjects.

Sentiments of American independence were fostered not only by the advent of Hessian brigades, but also by the growing realization that European aid would be extended only to a free people. The great powers were not disposed to interfere in a quarrel between an English king and his subjects while the latter were attempting to secure only more extensive rights as Englishmen. French Foreign Minister Vergennes told Americans in Paris that although France sympathized with the rebellion, no direct intervention could be undertaken by his nation while the colonists remained inside the British Empire. Of course, he pointed out, citizens of an autonomous American confederation engaged in active hostilities with Great Britain would be considered in quite a different light. When his opinion was reported back to Congress, many in that body perceived that independence was an imperative first step toward winning French assist-

[11] See pp. 54–55.

ance; and without European intervention, it was difficult to foresee total American victory.

Fortunately for those who were determined to slash all bonds with Britain, an expatriate Englishman named Thomas Paine had landed in America during 1774. Paine, "the Friend of Mankind," was a staunch enemy of oppression wherever it existed, and he embraced the patriot cause with ardor. His argument for independence was announced in his famous pamphlet, *Common Sense*, which forthwith became one of the best sellers in American history. The two and a quarter million colonials purchased over 120,000 copies; and most Americans, if not actual buyers, probably borrowed the pamphlet or had it read to them. Paine argued that reconciliation was impossible with "The Royal Brute, George III," who would always sacrifice American interest on the altar of British selfish advantage. Independence was, therefore, the only feasible solution to the dilemma. Paine's facile pen later rendered additional service. During the Revolution's darkest hour he wrote a second pamphlet entitled *The Crisis* in which he castigated fainthearted Americans as "summer soldiers" and "sunshine patriots." Washington and other Revolutionary leaders admitted the tremendous debt owed by the rebel cause to Tom Paine.[12]

JEFFERSON'S DECLARATION

Events of 1775–1776 had widened the rift between Great Britain and America to such an extent that there was little reason for surprise when Richard Lee of Virginia arose in the Continental Congress on 7 June 1776, to ask passage of a resolution stating that "These

[12] Paine remained in America until the somewhat more conservative days of the late 1780s. He then traveled to France, became a revolutionary there, was elected a member of the constituent assembly, and because of his affiliation with the Girondin faction was almost guillotined by Robespierre. Paine returned to Britain for a time and then came to America, where he died in poverty (1808). Conservatives never forgave his *The Age of Reason*, an attack on organized religion.

United Colonies are, and of Right ought to be, Free and Independent States." [13] The resolution was tabled for a few weeks while a committee composed of John Adams, the venerable Benjamin Franklin, and Thomas Jefferson worked on the proper literary form for a declaration of principles. Lee's motion was finally adopted on 2 July 1776, and that should be our Independence Day. Jefferson's Declaration of Independence was adopted on 4 July and sent to the printer.

The Declaration of Independence is a most important manifesto of human freedom, even if Jefferson's bold language described rather than caused the actual break with England. The words are Jefferson's, although he had the help of Adams and Franklin, who read (and toned down) his first draft. Yet the philosophy is John Locke's. Some of the language and most of the thoughts found in the Declaration are from Locke's *Second Treatise on Government*, although this should not suggest that Jefferson was a plagiarist. He had steeped himself in Locke's writings for so long that it was second nature to repeat them unconsciously.

Both Locke's *Second Treatise* and Jefferson's Declaration illustrate that the way of life changes first and that men form their philosophical and ideological justifications later. The Glorious Revolution of 1689 had already ousted the Stuarts when Locke wrote that men had instituted governments with restricted powers. If a government exceeded its delegated rights and moved toward absolutism, it was the duty of citizens to change that government, by force if necessary. In a similar manner Jefferson was itemizing the reasons why Americans had already risen against the Crown. Anthropologists feel that Locke's social-contract theory is incorrect. Rather than arising from free choice, primitive governments evolved as the strong imposed their rule

[13] Virginia had already proclaimed its independence (15 May 1776).

over the weak. But this is relatively immaterial. The genesis of eighteenth-century liberalism came largely from the belief that the ruled had unalterable rights—and the world is better for that creed.

The Declaration of Independence is divided into three parts. The preamble carries the clarion call that ". . . all men are created equal; that they are endowed by their Creator with certain inalienable rights . . . life, liberty, and the pursuit of happiness." The second portion falls under the heading of propaganda. Animosity is usually better focused upon an individual than upon either a group or an institution. For this reason, Jefferson attacked George III personally as if the King had been a divine-right monarch. Despite the fact that almost all disputes between 1763 and 1775 had been with Parliament, Jefferson itemized some twenty-seven specific charges against George III. The third and final segment repeated Lee's resolution calling for independence and went on to assert that "These United Colonies" had all the rights of any sovereign nation, including levying war, concluding peace, making alliances, and establishing commercial relations with other countries.

It took great courage to take the momentous step of dissociation from the 160 years through which America had been part of the British Empire. Ties of blood, ancestral memories, common literary and artistic backgrounds, economic bonds, and political unity made separation both a poignant and a serious move. The act of independence automatically made traitors of all who signed it; and they were indeed henceforth pledging, as Jefferson wrote, "our lives, our fortunes, and our sacred honor." Yet by the summer of 1776 the Continental Congress could hardly avoid independence. Almost fifteen months of warfare had forced the partial dissolution of the empire; the signatories of the Declaration were recognizing only that which had already been accomplished.

CHAPTER 4

The American Revolution

(1776-1783)

AMERICAN WEAKNESSES

❨ *The Congress and the Armed Forces.* The tasks facing the new American nation were herculean enough to dishearten the most starry-eyed patriot. A prime essential for any government, especially in wartime, is to have the power to act. Before the adoption of the Articles of Confederation in 1781 the Continental Congress had no real authority, and not very much after that. Prior to 1781 Congress lacked many basic powers. There was no executive, no administrative organizer to channel divergent efforts into a cohesive policy. Congressional committees acted in executive capacities in a few fields; but without centralized direction, true leadership was impossible. The Congress had no power to tax, although it could request financial assistance from the sovereign states. It had no right to assemble soldiers for the army—again the states were supposed to act. During most of the Revolution, Congress was simply a recommending body; and as often as not the states ignored its appeals. It is a wonder not that the Revolutionary Congress was so inefficient, but that it could have done anything at all.

Above all, the Continental government had to oversee as best it could the raising, equipping, and maintaining of an army. If the American Revolution is to be comprehended, notions about modern war's "nation in arms," with total mobilization and a regimented economy, must immediately be discarded. In a country of over two and a quarter million inhabitants enjoying the highest standard of living in the eighteenth-century world, George Washington was never able to command more than 25,000 men in the Continental army, and the average was close to 5,000. Conscription could not be considered at that time—contemporary Americans would not have tolerated it for a moment—and the army had to depend on volunteers. Those who enlisted usually did so in local militia units and often signed up for only ninety days. The unhappy General Washington would plan his campaign and start to carry it out, only to find that the enlistment period of perhaps half his army had been fulfilled, and back to their farms would go the discharged. Militia companies might turn out for the defense of their own locality; but as time passed, their enthusiasm to fight in other sections markedly lessened. Outright desertion from the Continental army was common, and discipline

51

practically nonexistent. Officers were elected after small political campaigns, and the victor could be ousted if action as a martinet destroyed his popularity. Raw, untrained American troops were fine for bushwhacking expeditions, but literally it took years before they could face British bayonets and give as well as take.

Before too negative a conclusion concerning the fighting ability of Revolutionary Americans is formed, the almost intolerable conditions under which Continental soldiers fought should be noted. While Congress procrastinated and bickered, the army was usually unpaid and often hungry. Supplies could not be requisitioned from civilians, and the horrors of a Valley Forge winter were heightened by the soldiers' realization that their malnutrition occurred in one of the richer agricultural areas of America. There was an abundance of food nearby, but hardhearted farmers sold their produce in occupied Philadelphia for British gold. Furthermore, there was no system of pensions or allotments for the families of Washington's men. Perhaps most desertions and short-term enlistments were caused by the soldier's natural concern for his family's welfare. Ill-fed, ill-armed, and most certainly ill-clad and ill-paid, the Continental regulars who endured privation and disease during a long and sometimes disastrous war must be deemed brave and dedicated men.

◖ *Finances.* The financial problems were as complex as the military. American colonials hated and feared taxation as the entering thrust of autocracy. They would not tolerate it; Congress could impose no tax on either citizen or state during the entire Revolution. Other means had to be uncovered. The chief method utilized was the simplest—to issue paper money. Americans had been used to paper currency during their colonial experience, and their printing presses had poured out new issues until the British government called a halt in 1751. Independence meant deficit spending, and paper backed only by the promise to redeem flooded the seaboard. American currency depreciated in value so rapidly that

the phrase "not worth a Continental" became a worn metaphor for the next century. Congress was not the only agency to utilize paper money; the several states did so as well.

There were other ways of getting money. Bonds were sold by the Continental government, but income from this source remained disappointingly small. The sale of confiscated loyalist property returned only a pittance. Late in the Revolution, France, Spain, and the Netherlands entered the war against Great Britain, and each lent money to the United States. Yet only $8 million was borrowed—although this was in real credits rather than paper. About $70 million worth of bonds were sold, and a total of some $450 million in paper was printed by Congress and the states. The financial picture somewhat improved after 1781 when Robert Morris of Pennsylvania became Congress's Superintendent of Finance. Under his direction the army was uniformed and armed better than before, the national revenues were organized upon a sounder basis, and a measure of financial stability was gained through the formation of the Bank of North America. Unfortunately Morris's record is shadowed by monetary irregularity. It appears that on one occasion he sold to his government supplies that had been given to it by France.

◖ *Patriot versus Loyalist.* Congress found it necessary to fight two wars: a revolution against Great Britain and a civil war against other Americans. John Adams described the degree of popular support accorded to the Revolution among the thirteen states as one-third patriot, one-third loyalist, and the remaining third impartial. Similar to so many revolutions, the American uprising was the work of an organized minority that knew what it wanted, acted with decision, and finally imposed its beliefs upon the more complacent majority. The old stereotype of stout patriot against cowardly, sneaking, tory traitor has long since been discredited as Revolutionary propaganda. Hundreds of thousands in America stayed loyal to the king and imperial tradition in a cause as fine as that of their patriot antagonists.

A historical truism states that what appears outwardly simple becomes complex once the surface is penetrated. The social-class alignment on both the patriot and loyalist side bears this out. Although *most* loyalists were from the colonial privileged classes and *most* patriots tended to be small farmers, sailors, and artisans who saw the possibility of their economic advancement in an independent nation, there were many exceptions. There was a tendency to find in the loyalist ranks such groups as the large landholders, men with positions in the royal governments, many of the merchants and wealthy farmers, the majority of the Anglican clergy, and a large portion of the more prominent professional men. On the other hand, minorities in all the above-mentioned groups supported the radicals and American independence. Many leading Southern planters, heavily in debt to English merchants, believed in the slogan, "Out of the Empire; out of debt!" In general, however, the conservative, the wealthy, and the aged tended to stay loyal; the more liberal, the less successful, and the younger were disposed to support the patriots.

Geographically the loyalists formed a large minority in most states and probably were an actual majority in New York, New Jersey, and Georgia. Such cities as Philadelphia and New York appeared to enjoy British occupation, and during the time that Washington's army froze at Valley Forge, Philadelphia belles had the time of their lives flirting, dancing, and attending the theater with young British officers. Loyalist devotion went beyond maintaining the social amenities and giving lip service to the Crown. Tory regiments were organized, although the royal government lost a golden opportunity by not using them on a wide scale until relatively late in the war. After 1779 the aspect of an American civil war became more noticeable than before, and the greatest atrocities occurred when tory and patriot forces clashed with the peculiar hatred of internecine strife.

The loyalists had a most difficult time, except when their locality was occupied by the British army. In patriot-controlled country, known sympathizers with the king were tarred and feathered, driven away, or sometimes even murdered by radical mobs. Loyalist property was confiscated throughout the states; and eventually, after years of abortive negotiations with the United States, millions of pounds had to be appropriated by the Royal Exchequer to compensate King George's loyal subjects for their devotion to his cause, which had ruined them. Naturally many who secretly opposed the patriots had sense enough to keep their mouths shut and were not molested. Nevertheless, enough loyalists so openly identified themselves with the king that after the Peace of Paris (1783) some 70,000 of them left their homes forever to sail away with the British armies. The majority of tory refugees settled in the province of Upper Canada (Ontario).

BRITISH WEAKNESSES

Considering the chaotic American conditions, the question might well be asked, "How could the British have lost the American Revolution?" The answer lies partially in the fact that London faced equally grave and in some instances worse problems of its own. The British war effort suffered from a lack of unity at home, inefficiency in the government and in the armed forces, the vast size of the American area in rebellion, and the need to win the war rather than merely to avoid losing it.

If Americans were divided into hostile camps, so too were the British. A large minority across the Atlantic sympathized with the original motives of American rebels. Included in this group were such famous Englishmen as Edmund Burke, the great orator; William Pitt, draftsman of victory over the French in 1763; and the Marquis of Rockingham, influential and conciliatory politician. Fearing that George III showed tendencies toward personal despotism, these English liberals held that Americans were fighting for the rights of all Englishmen. Naturally, American independence in 1776 lessened the fervor of such sentiments; but prior to that time, and to some degree even afterward, British war unity was affected adversely by split opinion.

British inefficiency in the government and in the army rivaled American and seems more inexcusable in a monarchy that had existed for centuries than in the United States, which had to assume all the problems besetting a new government. Yet British eighteenth-century rule was corrupt and incompetent under normal conditions, and it became positively scandalous through the maladministrations of Lord George Germain, Colonial Secretary, and the Earl of Sandwich, director of the Royal Navy. Germain controlled the military, despite the fact that he had once been cashiered from the British army for cowardice in action. The adjectives unintelligent, dilatory, and fatuously optimistic seem to describe him. The Earl of Sandwich tolerated such corruption in the navy that the fleet almost literally rotted away.

Perhaps these misfits in the upper echelons of the government might not have proved so disastrous if English officers in America had been given a free hand. Instead, they were allowed no liberty of action and were forced to await orders from London that far too often ignored American military realities. The sentiment in favor of the colonists that affected so many British politicians must have been contagious; some British generals seem to have caught the disease. The Howe brothers commanded English army and naval forces during some of the most critical days of the Revolution, and they seemed not disposed to win a crushing victory over their antagonists. General Henry Clinton, successor to General William Howe, was not much better. Even if a British general fought hard, war was a civilized matter to him. The eighteenth-century professional officer preserved "the rules and manners of polite society," looked after his own physical comfort at all costs, and seldom fought during the winter, preferring to wait for milder summer weather.

The very size of America operated against the British. The territory in revolt stretched over 1,000 miles along the coast and up to 300 miles to the west. The British never attempted to supply sufficient manpower to police this extensive tract occupied by well over two million inhabitants. The royal troops were usually numerous enough to capture any particular locale that they desired; but when strategy dictated a withdrawal to new arenas of conflict, the conquered section would revert to the patriots. The unfortunate loyalists who had exposed their hand during the occupation would be forced either to flee or to take their chances with vengeful mobs. The British also had trouble in manning their army. Recruitment lagged in the home islands, the German mercenaries proved to be rather undependable soldiers, and loyalist regiments were not formed early enough to make their presence decisive.

Finally, the British were opposing a foe who to win had only to stand firm and fight a defensive war. Before the United States could be compelled to establish residence in the empire once more, absolute conquest of the Continental army and occupation of the areas in rebellion were necessary—but they could never be realized. As long as Washington could retain some sort of a military organization he could afford to be beaten again and again, while time worked in his favor. Eventually the entrance of France and Spain into the struggle, and the growing British war weariness at home, motivated an English decision to end the conflict; and American independence was the price that had to be paid.

REVOLUTIONARY CAMPAIGNS

⟨ *New England and Canada.* In the military sphere, action centered in New England for the first year, shifted to the Middle States from 1776 to 1779, and ended in the South. Initial resistance to the government of George III occurred in Massachusetts, but New England was more fortunate than the other sections. After the British retreat from Concord on 19 April 1775, Massachusetts militiamen encircled Boston to await both the arrival of George Washington and the concentration of reinforcements from the other colonies. While the new commander was en route from Philadelphia, American troops occupied Charlestown Heights, north of the city across Boston Harbor. General Gage had enough naval strength to cut off the colonial forces simply by seizing the neck of the Charlestown peninsula, but the British commander decided to play the schoolmaster and educate the "Continentals" in the futility of resistance. On 17 June 1775, British regulars were moved to the foot of Breed's Hill ("Bunker Hill," the popular name for the battle, is erroneous), and in slow parade step they marched up the heights. The serried ranks of red-coated infantrymen ran into a hail of American fire at point-blank range, broke, retreated, re-formed, and again advanced. The same murderous volley flamed again from the colonial battlements with the same sanguinary result. On the third British advance, however, American ammunition was running low, and finally the British were able to bring their bayonets into play. The Continental forces were compelled to flee, but in view of its frightful casualty percentage, the British victory can only be judged pyrrhic.

During the winter and spring of 1775–1776 the colonial army around Boston was strengthened in numbers, and the arrival of heavy artillery allowed Washington to occupy Dorchester Heights overlooking beleaguered Boston from the south.[1] Concluding that his position was untenable, Gage ordered the evacuation of the city (17 March 1776). British soldiers and a thousand loyalists sailed to Halifax, leaving New England unvexed from enemy attack for the remainder of the war, save for an occasional raid along the coast and for sorties attendant upon Burgoyne's advance into northern New York during 1777.

While Gage was wintering in Boston, Congress attempted to persuade the Canadians to join the rebellion by the somewhat dubious argument of forcible invasion. Two expedi-

tions were sent forth; General Richard Montgomery traversed New York's Lake Champlain route north into Canada and actually captured Montreal. A second army under General Benedict Arnold, later to gain infamy as a traitor, struggled up the Kennebec River and through the almost impenetrable Maine forests with cannon and flatboats and after incredible hardships, proceeded all the way to Quebec. Montgomery and Arnold joined forces to attack the city (31 December 1775),[2] but Montgomery was killed, Arnold was

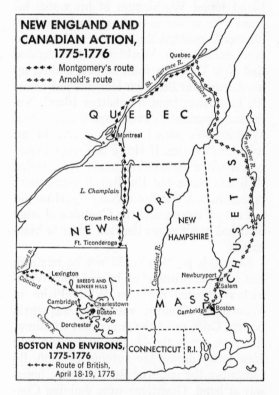

wounded, and after a short and abortive siege of Quebec, the Americans were obliged to retreat. Canada stayed loyal to the king during the entire conflict. Perhaps the dominating factor in this decision was the Quebec Act of 1774. Many French Canadians believed that their way of life was safer under the British than under the rule of a confederation in

---

[1] In May, 1775, the gigantic, voluble, and profane Ethan Allen had led his "Green Mountain Boys" against Fort Ticonderoga and captured it. It was artillery from the fort, dragged through the snow to Boston, that enabled Washington to fortify Dorchester Heights and drive the British from the city.

[2] Revolutionary generals faced many strange dilemmas. Montgomery and Arnold were practically compelled to attack Quebec on New Year's Eve, for many of their soldiers' three-month enlistments ended on 1 January.

which the radical Protestants of New England would play an important role.

❧ *The Middle States.* After New England had been cleared of British forces, Washington hurried with his army to New York City, confident that this would be the next battlefield. He was right; General William Howe, Gage's successor, soon arrived in New York with 32,000 troops, transports, and a protective convoy under the general's brother, Admiral Richard Howe. The following Battle of Long Island found Washington at his worst; his errors were so serious that only luck and British inertia enabled the Continental army to avoid annihilation. Washington had decided that New York City must be held and set up his defenses on Brooklyn Heights, just across the East River from Manhattan Island. Numerical superiority, clever English tactics, and Washington's blunders culminated in an American disaster. If Howe had moved energetically, the Revolution might have ended then and there; but the British commander procrastinated, the Royal Navy squadron did not cut off escape, and the Continental army managed to get across the East River to Manhattan.

Even this position could not be retained; and with the British close behind him, Washington retreated north to White Plains in Westchester County, where he was again beaten. Once more the Americans withdrew, this time across the Hudson and down into New Jersey during the autumn of 1776. By December the nadir of Revolutionary hopes was at hand. Desertions were draining Continental strength, the countryside was at best coldly neutral, and Howe had many reasons for his smug expectation of complete victory. The British general allowed his troops to celebrate the yuletide season. If Washington was inept during the New York campaign, he was magnificent at this dismal hour. On Christmas Eve he suddenly struck back, captured about a thousand sleepy and intoxicated Hessians at Trenton, New Jersey, and a few days later severely mauled three British regiments at Princeton. Following these successes, Wash-

ington retired into winter quarters and the British returned to New York to bask in loyalist affection there.

Across the sea the British War Office was busy with a grandiose scheme to end the war —a strategic masterpiece which looked most appealing when drawn on maps spread across a London desk, but which proved to be piteously lacking in consideration of such fundamentals as terrain, supplies, transportation, and coordination. Careful plans were itemized, involving three armies in America. General John ("Gentleman Johnny") Burgoyne was to proceed south from Canada with 8,000 men over the well-traveled Lake route.[3] Colonel Barry St. Leger was to bring his detachments east from Lake Ontario through the Mohawk Valley. General William Howe was to clear the Hudson River north from New York City. A junction would be brought about at Albany, and the United States would be severed along the Hudson. Burgoyne started south, St. Leger marched east, and Howe sailed—south to Philadelphia, acting upon previous orders. Not until under way did Howe learn of the scheme, and by that time he was unwilling to move north unless Washington retreated in that direction.

The results of the Albany campaign exceeded the most optimistic hopes of American patriots. Howe stayed in Philadelphia and St. Leger was turned back by General Nicholas Herkimer and some German-born militia at Oriskany, New York. That left poor Burgoyne, cultured playwright and epicure, to come wandering down through the woods with his army, artillery, and wagons, the last filled with linen napery, silver plate, and cases of champagne. The militia of upstate New York and western New England massed their forces and defeated segments of the British army at Bennington, Vermont, and Freeman's Farm, New York. Burgoyne lurched ahead as far as Saratoga,

[3] During the summer of 1776 a British force under Canadian Governor Sir Guy Carleton struck south along the Lake route. Sir Guy managed to defeat Benedict Arnold's forces at Valcour Island on Lake Champlain, but so heavy were his losses that he was compelled to retreat to Canada. Arnold had gained a valuable year for the United States.

New York, but there, cut off and outnumbered, he had no choice but to surrender his entire command to the American General Horatio Gates (7 October 1777). The Battle of Saratoga has been correctly called the most decisive engagement of the American Revolution, with the exception of Yorktown, for this was the victory necessary to bring France into the war against Great Britain.

While Burgoyne was still entangled in the wilderness, Washington had moved south to defend Philadelphia. Howe, sailing from New

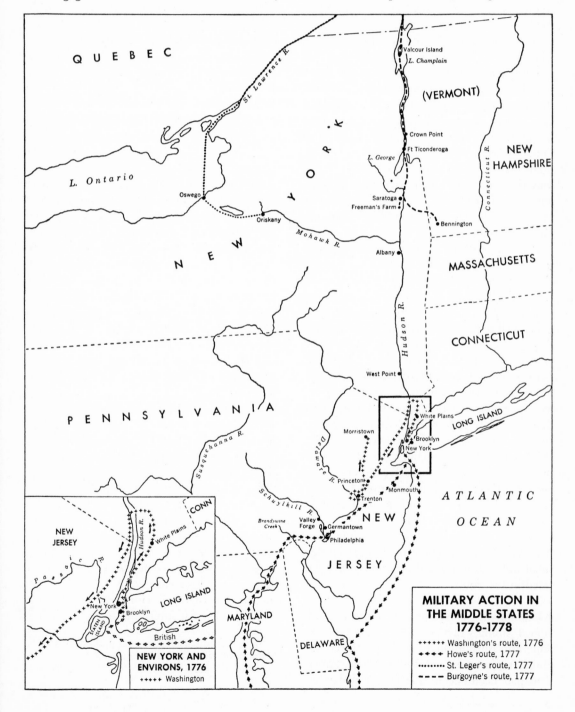

NEW YORK AND ENVIRONS, 1776
+++++ Washington

MILITARY ACTION IN
THE MIDDLE STATES
1776-1778
++++++ Washington's route, 1776
◄+++ Howe's route, 1777
·········· St. Leger's route, 1777
– – – Burgoyne's route, 1777

York into Chesapeake Bay, had landed on that inlet's upper shore and marched overland toward the Pennsylvania city. Attempting to defend it, the outnumbered Continentals were defeated at Brandywine Creek; and their surprise attack was unsuccessful at Germantown (4 October 1777). The disappointed Washington fell back to winter quarters at Valley Forge, some 20 miles northwest of Philadelphia, while Howe's army settled down to enjoy the urban delights of the City of Brotherly Love —and it certainly seemed well named during the winter of 1777–1778. The Continental encampment was quite the reverse; Valley Forge has become a symbol of disease and malnutrition. Washington's command gradually drained away until a scant 2,000 remained, and only the indomitable character and the unrelenting will of the Virginia planter were able to keep together even the semblance of a military organization.

With the advent of spring, Howe decided to return overland from Philadelphia to New York. With reinforcements, Washington attempted to halt the British at Monmouth, New Jersey, during June, 1778. The battle was going well for the Americans and a major victory seemed in prospect when Continental strategy was ruined by the action of a renegade British officer, General Charles Lee, who had long disturbed Washington's equanimity. Without authorization, Lee suddenly withdrew 4,000 troops from the center of the Continental line, forcing the advance to stop. On the battlefield Washington assailed Lee with profane invective and the latter was eventually court-martialed and dismissed from the army. But Lee's intervention had been damaging; instead of a triumph, Monmouth was a split decision, and Howe was able to continue on to New York. This battle was the last real engagement in the North, for after 1778 the war centered in the South.

❡ *Diplomacy.* Developments abroad conditioned military action during most of the American Revolution. Even during the coldest and hungriest hours at Valley Forge, Americans had been encouraged by the realization that the fight was no longer a battle between an upstart republic and the most powerful nation on earth. France had entered the war as America's ally in 1778. Ever since 1763 the French had waited for an opportunity to avenge their catastrophic defeat in the Great War for the Empire. The outbreak of hostilities between Great Britain and its American colonies was watched with grim satisfaction in Paris; and from the first shots at Lexington and Concord, French sympathies were strongly on the American side. But compared with the might of Great Britain, French strength was still weak. *Officially,* France could do nothing to aid the Americans until 1778. Nevertheless, considerable unofficial assistance was sent.

Both Frenchmen and Americans played important roles in this unofficial assistance. Even before independence had been declared, Congress recognized the importance of French aid by appointing Arthur Lee and Silas Deane to open negotiations with the French Foreign Minister, the Comte de Vergennes. The American envoys were soon collaborating with a most bizarre individual, Pierre Augustin Caron de Beaumarchais, *bon vivant,* lady's man, and eminent dramatist.[4] Beaumarchais became enamored of the American cause and supported it zealously. He set up a dummy corporation called Rodrique Hortalez et Cie. to serve as a front for French exports of war matériel to America. Although the French government tacitly utilized this company, it was able to profess the deepest official ignorance when the infuriated British Minister protested against such unneutral Gallic assistance to American rebels. Beaumarchais and his company were instrumental in supplying the Continental army from France; it has been estimated that nine-tenths of the American shot and powder used to capture Burgoyne's forces at Saratoga came across the Atlantic in the ships of Rodrique Hortalez et Cie.

Official French intervention in the Ameri-

---

[4] Beaumarchais wrote the successful comedies *The Marriage of Figaro* and *The Barber of Seville,* which were later the bases of the famous operas of the same names.

can Revolution was given impetus when the
great Benjamin Franklin arrived in Paris (September, 1776). Although he was in the sunset
of his astonishing career, Franklin's diplomacy
and tact remained unimpaired. During his
French sojourn he capped with the merited
title of statesman his previous accomplishments as politician, scientist, author, editor,
printer, inventor, patron of the arts, philanthropist, intellectual, and, beneath his carefully cultivated air of naïveté, sophisticate.
The astute Franklin quickly adopted the garb
and mien of a backwoods sage—complete with
fur cap—and the delighted French, immersed
in Jean Jacques Rousseau's stereotype of the
noble savage, fell over themselves doing him
homage. Portraits of Franklin adorned snuffboxes, medallions, and cameo brooches worn
by the finest ladies at the court of Louis XVI.
Behind all this façade, however, Franklin was
serving his country with conspicuous ability,
working with Vergennes to bring France into
the war.

The French Foreign Minister sincerely believed that the interests of his nation would be
best served by openly siding with the Americans, but he faced three difficult problems.
First, he had to await American independence.
Next, he had to delay intervention until a
brilliant Continental victory would prove that
the new country could both fight and win.
Saratoga settled the latter question, and Vergennes was able to step up his appeals to the
somewhat stupid Louis XVI that the time to
strike was at hand. The final problem was indeed thorny. Vergennes did not want to lead
his nation into war with so formidable an adversary as Great Britain unless Spain should
ally itself with France. Spain had every
reason to hate England, and the continued
British possession of Gibraltar was a festering
sore to the proud Iberians. Yet Spain, as conservative and autocratic a monarchy as existed
in the world, feared and detested the republican liberalism in the United States and was
apprehensive lest this contagion infect its own
American dominions. Consequently, Spain
hesitated to line up beside the new nation.
Vergennes tried to delay France's entrance

into the war until Madrid was ready, but the
tidings that Britain was considering generous
concessions to its American rebels forced the
French diplomat to act.

Anticipating the later entrance of Spain into
the war, Vergennes and the American envoys
to France signed two treaties on 6 February
1778. The first was a pact of "Amity and Commerce," which established trade relations between the two nations. The second was the
Franco-American military alliance [5] pledging
common effort for victory and promising to
conclude no separate peace with England. The
allies agreed about possible territorial acquisitions. The United States would receive any
territory on the North American mainland that
might be won (the French thereby renounced
any claims to Canada), and France would keep
any islands captured in the West Indies. Perhaps the alliance was signed just in time. British plans to grant concessions to the Continentals dawdled throughout the Christmas
holidays and well into the new year. Precisely
thirty-one days after the Franco-American
alliance had been signed, Parliament surrendered to every demand that had led to
revolution, if America would rejoin the empire.
It was too late for half measures, however.

As Vergennes had hoped, Spain entered the
war against Britain (1779). His Most Catholic
Majesty signed the Treaty of Aranjuez with
France, although Spain persistently refused to
ally itself with the United States or even to
recognize the latter's independence.[6] The
terms of the Franco-Spanish agreement are
interesting. Vergennes promised to continue
the war until British-held Gibraltar had been
returned to Spain. Since the Franco-American
alliance pledged no separate peace, and the
Franco-Spanish pact carried the same provision, in effect the United States was sup-

[5] The Franco-American military alliance was of
course the first such agreement in American history.
The alliance lasted for twenty-two years (1778 to
1800), and not until the United States ratified the
North Atlantic Treaty in 1949 did the nation belong
to another peacetime military alliance.

[6] John Jay, American Minister to Spain, was constantly and icily rebuffed by the court at Madrid. The
same fate befell other American envoys in the Netherlands, Prussia, and Russia.

posed to continue fighting until Gibraltar, probably the most powerful fortification in the world, had been captured.

Other Europeans showed their hostility toward Great Britain, if not their sympathy for colonial rebels in America. The Dutch, ever alert to economic opportunity, turned their minuscule Caribbean island of St. Eustatius into a depot for goods from Europe en route to America. Britain resented bitterly this unfriendly action and declared war on the Netherlands in 1780. Russia, Sweden, and Denmark, although never declaring war against Great Britain, entered the so-called "Armed Neutrality," which maintained amicable relations with the Franco-American allies. England was faced by an unfriendly world, and these altered circumstances naturally greatly encouraged Americans. France's entry was the pivotal step; material aid was dispatched practically throughout the war, and after 1780 military and naval assistance as well. Troops under French General de Rochambeau and particularly the fleet

commanded by the Comte de Grasse were instrumental in forging the joint victory at Yorktown, Virginia, which was the final major military action of the American Revolution.

❲ *Maritime and Western Aspects.* During the entire Revolution, action occurred on the high seas as well as on land. The Continental navy was too small to challenge the awesome British fleet (which was still the world's greatest, despite its corruption under the Earl of Sandwich), although some single-ship duels were fought. Especially noteworthy was the American Captain John Paul Jones, who won a bloody struggle in his *Bonhomme Richard* against the British frigate *Serapis* (1779). Considerably more important than the regular navy were the myriad American privateers. Terrible havoc was spread through the English merchant marine by these predatory raiders. Almost every port along the American Atlantic Coast dispatched privateers strong enough to capture merchantmen and swift

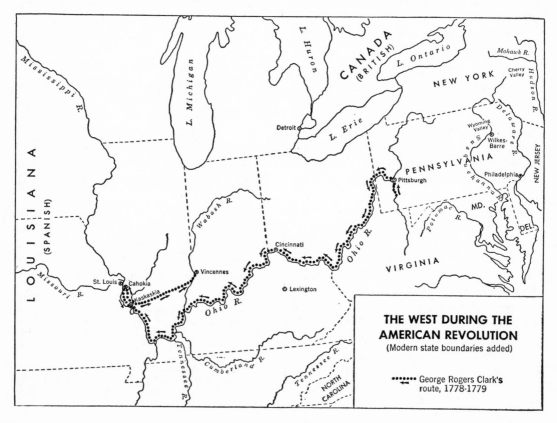

THE WEST DURING THE AMERICAN REVOLUTION
(Modern state boundaries added)

••••••• George Rogers Clark's route, 1778-1779

enough to outsail the more cumbersome frigates of the Royal Navy. The audacity of these American commerce destroyers was legendary, and prizes were taken within sight of the cliffs of Dover. British commerce suffered dreadfully, insurance rates soared, convoys had to escort merchantmen on the Irish Sea, and the appeals of British traders facing ruin from American depredations influenced considerably the Crown's decision to bring about a negotiated peace.

Meanwhile the war dragged on in America, and by 1778 Western conditions had become important. Colonel Henry Hamilton, British commander in the Northwest, stirred up Indian attacks along the frontier. Loyalist regiments, among them Walter Butler's Tory Rangers and Barry St. Leger's Loyal Greens, perpetrated some bona fide massacres at Cherry Valley in upstate New York and in the Wyoming Valley in northeastern Pennsylvania. Americans were busy in the trans-Appalachian area as well. Governor Patrick Henry of Virginia authorized George Rogers Clark to relieve as best he could both British and Indian pressure in that quarter. This would not only aid back-country settlements, but also strengthen Virginia's western claims. Clark led a force down the Ohio River and, after considerable hardship, captured British posts at Kaskaskia and Cahokia (Illinois) and at Vincennes (Indiana). Nineteenth-century historians pointed to Clark's exploits as the chief reason for America gaining the transmontane west at the end of the war, but there is no evidence that the negotiators in Paris even knew of his deeds.

❰ *The South.* Convinced that New England and the Middle States were too powerful to conquer, Howe's successor, General Henry Clinton, decided to utilize the strong loyalist sentiment in the South and moved to attack that sector.[7] Savannah, Georgia, surrendered to Clinton in December, 1778, but for about a

[7] There had been some earlier fighting in the South. During 1776 patriot militia had defeated some loyalists at Moore's Creek in North Carolina, and the British had been repelled in their attempt to capture Charleston.

year little further action took place until the British moved against Charleston. In May, 1780, South Carolina's metropolis fell, and in this debacle 5,000 Continental troops under General Benjamin Lincoln were captured. The British then headed for the Carolina hinterlands. Although American irregulars almost

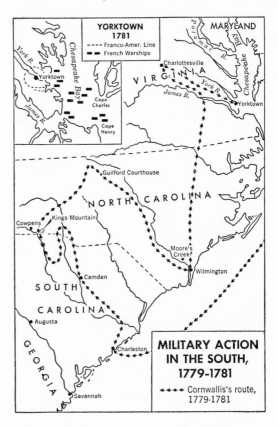

wiped out loyalist forces on Kings Mountain (October, 1780), the Continental armies were usually thrashed by Clinton and his successor, General George Cornwallis. Especially galling was the disaster at Camden, South Carolina, where General Horatio Gates,[8] who had received credit for the victory at Saratoga better merited by his subordinates, was utterly routed by the British. Cornwallis marched on to the Guilford Courthouse and gained an indecisive victory over the able General Nathanael

[8] Gates was overrated during the American Revolution. A group in the Continental army called the "Conway Cabal" attempted to oust Washington and replace him with Gates. Luckily for America, the plot failed.

Greene, but in so doing took quite a hammering. In addition, pressure from guerilla chieftains such as Francis Marion, "the Swamp Fox," was reaching a crescendo. Cornwallis decided to proceed toward Virginia to meet a British armada with supplies and reinforcements. His advance was slowed by a small American force under the youthful French Marquis de Lafayette. Although Lafayette could not stop Cornwallis, he skillfully retreated before him to the peninsula at Yorktown.

While these Southern episodes were taking place, Washington had remained at New York keeping a watchful eye on the English regiments still occupying the city; the unhappy American commander was trying to regain both his composure and his faith in his fellow man after the treachery of Benedict Arnold at West Point.[9] The news that Cornwallis was in Virginia awaiting reinforcements opened golden vistas for the American commandant. Washington persuaded the French General de Rochambeau, who had been resting with his army in Rhode Island for almost a year, to join him. The combined Franco-American army hurried down the coast to Virginia.

The situation at Yorktown was dependent upon sea power, and luckily for the allies a French fleet under the Comte de Grasse arrived off the Chesapeake Capes. De Grasse was just in time; a British squadron showed up, studied the situation for a while, and sailed away. Cornwallis had established himself on the Yorktown peninsula to meet the British fleet; and when it disappeared over the horizon, his prospects vanished. Yorktown saw some of the most brilliant strategy of the entire war, and the coordination between French and American armies and between the French fleet and both armies were almost beyond reproach. Completely cut off from any help, Cornwallis held out for a few weeks, but eventually had to surrender his entire command of 7,000 men (17 October 1781).

PEACE AND VICTORY

In London the distrait Lord North, hearing of Yorktown, threw his hands into the air and shouted, "Oh God, it is all over!" Actually, it was not necessarily so; the British still could have fought effectively. Not only did they control New York City, Savannah, and Charleston, but their naval power was sufficient to land almost anywhere along the Atlantic Coast. Furthermore, American enlistments had practically ceased once French troops were on hand. Nevertheless, British apprehension over the international situation, the temporarily bleak naval picture,[10] heavy financial costs, and growing war-weariness at home caused the North ministry to resign. After a threat to abdicate, George III found it necessary to appoint the pacifistic Marquis of Rockingham (who had repealed the Stamp Act in 1766) to head the government. Rockingham soon died, but Lord Shelburne, his successor, continued a conciliatory policy to end the war.

As early as April, 1782, Britain let it be known that peace would be welcomed. This met with a warm American reception; and negotiations were started between the English and United States representatives in Europe: Benjamin Franklin, John Adams, and John Jay. Jay's role was important. He had become highly suspicious of both France and Spain, and he was perfectly willing to sign a separate

[9] Benedict Arnold's career was most unusual. One of the great American generals during the Revolution, he had suffered wounds and won accolades for his heroism at Quebec, Valcour Island, and Saratoga. His marriage to a loyalist sympathizer and a rebuke from Congress that he felt was unwarranted soured him on the American cause. He persuaded Washington to assign him to command West Point, defense bastion of the Hudson River, and then negotiated with the British to turn the stronghold over to them. Arnold's messages were intercepted, and the American barely had time to escape, although his courier, the young English Major John André, was executed. Arnold fought for the British in the Carolinas, Virginia, and Connecticut. Eventually he died in England (1801).

[10] Britain was saved from a crushing defeat in the war by an overwhelming naval victory in the Caribbean. In this "Battle of the Saints" (1782) the great Admiral Rodney defeated De Grasse and regained British naval supremacy, which had been lost a year before.

THE UNITED STATES AFTER
TREATY OF PARIS, 1783

——— United States boundary

- - - - Disputed United States boundary

········· Boundary of Thirteen Original States

Anglo-American peace, despite the terms to the contrary in the Franco-American alliance. Jay suspected, with good reason, that neither France nor Spain desired a strong United States and that the Bourbon allies hoped to contain the new nation in a coastal strip east of the Appalachians, permitting Great Britain to keep the land north of the Ohio River and east of the Mississippi, and giving to Spain all the rest. Adams agreed with Jay, and together they persuaded the vacillating Franklin to go along with them on separate negotiations. Several meetings between Britons and Americans culminated in the preliminary treaty of peace that was signed on 30 November 1782, although its terms were not to go into effect until France eventually signed a definite treaty. The stipulations of the preliminary agreement were strikingly generous to the new republic, considering not only the lack of martial enthusiasm in the United States, but also continued British occupation of much American territory. The United States gained its chief demand—complete independence—and was awarded all the land south of Canada and the Great Lakes, north of Florida, and east of the Mississippi. The northeastern and northwestern boundaries were described so vaguely, however, that years of controversy with Great Britain were necessary before final frontiers could be drawn. Indecisive wording also characterized the treaty terms regarding compensation for the loyalists. This dispute was certainly not settled by the insertion of the weasel statement that Congress would "strongly recommend" to the several states that confiscated tory property should be recompensed. Both Britons and Americans knew that this specification would never be carried out, but its inclusion was imperative to placate English home opinion so that the treaty could be ratified.

Thanks to John Adams's stern insistence, New England fishermen were granted the vital right to fish Canadian waters and to dry and salt their catch along unoccupied Canadian shores. Yet future disagreements over fishing rights formed the most persistent controversy in American diplomatic history—not for a century and a quarter was the problem to be satisfactorily solved. All in all, the preliminary treaty (which was adopted into the final Treaty of 1783) was a tremendous victory for

America, far more extensive than any that had been gained on the battlefield. Naturally the American diplomatic triumph was due to no British love for "rogue colonials," but rather to British discouragement over the possibility of winning a complete victory over their cantankerous trans-Atlantic relatives.

What of France while Anglo-American conferences were meeting? According to the provisions of the Franco-American military alliance of 1778, neither ally should make a separate peace, and the United States was doing precisely that. The evidence shows that Vergennes knew what was going on (his espionage system was excellent) but rather than turning livid at this "treachery," he was quietly using it to further his own aims. By 1783 it was obvious that British Gibraltar was impregnable, and France simply could not carry out its promise made at Aranjuez to return the fortress to Spain. American negotiations at London enabled Vergennes to show the Spaniards that the defection of the United States from the alliance made a continuation of the war impossible.[11] Spain reluctantly agreed and joined France, Great Britain, and the United States in signing the definitive Treaty of Paris (2 September 1783). The United States received the territory promised in the preliminary agreement, Spain took Florida and the Mediterranean island of Minorca, but France gained little save a ruinous public debt (which was to be important in wrecking the Bourbon monarchy) and the satisfaction of having humbled the haughty British. Despite territorial exchanges and a temporary lessening of British world influence, the most vital measure accomplished at Paris in 1783 was the creation of a new republic, the United States of America.

[11] Vergennes protested to Franklin about the Anglo-American meetings, but concluded by lending additional money to the United States. This would appear to support the contention that Vergennes was secretly delighted that he could wriggle out of his Gibraltar obligation to Spain.

CHAPTER 5

Toward a National Government

(1783-1787)

POST-REVOLUTIONARY AMERICA

❰ *General Developments.* The American Revolution did not begin with the pealing of the Liberty Bell in 1776, was not limited to the maneuvering of the armies in the field, and did not end with the signing of a peace treaty in 1783. Military and diplomatic developments were but the most visible evidences of a changing society—of the end of one age and the beginning of a new. Very possibly even the political separation from England was the lesser part of the story. The English colonists for over a century and a half had been transformed by American geography. They had matured from dependent children of the empire to young men who felt aware of their individuality and eager to show that they were adults, with independence of judgment and action. The old family home was too restricted for their growing ambitions.

Americans were altering their institutions in dozens of ways that reflected not only unique American conditions but also liberal world thought, for the aspirations of Americans were related intimately to the thinking of the rest of the world; many cosmopolitan American leaders such as Jefferson and Frank-

lin were closely in touch with world movements. The West was opened to settlement, loyalist estates were confiscated, and relics of feudal land tenure were abolished, thus smoothing the path of American small-farmer civilization. Freedom of religion increased. State churches came into increasing disfavor, being in many cases disestablished. Church governments became more American, severing at least in part their ties to Europe. Criminal punishment became milder; the death penalty became less common, while the number of prisons increased. Personal freedom was guarded more tenderly; efforts were made to stop the slave trade, and even to free the slaves. In dozens of ways America demonstrated the all-embracing nature of the forces that produced political independence.[1]

❰ *State Developments.* The American Revolution transformed the colonies into sovereign states, and only Rhode Island and Connecticut felt satisfied to retain their colonial charters with but minor changes. All the other states produced completely new constitutions, although their methods varied widely. Some states, like Virginia, enacted the new charters

[1] See pp. 110–112.

exactly as though they were regular laws. Others gave specific authority for drawing the new constitutions, and a few provided for popular ratification, but only Massachusetts and New Hampshire used what was later the standard procedure of a constitutional convention for the specific purpose of drawing the new charter, which was then subject to a popular referendum.

The revolutionary state constitutions were in many ways not very revolutionary, being based on long-established precedents. Quite generally, they provided freedom of elections and rotation in office. Each contained a bill of rights, guaranteeing against any kind of governmental action such personal rights as a fair trial and freedom of speech and conscience. Although lip service was given to Montesquieu's concept of the separation of powers between executive, legislative, and judicial organs, the actual fact proved less impressive than the theory. Any strong government was viewed with suspicion, for stout patriots who had risked the hangman's rope to object to acts of Parliament and decrees of the Crown had no desire to exchange one tyranny for another. A powerful executive was generally abhorrent, and the powers of the governors were so strictly limited that only in one state—Massachusetts—was the executive given the power to veto legislative acts.

The power taken from the governor almost inevitably went to the legislature. All the states adopted a two-house legislature with the temporary exceptions of Pennsylvania and Georgia, which experimented with unicameral bodies. In four states the legislature or a special council elected the governor, while quite universally the legislature elected the judges. Judges ordinarily held their jobs for life or good behavior, although three states limited their terms to between five and seven years. The voters chose both legislative houses directly, except that Maryland and Georgia provided for the election of the upper house by the lower. Ordinarily, members of the lower house were elected for only a single year, while members of the upper house served longer. A governor also held office for one year, except

that South Carolina provided for two; and New York, Pennsylvania, and Delaware for three.

Clipping the wings of the executive and talking of popular sovereignty did not mean that Americans had overwhelming confidence in the bulk of mankind. In fact, extreme limitations were placed on the common man, particularly in such states as New York and South Carolina, which ensured aristocratic control. Every state limited the electorate to white males who held property or paid a poll tax. Officeholders were still further restricted in terms of property and religion and frequently had to take an oath of office that Roman Catholics found impossible to accept. Eighteenth-century Americans were convinced that a man should have a stake in society in the form of property before he could be permitted to vote and that officeholders should have an even greater material interest in the society that they controlled. Even ardent Jeffersonian liberals viewed with distaste any grant of political power to landless city artisans. The majority of American men did not obtain the right of suffrage until the advent of Jacksonian Democracy, while women waited much longer. Perhaps it was symbolic of frontier ideals that the state of Vermont was the first to grant universal male suffrage. Certainly Revolutionary democratic ideals were not those of modern times.

CONTINENTAL CONGRESS

In contrast to the carefully formed state governments, the Federal government was largely a matter of accident. The First Continental Congress (1774) was nothing more than a convention of delegates elected by state legislatures or popular assemblies to consider common grievances; every colony but Georgia was represented. The gathering was of course extralegal. Its membership was a cross section of American opinion, except that tories were not included. True, there were radicals such as Sam Adams and Patrick Henry, but there were also men with views as conservative as those of the aristocratic John Jay. The extent of the body's conservatism was demonstrated when it voted upon the proposal of Joseph Galloway (Pennsylvania) for home rule in the empire through a continental legislature that would have coordinate power with the British Parliament in any measures affecting America. The proposal lost by a single vote.

The Second Continental Congress (1775) was more distinguished in personnel than its predecessor and again represented a broad sampling of American points of view. Although this body took the responsibility of declaring independence, it realized that it had no proper authority for governing the new nation and so immediately (1776) prepared a scheme of government. The fact that this first plan granted considerable authority to the Federal government indicated a realization of the need for centralized power to fight a successful war, but also demonstrated the large proportion of conservatives in the Congress. The radicals looked askance at such centralization and before the document was sent for state ratification (1777) were able to amend it in such ways that the states remained dominant. Unfortunately for the successful prosecution of the war, the new Articles of Confederation dangled before the states for four years. The prime cause of the delay was the problem of Western lands. Loosely drawn colonial charters had given various colonies conflicting claims to Western empires, and the states without such claims, particularly Maryland, felt that the lands should be transferred to the nation as a common heritage before a Federal government was accepted.

While the Articles hung fire, the Continental Congress was forced to continue its operations, even though it possessed no legal power. It was a conference of delegates of independent nations engaged in a common war, and it passed resolutions rather than laws. It assumed control of the army and raised troops; but although Washington insisted that "to place any dependence upon militia is assuredly resting upon a broken reed," troops were still levied from the states. With no power

to tax, Congress could only ask humbly, hat in hand, for money and supplies, which arrived in varying amounts. It issued paper money, which soon became practically valueless, and obtained foreign loans that did little more than pay the interest on domestic obligations. Probably the most successful efforts of the Continental Congress were those leading to the French alliance. Although Franklin has properly been credited for effective American propaganda in France, the alliance resulted even more from the old and overwhelming desire of France to beat England at all costs. Spain was drawn into the war reluctantly upon the pressure of France, and Holland was involved involuntarily, Congress having little influence in either case.

SHIFTING ECONOMIC PATTERNS

Congressional troubles were no implication that the country as a whole was poverty-stricken during the war. Regions overrun by the contending armies, particularly the South during the last few years of the war, suffered considerable devastation, but they were the exceptions rather than the rule. The end of British trade and of empire controls inspired the Americans to produce more goods at home. Some of the states offered bounties for local manufacturing, while private societies offered prizes and premiums. Infant linen, wool, and cotton mills appeared in Massachusetts, Rhode Island, Connecticut, and Pennsylvania, although at the end of the war most of them were to go bankrupt. Ironworks, hat factories, and other establishments found business profitable in the war years. American stores by 1779 were displaying extensive stocks of goods, particularly for the lucky speculators, and the papers noted splendid balls, French dancing masters, and big races for large stakes. Profits from the depredations of hundreds of privateers poured into America as the ships reoutfitted and the sailors spent their pay— sometimes on riotous shore leaves. British pounds, and to some extent French livres, enriched American merchants and farmers. The military demand for farm products was extensive, while floods of paper money pushed prices to astronomical heights; as usual with inflation, the farmer benefited both as producer and as debtor.

The end of the war brought inevitable confusion, which led the conservatives to feel that the country was going to the dogs; but actually conditions were not impossibly bad, and most men looked toward the future with hope. Foreign trade improved as peace came to the seas and new markets were made available. England had never been very enthusiastic about the American war and now listened to its manufacturers and shippers by giving American ships preference in English ports. Only in the West Indies trade did Americans experience serious limitations, for by a royal proclamation of 1783 the British West Indies were closed to American ships, and certain American products barred completely. This British policy brought loud protests from America. United States manufacturers belied their few numbers and small production by the vociferousness of their complaints that British products were dominating American markets and should at least be restricted by tariffs; American shippers, joined by West Indian planters, moaned bitterly over the trade limitations, even though they realized how easily the restrictions could be evaded. Any possible loss was more than compensated in a short time by the opening of the French West Indies and by concessions from such countries as Holland and Sweden, while additional areas were increasingly opened to American ships. The shipping outlook was by no means depressing.

(*Farm Discontent.* Farmers were definitely less happy with the postwar world. Military markets disappeared. The end of British subsidies on indigo, rice, pig and bar iron, tar, pitch, resin, and lumber was a blow to the farmer as it was to certain other producers. But more important, the end of the war introduced a period of deflation produced by a real lack of currency. Foreign gold and silver were no longer being spent in the United States. The practically worthless domestic paper was no longer being issued and had stopped circulating. The resulting paucity of money in circulation increased the purchasing power of the little that remained, which in practical terms meant that prices fell. Debtors who had borrowed money when it was cheap and had little purchasing power now had to repay the same number of dollars when their purchasing power was greater. One type of debt that bore on every property owner was taxes, which had a depressing habit of staying high while other prices went down. The taxpaying farmer discovered that each year he had to sell more wheat or cotton or corn to meet his tax bill. Furthermore, practically all taxes were levied on land and its improvements, which meant a particularly heavy burden for the farmer, while many states collected a poll tax, which obviously hurt the small-income receiver more than the large. The farmer was in further difficulties because as usual in such periods the prices of the products he sold declined more rapidly than the prices of what he bought. His wartime prosperity faded before his eyes. With increasing frequency taxes were unpaid and farm mortgages foreclosed.

Farm troubles brought the historically inevitable rural demand for more money to recapture the prosperity of previous inflation. Seven states acceded to this demand, and the motivating force became entirely clear when five of them allowed loans on farm mortgages in the new currency. Most of these state issues turned out to be reasonably sound and useful, but there were exceptions. In Rhode Island, creditors objected strenuously to the new money, suspecting with good reason that it might soon become worthless. Since it was legal tender, which meant that it must be accepted for all public and private debts, the only recourse for the creditor was to hide. Instead of the usual picture of the poor but honest debtor hiding from the cruel and rapacious creditor, in Rhode Island the terrified creditors were in full flight with debtors in hot pursuit.[2]

[2] In the case of *Trevett v. Weeden* (1786), a refractory Providence butcher had refused to accept the

The farmer protest attained the status of armed rebellion in one state—Massachusetts. Led somewhat reluctantly by Daniel Shays, a Revolutionary veteran, mobs of western farmers averted further judgments for debt by preventing the sitting of county courts (Shays' Rebellion, 1786). Rumors flew of a possible march on Boston, including an attack on the state house. The conservative governor, James Bowdoin, immediately outlawed the leaders and ordered the mobs to disperse. An effort of the farmers to obtain arms from the Springfield arsenal was repulsed with grapeshot. Militia dispersed the rioters and hunted them into the hills like wild game. Many Bay State residents clamored for the death sentence for the revolutionaries; but calmer counsels in time prevailed, and they were pardoned. The incident was symptomatic of current economic ills and was particularly important in its wide repercussions throughout the nation. News of the Massachusetts disorders sent a thrill of horror and apprehension through the propertied classes in all states and strongly spurred the feeling that private property in general was under attack and that the only effective defense was the creation of a strong Federal government—a feeling that can be understood only against the background of the weaknesses of the Articles of Confederation.

THE ARTICLES OF CONFEDERATION

❨ *Step toward Union.* The Articles of Confederation had at long last been adopted in 1781 when Maryland's reluctance was overcome. Although Maryland had held out for state cessions of Western land to the Federal government, she finally was willing to accept even a minimum and token move in that direc-

tion rather than keep the Articles any longer in suspension. Actually only New York had acted, and her small gesture of offering (1780) to cede a rather tenuous claim based on Indian treaties had not yet been accepted by Congress. Most states had taken no action, particularly the important claimants, Virginia and North Carolina. Actually the last state cession (Georgia) did not come until 1802.

The Articles constituted a league of independent states, with the old Continental Congress maintained almost intact. Each state sent to Congress somewhere between two and seven delegates, who debated each measure among themselves to decide how to cast the one vote to which each state was entitled, regardless of size. If the delegates split evenly, a state lost its vote. Two-thirds of the states had to approve a bill before it became law, and the Articles could be amended only by unanimous agreement of the states. On two occasions an amendment received twelve votes, but in one case Rhode Island refused to agree, and in the other New York, so that none was ever adopted.

Congress had executive as well as legislative functions. The executive duties were performed, not by an official who was grandiloquently called "The President of the United States in Congress Assembled" and who was only a presiding officer, but by congressional "departments" of foreign affairs, finance, and war; these were run at first by committees, but their obvious inadequacy soon lead to the substitution of individual men. Congress had power to establish courts with appellate jurisdiction over disputes between the states and over cases concerning piracy and other crimes of the high seas. Each state agreed to give full faith and credit to the records, acts, and judicial proceedings of every other state; to give to citizens of other states all the privileges and immunities of its own citizens; and to extradite all criminals.

To men with a modern background, the absence of congressional power under the Articles is notable. The power to tax was conspicuously lacking. Congress could requisition the several states for money, apportioning its

---

new state money. Immediately he had been dragged to jail, but the Supreme Court refused to punish him, saying that it lacked jurisdiction. Indirectly it was really calling the law unconstitutional. The justices were reprimanded by the House, and four of the five were not reappointed, but the decision stood. More important than the immediate issue was the precedent that the courts had the power to consider the constitutionality of laws.

requests on the basis of the assessed valuation of state-surveyed lands, together with the buildings on them, but such funds were impossible to collect if the states should prove recalcitrant. Furthermore, Congress lacked authority to regulate foreign trade, even by imposing a tariff, and had no control over interstate commerce.

Despite serious limitations, the Federal government of the United States in the years after 1781 was by no means without authority. In foreign affairs, Congress was permitted— and the states specifically forbidden—to raise and equip an army and navy, to declare war, and to sign treaties with other nations. In domestic affairs, Congress could regulate Indian relations, establish a system of weights and measures, control the coinage, administer a postal system, and manage the Western lands as the states ceded their claims to the Federal government.

The task of the new Congress under the Articles seemed at first almost impossibly difficult. The war was still in progress, being prosecuted by a badly equipped and largely unpaid army. Congressional money had declined in value to the point at which it was not worth printing, and demands on the states for money produced only small amounts, which were obviously unfairly levied; they had to be apportioned on the basis of taxable land values, and quite notoriously assessments were vastly different in basis from state to state. Congress asked the power to levy a tariff, but first Rhode Island and then New York refused to agree to the proposal.

Congress survived its overwhelming difficulties sufficiently to bring the war to a successful conclusion. Greatest individual credit must go to Robert Morris, whose manifold duties included control of finance, supplying the army, and even corresponding with foreign ministers. The fact that he and his friends profited personally from some of his official actions should not obscure the much more important consideration that his tremendous energy and ability were largely responsible for keeping the government on its financial feet and fighting a war. Ultimately, congressional

peace commissioners were able to conclude a satisfactory treaty.

The end of the war was by no means the end of congressional troubles, particularly because the disappearance of the emergency inspired many of the abler members of Congress to return home to attend to their neglected personal affairs. Weeks would pass without even a quorum present to transact business; only twenty-three were available to ratify the treaty of peace. Federal currency had stopped circulating, while debts continued to mount. The unpaid and discontented army encamped at Newburgh, New York, appeared to threaten real mischief until Washington's calming influence moderated their bitter protests to a relatively mild petition by the officers to Congress. In fact, the rioting of Pennsylvania troops who were supposedly guarding Congress so alarmed the members that they moved their meeting place from Philadelphia to Princeton; later peregrinations included Annapolis and New York (1785).

❪ *Congressional Triumphs.* Faced with these unpleasant prospects and limited by its small powers, Congress under the Articles of Confederation did a surprisingly good job. The army was finally demobilized after being placated with three months' pay and the promise of a bonus, even though lack of funds and failure to provide for coinage postponed any bonus to the somewhat problematical future. Foreign affairs were prosecuted with moderate successes, including commercial treaties with Russia, Prussia, and Sweden. French relations remained good, and trade grew. Relations with England were probably as pleasant as the circumstances permitted, even though there were troubles over loyalist claims, over English retention of the Western posts, and over the limitation of trade with the West Indies.

Spain presented a really difficult problem since she had never felt any enthusiasm for the United States with its example of colonial revolt; yet it was a source of lucrative trade that beckoned to Americans and also controlled the mouth of the Mississippi, so vital to the American West. Spain was willing to make

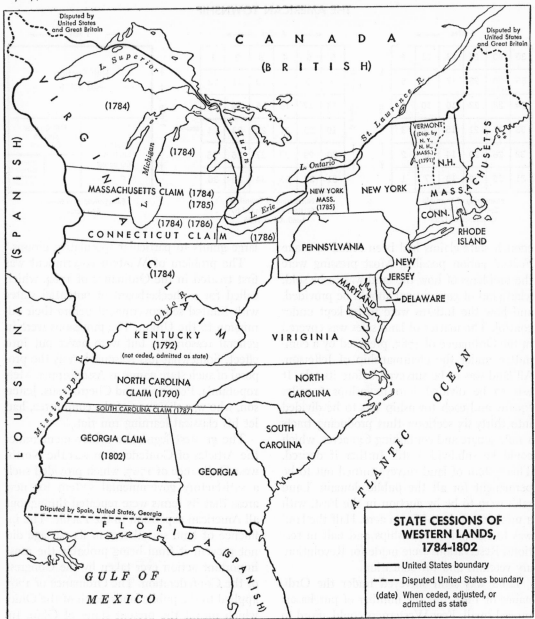

STATE CESSIONS OF
WESTERN LANDS,
1784-1802

——— United States boundary
- - - - Disputed United States boundary
(date) When ceded, adjusted, or
admitted as state

certain trade concessions, but she was far from anxious to encourage American expansion to the West. When Don Diego Gardoqui arrived in 1785 as minister to the new country, he followed time-honored diplomatic technique by providing presents for top officials and by making himself a devoted companion of Mrs. John Jay, whose husband was secretary of foreign affairs. His proposal that Americans accept the closing of the Mississippi in return for trading concessions elsewhere was placed before Congress and favored by a vote of 7 to 5, all the favorable votes being Northern. Although the vote was not sufficient to pass the measure, it was adequate to anger deeply the South and West.

The greatest opportunity of Congress lay in the control of Western lands, for by 1784

THE AMERICAN TOWNSHIP

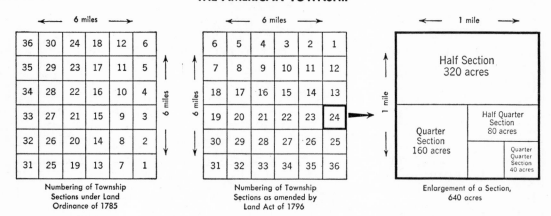

Numbering of Township
Sections under Land
Ordinance of 1785

Numbering of Township
Sections as amended by
Land Act of 1796

Enlargement of a Section,
640 acres

enough state claims had been ceded to make Federal action possible. Most pressing were the problems of how the land was to be sold, what kind of government should be provided, and how the Indians were to be kept under control. The matter of land sales was covered in the Ordinance of 1785, prepared by a committee under the chairmanship of Jefferson. All land was to be surveyed before its sale. It was to be divided into townships 6 miles square, and each township was to be divided into thirty-six sections, thus producing tracts 1 mile square and containing 640 acres, which could be subdivided still further if desired. This system of land surveys turned out to be permanent for all the public domain. Land sales were to be by auction in the East, with a minimum price of $1 an acre. Half the land was to be sold in townships and half in sections. Reservations were made for Revolutionary veterans and for education.

Land was soon surveyed under the Ordinance of 1785, but the number of purchasers proved small. Few Westerners could afford to attend Eastern auctions, and then they found the proffered tracts too large for their financial resources. The proponents of the law had realized that the purchase of a township could appeal only to a speculator, but from the standpoint of the Federal government the result was greater revenue with smaller costs of sale. This preference for the speculator was exaggerated when Congress began to make really

large grants to particular speculative groups.[3]

The problem of Western government was first treated in the Ordinance of 1784, which called for a checkerboard of potential states with limited self-government before their admission to the Union. The provisions were in general reasonable, but were never put into effect. Somewhat less reasonable was the proposal of such state names as Assenisippia, Metropotamia, Pelisippia, and Cherronesus. Jefferson, who was chairman of the committee, had let his classical learning run riot.

The greatest legislative achievement under the Articles of Confederation was the Northwest Ordinance of 1787, which provided such a satisfactory governmental system for new areas that its terms were repeated throughout all American expansion to the Pacific. The influence of land speculators in its passage did not prevent it from being probably the most important action ever taken by the Congress of the Confederation. The Ordinance of 1787 applied to the public lands north of the Ohio, which meant the present states of Ohio, Indiana, Illinois, Michigan, and Wisconsin, plus a small segment of Minnesota. Three stages of development were predicated. Initially, Congress passed all laws and appointed the necessary officials of governor, clerk, and three judges. When the territory contained 5,000 free, white, adult males, they could select a legislature and elect a congressional represent-

[3] See pp. 117–120.

THE NORTHWEST TERRITORY,
ESTABLISHED BY NORTHWEST
ORDINANCE OF 1787

Northwest Territory, including modern
states taken from it in whole or in part
---- Disputed boundary

ative who sat in the House and could speak but not vote. The third step came when the population reached 60,000, at which time a constitution might be adopted and the region admitted as a new state that would in every way be the equal of older members of the Union. The ordinance also guaranteed individual rights, encouraged education, and prohibited slavery.

Land sales and government were meaningless unless the Indians could be persuaded to move. Immediately at the end of the war, Congress permitted its elated spirit of victory to overwhelm its common sense and declared all Indian land claims forfeited. Whether or not such an assertion was properly founded in law, it was completely unenforceable; and Congress soon retreated to the slow business of arranging treaties for friendship and land ces-

sions. The administration of Indian affairs was placed in the hands of two departments, one north and one south of the Ohio River. Indian friendship was particularly difficult to maintain because white settlers continually disregarded Indian rights and settled where they pleased. Congress removed some of these unauthorized settlers, but had insufficient military forces to keep adequate control. Indian relations continued to remain unsatisfactory.

(*Congressional Failures.* The weakness of the Confederacy was a reflection of the real lack of national unity. Men might be bumptiously cocky over their successful war, but they still thought of themselves primarily as residents of their own states. Conflicts such as that between "Yankee and Yorker" died hard. Since business was no great respecter of either political or geographic lines, certain conflicts of interest arose inevitably. Some of them were settled quite amicably, such as the one between Pennsylvania and New Jersey over the navigation of the Delaware; between Virginia and Maryland over the navigation of the Potomac; between Virginia, Maryland, and Pennsylvania over the construction of a road to the West; and between Massachusetts and New York over their joint boundary.

Other state disputes did not end so happily, sometimes degenerating into outright conflicts. New Hampshire, New York, and Massachusetts clashed repeatedly over the "New Hampshire Grants," as Vermont was called, while land speculators headed by the Allen brothers capitalized on the situation by maintaining themselves for some years as an independent nation; the conflict was not solved until the admission of Vermont to the Union in 1791. Much worse was the heated dispute between Connecticut and Pennsylvania over the beautiful Wyoming Valley surrounding the modern city of Wilkes-Barre in northeastern Pennsylvania. By colonial charter Connecticut had a claim to this area; and even before the Revolution, settlers set up a little Connecticut along the Susquehanna. Pennsylvania resentment led to armed conflict in 1769 and again in 1776; but the states then listened to congressional appeals to devote their energies to fighting the British, and the issue lay dormant until after the war. A commission of 1782 followed the dictates of common sense rather than worrying about narrow legality and awarded the region to Pennsylvania, whereupon Pennsylvania celebrated its victory by voiding Connecticut claims and ousting Connecticut settlers. Once again the fat was in the fire, and only after further bloodshed was a compromise arranged by which the New Englanders were permitted to keep their individual holdings.

Another prolific source of confusion was the control of foreign trade, which was retained by the states and denied to Congress. A tangled web of levies, duties, harbor charges, and tariffs was the result. Naturally the Southern states, as farming areas, had few restrictions, while the Middle and Northern states tried to foster trade and manufacturing. Massachusetts, Connecticut, Rhode Island, New Hampshire, New York, and Pennsylvania all embraced high-tariff policies. Massachusetts, for example, levied ad valorem rates as high as 25 per cent on some imports, while Pennsylvania assessed incoming goods at almost 20 per cent. Although tariffs in a number of cases were levied only against foreign imports and reciprocity was practiced with neighboring states, even this policy brought difficulties. New York, for example, felt the necessity of taxing any foreign goods arriving through the neighboring states of Connecticut and New Jersey, and in fact tended to put somewhat higher rates on such articles. When New York placed high taxes on New Jersey farm products, New Jersey retaliated by placing a high tax on the Sandy Hook lighthouse built by New York. Not unknown was the kind of situation existing in Connecticut, where the state taxed Massachusetts products higher than she did comparable objects from England.

The trade-regulation situation was one of the most obvious indications of the weakness of the Federal government under the Articles of Confederation, and yet such difficulties should not obscure its positive achievements. Particularly in foreign affairs and in the handling of the Western lands did the Congress of the Articles perform valuable services. In addition it trained a body of public officials—for the army and navy, the post office, finance, and foreign affairs—that later was to operate under the new government of the Constitution.

The Congress of the Confederation was certainly an improvement over the Continental Congress and probably represented as strong a Federal government as most people would have accepted at that time. Certainly it was as strong as the radicals, who were the driving force of the Revolution, would countenance. Increasing nationalism, together with greater dominance by American conservatives, made possible a much stronger Federal government in 1787; and that government itself increased in strength through the years by both amendment and interpretation. But the America that had revolted against what it considered centralized tyranny required many years before it was willing to accept a much stronger government than the British rule which it had found sufficiently objectionable to inspire it to revolution.

CHAPTER 6

The Constitution

(1787-1789)

THE PHILADELPHIA CONVENTION

The troubles of the Confederation period, highlighted by Shays' Rebellion, raised the specter of civil disorder and confiscation in many American minds. Particularly did the wealthier and more conservative members of American society fear lest the institution of private property not survive against the egalitarianism of the lower economic groups. They doubted the possibility of any coherent foreign policy. They foresaw the possibility of disunity and of the appearance of three local federations arising from the ruins of the national government. They felt deeply that there was a crying need for a stronger national government.

An opportunity for reconsidering the Federal government arose when representatives of five states met at Annapolis, Maryland, in 1786 to decide problems of navigation rights on the Potomac River. Guided by the conservative Alexander Hamilton, they decided that the pertinent problems were really national and that there should be a general meeting of all states the next year. Congress harkened to their proposal and asked the states to elect delegates to a Philadelphia convention in 1787 to amend the Articles of Confedera-

tion. The convention met at the Pennsylvania metropolis during the late spring of 1787 and labored for over three months. Of the sixty-two delegates appointed formally by the states, only fifty-five attended any meeting, while the average daily attendance was nearer thirty. Thirty-nine signed the final draft.

The delegates to the Philadelphia convention were elected by the state legislatures; and since most state governments were controlled by the conservatives, they were almost exclusively members of the upper classes: shippers, speculators, bondholders, plantation owners, merchants, and lawyers. They were generally young, with such notable exceptions as the dignified Washington and the venerable Franklin; the latter was assigned a companion to be sure he did not indiscreetly divulge important secrets over his port. But they were conservative youngsters. Sam Adams was not elected. Patrick Henry refused to go because he "smelt a rat." Thomas Paine had moved to Europe. Jefferson and John Adams were abroad on official missions. These radicals were worried at the possibility of a very strong national government and preferred a federal arrangement by which considerable power could be retained by the states. Possibly significant is

76

the fact that Luther Martin of Maryland, who might be considered a representative of the mass of small farmers and artisans, refused to sign the final document and returned home to lead the opposition in Maryland.

The caliber of the delegates who assembled at Philadelphia was very high. In spite of the absence of Thomas Jefferson, John Adams, and John Jay, there was a plethora of former governors, members of Congress, signers of the Declaration, and diplomats. Their names form almost a *Who's Who* of famous Americans of the late eighteenth century. In wealth they belonged largely to the more privileged groups. In education they were extraordinary, almost half of them being college graduates. Obviously conservative, these delegates were intelligent conservatives, ready to make important concessions to more radical opinion so that their document might gain the support necessary for its adoption.

Outstanding among the multitude of luminaries were George Washington and Benjamin Franklin. Washington had left his beloved Mount Vernon to offer his sterling character, his unrelenting acceptance of public duty, and, it must be admitted, his glacial dignity to the movement for stronger government. The aged and erudite Benjamin Franklin, covered with renown from his successful French mission during the Revolution, was on hand to perform his last great public service: the application of his abundant fund of wisdom and tolerance to the cause of conciliation and amity. There were many others who added luster to their names. The Virginia delegation was crammed with able men. Not only Washington, but the indefatigable and acute James Madison was there to participate actively in the debates as well as to write his impressions of the meetings. Madison's notes are the most valuable record we have of the convention, for the minutes of the official secretary were scanty and almost illegible. Others from Virginia were George Wythe, a legal titan of his day; the prominent liberals James Monroe and George Mason; and the well-bred, well-meaning, but vacillating Edmund Randolph from the upper echelon of the state's society.

The most active members of the Pennsylvania delegation apart from Franklin were James Wilson, a canny and industrious Scotsman who labored very effectively; Gouverneur Morris, whose conservatism verged on reaction; and Robert Morris, financier of the Revolution. From New York came the youthful Alexander Hamilton, who was to play a vital role in the presidential administration of George Washington; his part in the convention was relatively unimportant, since he overlooked utterly the essential problem of Federalism by urging the establishment of a national government so powerful that the states would have been crushed.

Able spokesmen for the planters were the South Carolinians Charles Pinckney, his cousin Charles Cotesworth Pinckney, and John Rutledge. William Paterson of New Jersey became the nominal leader of the small-state forces, and Oliver Ellsworth and Roger Sherman of Connecticut were instrumental in arranging the "Connecticut Compromise," which solved the major problem of representation in the legislative branch of the government. Delaware sent the conservative John Dickinson, author of the influential, pre-Revolutionary *Letters from a Farmer in Pennsylvania.* . . . The Rhode Island delegation was conspicuous by its absence, since Rhode Island was the one state to refuse to send representatives.

DISCARDING THE OLD ARTICLES

Almost immediately upon convocation in Philadelphia, the members decided to ignore their specific instructions to amend the Articles of Confederation. They wrote a completely new document. Certain portions of the Articles, however, were adopted bodily into the new Constitution. The delegates realized that this maneuver would probably worry the radicals, who feared a strong national government, and so they made every effort to keep their meetings strictly secret. No outside observers were allowed, sentries guarded the closed doors, and dirt was spread on the street so that the deliberations might proceed unvexed by the noise of passing wagons. When the word of such procedures reached the back country, considerable suspicion was engendered; and this suspicion hardened into opposition when the final document appeared.

The convention generated inevitable personal and sectional differences that, intensified by the unrelenting humidity of an Atlantic seaboard summer, produced periodic occasions upon which the meeting appeared ready to disband with its work unfinished; and yet basically the delegates were agreed on certain broad and fundamental principles. These men of property and social responsibility desired a national government that would be sufficiently powerful to preserve order, against both foreign enemies and domestic insurrection, and to control both foreign and interstate trade—powers that inevitably meant restrictions on state sovereignty. They wanted property to be secure, which meant giving the Federal government power to lay and collect taxes, to obtain the return of "fugitive servants" (slaves), to guarantee the sanctity of contracts, and to prohibit state issues of money. They also desired intensely a limitation of current democratic trends, for they feared that propertyless people might seize control of the government and confiscate the wealth that they considered the basis of social order and progress. Not finding a practical method for limiting the suffrage to exclude the small and radical landowner, they developed other checks. Separation of power between the executive, legislative, and judicial branches of government was a restraining influence on controversial legislation. Indirect elections reduced the influence of the mass of the electorate. Long terms of office, and particularly of judges, lessened their responsiveness to public clamor.

❲ *The Representation Dilemma.* Of the points in dispute, the most argued was the composition of the legislative body; its final settlement has been called the "great compromise." The large Virginia delegation had

met before the convention opened and had drawn up the Virginia or "large-state" plan, by which there would be national executive, judiciary, and legislative departments, the last composed of two houses of which the lower would be elected by the people in proportion to population, and the upper by the lower. This system would have given control to more populous states such as Pennsylvania, Virginia, and Massachusetts and naturally met the opposition of numerically smaller states such as New Jersey, Delaware, and Maryland. After some delay the less populous states found their leader in William Paterson of New Jersey, who proposed the "small-state" plan of one house with equal representation for all the states. Paterson also suggested a plural executive for an unstated number of years. The small-state plan would have meant the reimposition of the Articles of Confederation and was quite unacceptable to most of the delegates.

The ensuing deadlock produced the most heated strife of the convention. Benjamin Franklin suggested an appeal to the Almighty lest the meeting adjourn in dismal failure, but Alexander Hamilton cynically objected to such intervention by a "foreign power." A committee was formed, and its recommendations, presented by Oliver Ellsworth in what has been designated the Connecticut Compromise, were finally adopted. The lower house—the House of Representatives—was to be elected on a basis of population, and an upper house—the Senate—was to be elected by the state legislatures, with equal representation among the states. This quarrel at the convention might seem to have presaged a continuing struggle, but the issue had no vitality. States have wailed that the Federal government intrudes into their own domains, geographical sections have clashed, and economic groups have collided head on, but the nation has never been plagued by a controversy between large and small states.

❲ *Other Compromises.* Another constitutional compromise settled the question of enumerating Negro slaves for purposes of taxation and representation. Because the number of representatives was determined by population, states with many slaves wished them counted for that purpose, while states with few or no slaves objected. Furthermore, the Constitution provided that taxation was also to be on the basis of population, whereupon the slave states felt that slaves should not be counted, and the free states that they should. After some debate a compromise was taken from a proposed amendment to the Articles of Confederation whereby three-fifths of the slaves were to be counted for both taxation and representation. Constitutional historians writing during the mid-nineteenth-century slavery controversy read a vast sectional clash into this dispute, which actually had little contemporary importance.

Several other controversies deserve mention. One concerned the executive branch of the government. The Virginia plan called for a single executive, and the New Jersey plan for a plural administration. Alexander Hamilton proposed that the President (as well as the Senators) be elected for life, but little attention was paid to this attempt to impose a monarchical system on America. Finally, it was decided that there would be one executive —the President of the United States—elected for a four-year term, with nothing said about reelections. No direct vote by the people was permitted, however; the unwieldy electoral-college method was installed.

Since the South was largely a producer of raw materials, certain compromises were necessary with the Northern shipping and manufacturing interests. The Southern demand that there be a prohibition of a Federal tax on exports was heeded and written into the Constitution. In addition, Georgia and South Carolina representatives were able to persuade the other delegations to prohibit any ban on the slave trade for twenty years after the adoption of the Constitution. In return for these concessions, the South dropped its advocacy of a plan whereby a two-thirds vote (implying a sectional veto) would be required on any act

regulating commerce. Southerners were to rue this decision during the nineteenth century, when they considered tariffs as primarily taxes on themselves.

A great deal of debate hinged on the question of the admittance of new territories to the Union. Such conservative Easterners as Gouverneur Morris were apprehensive about the future of the seaboard as population moved west. Their gloomy prognostications were finally ignored, and Congress was accorded freedom to deal with the problem as it saw fit. The general philosophy behind the Northwest Ordinance of 1787, and behind later legislation that carried its ideas farther west, ensured one of the happier developments under the Constitution: orderly progress from wilderness into settled state with privileges and responsibilities equal to those of the original members of the United States.

THE LIVING CONSTITUTION

❮ *Federalism and Nationalism.* The most important aspect of the completed Constitution was its division of powers between the Federal government and the states. The resulting Federalism gave very considerable powers to the Federal government, but also retained for the states larger powers than any other comparable constitution, while certain individual rights were guaranteed against any government. A somewhat curious system of dual citizenship was created, whereby an individual was a citizen of both state and nation.

The powers of Congress were stated in broad terms. It had the right to lay and collect taxes, duties, imposts, and excises, with the provision that they "be uniform throughout the United States," which has been interpreted by the Supreme Court in such a way that a constitutional amendment was necessary to permit an income tax. Although in general either house of Congress could originate legislation, only the House of Representatives could propose money bills. Congress had the right to borrow money, regulate foreign and interstate trade, pass naturalization and immigration laws, coin money, punish counterfeiters, establish a postal service, issue patents and copyrights, establish inferior courts, punish crimes on the high seas, declare war, call out the state militia, and raise and support an army and navy. Carefully written into the final point listed above was the requirement that no military appropriation should be for more than two years. This restriction was the product of a pervasive fear of military despotism and forced each Congress to reconsider military appropriations; presumably any possible danger to the Republic from the armed forces would thereby be stopped.

Some of the congressional powers were made clearly exclusive by their denial to the states— these prohibitions ordinarily came directly from the Articles of Confederation. The states were forbidden to wage war, to ally themselves with foreign nations, and to tax either imports or exports except under strict limitations. Particularly annoying both to state-rights advocates and to the debtor class was a constitutional bar against the state's power to "coin money" or to "make anything but gold and silver coin a tender in payment of debts." A ban on any interference with the "obligation of contracts" reiterated the conservative desire to protect property.

Both Congress and the states were denied the right to bestow titles of nobility or to pass either ex post facto laws or bills of attainder.[1] Congress alone was forbidden to interfere with the writ of habeas corpus (the accused must know the crime with which he is charged, and a reasonable date must be set for trial), to tax exports from any state, and to favor one state above another in commercial regulations or duties assessed.

In spite of the wide powers given Congress

and the limitations on the states, the states still retained a wide field of activity, either through the inclusion of a definite statement to that effect or because the Federal government was given no such right. States controlled the franchise and settled the vital question of who shall vote. The whole educational system was state-controlled. Such economic matters as the chartering and regulation of corporations and the control of factory and labor legislation were either shared with the national government or administered alone. Criminal administration remained primarily a state matter. Such powers have at times influenced foreign relations. Trials of foreign citizens in state courts and the expulsion of foreign students from state or local educational systems have occasionally produced diplomatic crises with other nations who find great difficulty in understanding why the United States cannot control its component parts in matters affecting foreign relations.

◖ *The Legislative Branch.* The legislative branch of the Federal government was called the Congress and consisted of a House of Representatives and a Senate. The House was apportioned according to the number of free adult males plus "three-fifths of all other persons" (mainly slaves); Indians not taxed were excluded from the enumeration. The House was elected by the votes of those who were eligible to cast ballots for the most numerous branch of the state legislature, and consequently disfranchisement in the state meant disfranchisement in the nation. The Senate consisted of two members from each state, regardless of population, elected by the state legislatures.

The House of Representatives was elected in full every two years. It had the sole power to originate money bills and was granted the right to impeach.[2] The Senate was divided for purposes of election so that one-third of its

[1] These prohibitions were included because of unfortunate experiences with both in Tudor and early Stuart England. Ex post facto laws retroactively make crimes of deeds that were legal when they were committed. A bill of attainder is a legislative act declaring an individual guilty of a crime. Since no trial is held, the accused has no opportunity to protect himself by using evidence in his favor.

[2] Some confusion exists concerning the impeachment process. The House of Representatives impeaches, in other words, brings charges against some government official. It is similar to an indictment in criminal law. The Senate, sitting as a court, then tries the individual impeached by the House.

members were chosen every two years. The Senate was granted equal legislative powers with the House and shared treaty-making and appointive powers with the President. According to the Constitution, the President was to have "the advice and consent" of the Senate in such matters; but in practice only the consent has been important.

(The Executive Branch. The executive authority of the new government was considerable, for the conservative delegates at Philadelphia were determined to avoid the errors of the Articles in this respect. The President of the United States was presumably removed, at least in part, from temporary popular excitement by the use of a cumbersome system in his selection. An Electoral College was created in which each state had representation equal to the total number of its Senators and Representatives. The electors were to ballot for the President and Vice-President, although originally no distinction was made between votes for the two offices. If no candidate had a majority in the Electoral College, the choice devolved upon the House of Representatives to elect a President from among the five top candidates. Twice in American history (1801 and 1825) the House has elected a President. With the two-party system firmly established, the present likelihood of a similar happening is remote.

The electoral system has usually worked fairly well, although there have been times in the nation's past when the candidate who received the majority of the popular votes lost the election in the Electoral College. Samuel Tilden in 1876 and Grover Cleveland in 1888 were the majority choices of the people, but in both cases the opposition candidates became President. There have been instances in recent times—such as when certain Texas delegates elected in 1944 on the Roosevelt ticket threatened to vote the other way, and when one Truman elector of 1948 voted against the man whom the voters expected him to support— that have caused many to fear that the electoral system might some day lead to a real crisis in American politics.

The powers granted to the President were considerable. He was made Commander in Chief of the armed forces, and in time of war he assumed tremendous responsibility that has never yet been limited or defined in a satisfactory manner. All bills passed by Congress had to have the presidential signature before they became law, unless he failed to return the bill within ten days and Congress had not adjourned within the period. A presidential veto required a two-thirds vote of both houses of Congress to override. The President made treaties, with the advice and consent of the Senate, provided that two-thirds of the Senate agreed. Although according to the Constitution the House of Representatives has nothing to say about treaty making, in actuality the House can kill a treaty simply by refusing to appropriate money to carry out its provisions.

Under the vague permission of the executive to appoint heads of departments and to ask their advice, the Cabinet system has developed. Three such chiefs were originally appointed in the first Washington administration, and others have been added through the years. The President's position is quite secure between elections. He can be removed only by impeachment proceedings, but the one such case in American history (Andrew Johnson in 1868) failed. Whereas the Vice-President normally presides over the Senate when the House brings impeachment charges, the Chief Justice of the Supreme Court occupies the chair at the trial of the President. Obviously the delegates at Philadelphia feared that the Vice-President might be tempted to use unfair methods against the President to obtain his job.

(The Judicial Branch. The third main branch of the constitutional government was the judicial. Judicial power was vested in a Supreme Court of unspecified size, with life tenure for the judges (subject to impeachment), and in whatever lesser courts Congress might establish. Cases over which the Federal courts had jurisdiction were those involving laws or treaties of the United States, those concerning admiralty law, those to which the United States was a party, those between citizens of different states, and those concerning states and citizens of another state or a foreign nation. The last point was changed by the Eleventh Amendment to the Constitution (1798), which returned the jurisdiction to the state involved. In cases involving foreign diplomats or controversies to which a state is a party, the Supreme Court was given original jurisdiction. In all other cases it had appellate jurisdiction; that is, it could hear appeals from lower courts.

The right of trial by jury was guaranteed, and a very careful definition of treason was written into the Constitution. Treason was to consist of "levying war" against the United States, "or in adhering to their enemies, giving them aid and comfort," and conviction could ensue only after open confession of the accused or the testimony of two witnesses to the "overt act." Although nothing precise was said about the doctrine of judicial review (the process by which the Supreme Court can declare an act of the United States unconstitutional and therefore null and void), there is no reason to doubt that the delegates assumed that this power would be used. The tradition of judicial review was deep in colonial experience; and John Marshall, who later was Chief Justice from 1801 to 1837, was instrumental in gaining general recognition of the theory.

⟨ *The Amending Process.* Changes in the original Constitution have come both from interpretations and from amendments, of which the former are much the more important. The founding fathers descended from no mountain above the Schuylkill River bearing the Constitution on tablets of stone as the word of God to apply for time everlasting. The document was not, as the eminent British statesman William Gladstone said, "the greatest work ever struck off at a given time by the brain and purpose of man." Rather it was a useful charter based on past experience and needing change in the future. Luckily it was worded loosely enough to be molded, altered, and adapted as a dynamic society grew to maturity

under evolving conditions that made changing interpretations mandatory.

The Constitution was fortunate in being brief and at times vague. Instead of spelling out an answer for each small problem, a good deal of leeway was made possible. For example, the permission granted to the President to consult departmental chiefs inspired the Cabinet system, while the short judicial section has enabled many changes to be made without formal amendment. Possibly more important was the permission given to Congress "to make all laws which shall be necessary and proper" to carry out its specific grants of authority. This "elastic clause" was the increasingly important source of authority for all sorts of Federal actions, while other clauses, such as the power to make appropriations, have been almost equally productive of new functions. Objections to the expanding powers of the Federal government have been frequent and bitter, but certainly the application of narrow eighteenth-century concepts to twentieth-century conditions would have been considerably worse.

The technique for adding to or altering the original document was deliberately made difficult and time-consuming by the constitutional fathers. An amendment could be proposed either by two-thirds of both houses of Congress or by a convention called by two-thirds of the states. The amendment was considered adopted when it was accepted by three-fourths of the states—sometimes the Constitution seems a study in fractions—either by act of the legislature or by special convention (invariably the former). The amendment immediately became a part of the Constitution and had equal force with any section of the original document. An amendment can be changed or repealed only by a new amendment.

The difficulties of the cumbersome and unwieldy amendment process have been proved by the fact that the Constitution has been amended only twenty-two times in our history, and of these, a block of ten came almost at once. Only twelve have been adopted since 1791, although literally thousands have been suggested. Actually, the first ten may be considered as practically an integral part of the original document. The Philadelphia convention had failed to include a Bill of Rights in its production and found necessary a guarantee that this omission would speedily be remedied. That promise was kept in 1791. Such vital rights as freedom of speech, of the press, of peaceful assembly, of petition, and of worship were included. The privilege of the people to keep and bear arms was guaranteed. Private dwellings were protected against the quartering of troops and against the search and seizure of papers and other property, except under strict limitations. The rights of the accused in criminal action were precisely enumerated in four articles. The final two amendments of the Bill of Rights reflected some distrust of the national government. Article IX stated that because certain rights were listed in the Constitution, it was not to be assumed that other rights were not retained by the people. Article X reserved to the states or to the people the powers not delegated to the United States.

Of the amendments adopted since 1791, one (XI), discussed earlier, concerned legal procedure. Five were concerned with voting and office holding—the election of President and Vice-President (XII), the election of Senators (XVII), woman suffrage (XIX), the terms of office of President and Congress (XX), and the length of the presidential incumbency of a single man (XXII). The remaining six dealt with slavery, the income tax, and prohibition. Slavery was eliminated (XIII); the freedmen were declared citizens (XIV); and states were forbidden to restrict voting rights for reasons of "race, color, or previous condition of servitude" (XV). An income tax was permitted (XVI). Intoxicating liquors were outlawed (XVIII), and then the prohibition repealed (XXI).

◗ Some Constitutional Faults. Changes, either by interpretation or amendment, indicate that the American people have not found the original Constitution perfect. The desirability of a bill of rights was recognized immediately. The cumbersome Electoral College system was soon modified in practice. The democracy that was suspect to the fathers be-

came increasingly common and was reflected in several amendments. The sanctity of property was so strongly embedded in the Constitution that even moderate controls proved difficult to apply. The drawn-out amendment process, the tortuous course of judicial review, the indirect system of elections and appointments—all proved to possess certain difficulties in the long run.

One distinctive feature of the American system—the chronological rotation of elections—has produced difficulties. Contrary to most other systems of popular government, American elected officials have terms stated in specific numbers of years, and elections are held at stated intervals whether or not any particular issue exists. The case of the President is a good example. Once every four years the people vote for the Chief Executive, even though there may be no particular issue; or, at the other extreme, the President must interrupt his vital activities during a major crisis to campaign for reelection. In the years between elections it is almost impossible to get rid of a President, no matter how bad he may seem. The situation obviously is different in Great Britain, France, and other Western democracies. Moreover, the President is not a member of the legislative branch and may well find himself, with our election system, in the almost impossible situation in which his party controls only one house of Congress, or even neither house. The result may well be practical stagnation in legislative affairs, with the President and Congress fighting each other bitterly.

◗ The Essential Success of the Constitution. Possible adverse criticism of certain provisions of the Constitution should not obscure its epochal character. Almost incredibly, an eighteenth-century charter has proved adaptable to twentieth-century conditions with only minor changes. If conservatives wrote the Constitution, they were enlightened conservatives, willing to compromise, to make concessions to somewhat more democratic opinion, and to leave in abeyance or in guarded vacuities problems that needed the passing of time before solutions could be found. A strong national government had been formed without destroying the dual citizenship of state and nation that is the basis of federalism. A republican form of government was instituted in a day when monarchy was almost universal. Property rights were accorded full protection, yet human liberties were not forgotten. Strong executive and judicial branches were instituted, but the legislative arm, more responsive to popular opinion, was granted some power to bring the others to heel. The system of checks and balances kept a degree of equilibrium among the governmental sections. When the Constitution of the United States is compared with contemporary governments in Europe or Asia, it stands as a remarkably liberal charter. Perhaps the final proof is that the American people have been able to grow and prosper under it for the better part of two centuries. Only an intelligently patriotic and politically wise group could have accomplished the task so magnificently.

THE RATIFICATION BATTLE

It must have been with fear and trepidation for the future of the Constitution that the delegates returned home to answer the charges of irate and suspicious fellow citizens that the secret meetings in Philadelphia had undone the work of the Revolution. Even before the convention adjourned, storm clouds shadowed the horizon. Only thirty-nine delegates signed the completed document. Luther Martin, champion of the debt-harassed farmers, had long since left, vowing eternal opposition. Elbridge Gerry of Massachusetts, Edmund Randolph of Virginia, and John Lansing and Robert Yates of New York were among others who refused to sign. Such Revolutionary war horses as Sam Adams and Patrick Henry were sniffing the smoke of controversy and donning their armor. George Clinton of New York and Willie Jones of North Carolina were numbered among the important state politicos known to be opposed.

When the Constitution was published, the storm broke. As its stipulations were spelled out in Western taverns or mulled over in the flickering light from farm firesides, popular resentment increased. Where was a bill of rights? Where were the safeguards for state sovereignty? Where were effective checks on the President lest a ruthless "man on horseback" impose a military despotism? Where was the jealously guarded legislative supremacy that had been the shield against autocracy? Where were the interests of the poor man upheld against the greed of the wealthy? The myriad facets of American discontent found a leader in Richard Henry Lee of Virginia, whose influential pamphlet, *Letters from a Federal Farmer to the Republican*, warned of dangers inherent in a government too powerful. Higher rose the clamor as the embattled conservatives hastened to the fray.

No worthwhile statistics concerning popular opinion about the Constitution have remained for the historian to study. It was long before the coming of public-opinion polls; and eighteenth-century opinion must be winnowed from diaries, letters, and editorials in the press. Since the upper class is usually the more articulate and literary, a true picture is difficult to draw. Recognizing a possibility of error, most authorities conclude that a majority of American citizens in all probability opposed ratification of the Constitution; and it seems quite likely that if the lower class had enjoyed the franchise, the Constitution would not then have been adopted.

The drive of the conservatives, however, was able to carry the day against the more mute and ineffective, if larger, opposition. Most of the wealthy, learned, and landed men were in favor of ratification. The lawyers turned out in considerable force; the merchants, happy to see a vision of trade and commerce free from state restrictions, welcomed the Constitution; and the owners of large Southern plantations fell into step. But it must not be assumed that only the upper classes favored the stronger national government. Some farmers, particularly those a little better off than the average, approved; and the conservatives picked up some valuable allies in the Northern cities among the sailors and artisans who hoped for new economic opportunity. Some Westerners shunted aside their natural abhorrence of a centralized rule because a stronger nation might deal effectively with the Indian problem and adopt a firmer tone in speaking to Briton and Spaniard. The universal expectation that George Washington would be the first President helped. The most important asset to those favoring the Constitution, however, was the fact that the groups naturally opposed to it—the lower economic classes—did not have the vote.

The supporters of ratification adopted the name Federalists and forced the opposition to take the negative appellation of Antifederalists. The Federalists had more impressive personnel than their antagonists. George Washington, George Wythe, James Madison, John Marshall, and Edmund Randolph (who had been converted after refusing to sign the document) marshaled the Virginia Federalists. If Benjamin Franklin's rich experience of over eight decades brought only wavering support in Pennsylvania, able assistance came from Gouverneur Morris and James Wilson. Alexander Hamilton, who had feared that the Constitution was far too democratic, philosophically accepted it as better than nothing and moved to the front in New York. In other states, Federalists of equal ability if not of similar fame guided and directed the drive for ratification.

If the writings of Richard Henry Lee thrilled the opposition, the collective efforts of Alexander Hamilton, James Madison, and John Jay channeled the Federalist arguments in a series of letters called the *Federalist* papers appearing in the New York City press. These essays are among the most effective political writings extant. Couched in clear and exact rhetoric, a carefully dispassionate and rational logic stressed the advantages that would follow the establishment of the constitutional government. Fears that the new rule might crush human liberties were deprecated, and a lessening of the "factionalism" rampant in the Articles of Confederation guaranteed. Particular emphasis was placed upon claims that prosperity would ensue if the Constitution were ratified and that a firm and united foreign policy would compel respect abroad. The *Federalist* papers were only the more prominent of a flood of pamphlets, editorials, and speeches that upheld the ratification side.

Even with the thunder of brilliant oratory and the charming persuasiveness of polished literature, the Federalists found it necessary to resort to compromise and occasionally to stoop to trickery to gain the approval of the nine states that had to ratify the Constitution before it could go into effect. In some states Federalist victory was easy. There was little or no struggle in Delaware, New Jersey, Connecticut, Maryland, South Carolina, and Georgia, but considerable strife marred tranquility in others. Pennsylvania Federalists, whose stronghold was Philadelphia, lowered themselves to use most dubious tactics. A convention was hastily called, and it voted acceptance before the strong Antifederalists from the western counties arrived.[3] After a hot contest in Massachusetts, the Federalists won a narrow victory only by the definite pledge that a bill of rights would be immediately written into the Constitution. The ninth state to ratify the Constitution and thus make it the law of the land was New Hampshire. Two meetings were called; the first was filled with Antifederalists and no vote was allowed. A second meeting gained a ten-vote victory for the constitutional supporters.

The Constitution may have been legally adopted, but it was worthless without the acceptance of Virginia, the largest state, and geographically vital New York. In Virginia the "tidewater" and the conservative farmers of the Shenandoah Valley combined against the more radical back country. A long and involved contest took place, the Federalists winning a ten-vote majority in a total of 168. The hottest fight was in New York, where the division was so deep between the inland Antifed-

---

[3] The Pennsylvania legislature wished to call a special convention to ratify the Constitution, but because of the deliberate absence of Antifederalist members no quorum was present. A Federalist mob forcibly carried two delegates into the legislature, and the quorum was announced.

eralists and the New York City Federalists that threats of secession were freely hurled. Governor George Clinton was staunch in opposition, but the Federalists cleverly made him chairman of the convention, and the scrupulous Clinton refused to use his authority unfairly. The untiring efforts of Alexander Hamilton and others (Hamilton is suspected of buying the votes of some rural delegates) finally achieved success by a 30 to 27 vote. Opposition continued unabated in North Carolina and Rhode Island. The former did not ratify until 1789, and the obstinate Rhode Islanders (who had sent no delegate to the Philadelphia convention) refused to join the Union altogether. It took the combined efforts of Massachusetts and Connecticut, through threats to establish customs houses along the border, before a grudging ratification was given in May, 1790,

almost two years after the Constitution had been officially adopted.

Despite the victory of the Federalists, the opposition had not been in vain. From Antifederalist endeavors, the American people gained the Bill of Rights. The conservatives learned that persuasion was necessary and that even with all the restrictions on voting power, popular opinion must be heeded, assuaged, and counseled—it could not be ignored. It had been a long and hard fight, both to write and to ratify the new charter; and, with the usual acquiescence of the loser in the democratic political game, the Antifederalists settled back to see how the constitutional government would work. To use a metaphor popular in the Federalist press, the American ship of state had trimmed its sails and tacked upon a new course.

CHAPTER 7

Continuing Economic Colonialism

(1789-1815)

A NATIVE POPULATION

Successful political revolution no more produced a cohesive nation than would dressing nine men in similar uniforms produce a baseball team. At the end of the American Revolution "these" United States were little more than thirteen independent units that had been cooperating to a limited extent against a common danger, and even after the adoption of a Constitution they still lacked economic, social, and intellectual understanding and unity. Colonialism did not disappear overnight. Unified national life required something more than a successful revolution, or even a good central government.

The United States of 1790 was approximately a quarter the size of the present continental United States and was almost encircled by more or less unfriendly powers. Its fabulously rich natural resources remained largely for the future to discover, but obvious at the time were the rich farming lands, the majestic rivers, and the magnificent and widespread forests. The American population of some four million was located almost entirely east of the Appalachians, fading into nothingness toward the north into the present Maine and toward Florida in the south.

The spectacular growth of American population was a basic contribution toward national power. Intelligent guesses indicate that the English settlements doubled in population about each twenty to twenty-five years and that this magnificent expansion continued during and after the Revolution. The usual estimate for 1775 is under three million; the First Census of 1790 showed slightly under four million; and the enumeration of 1810 indicated something over seven million. The relative importance of the birth rate and of immigration can only be guessed; but certainly the number of arrivals during the troubled period of the Revolution was small, while even as late as 1820 the first official figures showed only 8,385 immigrants. America's new citizens must for the most part have been born in America, with the splendid fertility of American parents more influential than foreign migration.

THE AGRICULTURAL WAY OF LIFE

America, from its earliest settlements until well into the nineteenth century, was above all a nation of farmers. As late as 1790 no more

87

THE UNITED STATES
ABOUT 1790

—— Boundaries

▪▪▪▪▪ Canals (only canals mentioned
in text are shown)

than a dozen towns could boast as many as 5,000 people, while twenty years later the number had reached only twenty-eight. And even the towns had a definitely rural aura, since they functioned mainly as purchasing and distributing centers for the surrounding countrysides. The average American talked with greatest authority on such agricultural essentials as the raising of corn and hogs; his diary was likely to be filled with daily notes on the weather. Scratch almost any town dweller and one found the farmer underneath.

Farming during the colonial and early national periods was of the individualistic and independent type that appealed to Thomas Jefferson as the ideal way of life for a democratic nation. Ordinarily land was owned in fee simple and in relatively small tracts. Although the number of big plantations increased in the South during the eighteenth century, the large farm remained the exception rather than the rule. Outside of New England there had been almost universal attempts at some sort of feudal tenure, but these relics of medieval

Europe proved objectionable to Americans, and very soon the few survivals, such as the estates along the Hudson, were startling anachronisms.

The investment of the average farmer was small. His land remained modest in price because of the competition of millions of unoccupied and fertile acres almost at his back door, and this profusion of potential farming land was kept constantly before the farmers' eyes by the omnipresent activities of the land speculators, who were to remain an outstanding feature of American civilization. Practically every prominent American, including such men as Washington, Henry, and Marshall, speculated in Western land. The outstanding operator in the postwar period was the well-known financier Robert Morris, whose 6 million acres in seven states included a goodly portion of the future national capital; like many other speculators, Morris ultimately went bankrupt. Such men called the attention of the farmer to potentially competing land, and hence very possibly encouraged the slovenly farming methods that were so usual. With new and rich acres almost for the taking, the incentive toward intensive farming declined.

The American farmer had not only relatively cheap land, but also simple and inexpensive tools. The ancient Egyptian would have understood the equipment of the American farmer during the two centuries from 1620 to 1820 much better than the early American agriculturalist would have understood the tools of the twentieth century. It was said that the average farmer could shoulder all his implements except his harrow and oxcart. Most tools were constructed of wood, although iron was sometimes used for the plow edge, for plating the spade, and for a two-tined fork; possibly the local blacksmith shaped the metal, but it is even more likely that the farmer was his own blacksmith. Hand labor was the usual motive force, horses and oxen being used only as supplements. For example, grain was strewn by hand, cut by scythe, and threshed with a flail.

The ordinary farm in the first two centuries of American history was something of a factory community in which the family performed the labor, since agricultural employees were scarce and hence expensive. Father not only planted and reaped, but also acted as toolmaker and repairer, carpenter, mason, mechanic, and even at times shoemaker. Mother was at least as fully occupied in her manifold functions of cook, washing and cleaning woman, candlemaker, textile worker, lye-soap producer, baker, gardener, dairymaid, and even doctor and nurse. Her services were vital for a successful farm, and if she died from overwork and excessive childbearing, she was replaced as soon as possible; in time the family burying plot might contain two or three such exhausted wives encircling their lord and master. Children were quite naturally pressed into service as soon as they could toddle. By adolescence the boy was doing full-time plowing, while the girl was working side by side with her mother in the kitchen.

Isolated and relatively self-sufficient farms had certain obviously unpleasant features. Food was simple, monotonous, and usually poorly cooked—a year-round diet of corn bread and salt pork is hardly inspiring. Fruits and vegetables were available in season, but modern canning methods were unknown; salting, drying, and burying in sand could be praised only as better than nothing. Water from well or brook or spring was frequently polluted by the barnyard or outhouse. Flies and other vermin were accepted as inevitable; one became hardened to bedbugs and merely brushed the cloud of flies away from each bite of food. The inevitable result was sickness, including frequent epidemics. Doctors ordinarily were not available, but their absence was not necessarily a calamity, since they did not know the origin, the nature, or the proper treatment of almost any disease.

Low farming income naturally circumscribed cultural opportunities. Schools were few and poor, and the rate of illiteracy was high. Churches were often remote, while theaters and museums were nonexistent.

Newspapers, magazines, and books were too expensive to be purchased in large numbers, even if the family could read. The news—chiefly local gossip—was brought home by father from his periodic trips to a neighboring small town to exchange his surplus for salt or cutlery or other articles not produced on the farm.

The advantages of farming life were as real, although not as apparent, as the disadvantages. Each farmer was an independent, self-respecting man who recognized his stake in the community and nation and who consequently was a responsible citizen, giving long and sober consideration to proposals that affected public policy, even though he had scanty information at his command. His relatively low standard of living was not the occasion for bitter repining, since the overwhelming bulk of the country was no better off. His near economic self-sufficiency made him less dependent on transportation, markets, and finance than were his successors of a later date. War inflation during the Revolution had brought high prices and plentiful demand, so that the confusion and falling prices at the end of the war seemed particularly distressing to the farmer as the prices of crops declined, taxes were difficult to pay, and farm mortgages were foreclosed; yet conditions were relatively better than those of a century or more later. Since most farmers had no mortgages and produced the bulk of their food and other necessities, large numbers merely tightened their belts and waited for better times.

Into this stable world of the farmer new ideas made their way but slowly. Throughout the colonial period and even into the nineteenth century, changes were few. The farmer was conservative by nature. He had learned his job from his father, he traveled but little, and his reading was meager even if he were literate. The plenitude of cheap, virgin, fertile acres acted as a deterrent. Hence, although farmers everywhere complained that their land was wearing out, newfangled ideas of cultivation were accepted slowly and reluctantly. Gradually the traditional three-crop rotation

was modified. The use of manure increased, so that the farmer less frequently moved his barn to avoid it. Around 1800 new breeds of stock were being introduced, including the "Patton cattle" (Durham) of the 1780s and Merino sheep after 1800.

Agricultural innovations came largely from "gentlemen farmers" who had sufficient leisure to investigate the best current European practices and adequate funds to risk loss in their own experimentation. Typical of this group was George Washington. Washington tried various seeds in different soils. He experimented with new breeds of cattle and with a variety of feeds and fertilizers. He plowed in such a way as to lessen erosion. He investigated numerous types of crop rotation, including one which involved seven crops. Like so many men of his class, he lost money on his experiments, and yet his efforts advertised a number of ideas that later became important.

The results of experimentation such as that of Washington were relatively unimportant when circulated only by letters and conversations. Some of them found their way into the various books of agriculture that were produced during colonial days; but not until 1784 was there formed at Charleston the first Society for the Promotion of Agriculture, designed to discuss and publish agricultural ideas. Once the way was opened, other similar societies came into existence rather rapidly—Philadelphia, 1785; New York, 1791; Massachusetts and Connecticut, 1792. The schools were quite inactive in agricultural instruction, since most people scoffed at the idea that farming could be taught from books. Spectacularly rare was the introduction by Columbia in 1792 of a chair of natural history, chemistry, and agriculture, even though the amount of agriculture taught by its occupant is a dubious matter, while, of course, very few potential farmers went to college.

◖ *Southern Farming.* The usual varied farming of the United States found its most numerous exceptions in the South, although even here traditional farming was the majority procedure until well into the nineteenth century. The great staples of Southern colonial farming were tobacco, rice, and indigo; and all three were exported in large amounts. Tobacco was indigenous to America, but as soon as its delights were discovered by the Virginia colonists, its cultivation became a profitable business. Tobacco was hard on the land, wearing out much soil in Virginia and Maryland even in colonial times; farmers found it cheaper to move to new areas than to restore the fertility of land that had grown tobacco too long. Rice became an important crop of the coastal lands, particularly of South Carolina, in the years around 1700. About the middle of the eighteenth century, indigo, a plant dye, was introduced successfully and proved particularly attractive because the nature of its culture permitted it to be grown on the same lands as rice, with the same labor force and in alternate periods.

Southern staples changed markedly in the period after the Revolution. Rice culture moved farther west and for a time lost its importance. Indigo disappeared from the American scene with the end of the British colonial bounty. Tobacco pushed into the Piedmont and across the mountains into Kentucky, being replaced in part by wheat, which moved down into large areas of Virginia and North Carolina. Sugar became practical in Louisiana in the years around 1800 and soon expanded magnificently.

The staple that soon was to dominate Southern agriculture and fix the character of Southern life was cotton, which had been of no importance in colonial times because of the difficulty of removing the seeds. The first solution of the seed problem came in the 1780s with the development of long-staple, sea-island cotton, from which the seeds could be ejected merely by passage between rollers. Although this cotton was excellent and was grown in large amounts, the plants were tender and difficult to cultivate and could be grown only in limited, humid areas. The more important answer to the seed problem was evolved by an ingenious Connecticut Yankee, Eli Whitney, a Yale graduate who was teaching in the South. Impressed by talk of the need for some machine to remove the seeds from cotton, his inventive imagination needed only ten days to produce (1793) a small and crude cotton gin that would remove the seeds from about 50 pounds a day if operated by hand, or 1,000 pounds if powered by water. The results were revolutionary. Within the next decade came an almost eightfold increase in the cotton crop, and the domination of Southern agriculture by cotton was in sight.

❪ *The Southern Labor Supply.* Southern emphasis on staples brought a pressing demand for labor, which was scarce and expensive everywhere in the colonies. The first important source, available only in colonial days, was found in white indentured servants. Many Englishmen and other Europeans looked hopefully to the New World for a fresh start in life, but had not the funds for the trip. Planters wanting labor, ship captains, and other speculators advanced passage money if the immigrant promised to work a given number of years—ordinarily between two and seven. This arrangement might have been completely advantageous for all concerned had not many profit-minded men been overly eager for returns. Sometimes men, women, and children were actually kidnapped, while almost always they were packed too tightly in the ships and fed inadequately, with a consequently high mortality rate. Furthermore, a good many criminals were sent to America as indentured servants—a cheap way of getting rid of undesirables.

The second answer to the labor problem was the Negro slave, but during the seventeenth century the Dutch maintained an almost complete monopoly of the slave trade and found their best markets in the West Indies, so that relatively few Negroes were transported to North America. The eighteenth century saw the English and Americans, spearheaded by the Royal African Company (incorporated in 1672), break the Dutch monopoly. An ever-increasing flow of Negroes came to North

America. Although slaves appeared in all the colonies,[1] the Southern planters found them particularly useful. The Negro was cheap and usually docile, physically strong, undemanding about living conditions, and available for life rather than for a short term of years. His great disadvantage was that he had no background for farm labor, although the frequent assertion that slave labor was the cause of land exhaustion is not accurate; the thin Southern land, devoted year after year to a single crop, was bound to deteriorate, regardless of the color or efficiency of the labor supply. Slave labor did, however, immobilize large amounts of capital, increase the difficulties of diversifying crops, displace white farmers, discourage white immigration, and retard the advance of general Southern culture.

The availability of the Negro slave undoubtedly had some influence in encouraging large plantations during the eighteenth century; and as plantations expanded, the demand for slaves increased. But in spite of this trend, the South was far from being an area of large plantations before the Revolution, and the expansion of the large estate seemed limited by the potential market for existing Southern staples. A complicating factor was the general acceptance of eighteenth-century ideals of freedom and the inherent rights of man. Most outstanding Southerners, imbued with the current ideology and well aware of the economic and social problems inherent in slavery, began to look for ultimate freedom for the slave, even though they appreciated the difficulties of the transition to freedom. This point of view received its deathblow rather ironically from a Northerner, Eli Whitney, whose cotton gin made cotton culture a profitable business that could use slave labor satisfactorily. Social idealism felt the force of economic facts. Within another generation Negro slavery was to be accepted quite universally in the South, even though in the years shortly after 1800 it remained in public opinion something more of a sad necessity than a positive good.

[1] Massachusetts was the only state to report no Negro slaves in the First Census of 1790.

EARLY INDUSTRIES

《 *Colonialism Still Remains.* Economically, America remained essentially a colonial area until well after 1800. It was originally a debtor region producing raw materials, and this status was reinforced by British policy, since England saw her colonies as supplementing her own economy and not as potential rivals. By subsidies on one hand and prohibitions on the other, England tried to keep America primarily a producer of raw materials that would be processed in the homeland. The results of such policies were apparent for many years after the pressures were removed.

Outstanding industries before the Revolution included the fur trade, the production of lumber and naval stores, and fishing. Every colony profited from the fur business; and although New York was preeminent, the Southern colonies found the trade particularly lucrative. This business was a potent factor in creating friction between the English and French empires in America. Lumber was available in large amounts throughout the colonies, and the sawmill was one of the earliest commercial establishments. Naval stores such as tar, pitch, and turpentine were highly desired colonial products from the standpoint of England and hence were paid bounties throughout the first half of the eighteenth century. Part of colonial lumber was used for shipbuilding, which was particularly important in the Middle and Northern colonies, but which also existed along the entire seaboard. Ships meant sailors and a fishing industry, particularly in New England. Every New England boy seemed a potential sailor, and fishing boats put out of every New England port; conflict with the French off the Newfoundland banks was one of the results of the business. With reason was the image of a cod put above the Massachusetts statehouse. A specialized type of fishing was whaling—particularly for oil for lamps. New England whalers, starting operations in the seventeenth century, were eventually found in almost every part of the world.

Industrial production in the modern sense was almost nonexistent in colonial America. Cloth was made at home, except for choice varieties that were imported. In the early years the entire process was domestic, but the more difficult jobs of carding, fulling, and dyeing began to be commercialized by the mid–eighteenth century, while professional spinners and weavers offered their services. Iron was widely existent in America. Colonial iron mills soon appeared from Massachusetts to Virginia, whereupon England tried (1750) to limit the colonials to the production of pig iron. Among other colonial products were furniture, grist, glass, bricks, leather, candles, beer, and small metal articles such as nails. The greatest centers for distilling rum were Philadelphia; New York; Boston; Newport, Rhode Island; and Medford, Massachusetts. Lynn, Massachusetts, was said to produce 80,000 pairs of shoes and boots in 1768, but most shoes were made either at home or by itinerant shoemakers; increasingly, factories furnished the materials for home production. English efforts to restrict these colonial manufactures were generally ineffective.

(*Post-revolutionary Industrialism.* Numerous profit-minded Americans longed for prosperous American manufacturing, and these aspirations became more intense when the patriotic impulse to attain national self-sufficiency was added. Organizations such as the Pennsylvania Society for the Encouragement of Manufactures and Useful Arts (1787) propagandized the virtues of factory production, and this particular society established, with state aid, a cotton mill that soon failed. But although the United States was blessed with plentiful raw materials, it lacked good transportation, cheap and skilled labor, large markets, trained engineers, and experienced managers. Although Americans tried more or less frantically to develop manufacturing, the results were disappointing, at least through the War of 1812.

Among American enthusiasts for manufacturing, none was more influential than Alexander Hamilton. In his private capacity he was active in the Society for Establishing Useful Manufactures (1791), chartered in New Jersey to make a great variety of products, including paper, textiles, hats, shoes, and metalware. This group established the first real American factory town at Paterson, New Jersey, but its plans were too ambitious for its resources and abilities. It failed in the middle 1790s.

Hamilton was also influential as Secretary of the Treasury, particularly through his "Report on Manufactures" in 1791.[2] Hamilton insisted upon the advantages of manufacturing as compared to farming and held that inadequate male labor could be replaced by women and children, while capital could be made available by chartering banks. He hymned the praise of division of labor because it developed habits of hard work, added to and diversified employment, and improved farmers' markets. Government should encourage manufacturing, and a considerable portion of the entire Hamiltonian legislative program buttressed these ideas. The funding of the public debt strengthened the capitalistic investing class, the chartering of a national bank produced more credit, and the levying of a tariff gave at least minor protection to infant manufactures.

Hamilton was but one of many men who saw the development of factories as desirable, not only for general American prosperity, but also for their own profit. The first specialized woolen mill appeared before 1790, which was the year of the opening of the historically famous Samuel Slater cotton factory at Providence; practically all such mills used water power, the steam engine being introduced very slowly. Iron production increased, and Americans proved particularly ingenious in making small metal objects; for example, a nail machine was put into operation about 1790. Other manufacturing, such as furniture, harnesses, and distilled liquors, also continued to expand. Particular industries tended to concentrate in certain localities, such as iron at Richmond and Pittsburgh; hats at Reading,

[2] See p. 133.

Pennsylvania, and Danbury, Connecticut; shoes at Lynn, Massachusetts; and clocks at Waterbury, Connecticut—the name of Seth Thomas was well known even at that time. But in spite of such developments the United States was still not an outstanding country for manufacturing. English products such as textiles and cutlery were superior, and American production was confined heavily to the cheaper and rougher articles designed for domestic markets and for less advanced areas like the West Indies.

Probably the greatest single American contribution to manufacturing was the idea of interchangeable parts developed by Eli Whitney. Whitney's hopes for wealth had not been realized with the cotton gin, so he turned to other projects, which included (1798) a contract for government muskets to be made on a "new principle." This new principle proved to be a system whereby any part of one gun could be exchanged for the same part of any other gun. Here was the essential idea upon which was built later American superiority in manufacturing. If any one man should be selected as outstandingly influential in the United States, at least serious consideration should be given to Eli Whitney with his two major inventions.

THE AMERICAN WORKMAN

The rise of manufacturing necessitated a class of industrial labor that was almost nonexistent in colonial days. Relatively few boys were willing to be apprenticed under the relics of the medieval guild system as a first step toward becoming skilled artisans, and certainly few farmers' sons were eager to take even well-paying factory jobs—and labor scarcity meant that wages were high—when farms of their own were well within their grasp. The main alternative of the manufacturer was to use women and children; and the general sentiment, as expressed by Hamilton and others, was that women and children had long worked in the home making such things as textiles and

that factory work would probably be easier and better paid, while at the same time it would deter them from vice and encourage habits of industry that would be valuable throughout life. While modern thinking rejects indignantly the prospect of a girl of seven working a twelve- to fourteen-hour day, that idea was generally accepted in the early Republic.

Industrial workers early acquired the feeling that they were being exploited by "those inevitable leeches, who fatten and are bloated by the blood of the honest mechanic, and hard working laborer" (1785). Rather tentatively they produced at least scattered unions before 1800, notably in the skilled occupations; for example, in 1794 were formed the Federal Society of Journeymen Cordwainers (shoemakers) of Philadelphia and the Typographical Society of New York. Now and then strikes, collective bargaining, and even a closed-shop contract were in evidence as early as 1794, but generally these early unions were interested primarily in fraternal aid, such as to sick members. Their successes were extremely limited, partly because they lacked a monopoly of labor and partly because of the generally antagonistic attitude of society, including the courts. Many years were to elapse before effective labor organizations came into existence.

TRANSPORTATION

⟨ *Overland Travel.* The prosperity of both agriculture and manufacturing was severely limited by the lack of good transportation, particularly on land. Until the mid–eighteenth century no roads connected the seaboard cities, while elsewhere land travel had to proceed by foot or horseback, with considerable danger of losing the badly marked trail and sorrowful experiences in the local inns, characterized mainly by vermin and bad food. In 1697 Philadelphia could report only thirty carts or other vehicles, while other towns, such as Boston and New York, were even more backward. Gradually roads were improved sufficiently to permit stagecoach travel between the larger towns, provided that the passenger had a sufficiently hardy constitution. Rapid transit in 1764 meant a five-day trip from New York to Philadelphia and return, including a day to transact business in Philadelphia. As late as the 1790s the traveler took eight to ten days from Boston to New York and at least another ten days if he continued to Washington. The fastest-known transportation was the express rider who covered the New York–Boston run in ninety-six hours.

Passenger traffic implied the transportation of mail. The individual colonies had established their own systems, and these were united by Parliament in 1710, even though at that time the amount of mail moving from one colony to another was negligible; Benjamin Franklin was one of the two men who jointly reorganized and expanded the system in 1753. Business increased gradually: in 1789, the year of the new constitutional government, there were seventy-five post offices; and in 1810, an impressive two thousand. The amount of the mail business was limited in part by the slowness of the service, but also by the price. The new government charged the recipient 10 cents for a "single letter" (one-quarter ounce) from New York to Philadelphia, and more for longer distances.

The use of roads for carrying freight was distinctly limited. Even as late as the 1780s almost all roads were practically unimproved. The better roads had the trees and shrubs removed, but remained ungraded and undrained; a heavy snow or rain practically brought traffic to a halt. The handling of heavy freight was too slow and expensive to be practical over any considerable distance. The result was that each town retained a virtual monopoly of its back-country business.

Road improvements might be either public or private, since people did not necessarily look first to government. Most local communities took some responsibility; each resident provided a few days of road work every year. The results were hardly spectacular—even after the work was transmuted into money payments. Various states, starting with New York in the 1780s, gave financial aid to local roads, but

the sums were small and frequently misused. The Federal government entered the scene as a star performer shortly before the War of 1812 by planning a great National Road to provide a link between East and West, but that is a later story.[3]

Private hopes of profit inspired most of the improved roads in the years around 1800; the first American example was the Philadelphia-Lancaster Turnpike,[4] built between 1792 and 1794 at a cost of $465,000. The road was constructed on the principles exemplified by the Englishmen John L. McAdam (source of the word macadam) and Thomas Telford, but was not black-topped as would be the case today. It was made of crushed rock, graded from large pebbles at the bottom to sand at the top with the pious hope that it would pack hard under the traffic. The center was raised, ditches provided for drainage, and bridges replaced the earlier ferries and fords. Even though a turnpike soon became rutty and bumpy it was such an improvement over any preceding road that men would drive miles out of their way to enjoy its relatively smooth surface. Bridges were also a matter of importance, with perhaps the greatest popular interest focused on the one opened in 1786 over the Charles River at Boston. Bridge construction improved with the development of the wooden truss bridge; its first American exemplification was the bridge at Bellows Falls, Vermont (1792), but its outstanding use was the long span across the Schuylkill at Philadelphia (1801).

The Lancaster Turnpike and similar roads were private, money-making ventures; and although the advantages of the roads were obvious, many users protested bitterly at what they considered unnecessarily high tolls. The answer in various states was for the government to place limits on the possible charges—a practice later to be used and expanded with canals and railroads. Although turnpikes were a transportational improvement, they produced no economic miracle. If mail, passen-

[3] See p. 202.
[4] The usual explanation of the word "turnpike" is that an attendant stopped traffic with a pike until the toll was paid and then "turned the pike."

gers, or freight were proceeding toward places served by new roads, faster delivery at less cost resulted, but for most of the United States conditions remained much as before.

❨ *Water Travel*. The most obvious effect of bad roads was that all possible traffic went by water, and this situation was so well accepted that there was little effort to make overland connections between towns that were joined by water. Internally, the many American rivers provided attractive alternatives to road travel, provided of course that the river connected the two desired towns. Early river travel was limited mainly by the means of transportation, since sailing vessels were of only limited utility, while barges and rafts could go only in one direction. Many ingenious Americans worked to overcome the problems of wind and current. The obvious solution was to install a steam engine on a boat, and as early as 1790 John Fitch was operating a steamboat commercially on the Delaware River between Philadelphia and Trenton. Despite such early ventures, however, the continuous development of river steamboating started only when Robert Fulton sailed his *Clermont* up the Hudson in 1807. Fulton was no great innovator; his importance rests partly upon his popularization of the steamboat and partly upon the monopolistic privileges that he and his partner Robert Livingston obtained on the Hudson and Mississippi from the state legislatures of New York and Louisiana. Although these monopolies in time collapsed in the face of judicial decisions, they did provide the first steam transportation on the Hudson and the Mississippi and for a time gave promise of dominating American water transportation.

The possibilities of improving rivers and of building canals were not overlooked, in spite of the almost insoluble difficulty of finding the necessary funds. Among river improvements were those of the Potomac and James, which were begun with state aid during the 1780s but not completed for some years. Important early ventures in canal building occurred in North Carolina, where the Dismal Swamp was connected with the Elizabeth River; in South Carolina, where the Cooper and Santee Rivers were joined near Charleston; and in Massachusetts, where Boston was connected with the Merrimac River near Lowell. Other projects were carried to various stages of completion.

Although steamboating developed rapidly on American rivers, it had no value on the ocean for over thirty years after the sailing of the *Clermont*. Inefficient engines required so much fuel that inadequate space remained for paying cargo, and they might fail embarrassingly in mid-Atlantic—in fact, all early steamships had auxiliary sails. Ocean commerce was dominated by the sailing ship until well after the middle of the nineteenth century. In the years around 1790 New England was active in shipbuilding, but so also were other parts of the nation, the "Baltimore clipper" being the best and most favorably known of American ships. These vessels were registered rather evenly in all the ports from Portland, Maine, to Savannah, Georgia, and even the smaller towns did a booming business. A little later, concentration was to become evident.

FOREIGN TRADE

American foreign trade in the colonial and early national periods was an extremely important part of the American economy as surplus American raw materials and farm products were exchanged for manufactured goods and exotic delicacies from the rest of the world. Because America was a relatively undeveloped country its capital came largely from Europe, with the result that interest and profits had to be met from a surplus of exports over imports. Colonial exports included most importantly tobacco, wheat and flour, fish, lumber, indigo, and rice, but also a great variety of other products such as beef, pork, poultry, horses, sheep, and hogs. A favorite variety of trade saw New England ships carrying rum to Africa to trade for Negroes, who were sold in the West Indies for molasses to make more rum. All colonial trade was of course limited and directed by English legislation, including particularly the Navigation Acts.[5]

Independence opened new markets to American shippers, but the nature and destination of American trade changed very slowly. Two-thirds of the foreign trade of 1790 was with Britain and British possessions, and half a century later over half was still with areas under the British flag. England continued to give preference to American ships, with the one exception of easily evaded restrictions on the trade of the West Indies—a limitation that produced such loud American howls of anguish that an impression of general restrictions was created. The eternal urge for more and more business led American captains, who were frequently at least part owners of the ships they sailed, to seek ever new areas for trade. The region of the Mediterranean proved attractive, and American captains regularly forged British passes to avoid the pirates. South America was an increasing possibility as its ties with the Spanish empire decreased and finally were severed. More exotic and exciting was the China trade, which was opened for the United States when Captain John Greene sailed his *Empress of China* from New York to Canton in 1784. Four years later Captain Robert Gray made the trade three-cornered by including the Far Northwest. As this business developed, New England cutlery and trinkets were traded in the Northwest for furs, particularly seal and otter, which had a regular market in Canton, where they were traded for silk and spices to be returned to New England. In the process the United States developed a certain degree of Chinese friendship, laid a claim to the Oregon country, and attained an interest in Hawaii, where ships took on water and other supplies. Possibly even more apparent was the littering of the New England coast with Chinese curiosities as New England sailors remembered their families and girl friends.

After the Revolution the general pattern of American foreign trade remained undisturbed in spite of variations in detail. Exports continued to consist largely of raw materials, such as meat, rice, ginseng root (a supposed "cure-all"), fish, flour, tobacco, lumber, and whale oil; cotton increased rapidly in importance after 1800. Imports tended toward the category of "finished manufactures" and included such goods as cotton, woolen, silk, and linen textiles; cutlery and other metal products; china and earthenware; and wines and liquors. Added to these necessities of life were such rare products as currants, raisins, nuts, figs, cloves, black pepper, ginger, citrus fruits, tea, and coffee; bananas and pineapples were added shortly after 1800.

MONEY AND CREDIT

American business, both domestic and foreign, suffered from a very real lack of money—a condition that was to prevail from the first settlements down through much of the nineteenth century. So great was this lack that various commodities, including tobacco, corn, wheat, cattle, hemp, rye, and port—or rather, certificates based upon them—were used at various times as mediums of exchange. English coins were rare, since England prohibited their export, and hence coins from all over the world circulated at various values, depending on local laws and customs. From 1728 the usual standard of value was the Spanish milled dollar or "piece of eight"; in time (1786) it was accepted by Congress. Possibly more important, however, was the fact that America was a debtor area, and hence all coins tended to drain back to Europe. The result was that all the colonies but Virginia issued paper money, and such certificates continued to circulate in spite of British restrictions. Several colonies, including Pennsylvania, South Carolina, and Rhode Island, also went into the lending business to provide merchants with the credit that otherwise was unobtainable.

The period of the Revolution brought worse financial conditions. Foreign trade was disrupted, and metal coins disappeared rapidly from circulation. Congress struggled somewhat despairingly and certainly ineffectively to provide necessary equipment and supplies for

[5] See pp. 38–40, 44–47.

the army. By the end of the war Congress had issued about $241,000,000 in paper money, while the states had issued some $210,000,000. Congress had also borrowed $67,000,000 at home and received a French gift of $1,800,000, a French loan of $16,352,000, and Spanish loans of $150,000; during the peace conference Adams had borrowed another $1,304,000 from Netherlands bankers. These large debts of a government that had no power of taxation naturally produced considerable American skepticism, American suppliers much preferring British or French gold and silver to congressional paper money. The Continental issues soon dropped rapidly in value. Whereas $100 in paper would have bought as much as 100 silver dollars in 1777, the rate became 300 by July, 1778; 600 by December, 1778; 1,600 by August, 1779; and 4,000 by March, 1780. A year later (31 March 1781), the Continental issues stopped circulating as currency and were of value only to speculators, who dealt in them in a desultory fashion at rates of between 500 and 1,000 to 1. Obvious evidence of the worthlessness of money was the very high prices that were normally charged.

The years of the Confederation brought frantic and not very successful efforts to improve America's financial conditions. Congressional money no longer circulated, although it could still be used to a limited extent for taxes. State issues had become almost worthless, and some states followed policies of partial repudiation by either collecting their paper money in large special taxes or exchanging it for bonds of a much lesser face value. For the moment there was more specie in circulation as it was imported or brought from hiding, even though Congress made no provision for domestic coinage and merely accepted the Spanish dollar as the standard of value. Seven states tried to meet the situation by issuing paper money of their own, and in most cases the results were satisfactory. Most of these states used their new money in part to lend to farmers on the security of mortgages, while Rhode Island provided potential loans to each freeman. Banks were opened in Philadelphia, New York, and Boston in that order,

with Robert Morris active in the Philadelphia bank and Hamilton in the New York institution; the Philadelphia bank (Bank of North America) had particularly wide subscriptions, including one from the Federal government.

Financial uncertainties inspired large-scale speculation, as such men as Robert Morris, Alexander Hamilton, William Duer, and Patrick Henry bet on the future. Two gambles were most common—land and government securities. With land, the speculator was betting on the future growth of the United States —its amount and place. Would it be Maine or Georgia, Charleston or New York, Ohio or Tennessee? With government securities, the gamble was whether the United States would survive as a nation, and whether both states and Federal government would pay their past debts in part or in full. At least as early as 1785 agents of wealthy New Yorkers were buying Continental and state certificates with the hope that some day they would be valuable.

The wealthy investors and the speculators were rewarded when Alexander Hamilton developed his financial program for the new nation.[6] State and Federal debts were paid in full. Continental currency was brought back to its original value. A law of 1792 established a mint to produce currency on the decimal basis with which we are familiar today. Both gold and silver were to be coined at the ratio of 15 to 1; but in practice gold was worth commercially something more and hence was not presented for coinage. Furthermore, a Bank of the United States was established to increase and to some extent to control American credit. Obviously the entire Hamilton program was to the advantage of the wealthy (including the speculator), of which Hamilton himself was one. This result was not obtained slyly by indirection; Hamilton believed firmly and stated time after time that the new government could only succeed if it attracted the loyalty of the wealthy and that this was his aim. The justice of his program has been questioned both then and later, but there can be little doubt that Hamilton's measures contributed materially to development of a strong, stable government.

[6] See pp. 131-133.

CHAPTER 8

Producing an American Culture

(1789-1815)

CITIES IN THE WILDERNESS

The development of United States culture in a period of poor transportation was retarded by a lack of cities. All the most important towns in 1790, as throughout colonial history, were on the Atlantic seaboard; thus in a very real sense America faced the Europe that produced it. Since manufacturing remained relatively insignificant, all towns depended primarily on commerce for their importance. They also needed rich and available hinterlands if they were to retain and improve their situations. Inland towns as yet had inadequate transportation to make large size possible and acted mainly as trading centers for their districts.

(*Major Cities.* The top American city of 1790, as it had been during much of the colonial period, was Philadelphia, with a population of 42,520. Philadelphia had a satisfactory port, but was particularly blessed with its hinterland: the very rich country of the Pennsylvania Germans. Indeed, Lancaster County was long to boast that it had the greatest per capita agricultural production in the United States. Philadelphia was the leader in foreign trade until very late in the eighteenth century, profited

from British gold during the Revolution, sired and provided home offices for the first and second Banks of the United States, and in 1800 gave birth to the most important stock exchange in the United States. Philadelphia was prosperous, and its elaborate and toothsome public markets provided assurance that the prosperity was transmuted into rich living.

Philadelphia was notably an abode of peace and quiet—an orderly, well laid out, and attractive city with paved streets, brick sidewalks, and trees to dapple the streets with shade. Visitors, however, often found the checkerboard pattern of the streets dull and monotonous, while the reputed cleanliness of the city was much deflated when the yellow fever epidemic of 1793 disclosed large quantities of filth in the poorer sections. The "plain people" (Quakers) and such small groups as the Mennonite, Dunker, and Amish sects were potent forces in making the atmosphere of the city decorous and religious. Sunday was observed scrupulously, all business being closed and a Sabbath calm permeating the air.

Philadelphia possessed more than peace and quiet, however, and more than economic prosperity. Here was the artistic and literary center of its day, famous for its books, magazines,

99

and newspapers. Charles Willson Peale opened his famous museum in 1794, and the Pennsylvania Academy of the Fine Arts was established in 1805. Here was a center of political interest and liberalism that afforded a home for the Federal government in the years before the capital was moved to the new and raw city of Washington. Here was a breeding ground for liberal religious thought, for the rational deism of the period. Here was the most important scientific center in America; quite naturally Joseph Priestley, famous chemist and discoverer of oxygen, when he fled from England with his Unitarian friends, settled near Philadelphia. This scientific primacy traced partly to Franklin, who among other things had helped establish a scientific organization which, reorganized as the American Philosophical Society (1769), was the most important in America. Truly, Philadelphia could be proud of its many accomplishments.

The second American city was New York, with a population of 33,130 in 1790; growing more rapidly than Philadelphia, it was to attain population leadership shortly after 1800, never again to be exceeded. New York's harbor was the best on the Atlantic Coast, but its back country of the Hudson Valley was comparatively small, and the real rise of the city did not occur until adequate connections were made farther west. New York always impressed its visitors as being more highly commercial than Philadelphia, with more bustle, noise, confusion, and dirt. In fact, dirt was probably its most obvious characteristic; the unpaved streets were ankle-deep in filth, which the freely roving pigs did little to dissipate. Possibly symbolic of New York was its opening of a primitive stock exchange some eight years earlier than did Philadelphia. But stress on commercialism should not obscure New York strivings for culture, as indicated, for example, by the formation of the Columbian Academy of Painting in 1792. In time the city was to be a literary and cultural center of first-rate importance.

The third American city was Boston, but its population of 18,138 was growing altogether too slowly for the ambitions of its mer-

chants. The center of Boston's economic life was the harbor, into which Long Wharf jutted a third of a mile. As sailors left the harbor they lost themselves in the narrow and winding streets, which sometimes were paved with rounded beach stones and which were lighted faintly with oil lamps that were altogether too far apart. Beacon Hill remained a rough, unkempt wilderness from which one could see cows grazing on the common. Boston stressed its cultural advantages. Large and impressive churches, mostly Congregational, dotted the town. The Massachusetts Medical Society had been formed in 1781. Libraries were relatively good. The influential American Academy of Arts and Sciences had been organized in 1780 under the presidency of James Bowdoin. Painters such as Gilbert Stuart and Washington Allston brought credit to the city, as did the great architect Charles Bulfinch. George Cabot expressed the common feeling of his fellow Bostonians when he said that there is in Boston "more wisdom than in any other part of the United States"; other Americans, however, expressed some skepticism that Boston was the center of American culture and learning.

Charleston was the fourth city, with a population of 16,359, and it was the most populous Southern city, for it was apparent even by the late eighteenth century that Southern cities were lagging behind their Northern rivals. This lag has various possible explanations, but most obvious in the case of Charleston was the difficulty of making connections with the interior, particularly to the West. The city tried long and hard to remedy this situation, but with little success. Charleston's impressively large, pillared mansions were occupied by the slaveholding aristocracy, for whom the height of the social season was in January and February. Wealth was accepted as normal, dinner parties were elaborate and gracious, and balls were impressively magnificent. Everyone of social importance belonged to the Jockey Club and attended the balls of the St. Cecilia Society. Possibly Charleston schools lagged, but the opening of a museum as early as 1773 indicated a real interest in culture. Outsiders accused Charlestonians of sometimes drinking excessively, of gambling continuously for too high stakes, and of too great a sensitivity about their code of honor, but had to admit that they were hospitable, well-mannered, charming, and cultivated people.

The fifth city was Baltimore, with 13,503 residents in 1790. Baltimore was in one sense a border city, with something of the bustle and rush that characterized more northerly communities, but also with a great deal of the charm of a Southern town. Baltimoreans were proud of their traditions of leisure and culture, of their beautiful women, and of their gracious entertaining. Economically the city was troubled by its considerable distance from the open sea, but even more by a limited back country and by great difficulties of communication with the West. Baltimore merchants were to spend the next generation trying almost frantically to improve connections with the West, but with nothing like complete success.

No other city in 1790 had as many as 10,000 inhabitants. Pittsburgh was a small hamlet; and Cincinnati, the future queen of the Ohio Valley, a few cabins. Detroit was a frontier trading post, while Buffalo and Chicago were not even dreams. Old Spanish and French towns, such as Mobile, St. Louis, and New Orleans, were not in American territory, any more than were Los Angeles and San Francisco. Most hopeful for the future was New Orleans (annexed in 1803), since its position at the mouth of the Mississippi River seemingly assured it of being the commercial center of almost half the continent. By 1810 it had gained sixth place among American cities, and ten years later it had passed Charleston to rate fourth; but unfortunately for New Orleans' hopes this was the highest relative ranking it ever attained.

❴ *City Characteristics.* The word city as used before the War of 1812 is misleading to modern ears. As communities grew they merely sprawled over the landscape with nothing like the present concentration. Buildings were low and usually of wood, subject to frequent devastating fires that the private fire companies with their hand engines could seldom control. Stores tended to be unspecialized, and factories were few. So-called "cities" were merely overgrown farming towns. Streets ordinarily were unpaved, uncleaned, unlighted, and unpoliced; those in the business district were lined with gambling houses, saloons, and brothels. At night a man alone felt himself lucky if he were only accosted and not beaten and robbed, for the handful of night watchmen never afforded any real protection. The first city to clean its streets regularly was Philadelphia in the years after 1790. Water was furnished by wells, rain barrels, and cisterns, although Philadelphia provided public pumps and in 1801 finished the greatest engineering achievement of its day—a pumping system that took untreated Schuylkill water and distributed it in the city. Throughout the nineteenth century the cities improved gradually in such matters as lighting, paving, policing, garbage disposal, and water supply, but the improvements hardly kept pace with the ever-increasing congestion. Not until after 1900 did real signs of improvement appear.

The jerry-built squalor of the city was offset to some extent by its cultural opportunities. Here were not only the poverty-stricken and the miserable, but also people of wealth, taste, and leisure, living closely enough together to know each other and to work in common. For obvious reasons painters and writers tended to concentrate in the city. Here were the publishing houses, and here were the magazines and books. Here was the bulk of newspapers, museums, and theaters. To a very real extent the culture of the period was concentrated in the cities.

THE CLIMATE OF AMERICAN OPINION

The loudest and most raucous voices in the post-Revolutionary United States were bumptiously boastful of victory over the world's greatest empire. They celebrated American prowess in both peace and war and held that "this country is reserved to be the last and greatest theater for the improvement of mankind" by furnishing a shining example to the effete nations of Europe and by affording a refuge for the oppressed of the world. But such loud boasting could not divert all attention from the great differences in American opinion. Many of the Revolutionary patriots had been desirous of nothing more extreme than home rule and had been pushed along the road to freedom. Now they looked with amazement and distress at the mob shouting for equality and democracy. These conservatives were joined by large numbers of loyalists who during the war had found the radicals taxing their property heavily, releasing their debtors, confiscating their estates, and removing their political rights. After the war their conditions improved as state proscriptions were relaxed, and many who had fled the country returned. In consequence American ideologies of the 1780s ranged from the beliefs of unregenerate tories and supporters of a military dictatorship to the equalitarian doctrines of the enthusiastic followers of Tom Paine.

Differences in belief were to a considerable extent the reflection of differences in wealth, education, and ways of life. A wide and deep gulf separated the leisured Charleston planter from the back-country farmer of Pennsylvania, and the wealthy Boston merchant from the New England boy shipping before the mast to Canton. Regardless of theory, there was an identifiable native aristocracy. The new President, George Washington, with his establishment of eighteen liveried domestic servants, was hardly representative of the average American. Rich planters and merchants, influenced to some degree by refugees from the French Revolution, thought of themselves as definitely superior to the common man. Their impressive town houses and country estates and their luxurious living placed them in a class apart. During the summer they were apt to congregate in such resorts as Saratoga Springs, which grew rapidly during the 1790s. Even in their clothes and in the way they did their hair they were distinctive.

Americans during the years after the Revolution were above all citizens of their own states, with a somewhat tenuous grasp of the larger and vaguer concept of the United States as a nation. If they looked beyond their own communities, their sentimental attraction might be more to England than to the United States. They might thrill more over the white cliffs of Dover or the houses of Parliament than over New York Harbor or Niagara Falls. Patriotism of the modern variety remained a long way in the future.

Energetic men of vision, regardless of social class, realized that national success depended heavily on the production of common traditions and common loyalties. Political unity was but one phase of the matter. A strong central government was necessary, but at least equally vital were common economic, social, and cultural institutions to develop the feeling that Americans were a unique and closely knit people. To gain these ends the United States had to mature economically and develop distinctive cultural traits that would set her apart from her mother country, England.

EDUCATION

《 *Colonial Education.* The nature of American culture depended heavily on the important formative influences of education. The earliest of American colonists had frequently been well educated, but had found difficulty in transmitting their accomplishments to their children when confronted with the economic problems of survival. The late seventeenth century was probably the low point in American education, although there was little in that field to point to with pride during the entire colonial period. The evidence of public petitions indicates that at about 1700 roughly 10 per cent of New Yorkers had to make their marks rather than sign their names and that the proportion in certain parts of the South and West ran a good 50 per cent, women on the average being much less literate than men. Colonial leaders appreciated the virtues of education, and many felt a strong urge to buttress their own religious faiths by enabling everyone to read the Bible and by providing facilities for young men to enter the ministry. At least moderate efforts toward general education were ultimately made in every colony.

Colonial educational efforts were greatest in New England, although even here conditions were far from ideal. Early Massachusetts schools received some aid from the towns or General Court and were open to all children, but parents were supposed to pay if they could. By 1642 Massachusetts required that all children should be educated, although without specifying the agency; and a few years later it legislated that each town should provide a school. Other New England states followed a similar pattern, but the results were disappointing. Many towns had no schools or else extremely poor ones with short terms, while large numbers of parents made the frugal assumption that they could educate their own children. New York schools were commonly described as poor. Pennsylvania, like Massachusetts, provided that parents were responsible for their children learning to read and write. Maryland required a school in each county, but the provision was not well honored. Maryland, Virginia, and the Carolinas leaned on the broken reed of private schools, while wealthy parents employed tutors.

Education beyond the elementary level was designed primarily to train ministers. Of the various secondary schools scattered throughout the colonies, probably the best—at least in New England—was the Boston Latin School. Many schools presented the classics and mathematics necessary for college entrance, although the same job was often done privately by various ministers. Colleges, being designed primarily for ministerial training, were ordinarily attached to the various churches. Among the colleges established in colonial days were Harvard (Congregational), which started the procession in 1636; William and Mary (Episcopalian); Yale (Congregational—to offset Harvard liberalism); Princeton (Presbyterian); Brown (Baptist); Rutgers (Dutch Reformed); and Dartmouth (Congregational). In some cases, as with William and Mary, the bulk of their early work was really secondary rather than collegiate. Boys were admitted quite young—between eleven and fourteen—which explains why discipline was of a juvenile variety, including even whipping. Every college was highly religious and emphasized the classical curriculum, with recitations from assigned texts. Science received little attention, even though Harvard was presenting lectures on anatomy as early as 1647.

⟨ *Postwar Education.* American leaders of the Revolutionary period were well aware of the importance of education in the future of the nation, even though their specific plans varied greatly. The idealistic Jefferson dreamed of a complete national school system culminating in a great university, to be open equally to everyone possessing the necessary ability. The more practical Hamilton talked merely of educating the well-to-do for leadership. The postwar period found patriotic orators blaring the advantages of universal education, but more to cultivate desired beliefs and moral standards than to advance some sort of abstract intellectual development. Noah Webster (1790) expressed an ordinary point of view in describing the education of a child: "As soon as he opens his lips he should rehearse the history of his own country; he should lisp the praise of liberty, and of those illustrious heroes and statesmen who have wrought a revolution in her favor."

The shining beauty of educational idealism made the actuality particularly drab. Schools had suffered during the war, some of them even being abandoned, and recovery was slow. Various states provided comprehensive school systems that existed only on paper. In fact the smallness of government aids left education primarily the responsibility of the family or of charity. Schools might be free, but they never were compulsory; and the poor man who accepted a free education for his child thereby acquired the social stigma of poverty. The first American Sunday school was opened in 1791 as a charitable aid to the education of poor children. Another effort to lower the costs of education was the Lancasterian system, in which the master taught only a selected group of students, who then taught the others. But no matter what approach was used, the main costs of education tended to fall on the family at the worst possible time; and altogether too frequently father decided on a new barn rather than a school term for his ten-year-old daughter, or a flock of sheep rather than Latin for his twelve-year-old son. Very possibly, elementary education was poorer than a generation earlier; and it seemed as though illiteracy were increasing, even in the favored New England States.

Children continued to be considered, as during the colonial period, primarily as unruly sinners to be disciplined, and stress was placed on obedience and on rote learning of essentials. Children were expected to meditate deeply on the sadder sides of life:

> Tell me, Mamma, if I must die
> One day as little baby died,
> And look so very pale and lie
> Down in the pit-hole by its side.

The idealism of the late eighteenth century was having its effect, however, and increasingly the child was being lured with rewards rather than threatened with hell-fire. The newer spirit was best represented by the very famous poem " 'Twas the Night before Christmas" (1822), written by a New York educator for his own children.

Secondary schools and colleges at least increased in numbers, although whether more rapidly than population may be doubted. Advanced education was most available in the Northern and Middle states, tending to become less as one went South or West. Among the newer preparatory schools were Phillips Andover (1778) and Phillips Exeter (1781). Among the colleges established in the twenty years after 1780 were Bowdoin, Georgetown, Franklin and Marshall, Transylvania, University of Vermont, University of North Carolina, and University of Georgia. Although the number of colleges increased, the contents of the curriculum remained about the same, stand-bys being the classics, mathematics, rhetoric and moral philosophy—the last taught ordinarily by the ministerial president.

❡ *Textbooks.* Most significant educationally was a self-conscious effort to Americanize the current texts. The young schoolmaster Noah Webster expressed the ideas of many Americans when he wrote in 1783, at the age of twenty-five: "America must be as independent in *literature* as she is in *politics*, as famous for *arts* as for *arms*." Webster himself performed valiant service toward the attainment of his ideas. His popular blue-backed speller, *The American Spelling Book* (1783), was filled with distinctively American religious and patriotic selections to perform its double function of speller and reader. Obviously the book filled a deeply felt need, because some fifteen million copies were sold before Webster's death, and ultimately some sixty million. Webster followed the speller with a *First Reader*, which also emphasized American quotations and ideas, but which went even further as it utilized distinctive American words and grammatical forms. Webster hoped to authenticate a truly unique American language and even for a time supported a simplified, phonetic system of spelling. Ultimately his *A Compendious Dictionary of the English Language* (1806), a tremendous and even magnificent work of painstaking scholarship, made a significant contribution to the stabilization of American word usages.

The patriotic concepts of Webster were far from unique, and other men used similar ideas for readers, spellers, grammars, arithmetics, science books, and geographies. Outstanding was Jedidiah Morse, who published his *Geography Made Easy* in 1784 and his *The American Geography* five years later. For the first time America became the center of the young student's textbook world; and although Morse recounted several tales of dubious truth, he gave the youthful scholar a much improved understanding of his own country. Today, however, he is remembered less for his geographic contributions than for his brilliant painter and inventor son, Samuel F. B. Morse.

The growing Americanization of education did not, of course, mean the elimination of all European influences. After all, the basic language was English, and English texts continued to be read commonly. For many years the most popular grammar was that of the Englishman Lindley Murray. Newer ideas, such as the Lancasterian system and the Sunday school, were British in origin. But dependence on England was becoming less. Citizens of the New World were more and more thinking of themselves as Americans, with ideas and ways of life that were distinctively their own.

LITERATURE

⟨ *Newspapers.* Literature also felt the force of self-conscious Americanism in the postwar generation after a very slow development during the colonial period. The newspaper, which was later to become the standard reading material of most Americans, was actually late in appearance, since it needed a large and literate clientele, which in turn required the non-existent large city, good transportation, and adequate schools. Even printing presses were not available in the early days—there were none in Virginia in the entire seventeenth century. The first newspaper—provided that one should not really call it a pamphlet—titled *Public Occurrences, both Foreign and Domestick,* was quickly suppressed by the Boston authorities of 1690. The first regular newspaper was the *Boston News-Letter* of 1704, a dull little publication. Much more sprightly and literary was James Franklin's *New-England Courant* (Boston, 1721) from which Benjamin Franklin obtained ideas for his own *The Pennsylvania Gazette* (Philadelphia, 1729), the most entertaining paper of its day. New papers were established rather rapidly, but their high mortality left few survivors in any given year; it has been estimated that only about thirty papers were being published in 1775 and that these were all four-page weeklies, devoted largely to such prosaic matters as re-

prints of European news items, shipping news, and legal notes.

Important for the future was the growing tradition of freedom of the press, marked particularly by the trial of John Peter Zenger in 1735. Zenger published the New York *Weekly Journal* and, when he printed the letter of a man who had been dismissed as chief justice, was accused of uttering false and scandalous libel. His very able lawyer took the novel position of arguing that there was no libel because the statements were true; the jury accepted this line of reasoning and called Zenger "not guilty."

The war produced difficulties for struggling newspapers, and only about 40 were in existence at the coming of peace. But then the number grew rapidly, with 90 in 1790 and 350 in 1810. These papers printed more and more American news, from necessity as well as from desire. With a fixed date of publication the editor could not wait for the next boat from Europe but had to depend on politics, ship disasters, and other local events; whenever possible he filled his four small pages each week with material clipped from other papers. The most vigorous writing was political disputation, which increased with the Revolution and became really violent in the early days of the Republic. Editorials and articles became vituperous and slanderous, with practically no limitation on invective, and such writing seems to have been accepted by most readers as quite proper to add spice to an otherwise dull paper. Among the better newspapers about 1800 was the New York *Evening Post,* a conservative Federalist sheet founded by Alexander Hamilton, and the Philadelphia *Port Folio,* which editor Joseph Dennie filled with an unusually wide selection of literature, law, art, drama, music, poetry, and fashions. The daily paper, starting with the *Pennsylvania Packet and Daily Advertiser* (Philadelphia, 1784), emphasized the current trend toward more local news and wider coverage.

⟨ *Magazines.* Magazines were developed later than newspapers. The first was founded by Franklin in 1741 under the intimidating title

The General Magazine and Historical Chronicle for All the British Plantations in America; it contained a wide variety of American material. This opening wedge encouraged no flood of periodicals; in fact there were many succeeding years in which no magazine was published in America. After the Revolution the number increased gradually, including such noteworthy periodicals as *The American Magazine* of Noah Webster and the *American Museum* of Mathew Carey, the versatile Philadelphia publisher and economist. The market for magazines was small, most publications teetering perpetually on the rim of financial disaster. A small market meant that editors could not afford to pay for contributions and depended heavily on copying. Even more disastrously, they assumed that their public could contain only the most highly educated and sophisticated, and therefore imitated English and Scottish reviews by filling their pages with long and usually tedious essays inspired by some book; the results were something less lurid than reports of congressional debates. But gradually, inspired by growing nationalism, the magazines began to use more American material, many an editor feeling a real mission to encourage independence in the literary field.

❧ *Books.* Publication of books was also difficult for a young America. Although a scattering was published during the colonial period, there was no considerable market for American writers except ministers who collected their sermons. The poorer family, even if literate, might possess little more than a Bible and an almanac. Richer booklovers sometimes collected considerable libraries, usually including many of the classics, which they often could read in the original Latin and Greek, and selections from current English authors. Since American poets, novelists, and playwrights did little more than copy English styles and materials, the book buyer realized that without an international copyright law he could buy the better English author more cheaply and was hardly encouraged to patronize local efforts.

The Revolutionary period encouraged distinctive American production in literature. Particularly was there a market for political disputation, and in time *The Federalist* exhibited some of the finest of American writing. American poets and novelists became better known; they turned increasingly to local themes, and before long every American writer talked about Indians, Revolutionary heroes, and other domestic matters. Among the poets Philip Freneau was clearly outstanding, his writings breathing a sensitive and passionate love for things American. William Cullen Bryant was an outstanding lyricist before he turned to the newspaper business. The so-called "Hartford Wits," a group of writers for whom the adjective witty is certainly a misnomer, tried self-consciously in both poetry and prose to emphasize American patriotism of a conservative character. Typical was the work of its best-known member, Joel Barlow, who in 1787 published his long epic *The Vision of Columbus*, which sought to express a noble idea but which succeeded in being little more than extremely tiresome.

The first American novel did not appear until 1789 with the publication of *The Power of Sympathy*, frequently credited to Sarah Wentworth Morton. Much more important, however, was Susanna H. Rowson's *Charlotte* (1791), a sickly sentimental production that for many years was one of America's most popular books. The first professional American novelist was Charles Brockden Brown, a social and political radical whose writings exhibited extreme patriotism.

THE FINE ARTS

The American theater developed slowly for rather obvious reasons. Although professional companies appeared early in the eighteenth century, as at Charleston and New York, even the residents of the larger cities could not see dramatic performances more or less regularly until after 1750. The favored dramatists were English, and Shakespeare was particularly admired. Seldom could the theatergoer—and many Americans were deterred by religious scruples—see an American play, which was probably on the whole a fortunate circumstance. Political independence inspired patriotic citizens to dramatize American glories; typical of the early playwrights was Mercy Otis Warren, whose *The Group* dealt with the American Revolution. Best known was Royall Tyler, whose play *The Contrast* (1787) compared English class distinctions with American democracy, of course to the great disadvantage of the English; today the play seems like bad theater, but it was greatly appreciated in its time. After all, the author was American, and patriotic citizens were pathetically desirous of glorifying any local dramatist, no matter how poor.

The other arts also showed in varying degrees the tendency toward Americanization, architecture being the least affected. The colonial period produced no professional architects, and local craftsmen quite naturally copied the well-known Georgian buildings of England. The results were beautiful and often well designed for charming and gracious living. The end of the Revolution found in England a trend toward the Gothic, but luckily it reached the New World but little. The first important American architect, Charles Bulfinch, was beautifying the Georgian by the 1780s. Americans who sought a style particularly fitting for American democracy went back to the classical Greek and Roman. Inspired by Thomas Jefferson, as illustrated by both his own home and his University of Virginia, Americans began to strew Greek and Roman temples over the countryside. In some ways the most functional American building was the log cabin, but even here the model was European—Swedish. As for sculpture, the only Americans with any pretensions were the artists who produced tombstones and ship figureheads.

Music of colonial and early national days was hardly a sophisticated art. Individuals owned and played such instruments as flutes, violins, spinets, and virginals even in colonial times, and the pipe organ was available by the early eighteenth century. Concerts could be attended by music lovers in the larger cities by the 1730s, and the oratorios of such masters as Handel and Haydn were being given by the end of the century. The Moravians of Bethlehem, Pennsylvania, began their Bach festivals in colonial days. In fact, Americans loved all kinds of group singing, including congregational singing. When native composers began to be active in the late eighteenth century, their major efforts were devoted to hymn and psalm tunes. Even more significantly, the Americans produced a flood of passionate but often mawkish patriotic yearnings. "Yankee Doodle" had become almost a national symbol during the Revolution, but considerably more patriotic were "Hail Columbia," a pro-Federalist song that later was much modified, and "The Star-spangled Banner," which was a product of the unsuccessful British effort to capture Baltimore. Rather ironically the music for "The Star-spangled Banner" was English, as was also that of the later "My Country 'Tis of Thee."

The work of American painters showed the effects of patriotism as much as that of musicians. Colonial painters had stuck to portraits almost entirely and in many ways filled the function of later photographers. The most fashionable Boston portrait painter of the 1760s was John Singleton Copley, whose great accuracy was properly a forerunner of the candid camera; his portrait of Paul Revere in his shirt sleeves is typical of his best work. Copley was a neutral in the pre-Revolutionary troubles and was but mildly sympathetic to the Revolutionary cause after he moved to London in 1774. Most influential of American painters was Benjamin West, who spent almost his entire adult life in England; he was president of the Royal Academy for over a quarter century and acted as sponsor and teacher for many Americans, including Copley and Gilbert Stuart.

Indicative of increasing American nationalism was the formation in the years after 1790 of art associations in Philadelphia and New York. Marking the same trend was the return (1792) of Gilbert Stuart to America, primarily to paint George Washington. He was responsible for the American stereotype of Washington as a delicate and patrician figure; his overly sentimentalized and stylized portraits had little relation to the real Washington, whom Stuart never saw. Much more realistic Washington portraits were the work of the native-born and trained Charles Willson Peale, a student of the Copley technique and of West. Peale painted Washington from life as a real, living man—big, rawboned, slightly awkward, and powerful. In addition to painting, Peale was extremely active in forming artistic groups, and his Philadelphia museum was the best of its kind. Most patriotic of all American painters was John Trumbull, another pupil of Benjamin West. His best-known works after the Revolution were great in size as well as in theme, including such scenes as the Battle of Bunker Hill, the surrender of Cornwallis, and the signing of the Declaration of Independence.

SCIENCE

Science also showed a similar process of Americanization. Although many early American scientists, such as Joseph Priestley, were foreign-born, native-born Americans were frequently conversant with the latest European discoveries and at times made additions of their own; the versatile Franklin and Jefferson, for example, did much to encourage scientific advance. Since North America was largely unexplored, the first contributions were geographical discoveries. Each explorer, including each fur trader, pushed back the frontier of scientific knowledge, and it was no accident that the scientifically minded Jefferson was responsible for the first American expedition to cross overland to the Pacific. The Virginia planter William Byrd and the Quaker William Bartram wrote particularly excellent accounts of their observations; the latter's father John gave his name to the Philadelphia botanical gardens. Observation was followed by classification, as when Alexander Wilson pub-

lished his first volume on ornithology in 1808. Other men were busy describing and classifying plants, animals, snakes, and rocks.

Agriculture naturally attracted ingenious Americans who experimented with varying crops and methods and described the results. The sea received its quota of interest; and quite naturally a New England man teaching mathematics at Harvard, Nathaniel Bowditch, published (1802) the very significant *The New American Practical Navigator*. Dr. Benjamin Rush was outstanding in medicine. A vast amount of sickness, including such epidemics as the yellow fever that took 10 per cent of the population of Philadelphia in 1793, furnished much scientific material. Unfortunately the results of scientific inquiry in the field of medicine were negligible in terms of cures. Americans were also active in more abstract work. The first American chemical society was organized at Philadelphia in 1792 and was the precursor of various groups in other American cities. Over-all excellence went to the American Philosophical Society, which became increasingly active after the return of Franklin from Europe in 1785. Similar was the American Academy of Arts and Sciences at Boston; James Bowdoin was its president, and John Adams was very active in its affairs. The best scientific journal of the years around 1800 was the *Medical Repository*. Among American scientific inventions was the oxygen blowtorch by Robert Hare, a Philadelphia brewer. The most noted scientist of his day was Benjamin Silliman, who started his work at Yale in 1802.

The field of mechanical invention was one in which European-born inventors were soon to be replaced by ingenious Americans. Examples of early foreign influences were the textile machinery of Samuel Slater, who had worked for Richard Arkwright in England, and the Philadelphia waterworks, which were the product of the engineering genius of the foreign-born Benjamin H. Latrobe. But natives such as James Rumsey, John Fitch, John Stevens, Robert Fulton, and Eli Whitney proved prolifically inventive as they worked on such ideas as steamboats, propellers, submarines, torpedos, diving bells, and cotton gins. Foreign influence, of course, did not disappear—for example, Fulton used an English engine on his first boat—but American inventors were increasingly able to stand on their own feet.

RELIGIOUS PATTERNS

❨ *Colonial Religion.* Growing nationalism inevitably affected religion and the church, and the resulting changes were particularly disturbing to most people because they concerned beliefs and emotions that were deeply held and dearly cherished. Colonial Americans were extremely religious; general support of the churches by taxation indicated the vital importance of the church. Ministers were highly respected and exercised important temporal as well as spiritual influence, even though they did not always conform in personal deportment to modern ministerial standards. Members of the Virginia clergy were accused of swearing, using obscenity, fighting, and staggering with drink, while Puritan divines were not beyond reproach. One must remember, however, that the day was one of crude manners and that excessive drinking was characteristic of all classes of society.

The Sabbath was observed strictly throughout the colonies. In New England the Puritan fathers expected their flocks to spend the day in meditation, prayer, and Bible reading, and they were willing to punish such diverse activities as driving cattle, making beds, cooking, fishing, playing games—and even walking with, conversing with, and kissing one's spouse. Blasphemy was everywhere punished severely; seventeenth-century Maryland provided penalties ranging from a hole in the tongue for the first offense to death for the third. Such attitudes have been well advertised in more recent years, but what is less known is that the Middle and Southern colonies were little if any less strict than New England in religious observances and that even in New England there were frequent and obvious lapses from the presumed code. As a single example, there

was a good deal of illegitimacy, and various churches insisted that parents confess their error if their first child was born less than seven months after their marriage.

Deeply held religious sentiments were reinforced by regular attendance at long church services and periodically quickened by highly emotional meetings. During the 1740s there were widespread revival services in which the leading minister was George Whitefield (English). His work was preceded and supplemented by a number of Americans, including most importantly Gilbert Tennent and Jonathan Edwards. This wave of religious emotionalism, commonly called the Great Awakening, brought an ever greater awareness of spiritual matters to thousands of Americans.

Americans were almost entirely Christian, even the Jews being small in number; here and there were synagogues, as at Charleston, New York, Philadelphia, and Newport. The great bulk of Christians were Protestants, the Catholics being vastly outnumbered even in Maryland, where they were most numerous. Generally speaking, people of the same faith had settled together and thus dominated particular regions. New England was Congregational except for Baptist Rhode Island. New York was Dutch Reformed, although with English control an effort was made to swing it to the Church of England (Episcopal). Pennsylvania was dominated by the Quakers, and the South was generally Church of England. The Presbyterians and Methodists were not so well concentrated, but both were most numerous in the South. The latter group had started in England about the mid–eighteenth century as an effort to reform the Church of England and by the outbreak of the Revolution claimed some 3,000 members in America.

Variety of sects did not imply religious toleration. Each state church approved limitations on other faiths, and all of them agreed on limiting the Catholics. Roman Catholics were frequently disfranchised, excluded from public office, debarred from holding public church services, and otherwise discriminated against. Sometimes even their rights to give or receive property or to testify in court were limited. Apparently they were most free in Rhode Island and Pennsylvania. Throughout the eighteenth century, toleration tended to increase, reflecting the contemporary trend in Europe.

◖ *Changing Religious Characteristics.* With the coming of political revolt in the colonies, the church and religion also came to be questioned—not an unusual situation. The same spirit that inspired doubts about long-established political institutions also brought questions about religious orthodoxy, particularly when it was apparent that the ministry in general, and that of the Church of England in particular, was conservative in outlook and generally in favor of the political stability that had been so good for them. Most prevalent of the more radical religious beliefs was Deism, which had been quite popular earlier in Europe. The Deists believed that God had created the world, but then had not interfered with the running of the machinery. For the Deist, God accordingly was transformed from a loving father to a remote, impartial force, thus excluding all direct divine interference in the affairs of the world. Deism spread rapidly in America, affecting such leaders as Washington, Jefferson, Madison, and Franklin. Ethan Allen wrote his famous book *Reason, the Only Oracle of Man* (1784), and traditionally minded Americans felt that it was the judgment of God when fire destroyed all but thirty copies. More important was Tom Paine's *The Age of Reason*, which had a large sale in the United States; its publication date of 1796 indicated the continuation of such ideas after the American Revolution. Deism in time lost ground; and the more conservative viewpoint, which had always been maintained by the great majority of Americans, regained its practical universality.

Religious ferment, as it occurred in a postwar world, brought certain relaxations in traditional religious and moral concepts. Puritanism became not quite so grim. Sunday was observed less strictly, some boys and girls hurrying home after church to play games. Profanity was on the rise. More important in its long-

run implications, the gloomy doctrines of Calvin as taught in New England were subject to attack by a young and hopeful generation. The major onset came in the form of Unitarianism (originally English), which insisted on the unity of God instead of the concept of the trinity and which emphasized the loving kindness of God, the nobility of man, and the joy of religious life. These ideas spread widely, particularly in the neighborhood of Boston; in time (1805) the Unitarians captured Harvard —a victory signalized by the appointment of one of their number as professor of divinity. Congregationalism fought back, partly by establishing Andover Theological Seminary in 1808 to buttress the more conservative point of view. A plan of union (1801) with the Presbyterians divided missionary work between the two churches; although it left the Congregationalists in control of the East, it meant a severe blow to their Western expansion.

Also during the post-Revolutionary period Methodism spread rapidly, particularly in the South, where there were notable revivals in Virginia during the late 1780s; by 1787 the Methodist Church claimed 25,000 American members. The Methodist doctrine of salvation through individual faith and works appealed to Americans. Much more radical were the Universalists, of which the American group was organized formally in 1794. Under the leadership of Hosea Ballou they repudiated the doctrines of human depravity and the deity of Jesus and approached the philosophy of deism by picturing a rational world. They played down hell-fire, and their very name indicated their belief in the possibility of universal salvation.

The newer religious trends, with their greater emphasis on the chances of human conversion and salvation, afforded the basis for an ever-increasing emotionalism. If a man might be saved by the single act of conversion, then was it not the duty of the church to provide such strong emotional pressure that the sinner would see the error of his ways? Various waves of revivalism had previously swept the country, but now the Great Revival, with its peak in Kentucky in 1801, stirred thousands of men and women to the depths of their natures. Protracted meetings were held in churches in the East and in open clearings in the West, where emotional fervor was whipped into ecstasy by a succession of ministers who dwelt on the pains and horrors of eternal damnation rather more than on the glories of golden streets and milk and honey. As excitement grew, men and women were sometimes seized by uncontrollable jerks; they laughed, shouted, ran, "talked in tongues" (incomprehensible jargon), or even fainted or entered trances. Those who felt most powerfully the working of the spirit came down front, confessed their sins, and promised reformed lives.

The Revolutionary period, with its emphasis on individual freedom, brought successful attacks on the linking of church and state. Everywhere throughout the new nation the Church of England was removed from its preferred position; but somewhat more surprising and significant, other churches were also disestablished. Although the process at first went rapidly it was not completed in New Hampshire until 1817, in Connecticut until 1818, and in Massachusetts until 1833. Along with disestablishment went increasing pressure toward religious toleration, for, as the Virginia constitution of 1776 proclaimed, "all men are equally entitled to the free exercise of religion, according to the dictates of conscience." A similar idea, as applied to Congress, was placed at the very beginning of the First Amendment to the Constitution. In most states, however, although a man had freedom to choose the specific church to which he would belong, only a Christian could vote and hold office, while in New Jersey and the Carolinas he had to be a Protestant.

Americans also expressed their growing nationalism by objecting strenuously and successfully to the foreign control that was so evident in several churches. The Episcopal Church provided an American bishop, Bishop Seabury, in 1784. During the same year the Methodist Church, also English in control, was given an independent American organization. Also in 1784 the Catholic Church made Father John Carroll head of the American church and six years later advanced him to the rank of bishop. Other churches, such as the Congregational and Presbyterian, had long been controlled domestically. Clearly, nationalism had invaded the church.

RISING HUMANITARIANISM

Closely associated with religious sentiment were several social reforms that gathered impetus during the late eighteenth century. A missionary movement, both national and foreign, showed signs of vigor in the 1790s. Whereas America had once itself been primarily a field for missionaries, now Americans felt it their duty to help convert the rest of the world, which included the American Indians. The very important American Board of Commissioners for Foreign Missions was established in 1810 and two years later was responsible for the first American work abroad—in India.

The treatment of the criminal was liberalized. Although the colonies valued life somewhat more than did England and hence imposed the death penalty less frequently, they still believed that the more severe the punishment, the greater the deterrence to crime, and that immediate physical pain was more effective—and also cheaper—than imprisonment. The result was a plethora of branding, slitting the nose, boring the tongue, slicing the ear, whipping, pillorying, and hanging. Now, during the late eighteenth century, the tendency was to decrease the number of punishable crimes and to lessen the severity of punishment. Furthermore, prison incarceration increasingly was substituted for physical torture. The change was of doubtful advantage to the convicted person, since prisons were filthy holes where men, women, and children awaiting trial or convicted of all varieties of crime were subject to the whims of sadistic and grafting guards. Various private groups, of which the Society for Alleviating the Miseries of Public Prisons (Philadelphia, 1787) was best known, worked hard but not very successfully to ameliorate the sad conditions of convicted criminals.

A problem that sounds anachronistic in a rich America was that of the poverty-stricken. In colonial days a man with debts he could not pay might have been imprisoned in most colonies, but also he could have taken the pauper oath and retained his freedom, with possibly a provision for later payments in case he again acquired property. Agitation against imprisonment for debt increased during the late eighteenth century, but with few positive results. The bulk of aid to the poverty-stricken of the colonies came from private charity, but even this early some social provision was necessary. In the Northern and Middle colonies almshouses were frequently established in the larger communities, while elsewhere the poverty-stricken individual might be auctioned off to the lowest bidder. In the South they were sometimes given licenses to beg, but usually able-bodied vagrants were bound out to service, and such a person found without a master might be whipped. As to the indigent sick, the first regular provision for them was in the Pennsylvania Hospital (1751), supported in part by public funds. This hospital by charter gave equal treatment to everyone and had to treat the poor free of charge as long as its money held out; it had power, however, to exclude incurables and people suffering from contagious diseases. In periods of epidemics pesthouses were sometimes constructed to isolate the sick. These general conditions were modified but not changed radically in the early nineteenth century, in spite of the fact that humanitarian sentiment was on the rise.

Other charitable enterprises had surprising variety, even if usually inadequate funds. Philanthropic societies helped strangers and raised money for education and for the insane. Various groups tried to help immigrants to adjust themselves to the New World, usually working with specific nationalities such as the Welsh, English, and Germans. "Humane" societies specialized in lifesaving training and equipment. Disabled seamen were the subject of private solicitude. Library societies provided facilities that otherwise were lacking. Temperance had its supporters, like, for example, a group of Litchfield men who in 1789 pledged that they would not use liquor in their businesses and would serve only beer and cider to their workingmen.

Slavery came under increasing attack during the late eighteenth century in harmony with the current emphasis on the rights of man. The slave trade was either strictly limited or entirely abolished in every state, both North and South, before 1800, although Congress, according to the Constitution (Art. 1, Sec. 10), was prohibited from ending it nationally before 1808. Slavery itself was outlawed by gradual emancipation in all Northern states and generally opposed in the South. Jefferson wrote: "I tremble for my country when I reflect that God is just; that His justice cannot sleep forever." The Southern problem was obviously very much more complicated and difficult than the Northern, with the result that although several Southern states encouraged masters to free their slaves, there was no general emancipation.

Would more rights for all men, however, apply also to all women? A small group of Americans took the very radical position of advocating something near equality for women: among them was the novelist Charles Brockden Brown, who propagandized his beliefs widely through his writings. The famous and radical book of the Englishwoman Mary Wollstonecraft, *Vindication of the Rights of Women*, was reprinted at Philadelphia in 1794. Most Americans, however, did not see the point of the arguments. Steeped in the traditions of the common law, they felt that men and women were created to occupy different fields of activity, and that this division had scriptural authority. To have women invade men's spheres, such as politics and business, was to try to create a type of equality that God had never intended. To them, difference of function by no means implied inequality. The best they would grant was that women might be better educated along traditional lines and might enter such fields as the writing of didactic novels and treatises, particularly for the edification of the young. They raised little objection when the first American novels were written by women.

SPECIFIC NATIONAL PROBLEMS

The American trend toward a distinctive nationalism in the period immediately following the Revolution was partly a self-conscious striving for real independence and recognition, but also came in part from sheer necessity, since certain American problems were unique by their very nature, with little European precedent for their solution. For example, the war had ended not only British colonial restraints but also the protection of the British navy. From these changes came immediately a sensation of more freedom and less taxes, but very quickly the discovery was made that the mild English control had carried with it numerous trading rights and protection, which now disappeared. Immediately obvious was the necessity for the United States to provide a complete set of commercial treaties, a tariff policy of some sort, and armed protection. Such problems were not unique to the United States, but they had to be solved with reference to purely American conditions and desires.

Another unique problem was that of land disposal. Americans had long been land-hungry and had seized the opportunity of the Revolution to confiscate tory estates; later efforts to compensate the dispossessed loyalists were doomed to almost certain failure. Such objectionable English institutions as quitrents and entail were abolished. The practice of primogeniture was generally outlawed, and every state but two (New Jersey and North Carolina) provided that daughters should inherit equally with sons. These changes, which were pet ideas of Jefferson, were in general accomplished before 1790, even though certain relics lingered for many years.

Seemingly endless acres of rich Western land represented another distinctive American problem. England had tried to stop colonial expansion by means of the Proclamation of 1763, and now this measure went on the scrap heap. But who really owned the land? And who would buy it, in what amounts, and for how much? Would the new areas become in time integral parts of the Union? A complete land and colonial policy had to be developed. Experiments over the next century produced no complete and perfect solution, but they did bring results that were uniquely American.

Use of the Western land that was such a lodestone for American eyes was hindered by the fact that it was actually not open for immediate settlement. It was held by a native population which did not follow the white man's traditions of dress, agriculture, and government and which, although sparse, was self-reliant and warlike. Something had to be done about these Indians, and again there was no easily available and pertinent European solution. Any action must perforce represent a distinctively American contribution to racial relations.

The whole frontier experience itself furnished a uniquely American bond for the new nation. Here was a common experience that set off the United States from the rest of the world. Nothing like it had occurred in Europe or Asia within historic years, for even the eastward expansion of Russia was not parallel. The only comparable developments were in South America, Africa, Australia, and New Zealand; but conditions were not entirely similar, even if the experiences had been available for Americans to compare.

Viewed generally, the war of the Revolution had been only one step in the creation of a new and unique nation. The old colonial status and frame of mind changed but slowly under the influence of peculiarly American conditions, and real independence appeared in one phase of life after another. As a part of the world community, the United States influenced and was influenced by the rest of the world, but increasingly it came to have a distinctively national character and individualized ways of life. Along with these changes appeared an increasing nationalism or patriotism that was of relatively small importance in the intellectual world of the Revolutionary generation. Americans came to boast loudly of their differences, which they assumed to be superiorities. The Revolutionary fathers came to be practically deified, and George Washington was beyond even the most minor criticism. Independence became the great national celebration. It

is from this point of view that the War of 1812 has long been described as our second war of independence. Not until this time was it possible for a Stephen Decatur to state the creed: "Our country! In her intercourse with foreign nations may she always be in the right; but our country, right or wrong!"

CHAPTER 9

Beyond the Appalachians

(1789-1815)

TRENDS IN WESTERN MIGRATION

Thousands of land-hungry Americans greeted the end of the Revolution as providing the opportunity for occupying the rich lands beyond the Appalachians. British opposition to such expansion, as expressed in the Proclamation of 1763 and in the Quebec Act, was no longer a deterrent, while the coming of peace provided favorable circumstances. Whereas during the Revolution Western settlement had contracted, so that Kentucky was almost abandoned and settlers farther north had retreated to the neighborhood of Fort Pitt (Pittsburgh), now the way seemed open for peaceful expansion. Thousands of individuals and families began to flock toward the West.

The new Westerner above all had to be optimistic if he were to face with equanimity the conditions confronting him. Strong Indian tribes viewed the new arrivals with anything but enthusiastic hospitality; they had been fighting the white invasion and could see no good reason for ending the war. Even the basic characteristics of civilization, such as government, satisfactory land titles, roads, schools, and churches, were missing. To the north the boundary with British Canada was vague, and

England continued to hold important trading posts on United States territory. To the west and south lay the outposts of the widespread Spanish empire. Madrid's control of the mouth of the Mississippi, with its threat to Western economic life, was only a part of the story. The British-American treaty of 1783 had given the United States the area as far south as the 31st parallel, with the secret proviso that if Britain retained Florida its boundary should be parallel to the mouth of the Yazoo River, about 100 miles to the north. No such statement had appeared in the Spanish-British agreement by which Florida went to Spain, and naturally Spain insisted on the old British boundary; in fact she was in at least partial occupation of the region north to the Yazoo and claimed even more territory to the north as the spoils of her joint action with the United States. The result was that in a very real sense the West—and in fact the entire United States—was almost encircled by stronger powers of dubious friendship. And the weak American government under the Articles of Confederation was in no position to take any drastic and effective action. Certainly the future was darkened by ominous clouds.

Western troubles may have slowed migra-

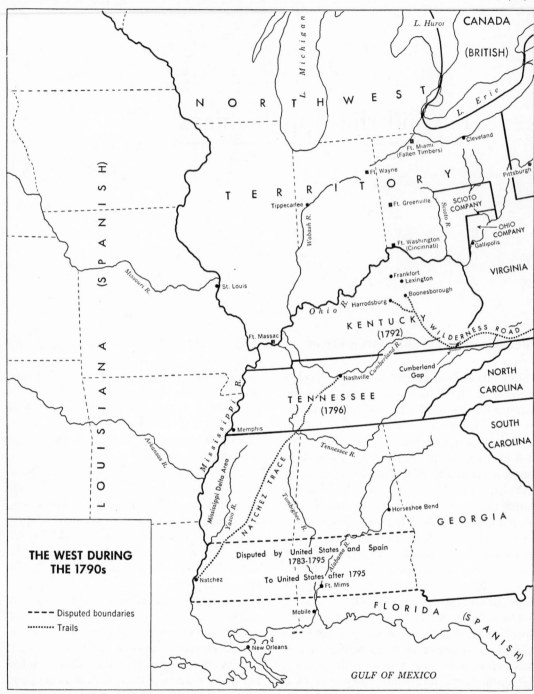

THE WEST DURING
THE 1790s

– – – – Disputed boundaries

••••••••• Trails

tion, but they certainly did not stop it. Increasing numbers of people proved willing to hazard
the dangers of a new life beyond the mountains. These migrants had seldom made notable successes in the East, and a certain number were undesirables who were only a step
ahead of the sheriff, the letters "GTK" (Gone
to Kentucky) being quite generally understood; but the great majority was composed
of young people seeking their fortunes. The un-

married farm boy who had just attained his majority was perhaps the most typical settler. His legal and social obligations to his father had been fulfilled, and he was free to seek greater opportunity than was represented by a small fraction of the old family farm. Often he would go West for a few years to collect a little nest egg and to locate good land and then return East for a bride before he settled down to farming. Part of the migrants were young married people anxious to improve their fortunes faster than seemed possible in the East.

Movement to the West, like any migration, tended to be greater in prosperity than in depression. If a young bachelor went West his earning opportunities were much better in good times. If a family moved it needed to sell most of its possessions and probably borrow money from relatives and friends. The trip west was by no means cheap; and even if father did not at once buy land, the family still had to continue to eat for the best part of a year before a crop could be harvested. Even under the most favorable circumstances and with the greatest frugality every settler needed the financial backlog that was more possible in good than in bad times.

The hopeful migrant tended to travel by the shortest possible route, which in the majority of cases meant due west. He was influenced by distances, but also by a desire to obtain the climatic conditions with which he was familiar. New Englanders, provided that they did not go to the frontier regions to the north, tended to fill central and western New York State and then push out along the southern shore of Lake Erie; Cleveland originated as a New England town. Pennsylvanians and other residents of the central states moved west through Pittsburgh to occupy the present state of Ohio, spilling over into the future Indiana. Southerners followed the Wilderness Road into Kentucky, spreading from there over the Ohio River to the north and into Tennessee to the south, a few adventurous souls pioneering to even more remote areas. As yet little migration went around the southern end of the Appalachians because of the strength of the Indian tribes.

THE FRONTIER FARM

The trip to the West ordinarily began in the spring, as soon as the grass would support the stock. At first travel was by horseback, but in time the roads were broadened so that they could take wagons, either the oblong-box Pennsylvania or the tipped Conestoga type. In either case a tarpaulin was stretched over curved wooden poles to keep out most of the weather. Movement was at walking speed, for both humans and horses walked, and the parties camped at night. Those who went through Pittsburgh frequently had flatboats constructed for the trip west from that city and floated down the Ohio to as near their prospective homes as possible. The boat was then torn apart for the valuable planed lumber and nails.

Picking the location of a new home was a decision of vital importance. Normally the new settler preferred to be near people he had known in the East; very possibly he had been impressed by the letters they had written home, but in any case it was pleasant to see friendly faces. He wanted human companionship not only because man is a friendly animal, but for protection against the Indians, for the construction of churches and schools as rapidly as possible, and because his future prosperity depended on improved transportation and marketing, which could come only with more people. Water was also a vital matter, both for drinking and to furnish transportation before roads could be improved.

Top consideration in picking a new farm went to good land. If possible the farmer obtained land that had been at least partially cleared and improved, but ordinarily his funds were not sufficient for such luxury. His tests of fertility were whether the land supported vegetation and whether it looked similar to Eastern land that he knew by experience was fertile. The test of vegetation meant that the settler in the early years skipped the prairies and took the wooded land along the streams; the obvious results were the inevitable sound of the woodsman's axe and multitudinous kinds of sickness, particularly malaria. The test of similarity also produced mistakes, as when the Pennsylvanian, accustomed to the rich, reddish soils of southeastern Pennsylvania, picked reddish western soils that turned out to be clay.

Once having chosen his land, which he might or might not buy immediately, the new settler's first job was to clear enough ground to build his house and to plant his first crop. Brush was grubbed out and burned, but the cutting of trees proved a larger job than most men could accomplish completely; consequently many were girdled and allowed to die, while others were burned. In any case the results were not very satisfactory. Plowing the root-filled ground with a wooden plow and raising corn in a partially shaded field did not produce first-rate results.

Permanent housing was a necessity before the snow began to fly. In the summer a family could live in a rough lean-to of saplings or accept the hospitality of neighbors, but by fall better quarters were required. Logs that had come from land-clearing operations were moved and put into place by community effort. Shingles for the roof were held in place by pegged saplings. The fireplace was constructed of field stone or of wood covered with clay. The floor was either dirt or puncheons, which were half logs with the moderately flat side on top. Seldom was more than one window provided, and that was often small and barred to keep out wild animals, with oiled paper to permit light to enter; glass was very rarely used.

Inside the house were the simplest furnishings. A bed in a corner might be supported on two sides by the walls and on the other two by a stick driven into the earth; rope springs, a husk mattress, and covers of animal pelts were usual bedding in the early days. Stools were three-legged to stand on the rough floor. Clothes hung on pegs. An attic was used for storage and for the children's beds. Cooking was done at the fireplace, the principal utensils being a crane and pot, a big frying pan, and a Dutch oven; reputedly most food swam in grease. Dishes were frequently of wood carved

by father in the evenings. Their contents tended toward corn bread and salt pork the year round, although fruits and vegetables were possible in season. Practically everything used by the family was homemade, including such items as tools, clothes, soap, candles, and even shoes.

WESTERN PROBLEMS: THE PUBLIC LANDS

The new Western settler was faced with almost innumerable problems in his effort to convert a wilderness into a source of fame and fortune, but none was more basic than that of getting proper title to the land that he farmed. True, he could at first "squat" on the land without obtaining title, but in that case he might one day find years of backbreaking labor lost to some newcomer with a better legal claim. Immediately at the end of the Revolution he could buy only from a state, or from a prior owner who had obtained his rights from a state. The situation was unsatisfactory since state land systems were poor, locations were vague, and state conflicts made many purchases of dubious validity.

Congress under the Articles urged ardently that all state claims should be ceded to the central authority, thereby ending conflicts and giving the government one of its few valuable assets, but was in no position to exert any great pressure in this direction. The states, at times with considerable reluctance, gradually came to feel that Western land was more a liability than an asset, because of the expensive demands of the new Western settlers and the overlapping claims with other states, and gradually began to make cessions. The procession started with the New York gift of rather shadowy rights in 1780 and was completed with the unloading by Georgia of her almost insoluble troubles in 1802. The results were rather mixed. Some states, such as Connecticut and Virginia, made important reservations. Cessions south of the Ohio River meant very little, since practically all the land had already been granted; in fact Georgia had granted more land than existed, and the cession actually cost the Federal government money to disentangle. But at any rate considerable areas of Western lands came into the hands of the Federal government for disposition.

❨ *Land Companies.* The first reaction of Congress to its Western domain was to try to make it produce the maximum financial yield, for the government was desperately in need of money. The Ordinance of 1785 [1] unfortunately produced but little revenue, and the first big land sale came as a result of the demands of a group of Revolutionary soldiers who could see that their war services were unlikely to be rewarded in cash and hence looked hopefully to Western land. Forming the Ohio Company (1786), they sent lobbyists to plead the soldiers' case before Congress, although prospects were anything but hopeful, since Congress seldom even had a quorum present to do business and was more or less marking time to learn the results of the Constitutional Convention. Nothing daunted, the second lobbyist, the Reverend Manasseh Cutler,[2] exercised all possible pressure, did a little logrolling, and ended with a grant of about 1,500,-000 acres of Ohio land priced at something like 8 cents an acre. One of the concessions that made this law possible was the inclusion of an even larger grant (some 5 million acres) for a group of congressional speculators usually labeled the Scioto Company. Also at about the same time a third large grant was given to another speculator, one John Cleves Symmes. To get a trifle ahead of the story, no one of the three purchasers was ever able to pay for the land in full, and ultimately each grant was reduced.

These early congressional grants bring into focus the importance of land speculation in the settlement of the West. The Ohio Company venture was in large degree speculative. These speculators happened to be Easterners,

but Westerners were bitten by the same bug. Any list of outstanding Westerners such as George Rogers Clark, John Sevier, and William Blount tends to be also a list of speculators. And this motivation was by no means limited to the wealthy. The average farmer saw more chances for wealth in the increase of the value of his land—particularly if it might be the site of a future city—than in the profits from farming. He tended to buy all the land that he could possibly acquire, with the hope that some day he would be able to sell at least the surplus at a handsome profit to himself.

One very nice illustration of the speculative urge is a deal involving the Scioto Company, which was interested not only in Western land but in all kinds of investments, including stock purchased on margin. Its congressional land grant was only an option to buy, and the company hoped to raise foreign loans on the land and then exchange these loans, or possibly the land itself, for other securities. As its representative in Paris it sent the well-known author Joel Barlow, who only lost money until he was joined by the English soldier of fortune William Playfair. The two men organized the French Scioto Company, presumably to buy land from the American company and to retail it to French purchasers. Basically such a plan was fraudulent, since the American company did not own the land, and Barlow had no instructions to sell it in this fashion.

Scioto land was advertised in France as of fabulous fertility, well on the way to settlement, and the probable location of the future capital of the United States. Frenchmen flocked to the company's office and bought freely, although whether or not for cash is a little uncertain since the company's books became hopelessly muddled, particularly after Mayfair decamped. Meantime the American company heard rumors of the sales and tried fruitlessly to raise money so that some land would be available; its drafts on Barlow were not honored. While American officials were rushing around frantically and fruitlessly, about 600 Frenchmen, mostly of the middle class, set sail for America early in 1790. After

[1] See p. 72.
[2] General Samuel H. Parsons was the first and unsuccessful representative of the company. His successor, Reverend Manasseh Cutler, obtained the grant.

some delay, agents of the company met them and took them to the Ohio wilderness, where eighty log cabins had been constructed hastily for their reception. The newborn town on the Ohio River was called by the impressive name of Gallipolis, but French lawyers, hairdressers, watchmakers, and confectioners were obviously unfitted for frontier life. Many of them soon left the town, while those who remained discovered that they had no legal title to their land; ultimately Congress took pity on them and gave them land elsewhere. As for the Scioto Company, it went bankrupt, and its head died in debtors' prison.

The Scioto Company had no great intrinsic importance, but it well illustrated the current land speculation. It was reasonably typical in going bankrupt, for while a few speculators succeeded in making their fortunes, a greater number failed. But whether the individual made or lost money, his social service should not be overlooked. The Scioto Company was typical in that it advertised Western land and actually attracted settlers who otherwise might well not have come. An imposing list of Western cities, including Cleveland, Cincinnati, and Nashville, originated as land speculations. The speculator certainly gave a return for his somewhat dubious profits.

Neither the Ordinance of 1785 nor the large congressional grants satisfied the Western settlers, who found the purchase of land almost impossible except from speculators who might or might not own the desired tracts. Perhaps just as important, the receipts of the Federal government were unimpressive. After much discussion both inside and outside Congress a new Land Act was passed (1796), which ultimately was expanded and improved in the more famous act of 1800. Land was still to be sold at auction, but the minimum price was raised to $2 an acre. But now the sales were to be made at Western land offices, the amount which might be purchased was as small as a half-section (180 acres), and payment could be spread over four years. Although the higher price was certainly no boon to the settler, the small down payment meant that he could obtain a claim on more land than

before for the same money. The Westerner was always optimistic and expected that good fortune would come his way before he was called upon for additional payments. Unfortunately his hopes were not realized in many cases.

WESTERN PROBLEMS: DOMESTIC AND FOREIGN INTRIGUES

❨ *Domestic Troubles.* An organized government was at least as great a need of the West as the ability to acquire land. Immediately at the end of the Revolution most Westerners were left largely to their own devices in government. Congress had no power, and the states had no money. Most of the Westerners lived either in the present Kentucky, claimed by Virginia, or in the present Tennessee, claimed by North Carolina; the only answer to their pleas for government was the formation of Western counties. The people of Kentucky were the more numerous and started to petition Virginia for statehood in 1782; ten years passed before their desires were gratified. Kentucky then became the first state west of the mountains, but actually it was number fifteen in the national roster, for Vermont had been admitted to statehood in 1791.

The people of Tennessee were also restlessly impatient for government, but found themselves badly involved in land troubles, the outstanding citizen of the area, John Sevier, being also a top land speculator. Moreover, North Carolina could not seem to make up its mind whether or not to cede its Western land to Congress, and the hesitation was produced at least in part by conflicting groups of speculators. Finally Tennessee impatience became so great that the Western area declared itself independent (December, 1784) as the nation of Franklin. A brand-new constitution was adopted, with an elaborate bill of rights. Officers were elected; and the governor, as elected by the legislature, was none other than John Sevier.

For several years the state of Franklin exercised a rather precarious sovereignty. It made and enforced laws, collected taxes, fought Indian wars, and made treaties, even though it failed to obtain recognition from either Congress or North Carolina. Its death in some five years was the result more of compromise than of conquest. By this time North Carolina had ceded her Western claims to Congress. All Franklinites except Sevier were pardoned, but this exception proved meaningless when Sevier was permitted to attend both the legislature and the Constitutional Convention. When the Southwest Territory was created by Congress in 1790 Sevier's friend William Blount became governor, and Sevier became brigadier general of the territorial forces. When Tennessee became a state in 1796 Blount was elected its first Senator, while Sevier spent two terms as governor and then moved to the Senate.

The state of Franklin was a fine example of the willingness of the West to seize the bit in its teeth and act independently when it felt that it was not being given proper consideration. Throughout its history, the West time after time refused to wait with docility until the East got around to acting. This propensity, plus the real physical isolation of the transmontane West in the early years, led such Easterners as Washington to fear that some day the West might break away and form an independent nation.

With the cession of the state land claims to the Federal government, even the rather impotent Congress of the Articles of Confederation felt inspired to make some provision for the government of the territory obtained. The abortive Ordinance of 1784 was succeeded by the Ordinance of 1787, which, in spite of being involved in a complicated web of compromises and logrolling (including the Ohio Company grant and the promise that the president of Congress, Arthur St. Clair, should be governor of the new territory), emerged as the most important and successful law of the Confederation.[3] The Northwest Ordinance provided that ultimately the Old Northwest should be divided into between three and five states, and

[3] For its terms, see pp. 72–73.

as population grew additional regions were cut away until the maximum number of five was in existence. The first of these regions to attain statehood was Ohio (1803), which consequently was the first of the public-land states and the first to follow the pattern of political development that was to be customary in the American march across the continent.

❡ *Foreign Plots.* A tale of the orderly development of Western states along the lines specified by Congress hardly gives a true picture of the situation during the late eighteenth century. Nationalism in the modern sense of the term was little more than an embryo, and Westerners even more than Easterners thought of government less as the center of their loyalties than as an agency to satisfy their desires. If one government did not do a satisfactory job, why not change to another, even if the change meant independence or foreign allegiance? More specifically, Westerners frequently felt neglected by the government of the Confederation and antagonistic to the aristocratic Federalist administration of the young constitutional republic. Quite a few of them felt that independence offered attractive possibilities for personal and group advantage, while still others eyed Spain speculatively and hopefully. After all, Spain had millions of vacant and attractive acres, as well as control of the Mississippi, which was the basis of Western prosperity.

To the average Westerner Spain looked strong in the period just after the Revolution. She expanded her garrisons up the east side of the Mississippi as far as the present Memphis (1795) and reinforced St. Louis. She cultivated friendship and trade with the Indians and closed the river (1784) to American trade for a short time. Although this apparent strength impressed many Americans, a real weakness was more obvious to Spain herself. The long frontier around American territory contained not over 25,000 people (excluding Indians)—largely Negro, French, and English —while American frontiersmen were at least three times that numerous (1786). Spain's poor financial circumstances did not permit large expenditures on colonies that had few advantages, either economic or military. In 1784 the Governor of Louisiana could muster fewer than 1,400 effective soldiers and often had trouble getting funds to pay them; the idea of large-scale reinforcements was chimerical.

The greatest problem of the Spanish Governor of Louisiana was the attitude he should take toward the restless and aggressive American frontiersmen who began to seep into his territory. In many cases he found them undesirable residents who might well create discontent and disorder; in one report (1785) he described them as "vagabonds, dregs of Europe and America, . . . abandoned to all vices and capable of committing any crime." But on the other hand the effort to exclude Americans might inspire outright invasion against which he had no adequate defense. In consequence his policy fluctuated. Most of the time, however, he chose the lesser of the evils and welcomed American migrants. For example, he offered liberal terms to all Franklinites to make their homes in Spanish territory.

Western uncertainties about domestic government and about the attitude of Spain inspired a long series of intrigues and land speculations that included such outstanding men as Sevier, Blount, and Clark. Throughout the West rumors were spread of possible independence, of an attack on Spain, of an alliance with Spain (or even of joining the Spanish empire), and of grandiose plans for land speculation. Many of even the wildest rumors were based on at least a minimum of fact. And no Westerner enjoyed the situation more, or tried harder to take advantage of it, than one James Wilkinson.

James Wilkinson was no penniless adventurer. Born in a well-to-do Maryland family, he had been trained as a doctor; but the Revolution interrupted his career before it was well started, and he enlisted in a rifle corps. Advancing rapidly, he soon became "Clothier General" of the Continental army. His record was generally satisfactory if one overlooked a propensity toward devious plots and toward too much talking and too many quarrels. Upon

leaving the army he settled in Pennsylvania, where he sat for a time in the legislature; but his income did not satisfy his desires, so in 1783 he sought his fortune in Kentucky as an agent of various Philadelphia merchants. Here this young, energetic, and plausible Revolutionary hero soon became a man of importance. He traded and speculated in land, and his big home was always open to his many friends.

Plotting and intrigue were lifeblood to Wilkinson, and soon he was up to his neck in all sorts of plans. In the very year (1784) in which Spain closed the Mississippi River to American trade he loaded two flatboats with produce and floated them down to New Orleans, where he emerged from an earnest talk with the governor as a paid Spanish agent. His exact personal desires, except financial, remain uncertain. For home consumption he talked of independence and an alliance with England if Spain would not open the river. For Spanish consumption he advocated independence and an alliance with Spain and urged that the river be kept closed. To appeal to the English he proposed that he be made an agent to promote Western independence and an attack on New Orleans. Between these plots he found time for certain private speculations, such as an expedition proposed by a brother-in-law of George Rogers Clark to seize the disputed land along the Yazoo; in this case, however, the chief plotter was a little skeptical of "our friend the General" and did not give him full confidence. All these plans lost much of their appeal when Kentucky became a state in 1792, whereupon Wilkinson returned to the army.

New opportunity came upon the arrival in 1793 of Citizen Edmond Genêt with grandiose plans for lining up the United States on the side of France. His Western agent, André Michaux, appointed George Rogers Clark as commander in chief of a "Revolutionary and Independent Legion of the Mississippi," with plans for a three-pronged attack on Spanish territory. The resulting excitement was delightful to Wilkinson, who immediately informed the Spanish government and asked

for pay; the pay turned out to be a keg of Spanish dollars that was seized by bandits on its
way north. President Washington was tremendously concerned and issued a proclamation (March, 1794) against any armed force
in the West; he also had Wayne establish
Fort Massac on the lower Ohio—an act that
worried the Spanish governor more than the
French plans. Ultimately the intrigue collapsed, and Wilkinson joined Wayne in
fighting the Indians. When Wayne died,
Wilkinson became head of the Western
army, even though he still remained in the
pay of Spain.

The mid-1790s should theoretically have
seen the end of Western intrigues. Government had been provided for the West, and
the Indians had been defeated. England had
given up its Western posts as a result of the
Jay Treaty (1794). Spain had settled her
boundary dispute and opened the Mississippi
in the Pinckney Treaty (1795). And yet some
of the most fascinating plots came in the following years, the most exciting of all coming
even after the purchase of Louisiana. William
Blount, prince of land speculators, governor
of the Southwest Territory, and soon to be
United States Senator, projected in 1796, with
British aid, an attack on Spanish territory.
After the expected success, England was to receive Louisiana and Florida, while the conspirators were to be rewarded by public funds
and large gifts of land. Unfortunately a
drunken colleague talked too much, and
Blount was expelled from the Senate. Alexander Hamilton sponsored a similar plot by
which he was to win the military glory he had
long desired by leading an army to take
Louisiana and Florida and then possibly continuing into Mexico and Central America;
the plans involved an alliance with England
and war with France and Spain. Another
schemer, William Bowles, actually invaded
Florida twice in the years 1799 and 1801, but
without success.

The extent to which Wilkinson participated
in, or even was aware of, these later plots is a
trifle uncertain. The only certainty is that he

remained in Spanish pay. Apparently his attention was being drawn more and more toward Texas, for starting with the Texas filibustering expedition of his protégé Philip
Nolan in 1800 there are numerous indications
that his interest was turning toward the Southwest. All this fitted well with the plans of his
friend Aaron Burr, whom he had known since
the days of the Revolution. Burr's Western
plans of 1806 remain more than a little uncertain, but there is no inherent impossibility in
his own later explanation that he envisaged a
Mexican empire. At any rate, it is clear that
he consulted long and earnestly with Wilkinson, the head of the Western army. Wilkinson's ambitions also remain somewhat vague,
but after apparent indecision he denounced
Burr to the government. Wilkinson's reputation was considerably tarnished by his association with the New Yorker, even though he had
turned him in, and even though Burr was acquitted on the charge of treason. Nevertheless,
Wilkinson remained commander of the army
in the West.

The Western intrigues of the late eighteenth century had both temporary and permanent implications. In so far as they involved
independence for a part of the United States
and agreements or alliances with foreign
powers, they were temporary; within a generation such ideas were as dead as a dinosaur. In
so far as they represented sectional stirrings
and frictions, they were indicative of the future. In so far as they pertained to land-craving
and a willingness to use forceful and aggressive
action to attain their desired goals, they remained the same. During the next half century American covetousness for newer and
greener pastures apparently knew no limitations, and the means utilized included any
type of action that promised success.

WESTERN PROBLEMS: THE INDIAN

The third great problem facing the West was
that of the Indian. To most Americans the

Indian was something of an intellectual anomaly. Obviously God could not have intended an entire continent to be monopolized forever by partially clothed and backward pagans, but why then did He make them so strong and war-like? Truly, the ways of God were inscrutable, and the only immediate answer was to push the aborigines aside from the land that the whites wanted immediately.

During the Revolution the Indians had fought on the side of the British, but for different reasons. When the United States won the war it assumed, in the white tradition, that the Indians were among the losers, and in a moment of victorious jubilation declared that all Indian land was forfeit and would be returned only at the pleasure of the whites. This frame of mind was rudely disturbed by the failure of the Indians to recognize any defeat and their continued harassment of undesired settlers who entered their country, whereupon the United States was jolted back somewhere nearer reality, established two Indian departments (north and south of the Ohio River) under the Secretary of War, and tried to make treaties of peace and friendship.

Indian agreements had to be in the form of treaties because the law considered the various tribes as independent nations—and therein lay manifold troubles. White commissioners professed to believe that the Indian tribes were bound by a signed agreement even if the signatories were random braves who had been made drunk, plied with presents, and overawed by force. And Western white Americans continued to hold the treaty valid even though the Senate changed its terms and the government failed to live up to it. Under such circumstances the Indians had a marvelous record of obedience to treaties, and only gradually did they learn that the white man's word could not be trusted. Annuities and gifts did not materialize in the promised amounts, and whites were not removed from the land that was reserved for the Indians. After all, the whites had votes and the Indians did not.

❮ *Indian Wars.* The first real Indian wars of the new government under the Constitution were with the tribes north of the Ohio River. These Indians were largely Algonquian and included such tribes as the Shawnee, Wyandot, and Miami. All told they numbered possibly 50,000, but they probably never had more than 3,000 warriors in the field at the same time. They were in the stone age of human development and had few guns, but their bows and arrows made effective weapons in the forests where they did their fighting. They had regular towns, but their dependence on hunting meant that they moved a great deal. By nature they were generous, hospitable, friendly, fun-loving, and even loquacious, but the whites received a different impression on the battlefield and in the council meeting with its strict decorum; with continued white contacts, the friendliness and hospitality of the Indians declined. After all, they were engaged in a war for the preservation of their home country from the invading whites; and although they had no concept of individual land ownership in the white sense, they were even more passionately attached to the lands of their fathers.

The failure of the Federal government to negotiate satisfactory treaties with these Northern tribes led to a series of military actions to conquer or at least to overawe them. In the fall of 1790 General Josiah Harmar moved north from Fort Washington (Cincinnati) with a rather unprepossessing army composed largely of relatively untrained militia; near the present Fort Wayne he was attacked by the Indians, and only because of the red men's desire to collect plunder did a good share of the whites manage to get back to civilization. The next year Arthur St. Clair, governor of the Northwest Territory, took personal command of an expedition that was almost a carbon copy of that of the preceding year, with the minor exception that it did not get so far before it was defeated by the Indians. Naturally the Indians became arrogantly certain of their power to defeat any white troops that were sent against them.

A third expedition was gathered in 1792 under Anthony Wayne of Revolutionary fame. Quite remarkably it spent the better part of two years in training before it launched itself into the wilderness—the delay being caused, it should be said, not by the desire of Wayne but by strict orders from the War Department, which clung stubbornly to the faint hope of a peaceful solution. Whatever the cause, the army that started its advance from Fort Washington in July, 1794, was the best trained that the West had ever seen. Advancing cautiously along the route of Harmar and St. Clair it finally met the Indians in force at Fallen Timbers, not far from Lake Erie. The resulting battle was no clear-cut white victory, but the Indians were tired of war and impressed by the failure of the British to come to their support. Consequently they were ready to sue for peace, and the Treaty of Greenville (1795) ceded to the whites roughly the southeastern two-thirds of the present Ohio and the southeastern corner of the present state of Indiana.

Indian power had not been broken by Wayne, and hence there can be no surprise that further troubles arose as more and more whites pushed into the Indian country. Affairs approached a climax with the arrival in 1801 of William Henry Harrison as governor of the new Territory of Indiana, which had been created the previous year as part of the preparation of Ohio for statehood. Harrison had fought with Wayne at Fallen Timbers and had a high opinion of his own military abilities; spurred by the Federal government he began to buy more land for future white settlement. His opponent was the very able Tecumseh, who had been a young brave at the time of Fallen Timbers and who was the spearhead of Indian hostility toward any further land cessions to the whites. He envisioned a widespread Indian confederation to stop white expansion, and to forward this vision he traveled widely, both north and south.

While Tecumseh was consulting with the Southern tribes in the fall of 1811, Harrison seized the opportunity to lead an expedition into the Indian country. At Tippecanoe he barely averted defeat, but the results of his action were almost as impressive as if he had actually won the brilliant victory he claimed. Tecumseh's prestige was undermined, and in fact Tecumseh died not much later in the War of 1812. The prospective Indian confederation never materialized, and the Indians were discouraged by the obviously growing white power. Never again in the Old Northwest was there to be serious Indian resistance to the all-conquering surge into Indian country of the pioneer farmer.

South of Kentucky lay the country of the Five Civilized Tribes—Creek, Cherokee, Seminole, Choctaw, and Chickasaw. These tribes were further advanced in civilization than their Northern brothers. Generally they lived in permanent villages, owned considerable livestock, and practiced settled agriculture, raising such crops as corn and beans. Like the Northern tribes, they resented the intrusion of the white man, but also like their Northern contemporaries they seldom furnished unified resistance since there was no tradition of common action; the nearest approach to real union came in a Creek confederation during the years just after the Revolution. Clashes between the redskins and the whites occurred from time to time, and white expeditions such as those of Sevier periodically entered the Indian country, but by and large the Indians remained powerful and in control of the country that they occupied.

The increasing Indian resentment against encroachments was fanned into white heat by the visits of Tecumseh; and finally on 30 August 1813, the Creeks attacked and massacred the inhabitants of Fort Mims (at the junction of the Alabama and Tombigbee Rivers) as a part of a larger plan to drive all whites from the Indian country. Terrified pioneers fled to the larger and stronger settlements, and immediately three columns of troops took the field. The strongest of the three was under Andrew Jackson, and early in March of the following year it met a sizable Creek force at the Horseshoe Bend of the Alabama River and defeated it decisively. The ensuing treaty naturally removed much of the Creek land, but not so naturally also took much land from the Cherokee, who had fought with Jackson. This campaign broke the power of the Southern Indians, even though another quarter century was to elapse before the tribes were to be removed completely to make way for the whites.

WESTERN DREAM AND WESTERN REALITY

The elimination of the Indians, like the land-purchase system and the formation of government, was for the Westerner merely the precursor of the real business of life. What he really wanted was success according to Eastern standards, which meant first of all wealth and opportunities for its enjoyment, including moral and artistic advantages. He was trying not to escape a civilization, but to carry it with him. Basically he accepted conservatively the goals that seemed important to the seaboard and only sought to achieve them more rapidly by meeting the hardships of the West.

❲ *Economic Factors.* The easiest evidence of success was economic well-being, and each Western farmer tried to make money that could be spent for such impressive items as a frame or brick house, improved stock, a span of fine horses and a beautiful carriage, a silk dress for his wife, a fiddle for his son, cigars and wine for himself. His original self-sufficiency had been a necessity, not a desire, and increasingly he exchanged his surplus production for goods that could be produced more satisfactorily by experts. Quite early in the West appeared such industries as flour and lumber milling, tanning, glass- and ropemaking, distilling, salt mining, and shipbuilding.

As the Western farmer bartered his surplus with the local storekeeper, a rather complicated system of trade soon developed. The storekeeper obtained his own stock from an Eastern city, ordinarily Philadelphia, on credit; then he swapped these goods for his Western patrons' produce. The farm products were shipped down the river to New Orleans, where they were ordinarily paid for by a draft on an Eastern bank, which could be used to meet the original cost of the merchant's goods. The whole transaction was conducted by credit.

And in truth there was very little cash in the West, the usual farmer seeing only a few actual dollars in the course of a year—possibly several Spanish dollars and maybe a little of the cash brought to pay the soldiers at some nearby fort. Paper money from various Eastern banks circulated a little, but its value was dubious, while a few Western companies such as the Kentucky Insurance Company (1802) issued notes of their own. Altogether, however, the West lacked money and as a debtor community supported any possible device to increase the amount of the circulating medium.

Trade implied transportation, which was another thorny problem for the West. Overland transportation improved gradually as roads were cleared and widened, but none was improved in the modern sense of the word; being "up a stump" had real meaning in the West. Wherever possible the traveler or shipper used water. Down the rivers floated thousands of flatboats, which were little more than crude wooden boxes with oars for steering. After floating down the river to New Orleans such a boat could be taken apart, and its component materials sold; the men would come back over the Natchez Trace, with danger of highwaymen—but then the river itself was no safer. The most common upstream conveyance was the keelboat, which used wind, oars, poles, and even towropes for propulsion; goods shipped by keelboat were so expensive that they were in the luxury class. Shortly before the War of 1812 appeared the steamboat, which was to revolutionize river transportation, but its influence was not felt until after the war.

Transportation and trade inevitably meant cities, and here New Orleans had unquestioned dominance, with a population of over 17,000 in 1810. It had every hope that the future would make it the greatest metropolis of the New World because of its position at the mouth of the river that drained two-thirds of the United States. Much smaller were such towns as Pittsburgh, St. Louis, and Cincinnati; in fact, Cincinnati numbered only 2,540 in 1810. These towns originated largely as trading centers, but they naturally attracted early manufacturing, which meant that they were the homes of the artisans of the period. Since labor was relatively scarce in the West, wages were high; in hard times the average workman could if necessary return to the farming that probably had been his original occupation. Also in the towns were professional men —doctors, lawyers, and ministers. Quite notoriously, few of them were highly trained. Doctors and lawyers received their technical education by a system of apprenticeship, while a good many of the ministers had extreme piety as their only recommendation. Many a professional man pieced out his income by doing a little trading, land speculating, or farming on the side.

(*Cultural Factors.* The town was a natural center for developing the culture of the West. Most important in the years after the Revolution was Lexington, Kentucky, which was considered the Athens of the West. As time passed, other towns took the lead, particularly Cincinnati, with its greater population and wealth. Here were the centers of publishing, the homes of theaters and museums, the locations of the best schools. As always, the urban centers had the wealth with which to lead in the cultural activities of the times.

One of the earliest cultural activities to take place in the average town was the founding of a newspaper. *The Kentucke Gazette,* for example, came into existence at Lexington in 1787. Such a paper was commonly a four-page weekly, and very dull to most moderns. Seldom did it print much local news, depending rather on material it could clip from Eastern papers. Shortly later came magazines, which died with great rapidity; in a few cases they tried to exploit Western material. In time came the publication of books, and even of books written by Western authors. Here and there a school or a well-to-do citizen of studious tastes collected a little library.

Educational facilities appeared rather slowly, primarily because of the lack of funds, and illiteracy long remained high in the West. The average farmer approved of education in the abstract, but when it was time for his John or Mary to go to school he frequently concluded that a new barn or a blooded cow was more immediately important. Only gradually did the number of schools increase; instructors remained difficult to obtain, and frequently a New England boy would earn his stake in the West by teaching school for a time. Secondary schools also gradually came into existence, their prime objective being training for college entrance. The first Western college, Transylvania University at Lexington, Kentucky, opened before 1800, but it was not until after that year that colleges really got their start.

Amusements before the War of 1812 tended toward the crude and homemade; for example, no professional theatrical company toured the West before 1810. Horse races, shooting matches, and wrestling required no elaborate preparation; local wrestling champions toured the immediate countryside chewing off fingers and gouging out eyes. Many of the amusements were sublimations of work, as in house raisings, corn huskings, and quilting parties. Many participants ate too much, drank too freely, and made love too vigorously. Fun was on the boisterous and earthy side, for this was before the day of Victorian prudery. Westerners were on the whole poorly educated and hard working, and they took their fun with rude gusto.

To most Easterners the West seemed irreligious and headed for damnation, particularly because of the lack of churches and church memberships, the prevalence of blasphemy, and the more lenient observance of the Sabbath. In consequence the East began to form home missionary societies to save the West from the devil. Actually, Eastern fears were at least exaggerated. True, the Westerner swore rather freely and could hardly join or even attend nonexistent churches, but he really carried a basic piety with him to the West. Many a literate family had at least a Bible and a religious magazine in its slim library, while churches were built as rapidly as each community could find the funds. Any impression of irreligion was quite superficial.

The favored faiths of the early West were Methodist, Baptist, and Presbyterian, the Roman Catholics being fairly unimportant numerically before 1815. Methodism was possibly best adapted to frontier conditions, with its optimistic doctrines of free grace and individual responsibility, its favoring of the emotional type of religious experience, its refusal to worry about formal education for the ministry, and its use of the circuit rider. The Baptists had similar beliefs, but supplied local preachers rather than circuit riders for the scattered Western communities. Slightly less well fitted was the Presbyterian faith, which tended to be more gloomy, to emphasize an educated ministry, and to look askance at religious emotionalism. The result was a secession (1810) of the Cumberland Presbyterian Church, with doctrines that more closely approximated the beliefs of the average Westerner. More happily, the Presbyterian emphasis on an educated ministry led to the obvious deduction that more Western colleges were necessary, and the Presbyterians were very active in their establishment.

Distinctive in the Western religious picture was an emphasis on emotionalism. Starting in the 1790s the revivalist type of meeting became more and more frequent, until it outgrew the small country churches and moved into tents, and until it increased to a duration of four or five days. Entire families came from many miles around with their supplies and even furniture; they settled down to an orgy of emotionalism, interspersed with neighborly conversations, gossip, and love-making. Meetings at night were particularly impressive as flaring pine knots emphasized the darkness of the surrounding forest, and as a succession of ministers thundered impressively of the dangers of hell-fire. Even hardened sinners shouted, shook in every limb, gibbered, fainted, and pled with God for salvation. Whether or not conversions under such conditions were of lasting value has been long debated, but there is no question that these camp meetings filled an important place in the social life of the West.

In some ways the Western settler recapitulated in a few years the long progress of mankind from a nomadic hunting life to a high-speed urban civilization, but in a more important way he carried a civilization with him to the West. He endured the hardships and deprivations of frontier society only as a short cut to the kind of success and of living he had known while growing to maturity. Whether or not he hoped ultimately to return to the East to enjoy an expected success, he certainly had every intention of attaining the most luxurious conditions of which he had knowledge. In no sense was he a man with a mission to build a new and different civilization. His objective was to make his life in the West similar to, and if possible better than, that of successful Easterners. He was the cutting edge of American civilization as it progressed in its conquest of North America.

The Federalist Ship of State

(1789-1800)

THE FIRST ADMINISTRATION

The blueprint for the stronger American Union had been drawn at Philadelphia in 1787, but the first Congress had to turn to a more prosaic carpentry before the architects' vision could become reality. The problem of establishing precedents was basic. Any decisions initially taken were likely to have deep significance, for governments as well as other institutions and individuals tend to become creatures of habit. Washington and his colleagues recognized that any courses of action adopted during the first months of the new government were likely to become accepted methods for the future until particular conditions changed so radically that new channels would have to be dredged. Inside the general framework of the Constitution specific legislation was vital. The Constitution, after all, merely listed certain rights of the Federal government that had to be implemented by acts of Congress. Some six areas were especially important: a corps of Federal officials had to be appointed and the main advisers of the President selected; a judicial system constructed; the promised Bill of Rights written and adopted; government revenues provided; the

authority of the nation manifested internally; and foreign affairs conducted.

❨ *George Washington.* According to the Constitution the President wielded the executive powers, and this position of deep responsibility fell to George Washington. No other man was considered for this powerful office. Washington was respected by all groups and factions—and deservedly so. His courageous and self-sacrificing Revolutionary career had merited him enough popularity so that he might have accomplished a *coup d'état* to make himself military dictator, but he angrily spurned veiled hints in that direction. True, George Washington was no democrat. He maintained a strict decorum and accoutered himself in such ornate fashion that he was accused of fostering monarchical ambitions. But Washington's republicanism was sincere, and he never subverted it for personal advantage. He leaves no decided impression of genius or even unusual brilliance, but rather one of logic; sober, farsighted judgment; self-sacrifice; and high moral ideals. If his fellow countrymen have not remembered him with the unstinted affection that has been reserved for Abraham Lincoln, George Washington's greatness of character has come down to the present undimmed.

This austere Virginian was fifty-seven years old when he became President of the United States. He considered himself an old man who deserved retirement after a crowded and hectic life. Years of military and political service had left him with a passionate desire to live in peace at Mount Vernon, but an abiding sense of public responsibility impelled him to heed the nation's call. Washington detested the political limelight, for behind a façade of icy reserve he was a shy, reticent, and sensitive man. Political attacks caused him acute agony. In addition, he faced a disheartening financial problem. His personal affairs were in chaos, and he even had to borrow money for his inaugural trip to New York. The heavy expenses incidental to the executive office ensured continuing difficulties. He faced the future with foreboding; but duty was his lodestar, and he was obliged to follow it.

❲ *Washington's Cabinet.*   As a first President, Washington needed assistance. After some deliberation he implemented the executive powers by appointing at first three (later four) department heads who soon formed a recognizable Cabinet. Thomas Jefferson was accorded the portfolio of the Secretary of State. Tall, rangy, light-complexioned, and blue-eyed, Jefferson combined a pleasant if undistinguished appearance with a shy air that some thought to be cold withdrawal. Actually he was warmhearted and affectionate, modest and courteous. His reputation was world-wide, and he numbered his friends on both sides of the Atlantic, for he was equally at home in a French salon or a Virginia dining room. His versatility rivaled Franklin's. Jefferson was an architect, scientist, author, inventor, farmer, humanitarian, philosopher, diplomat, and to a lesser degree musician (he was an ardent violinist).

Jefferson's oratory was hesitant and unconvincing, but his literary style was magnificent. His *Notes on Virginia* commanded an overseas as well as an American audience, and the thrilling prose of the Declaration of Independ-

ence sounded liberty's bell. Although some of his intellectual accomplishments were meager (he never understood theoretical economics, especially finance) and although he aimed at an impossible ideal—a pastoral nation of yeoman farmers—Americans have found in Thomas Jefferson a fountainhead for the democratic impulses that coalesced into action a quarter century after his administration. Jefferson did not personally bring a considerable increase in democracy to this nation, but his liberal influence working in the political imagination of his later followers certainly did.

Alexander Hamilton became Secretary of the Treasury and almost the unofficial prime minister of Washington's administrations. Increasingly the elderly Virginian depended on the cold logic and hard intelligence of his former aide-de-camp during the Revolution. Hamilton was only thirty-two when he sat in the Treasury chair, but already he enjoyed a national reputation. He had been born on the island of Nevis in the British West Indies, the illegitimate son of a Scots father and a French mother. Relatives paid for his passage to New York when he was fifteen; he entered King's College (Columbia University) and soon dazzled the faculty of that staid institution with his precocity and clear-sighted ambition. Hamilton served in the Revolution, but circumstances prevented him from achieving great renown in battle; and there is evidence from his later career that he remained a frustrated soldier all his life. Marrying into the socially prominent Schuyler family, he soon entered the legal profession in New York and quickly made a name for himself. His friendship with Washington and his legal reputation secured him election to the Constitutional Convention. He had little influence there, but contributed invaluable assistance in the ratification struggle.

Hamilton was a small-statured but impressive figure. Handsome, charming, vigorous, and perceptive, yet vain, sometimes impetuous, and occasionally amoral, the new Secretary of the Treasury was able to command respect and sometimes obedience by the masterful logic that he utilized in debate. His vision of a commercial and industrial America was far closer to the reality of the nation's future development than was Jefferson's anachronistic agrarianism. Hamilton, however, never fitted into the pattern of American democracy. His distrust of the people ("a great beast," was his term), his monarchical tendencies, his pro-British conservatism, his lavish favors to the upper economic classes at the expense of the lower, and his occasional treachery toward associates have lessened Hamilton's reputation among recent historians. Hamilton was a great American, but he is not remembered with love. The people whom he never quite trusted could never completely trust him.

The other two members of the first Cabinet were below Jefferson and Hamilton in intelligence and influence. Washington's artillery chief, General Henry Knox of Massachusetts, became Secretary of War and, in Cabinet meetings, practically the echo of Hamilton. A rather dull, unoriginal mind was encased in a massive 300-pound body. The term ponderous describes him physically and mentally. Edmund Randolph of Virginia was the first Attorney General. Supposedly Randolph was a liberal and sometimes sided with Jefferson, but the constant vacillation that plagued him all his life made his value as an ally dubious. As time passed, Hamilton's ascendancy in the administration became greater; Jefferson found himself more and more often a minority of one until he disgustedly resigned in 1793 to oppose the Hamiltonian influence.

FIRST DAYS OF THE CONSTITUTIONAL GOVERNMENT

Only after many vexatious delays during the spring of 1789 was the new government able to assemble in the little city of New York, huddled at the southern tip of Manhattan Island.[1] Amid cheering crowds and considerable pag-

[1] New York remained the seat of the government for only one year. Philadelphia became the capital in 1790 and remained so until the new Federal city of Washington, D.C., was ready for occupancy in 1800.

eantry, George Washington took the first oath "to preserve, protect, and defend the Constitution of the United States." After some time spent in filling governmental positions— Washington made sure that most of the appointees had supported the Constitution— the administration sponsored an important piece of legislation that passed Congress and received the Executive signature.

This was the Judiciary Act of 1789 which provided for the personnel of the Supreme Court and established lesser Federal courts. The Supreme Court was to be composed of a Chief Justice and five Associate Justices (the Constitution does not specify how many and the number has varied from time to time). Eleven Federal district courts were organized. In addition, this act created three circuit courts composed of both Federal judges and Supreme Court Justices. All judges and Justices enjoyed tenure for life, subject only to "good behavior," and they could be removed from office only through the difficult impeachment process. The principle of judicial review of legislation was written into the law, and John Jay, the first Chief Justice, delivered decisions based on this provision. The bitter quarrel about judicial review came later when John Marshall made the Federal courts beleaguered fortresses for more conservative opinion.

True to its solemn avowals made during the battle for ratification of the Constitution, Washington's administration sponsored the Bill of Rights. Many amendments were proposed, but after considerable debate only those which became the first ten amendments to the Constitution were passed by Congress and ratified by the necessary states. These safeguards for personal liberties, rights of the accused, and privileges of the states became effective in 1791.

HAMILTON AND FEDERALIST FINANCES

The main political controversy of the early Republic attended Alexander Hamilton's financial program. Responding to a directive from the House of Representatives to provide for the "public credit," early in 1790 the Secretary of the Treasury presented a four-point program: to pay the foreign debt, to pay the domestic debt, to "assume" the state debts, and to found a "Bank of the United States." There was little difficulty over the first item. All admitted the necessity of paying off the European debt of almost $12 million that had been loaned in cash or credits to enable us to fight the Revolutionary War.

More opposition came on the second point, the amortization of a national domestic debt of about $42 million. This debt was chiefly in the form of Revolutionary certificates that had been purchased years before. One might well ask: Why was there any opposition to the government meeting its just obligations at home as well as abroad? The answer lies in the fact that these certificates had steadily depreciated over the years and by 1790 were selling for as low as a fifth of their face value. Some citizens sold below par because they believed that the certificates would never be redeemed, and others were forced to sell during the depression of 1785–1786. Speculators had bought up the certificates and most were no longer owned by the original purchasers. Furthermore, someone in the Treasury Department let it be known that Hamilton was going to urge payment at face value. Hamilton was not personally responsible for this unfortunate loquacity, but close associates were. The rumor spread among the speculators of New York and Philadelphia, who promptly headed for the hinterlands and bought many certificates from unsuspecting holders.

When Hamilton proposed that the certificates be paid off in full to the present owners, the opposition was loud and clear. Hamilton stood firm, refused to countenance various suggestions by Madison and others that any rewards accruing to this policy be split between the original purchaser and the present holder, and engineered passage of his program through Congress. When the news was officially given that the government would redeem the certificates at 100 cents on the dollar, the emotions

of those who had sold for 25 cents on the dollar can easily be imagined.

Hamilton's third point was the assumption of state debts, which totaled approximately $25 million. He argued that this debt had been incurred in a common cause and that therefore it should be paid in common. Although he did not admit it, the Secretary of the Treasury wished to reward his friends in the upper economic group, since many states had been remiss in paying their obligations. Again a question might be asked: Why should the states object to the Federal government assuming their own debts? Two reasons seem primary. States that had good financial records naturally showed no pleasure at being taxed to help their more improvident sister-states. Also, the opposition suspected correctly that Hamilton was using this bland and persuasive scheme to promote the authority of the nation at the expense of the states.

Jefferson headed the opposition to assumption of state debts, and Hamilton appeared to be facing defeat. The New Yorker managed to trick his adversary, however, as Jefferson later admitted. The shrewd Secretary of the Treasury persuaded his opponent to compromise on a "you scratch my back and I'll scratch yours" arrangement whereby Hamilton's supporters would vote for the new capital to be placed on the Potomac between Maryland and Virginia. In return the Southern Jeffersonians would support the assumption of the state debts. This was duly arranged, but Jefferson soon realized that his bargain was unfortunate. The location of the capital was meaningless—the other issue was vital.

The last item on the Hamiltonian program was the establishment of a Bank of the United States. There is no exact counterpart to this institution in modern America, although it is an old story in Europe. This "National Bank" was modeled on the Bank of England and the Bank of France. It was partly public and partly private and served in place of a Treasury as the depository for Federal money. Twenty per cent of the Bank's stock was held by the government, and 80 per cent sold to private individuals. Obviously a bank of the quasi-public nature of Hamilton's creation with the full authority of the nation behind it would be a Gargantua in credit and finance, and such proved to be the case. The financial policy of the Bank of the United States as reflected in its home office at Philadelphia and its branches scattered throughout the country tended to be identical with the policies of the United States.

Objection to the bank was prolonged and vociferous. There was no precise authorization in the Constitution for a national bank, and those who favored strict limitation of Federal power feared any usurpations that might establish precedents. Moreover, it was quickly realized that such highly centralized governmental finances would be controlled by the mercantile, commercial, and speculative classes in the Eastern cities. Small farmers and artisans joined planters in suspecting the motives of their economic adversaries. As usual, the agrarian debtor group wished for easy credit, and a centralized banking system such as Hamilton proposed might stand in the way with strict collateral requirements. Despite the efforts of the Jefferson-led opposition, the Secretary of the Treasury mustered enough support to engineer his bill through Congress. When the bank stock went on sale, wealthy seaboard and foreign speculators snatched it up inside of two hours. Their gamble was a good one; the bank paid average annual dividends of 8 per cent during its twenty-year existence.

For a fuller understanding of what Alexander Hamilton was attempting to accomplish, his "Report on Manufactures" should be read in conjunction with his financial program. When this is done, the Hamiltonian thought pattern becomes doubly evident. In his treatise the Secretary of the Treasury argued for an industrial policy to aid the nation, itemized the mineral and other resources of the United States, and boldly called for direct governmental intervention in favor of the manufacturer. Hamilton was no advocate of unrestrained *laissez faire*. He wished "private enterprise" to be publicly fostered—not merely let alone. Protective tariffs, bounties for essential manufactures, land grants, and light taxation loads were either stated or implied to enable the American industrialist to compete with foreign rivals. Later, Hamilton's policies were continued and expanded by Henry Clay and others in the "American System" shortly after the War of 1812, and they became the philosophical bases of the Whig party during the 1830s.

When one surveys Hamilton's economic program, aspects both benevolent and malevolent for the national welfare are evident. In its stated purpose to stabilize the credit of the United States, success was spectacular. From the depths of the 1780s, the foreign and domestic credit of the nation became by the next decade as solid a financial rock as existed in the world. Foreign obligations were satisfied, domestic credit was augmented, financial supremacy of the United States over its component parts solidified, and a centralized depository set up. As Daniel Webster later said of Hamilton, "He smote the rock of national resources, and abundant streams of revenue gushed forth. He touched the dead corpse of Public Credit, and it sprung upon its feet."

The reverse side of the Hamiltonian coin is somewhat different. His end was to strengthen the national economy, and this he did. The means that he utilized, however, divided the country. The anticonstitutional flames of opposition had died down for a time while the new government was getting under way, but the embers were rekindled by the Secretary of the Treasury. He deliberately favored the upper classes—the wealthy property owners—by bestowing special privileges upon them. He wished to tie the moneyed groups to the United States so closely that the skein could never be unraveled. The amortization of certificates at face value and the financial centralization accomplished by the Bank of the United States sold the Federalist cause particularly to those who were already sold—the merchants, the shippers, the manufacturers, and the speculators. The natural antipathy toward a strong national government that characterized colonial Americans was resurrected and strengthened by the resentment and dismay which greeted the alliance between wealthy citizens and the Federal government. The party split during the

1790s was caused in part by the financial and economic policies of Alexander Hamilton.

TAXATION AND REBELLION

To pay for such an ambitious program, Hamilton promptly sought tariffs and excise (internal) taxes to augment the small income derived by the government from the sales of land. Although the Secretary of the Treasury earnestly called for a protective tariff (taxes on imports high enough to enable the American producer to undersell his foreign competitors), the manufacturing interests at that time were too weak to offer much assistance. Instead, a small tariff for revenue was passed, with duties averaging around 8 per cent.

Hamilton was more successful in pushing through Congress an excise tax on distilled liquors, although he must have known that he was using kerosene to start a fire. Resistance was inevitable to such an excise as the whisky tax. In that day of bad roads and slow water transportation, the corn that was the basic commodity of the West could find purchasers in only two practicable ways. Corn could be fed to hogs; the potential ham, pork, and bacon walked across the mountains to market. It could be distilled into whisky and barreled; the resultant "white lightning" was rolled or carted to the consumer. When the government announced that it was going to tax their best means of ready cash, the astonishment and fury of Westerners was unrestrained. The "Whisky Rebellion" centered in western Pennsylvania, where lynching parties tarred and feathered revenue officers. Federal authority temporarily came to an end, and talk of secession was widely heard in the Pittsburgh environs.

Washington and Hamilton decided that such an affront to national prestige could not be tolerated; and militia detachments from Virginia, Maryland, Pennsylvania, and New Jersey were assembled. Early in the autumn of 1794 Hamilton took personal command of the army and marched it through the rolling hills of Pennsylvania. Resistance promptly collapsed, a few ringleaders were seized, and the expedition triumphantly tramped back to Philadelphia. Two rebels were convicted of treason but were promptly pardoned by the President. The whole affair had a slightly comic-opera flavor, but the Federal government had clearly demonstrated that its authority was real—that it could act when threatened. Nevertheless, the popularity of the administration sank to a new low in the hinterlands, and thenceforward what small Western support the Federalists had commanded vanished almost completely.

RISE OF THE TWO-PARTY SYSTEM

Even before taxation programs and the Whisky Rebellion had further widened the schism between supporters and antagonists of the administration, the two-party system, characteristic of American politics, had come into being. The delegates at the Philadelphia convention in 1787 had feared political partisanship, which they considered to be anarchistic. During the ratification controversy the *Federalist Papers* of Hamilton, Madison, and Jay had effectively played upon the fear of "factionalism," as they called political activity. Despite their cry for unity, however, the new government was barely two years old before partisanship became noticeable. Those who favored the administration continued to use the name Federalist, which had originally designated a supporter of the Constitution. Titularly headed by the august George Washington and numbering in its ranks such luminaries as John Adams, John Jay, and John Marshall, actual party leadership was in the hands of Alexander Hamilton. The Federalists advocated a relatively strong central government, utilized a "loose construction" of the Constitution based upon the "implied powers" clause in order to allow the government to take decisive action not precisely granted, tended to view Great Britain through rose-colored glasses in foreign affairs, and in general accepted Hamilton's solicitude for the property rights of the commercial, speculative, and manufacturing classes.

The opposition to the Federalists shelved the unwieldy title of Antifederalist and gradually adopted the name "Democratic-Republican." In common parlance it was entitled "Republican," since the term democratic carried the contemporary connotation of mob rule. The Democratic-Republicans were disciples of Thomas Jefferson and carried on their roster such names as James Madison (ardent supporter of the Constitution who joined the party in opposition to Hamilton's program), James Monroe, Aaron Burr, and the eccentric John Randolph of Roanoke. The party had been created in 1791 when the Virginians formed an alliance with varied elements in New York State. A strong back-country organization was constructed to oppose the "monarchical" tendencies of the Federalists. The urban lower classes also tended to cluster about the Jeffersonian standard.

The Democratic-Republicans argued for a strict interpretation of the Constitution lest the rights of the people be transgressed by a central government too powerful to be controlled. Great Britain was viewed as the real enemy of the nation, and the disorders attending the French Revolution were glossed over. Particular emphasis was placed on the rights of the agricultural elements; the Southern planter was favored over the Northern speculator. Human liberties were mentioned more often in Democratic-Republican circles than in Federalist councils. The Jeffersonians were perhaps the purer advocates of *laissez faire* and decried such legislative favoritism as Hamilton was showering upon commercial and manufacturing interests.

Although the schism was well under way before the first administration was over, both parties united behind Washington for reelection in 1792. The Federalists needed the awesome prestige of the general, and the Democratic-Republicans were not yet ready to compete against him. Once more Washington received a unanimous vote in the Electoral College. By 1793, however, the party split had

become open and bitter. As Washington gravitated into the Hamiltonian orbit, Jefferson resigned his Cabinet position to prepare for future jousts. He solidified his machine through alliances with the pro-French "Jacobin" clubs, which, in imitation of their more famous Gallic counterparts, were springing up in many of the cities.

Federalists and Democratic-Republicans vied with one another for the more outrageous billingsgate. Perhaps the political press of the 1790s was the most partisan in the nation's history. William Cobbett in his newspaper called *Porcupine's Gazette* ("Peter Porcupine" was his pen name) referred to Jeffersonians as "Cut-throats, Brigands, Debauchers, and Madmen," to mention a few of the more printable epithets. The opposition answered in kind. Typical Democratic-Republican fare used a quaint metaphor in calling Federalists "dirty hedgehogs . . . vomiting forth malicious abuse." Even the Olympian reputation of Washington did not spare the President from journalistic attack in the pages of the Philadelphia *Aurora*.[2] Political battles over both domestic and foreign issues raged white-hot.

The clash was, nonetheless, partly storm and fury. When Jefferson said in his first inaugural address, "We are all Federalists, We are all Republicans," he was essentially correct. Despite the frantic name calling, agreement on the basic points so essential to a democratic government remained. Even an ardent Philadelphia Jacobin could be roused to anger when his beloved France took steps against America. The crustiest and most reactionary Boston merchant could blast his foreign favorite, Great Britain, when domestic commercial prosperity was at stake. Although the word "pro-French" is used to describe the Democratic-Republicans, and "pro-British" for the Federalists, both parties usually acted for the United States. Ideology tended to be placed in escrow when the showdown came. There was biparty accord on a republican form of

[2] Even Jefferson forgot himself sufficiently in the heat of political controversy to allude to Washington as one of the men "who were Samsons in the field and Solomons in the council, but who have had their heads shorn by the harlot England."

government and on the importance of both human and property rights; the difference was in emphasis and degree.

WESTERN DIFFICULTIES

Although foreign affairs of the early Republic will be discussed in later chapters, entanglements abroad must be mentioned here because of their direct influence on the American West. From the end of the Revolution until the ratification of the Jay Treaty over a decade later, Great Britain refused to abandon several of its forts on American territory, claiming that the United States had been remiss in carrying out some of its treaty obligations and that Britain should not be expected to behave differently. Westerners angrily charged that the Indians were being supplied from the arsenals of His Britannic Majesty. Federal troops joined with Western militiamen in chastising the Indians both in the Northwest Territory and in the South, although some defeats were suffered before victory was gained.[3] After treaties had been concluded with Britain and Spain by 1795, Westerners breathed more easily.

Washington's second administration concerned itself with another Western problem— that of land disposal. Especially pressing was the disposition of territory in the Ohio country, acquired from the Indians by the Treaty of Greenville (1795). Two conflicting American viewpoints had to be reconciled. Eastern conservatives followed Alexander Hamilton's reasoning that settlement should proceed slowly. Hamilton wanted to award his friends speculative opportunity by making it easy for them to pick up vast tracts for eventual resale. Furthermore, restrictions on migration would ensure an adequate labor supply in the East, so important in fostering industrial growth. To more liberal opinion, the crux of any land policy should be the facilitation of migration and occupancy.

The Land Act of 1796 tried to provide for both sentiments, although it was tipped in favor of the speculator. The township, comprising a square 6 miles on each side (thirty-six 640-acre sections), was taken from the Land Ordinance of 1785. In the act of 1796 every other township was reserved for speculators by making eight sections the minimum purchase. Intervening townships were supposed to attract actual settlers by allowing individuals to buy a single section of 640 acres. Relatively stiff credit terms and the high minimum price of $2 an acre appealed to few, however, and in four years only 48,000 acres were sold. In 1800 a new act allowed purchases of half-sections (320 acres), and in 1804 the amount was lowered to 160 acres. Some increased settlement followed these liberalizations, but during the whole period land was cheaper in the states' undeveloped areas than in the Federal domain.

Westerners were delighted when the government adopted the sensible policy of admitting new states on terms of absolute equality with the original thirteen. Three were added to the United States during Washington's administrations: Vermont (1791), Kentucky (1792), and Tennessee (1796). Pioneer democracy was exemplified in the constitutions of these new states. Vermont and Kentucky granted relatively universal manhood suffrage, and Tennessee did almost as well.

It must have been with the strongest possible sense of relief that General George Washington concluded his two terms as President of the United States. He had some advice for his compatriots. His famous Farewell Address, written with considerable assistance from Alexander Hamilton, offered a warning to desist from the factionalism that had become so rampant during recent years and recommended an essentially independent American policy in foreign affairs.[4] Washington returned to the simple pleasures of a Virginia squire until his death in 1799. He was widely and sincerely mourned, for by any criterion he had given far more to the nation than it could return.

[3] For a more complete discussion of difficulties with the Indians, see pp. 123–125.

[4] See pp. 151–152.

THE LAST FEDERALIST ADMINISTRATION

Once it became obvious that Washington would not run again in 1796, political loins were girded for battle. By this time the formerly chaotic Antifederalists had become the powerful Democratic-Republican organization, ready to fight for the candidacy of Thomas Jefferson. The Federalists were split. Hamilton had retired from the government in 1794 to practice law in New York, although Washington had continued to avail himself of his former Secretary of the Treasury's services through regular correspondence. Still a vital cog in the Federalist machine, Hamilton had been sufficiently ruthless and tactless when in power to alienate many even in the Federalist ranks. His party turned against Hamilton to nominate John Adams. The New Yorker personally disliked the latter, and the aggressive New Englander returned the sentiment. Nevertheless, in the campaign of 1796 Adams was able to overcome the handicap of Hamilton's lack of enthusiasm, and he inched past Jefferson by the slender margin of three votes in the Electoral College. Enough disgruntled Hamiltonians threw away their second ballots, however, to allow Jefferson, with the united support of the Democratic-Republicans, to win the vice-presidential contest. The United States found itself in the strange position of having a Federalist President and a Democratic-Republican Vice-President.[5]

John Adams was the first member of a famous family to step into the national limelight. Although the Adams clan had been in Massachusetts for many years, it remained undistinguished until the second Federalist President started it on four straight generations of well-known political and literary figures.[6] John Adams was short, corpulent, and nearly bald. Adjectives describing him are intelligent, honorable, industrious, and self-sacrificing, but at the same time tactless, vain, and occasionally vindictive. He and his equally famous son, John Quincy Adams, were notable diarists and letter writers. Motivated by a stern sense of public service and an unyielding New England conscience, John Adams found himself unable to compromise. Unwilling or unable to make the concessions that are so integral a part of American political life, he could not maintain unity in his own party.

A deep schism in the Federalist party embroiled the President in difficulties. Late in the 1790s it appeared that a bona fide war with France was imminent, and indeed, an unofficial naval struggle was already under way. Federalist extremists, operating under war hysteria, led Congress to pass some highly controversial legislation in 1798, despite the objections of both Adams and Hamilton. First were three Alien Acts. The ultrafederalists had noticed that most French and Irish immigrants promptly became Jeffersonians, and they resolved to stop this influx that was aiding the opposition. The Alien Acts empowered the President to deport unwanted aliens and raised the naturalization time for residence in America from five to fourteen years. Although the President was unwilling to take such action, some aliens fled abroad in fear of prosecution.

The second point of the ultrafederalist legislation was embodied in the Sedition Act. This restricted freedom of speech and of the press by calling for fining and/or imprisoning any individual for "writing, printing, uttering or publishing any false, scandalous and malicious writing or writings against the government of the United States." Additional sections inflicted punishment for bringing the President or Congress "into contempt or disrepute." The Sedition Act was at least par-

---

[5] This situation was able to come about through the Constitution's lack of specifying separate ballots for the President and the Vice-President. The Twelfth Amendment (1804) corrected this omission.

[6] John Adams was, of course, the luminary of the first generation. His son, John Quincy Adams, was another President of the United States. The third Adams generation was highlighted by Charles Francis Adams, railroad president and Minister to Great Britain during the Civil War. The fourth gave American literature the eminent writers Henry and Brooks Adams.

tially enforced; a few Democratic-Republican editors and orators were arrested, tried, and convicted. One Vermont newspaperman named Matthew Lyon ran for and was elected to Congress while serving his jail sentence. So vindictive were such jurists as Associate Justice of the Supreme Court Samuel Chase that angry Jeffersonians grimly awaited the day when they could settle accounts with judges who acted like prosecuting attorneys rather than as disinterested and impartial arbiters. Perhaps the height of silly enforcement of the Sedition Act occurred when one Jerseyite was fined $100 for expressing the pious hope that wadding shot out of a cannon might strike His Excellency John Adams in the executive posterior.

The shocked Democratic-Republicans did not remain silent in the face of these arbitrary actions. Protests roared from Eastern cities; once more the West was aflame. In 1798 organized opposition found formal utterance in the resolutions passed by the Virginia and Kentucky legislatures. James Madison wrote for the former and called upon the other states to join Virginia in protest against Federal usurpation of authority. Jefferson spoke in a more radical vein for Kentucky, declaring that the Alien and Sedition Acts were "null and void" inside the boundaries of that state. These twin resolutions went beyond mere philosophical observations on the relations between the Union and its component parts. They evinced a real fear that unless the states either offered vigorous objection, as did Virginia, or took the direct action of nullification, as did Kentucky, American liberty might be engulfed by swollen national despotism. Once these resolutions were published, however, no further moves were necessary at that time. The offensive Alien and Sedition Acts expired with the end of the Adams administration, and the Virginia and Kentucky Resolutions remained dead letters until their concepts were resurrected by bitterly angry South Carolinians a generation later.

CHAPTER 11

"The Revolution of 1800"

(1800-1812)

TWILIGHT OF THE FEDERALISTS

⟨ *The Election of 1800.* The Federalists looked toward the campaign of 1800 with scant enthusiasm. Not only were they unpopular because of the Alien and Sedition Acts and the imposition of increased taxes passed during 1799, but John Adams had barred the easy exit through foreign war that might have saved them. What Federalist hopes remained were blasted by an unseemly quarrel at the highest party level. Alexander Hamilton's natural antipathy for John Adams had been heightened by an abiding disappointment; the President's action in regard to peace with France made it impossible for "General" Hamilton to lead American forces. The New Yorker considered Adams little more than a party turncoat. The split between these two top-ranking Federalists became open when Adams fired three Cabinet members who had been acting as spies, trotting to Hamilton's New York law office to spill administration secrets into the latter's eager ears. Hamilton angrily wrote a pamphlet for circulation among close friends stating why he considered John Adams unworthy to hold his high office. This explosive document fell into the hands of the elated Jeffersonians, who circulated it broadside.

Even with their ranks riddled by dissension, the Federalists waged a strong fight against the Democratic-Republican candidate. All the party batteries were wheeled into line and discharged. Conservative editors gravely warned of the impending collapse of private property if Jefferson were victorious. Leading citizens wrung their hands over the leveling spirit of "mobocracy," which was sure to destroy the nation. Impassioned clerics thundered from New England pulpits that if Adams lost, "Jacobin phrenzy" would debauch all the wives and daughters of the land and that horses of "dragoons" would be stabled at the "Altars of Christ." Jefferson was painted as a blood-drenched atheistic libertine slavering for the American throat. By pen and word Adams and Hamilton were subjected to villainous personal abuse as a barrage of equal intensity was leveled from the other side. The Federalist leaders were accused of being prancing minions of the British, plotting to establish a monarchy and/or turn the country over to King George.

Important to the Democratic-Republican surge to victory was the political marriage of convenience between Virginia and New York in the persons of Jefferson and Aaron Burr. The latter was strong enough to swing by the merest handful of votes New York City and thus the Empire State to the Virginia liberal. In a close national election the Democratic-Republicans were able to defeat the drum beaters of doom in the Federalist camp. Hardly had the election dust settled, however, when a new crisis arose. The Constitution had not permitted presidential electors to stipulate which man they preferred for the President and which for the Vice-President. The total ballots were simply added; the presidency went to the first man and the vice-presidency to the second. All the Democratic-Republicans voted for both Jefferson and Burr; hence they tied, and the choice had to devolve upon the lame-duck House of Representatives, which still contained a Federalist majority elected during the war scare of 1798. Burr adamantly refused to give way, although the rank and file of his party did not want him to head their administration. Under the motto of "anyone but Jefferson" embittered ultrafederalists talked of throwing the election to Burr.

At this point Alexander Hamilton stepped forward. Still influential in Federalist councils, he said in effect that he hated Jefferson, but he feared Aaron Burr as a potential "Catiline" who might destroy the Republic. This intervention was decisive, and Jefferson was elected.[1] Needless to say, Burr looked upon Hamilton as the person who had robbed him of the presidency, and this feeling played no small part in the smoldering quarrel between the two, which culminated at Weehawken, New Jersey, four years later.

THE FEDERALISTS

❪ *An Assessment.* The Federalist party had elected its last President in John Adams. It never recovered from the defeat in 1800, although it lingered on in powerless opposition until something of a party renaissance occurred

---

[1] This was the last time such a situation was able to occur. Four years later, the Twelfth Amendment to the Constitution provided for separate ballots for the President and the Vice-President.

thanks to the unpopular commercial policies of Jefferson and Madison from 1807 to 1814. The Federalists became more and more reactionary under the influence of a Massachusetts bloc called the Essex Junto. Timothy Pickering led this group practically to treason as they intrigued with Great Britain and worked for the secession of New England from the Union. Perhaps their philosophy was summed up with precision by Fisher Ames, who protested that the United States was "too big for union, too sordid for patriotism, too democratic for liberty." With such individuals important in party policy, even the opportunity opened by frantic hostility to the Embargo during 1808–1809 meant only a brief Indian summer for the Federalists. The collapse of its machinations during the War of 1812 smashed the party once for all, and it never nominated another presidential candidate after 1816. The Federalists had not understood the people. Fearing and distrusting them, they could expect only their own coin in return. They were the spokesmen for the minority; and when the majority was heard, defeat became permanent.

By another criterion, however, the Federalists were not defeated—they continued to play an influential role in national history after a temporary eclipse. Most of them gradually drifted into the victorious Democratic-Republican party and helped to move the Jeffersonians to a more Hamiltonian position. The Whigs of the 1830s, opposing Jacksonian Democracy, also adopted many of Hamilton's favorite tenets, although in a somewhat different guise. The Whigs tried to bring about national prosperity through favors for the upper classes. Protective tariffs, bounties for manufacturers, a Bank of the United States, and Federally financed internal improvements all attested to the lasting effect of the Federalist party, fountainhead of the conservative tradition in American life.

It is true that the party of Washington, Hamilton, and Adams never understood the deeper aspirations of the people, but within its circumscribed frame of reference its contributions were impressive. A stronger and more respected nation existed in 1800 than in 1790, and certainly Federalist policies were instrumental in achieving this happy result. A mighty financial edifice had been reared, and the credit of the United States was solid throughout the world. A strong judiciary had been established to act as a check on premature or overenthusiastic social reforms. War with England or France, ruinous to a nation of a few million, had been avoided, and the United States had been given time to grow. Manufacturing, trade, and transportation had been strengthened. Important precedents had been set. For all the accusations of dictatorial or monarchistic ambitions by the opposition, the Republic had prospered under Federalist rule.

JEFFERSON'S "REVOLUTION"

On the morning of 4 March 1801 Thomas Jefferson walked from his boardinghouse along the clearing that was Pennsylvania Avenue through a swamp to the Capitol. The new Federal center of Washington, D.C., set the background for the inauguration. The city had been planned by the French Major L'Enfant and featured impressive distances. Broad avenues emanated from a central focus so that artillery could easily check civil insurrection— with which a Frenchman of the late eighteenth century might well be familiar. Depending on atmospheric conditions, the new capital was ankle-deep in either dust or mud. A few half-finished public buildings, some taverns, a handful of private homes, and vast sweeps of woods, clearings, and bogs composed the city. Since accommodations were lacking, Congressmen usually left their families at home and lived in crowded boardinghouses during the short sessions. Congress met only a few months a year in sharp contrast to the marathon sessions which are typical of our own time.

As Jefferson stepped forward to read his inaugural address, what has been called the "Revolution of 1800" officially commenced. Would the dire forebodings of the ultrafederalists be consummated? Would anarchy, atheism, and immorality sweep over the nation? Most assuredly not. The revolution was no deep ground swell, but more a light surface agitation. Perhaps it can best be described as the exodus of a group of educated, conservative, upper-class merchants, shippers, and financiers, and the advent of educated, conservative, upper-class agrarians. If the breath of liberalism was more noticeable under Thomas Jefferson, the new administration's similarities to the policies of its predecessor were even more striking. "Gentlemen" still governed the United States, and it was not until Jacksonian Democracy a generation later that what has been designated the "Century of the Common Man" was instituted. Throughout the nation's history the upper classes have retained a larger share in government than their numbers might warrant, but since 1830 they have had to play a more intense political game to keep their influence strong. In Jefferson's time a different faction of the same economic and social group moved into control.

Nevertheless, the Jeffersonian dream of liberty, even if it lagged after its protagonist became subject to the dreadful responsibilities under which an American President labors, was a contribution uniquely personal. The new President was a great liberal. His magnificent advocacy of religious liberties; his insistence on human rights, which he expressed in the Declaration of Independence; his hostility to feudal anachronisms and the blind rigidity of English common law have made Jefferson the prime arbiter of the democratic tradition during the late eighteenth and early nineteenth centuries. If socially Jefferson was no democrat, if intellectually he placed too much reliance on the moral superiority of the yeoman farmer ("Those who labor in the earth are the chosen people of God"), if politically he allowed exigencies to govern his actions, emotionally and philosophically he was able to capture the popular impulses of his time and contribute vitally toward creating a democracy in the Republic.

THE JUDICIARY

◖ *Fortress for Federalism.* Jefferson faced stern prospects, some immediate and others latent. Important problems were Federalist incumbents, especially in the courts; governmental economy; unpopular laws that cried for repeal; party disunity; domestic treason; and weighty decisions coincident to a neutral in a world at war. The Virginia liberal pondered about his first dilemma: Federalist holdovers from the previous administration.

John Adams had spent the last weeks of his term appointing Federalists to positions in the governmental bureaucracy. While the phrase "midnight appointments" is technically a misnomer, it essentially describes what was done. The judiciary was particularly affected. Both in the Constitution and as implemented by acts of Congress, the judiciary was the one agency of the government largely removed from popular control. Jefferson saw the danger that his whole program might be defeated by hostile judges, appointed for life. The President querulously stated that "removals by death are few, by resignations none." Therefore, during the next few years, the President moved against the judiciary—against the Supreme Court itself—brandishing impeachment as the only weapon in his arsenal. He looked first toward Portsmouth, New Hampshire. In that citadel of New England Federalism, Judge John Pickering had made himself notorious. A confirmed drunkard, his mind had degenerated to outright insanity, and he had made his decisions from the bench a travesty on judicial behavior. Pickering was impeached, convicted, and removed from office.

Next the Jeffersonian net was cast for a bigger fish, Associate Justice of the Supreme Court Samuel Chase. This reactionary Federalist of the Essex Junto type had harangued defense lawyers and actually dictated decisions to juries while judging cases under the Sedition Act. Although Chase had clearly demonstrated his extreme partisanship, removal by impeachment depends on proving "high crimes and misdemeanors," not partisanship. In his impeachment trial Chase was found not guilty, and the disappointed administration had to abandon its planned move against Chief Justice John Marshall.

◖ *John Marshall and the Early Judiciary.* Freed from the shadow of impeachment the Supreme Court proceeded to interpret the Constitution according to the tenets of the Chief Justice, an Adams appointee. Scion of Virginia aristocracy, John Marshall became one of the most important and influential Americans. He ruled the Supreme Court for thirty-four years (1801 to 1835) and burned his brand of legalistic interpretation deep into the national fabric. In his youth an ardent supporter of the Revolutionary cause, Marshall steadily became more conservative and property-conscious as he grew older. Presidents from Jefferson to Jackson broke against this sea wall of Federalism. Again and again supposedly liberal justices would be appointed; again and again they would become satellites to Marshall's sun. The justices used to board together while the Supreme Court was in session, and such was the charm of Marshall's personality and so persuasive was his legal reasoning that gradually all fell under his sway. From 1801 to 1835 the Court made 1,106 decisions. The Chief Justice dissented from the majority in precisely eight.

No fireworks between the executive and judicial branches of the government detonated until 1803. In that year Marshall gave his first important decision in the case of *Marbury v. Madison.* Marbury was one of Adams's "midnight" appointees, and the new Secretary of State James Madison refused to issue his commission. Marbury appealed to the Supreme Court to force the issuance of his commission, but Marshall decided that there was no such power under the Constitution. Since Congress had specifically given the Supreme Court this power in the Judiciary Acts of 1789 and 1801, Marshall declared these acts null and void on the grounds that they were unconstitutional: "A legislative act contrary to the Constitution is not law. . . . It is emphatically . . . the duty of the judicial department to say what the law is. . . ." Since the decision restricted the power of the Court, Jefferson was naturally pleased. Although the decision in *Marbury v. Madison* was not the first to claim the right of judicial review for the Federal courts, the point was emphasized and popularized. Usually this case is declared to have established a precedent, and perhaps it did, but its trail blazing in respect to the power of the Supreme Court to throw out acts of Congress seems a little dubious. Fifty-four years elapsed before the Supreme Court again nullified a national law (*Dred Scott v. Sanford*, 1857).

Marshall delivered another important decision before the War of 1812 in the case of *Fletcher v. Peck* (1810). A land company had acquired vast tracts of land along the Yazoo River in what is now Mississippi. It had received a charter from Georgia in 1795 by the simple and effective device of bribing most of the state legislature. Meeting the next year, a new legislature, aghast at the corruption exposed, promptly annulled the Yazoo grants. The decision of the Supreme Court was that the initial charter was legal, even though it had been procured through fraudulent means, and the Georgia act nullifying it was thrown out. This case was important not only in the question of sanctity of contracts but also in the question of the Supreme Court's right to invalidate acts of state legislatures. Marshall continued his rule over the Federal judiciary until well into Jackson's day, but the important later decisions will be discussed in their proper chronological place.

JEFFERSONIANISM IN ACTION

Both Jefferson and Albert Gallatin, his Secretary of the Treasury, had protested vehemently against the extravagance of the Federalists. Once they were in power, however, they continued many of Hamilton's financial policies, although the national debt was reduced through sharp cuts in military and naval appropriations. One of the amusing sidelights of the Democratic-Republican regime was in connection with the navy. Jefferson considered a professional navy dangerous to the public safety as well as too costly a luxury. In place of frigates he called for a bizarre program to construct many small boats, each mounting a single gun. The strange vessels were to be drawn up on beaches until a dauntless naval militia would push them out to sea to repel an invading fleet.

The first gunboat under this program sailed into Savannah Harbor in 1804, was caught in a terrific hurricane, and when the winds finally died down was found, after a search, some eight miles inland, comfortably ensconced in a cornfield. Delighted Boston Federalists proposed a toast: "Gunboat Number 1: If our gunboats are of no use upon the water, may they at least be the best on earth." Foreign disturbances caused the disgruntled Jefferson to order that new frigates be built, but he doggedly continued his beloved gunboats until 176 were eventually constructed. They played little part in naval action.

True to its campaign promises, the new administration released those imprisoned under the hated Sedition Act and lowered the time required for a foreigner to become naturalized from fourteen to five years. Western Pennsylvania hailed the repeal of the whisky tax, although it meant that governmental revenues were dependent upon land sales and the small tariff. Jefferson accomplished one of the most epochal feats in American history when he acquired the Louisiana Territory from Napoleonic France.[2] The President soon dispatched an expedition under Meriwether Lewis and William Clark to ascend the Missouri River to its source, cross the continental divide, and follow a westward-flowing river to the Pacific. Lewis and Clark accomplished their lengthy and perilous journey between 1804 and 1806. Their reports called attention to the vast distances and unexploited resources of the far Northwest. The Louisiana acquisition meant that the United States had doubled in size. Jefferson had brushed aside his own constitutional scruples and the wails of Northeastern

[2] See pp. 154–158.

reactionaries who feared that the admittance of new states from the mighty Louisiana domain would mean relatively less sectional influence for New England.

BURR'S MACHINATIONS

Aaron Burr again occupied the national spotlight in 1804 and became involved in a strange sequence that finally led him late in Jefferson's second administration to face a treason charge. The President had never forgiven Burr for what he considered a base attempt to steal the election of 1800. Burr received no Federal patronage, although it was freely bestowed upon his New York enemies in the Democratic-Republican camp. Burr soon found himself a man without a party. Essex Junto Federalists decided that the influential New Yorker might be able to bring his state into a confederation with seceded New England, and they offered him the Federalist nomination for Governor of New York. Burr eagerly accepted, although he still had a year to serve as Vice-President. Alexander Hamilton emerged from retirement to fight against Burr's candidacy, and the latter was decisively defeated.

This latest opposition from Hamilton was too much for the angry Burr. Time and again his fondest ambitions had been shattered by what he saw as the sly and sometimes disreputable tactics of Hamilton. Burr resolved to kill him. He started exchanging with Hamilton the usual letters preliminary to a duel, solicitously polite in salutation and conclusion, with venom sandwiched between. Even though Hamilton had proved his courage repeatedly, and even though he abhorred the senseless custom of dueling that had killed his son two years before, Hamilton felt obliged to accept Burr's challenge. Evidence suggests that Hamilton thought the American people would construe a refusal as cowardice, which would end forever any future political hopes. The mortal conclusion occurred on a pleasant July morning in 1804 at Weehawken, New Jersey. Burr shot his adversary through the chest, and

after many hours of agony Hamilton died on the next day. In remembrance of the noted financier, Eastern conservatives mourned him in funeral processions, memorial dinners, and eulogistic editorials.

The death of Hamilton finished Burr's career in the East, but impelled him toward the West. Many of the more unruly frontiersmen hailed him for killing Hamilton, whom they had considered an archenemy of their sectional interests. Burr soon involved himself in a series of intricate cabals with Britons, Spaniards, and fellow Americans.[3] His intrigues ended in disaster; he was soon apprehended and brought back to Virginia to face a treason charge. Jefferson did everything in his power to convict Burr, even to the point of almost dictating the decision to John Marshall, but the Chief Justice refused to concur. Pointing out that intent of treason was not sufficient for conviction and that no overt act had been proved, Marshall ordered Burr freed. The latter engaged in shady political intrigues later in Europe, returned to New York, suffered a tremendous personal loss in the death of his beautiful daughter, and finally died in 1836, almost a forgotten man.

SECOND-TERM TROUBLES

Despite his defeat by the judiciary and some minor setbacks, Jefferson retained his national popularity and easily won reelection in 1804, crushing his Federalist opponent, Charles Cotesworth Pinckney, 162 to 14 in the Electoral College. Yet the skies darkened for the Virginia liberal during his second term. His own Democratic-Republican party began to divide. John Taylor, sage of Southern agrarianism, turned against him, claiming that Jefferson could no longer be considered a true liberal. In Congress, John Randolph of Roanoke, fit subject for Freudian psychoanalysis, attacked the President with abandon, charging that he had wandered from the paths of pure Republicanism to become little more than a

[3] For details, see p. 123.

Federalist in disguise. Although Randolph and his fellow "Quids" (from the Latin word meaning "essence") remained a small minority, any opposition that contained Randolph's virulent wit and caustic tongue was sure to be aggravating.

The difficulties attendant upon a neutral nation when most of the world is at war hit hard from 1805 to 1809. Jefferson attempted to follow a course of commercial self-abnegation to enforce the belligerents to respect American rights. In 1807 he sponsored the noted Embargo Act, which forbade the United States to engage in any foreign trade. The nation forthwith sank into a terrible commercial depression, and the fury of maritime areas was maintained at a high pitch. Just before Jefferson stepped aside for his successor James Madison, the Embargo had to be repealed. The second term was in sorry contrast to the first.

Throughout his eight years in the White House, Thomas Jefferson had been forced by circumstances to adopt many policies that he had originally opposed. He believed in a decentralized Federal government and a "strict" interpretation of the Constitution. Yet the unparalleled opportunity offered by the Louisiana Purchase forced him to buy it, even if there were no such privileges specifically granted in the Constitution. He favored economy, especially in regard to the armed forces. Nevertheless, the Tripolitan War in North Africa compelled him to undertake expensive improvements in the martial field. He loved and admired the French, only to turn to Great Britain when Napoleon became menacing. He was a great liberal, but little direct increase in democracy was recorded from 1801 to 1809. He was hamstrung by the judiciary and embarrassed by Congress. Such enemies as Samuel Chase and Aaron Burr escaped what he considered well-merited punishment. His Embargo had been ruinous to national maritime prosperity.

Despite this grim recapitulation, Jefferson remains one of our finest Presidents. Later generations would turn to his writings to find renewed faith in liberalism and democracy.

He maintained unruffled moderation and tolerance; there had been no cataclysmic overturn of American institutions as a new party took over, and no persecution of the Federalist minority had taken place. Although with difficulty, war with Great Britain and France had been avoided, and invaluable years of peace obtained. Some acts inimical to the public welfare had been repealed. Jefferson's administrations were marked by almost a decade of population growth, geographical expansion, and to a lesser degree industrial aggregation.

The great Virginian enjoyed a happy old age, although he was sometimes beset by monetary difficulties. Retiring to Monticello, his magnificent estate, much of his time was occupied by the University of Virginia, for Jefferson was the founder of that educational institution. One of his amusements was to watch through a telescope from his lawn the construction of what has been called the most beautifully planned campus in the United States. Jefferson's correspondence reached awe-inspiring proportions, and he sometimes wrote twenty long letters a day. Shortly after the War of 1812 his lapsed friendship with John Adams was resurrected. These Revolutionary cronies had quarreled during the party battles of the 1790s, and Adams had not even attended Jefferson's inauguration. But ancient enmities were forgotten, and the two men exchanged verbose letters commenting on contemporary events. In an amazing coincidence both Jefferson and Adams died on the same day, 4 July 1826, precisely fifty years after the adoption of the Declaration of Independence, written by one with the help of the other, and signed by both.

Although some important domestic events happened during the succeeding administration of James Madison, foreign affairs were temporarily in ascendance. The results of over twenty years of controversy and agreement, crisis and settlement, finally erupted in the War of 1812. The foreign relations of the United States from 1789 to 1812 deserve separate study to conclude these first decades of the Republic.

CHAPTER 12

Federalist Foreign Policy

(1789-1800)

EUROPE'S STEPCHILD

The United States had won political independence by revolution, but economic and social freedom from Europe was far in the future. Because of powerful ties across the Atlantic, foreign affairs would play a large role in the over-all pattern of the Republic's early years. Perhaps only during the second quarter of the twentieth century did diplomatic relations with great world powers influence American policies to the extent that they did during the first thirty years under the Constitution.

The precarious international position of the United States in 1789 should be emphasized. Far from its present status as one of the world's colossi, at that time the nation was, although large in area, small in population, lacking in military and naval strength, and laboring under the added onus of international opprobrium because of the new government's revolutionary origins and republican principles. The European continental powers of France, Austria, Prussia, and Russia and the international empires of Spain and Great Britain looked with contempt upon the impotence of the American nation. Their derision was mixed with fear lest the liberalistic forces settled in

the United States prove contagious. It was indeed fortunate for the new nation that almost coincidentally with the inauguration of George Washington, Europe became embroiled for over twenty years in the far-reaching struggles of the French Revolution, which merged with the Napoleonic wars. With their energies expended on European matters, the great powers were able to offer little opposition to the growth and increasing prosperity of the United States.

Washington had been President only a short while before the first diplomatic difficulty appeared from the distant Northwest. The decadent Spanish Empire suddenly sprang into a flurry of activity during the reign of Charles III, although it was a spasm of *rigor mortis* rather than any basic resurgence of Iberian power. In 1790 a Spanish ship from California seized some Englishmen on Nootka Sound off Vancouver Island, and trouble was immediately precipitated. In this Nootka crisis Washington had to face the possibility that America could become a battleground if British troops moved down the Ohio and Mississippi Rivers to attack Spanish Louisiana. Under such conditions the American government would have to resist. Luckily Spain soon retired from the

Northwest, aware that it could not hope to defeat Great Britain. The American administration could sigh with relief that tensions had relaxed. Britain, during this controversy with Spain, saw that American intervention would have been at best embarrassing and opened diplomatic relations with the United States by sending a minister to Philadelphia.

FRENCH REVOLUTIONARY REPERCUSSIONS

Despite its alarming implications, the Nootka crisis had not aroused American public opinion. Such was not the case, however, when the tidings arrived from Europe of the tremendous political and social upheavals attendant upon the French Revolution. Here the emotions of Americans were directly concerned, and from initial unity a later division of opinion was partly responsible for the growth of the two-party system. At first the vast majority of Americans cheered when the Third Estate defied the King's order to disperse and dramatically pledged to remain united until a constitution for France had been written. Even the bloodshed resulting from the fall of the Bastille and additional disorders throughout the French countryside when peasants celebrated their liberation from feudal servitude in the light of burning châteaux failed to allay American enthusiasm. Quite naturally most citizens of the United States assumed that the French were paying them the supreme compliment of imitation and that the American Revolution had been the blueprint for Gallic action. Was not the immortal Lafayette involved? The initial wave of pro-French sentiment continued among the majority for at least two years and among many for much longer.

During the heyday of revolutionary affection, enthralled Americans manifested in strange ways their good will toward France. The cumbersome salutations of "Citizen" and "Citizeness" began to be exchanged by worthy burghers when they met on the streets of New York and Philadelphia; one cynic suggested querulously that the term "biped" would be more appropriate. Long pants started to supersede the more refined knee breeches. Testimonial banquets, pledges of monetary assistance, and enthusiastic pamphlets hailed each new development in Paris. In 1791 general American approval greeted the French Declaration of the Rights of Man, considering it to be a later reissue of Jefferson's Declaration of Independence. By 1793 American as well as French "Jacobin clubs" were in existence.

Not all Americans joined in this exultant chorus. More conservative individuals echoed the sentiments of the liberal Englishman Edmund Burke, who feared that the forces set in motion by the French Revolution could not be controlled. During 1792–1793 this opinion solidified as the French Revolution veered sharply to the left. War pitted France against Austria and Prussia; later Great Britain and Spain joined the Teutonic allies. King Louis XVI was first deposed and then guillotined under the nom de plume of "Citizen Louis Capet." [1] After all, said some Americans, didn't he help us win our Revolution? The French monarchy was abolished, and the Republic "One and Indivisible" was proclaimed. Many Americans who had rejoiced when the Bastille was captured in 1789 were filled with revulsion by 1793. Gradually the Federalists became the party that opposed the French Revolution and looked upon Great Britain as the world's shield against anarchy. The Democratic-Republicans continued the laudation of France and steeped themselves in Anglophobia. European events had widened party division across the Atlantic.

Once revolutionary France faced in war a hostile Europe, the Washington administration was confronted with a grave dilemma. The Franco-American alliance of 1778 was still in effect, and under it we were pledged to defend the French West Indies. The Cabinet argued about whether the alliance was actually

[1] Some pro-French enthusiasts in the United States definitely exceeded the bounds of good taste. On several occasions Louis was decapitated in effigy; and at one banquet a pig, designated as the unhappy monarch, was hacked to pieces by the guests. A Western paper exulted, "Louis Capet has lost his caput."

binding; Hamilton claimed that the pact was only with the French monarchy and not applicable to the French Republic. Jefferson opposed this contention, maintaining that any alliance was with the French people. For once Washington agreed with his Secretary of State, and the alliance was not abrogated. There was no question of American entry into the contest on the side of France; the entire Cabinet was united behind Washington's Proclamation of Neutrality (April, 1793).

❦ *"Citizen" Genêt.* Luckily the French did not particularly want the United States to fight on their side. They hoped for a benevolent neutrality that would enable economic assistance to reach them, but it was generally recognized that the United States was militarily too weak to wage war. To ensure America's continued amity, Paris sent to the United States a new Minister, the volatile, generous, enthusiastic, and rattlebrained Edmond Charles Édouard Genêt. Few governments have been served worse by a diplomatic representative than was France by "Citizen" Genêt.

Afire with revolutionary zeal, the new emissary sailed directly to Charleston, South Carolina, and promptly began to outfit and to commission French privateers. Sailing from American ports, these commerce raiders would bring their prizes back to Charleston and other cities, and the French minister would recommission them as additional privateers. Not content with this, Genêt looked toward Spanish Louisiana. Ambitiously dreaming of a mighty French-controlled Louisiana wrested from Madrid, Genêt entered into discussions with George Rogers Clark. This disappointed and resentful Westerner had won the Ohio country during the American Revolution and considered that his government had rewarded him poorly. Genêt and Clark plotted to attack Spanish New Orleans, Clark's Western supporters furnishing the man power. Just when the situation looked most promising, Genêt ran out of money and had to procrastinate with glittering promises and no cash. The

entire affair was dropped quite naturally by Genêt's successors, since Spain had switched to the side of France.

After outfitting privateers and intriguing with Clark, Genêt plunged into the American back country, proceeding overland toward Philadelphia. His trek through the hinterlands was a continuous triumphal march. Hosannas of praise, wild cheering, and frantic applause marked Genêt's progress through the pro-French rural settlements. Naturally he assumed that the rank and file of the American people were solidly behind his mission and that contrary opinion did not reflect the true sentiments of the United States. Genêt resolved to solidify his position by increasing pressure upon the Washington administration.

On arrival in Philadelphia, Genêt met the President, and that dignitary subjected the unhappy Frenchman to the frostbitten treatment that the Virginian could use with such devastating effect. Washington was furious at Genêt's privateering commissions, which violated American neutrality. Even Jefferson was worried and extracted from the French Minister a promise that the captured British ship *Little Sarah* would not be commissioned to attack British shipping. Genêt promptly renamed the vessel with the ringingly liberal appellation of *Little Democrat* and sent it to sea as a French privateer. Jefferson's anger promptly matched Washington's. The Secretary of State could see that Genêt's headstrong impetuosity was harming the Democratic-Republican party and thus seriously weakening the pro-French cause. Jefferson joined the rest of the Cabinet in demanding the recall of Genêt.

This placed poor Genêt squarely in the frying pan. Revolutionary tides had shifted in France, and the more moderate Girondin faction, of which Genêt was a member, had been ousted and guillotined by Maximilien de Robespierre's radical Jacobins. Not only was the French Minister on the wrong side at home, but the Jacobin government was aghast at the harm that he had done to the initially great American enthusiasm for France. When Washington demanded Genêt's recall, Robespierre was delighted to oblige. The luckless Frenchman knew that decapitation would be his European destiny, and he threw himself upon Washington's mercy for asylum. He was permitted to remain in America, and the emotional fervor that served him ill as a diplomat won him a wife in the person of New York Governor Clinton's daughter. Head firmly in place, Genêt lived until 1835.

Coincidental to Genêt's recall, the French government asked the United States to extend the same courtesy by recalling the American Minister to France. Gouverneur Morris was a crusty reactionary who had been as impossibly partisan in France as Genêt in the United States. Morris had made no secret of his royalist sympathies, shielded nobles from revolutionary chastisement, and actively conspired with Bourbon supporters to arrange for King Louis XVI to escape. Morris for Genêt was an exchange that benefited both governments. Succeeding French ministers to the United States perpetrated almost as many unneutral acts as Genêt, but at least they were more circumspect in doing so.

ANGLO-AMERICAN TENSIONS

If relations with France were strained during the early 1790s, those with Great Britain tightened almost to the breaking point. For one thing, old wounds still festered. Since 1783 British garrisons had manned forts on American territory. Three strongholds controlled the border region from the Great Lakes to Lake Champlain; and strategically located outposts at Niagara, Detroit, and Michilimackinac made the inland seas British lakes. Westerners charged that from King George's magazines the Indians received muskets, bullets, and hatchets with which to accomplish the bloody work incited by British rum. Repeated American demands that the redcoats withdraw from United States territory were invariably refused.

The British would not retire until satisfaction had been received on the Treaty of Paris requirements that America both compensate the loyalists and pay colonial debts to English merchants.

A new grievance topped this perennial difficulty. When the European war broke out, the British navy drove much of the French merchant marine off the seas, leaving the French West Indies dependent upon the United States for food and other commodities. In a matter of months a huge trade had been built up between the American mainland and the French insular dependencies. In 1793 two British Orders in Council (roughly corresponding to Executive orders in the United States) suddenly cracked down upon this lucrative commerce. Applying the Rule of 1756, which stated that trade illegal in time of peace was illegal in time of war, the British pointed out that this commerce had been a French monopoly before hostilities started and hence could not, under the iron hand of adversity, be opened to the United States.

Applying these Orders in Council, British frigates sailed into the Caribbean, seized scores of American ships, confiscated their cargoes, and either imprisoned their crews or impressed them into the Royal Navy. The uproar in the United States was considerable. Even Boston Federalists, who usually cheered English success, were quick to denounce this activity that nipped their pocketbooks. Naturally the pro-French Democratic-Republicans were beside themselves with fury. A noticeable drift toward war became obvious.

❡ *The Jay Treaty.* Knowing that his nation was unprepared for such hostilities, Washington decided to negotiate. He appointed John Jay, first Chief Justice of the Supreme Court, as Minister to Great Britain. His instructions were clear. Jay was to attempt settlement of the controversies still outstanding from the Treaty of Paris in 1783, secure compensation for the illegal seizures of American ships in the Caribbean, and acquire the right to trade with the British West Indies. If possible, he was to discuss both impressment and British machinations with the Western Indians. Jay's selection was unfortunate. He had made a poor impression as a negotiator with the Spanish envoy Don Diego Gardoqui in 1785 and had seemed willing to sell out Western rights on the Mississippi for a trade agreement with Spain. Jay was honest, upright, and intelligent; he was also rather overconciliatory and quite vain.

In 1794 the American Minister arrived in London, where he was wined, dined, and flattered by sagacious English diplomats. After long-drawn negotiations, the Jay Treaty was signed with Great Britain on 19 November 1794. In view of Jay's instructions, the treaty was unsatisfactory, although the American envoy was not entirely at fault. In a casual chat with George Hammond, British Minister to the United States, Alexander Hamilton had remarked that under no circumstances would the United States join the Armed Neutrality, a combination of Baltic maritime powers maintaining a cold neutrality in the war. This was glorious news to Hammond, who promptly communicated it to his government. When Jay tried to use the threat of joining the Armed Neutrality as a lever to pry better conditions from the British, they smiled quietly and ignored it. Hamilton had trumped his partner's trick.

The Jay Treaty granted to the United States a stipulation agreed upon eleven years before: the British were to abandon their forts on American territory by 1 August 1796. Disputes concerning the northeastern boundary, American debts owed to British merchants, compensation for loyalists during the Revolution, and damages for American ships confiscated in 1793 were put aside for future negotiation.[2] Nothing was said about impressment or the Western Indians. Jay surrendered on an im-

[2] The northeastern boundary was not finally settled until the Webster-Ashburton Treaty (1842). In 1800 a mixed commission awarded British creditors £600,000 (about $3 million) for debts outstanding since the Revolution. Britain had to compensate the loyalists itself, but another mixed commission granted almost $11 million to Americans for merchantmen seized in the Caribbean.

portant point when he agreed that the British could seize cargoes of foodstuffs bound for the French West Indies if compensation were paid. The only advantageous commercial privilege (and it was small enough) gained by the United States allowed ships of under 70 tons to trade with the British West Indies. Jay paid for this dubious benefit by an amazing concession. He agreed that such tropical products as ginger, molasses, cocoa, coffee, and cotton could not be exported by the United States to *any part of the world*. Eli Whitney had just invented the cotton gin, and it is simple to see how ruinous that provision could have been. The Senate, however, removed this ban on tropical exports before it would accept the agreement.

A howl of execration greeted the Jay Treaty when it was published in the United States. Federalists either remained silent or offered feeble apologies. Thomas Jefferson was so indignant that he referred to Washington with the statement, "Curse on his virtues; they have undone the country!" Evening skies were colored by the flames of Jay's effigies as they were cast into bonfires. Alexander Hamilton, attempting to speak in favor of the treaty, was stoned and driven indoors from a New York balcony with blood pouring from his face. One apoplectic Francophile demanded that all Americans "kick that damned treaty to hell!" Myriad Democratic-Republican editorials referred to "the Arch-traitor, Sir John Jay."

Washington and the other Federalist leaders recognized the unfortunate aspects of Jay's pact, but they decided it was either the treaty, bad as it was, or war with Great Britain. The Federalists enjoyed majorities in both the House, which had to appropriate the funds to carry through the treaty, and the Senate, which had to concur by a two-thirds majority. Despite the almost frantic efforts of the opposition, the treaty was approved by narrow margins. Hindsight can see that the Federalists were correct. The Jay Treaty may have been appeasement, but it was an appeasement that gave to the United States the additional strength of almost twenty years' growth before war with Great Britain finally came.

AGREEMENT WITH SPAIN

To make poor Jay's discomfiture even more extreme, a Federalist colleague was almost completely successful in negotiations with Spain. Ever since the end of the American Revolution, Spain and America had quarreled over the lower Mississippi. In 1785 Spanish demands had been unacceptable, but a decade later a new attempt was worth making. Westerners had become increasingly angry at the Federal government's seeming lack of concern about their interests. To the trans-Appalachian citizens, foreign control of the great river was intolerable; the Mississippi was their economic artery. Roads across the mountains to the East were miserable, and it was still well before the day when canals and railroads could alleviate economic stagnation. Most Western produce had to pass through New Orleans, and it was unbearable to have that essential traffic subjected to Spanish whim. So prominently was Western attention focused on this problem that any faction, foreign or domestic, that promised solution was sure to find ready support. Backwoods cabals were as common in the late-eighteenth-century West as razorback hogs. Suspicion was strong in the Mississippi Valley that the Federalist administration was more devoted to the interests of Eastern financiers than transmontane empire builders.

❰ *The Pinckney Treaty.* Washington saw a chance that the West might be more firmly attached to the Union if the Mississippi problem were solved. He sent Thomas Pinckney as special negotiator to Madrid. Pinckney was assisted by the European situation in 1795. Spain had originally joined the alliance against revolutionary France (1793); but a combination of military reverses, the old Franco-Spanish amity, and Britain's sudden interest in Spanish-American colonial trade caused Spain to switch sides two years later. Fearing that Britain would attack its possessions in the Americas, the Madrid government decided that one enemy in the Western Hemisphere was enough. Furthermore, the Spaniards did not know whether the Jay Treaty forecast an Anglo-American military alliance. The result was that the chilly court of Charles III thawed perceptibly, and Pinckney was able to return home triumphantly bearing with him the Treaty of San Lorenzo (the Pinckney Treaty).

American demands that had been denied *in toto* a decade before were recognized in 1795. Citizens of the United States were given free access to the port of New Orleans and the right to store goods without taxation in that city for as long as three years. The latter point was important. Sailing schedules were notoriously unreliable, and the shipper wanted to keep his goods in storage during a temporary glut on the market that had depressed prices. In addition, Spain abandoned its claim to a 100-mile belt north of the present Florida line, thus accepting the boundary along the 31st parallel. So enthusiastic was the reception of the Pinckney Treaty that the Senate approved it unanimously, a circumstance which has happened very seldom in American history.

WASHINGTON'S FAREWELL ADDRESS

When George Washington relinquished the presidency to revel in his well-merited retirement, he took the opportunity to impart counsel to his fellow Americans. Although much of the memorable Farewell Address applied to domestic matters, the sections on foreign policy are especially noteworthy. Washington objected to American political factions that "open the door to foreign influence." He appealed to Americans to utilize their advantageously isolated geographical position and have with European nations "as little *political* connections as possible." He warmly advocated a detached policy in foreign affairs and decried "excessive partiality for one foreign nation and excessive dislike for another. . . ." The President admitted that short-term alliances for "extraordinary emergencies" were sensible, but warned his compatriots to eschew permanent alliances with European powers, which, he maintained, never have American interests at heart but are solely motivated by "ambition, rivalship, interest, humor, or caprice" on a purely selfish basis.

Washington was probably referring to a contemporary situation that worried him. It should be recalled that the Franco-American alliance of 1778 was still in effect. Once the wars of the French Revolution erupted, the pact had proved both embarrassing and potentially dangerous to the United States. The President fervently hoped that his country might rid itself of that alliance and be able to embark upon the unilateral foreign policy so dear to the General's heart. Americans followed his advice rather quickly. In 1798 the United States terminated the French alliance, and two years later the Convention of 1800 with France permanently severed the formal tie between the two republics.

It should be emphasized that Washington was offering sagacious advice to Americans living in the late eighteenth century. Perhaps he had no desire to draw a blueprint that would have to be followed by a different United States in a different world. Washington spoke at a time when Europe and Asia were many weeks away in time. It should not be assumed that Washington was necessarily wrong in his advice. It is rather that each generation must adapt itself to its global environment. American politicians are not prophets. Very seldom can they be considered divinely inspired to make rules in one day to apply to another.

JOHN ADAMS AND FRANCE

John Adams, the next President, must have often recalled the words of the Farewell Address, for he became constantly involved in difficulties with our French ally. By midsummer of 1794 the radical phase of the French Revolution had come to an end when Robespierre and his colleagues were hauled in carts through yelling crowds to the guillotine. During the next year radical impulses notably lessened, and in 1795 a new French government

called the "Directory" assumed power. Handling its foreign relations was the astute and slippery Charles Maurice de Talleyrand-Perigord, almost a stereotype of the suave, polished, unscrupulous European diplomat. It was a sensible choice for one of his biographers to entitle his work in the plural, *The Lives of Talleyrand*, for the ex-Bishop of Autun served six French governments and betrayed them all but the last—cynics have claimed that he died before he could take care of the latter point. Forced to flee from France during the rule of Robespierre, Talleyrand had lived in Philadelphia for a while, but this experience seems to have kindled no flames of affection in him for the country that granted him asylum.

By 1797 Franco-American relations were in turmoil. France had been most disturbed by the Jay Treaty. The American Minister to Paris at that time was James Monroe, a warm sympathizer with the revolution. Monroe had not been kept in touch with the developments that led to the *rapprochement* with Great Britain, and he made the mistake of assuring the suspicious French first that the treaty would not be signed, and secondly that it would not be ratified. When the Jay Treaty became effective, the French sent Monroe packing. In retaliation Pierre Adet, French Minister to the United States, was dismissed. He had been interfering in domestic American politics and plotting Western secession with sectional extremists.

Adams tried to attain amity with France, but the two official allies were closer to war each day. He sent to Paris a commission composed of Elbridge Gerry of Massachusetts, Charles Cotesworth Pinckney of South Carolina, and John Marshall of Virginia, the future Chief Justice. The three envoys cooled their heels in Paris for a time before contact was made by emissaries of Talleyrand.[3] The French proposition was interesting. Before a meeting with the French Foreign Minister could be ar-

[3] In the finest traditions of eighteenth-century European diplomacy, a beautiful woman was included among the French negotiators. John Marshall thought her fascinating.

ranged, an apology would have to be offered for some harsh things that John Adams had said about France, a large loan tendered to the Gallic ally, and a considerable bribe paid to Talleyrand himself.

Bribery was an integral part of that day's diplomacy, and Americans whose nation regularly sent tribute to the pirates of North Africa had no reason to be shocked by such mendacity. Yet the amounts involved were expensive, and the American commissioners had no authority to spend anything. Pinckney snapped, "No, no, not a sixpence," which was soon corrupted into the popular slogan "Millions for defense, but not one cent for tribute!" Pinckney spent the rest of his life denying authorship of this ringing prose, but it was too good to disbelieve.

When the terms offered by the French were sent to President Adams, he recalled Gerry (the other two had left immediately) and shrewdly published the complete documentation of the episode, referring to the three agents of Talleyrand by the cryptic letters "XYZ." The nomenclature was catching, and the whole controversy has carried that name ever since. Capitalizing on a wave of anti-French sentiment, Adams proceeded to take strong action in 1798 with a relatively unified nation behind him. Stating that no minister would be sent to France unless assurances were given that he would be welcomed, Adams recommended and Congress enacted a suspension of commercial intercourse with France, and the abrogation of the Franco-American alliance.

With neither country represented in the capital of the other, France and the United States drifted into an undeclared war. From 1798 to 1800 French and American ships exchanged shots on sight, privateers of both nations took many armed prizes (attacks upon unarmed merchantmen would have been open war), and in a pitched battle the American frigate *Constitution* smashed the French *L'Insurgente*. By 1800 the ultrafederalists were eagerly anticipating the full-scale war that

seemed sure to come, but suddenly John Adams personally intervened for peace.

❲ *The Convention of 1800.* Hearing that Talleyrand wished no war and would welcome an American envoy, the President sent to the Senate the name of William Vans Murray as Minister to France. Adams' fellow Federalists were struck with consternation; they knew that his action would destroy the best chance their party had to regain its lost popularity. But there was little they could do. Open opposition to Vans Murray would give credence to the Democratic-Republican allegation that the Federalists were warmongers. They had to satisfy themselves with procrastination and a demand, accepted by the President, that two others be appointed to accompany Vans Murray. True to Talleyrand's hints, the commissioners were treated with courtesy in Paris. By this time Napoleon Bonaparte was First Consul in France and was busy preparing for the *coup d'état* that would establish his personal rule. Furthermore the Corsican wished no American difficulty to interfere with his tortuous negotiations to get the Louisiana Territory from Spain. Amid such an atmosphere, settlement was easy.

The Convention of 1800 with France verified the action taken by the American Congress two years before; France agreed to terminate the Franco-American alliance of 1778. In addition, claims owed to American citizens by France would be assumed by the United States. Although our original bill to Paris called for claims amounting to about $20 million, Congress eventually appropriated only a fifth of that sum. The settlement of the French difficulty freed the United States from an embarrassing alliance, yet made it possible to avoid war and to clear the decks for the Louisiana Purchase three years later. Luster was added to the name of John Adams, and it is eminently fitting that he selected as his epitaph: "Here lies John Adams, who took upon himself the responsibility for peace with France in the year 1800."

Jefferson's Foreign Policy

(1800-1809)

THE LOUISIANA PURCHASE

⟨ *Napoleon and Spain.* The so-called Revolution of 1800 that turned the Federalists into the political limbo caused no greater convulsion in American foreign policy than it did in the domestic sphere. One might suppose that the Francophile Thomas Jefferson, leader of the American Jacobins, would maintain the warmest relations with France. Yet both Jefferson and his Secretary of State James Madison wished to conduct a foreign policy relatively free from foreign influences. In fact, Jefferson's Gallic sympathies went only to a point—the point at which American interests were threatened. Right there Jefferson would oppose France as well as any other nation.

Early in Jefferson's first administration, disquieting rumors drifted across the Atlantic from France. Napoleon Bonaparte, the imperial Corsican, had wheeled to face west. The reasons why Napoleon developed such a keen interest in North America are complex. Some claim that his decisions were molded by altered circumstances and that his plans were therefore carefully formulated. Others maintain that impulse and whim impelled the future Emperor to stumble into possession of Louisi-

ana. At any rate the Peace of Amiens (1802) ended ten years of war and inaugurated fourteen months of uneasy peace. It was during this breathing spell that Napoleon was able to bring into fruition his plans for Louisiana. The territory was a magnificent expanse that extended from the present state of Louisiana along the west bank of the Mississippi, broadening as it went north, all the way along the eastern slopes of the Rocky Mountains to approximately the present Canadian-American border.

The manner in which Napoleon gained Louisiana is illustrative of his double-dealing. Spain had owned the territory from 1763 to 1800; but weak and impoverished, Madrid was usually unable to administer the great domain west of the Mississippi. Spanish control remained practically nonexistent, except for New Orleans, St. Louis, and a few other sites. Increasing pressure from westward-moving Americans caused the Spaniards to fear that they might lose all by default. Furthermore, Great Britain and Spain were so often on opposite sides during war that an English fleet might sweep up the Mississippi and take everything. Capitalizing on such Spanish apprehensions, Napoleon persuaded the King of Spain to exchange the Louisiana Territory for the Italian Duchy of Tuscany (Treaty of San Ildefonso, 1800). Hoots of derision have greeted this barter of over one-third of the United States for a tiny Italian dependency. Yet in 1800 sprawling Louisiana was a liability to Spain, draining the royal treasury, and militarily most difficult to defend by land or by sea. Tuscany had declined considerably from its Renaissance heights, but was still economically valuable and would be a source of revenue to the Spanish crown. A deal that soon became ridiculous was quite sensible when it was consummated.

That this exchange was an extremely attractive proposition for France cannot be denied. Napoleon received Louisiana for precisely nothing; he *never* ceded Tuscany to Spain. There was no immediate exchange of territory in the Treaty of San Ildefonso, and Louisiana was to remain Spanish until Tuscany was received. Despite the fact that Napoleon had not fulfilled his Tuscany pledge, his bluster and cajolery successfully persuaded King Charles IV to cede Louisiana to France in 1802. Later Spanish complaints were brushed aside. Moreover, Napoleon swore that Louisiana would never be sold or ceded to a third power without Spanish acquiescence. Seven months *before* France occupied New Orleans, Bonaparte sold the entire territory to the United States. Such were the ethics of the French dictator.

❨ *Haitian Phase.* The French West Indies, particularly Haiti (the western third of the island bearing the same name), were closely connected with any French plans for the North American mainland. Long the heart of the French Caribbean empire, Haiti had fallen upon evil days. The island had faced an almost impossible racial situation since the time of its first French occupancy. Negro slaves had been imported in large numbers, and by the late eighteenth century the French owners were heavily outnumbered. In deadly fear of a slave insurrection, the French controlled their Negroes with unbelievable brutality. A strong case can be made that Haitian slavery was perhaps the worst in the history of that abominable institution. Sustained floggings, frightful mutilations, and executions by torture featured French mastery of the colony. In addition, sugar was widely grown, and the very nature of that crop made laboring conditions inhuman. Haiti was a time bomb.

The simmering hatred of the Negroes for their overlords erupted into violence when the news of the French Revolution reached the island. In kaleidoscopic sequence, white colonists, mulattoes, and Negroes fought one another in shifting alliances, until finally the Negroes emerged on top under Pierre Toussaint L'Ouverture, a great military chieftain. Establishing his personal rule, Toussaint L'Ouverture defended his domains successfully against French, Spanish, and British armies invading the island. Foreign authority in Haiti had come to an end.

While engaged in hoodwinking the Spanish monarch over Louisiana, Napoleon had studied the Haitian situation and concluded that the recapture of the island was imperative both for French prestige and for the economic health of Louisiana. The tropical resources of Haiti would dovetail admirably with the produce of the Mississippi Valley. In Bonaparte's mind Louisiana and Haiti formed an economic unit; the value of the first being conditional upon regaining control of the second. This possibility was pregnant with future Franco-American hostility; French military power firmly planted on the North American continent, nurtured by West Indian riches, would have been most inimical to the welfare and security of the United States.[1]

With Europe still at peace, the Corsican planned a two-pronged expedition during the winter of 1802. He assembled one army in the Netherlands for transportation to Louisiana; the other force would go to Haiti. The first delayed so long and was so hampered by bad weather that it never sailed. Despite this setback, Napoleon continued with his plans to reconquer Haiti. His brother-in-law, General

[1] Some students of this period have suggested that Napoleon had in mind conquering the Southern United States, perhaps with trained Negro troops from Haiti, once that island had been recaptured.

Charles Victor Leclerc, arrived with a large army, and at first all went well for the invaders. Toussaint L'Ouverture was granted a free-conduct pass to negotiate with the French, who treacherously seized him and shipped him back to France. Napoleon was able to wreak his vengeance against this "gilded African" as he called him. Locked up in a damp and frigid cell high in the Jura Mountains, Toussaint L'Ouverture soon sickened and died of tuberculosis.

The news of the underhanded treatment of their leader aroused the Haitian Negroes to frantic resistance. Leclerc could take cities, but he could not control the back country. Such was the fanaticism with which Negro guerrillas fought that on one occasion 173 of 176 who were captured committed suicide so that they could not be tortured into revealing secrets. Haiti became a charnel house for French ambitions. Not only did casualties mount from the unrelenting opposition, but also yellow fever and malaria decimated French ranks. Inside of a year, Leclerc and thousands of his troops were dead, debts were soaring, public opinion in France was increasingly hostile to the venture, and Napoleon finally concluded that Haiti was unconquerable. Moreover, the Peace of Amiens was approaching its end, and a general European war was sure to be forthcoming. Without the Caribbean colony, Louisiana was of little value to Bonaparte, and New Orleans could easily be taken by British frigates. Napoleon dramatically decided to rid himself of his American mainland domains. The future Emperor's word was law in France, despite considerable opposition to his whim.[2]

(*American Aspects.* While these portentous events were occurring in France and the West Indies, what of the United States? Obviously the accession of Louisiana by so strong a power as France and the prospect of Napoleonic legions on the west bank of the Mississippi were intolerable to America. If the French had taken permanent possession of Louisiana, squarely

athwart America's westward movement, eternal hostility between the two nations would have been an almost certain destiny.

Vague rumors concerning some sort of Franco-Spanish transaction in regard to North America had bothered Jefferson from the start of his administration. Confronted with the possibility of Napoleon as a next-door neighbor, the leader of the pro-French forces in the United States made one of his most startling observations: "The day that France takes possession of New Orleans . . . we must marry ourselves to the British fleet and nation." Additional confirmation of the President's fears appeared to be furnished in 1802 when the Spanish intendant at New Orleans suddenly suspended the rights of free transit on the Mississippi and of storing goods without taxation —rights that had been granted in 1795. We now know that Spain took this action on its own initiative, but Jefferson did not know this, and it seemed to presage the shadow of Napoleon.

Jefferson decided that every exertion must be expended for the purchase of New Orleans and its immediate environs. He notified Robert Livingston, American Minister to France, to open negotiations with Talleyrand (this foxy diplomat had landed on his feet during the Napoleonic coup and was Bonaparte's foreign minister off and on until he switched to the Bourbons). Jefferson also sent James Monroe to assist Livingston. The President instructed his envoys to offer France as much as $10 million for New Orleans and West Florida —the territory between the Mississippi River and the western boundary of the present state of Florida. Livingston was doggedly attempting to persuade Talleyrand to sell New Orleans and was delightfully thunderstruck when the Frenchman, acting on Napoleon's orders, calmly asked how much the Americans would pay for the entire Louisiana Territory. When Monroe arrived, the negotiations were quickly concluded. The United States agreed to pay

---

[2] So upset were two of Napoleon's brothers about the disposal of Louisiana that they broke into his bathroom while the Corsican was bathing. They re-

monstrated with him so forcefully that he could only silence their protests by throwing himself back in the tub, soaking them with perfumed bath water.

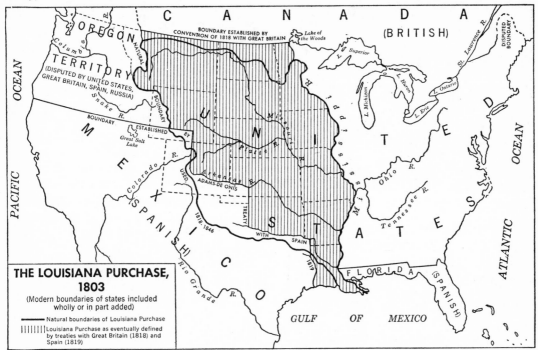

THE LOUISIANA PURCHASE, 1803

(Modern boundaries of states included wholly or in part added)

━━━ Natural boundaries of Louisiana Purchase

|||||||| Louisiana Purchase as eventually defined by treaties with Great Britain (1818) and Spain (1819)

France $15 million (60 million francs) and to assume claims in the neighborhood of $3 million owed by France to individual American citizens.

When the elated envoys notified Jefferson of their mission's astounding success, the Virginia liberal was overjoyed but doubtful. He had always preached the doctrine of strict constitutional interpretation, and he wore out the pages of that document trying to find the Federal government's specific power to purchase territory. The Constitution is loud in silence on this point. For a time the President played with the notion of a constitutional amendment, but that process was so time-consuming, and the Napoleonic whim was recognizably so capricious, that the worried Jefferson dared not delay.

Swallowing his philosophical objections, the President sent to Congress his recommendation that Louisiana be purchased. After some debate this was duly accomplished. On 20 December 1804, only twenty days after Spain had officially ceded Louisiana to France, a colorful scene took place in the small creole city of New Orleans. The tricolor was lowered, the American flag raised; soldiers fired a volley, and a small crowd cheered the announcement that Louisiana had become American territory. Livingston's joyous announcement that "From this day the United States take their place among the powers of the first rank" was, if premature, eventually destined to be true. Not only had the Louisiana Purchase more than doubled the size of the United States, but a potential source of continuing friction between France and America had been removed by diplomatic action—and considerable luck.

The acquisition of the vast Louisiana territory was a delight to Jefferson—not only because of the vast expansion of the United States, but also because it gave him an opportunity to satisfy a long-held scientific curiosity as to the nature of the western half of the continent. Following his suggestions, Congress authorized several explorations, of which the most important was to be to the Pacific Ocean. For the leadership of this latter expedition Jefferson appointed two personal friends, Captain Meriwether Lewis, a former private secretary, and William Clark, brother of George

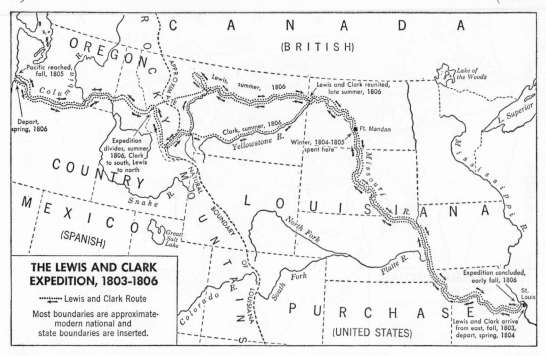

**THE LEWIS AND CLARK
EXPEDITION, 1803-1806**

┅┅┅ Lewis and Clark Route

Most boundaries are approximate-
modern national and
state boundaries are inserted.

Rogers Clark. After collecting men and supplies the party made its real start in 1804. The
first winter was spent near the present Bismarck, North Dakota. After much necessary
exploration to find the best route, the party
crossed the Rockies in the fall of 1805 and
finally sighted the Pacific Ocean on 7 November 1805. The return journey was more rapid,
in spite of many exploratory side trips, and
St. Louis was reentered in the fall of 1806.

The Lewis and Clark trip was not the first
across North America, since Alexander Mackenzie had been successful a decade earlier,
but it was the first through present United
States territory. The hardships were almost
incredible when one considers that the small
party of some thirty men was traversing thousands of miles of wilderness, including the passage of the main ranges of the Rockies in the
fall, with inadequate or nonexistent directions,
and surrounded by Indians who were suspicious and sometimes hostile. But the results
were worth the effort. Each man made notes,
and in time the collected information concerning physical features, plants, animals, and Indians became available generally to Americans.
Certainly the expedition marked the real be-

ginning of American conquest and occupation
of the trans-Mississippi country.

NORTH AFRICA AND NORTH AMERICA

While the fundamental decisions about Louisiana were being formulated, the bothersome
rather than vital trouble with North African
pirates approached a climax. The four "Barbary states" of Tripoli, Tunis, Algiers, and
Morocco were supposedly under the Ottoman
Sultan, but as long as that potentate received
tribute, he permitted them relative freedom
of action. These North African states gained
their economic livelihood by extortion—if a
nation paid regular tribute, its shipping would
not be molested. For years the great powers
had contributed annual stipends as a policy
less expensive than fullfledged naval expeditions against the Barbary nations. Actually,
Great Britain was by no means averse to Mediterranean pirates harassing its smaller maritime rivals. Ever since the days of the Articles
of Confederation the United States had paid

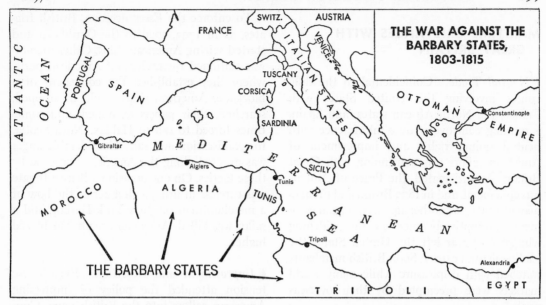

THE WAR AGAINST THE
BARBARY STATES,
1803-1815

THE BARBARY STATES

protection money. As a weak naval power America was treated with a contempt best exemplified when the Dey of Algiers forced the frigate *George Washington* to sail under the Algerian flag to Constantinople with presents for the Turkish Sultan.

In 1801 the Pasha of Tripoli learned the grievous news that Algiers received more blood money from the United States than he did. Aghast at this frightful favoritism, the Pasha declared war by the simple expedient of chopping down the flagpole outside the American consulate. The Tripolitans began attacking American ships, seizing their cargoes, and enslaving their crews. Despite the crimp it put in his budget, Jefferson was compelled to enlarge the American fleet and order it into the Mediterranean.

A desultory war followed for about three years. Before partial victory was won there was a shocking loss for the fledgling navy. The *Philadelphia*, crack American frigate, went aground while chasing a pirate ship outside Tripoli Harbor and was captured intact. The brilliant officer Stephen Decatur first gained his reputation by boarding the *Philadelphia* and burning it. Brave as was his action, the net result was that both the United States and Tripoli lost a fine ship. In 1804 a combined naval attack and overland expedition led by

Captain William Eaton, consisting of a handful of Americans, some Greeks, and a few hundred Arabs, managed to put a pincers movement on Tripoli, and the Pasha sued for peace. The United States managed to write a somewhat more satisfactory treaty with him. Payment of tribute to Barbary pirates did not die out, however, until after the War of 1812.

Perhaps the least attractive aspect of Jefferson's diplomacy was his inept attempt to extract West Florida from Spain, specifically the area between the modern cities of Baton Rouge, Louisiana, and Pensacola, Florida. Cognizant that Spain was in trouble overseas, Jefferson tried to get Napoleon to force Spanish cession of the territory. Napoleon would do nothing, and the net result of Jefferson's meddling was to arouse the ire of Spain and the jeers of Federalist opponents at home. During Madison's administration part of West Florida was seized when some Americans rebelled against Spain and were promptly recognized by and then annexed to the United States (1810). It was all rather sordid. When our discomfited Minister to Russia was trying to explain such a naked land grab to the Tsar, Alexander suavely stopped the American's lame excuses with the sophisticated observation, "Everybody is getting a little bigger nowadays."

MARITIME GRIEVANCES WITH GREAT BRITAIN

⟪ *Neutral Trade.* Coincidental to the difficulties involving the United States with France, the North African states, and Spain, a running controversy over interference with neutral sailing rights and impressment of American sailors was continuing with Great Britain. As anticipated, the Peace of Amiens was ephemeral, and in 1803 Briton and Frenchman were at one another again. American commerce promptly boomed as the widening whirlpool of war left the United States the leading neutral carrier. Soon British merchants watched with displeasure while many world markets were preempted by their overseas rivals.

Britain finally reacted in 1805 with the celebrated *Essex* decision. With this order, the British tried to stop the "broken voyage" between the French West Indies, the United States, and France. A prosperous trade had sprung up between the islands of Martinique and Guadeloupe and the American mainland. French Caribbean goods found their entrepôt in Europe by sailing as neutral goods protected by the American flag. It was legal for French colonial noncontraband exports to be carried to the United States. It was also proper for noncontraband American goods to be shipped to Europe. It was, of course, illegal for colonial French produce, contraband or not, to be shipped to France. The broken voyage tried to circumvent this restriction by a procedure closely akin to seventeenth-century violations of the Navigation Acts. Typical early-nineteenth-century procedure might be as follows: an American ship would pick up a cargo at Martinique and transport it to New York. The cargo would be landed, and a duty paid. The cargo would then, however, be reloaded, the duty refunded, and as American goods the cargo carried to Europe. The *Essex* decision interpreted this as a continuous rather than a broken voyage and insisted that a bona fide duty must be paid before French goods could be considered American.

To enforce the *Essex* decision, British frigates, as in 1793, sped to the Caribbean and started seizing American ships. Other men-of-war stationed themselves off American ports, where they established the equivalent of a blockade. American ships would be stopped, searched, their papers examined, and sometimes forced to sail to Halifax, Nova Scotia, for confiscation and sale. Considerable anger was aroused along the American coastline by these tactics. On one occasion a British frigate was careless in firing a shot across the bow of a merchantman off New York Harbor, and a sailor was killed. American resentment blazed higher.

⟪ *Impressment and Desertion.* Even worse tension attended the policy of impressing American sailors into the British navy. Conditions of able seamen in the Royal Navy were almost literally unbearable during the eighteenth and early nineteenth centuries. Food was abominable, quarters atrocious, pay almost nonexistent, and discipline sadistic. The rawhide cat-o'-nine-tails, each lash often knotted at the end or tipped with metal studs, was a truly murderous weapon. In the hands of a skilled bosun's mate, a few dozen lashes could cripple or even kill a man. The ship's captain had completely dictatorial powers, and there was no appeal from his command. Under such conditions it is not surprising that desertion was common on all British warships, even though death was the customary punishment. Frigates had been known to founder during heavy weather because desertions had so whittled down the crew that quite literally there were not enough men to reef the sails when a gale suddenly blew.

Food and pay were better and discipline less harsh on American merchant ships, and most British desertions took place in American ports. Deserters usually applied for and received certificates of American nationality—which could sometimes be bought in waterfront saloons for as little as a dollar. The British slogan "Once an Englishman, always an Englishman" held that British citizenship was not revocable and paid no attention to American naturalization papers. Impressment was often distressingly casual. A British frigate would force an American merchantman to lie to, board her, and subject the crew to questioning by an officer. Cockney, Irish, or Scots vocal inflection was deemed sufficient evidence for impressment. If the British ship were really shorthanded, anyone might be taken. Portuguese, Germans, and Swedes—some speaking not a word of English—would be declared loyal subjects of King George and "requested" (a belaying pin across the skull might lend additional emphasis) to become able seamen in His Majesty's Navy.

Statistics of the numbers concerned in both desertion and impressment are notoriously unreliable, since both sides lied for partisan advantage. Perhaps in the neighborhood of 20,-000 deserted from the British navy, and about 10,000 were impressed from American ships in return, although probably nine-tenths of the latter were bona fide American citizens. New England was particularly affected by impressment, for that section was the commercial heart of the United States. Did most of the demand for American retaliation against this policy emanate from the Northeast? Not at all. The sailors did not like it very well, but wartime trade was so profitable that New England shippers would do anything to keep their vessels at sea. If an American merchant sent out three ships during the years from 1805 to 1807, one could be a total loss, yet the entire transaction would return a profit if the other two completed their round trips. Hence Boston merchants could meet the impressment of sailors with equanimity. It was usually the more individualistic Westerner who found British impressment and trading restrictions intolerable.

From the British viewpoint impressment, although unfortunate, was an absolute imperative. The fleet was its only line of defense against the Corsican who bestrode Europe, and mastery of the sea was all that kept him on the other side of the English Channel. Naval blockade of the Continent was the best trump in the British hand. Therefore London considered maritime matters to be life or death for the British Empire. Frigates had to be manned; naval squads in England impressed native Britons for service, and certainly the whining of English deserters or penny-pinching Yankees would not be countenanced. Britain simply would not give in on the question of impressment, and any attempted Anglo-American settlement dependent upon that question was foredoomed to failure.

Thus it was no wonder that Jefferson failed when he attempted to negotiate upon both impressment and British interference with American neutral rights. In May, 1806, the President sent James Monroe and William Pinkney to London for discussions. According to Jefferson's express directive, a clear renunciation of impressment must be a condition of any agreement. When Monroe and Pinkney signed a treaty that said nothing about impressment, the disgusted Jefferson refused to send it to the Senate. Diplomacy was unable to ease the tension.

THE VISE TIGHTENS

By 1806 the European war had reached a stalemate. Under the command of the battered, one-armed, one-eyed Horatio Nelson, Britain's navy hammered so thoroughly a combined French and Spanish fleet off Cape Trafalgar in southern Spain (1805) that English oceanic hegemony was assured for years to come. Only a month later Napoleon overwhelmed Austrian and Russian armies at Austerlitz in what is now Czechoslovakia, and Bonaparte stood supreme from the Baltic to the Adriatic. Neither Britain nor France could get at the other very well ("the whale versus the elephant"), and for the next several years both moved into the arena of economic warfare.

French policy was announced in the Berlin (November, 1806) and Milan (December, 1807) Decrees, which established the "Continental system," forbidding any European nations to trade with Great Britain and subjecting neutral ships to confiscation if they had engaged in traffic with England. The British retaliated with two Orders in Council that established a blockade of all Napoleonic Europe. Since even the gigantic Royal Navy did not have enough ships to police a continental shoreline, the measure resulted in what was in part a paper blockade.[3] Neutral ships were forbidden to trade with France or its European dependencies and were subject to seizure if they did. Thus nonbelligerent commerce was menaced from both sides—and the United States was the leading neutral carrier. If American ships cleared English ports they were subject to Napoleonic capture. If they traded with French domains, the King's navy considered them legitimate prey. Yet the more hazardous the commerce, the greater the profits. The coastline of the United States hummed with activity.

While affairs drifted in this situation and British frigates still patrolled off American harbors, a major Anglo-American crisis was precipitated by the famous Chesapeake-Leopard embroglio. His Majesty's Ship Leopard was on duty off Virginia when four of her crew deserted. Hearing that they had signed with the U.S.S. Chesapeake, the British captain decided to recoup his losses and maneuvered his frigate alongside the American man-of-war, which had just left Norfolk, Virginia, en route to the Mediterranean. Captain James Barron of the Chesapeake assumed that the British wished him to carry letters to Europe, a common courtesy of the time. When the announcement came that his ship was to be boarded, Barron could hardly credit his hearing, for the right to search a naval vessel was clearly contrary to established maritime practice.

The American captain tried to stall until his decks were cleared of cluttered gear and the matches to fire his guns were lit, but the Leopard suddenly poured a broadside into the unprepared ship. One heroic individual brought a live coal from the galley with his bare hands, enabling the Chesapeake to fire a single shot,

but then Barron had to strike his colors. A British boarding party found the four deserters: three Americans who were promptly reimpressed, and one native Englishman who was hauled from hiding for eventual hanging. The Chesapeake limped back to Norfolk with eighteen killed or wounded. In a subsequent court-martial Barron was found guilty of commanding an unprepared ship and was suspended from the navy for five years without pay.[4]

Americans were beside themselves with rage over this national humiliation. British officers on shore leave in American cities fled for their lives. Even New England Federalists were ready for war, and there seems little reason to doubt that Jefferson could have led a united people against Great Britain. The President wanted peace, however, and decided to negotiate. He might well have received satisfactory apologies and damages for the Leopard's brutal action, but he attempted to use the attack as an entering wedge to force British surrender on impressment and the question of American neutral rights. Once this had been done, all negotiations were plunged into a legalistic morass of conflicting claims and interests. It was several years before restitution for the Chesapeake was made.

THE EMBARGO

Even if Thomas Jefferson were unwilling to go to war, he decided to take strong economic action. This was embodied in the Embargo, which called for a complete ban on all exports both by sea and by land from the United States to any part of the world.[5] The President was positive that American foodstuffs were all-important to Great Britain and France; if they were withheld the European belligerents

---

[3] A paper blockade is one that is not effectively enforced. Now neutrals do not have to obey a paper blockade, but no such policy had been formulated in the early nineteenth century.

[4] Presiding at Barron's court-martial was Stephen Decatur, hero of both the Tripolitan War and the War of 1812. Barron never forgot what he considered Decatur's malevolent attitude, and in 1817 he shot and killed that famous officer in a duel.

[5] An embargo was no novelty. Congress had voted one for two months against Great Britain in 1794.

would be forced to acquiesce to American terms. Fervent protests from the maritime areas were of no avail, and the Embargo became law (22 December 1807). American seaports immediately tail-spinned into a dreadful depression, perhaps 50,000 sailors were thrown out of work, and allied industries such as ropewalks, sail manufactories, and purveyors of salt pork and hardtack went into bankruptcy. Although the whole nation was hard hit, discontent was centered in the Northeast; and there the Federalists, led by the Essex Junto, enjoyed a quick resurgence. More than fiery words opposed the Embargo; widespread smuggling operations started across the Canadian border in defiance of the national law. American ships that were at sea when the act went into effect stayed away to engage in the European carrying trade during the Embargo's fourteen-month course.

The Embargo must be considered a failure. It hurt the United States far more than it afflicted the belligerent powers. It effectively blanketed a thriving Atlantic seaboard and smothered a soaring domestic prosperity. Although it caused some belt-tightening in Great Britain, luckily for that nation its crops in 1808 were unusually good, and the lower class, which was hardest hit by the Embargo, could not vote to make their complaints politically effective. This "ostrich in the sand" retirement only played into Napoleon's hand. With cynical hypocrisy the Emperor announced that any American ships in France were obviously illegal, and since he wished to assist his good friend Jefferson, he would confiscate them (Bayonne Decree, 1808).

The Embargo, however, had its good side. Money earmarked for commerce was directed toward industry. The great expansion of New England textile manufacturing dates from this period, and scores of new enterprises were started. Actually the European belligerents felt sharply the pinch caused by drastically reduced American imports, and such pressure tended to become cumulative as the months passed. Perhaps the Embargo is assessed as a failure because it was repealed before its full weight could be applied abroad. The opposition from New England and other commercial areas became so acute, however, that Jefferson was forced to permit the repeal of this act only three days before he left the White House in 1809.

CHAPTER 14

"Mr. Madison's War"

(1809-1815)

MADISON'S COMMERCIAL POLICIES

James Madison was Jefferson's successor and inherited the headaches pertaining to the presidency of the largest neutral carrier in a war-torn world. Madison was small, slight, and studious. His mind was keen and perspicacious, his literary ability topflight, and his personality attractive enough to claim the great Jefferson as a close friend. Analytically the new President was above reproach, but by 1812 he tended to waver when decisiveness was imperative, and sometimes he allowed wishful thinking rather than concrete facts to condition his policy. Madison had been a Virginia Revolutionary, the busiest member of the Constitutional Convention, and an ardent supporter of the Constitution during the ratification battle. As an agrarian, he disliked Hamilton's financial program and became Jefferson's right-hand man in the Democratic-Republican party. In several instances Madison appears to have formulated important party decisions for which Thomas Jefferson received the credit. When the latter became President, Madison was rewarded with the appointment of Secretary of State. "Little Jemmy" was pushed forward when Jefferson decided not to run for a

third term. Despite a swing to the Federalist candidate, Charles Cotesworth Pinckney, that cost Madison all of New England save Vermont, Southern and Western support made him the new Chief Executive.

Naturally the tense relations with the warring powers occupied most of Madison's time. His primary responsibility was to administer a new law replacing the defunct Embargo. This was the Non-Intercourse Act (1809), stipulating that commercial restrictions be lifted against all nations except Great Britain and France. Furthermore, if either of the latter removed its interference with American commerce, the United States would follow suit and relax its economic coercion.

At this point Great Britain decided to try conciliation and sent the personable John Erskine to America for discussions to settle outstanding difficulties. Erskine and Madison found themselves congenial, and soon the President triumphantly announced that an agreement with Great Britain had been signed. The Non-Intercourse Act was declared no longer to apply against Britain; amid general exultation a mass exodus of 600 ships loaded with cargoes for England left American wharves. Unfortunately for Madison and his entire commercial policy, Erskine had exceeded his instructions. He had pledged revocation of the offensive Orders in Council that restricted American trade, and this provision had been written into the treaty. In return Madison had agreed to forget about impressment of American sailors. The British government disavowed the Madison-Erskine understanding, and the discomfited President had no choice but to reimpose the Non-Intercourse Act against the British. The damage had been done, however. Enough American goods had landed in England to alleviate its most acute shortages, and the whole job had to start all over again.

Still claiming to desire an amicable settlement, London appointed a new Minister to the United States, Francis Charles Jackson. It is difficult to imagine a worse choice. He was a loud, aggressive, obnoxious individual who had taken so prominent a part in the savage British bombardment of the Danish capital that his universal nickname was "Copenhagen" Jackson. He aroused intense resentment over here by his patronizing attitude, sneering at Madison's wife, the volatile Dolly ("Copenhagen's" considered judgment of her was "fat, forty, but not fair"), and finally making himself so impossible that the President announced that no further communications would be received from him. When this so-called diplomat returned home, Great Britain appointed no successor until Augustus Foster arrived two years later, only to score about as resounding a failure as Jackson. A war needless to both nations was creeping closer.

Apprehensive at the approach of hostilities, Madison decided to retreat from his policy of economic coercion. In place of the Non-Intercourse Act, the President supported the second of two bills sponsored in the House of Representatives by Nathaniel Macon of North Carolina. "Macon's Bill No. 2" removed nonintercourse from both Great Britain and France, but carried the proviso that if either nation repealed its restrictions against American commerce, nonintercourse would be applied against the other if similar friendly action were not taken within three months. Macon's Bill

No. 2 was made to order for devious Bonaparte trickery.

The Duc de Cadore, French Foreign Minister, wrote Madison that France was repealing the Berlin and Milan Decrees against American shipping because "His Majesty loves the Americans." There was a major restriction in the Cadore letter, however—Great Britain would have to repeal its Orders in Council or the United States would have to compel the British to do so. There was no way in which America could have forced this point, hence the French communication promised exactly nothing. At the very least Madison should have delayed until he saw whether Napoleon was acting in good faith; actually the Corsican continued to confiscate every American ship that he could find. But the desperate Madison, craving some diplomatic success after his fiasco with Erskine, allowed his hopes to override his judgment. In March, 1811, he reapplied nonintercourse against Great Britain. British anger was extreme; they looked upon Madison's act as outright hostility, especially since it was common knowledge that French seizures of American shipping continued unabated.

❨ *The War Hawks.* At about the same time that Napoleonic chicanery was plaguing the President, something of a political ground swell, conditioned in part by troubles with the Western Indians,[1] was under way in the United States. In the congressional elections of 1810–1811 a younger and more aggressive group entered the national government to receive from John Randolph of Roanoke the derisive nicknames of the "War Hawks" and the "Boys." The War Hawks, mainly from the South and West, were led by Henry Clay of Kentucky, who strode upon the American stage to commence his featured role that would last for forty years. John C. Calhoun, eventual shield of South Carolina home rule, was also a prominent member of this group. The War Hawks were early advocates of unrestrained expansionism, and these land-hungry young men looked calculatingly toward

[1] See pp. 124–125.

Spanish Florida to the south, while indulging in what Randolph called their eternal "whippoorwill cry" for British Canada to the north.

Immediately their pressure on the administration began. Elected to the House of Representatives, Henry Clay announced with greater local pride than accuracy that "the militia of Kentucky alone" would conquer "Upper and Lower Canada within six weeks." Scions of the more egalitarian frontier, the Western and Southern expansionists were angered at impressment and could not understand the economic motivation that led New Englanders to tolerate such a practice. The commercial depression existing since 1808 had toppled Western produce prices. British blockade and illegal searches filled the War Hawks with resentment. In addition they were thoroughly convinced that the Indian menace could never be abolished while Canada remained under the Union Jack. One of their members, Felix Grundy of Tennessee, had lost three brothers to Indian massacre. With such sanguinary memories common in their ranks, the War Hawks would not remain silent until an American Canada made possible concerted action against the tribes.

THE OUTBREAK OF HOSTILITIES

By 1812 Madison was sure that his and his party's political future was dependent on Southern and Western support. Gradually the President became convinced that Great Britain could be brought to terms only through hostile action by the United States. He adopted the point of view that the minimum condition for peace was repeal of the British Orders in Council against American shipping, but London had remained obdurate on that particular. If he could gain this concession, Madison was willing to forget about the impressment issue. Yet as the weeks passed, the President's patience rapidly ebbed away. In the spring of 1812 he recommended to Congress a declaration of war against Great Britain. He charged the British with inciting the

Western Indians to violence, impressing American seamen, illegally interfering with neutral rights, and maintaining an illicit blockade of American ports.

Despite Federalist attempts to procrastinate, the United States declared war on 18 June 1812. The vote in Congress is significant. The maritime areas were overwhelmingly for peace, and it took the combined efforts of Southern and inland expansionists to declare hostilities against Great Britain. Votes of 19 to 13 in the Senate and 79 to 49 in the House illustrated the split among the Democratic-Republicans, for the ballots were cast on sectional rather than party lines. A strange sidelight of the war resolution saw one Senator offer an amendment that France be included in the declaration, and his motion failed by the narrow margin of 18 to 14. Not content to restrict fighting to the greatest maritime power in the world, some Senators wished to add the strongest military machine as well.

In one of the many instances, good and bad, in which slow communications have had important historical consequences, Great Britain repealed her offensive Orders in Council only five days after the United States declared war. Thus, during the first week of hostilities, the primary stated cause for the war had been removed. Of course the bellicose action of the United States was unknown in England when the Orders were repealed.

The second war with Great Britain was unnecessary. If Madison had delayed a little longer, if England had acted with a bit more celerity, peace would have been assured. In reality, despite diplomatic impasse, relations between the two countries were better during the spring of 1812 than they had been for the past six years. Britain had apologized for the *Chesapeake-Leopard* affair, and American revenge over that humiliation had been satisfied when the frigate *President* blasted the British *Little Belt* out of the water in 1811. Shrewd observers could see that it was only a question of time before the Orders in Council would be repealed. English domestic conditions were desperate by the winter of 1811–1812, and certainly that nation had no desire to fight the

EUROPE DURING
HEIGHT OF
NAPOLEON'S
POWER (1812)

|||||||||| France
========= French puppets
▨▨▨▨▨ French allies
☐☐☐☐☐ Hostile or neutral
states

United States while the Napoleonic War was approaching a climax.

Although it is true that Great Britain had given America cause for deep resentment, it had committed no greater wrongs than Bonaparte had perpetrated. In fact, Madison admitted that more American ships had been confiscated by the French than by the British from 1807 to 1812. Despite Napoleon's obvious malice, the United States drifted into war, if not allied to, at least acting in consort with, the French dictator. The United States was not fighting on the side of liberalism or freedom from 1812 to 1815.

THE WAR OF 1812

❮ *The Rival Powers.* The United States entered the war with Great Britain almost hopelessly unprepared. Although the likelihood of hostilities had been present for many months, practically nothing had been done to make ready. Finances, an army, transportation, and leadership were lamentably missing. In addition, Madison led only a part of the nation into

war. Commercial areas, particularly in New England, were bitterly hostile to the whole conflict, and this initial animus steadily increased. The election of 1812 showed how deep was this cleavage. An antiwar faction of the Democratic-Republican party nominated De Witt Clinton of New York to oppose Madison and the war. Clinton received the united support of the Federalists as well. The older states of the Union split; all seaboard areas north of the Mason-Dixon line save Pennsylvania voted for Clinton and peace. The combined efforts of the South and the inland belt of states from Vermont to Tennessee supported Madison and swung the election to him. But the conclusion is inescapable; the War of 1812 was a sectional rather than a national conflict.

The financial story was shocking. The government was dependent on tariffs for most of its revenue; and once the British blockade became effective, income from this source almost vanished. Monetary levies on the states were sometimes ignored. New taxes, among them a stamp tax, brought little yield. Attempts to borrow money largely failed. Bonds could be sold in the Central and Southern states, but New England made little monetary contribution to a cause that it opposed. On the eve of the war (1811), the twenty-year charter of the Bank of the United States terminated, and no centralized financial depository existed during the whole conflict. By 1815 the American government was almost bankrupt.

The word ludicrous is none too strong to describe military conditions in 1812. The United States had something over 8 million inhabitants at that time. Yet its professional army numbered less than 7,000 officers and men; their hands were full patrolling Indian territory. There were some 694,000 enrolled in the militia companies, supposedly "The Swords of the Republic." These raw levies were untrained, undisciplined, and unready. Often they showed a reluctance to leave the confines of their own state and sometimes refused to fight even inside it. Few of the nearly 700,000 militiamen responded to Madison's call for volunteers; the United States never had more than 35,000 men under arms at any one time during the whole struggle. The majority of commanding officers were Revolutionary antiques who had gained reputations a third of a century before. Military transport was hopelessly disorganized and quite unprepared to supply armies over the trackless and difficult terrain along the Canadian border.

Conditions were considerably better in the navy. Its frigates were, gun for gun, the best in the world, and its personnel highly able and well trained. Excluding Jeffersonian gunboats, however, there were but thirteen ships in the United States navy. Great Britain had between 800 and 1,000 in the Royal Navy, and perhaps 200 could match the most powerful American ships. When the military and naval situation in 1812 is studied, a conclusion is reached that applies also to the American Revolution: it is a wonder, not that the United States fought no more effectively, but that it was not completely overwhelmed.

Certain advantages pertained to the American cause, despite the nation's startling weaknesses. The British and Canadians were heavily outnumbered, even including their In-

dian allies in the West. It was possible for Canada to fall; the United States could not be conquered completely. The British were little better prepared, and their war effort was equally hampered by the miserable transportation facilities. The greatest American advantage was found in the international situation. The North American conflict was an unimportant side show to the British; action with Napoleon was featured in the main tent. Just when the War of 1812 broke out, the European war was approaching its apex. Only four days after Madison's war recommendation was passed, Napoleon started chasing his will-o'-the-wisp down the endless Russian roads toward Moscow and eventual catastrophe. The year 1813 saw the beleaguered Emperor defeated in Germany, and his abdication followed during the spring of the next year. Only in mid-1814 could the British center their attention across the Atlantic. Even then the English masses were understandably war-weary after almost twenty-two years of French conflict.

MILITARY ACTION

❨ *Campaigns of 1812.* American hopes were high during the summer heat in 1812, but wintry blasts coincided with dashed ambitions. The campaigns of the first six months featured unbroken American defeat. Operating under the influence of Henry Clay's dramatic oratory concerning the ease of Canadian conquest, a three-column attack on British North America was planned. General William Hull was to advance from Detroit into Upper Canada (Ontario). General Stephen Van Rensselaer would attack the other end of the Upper Canadian peninsula from Niagara. General Henry Dearborn would march up the well-traveled Lake Champlain route from Plattsburg, New York, to occupy Montreal and perhaps Quebec. The over-all strategy was excellent; the results, abominable.

General Hull, commanding at Detroit, objected to attacking Canada without naval con-

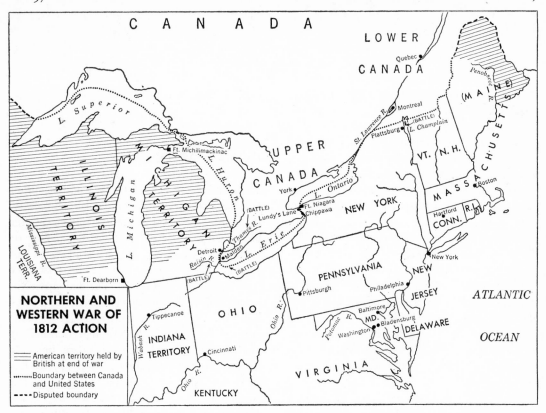

NORTHERN AND
WESTERN WAR OF
1812 ACTION

≡≡≡ American territory held by
      British at end of war
······· Boundary between Canada
      and United States
---- Disputed boundary

trol of Lake Erie, but he had to follow his orders. Timidly he advanced toward the Canadian hamlet of Malden. There the spirited British General Isaac Brock commanded a mixed army of whites and Indians considerably smaller than Hull's force. The aged American wavered and retreated to strongly fortified Detroit. His curiosity aroused by these strange tactics, Brock followed and decided that he might as well lay siege to the stronghold. The Briton suggested that the Americans surrender, hinting broadly that he probably would not be able to avert an Indian massacre if resistance continued. Terrified, the pitiful Hull did precisely that. A court-martial later sentenced Hull to be shot, but Madison pardoned him. The surrender of Detroit, the evacuation of Fort Dearborn (present Chicago), and the fall of Fort Michilimackinac, key to the upper Lakes, rolled back the Americans from most of the Northwest.

Catastrophe also attended General Van Rensselaer at Fort Niagara. Part of his army

was composed of veteran United States troops, but most of it was undisciplined militiamen from upstate New York. The regulars had crossed into Canada and were winning a battle against Brock (this able officer was killed in the fight) when Canadian reinforcements arrived. Despite Van Rensselaer's commands and entreaties, his militiamen came to the interesting conclusion that because they were New York troops they should not fight outside their state. From across the Niagara River they watched with fascinated absorption while their fellow soldiers were killed or captured. Not surprisingly, Van Rensselaer resigned his commission and went home.

At Plattsburg, General Dearborn, senior major general, commanded several thousand unruly recruits. Orders were freely debated and then decided upon by the men. Dearborn led his army north from Plattsburg some twenty miles toward Canada to attack Montreal. At this point the army decided that it was more fun in camp and demanded to return—General Dearborn marched them back to Plattsburg. Such was the three-pronged attack on Canada in 1812.

NAVAL ACTION

Happily for American morale, while the army was suffering such humiliation, the navy was covering itself with glory during the early days of the war, although its triumphs were only temporary. The *Constitution* smashed the *Guerrière* and later battered the *Java* into kindling wood off the coast of Brazil. The *Essex* captured the *Minerva* and defeated the *Alert*. Stephen Decatur added to his laurels when the *United States* brought the beaten *Macedonian* into port as a prize. The *Wasp* beat the *Frolic*, and the *Hornet* whipped the *Peacock*. Jubilation greeted each new victory. It is true that usually the American ship outgunned its English opponent, but the proud British navy for years had considered that odds of two to one against it only made a more interesting contest. To be defeated, as one London newspaper mourned, by a "handful of bastards" in "fir-built frigates" was intolerable to British complacency nurtured by some 250 years of almost continuous naval victory.

Unfortunately for the United States, these oceanic triumphs, impressive as they were, were flashes of individual achievement rather than decisive and sustained campaigns. Gradually the British blockade of the American coast tightened as more "ships of the line" appeared in American waters. Inevitably the number of American frigates was whittled down by capture or confinement. The unlucky *Chesapeake* was beaten, and the *Essex* and *President* forced to surrender. Others were bottled up in port by the blockade. By 1814 only the *Constitution*, "Old Ironsides," of all the frigates was at large on the high seas. If the navy's usefulness was destroyed, American privateers operated during the whole war and caused panic in British insurance circles. Over 1,300 prizes were taken, and, as in the Revolution, merchantmen were captured off London

Harbor. Insurance rates soared even for coastal shipping. Late in the war, however, convoying of merchant ships seriously reduced privateering effectiveness. Nevertheless, some impetus to end the war arose from the losses to these commerce raiders.

CLIMAX OF THE WAR

❨ *Campaigns of 1813.* In 1813 fighting along the Canadian border went a little better for the United States. The administration ordered Oliver Hazard Perry [2] to construct a fleet on Lake Erie, recognizing that control of the Great Lakes was the key to the entire frontier. Coincidentally the British decided upon the same policy, and the novel situation of a naval race on inland seas was under way. It was difficult on both sides. British matériel had to journey up the St. Lawrence and be portaged to the lake. Perry's ordnance and supplies had to be hauled over the mountains; and lacking trained naval personnel, he had to request Western frontiersmen to get their feet wet. Both fleets had to be constructed from keel to mast on the spot. In a sharp and savage battle between the fresh-water flotillas (10 September 1813), Perry's superior artillery won the day; he notified the government of his success with the laconic announcement, "We have met the enemy and they are ours: two ships, two brigs, one schooner, and one sloop." By this victory, control of Lake Erie reverted to the United States.

With American flanks secured by Perry's triumph, it was feasible to reinvade Canada. General William Henry Harrison advanced into Ontario and met a motley army composed of British regulars, Canadian militia units, and Indian braves. Commanding this aggregation was General Henry Proctor, who had offered no effective deterrence earlier in the year when his drunken Indians had butchered 500 helpless American prisoners at Raisin River. Dur-

[2] Oliver Hazard Perry was the brother of Matthew Perry, who opened Japan to Western trade during 1854–1855.

ing this Battle of the Thames Harrison extracted revenge; Proctor had to flee for his life; and Tecumseh was killed, his Indian confederation falling to pieces after his death. Harrison did not follow up his victory, however, although the ground lost by Hull was largely retaken.

Other action was not so successful from the American viewpoint. A limited attack toward Montreal was beaten back, Fort Niagara fell late in the year, and an engagement that marked a temporary American success was destined to reap a whirlwind. General Dearborn led a hit-and-run attack across Lake Ontario to capture York (Toronto), the capital of Upper Canada. In the fracas the city was burned, and the next year the British retaliated in Washington, D.C.

❨ *Campaigns of 1814.* The war climaxed in 1814. Under better leadership, Americans fought more effectively in the Niagara sector. Advancing into Canada, General Jacob Brown and his subordinate Winfield Scott won vigorous engagements at Chippawa and Lundy's Lane, although British reinforcements soon compelled withdrawal. This was the only major American offensive of the year, for national energies had to be channeled to repel invigorated British onsets. Freed from the menace of Napoleon, who was temporarily in exile on the Mediterranean island of Elba, London was able to send over new regiments of veterans, hardened in battle with the Corsican. For two years the British had fought to protect their Canadian territory; now they tried conquest.

Their offensive was embodied in a typical military plan of that day—threefold. One army was to proceed south along Burgoyne's old route toward Albany. The second was to be transported by sea to conquer the Chesapeake Bay area. A third was to sail to New Orleans and capture the mouth of the Mississippi. Triple or even double success would ensure a victor's peace.

The first offensive was under the command of General George Prevost, who marched his troops south along Lake Champlain, hoping to detach New England from the rest of the Union and perhaps persuade it to rejoin the British Empire. As at Lake Erie in 1813, naval action on an inland sea saved the Americans. Commodore Thomas Macdonough was ordered to control Lake Champlain, and that officer defeated a British squadron in freshwater naval action. With his flanks menaced by American ships which enjoyed freedom of movement, Prevost dared advance no farther and led his army back to Canada. The victory on Lake Champlain was to have important diplomatic as well as military repercussions.

Partially successful was the second British attack, which, it was hoped, would sail into Chesapeake Bay, capture Washington and Baltimore, and perhaps strike to the northeast toward Philadelphia and New York. When the tidings spread that the invaders had arrived, local militia units turned out in sufficient numbers so that Washington, D.C., should have been safe. The advancing British were met at Bladensburg, Maryland, near the national capital, with President Madison and many other dignitaries in attendance. The battle has carried the unflattering appellation of "The Bladensburg Races" ever since, for the recruits broke and ran for their lives on the first volley; only a small naval detachment, which was soon overwhelmed, offered much resistance.

The British sauntered on to occupy undefended Washington, almost capturing President and Mrs. Madison in the process. So hurriedly did they have to leave that Dolly had time to snatch up only a portrait of Washington and the Declaration of Independence. That evening British officers dined at the White House and, in retaliation for the burning of York in 1813, ordered that the Capitol and the White House be set afire. Leaving Washington's main public buildings in flames, the British proceeded toward Baltimore at the head of Chesapeake Bay. Here resistance was effective. Fort McHenry, defending the city, held out amid "the rocket's red glare," as Francis Scott Key described the scene in his national anthem, which was written during the bombardment. The British decided that further advance was impossible, and the whole expedition returned to Canada.

The British campaign against New Orleans had a prologue in 1813 when war against the Indians broke out in the Southwest. Elements of the powerful Creek tribe went on the warpath and perpetrated one of the worst massacres in American history when they slaughtered 500 settlers huddled for protection in Fort Mims, Alabama. Although the South had been somewhat lackadaisical before, this outrage aroused the section to more effective participation in the war effort. The indefatigable Andrew Jackson was given command of the area and fell upon the Creeks, routing them in a sharp contest at Horseshoe Bend. Jackson charged hither and yon after detachments of Creek warriors, marching into Spanish Florida on one occasion. Not only were its borders violated, but Spain also suffered the additional indignity of losing the only territory gained by the United States through the war that was supposed to conquer all Canada. The rascally James Wilkinson seized a small portion of West Florida around the present city of Mobile, Alabama. We never returned it to Spain.

When it became obvious late in 1814 that a British fleet was sweeping through the Gulf of Mexico toward Louisiana, Andrew Jackson hastened to defend New Orleans. A combat-hardened British army of 7,000 troops was landed outside the city and proceeded toward it. Jackson had erected defenses of earthworks and cotton bales, manning his lines with a variegated army of about the same size as the British. Pallid clerks, fur-hatted and bearded Tennessee frontiersmen, river ruffians, run-of-the-mill planters, and, most picturesque of all, wild pirates of Jean Laffite, a notorious Louisiana freebooter, waited behind their fortifications as the British drew near. General Sir Edward Pakenham made the same unfortunate decision at New Orleans that an English predecessor had made at Bunker Hill in 1775. Convinced that the Americans could not withstand a full charge, Pakenham ordered a frontal assault at Jackson's entrenched positions. Even against Napoleon, the red-coated infantry never experienced a day so awful as that at New Orleans. A murderous fire at point-blank range wiped out rank after rank. Pakenham and most of the officers were killed; and before the British had retreated to their ships, 13 American dead had been exchanged for 2,000 British casualties.

New Orleans was a glorious victory, and the nation went into ecstasies of delight over it. It had one drawback, however. It had been fought two weeks *after* peace had been signed between the United States and Great Britain. European communications were so slow that neither force at New Orleans knew that hostilities had officially ceased. For Americans, the Louisiana victory cast a pleasant glow over a losing war, but naturally it had no effect on diplomatic negotiations abroad. Its memory was strong enough, however, to help put Andrew Jackson in the White House fourteen years later.

⟨ *New England's Opposition.*   A striking feature of the War of 1812 was the attitude of New England. Bitterly opposing the war from its beginning, the Northeast dragged its heels throughout. New England governors refused to call the militia into national service; and wealthy citizens of Boston, Providence, and Hartford would not purchase United States bonds. For the first two years of the war, Great Britain left New England pretty much alone, apparently hoping that sectional secessionists might lead the area back into the empire. During this time Yankees profited through large-scale smuggling across the Canadian border. By 1814, however, the English attitude changed, and raiding parties had a fine time ransacking barns along the New England coast. Most of northeastern Maine was conquered, and an impenetrable blockade established offshore. The latter ruined what trading activity remained after the Embargo and the Non-Intercourse Acts. Once the war was over, major ports such as Boston and Salem quickly recovered their remunerative foreign commerce, but smaller towns never regained their great days of maritime glory.

Rather than resenting the British for these depredations, New Englanders vented their displeasure at the American administration that had dragged them into this unpopular struggle. New England's attitude seems to have been, "It's Mr. Madison's war, let Mr. Madison fight it!" Some arrant secessionists came out of hiding, and a few Essex Junto traitors actively conspired with Great Britain for re-annexation. Each month they grew in strength as New England's fury against Madison heightened.

To capitalize upon this unrestrained discontent, a convention was called to meet at Hartford, Connecticut, during December, 1814. Luckily for the nation, more moderate Federalists, led by Harrison Gray Otis and George Cabot, marshaled enough votes there to check the Timothy Pickering separatists. No motion to secede was passed. Instead, the convention dispatched not delegates but "ambassadors" to Washington with seven amendments which had to be added to the Constitution before New England's opposition could be quieted. Among these amendments were items calling for one-term Presidents; removal of three-fifths representation for Southern slaves; and congressional approval by two-thirds rather than simple majority for admission of new states, declarations of war, and commercial restrictions. Obviously New England wanted a sectional veto on these points. While the august ambassadors were en route to Washington, however, the end of the war was announced. The embarrassed legates had to scurry back to New England with the laughter of the rest of the nation ringing in their ears. This was the death rattle of Federalism. The party ran a presidential candidate against James Monroe in 1816, but suffered such a cataclysmic defeat that the Federalists never nominated another.

THE PEACE OF GHENT

The War of 1812 had hardly started when Madison first began to hope for peace. The Orders in Council had been repealed, and news from the Canadian border was grim enough to make the President anticipate a prompt end

to hostilities. Nothing could be accomplished during the remainder of 1812, however, for Great Britain had no desire to negotiate while all was going well. In 1813 intervention for peace came from a distant source. Tsar Alexander I of Russia had seen his land invaded by Napoleon, and this automatically made him brother-in-arms with King George. The Tsar hated to see any British energies diverted to North American conflict while European battles raged. He communicated to both belligerents his willingness to negotiate a peace.

Madison promptly sent to Russia James Bayard and Albert Gallatin, the latter recently resigned as Secretary of the Treasury, to assist our Minister in St. Petersburg, John Quincy Adams, son of the former President. Britain did not want the Tsar meddling in its own affairs, but, not wishing to offend the Autocrat of All the Russias, offered instead to deal directly with the United States. This was even better news for Madison, and he sent Henry Clay and James Russell to aid the three American envoys already in Europe. They were instructed to hold out for a ban on impressment (Madison later modified this stipulation) and condemnation of illegal blockades. No American territory was to be ceded, and the delegates were to keep alert to any possibility of annexing Canada. They should also try to receive compensation for property illegally seized. Actually the envoys were granted considerable liberty of action, for Madison recognized that changed war conditions would lead to altered circumstances.

So much time was expended in travel that it was August, 1814, before the five Americans were able to meet three British negotiators at the Belgian city of Ghent. Discussions dragged on for several months. Weeks would pass while the British delegates awaited instructions, for they were permitted to do little on their own. The upper echelons of British administration were busy in Vienna settling the vastly more important European questions. Viscount Castlereagh, the Foreign Minister; the great General Arthur Wellesley, Duke of Wellington (the "Iron Duke"); and Lord Bathurst, Colonial and War Secretary, could not be spared to talk about American situations. Therefore three relative nonentities with little diplomatic experience were ordered to act as messenger boys between Vienna and Ghent. The trio consisted of Lord Gambier, who had commanded the destruction of the Danish fleet at Copenhagen; Henry Goulburn, a supercilious and startlingly naïve young man; and a Dr. William Adams, supposedly an authority on international law, who did little more than occupy space.

What the British delegation lacked in ability it made up in sweeping demands. Confident that the invasion of New York would detach the Northeast and that Baltimore and the central Atlantic states would soon fall to the naval expedition in the Chesapeake, the British proposed a conqueror's peace. No American warships or fortifications were to be permitted on the Great Lakes. Northeastern Maine, the Niagara environs in New York, and parts of Michigan and Minnesota must be ceded to Britain. Even more shocking was the demand that a vast Indian "buffer state" be set up north of the Ohio River, stretching from the Appalachians to the Mississippi. When Gallatin inquired about what would happen to the 100,000 Americans already inhabiting that area, Goulburn had a ready answer: they must shift for themselves. They would be well treated, Goulburn assured the stunned Americans; he had once known an Indian personally and the latter was very intelligent. Infuriated at such cavalier behavior, four envoys from the United States prepared to go home. Only Henry Clay suspected that the British were bluffing, and he persuaded the others to remain for a time.

Clay was correct; the British were awaiting good news from America; but instead of the happy tiding they anticipated, reports told of Macdonough's resounding victory on Lake Champlain and the retreat of the invading army to Canada. Rather than capturing Baltimore, the British were forced to retire. Even though these setbacks were discouraging, the English commission soon brought up a new demand: peace should be arranged on the basis of *uti possidetis* (that which you possess). Since this would mean British accession of all

Maine east of the Penobscot River as well as Forts Niagara and Michilimackinac, the Americans insisted on the *status quo ante bellum* (conditions as they were before the war). With such a wide schism between the opposing viewpoints, once again preparations for disbanding the conference were made.

Behind the wrangling at Ghent, international forces were aiding the United States. The allies carving up Europe at Vienna were bitterly disagreeing, there was constant peril that the Corsican might return from Elba, and in England taxpayers were insistent that wartime levies be relaxed. The final straw that tipped the balance against continued pressure for a victor's peace was the attitude of the Duke of Wellington. There had been some talk in London of sending the Iron Duke to command British forces in America; but after studying the military situation in the Great Lakes–Champlain arena, Wellington not only felt that his rumored mission had little chance for success but also concluded that the American position was so strong that there was no justice in British demands for *uti possidetis*. He recommended that joint restoration of all territory was the only sensible way to end the war.

Just at the point when it seemed that all issues dividing the two nations had been settled, a well-timed British request split the American delegation internally; Clay and Adams had so sharp a disagreement that it appeared that all the laborious efforts of several months would be abortive. Many weeks of living together under cramped and harrowing conditions had grated on the nerves of the American commissioners. John Quincy Adams, like his father, had many virtues, but he was smug, tactless, irritable, and self-righteous. Adams openly showed his disgust at the cards, liquor, and late hours of Henry Clay, and the latter returned the hostility. The two were always bickering, and Albert Gallatin usually had to act as peacemaker. So thorny a dispute finally embittered the two men, however, that it appeared unlikely that even Gallatin's calm persuasiveness could soothe the animus between Clay and Adams.

The British proposal that set off all the fireworks inside the American delegation stipulated that its ships should have free navigation of the Mississippi in return for granting Yankee fishing rights off Newfoundland. To Adams, the staunch New Englander, fishing privileges were paramount, and navigation of the great river a bagatelle in comparison. Clay was perfectly willing to dispense with codfish, but fiercely maintained that shipping on the Mississippi must stay an American monopoly. After acrimonious debate, the course of conciliation narrowly won out when both fishing and inland commerce questions were set aside for future discussion.[3]

The Treaty of Ghent (24 December 1814) was a strange document. It said absolutely nothing about the causes, real or expressed, for which the war had been fought. All territory captured on both sides was returned. Knotty problems such as the Maine boundary, the western frontier between the United States and Canada, fishing rights in Canadian waters, and possible demilitarization of the Great Lakes and the frontier were left for future negotiation. No mention was made of impressment, although the end of the war made it an academic discussion. Rather than the sweeping annexations of Canada and Florida that had been envisioned, Americans rejoiced that the peace came with "Not one inch of territory ceded or lost!" British opinion was divided. Many looked upon Ghent as a surrender to Yankee aggression, but such talk was soon quieted by the news of the crushing defeat suffered by British arms at New Orleans.

POSTWAR SETTLEMENTS

Perhaps more important than the actual treaty itself were two settlements arranged by negotiations within the next three years: the Rush-Bagot Agreement (1817) and the Convention of 1818. In the first the American Secretary of State, Richard Rush, and the British Minister

to the United States, Sir Charles Bagot, arranged that both nations reduce their forces on the Great Lakes, since there was considerable danger of a naval race on the inland waters. Usually this Rush-Bagot Agreement is hailed as demilitarizing the whole Canadian-American border, but real disarmament did not come until after the Civil War. Both sides continued to build fortifications after 1817 and retained naval vessels in dry dock until the 1870s. At least, however, a fortunate precedent had been set.

The Convention of 1818 settled several points of contention between the two nations. The boundary between the United States and Canada was set from the Lake of the Woods in Minnesota west along the present line of the 49th parallel to the "Stony [Rocky] Mountains." Disregarding the claims of both Russia and Spain, Great Britain and the United States agreed to a ten-year joint occupation of Oregon Territory (the present states of Oregon, Washington, and Idaho, parts of Montana and Wyoming, and much of British Columbia). Later this Northwestern agreement was renewed annually until terminated by the United States in 1846. The fishing rights (dating from the Treaty of Paris, 1783, and so stoutly supported by both John and John Quincy Adams), which had been stopped by Great Britain on declaration of war in 1812, were restored, although certain technicalities less favorable to American fishermen were included.

Amazingly enough, the War of 1812 has sometimes been looked upon as a major American victory. Our greatest triumph, New Orleans, fought after hostilities had been concluded by treaty, became in the popular mind the reason for victory. The War of 1812 was at best a draw. Neither in the announced reasons for the war—impressment and interference with neutral rights—nor in the chief underlying cause—territorial aspirations—was satisfactory settlement reached. The cessation of European hostilities took care of the first, and failure in battle removed the other. It is true that this war was the last fought between Great Britain and the United States, but this

[3] Great Britain soon dropped her demand for shipping rights on the Mississippi River. Fishing matters were temporarily settled in the Convention of 1818.

was due to no settlement at the time, either by hostilities or the resultant peace moves. Anglo-American mutual detestation remained virulent and intact during the next half century. Periodic crises regularly disturbed tranquility. To Americans, Englishmen remained the eternal red-coated enemy; and to the British, Americans continued to be bumptious Yankee upstarts who must regularly be threatened with chastisement.

Sometimes the War of 1812 has been called the Second War for American Independence. This viewpoint must be accepted, if at all, with strong reservations. Political ties had been severed between 1776 and 1783, and economic and social bonds remained for many years after 1815. To be sure, there were a few increased manifestations of American nationalism arising from the war. There was some American industrial growth, particularly in cotton textile manufacturing, but so many went bankrupt in the five years following the Peace of Ghent that this growth can be characterized only as premature. Despite some advantages from the contest, the conclusion seems clear: the War of 1812 was futile in origin, meaningless in action, and of doubtful benefit for the United States.

The American Farm

(1815-1860)

RURAL LIFE

The United States during the first half of the nineteenth century remained preeminently a farming country. As late as 1860 nearly four out of five Americans lived in communities numbering less than 2,500. A city like New York, which boasted about 800,000 inhabitants in 1850, was a striking exception to the generally rural aspect of the nation. The great majority of men either were farmers or were engaged in occupations that depended immediately on the patronage of farmers. To be understood in common conversation, one had best talk of the weather, of the price of corn, of the value of the mangel-wurzel, or of the advantages of shorthorn cattle.

The typical farmer remained somewhat more self-sufficient than he desired. He would have been delighted to eat pineapples, oranges, and figs; to buy silk dresses for his wife; and to furnish his children with nice ruled paper for their schoolwork. He had no desire to wear homespun or to read his Bible by the light of a tallow candle. But slow and expensive transportation limited even the most progressive farmer, while the average agriculturist, handicapped by poor education and little travel, re-

mained not only ignorant of new ideas but suspicious of them; quite naturally he continued in the ways to which he had become accustomed as a boy.

The farmer worked hard, as did his wife and children. Diet was limited and unhealthy, emphasizing cornmeal and salt pork as year-round staples; fresh fruit and vegetables were limited to summer enjoyment. Drinking water was frequently contaminated, while flies and other vermin were omnipresent, since screens and insecticides remained in the unknown future. Medical attention was rare, even for major accidents and diseases, and each housewife had her favorite remedies for the more common ills of life. Perhaps a little sage tea or sassafras or pennyroyal was no less effective than the bleeding and purging that would have been used by the doctors, but in any case the morbidity and death rates were high. Later generations that regretted the passing of the good old days when people lived to ripe old ages should have counted the number of tombstones bearing the names of children. The man or woman who lived to enjoy old age was blessed with an almost miraculously strong constitution.

Early in the century the farmer's tools and methods remained largely those of earlier generations. He might well broadcast his seed by hand, cut it with a cradle scythe, flail it with two sticks connected by a strap, and remove the chaff by flapping a sheet; the only new process was the use of the cradle scythe instead of the sickle. Rotation of crops was in many cases practiced only incidentally, as when a farmer had more land than he could work each year and left part of it to lie fallow for pasturage; this pasture land was then put under tillage when the regularly used fields declined in yield. Fertilizer was used rarely—a popular story tells of the farmer who found so much manure collecting around his barn that he moved the barn to a cleaner site. Drainage tile was generally unknown.

The average American farm looked slovenly to the European visitor. The explanations are various. A great deal of land, such as in the Upper South and in New England, had been worn out by improper use. Even the better land was not all cultivated because of a lack of labor; manpower was scarce and expensive, the work of the family being seldom supplemented by more than a "hired hand," who usually was a neighboring farm boy trying to get a start in life. Millions of new and fertile acres in the West always loomed menacingly to the Eastern farmer. Was it profitable to experiment with new crops and methods that might fail? Maybe the right answer was to exhaust the fertility of the land and then move West.

The United States was primarily a grain country, with emphasis on corn and wheat. Corn was the outstanding food for both man and beast. Hog and hominy, both being derivatives of corn, were more usual than ham and eggs. Transformed into liquid dynamite, corn appeared as whisky in the city bar, on the river boat, and in the frontier cabin; in this form corn could be transported most easily and gave the greatest kick for the least money. Wheat was extremely important in the expanding West, but also in certain sections of the East, especially New York and Virginia; the Hessian fly plague of the late eighteenth century had been conquered by the introduction of new

wheat varieties. The great flour-milling centers were Baltimore, Richmond, Rochester, and Oswego, St. Louis gaining prominence in the 1840s; and at these cities model mills started the grain at the top, allowed it to descend by gravity through the milling processes, and finally loaded the finished product at the front door for either domestic or foreign sale.

Hemp was widely grown, although it centered in Kentucky and Tennessee. In time it appeared as cord, rope, and bags; the greatest number of ropewalks, or manufactories, were in the West. Flax was also grown in many areas, since it was vital for the production of the common linsey-woolsey cloth. Production of milk, butter, cheese, and poultry was almost universal throughout the United States, although especially prevalent in New England, which shifted to dairy and poultry farming when faced with Western competition in the great staples. Vegetables were grown by most farmers, although somewhat less in the South and West than in the Northeast. Among the newer vegetables were tomatoes (used largely as garden decorations), rhubarb, turnips, rutabagas, and artichokes, the last three quite sensibly being used primarily for cattle feed. Fruits included all the common varieties, but the average farmer had neither the time nor the knowledge to take proper care of his orchards; rather than market an inferior product, he converted much of it into brandy. Citrus fruits were imported delicacies, and efforts to grow such exotic products as dates, nectarines, and olives were unsuccessful. Wine making, as by Nicholas Longworth near Cincinnati, was said to produce a palatable product.

The greatest mania to overwhelm American farmers periodically was that of silk culture. During the 1830s, for example, successful silk production was reported as far north as Maine, nurseries specialized in mulberry trees, and several agricultural journals were devoted entirely to silk. Here and there appeared a man in a suit made entirely of domestic silk, while two French immigrants gave the House of Representatives a native-silk flag to be draped over the portrait of Lafayette. This particular boom collapsed with the panic of 1837, and mulberry nurseries were almost willing to give away their trees.

THE SOUTHERN FARMER

Various staples such as rice, sugar, tobacco, and cotton were confined largely to the South, although they by no means completely displaced the traditional varied farming. Particularly in the uplands, but also throughout the entire countryside, were small independent farmers who sometimes had one or two slaves to work beside them in the fields and who were much like their Northern counterparts. In the mountainous areas were "poor white trash" or "hillbillies," who to some extent resembled the earliest of frontiersmen with their poverty-stricken cabins and their scraggly fields of potatoes and corn. This group in time formed a reservoir of labor for budding Southern industrialization.

Of the distinctive Southern crops, rice was most usually found in the lowlands of South Carolina and Georgia, but was raised as far west as Louisiana. Sugar production was highly concentrated in Louisiana, and the arduous year-round labor brought great sorrow to the slave who was sold to work on a Louisiana sugar plantation. Tobacco was produced in largest amounts in Virginia, North Carolina, Kentucky, and Tennessee; the importance of Pennsylvania and Connecticut came later. Pipe tobacco was grown largely in Virginia, although Kentucky Burley entered the market by the late 1830s. The omnipresent chewing tobacco that bulged male cheeks was poorer in quality and came largely from Kentucky, although other areas made their contributions. The largest American tobacco market was Richmond, and the largest manufacturing center was Lynchburg.

King of Southern crops was cotton, which had its greatest concentration in the belt from central Georgia to northern Mississippi, although it was grown almost everywhere. Cotton dominated Southern life. Rising cotton prices meant general prosperity, while falling prices brought widespread distress. The great cotton planters tended to rule all of Southern life. They had the wealth and leisure to enter politics and to give direction to social and religious institutions. Immediately related and to some extent dependent groups such as lawyers, merchants, and bankers followed their lead. Poorer whites might at times view them with jealousy and even outright enmity, but their most usual emotions were respect and emulation.

NEGRO SLAVERY

The number of dominant big planters was never large, and in fact the total number of slaveholders was surprisingly small. In 1850 possibly 300,000 Southerners owned one or more slaves, which meant about one white family in four, and some 60 per cent of this number possessed fewer than five slaves apiece. For the small owner the slave was ordinarily a co-worker and at times ate at the same table with the master; obviously the usual descriptions of slave life on a plantation do not apply. Owners of over 500 slaves numbered but eleven in the entire South, while even those who owned 200 or more (254) would have filled no more than a moderate-sized auditorium.

The plantation of fiction approached reality in only a handful of cases. Here and there was the impressive, pillared family mansion, with its high-ceilinged rooms, its gleaming mahogany furniture, its opulent draperies, its deep-piled rugs, its rich silver service, and its large staff of smartly liveried servants to please the whims of a houseful of guests. Such an estate had its rows of slave cabins in the rear, a ginning mill, and other structures that included quarters for a variety of artisans; vegetable gardens for the family and slaves; and hundreds of acres of cotton and corn. But such estates were rare; the more usual establishment was a moderate-sized farm with the same kind of nondescript home that was common for all the United States.

The management of slaves rested basically on the obvious fact that the slave was an expensive piece of property that tended to increase in price as cotton culture expanded. A prime field hand reached about $1,000 in the 1830s and then almost doubled in price in the next generation, while individuals with special skills commanded even more. This valuable property had to be fed, clothed, and housed regardless of its productivity, in bad times as well as good, and in sickness and old age as well as in mature power. The usual owner, with human sympathy buttressed by economic urges, was reasonably careful of his human chattels, even to the extent that he and his wife might personally tend the slaves in sickness. Cases are recorded in which replaceable Irish labor was used for dangerous jobs in which the slaveowner did not want to risk his capital assets.

Care of the slave did not mean that he was cradled in luxury. Negro cabins were almost always small and frequently had dirt floors, no windows, scanty furniture, and only a fireplace for cooking and heating. Less commonly they were larger, better equipped, and either built of brick or whitewashed. Many masters made valiant efforts to keep clean the homes and persons of the slaves, but the inherent difficulty of the situation plus slave inertia tended to foil their efforts. Clothes, frequently made on the plantation, were reduced to a minimum. Food was plentiful, but lacked variety and was ordinarily badly cooked in the individual cabins. Such conditions were probably no worse than those of the poorest industrial and agricultural labor in other parts of the world, with the notable exception of the improbability of personal advancement by the slave.

The work of the slave was also roughly similar to that of agricultural workers elsewhere. The men generally worked in the fields in gangs, often controlled by Negro drivers, from sunrise to sunset. Rewards for good work were found more efficacious than punishment for bad, since a sullen and resentful laboring force is seldom efficient. Sometimes the stint system was used, whereby the slave was set a fixed requirement per day and could use the remaining time as he pleased. Not infrequently the slave was encouraged to have a garden and to sell vegetables and eggs to the master or in town. Holidays brought special rations and presents. Sunday was a day of rest, church facilities being provided for those who cared to use them.

Large numbers of slaves generally required the employment of a white overseer, coming frequently from the small-farmer class. Some of these men undoubtedly were able and kindhearted, but overwhelming evidence insists that they tended to be ignorant, uncouth, and brutal. Their situation was in many ways unsatisfactory, since they could not associate on terms of equality with either their planter employers or with the urban middle class. They were under great pressure to produce profits, and this pressure at times became unreasonable when the owner was not present to view the difficulties. Some of the owners were gone the year round, while many of them deserted Southern summer heat in favor of the more salubrious Northern climate of Saratoga or Newport.

Slavery inevitably implied the buying and selling of human beings as masters died, land wore out, and new areas were opened to cultivation. The business was generally under a cloud, even in the South, although there were exceptions. Selling men, women, and children like cattle was difficult to accept as proper. The more kindhearted masters tried to avoid breaking up families and to ensure that their slaves would not be taken to very bad working conditions; but although the dealers frequently made promises of this sort there was no insurance that the promises would be kept, and a Negro boy from Virginia might find himself taken to a sugar plantation in Louisiana while his sister ended in a New Orleans brothel. The sight of a chained slave coffle making its way overland by foot was not one to cheer the heart.

In general, it is possible to say that the average slave was no worse off than many farm and factory employees elsewhere, but such a statement excludes a considerable number of factors. The opportunity of the Negro to advance was practically nonexistent. Only a few were taught to read and write, and Southern hostility to such instruction increased with the years. Only a few were permitted to learn trades or were given industrial work, even though some owners found profit in renting them out for such purposes. Family life was unsatisfactory. Marriage ceremonies, even when performed, had no legal validity, and many sex relations were quite casual, a mother being often unsure of the paternity of her various children. Some owners frowned upon marriage between slaves on different plantations, and some were quite callous in breaking up families by sale. The children of a female slave were the property of her master, even when they were mulatto. The Southern contention that slavery provided a transition to a superior civilization had little meaning when most of that civilization was not available to the Negro.

The slave was almost completely at the mercy of the master, who frequently was neither kind nor generous. A certain proportion of masters and overseers held that Negroes were childlike and that just as to spare the rod was to spoil the child, so to spare the lash was to spoil the slave. Even worse, there were owners who were psychologically warped and who gloated sadistically at inflicting pain on the people under their control. Certain beatings and mutilations were unjustifiable by any normal human standards, even of that day. Theoretically the slave had legal recourse from such a master, but in practice the courts never decided in his favor. He could not testify against a white man, and the white judge and jury universally sided with the white owner. Even cases of murder and lynching brought no punishment to the whites.

The extent of Negro unhappiness with slavery is impossible to determine, but certainly it existed. A definitely desirable goal was the attaining of freedom, even though the situation of the free Negro in the South was extremely circumscribed. For many years philanthropically minded slaveowners had provided for the freeing of their slaves—upon an owner's death, for example—but increasing public hostility brought laws that made the process more difficult. Evidence of Negro desire for freedom came with their periodic escapes from the plantations, even though many cases implied nothing more than the desire for a vacation or to see a wife and children. Most fearsome to the South, however, was the periodic slave revolt, in which groups of Negroes broke loose to loot and murder before the ringleaders were killed and the others whipped. The white South continually felt that it was living on the top of a smoldering volcano, particularly in the many areas where the whites were outnumbered by their slaves. This fear of slave revolts and of possible black control was one of the prime reasons that the bulk of whites supported slavery and accepted the leadership of the planter aristocracy.

Slavery and the plantation system brought the South a reasonable measure of prosperity in spite of periodic collapses of cotton prices. The failure of the panic of 1857 to strike the South as severely as the North seemed to the Southerner a striking illustration of the virtues of a cotton economy. And yet later observers have raised grave doubts. Slavery necessitated large capital investments in manpower, consequently leaving but small sums available for industrial developments such as railroads and factories; the South always repined bitterly about the draining of its profits to Northern shippers, bankers, and manufacturers. Slavery probably was inefficient as a system of labor, although comparisons are difficult. Indirectly it deterred the poorer Southern whites by demeaning any labor ordinarily performed by Negroes, while immigrants generally avoided the South because of the competition of slave labor.

The profits of the slave-plantation system were highly concentrated, which had both advantages and disadvantages. A small leisured group traveled widely, entertained charmingly, and in general were the cream of Southern society; in fact, a larger proportion of Southern than Northern boys attended college. The smallness of this upper group and the failure of the South to develop urban centers limited the number of such cultural institutions as theaters, museums, and schools. Southern boys frequently went to Northern colleges, and even Southern schools were manned in part by Northerners. Southern writers had to find Northern publishing houses, while Southern artists were dependent on Northern markets.

Slavery was one possible way of handling race relations when one race was in a much lower state of cultural development, and certainly many Negroes were but little removed from the jungle. But while the whites contended that slavery provided an opportunity for the Negro to acquire white civilization, actually such acquisition was limited or made impossible in practice, many whites actually viewing the Negro as a lower order of animal and scarcely human. An extreme of this attitude was represented in the story told of an aristocratic young Southern girl who considered her male Negro bodyguard so little human that she had him sleep in the same room and dressed and undressed in front of him. More generally, slavery tended to produce whites who were intolerant, domineering, and often cruel. Quite possibly the South paid an unduly high price for the luxury of cultured planters sipping their mint juleps on Charleston verandas.

AMERICAN LIVESTOCK

Every American farmer had one or more cows, but usually of uncertain breed, scrawny, muscular, short on milk production, and tough to eat. Some towns such as Cincinnati used them as scavengers, while in much of the West they were belled and allowed to forage for themselves. The big Texas and California herds had little value except for their hides and tallow; the packing of beef was rare, since salted beef was not appetizing. Because of the lack of refrigeration the great bulk of the milk and beefsteak used in the larger towns came from rela-

tively close areas; driving Western herds to the East was a rare occurrence. Most farmers realized the advantages of blooded stock, but had neither the money to buy it nor the time to take care of it. Such breeds as Hereford, Holstein, Guernsey, and Jersey were all well known before 1840, but the greatest popularity went to the Durham Shorthorn; a cow with calf might sell in the 1830s at upward of $2,000, a figure that was of almost astronomical height. American stock improved quite definitely during the first half of the century, a fact that was illustrated by the doubling of the butter production of the average cow.

Sheep were also popular animals in the United States, but not so much for their meat as for their fleece, which was combined with linen to make the linsey-woolsey that clothed such a large proportion of Americans. New England was the great wool-producing area during the 1820s and 1830s, Vermont at one time boasting six times as many sheep as humans. In succeeding years the flocks moved west, where the land was cheaper and the grazing better. The most popular breed of sheep was the Merino, and for a good ram the farmer might pay as much as $1,000. Although many American sheep were unimpressive scrubs, there was coming to be a definite Merino appearance to most flocks.

Oxen, mules, and horses could be seen anywhere in the United States, although the greatest breeding center for both mules and horses was Kentucky. Oxen were favored by many for their strength and endurance; true, they were not speedy, but the driver could be sure that they would take him where he was going and that in extremity he could use them for food. Everywhere from the New England farm to the Western plains, oxen were a common sight. Mules were used extensively for freighting, on the grounds that they had more speed than oxen and more endurance than horses. But the horse was the aristocrat of American livestock. Every American youth envisioned himself as owning the fastest horse of his community, for nothing could be more heart-warming than to take your best girl for a ride and pass everything on the road. Since horses had prestige value as well as economic utility there was no limit to the price that might be paid. Even a well-bred Morgan horse or a sturdy Percheron ran into big money, while the speedy Arabian stock, introduced by Henry Clay, brought even better prices. The ultimate dream was to possess a stable of really fast race horses. Quite surprisingly, however, there were practically no trained veterinarians; each community placed its main reliance on one or more men who had the reputations of being particularly good in the management of horses.

THE CHANGING FARM

The quite evident improvement of American livestock during the early nineteenth century was but one part of a general advance in American farming practices. Such changes did not usually originate, however, with the practical dirt farmer, who had neither time, money, nor background for playing around with new ideas; such a man was likely to greet any innovation with scorn and to adopt it only after much persuasion. Neither did the schools and colleges make any great contribution. About the best they afforded was an infrequent course in agricultural chemistry. A private venture in the teaching of farming occurred at Gardiner, Maine, where the Gardiner Lyceum was chartered in 1822; ten years later it died from financial malnutrition. Not even the government gave much assistance. Now and then the states gave bounties on particular crops or subsidized private agricultural societies. The Federal government started sporadic gifts of free seeds and the collection of statistics in 1839 on the plea of the director of the patent office, but not until 1862 was there even a Bureau of Agriculture.

One great source of agricultural innovations was the gentleman farmer—the man, like Henry Clay, who had leisure, funds, and an inquiring mind; if the new idea failed the innovator did not starve, but merely wrote the experiment off to experience; if the new idea succeeded he was quite properly proud and told others of his achievement. Other supporters of progressive farming were the numerous farm papers; journals like the *American Farmer* and the *Farmer's Register* dingdonged month after month on such matters as the rotation of crops and the use of fertilizer. Sometimes the papers were wrong in their advice, but their over-all effect was undoubtedly good.

The most exciting of the farmers' sources of new ideas was the agricultural fair. The idea of the fair was very ancient, but the more modern American variety traces back to one Elkanah Watson of Massachusetts and his proud display of Merino sheep in 1810. From this beginning came the county and state fairs, frequently subsidized by the various states. The entire farming family looked forward eagerly all year to the great event. For the men, exhibits of cattle, grain, fruits, and farm machinery earned prizes for such excellences as the best pumpkin, the most grain per acre, and the strongest horse. For the women, prizes went to domestic products like jellies, quilts, and examples of hemstitching. Even the most skeptical farmer was bound to be impressed by a cow that produced twice as much milk as his own stock, or by a neighbor's horse that could pull his own completely around the lot. Inevitably he acquired new ideas concerning stockbreeding, crop rotation, and fertilization, while his wife picked up hints on making butter or grape jelly or better cloth. And along with this practical education went considerable amusement—not only the normal gossip, but also food, drink, gambling, horse races, and dramatic performances. Although the farmer frequently was cheated by the "city slicker" at some game of chance, his total receipts of education and amusement more than justified the cost.

Definite improvements in farming were visible by the middle of the century, as in stockbreeding and in new crops, which have already been discussed. But these improvements should not obscure the equally apparent fact that the typical farmer of 1860 was not tremendously in advance of his father and grandfather. Most farmers changed reluctantly, and the total progress was not startling. The usual stock remained scrubby, the usual fruit small and sour, the usual vegetables unprepossessing, and the usual yield per acre low.

Methods of cultivation improved but slowly. Rotation of crops became more common, but many of the more elaborate systems that ingenious men devised were seldom used; much of the West felt no need for rotation, while much of the South found it impractical with slave labor. Deeper plowing was propagandized, and here and there contour plowing slowed the erosion of the soil. A few fields were tiled, and here and there a swamp was drained. Irrigation was almost nonexistent until the Mormons ventured into the poorly watered areas of Utah. Fertilizers were used increasingly, not only manure, but also such materials as lime, gypsum, and marl. Marl (calcareous earth) was the pet idea of Edmund Ruffin, while chemical fertilizers were made known by the writings of the German Von Liebig. By the middle of the century guano (imported bird manure) was being used, and chemical fertilizers were being manufactured.

The most intriguing of the changes was the gradual introduction of machinery, with its obvious advantages where there are large amounts of land and a scarcity of labor. And yet in spite of the conditions favoring machinery, it was not introduced rapidly. Frequently a machine was expensive to buy, difficult to keep in repair, and none too effective at the best. Moreover farmers were conservative by nature and had to be convinced of the value of spending their hard-earned money. Some of the objections may have been a trifle emotional; for example, consider this reaction to an incubator, which was called an "eccaleobion": "This idea of substituting machinery for mothers excites in me some resistance. I should suppose the intelligent hens would get up a protest against being thus thrust aside from the use of creation." But in spite of such objections, the machines marketed by 1860 were impressive in number. They included not only such obvious improvements as mowing machines, rakes, tedders, balers, and fan mills, but even sausage fillers, lactometers, and stump pullers. Many of them were adopted

rather widely, as for example the drill, which almost entirely replaced hand planting.

The most basic of all farm machines was the plow, which historically had been made of wood. A cast-iron plow was marketed before 1800, but it was expensive, and some thought it poisoned the soil. Real popularity for the iron plow came when Jethro Wood in 1819 started the production of a cheap and effective standardized article with interchangeable parts. This plow, however, was ineffective in the deep, sticky mud of the prairies; and by the 1830s an Illinois blacksmith started production of a more effective steel plow, which in time was constructed along self-scouring lines.

The best advertised of all farm machines have been reapers, threshers, and combines. Credit for the first practical reaper goes to Cyrus McCormick, who demonstrated his machine in the Shenandoah Valley in 1830. His great rival in the early years was Obed Hussey of Cincinnati, who invented a reaper independently; Hussey was the first to patent his machine, and for some years was the only commercial producer. McCormick started production in 1840, and in time combined business genius with an able legal staff to blanket the field; his greatest fight came in the 1850s with an Illinois competitor, John H. Manny. The reaper was employed frequently before the Civil War, but its really widespread use developed after 1860. The first threshers were English and did not work very well. American machines appeared by the 1830s and were perfected in the succeeding twenty years, so that by 1860 they were doing the majority of American threshing; generally they included a fan mill run by steam power. The first combine—reaper and thresher—was patented in 1836, but had an unfortunate propensity for breaking down. Not until after the Civil War did the combine attain real importance.

THE DISCONTENTED FARMER

The farmer of the early nineteenth century should theoretically have been happy. He was an independent husbandman of the type eulogized by Jefferson, and his position improved year by year. Practically everyone, but particularly the politician who wanted the farm vote, proclaimed the farmer to be the basis of American civilization and culture. And yet the farmer was troubled. Greater production means lower prices, and the farmer was engaged in a perpetual race to keep his production advancing faster than prices fell. A vast increase in the number of farms (almost 50 per cent between 1850 and 1860) was accompanied by an almost equally great expansion of production, which in turn depressed prices. For example, wheat was generally low in price throughout the decade, except in 1854 when a drought emphasized the effect of the Crimean War; even this shot in the arm lost its effect with the crash of most prices resulting from the panic of 1857.

There were other difficulties for the harassed farmer. More blooded stock and more machinery meant a greater investment, which meant more dependence on market prices and more distress when a depression came. Farms remained fairly isolated. Farm children compared the quiet of their homes with the city's gold and glitter, and large numbers deserted a life that they felt to be stodgy, dull, and uninspiring in favor of urban opportunity. With wealth as the prime American test of success, what farmer could hope to attain the supreme rewards? Who had ever heard of a really rich farmer? He might indeed be the backbone of the country, but who wanted to be a backbone? The dashboard is always more exciting than the chassis.

Thoughtful farmers and their friends worried increasingly about the future. They talked solemnly of the dignity and importance of the agriculturalist, but impressed few besides themselves, while their children continued to leave for the cities. They talked hopefully of a distinctive code of ethics, similar to that of the doctors, but no such code appeared. They succeeded in forming a national society (1841), but their organization soon faded into oblivion, and the later United States Agricultural Society (1852) seemed unable to alleviate farm problems. Hope for a national weather bureau remained abortive. Some help came from the Patent Office, which introduced and distributed seeds, such as imported varieties of wheat, barley, and corn. The National Bureau of Agriculture (later the Department of Agriculture) was founded in 1862. Federal aid to railroad construction was inspired in large part by farmer pressure.

One increasing farm demand was for aid to agricultural education, even though much of the nation, including many farmers, laughed heartily at the idea that farming could be taught from books by professors. Nevertheless, Pennsylvania, Michigan, Maryland, and some other states supported agricultural schools during the 1850s. More important was the request for Federal action. Justin S. Morrill of Vermont was the congressional sponsor for national aid to agricultural education, but his apparent success in 1859 was thwarted by a Buchanan veto. Revived later, the bill was signed by President Lincoln in 1862. Under this Morrill Act each state received 30,000 acres of public domain for each Senator and Representative; the proceeds from the land were to be used to develop colleges of "agriculture and mechanic arts." Some aid went to existing colleges and universities, but in many cases wholly new institutions were created. Much of the assistance was dissipated unprofitably, but the resulting land-grant colleges in time became an exceedingly important part of the farming picture.

Another farming demand was for free land —a demand, incidentally, that appealed much more to Westerners and potential Westerners than to Easterners. During the late 1850s free land was supported by such congressional luminaries as Stephen A. Douglas and Andrew Johnson, but was stymied by President Buchanan's veto. The new Republican party gave the necessary authorization in the Homestead Act (1862), by which a settler on the public domain, having cultivated his claim for five years, could obtain a maximum of 160 acres for no more than a small title-registration fee. The results of the Homestead Act were extremely disappointing. Most public lands were never homesteaded; parts were marketed by way of railroad, swampland, or other grants, while much of the remainder was brought under special legislation to avoid the five-year-residence provision. Many of the homestead claims were obviously fraudulent, being based on token settlement and cultivation, while others apparently were only for speculation; barely a third of the homestead entries during the twenty years after the Act's passage were ever made final. Presumably numerous claimants were interested only in passing their

grants over to cattle companies, timbermen, or later farmers. In fact there came to be a regular market for initial homestead claims.

Despite the somewhat discouraging results of the Morrill and Homestead Acts, to some degree they alerted the American farmer to his political power. They showed that governmental favors might be forthcoming when agricultural pressure became sustained and aggressive. Increasingly after the Civil War, the American farmer turned to the national government for economic relief.

CHAPTER 16

Infant Manufactures

(1815-1860)

INDUSTRIAL GROWTH

The usual goal of the ambitious American of the early nineteenth century, if foreign observers can be trusted, was wealth. Perhaps inevitably in a young nation without hereditary nobility or an important professional army, the greatest prestige went to the man who could afford an impressive mansion, a stable of fast horses, and diamonds for his wife. A Stephen Girard or a John Jacob Astor had attained the peak of success as it was measured by most Americans. With wealth the goal, the means of its acquisition declined in importance, and success veiled such minor peccadilloes as sanded sugar, wooden nutmegs, spavined horses, and the sale of whisky to the Indians. Practically no one ended in jail—or even in disrepute—because his business practices did not conform to the highest ethics.

The path toward the mecca of great wealth was almost never normal farming. The ambitious farm boy tended to leave the farm for the city, with his eye on some such field as speculation, transportation, or merchandising. One of the occupations that caught his eye, and hence attracted some of the outstanding talent of the period, was manufacturing.

The Tariff. At the end of hostilities, infant American manufactures, which had just obtained a good start before the War of 1812, prefigured a splendid future if only a postwar slump could be avoided. Just as at the end of the Revolution, British merchants greeted the reopened American market with vast enthusiasm as an outlet for large stocks that had accumulated during the war. Immediately the United States was flooded with goods of high quality and low price, and American manufacturers howled that they were on the point of bankruptcy. Since the nation retained the patriotic fervor engendered by the war and still felt unkindly toward England, such ardent nationalists as John C. Calhoun and Henry Clay argued vigorously for a tariff to protect American industries. The most vocal opposition came from the shipping interests, as represented by Daniel Webster. The Calhoun group won, and the resulting Tariff of 1816 was designed to protect cotton and woolen textiles and iron products.

The "infant" industries that had received protection in 1816 never seemed to attain maturity, at least in their own eyes, and were soon joined by other hopeful infants. The result was the higher Tariffs of 1824 and 1828,

187

although by this time sectional interests had shifted. Calhoun now represented the Southern farmers in their hostility to any taxes that would raise the cost of what they bought, while Webster had swung over from the New England shipping interests to the support of the manufacturers in their desire for more protection. The West, under the leadership of Henry Clay, talked of an "American system" in which high tariffs would protect American industries as a market for the products of the South and West and also provide funds for internal improvements. Southern protests continued in the succeeding years and brought a moderate decrease in rates in the Tariff of 1832, and then again in 1833, after South Carolina had produced a national crisis by nullification and threatened secession. A slight upward trend in the Tariff of 1842 was reversed by the lower Tariffs of 1846 and 1857, a new period of protection starting in 1861 when the Republican party gained control of the Federal government.

The effect of the tariff on American manufacturing has been a matter of vigorous argument. Favorable opinion has insisted that the tariff permitted the establishment and growth of American industries, with a consequent increase of employment. The opposition has held that the tariff merely subsidized inefficient producers and raised the American price level to the disadvantage of consumers and exporters. Regardless of the virtues of the opposing arguments, the tariff certainly illustrated the lack of any complete subservience to the current doctrine of *laissez faire*. Most theorizers, as well as most businessmen, held that in general the government should stay out of business, but in actual fact most Americans were willing to call upon the government whenever they felt that they could be helped. The government was asked not only to build schools, poorhouses, and insane asylums, but also to furnish postal service, construct roads and canals, improve rivers and harbors, and control steamships—all of which might well have remained private operations. Later generations were to be more ingenious in their

demands for government aid, but Americans have always felt close to their government and willing to call upon it for desired services.

❴ *Currency and Banking.* No function of the government in relation to business was more important than provision for a sound currency. The first monetary act (1792) had provided for the coinage of both gold and silver at a ratio of 15 to 1, which meant that the smallest gold coin, a \$5 piece, would weigh one-fifteenth of the silver in five silver dollars. Unfortunately for the government standard, private dealers in the precious metals (such as for the making of jewelry) found gold to be worth a little more than fifteen times its weight in silver, and consequently practically no gold was presented to the Treasury, whereupon Jefferson stopped all gold coinage. Since money was scarce a new ratio of 16 to 1 was adopted in 1834, with the hope of obtaining gold to coin. This aim was achieved, but now the undervalued silver disappeared as money, so that the final result was no particular improvement.

Metal coins were supplemented by paper money, which was usually the promise of private banks to pay gold and silver on demand, and which in ordinary times could be issued in amounts considerably larger than the bullion reserve since most people would not present them for payment. These private banks were subject to varying and usually inadequate state supervision. The Suffolk system in Boston, whereby several banks joined together for mutual protection, was a rare exception. In addition, some states went into the banking business themselves with dissimilar results. The multiplicity of banks issuing paper money brought vast confusion. The notes of a sound bank might be accepted at face value near home, but were discounted at more remote places, while the issues of shakier banks obviously fluctuated even more. Further complications came with the appearance of many counterfeit notes. Each merchant needed a special magazine to help him to identify good money, while others made paper monetary speculation their lifework.

These state banks had come about largely as a reaction against two Banks of the United States, which had been chartered by the national government for twenty years, the first from 1791 to 1811 and the second from 1816 to 1836. Periodically the Bank of the United States would collect some notes of a smaller bank and present them for redemption; and if the latter could not redeem, it was forced out of business. Such threats tended to force smaller banks to keep their note issues somewhere within reason. The Banks of the United States tended to be a force for sound financial policies, but the farmers, relatively more numerous in the South and West, groaned bitterly; they wanted more money in circulation, realizing that new issues would bring about an inflationary rise in prices, from which they would benefit both as producers and as debtors. Their point of view led them to support Andrew Jackson in his successful fight against the second Bank.

During the 1850s the number of state and private banks increased fearsomely. Some were poorly supervised, and others, particularly those which were not incorporated, were inefficiently and even dishonestly run. Among their numerous activities banks sometimes lent funds to brokers anxious to speculate on new stock issues, and this banking practice was one of the causes for the depression that avalanched in 1857. The National Bank Act of 1863, as amended during the next two years, brought some monetary improvement. Paper money of the state-chartered banks was driven from circulation, being replaced by the notes of national banks, the latter chartered and supervised by the Federal government.

⟨ *Raw Materials.* Nationally sponsored tariff and monetary policies were only two factors important in the growth of American manufacturing. The availability of raw materials should be placed even higher on the list. The rich American soil produced immense quantities of grain, meat, leather, wool, linen, flax, and cotton. Tremendous forests, which originally had covered almost the entire area east of the Mississippi, provided buildings, tools, and heat; an America without wood was inconceivable. Minerals existed in great profusion, above all coal and iron, but also lead, copper, gold, and silver.

The development of American coal production did not come until the nineteenth century. Soft coal (bituminous) was widely existent and first used. Hard coal (anthracite) from Pennsylvania came on the market in the 1820s, when a gravity railroad carried it from the Mauch Chunk mines to a branch of the Delaware River, where it was loaded on barges for the Philadelphia and New York markets; the empty coal cars were hauled back up the hill to the mines by mule power. Once under way, the coal industry boomed magnificently. The total production of 50,000 tons mined in 1820 increased to 7 million by 1850 and then again doubled in the next decade. Practically every year from 1830 to 1865 saw more anthracite mined than bituminous, since coal was used but little industrially, even railroad locomotives clinging to wood. For domestic heating anthracite was preferred, although even here the adoption of coal encountered opposition; wood was cheap, while coal was a new problem for the household fireman and was rumored to be dangerous because it devitalized the air.

Iron had been mined widely in colonial days, but now the production areas tended to concentrate in western Kentucky and Tennessee; in the Hudson-Housatonic-Champlain basin; in New Jersey, eastern Pennsylvania, and Maryland; and in the valleys of the Lehigh, Delaware, and Schuylkill Rivers. Among the regions hopeful for the future was western Pennsylvania, and even as early as the 1820s Pittsburgh was said to be characterized by "immense volumes of smoke, and . . . an unusual quantity of cinders and dust" that "are continually falling in showers, to the great terror of strangers, and with manifest injury to the dresses of the ladies." The 1840s saw the discovery of the gargantuan iron deposits around Lake Superior, and these invaluable assets were quickly developed. While both anthracite coal and coke were used for smelting before 1837, charcoal was the usual fuel until well after the middle of the century. The resulting iron was used in hundreds of ways, from railroad rails to machine tools, and from steam locomotives to pins. It was also appreciated as a decorative material, being used for intricately twisted railings and balustrades, ornate tables and lamps, and figures (deer or dog) for the lawn. Steel was too expensive for large-scale use until William Kelly of Kentucky found a new process (1851) that anticipated the later findings of Bessemer in England, but huge production did not come until the introduction of the open-hearth method after the Civil War.

Copper was mined rather widely until vast deposits of almost pure metal were found in the upper peninsula of Michigan during the 1840s; ultimately the Consolidated Calumet & Hecla Company became one of the most prolific American organizations. Later years produced other great copper discoveries farther west, particularly in Idaho, Montana, and Arizona. Lead was largely a Missouri monopoly until the 1820s and 1830s, when the region that included Galena, Illinois, and Mineral Point, Wisconsin, was opened. The native galena (lead sulfite) was extraordinarily rich and easily worked, so that an adventurous miner, burdened with little more than a pick and shovel, might make his fortune. The result was a mining boom that compared favorably with the later California gold rush. A great deal of lead went into pewter ware, of which the American variety was quite soft because sufficient tin was lacking. Even more lead went into shot and bullets; hot lead was poured through a screen at the top of a shot tower and fell into water, after which it was polished into roughly rounded pellets.

American gold production first attained importance in the 1820s with discoveries in Georgia, Alabama, and Mississippi; and one of the results of the ensuing rush was the ejection of the Indians from the area. Later discoveries in California and then in other parts of the West were to have important effects both on population movements and on economic affairs. Silver production was small until the

opening of the rich Nevada mines in the 1850s and then other mines elsewhere in the West. Incidentally, the introduction of electroplating in the 1840s made small amounts of gold and silver cover much larger surfaces than had been possible earlier.

❧ *Other Factors.* Power was another matter of first-rate importance in the development of manufacturing. The prime American source of power until at least the middle of the century was water; leading manufacturing centers such as Lowell, Fall River, and Lawrence were located where water power was easily available. Most widely used before 1840 was the pitchback water wheel, which operated by the weight rather than the force of water; properly constructed it could attain as high as 75 per cent efficiency. The water turbine, which was known before 1800, did not attain popularity until the 1840s. The steam engine (originally developed in England, although an American model constructed by Oliver Evans appeared before 1800) was used ordinarily only when adequate water power was not available, as on steamboats and locomotives; the usual fuel was wood. By the late nineteenth century steam was dominant, but then it had to meet the challenge of the electric motor and the internal-combustion engine.

Other factors of importance in the development of American manufacturing were transportation, a labor force, markets, and technical and managerial skill. The first two will be discussed later. New markets were the product of less farming self-sufficiency and the growth of cities rather than the development of foreign trade. The factor of managerial skill is obviously difficult to estimate accurately, but technical ability and ingenuity were clearly American traits—there are dozens of easily available examples, notably in the fields of textile production, power, and transportation. Eli Whitney visualized the cotton gin and the use of interchangeable parts. Charles Goodyear pursued his enthusiasm for rubber through debtor prison and ultimately discovered the process of vulcanization, which made the modern rubber industry possible. Elias Howe patented his sewing machine in 1846, thus laying the basis for the ready-made clothing industry; a predecessor had refused to market a similar invention for fear of impoverishing tailors and seamstresses, but Howe felt no such reluctance. These developments were typical of "Yankee ingenuity"—a term which was first applied to New England and then to the entire United States.

Manufacturing also needed capital; a sizable factory was considerably more demanding than a small store or shop. To only a limited extent did a man with a small shop reinvest his profits until the enterprise became large. More frequently, factories were established by well-to-do men who had made their money in shipping or merchandising; for example, many of the New England factories came from the shipping profits of Boston and Providence men. Bank loans were a possibility, but the banking capital of the United States was not impressive, the resources of all New York banks in 1833 being estimated at $28 million. Moreover, bankers hated taking unnecessary risks and tended to look askance at any business that was only in the planning stage.

The most promising source of manufacturing capital was the savings of thousands of individuals, each of whom had relatively small funds. The most effective means of collecting these scattered savings was through a corporation, in which ownership was divided into small units and responsibility limited, but in which control remained concentrated. The early use of the corporation in the 1700s was largely in the fields of transportation, banking, and insurance; there was considerable public hostility to "chartered monopolies," but after 1800 an increasing number of manufacturing corporations came into existence, and the same objection was not raised. Individual legislative charters were replaced in the 1850s by charters granted under the authority of general state laws. Even in these early days various corporate abuses existed, like the use of nonvoting stock and the all-too-frequent control by minority interests; but corporations had such evident advantages that their number continued to increase rapidly.

SPECIFIC INDUSTRIES

The most important American manufacture was textiles, particularly the making of cotton cloth, which was consuming half a million bales of cotton a year by the middle of the century. Greatest credit goes to Francis Cabot Lowell, a scion of two of the best-known Boston families and a business genius of varied attainments. Lowell visited English mills and returned to the United States to reproduce and improve their machinery with the aid of a mechanic. He and his friends transferred some of their shipping profits into manufacturing, banking, and transportation, until they had a closely knit economic empire centering at Boston. Massachusetts became the center of the textile industry and had 20 per cent of all American spindles by the 1830s. The city of Lowell became the manufacturing capital of the United States. The unified ownership of numerous mills made possible a rough specialization of product, as at Waltham, Fall River, Lawrence, Lowell, and Chicopee. By 1845 cotton cloth was being made in as many as six colors and was being sold all over the world, including South America and the Far East. American textiles were always under the cloud of the popular impression that English goods were better. British mills encouraged the idea by sometimes labeling their inferior products as American, while American factories did nothing to help themselves when they called their better products imported.

Other textiles were made in much smaller amounts. The production of woolen cloth centered in Connecticut, but a lack of highly skilled labor kept production down; until after the middle of the century most woolen cloth was made at home, better quality goods being imported mainly from England. Linen was another cloth made but little in factories. The small American silk production centered at Paterson, New Jersey. Hemp was turned into rope and bagging at various places. Ingrain carpets became a fairly important American product after the invention by Erastus Bigelow in 1841 of an effective loom. As for the ready-made clothing industry, it was still largely a faint gleam of hope for the future. Except for a few garments made by tailors and seamstresses, particularly in the cities, the American family had mother make its clothes. The hat industry was concentrated chiefly in the three cities of Danbury, Connecticut; Paterson, New Jersey; and Reading, Pennsylvania; the ordinary felt hat was usually made of beaver during the first third of the century, but then rabbit and other furs took precedence.

Shoemaking probably showed the most interesting development of any single industry. Through the eighteenth century shoes were made entirely by individual craftsmen, but early in the nineteenth century there appeared a demand for large numbers of rough and cheap shoes, particularly for the West Indies and for the slave states. The result was a putting-out system that centered in Massachusetts. A merchant collected orders and passed them on, together with the necessary leather, to workmen who labored at home with the help of their wives and children; they paid little attention to size, and there was no distinction between rights and lefts. After the making of the shoes, the merchant packed and shipped them and then collected the payments. This system proved unsatisfactory to the merchants, who suspected that their workers were scamping on the leather and keeping some for themselves. The answer, in the years after 1815, was to have the cutting and the finishing done in a central plant, but to permit the remainder of the job to be done at home— which frequently meant in a small shed attached to the worker's house. The result was still none too good, being a miscellaneous collection of shoes that were dumped into a barrel for delivery. A demand for better shoes inspired manufacturers to complete the entire process in the factory, where expensive machinery was economically possible. Now there were better patterns, a distinction was made between rights and lefts, and each pair of shoes was packed in a separate cardboard container. The modern industry had arrived.

The manufacture of such small metal objects as cutlery, tinware, and buttons centered in Connecticut. As a result the omnipresent peddler of the early nineteenth century was ordinarily stocked—on credit—with "Yankee notions" in Connecticut: tortoise-shell combs, rings, bracelets, thimbles, gold and silver spectacles in shagreen cases, needles with gold and silver eyes, pencil cases, knives, scissors, purses, rouge paper, essences, oils, soap, hair oil, sewing materials, playing cards, picture bricks and puzzles, hats, shoes, clocks, guns, books, matches, suspenders, and even washing machines, spinning wheels, and organs. The peddler put his collection into a pack for his back or horse, or loaded it into a wagon, and started to the back country, particularly of the South and West. Often he was guilty of sharp dealing—selling shoddy jewelry that turned green overnight, wooden nutmegs, soapstone for soap, charcoal for indigo, or clocks that would not run; in his defense it might be remarked that he himself had often been cheated when he bought his stock. His questionable practices brought Yankees into disrepute in the South and West. However, not only did the peddler provide long-desired manufactured articles, but also brought news from the outside world and often furnished the first compliments that the harassed backwoods housewife had heard since her marriage. His advent was ordinarily viewed with pleasure.

Connecticut was also well known for its clocks and guns. Early in the century clocks with wooden works had sold for some $20 to $50, but because of the genius of Seth Thomas and Chauncey Jerome, who used improved machinery to make interchangeable parts, the better brass clock was reduced in price to under $10 by the 1830s, while twenty years later it could be purchased for less than $1. Consequently Connecticut clocks appeared on the mantels of the world. In the realm of small arms, the old muzzle-loading flintlock was clumsy, and even the introduction of the percussion cap in the early 1830s did not produce a utopia for the pistol-wielder. The hope of firing more than one shot without reloading led to various experiments, but several barrels proved cumbersome, while several shots in the same barrel tended to explode simultaneously.

A young and ingenious Connecticut Yankee, Samuel Colt, had the idea of the revolver and whittled a model of it in his spare moments while on a trip to Calcutta. His father advanced money for test models, but they were so poorly made that one exploded and the other would not fire. Father was discouraged, so Samuel tried to collect funds by touring the country as "Doctor" Colt, demonstrating nitrous oxide (laughing gas) and electricity. In 1836 he patented his revolver and started a manufacturing company at Paterson, New Jersey. Sales were negligible. After much lobbying, Colt persuaded the army and navy to test his product, but both organizations decided that the new device was too dangerous. Sam then went to hawking his wares on the streets, but even this drastic action did not prevent bankruptcy. Ultimately a few of his pistols proved so effective in the Mexican War that orders began to pour in, whereupon he was able to establish a Hartford factory that became very successful.

Other American industries were so numerous and varied that they almost defy statement. Several have already been mentioned, such as iron production, tanning, wheat milling, tobacco packing, and sugar refining; there were also distilling, Cincinnati being the great center by 1850, and meat packing, which used even the by-products for such desirables as brushes, candles, soap, and fertilizer. Printing offices existed in most towns; although type continued to be set by hand, the new rotary press, using steam power, increased production mightily. Furniture was largely the domain of the cabinetmaker, but tended to move toward factory production; the use of veneer began shortly after 1815. Shipbuilding was a major industry in certain areas. Wagons, carriages, and coaches were prime necessities. The Concord coach attained a world-wide reputation, while the Studebaker wagon got its start in gold-rush days. Names like Knabe and Chickering were known in the piano field, and Du Pont in powder. Porcelain was almost the monopoly of Trenton, New Jersey. Even the camera industry had its origin after Daguerre's invention of 1839 was carried from France to America, while the founding of the American Watch Company of Waltham, Massachusetts, in 1848 ushered in the American production of fine watches.

The growth of American manufacturing was impressive to the people of the early nineteenth century, even though it was to seem very small to a later generation. Every American was proud of the industrial growth of the nation, and thousands of individuals saw opportunities for personal wealth. Compared to a century later, certain conditions were distinctive. Ready-made clothing was rare. Common foods such as flour and crackers were not packaged and sold under trade names, but were retailed in bulk from barrels. Practically no company prior to the 1840s, except in the patent-medicine field, had really national distribution for its product, primarily because of poor transportation. There was a lack of national advertising, again with the exception of patent medicines, and a store generally listed a few articles, frequently running the same advertisement for months. Trade associations were practically unknown; agreements on prices and conditions of sale were rarities, save on salt and steamship fares. Banks were comparatively few in number and were weak and uninfluential, hence barter was a common process.

Retail selling was much less specialized than it was a generation or two later. Although the larger cities had stores devoted to specific items such as harnesses, hardware, or candy, the usual retailer handled almost everything, and his goods tended to be piled helter-skelter in magnificent disorder. The 1850s saw some improvement in this field. Urban stores became larger and more specialized; Marshall Field and Charles L. Tiffany founded thriving establishments still well known a century later. The greatest retailing prince of the day was Alexander Stewart, who erected on Broadway in 1848 a six-story pile of marble pillars and plate-glass windows that was considered the last word in luxury. Stewart typified to many Americans their country's existing economic opportunities. Starting as a penniless Irish immigrant boy, he was able by 1864 to boast of an annual income of $5 million. Stewart's success was, of course, distinctive, yet it was well merited because he was one of the first merchants to recognize the importance of efficient service and diversity of product in national retailing.

Although private enterprise was the most powerful stimulus to burgeoning manufacturing activity between 1815 and 1860, the Federal government obviously helped. Whenever government and business converged there was real danger of serious fraud and bribery, disclosure of which led to many scandals. When President Buchanan refused to accept railroad passes he was in a definite minority among governmental officials. In contrast, Lincoln accepted and utilized such favors freely, possibly in part because he had been a railroad attorney. Business wanted governmental concessions such as tariffs, franchises, and land grants, while public servants all too frequently were willing to use their official positions for private advantage. Questionable governmental practices were matched by questionable private-business practices—at least according to modern ethical standards. Acuteness in making money was generally admired, and at times sharp business practices verged on the rim of criminality, even from the contemporary standpoint of pre–Civil War America.

The existence of antisocial activities in business should not obscure the very real virtues and accomplishments of the mid-nineteenth-century industrialists. Such names as Cornelius Vanderbilt, Cyrus McCormick, Andrew Carnegie, John D. Rockefeller, Collis Huntington, Matthias Baldwin, and Peter Cooper denote much that is fine as well as much that is unethical. By and large such men were intelligent, hard working, buoyant, optimistic, and shrewd. If they considered business to be a catch-as-catch-can game with rather rough rules, many of them also felt a measure of social responsibility for the wealth they accumulated, and used much of it for socially desirable ends. More important, these men were industrial builders rather than merely speculators. From their work the United States acquired its railroads, its steel mills, its oil re-

fineries, and its myriad other economic assets. The average American tended to share in the riches amassed by their manufactories leaders. The highly individualistic search for wealth produced impressive gains. The United States was giving notice that it was on its way toward becoming the world's richest nation.

AMERICAN LABOR

❰ *Scarcity and Wages.* National economic strength was not the sole contribution of the American entrepreneur—the American wage earner played a commanding role. The rise of manufacturing meant an increase in the number of people working for wages. Nevertheless, at no time before 1860 did industrial labor become a majority of the total working population. The 72 per cent of the gainfully employed occupied in agriculture in 1820 fell to 64 per cent by 1850, but the remaining 36 per cent included large numbers of people who could by no stretch of the imagination be classified as industrial labor. Consequently labor, as we now use the term, had relatively small importance and was in no position to hope for governmental favors.

The central fact about American labor was its relative scarcity. The tremendous farming opportunities afforded by the expanding West meant that few farm sons and daughters were forced by necessity to enter industry. The rapid construction of canals and railroads, and the almost equally rapid growth of manufacturing, meant that in good times labor was in great demand, with the obvious corollary that businessmen were avid for new machinery.

The modern tendency to describe earlier working conditions as almost impossibly bad has been based on an unrealistic comparison with the present. A man can hardly feel himself mistreated if he does not enjoy improvements that do not exist. True, a workman labored from sunrise to sunset, often twelve to fourteen hours or even longer, but that was the usual working day all over the world, in both town and country. True, the factories had little ventilation, poor lighting, and improper sanitation, but they represented the normal conditions of the times and certainly were better than urban home working conditions, as when women made shirts and caps and lace at piece rates. Certain new industrial hazards appeared, like accidents from unprotected machinery and the diseases incident to such working conditions as the dampness and flying lint of the cotton factory, but their number and severity are difficult to compare with the dangers of ordinary farm work. Unemployment was a condition unique to the laborer, but in sickness and old age he had the same protection from families and friends that was customary in the day.

The matter of pay is difficult to state with accuracy. Quite obviously there were vast differences in pay and working conditions. Some employers were very generous, a few considering themselves as fathers of their workers; they gave their employees houses, stores, and parks and guarded their morals. Other employers were hard-boiled, paying as little as possible; for example, a day laborer on the Pennsylvania Canal in 1831 received bed, board, and $10 a month until bad weather arrived, whereupon the $10 was eliminated. Most employers considered their workers to be like any commodity, such as wood or cotton, which was to be bought as cheaply as possible and discarded when not needed. Free competition of this type might benefit the worker during good times, but was desperately harmful in periods of depression, when even the government took no responsibility for the completely down-and-out except to provide almshouses.

Rates of pay must be considered in relation to the living standards and prices of the time. Family incomes must also be taken into consideration, since in many families more than one person worked; and frequently there was additional income from a garden patch, perhaps. Wages should be related to working hours, which declined throughout most of the period. Allowing for such factors and recognizing that city slums grew, the wages of the early nineteenth century started high and improved, in comparison to those in Europe.

Daily unskilled labor at 75 cents to $1 could not be considered extremely low when board was $1.50 a week, and a room was only 50 cents. Visitors commonly noted the good clothes, the glossy hats, the gay watch guards, and the doeskin gloves of American workmen.

These pleasant labor skies darkened during the 1850s. Much of this shadow was probably cast by a gigantic spurt of immigration, originating largely from the British Isles, Germany, and Scandinavia. These newcomers tended to influence labor conditions adversely in the New England textile mills. Native farm girls were being displaced by immigrants, discipline became more severe, and wages sagged. Conditions became even worse when the depression of 1857 caused widening circles of unemployment. Yet despite the pre–Civil War slump, the average American workman was proud of his relative prosperity, his freedom, and his opportunity for advancement.

Several classes of labor were clearly evident. Lowest in the economic and social scale was the Negro slave agricultural worker. Although Negroes were at times used as domestic servants, mill hands, railroad labor, and even skilled artisans, the vast majority was kept at field labor because thereby came more profit for the owners. The Northern farm laborer—white—was scarce and therefore relatively expensive; the average "hired man" hoped in time to have a farm of his own. Also low in the scale were domestic servants, probably not so much because of their pay as because of the implied personal servility, which was considered degrading by the usual American. Negroes and newly arrived Irish furnished the great majority of domestic service, since native-born Americans were too difficult to handle. The story was told that the president of Harvard had a servant who was a major of militia; on muster day the servant sat at the head of the table, with the president on his right, after which he got up and served tea to the president's guests.

Common, unskilled labor generally received about $1 a day, although there were variations. Increasingly this field was dominated by newly arrived Irish, whom you could see anywhere from the Erie Canal in New York to Lake Pontchartrain in Louisiana. Contemporary opinion held them to be noisy, boisterous, and quarrelsome, drinking too much, living in filthy houses or tenements, and engaging in perpetual fighting and rioting. The same description has been given of other immigrant groups that entered industry from a simple, agricultural life and indulged their high spirits and newly acquired wealth in eminently natural ways.

Skilled workmen such as carpenters, cabinet-makers, blacksmiths, and whitesmiths received possibly twice or three times the wages of unskilled labor. Their skills were acquired through apprenticeship, the period of which depended on the trade. This apprenticeship system was being abused by many employers, who took excessive numbers of apprentices to be used mainly as cheap, unskilled labor or else subdivided jobs so that the apprentice never really learned the trade. In time labor obtained control of apprenticeships and went to the opposite extreme by hiring too few apprentices in the expectation of making skilled workmen scarce and expensive. At the end of his apprenticeship a man became a journeyman, with comparatively good pay and the hope of some day becoming a master running his own shop; actually this final step was disappearing, the artisan more frequently becoming a straw boss or foreman in someone else's shop.

The growing factories used both skilled and unskilled labor, with wages similar to those paid for comparable jobs elsewhere. A skilled patternmaker or mechanic would be quite well paid, while the machine tender, who needed but little training, would receive about the going rate for unskilled labor. The usual factory hired but few highly skilled and highly paid men, since after all the great advantage of a factory was the use of specialized machinery that would reduce the total labor bill.

White-collar workers included such people as salesmen, clerks, and bookkeepers, whose jobs were unmechanized, since letters were still written by hand and figures added mentally. Such a job was paid at about the rate for skilled labor. It had the advantage of social prestige, for a bookkeeper was a step up the ladder from the carpenter, even though he might receive the same or less pay. Many an ambitious boy hoped that by working in a countinghouse he would obtain the knowledge and experience to go into business for himself.

(*Women and Children.* During the mid-nineteenth century at least three-quarters of the gainfully employed were men (the 1850 census showed 76 per cent), but the lack of men inspired many employers to look toward women and children with at least half an eye to their lower rates of pay; there are cases on record in which an employer refused to hire a father unless the entire family worked. The use of women in industry did violence to the traditional concept that woman's place is in the home, but the theory had to give way to facts. Many women never got married; in fact, New England always had a surplus of women. Some were spinsters by their own desire, which seemed incredible to many people. Others were spinsters by male preference. Some were widows, for women married younger and lived longer than men. In addition, practically every girl had a free period between school and marriage. Very possibly she wanted to help her parents, or her brothers and sisters, or maybe she just desired a little fling at life and wished to collect a dowry before marriage.

Traditionally, unattached women had become boardinghouse keepers, milliners, seamstresses, laundresses, and scrubwomen and found themselves very badly paid because of excessive competition. A woman doing sewing at home might work sixteen hours a day and earn no more than a dollar or two a week; in thousands of cases the pay was less than 10 cents a day. Under such conditions, mill work offered a splendid opportunity to the woman worker. The agents of the New England textile mills scoured the countryside for available girls, and the girls flocked delightedly to such towns as Lowell, Chicopee, Waltham, and Fall River. By the 1830s New England textile mills employed some 400,000 women, who constituted possibly three-fifths of all cotton-mill operatives and one-third of all working women.

The mill towns were crowded with young, healthy, and attractive girls enjoying the excitement of city life and the companionship of their fellow workers. Most of them were under thirty, with hopes of early marriage. These hopes ordinarily were realized, and the labor turnover was probably between a third and a half each year. Most visitors, particularly male visitors, were impressed by the feminine charm and vivacity of these working girls —by their ringlets, shawls, calico bonnets, and parasols. They were also impressed by their bank accounts, by their heavy attendance at Sunday school and church, and by their cultural activities, which even included a sickly sentimental women's employee magazine, the *Lowell Offering*.

Working hours at the mill ran to as much as fourteen hours in the summer, not counting some tinkering with the clock, and this stint was broken only by two half-hour intervals for meals. The lighting and sanitation were poor; there were no fire escapes, and lint filled the air. The girls lived by necessity in large boardinghouses, and not infrequently six girls would occupy three double beds in a comparatively small room, an arrangement with obvious disadvantages when one of the girls became sick. Food was plentiful but simple. The private as well as the working lives of the girls were controlled narrowly, and in fact the two were interrelated. Strict rules limited leisure activity. A girl might be fired not only for theft or idleness, but also for gambling or keeping late hours, or even for card playing or dancing. And if she were fired she might as well go home, for an efficient black list prevented her from getting work in another mill.

Conditions in the mill towns seemed quite reasonable to the girls who experienced them. The strictly circumscribed behavior was not only normal, but absolutely essential if the average father and mother were to let their daughter work in town. For the farm girl the work seemed easier, the conditions more pleasant, and the hours no longer than she had known at home. Mill discipline tended to be lenient; the girls were allowed to visit back and forth, and even shopping expeditions were permitted during work hours. Superintendents were screened carefully to obtain substantial and honorable married men. Of course there were exceptions, but they were rare. The food was probably as good as at home, and sleeping with five other girls of a comparable age was to be preferred to the responsibility of caring for an equal number of younger sisters of miscellaneous ages. The pay was good—possibly $3 a week in the 1830s, when board and room cost $1.25—although it deteriorated somewhat in the 1840s with the hiring of many newly arrived Irish. High and strict moral standards were generally unobjectionable, and the girl might of her own volition change her clothes after a twelve-hour workday and trip down to town for a dry, two-hour moral discourse to improve her soul. Objections came ordinarily not from the girls themselves, but from men who felt strongly either that the traditional place of women was in the home or, more selfishly, that these girls represented labor competition which would depress the pay of the men.

Children were another source of labor, and the idea came as no shock to most Americans. Children had always worked on the farm, and great numbers of Americans had nodded their heads when Hamilton argued that children employed in manufacturing would learn industry and thrift rather than sloth; "as the twig is bent so is the tree inclined" was the verdict of many. Employers found the theory supported by economic greed, for a child worked the ordinary adult day at a fraction of the wage. In the early 1830s it was estimated that about two-fifths of all employees in Massachusetts factories were under sixteen, although the percentage for the entire United States was much lower. Superficially such labor was very cheap, but actually a boy of eight, for example, might be a luxury at 50 cents a week, depending on his efficiency, his strength, and the rate of his spoilage of material.

With the passage of time more and more people felt that childhood should be a time for education and play, rather than for gainful employment; undoubtedly the concept of labor competition was in the minds of many men who spoke entirely on idealistic grounds. State intervention began with a Massachusetts law of 1836 that prohibited the full-time employment of any child under fifteen who had not attended school for three months during the previous year, and other states soon followed with similar laws. This type of limitation obviously did not affect home employment, such as on a farm, but even more important it was not enforced, so that the results were negligible for many years.

❢ *Unions.* The increasing number of industrial workers, together with the progressive collapse of the apprenticeship system, led to a growth of labor organizations. In one sense this trend indicated a declining belief in American economic opportunity, since a worker who hoped some day to own his own business would not normally work toward a strong union that he expected some day to fight as an employer. The earliest unions—and some had existed before 1800—had been composed ordinarily of skilled workers and devoted largely to social and philanthropic ends. They encouraged technical skill, gave comfort to the sick, and aided orphans and widows; only rarely did they strike for better pay and working conditions. Typically they held meetings and drank toasts such as "Honesty and industry; the only sure foundation for the prosperity of the working man." As the nineteenth century unrolled, the objectives of the unions shifted, but the composition tended to remain the same. Most unions were composed of such skilled artisans as coopers, cordwainers, carpenters, and printers, who could possibly monopolize their respective skills and thus bring real pressure to bear on their employers. They were anxious not only to achieve higher wages and better working conditions, but also to reduce the use of women, children, and apprentices and to retard the increasing mechanization of the day; the hand weavers, for example, realized that unless they decreased the use of machinery run by relatively unskilled women and children, their own economic death warrants had been signed.

The great periods of active and expanding unionization were times of prosperity, when business was humming, interruptions of production would be costly, and labor would be difficult to replace. The first important years of union advance, in modern terms, were the late 1820s and the early 1830s, when possibly 300,000 men and women joined the unions. Most of the organizations were local and unaffiliated groups of single trades, but there were also national unions of single trades, as in printing; city centrals, as in Philadelphia and New York; a union embracing all workers, the New England Association of Farmers, Mechanics and Other Working Men (1831 to 1834); and even a feeble attempt to confederate all American unions in the General Trades' Union (1834). Labor unions collapsed with the panic of 1837, but returned to life with the resurgence of prosperity. By the 1850s there were several strong national trade-unions, as of printers, stonecutters, iron molders, hat finishers, and machinists. In fact, unions were becoming almost respectable.

To be successful, a union had to demonstrate economic power, which in many cases meant winning a strike—or "turnout" as it was called in the early nineteenth century. The most frequent objective of strikes was higher wages, an eternal and inevitable demand of labor. Almost as frequent was the demand for shorter hours, and specifically for the ten-hour day. In some cases wages and hours were one and the same thing, as when carpenters talked of a shorter day and really wanted overtime pay. Workmen argued that they needed time for family life and for civic duties, and that more rest would improve their efficiency. Employers' objections were that shorter hours would permit more vice and dissipation, with a subsequent decrease in work standards. Employers deplored particularly the effect on apprentices of "seducing them from that course of industry and economy of time, to which we are anxious to enure them" and insisted that the ten-hour day was an "evil of foreign growth" to be rejected indignantly by freeborn Americans. Actually the ten-hour day was gradually becoming usual. The Federal government specified it for civilian employees in the early forties, while numerous states established a normal ten-hour day in the late 1840s and the 1850s. Unfortunately, such laws always had loopholes—for example, that a longer day might be used by joint agreement—and actually had but little effect. Other causes for strikes were so varied as to be unclassifiable. Workmen objected to various conditions of work and in a few cases fought for a closed shop; even a jurisdictional strike occurred in the period.

The nature and results of strikes were various. At one extreme would be an orderly and city-wide strike of all skilled workmen for the ten-hour day. At the other extreme would be riots of stevedores or Irish canal labor, who battled with the police and militia for rather vague purposes. Now and then came a strike of girl mill workers, which might mean no more than a parade with flags and speeches, after which the girls returned to work and the ringleaders were fired. Most strikes failed because of the obvious lack of adequate organization and funds, but a smattering succeeded.

Labor organizations ordinarily found the government, with its desire to "preserve order," an obstacle. In particular, the courts long looked at labor unions with a jaundiced eye. Judges of the early nineteenth century had considerable doubts about whether any strike, or even any labor union, might not be inherently illegal under the common-law prohibition of conspiracy or combination in restraint of trade. A series of cases, starting in 1806 and involving particularly the cordwainers, brought a gradual liberalizing of judicial attitudes, even though the immediate effects seemed negligible. Whereas the earlier decisions seemed to make even the formation of a union illegal, the later decisions granted the legality of unions and of their requests for higher wages, but then seemed to outlaw practically any effective action, including the quitting of work in a body and the use of pickets. A decision of the Supreme Court of Massachusetts in 1842 (*Commonwealth v. Hunt*), based on a shoemakers' strike for a closed shop employing only union labor if available, provided a judicial landmark. The court stated specifically that unions and strikes were legal, including the strike for a closed shop, and held that individual acts of violence were not the responsibility of the union. Although all courts did not go this far, the future saw a continual loosening of judicial restrictions on unions.

Court decisions represented the attitudes not only of employers but also of many Americans who felt that unions were unnecessary in a free society and that most labor complaints were unjustified. When labor leaders insisted that their low wages meant poverty and squalor, many Americans were convinced by the argument of the employers that wages really were high. The exact facts are hard to recapture after the passage of more than a century, but certainly the stronger unions were not concerned with the worst trades and employments, such as industrial homework, in which individuals or even entire families ruined their health at starvation wages to produce such goods as men's trousers, caps, lace, and dress trimmings. Some labor theorizers went so far as to contend that all of the value of any product came from the work of labor, and that the capitalist merely sat at home in luxury and idleness while he exploited the real worker. Several efforts to apply this theory in practice included the "time store" in Cincinnati in 1827 of Josiah Warren, a pioneer American anarchist; products were exchanged in the Warren store solely in terms of the amount of labor consumed in the making of each.

Most employers professed to believe that unions were the idea of the least desirable class of workers: "Combinations among journeymen are usually set on foot by the dissolute, improvident, and therefore restless; and in the outset sustained by the second and third rate hands." They argued that prices adjusted themselves to a natural level and that, if a strike for higher wages were won, prices would be forced up; thereupon people would not buy, mills and shops would close, and labor would be made idle. In fact, labor pressures were practically impious: "All combinations to compel others to give a higher price or take a lower one, are not only inexpedient, but at war with the order of things which the Creator has established for the general good, and therefore wicked."

{ *Political Action.* Labor's failure to make rapid progress through direct economic means led some of the more active agitators to turn to politics, particularly in periods of depression when economic weapons were clearly useless. The usual result was a reforming party, which had varied aims designed to attract all the dissatisfied, and which hoped more to attain a balance of power between the major parties than to obtain dominance. Workingmen's parties were established at both Philadelphia and New York in 1828, and then at other places. Several had brief periods of local success, only to find their issues undercut and their leaders discredited; in truth such intellectual doctrinaires as Thomas Skidmore, Robert Dale Owen, and Frances Wright were too far advanced to hold for long the allegiance of the average worker. The actual aims of the parties they sponsored, however, would seem moderate today. These aims included preference for wages in case of bankruptcy; the end of imprisonment for debt; an improved militia system bearing less heavily on the poor man; abolition of lotteries; better courts and simplified laws; smaller bonds for officeholders so that the poor man might qualify; free public education; free land; a lower tariff; and less labor by prisoners, women, and children. Most of these aims actually were being realized in the period.

The labor vote was not impressive, partly because the number of workers was relatively small, but even more because the vote was always split. Many workers wanted no new party since they were enthusiastic over Andrew Jackson and then over Martin Van Buren as he headed the "Locofoco" or radical wing of the Democratic party, while still others continued to vote Whig. As for the leaders, a good many were dissatisfied with slow and prosaic work and floated away into various idealistic groups that supported utopian socialism. The idea of simple communal living and high thinking was tried at Brook Farm and elsewhere, but the results were not encouraging.

The hope for free land was of greater long-run importance to the American workman than idealistic communal societies. The former developed into the agrarianism of George Henry Evans, a New York labor leader, who argued that labor troubles would disappear if the government would offer each workman a Western farm, together with his transportation and the necessary tools. The practical embodiment of Evans's dream was a Homestead Act that was first introduced to Congress in 1845 by Andrew Johnson of Tennessee and then became an important principle of the Free Soil party three years later. In time (1862) the idea was enacted into law, but the results never operated as its sponsors hoped—as an outlet for distressed industrial workers. The best chance for the Eastern artisan was to find a similar occupation in a small but growing Western community. Aid from free land came only indirectly when surplus Eastern rural boys headed toward Western farms rather than to Eastern cities.

Political action by early-nineteenth-century labor was distinctly ineffective. Men of good judgment who were interested in the labor movement drew the seemingly clear moral that strong economic organization and an increased consciousness of unique problems must precede any hope of effective entry into politics. In fact, many years were to elapse before organized labor had any important political influence.

CHAPTER 17

A Shrinking United States

(1815-1860)

THE NEED FOR IMPROVED COMMUNICATIONS AND TRANSPORTATION

Every American, whether merchant or day laborer, peddler or farmer, soldier or missionary, was inspired with the desire for improved communication and transportation. Between 1815 and 1860 a veritable revolution was accomplished in the communication field. The Federal postal service continued to improve; the postage stamp was introduced during the 1840s, rates were cut, and deliveries were speeded by steamships and railroads. Better transportation created increasingly national circulation for weekly newspapers and magazines; ideas could move about more rapidly. By far the most important communicative development during this period was the introduction of the telegraph. The well-known artist Samuel F. B. Morse is given credit for this invention, and he sent his first message between Baltimore and Washington in 1844. With a keen sense of the dramatic, Morse wired, "What hath God wrought?" Telegraph lines soon sprouted all over the East, although a transcontinental system had to await the time of the Civil War. Late in the 1850s Cyrus

W. Field actually put into temporary operation his Atlantic cable. President Buchanan and Queen Victoria were able to exchange underwater telegraphic felicitations in 1858, but the cable broke within a few weeks. Almost instantaneous communication across the ocean was not finally and permanently accomplished until 1867.

In transportation, progress was steady if not so rapid. At the beginning of the period the need for improvement was obvious. The farmer wanted to market his crops and to obtain intensely desired mill products, the manufacturer wanted cheaper raw materials and wider distribution for his goods, the expansionist wanted easier access to new areas, and others had desires that were equally strong. Many of these aspirations were realized before 1860. Whereas the nation at the turn of the nineteenth century was relatively static, many a man spending his life in the region, or even the house, of his birth, a generation later America was on the move. Easterners established new homes in the West, Westerners sought education and economic opportunity in the East, Northerners taught and labored in the South, wealthy Southerners spent their summers at Northern watering places, and if no need for travel existed people moved about just for the pleasure of movement. Even the poorest Americans could afford a Sunday picnic or excursion, while the more prosperous could visit Niagara Falls or even Europe. America was restless, and the typical citizen cast his gaze on greener fields toward the horizon.

OVER THE ROADS

The simplest form of overland travel was by road, but even the best turnpike of that day was far from being the modern superhighway. Most roads were described kindly as being in a "state of nature," which meant that the trees had been cut and the brush removed, but that there was no drainage and no improved roadbed. One typical traveler described his experiences thus: "For two days and two nights was my body exposed to the thumps of this horrid road, and when I got to Pittsburgh (after having broken down *twice*, and got out *three* times during one night and broken down rail fences to pry the coach out of the mud) my body was a perfect *jelly*—without one sound spot upon it, too *tired* to stand, too *sore* to sit." And clearly this road was not the nation's worst, since the worst roads did not permit stage travel.

The usual American road during the first half of the nineteenth century was little more than a series of parallel ruts. In dry weather dust filled the air, and in wet weather the coach sank into the mud to its hubs; the worst bogs were avoided by detours through the fields. If the coach stuck, the male passengers took fence palings or cut saplings and waded in the soupy mire to pry it loose. If it hit a stump and broke a wheel or axle, and repairs were impossible, the passengers invited themselves to the nearest cabin or house while the driver went for help. Bridges were rare. Ferries often necessitated hunting the ferryman, who might be a neighboring farmer. Most streams were forded; when there was danger of the coach tipping or becoming stuck the pas-

sengers sometimes waded, with appealing scenes of gallantry as the men carried the younger, lighter, and prettier of the ladies.

Road building was ordinarily a function of local government, although private chartered companies constructed turnpikes in areas where toll payments promised profits. Road work was the duty of each citizen, but might be commuted into a money payment. Most states gave financial assistance to local communities, and the Federal government entered the picture by building a great National Road to connect East and West. Its eastern terminus was Cumberland, Maryland, from which there were connections to Baltimore and Washington. It was finished across the mountains as far as Wheeling, Virginia (later West Virginia), in 1818 and immediately was crowded with traffic. Plans for its extension called for a road through Columbus, Ohio, and Vandalia, Illinois, to St. Louis, Missouri. The Federal government succeeded only in grading and bridging the route as far as Vandalia. The upkeep of the road proved expensive, and presidential constitutional scruples prevented the collection of tolls, so in the 1830s the National Road was turned over to the states through which it passed.

The National Road, like other improved highways, was crowned and had drainage ditches on both sides. Streams were bridged. The steepest slopes were graded. The roadbed itself was of rock, ranging from a bottom layer of large pieces, broken by hammer, to sand on the top. The theory was that the rock and gravel would be packed into a smooth surface by the traffic. Actually it became extremely rutty almost at once and washed away on the hillsides, so that repairs were soon needed. But in spite of these difficulties, the improved road was greeted by travelers with enthusiasm.

The movement of freight by road was ordinarily the business of a private teamster, although organized companies were in existence. The teamster picked up his wagonload, drove it to its destination, and then hoped for a return load. Travel was only during daylight hours, and the average tavern had a room where teamsters cooked their own food and

ECONOMIC AMERICA,
1815-1860

- - - - Roads
········· Canals (only some of
main canals included)

rolled up in their own blankets. Failing to find a tavern, the teamster merely camped. Such transportation was slow and expensive, which made it practical only for fairly valuable articles that neither spoiled nor changed rapidly in price.

Travelers might use their own horses and carriages, but generally preferred coaches. Most coaches were operated by large companies, since the necessary equipment and livestock were too expensive for the individual. On a main road the traveler might prosecute his journey day and night, but the physical trials were so great that most people stopped overnight at the frequent inns, which meant late to bed and early to rise. With certain pleasant

exceptions the inns were crowded and uncomfortable. Every bed was filled to capacity, vermin were omnipresent, and bathing facilities were extremely limited. When the beds were filled the overflow slept on the floor. The one saving grace was the cheerful warmth of the bar, which usually occupied the best room of the house, and in which the traveler could fortify himself against the discomforts of his sleeping accommodations. Incidentally, the landlord of the inn usually acted as agent for the stage company to collect fares.

The usual stagecoach was one of the famous Concord coaches, built at Concord, New Hampshire, and was to be seen all over the country from New Jersey to the Western plains. The Concord coach was sturdily built and elaborately decorated, which meant that it was expensive. The body contained three seats, the front one facing the rear, and the middle one having a strap for a back rest. The normal complement of nine passengers might be increased by crowding or by sending some up front to the high driver's box. The leather straps used for springs had limited resiliency, while the leather curtains excluded only a portion of any bad weather. Baggage was tied to the top of the coach and not infrequently was lost. Mail and small parcels were put into the "boot" (compartment) at the back. Early in the century the cost of mail had been paid by the recipient, but gradually a system of prepayment was installed; the first regular government postage stamp was issued in the mid-forties. Too heavy a load of mail was sometimes lightened by jettisoning part of it in a vacant field.

The stage driver, in control of the top speed of the day, was the idol of all small boys along the road. It was said that he never accepted a tip and never refused a drink. He delighted in startling his passengers by racing the horses on dangerous portions of the road; and upon arriving in town he made the most of his glory by whipping up his horses and then reining them in fast, so that the coach slid to a stop with squealing of brakes and tooting of horn, enveloped in a cloud of dust. The close confines of a coach frequently produced a sense of good fellowship, particularly after a convivial dinner including much whisky. Less enjoyable were the breakdowns, particularly when—as not infrequently—the coach overturned with tremendous noise and confusion.

Efforts to improve the stagecoach, particularly by adding steam power, were not successful. The machinery broke down frequently on the rough roads, and the problem of finding room for both fuel and passengers seemed insoluble. Unsuccessful efforts were made to utilize sails, and a few people talked of air travel, by which they meant balloons with steam engines, a speculation little short of fantastic.

ACROSS THE OCEAN

Because of the slowness and difficulty of land travel people used water whenever possible— ocean, lakes, and rivers. For oceanic travel, the first half of the nineteenth century remained the day of the sailing ship. As the century became older the shipping of most seaports declined relatively in favor of New York, which became dominant. But New England continued to build a large proportion of American ships, which were then manned by men named Obadiah, Job, and Ezra who hailed from such towns as Truro, Harwich, and Hyannis. Their crews contained many a New England boy who wanted a trip or two to the far places of the world before he settled down to more prosaic farming. New Englanders manned the fishing boats and the whalers, as well as the cargo and passenger ships. They developed the clipper ship—in relation to speed, the finest cargo carrier of them all—which dominated the seas during the 1840s and 1850s.

(*Foreign Trade.* The total foreign trade of the United States, carried largely by American ships, rose very moderately in view of the general expansion of American business. During the early part of the period restrictions were placed on British vessels coming from colonial ports closed to American ships, but with the commercial treaty of 1830 British ports were opened equally to American ships and vice versa. Similar treaties followed with other nations, including the South American countries, which had recently won their freedom from the Spanish Empire. In all but twelve of the years between 1800 and 1850 American imports exceeded exports in value, a situation commonly called an adverse balance of trade. Accounts were evened by the rapidly expanding output of American gold mines, by shipping services performed by Americans, and by increasing loans from Europe, which were partly direct investments in the United States and partly the financing of international trade. Trade finance continued to center in London, since Britain remained the world's prime manufacturing and trading nation. Hence America had to follow overseas leadership to some degree. Britain's free-trade policy was reflected timidly in the American Walker Tariff (1846), and trade between the two nations boomed during the 1850s. In spite of the depression of 1857, American foreign commerce in 1860 was twice that of a decade before.

The nature of American foreign trade demonstrated the relative backwardness of the United States. The main exports were raw materials and food products: cotton, which dominated the world market and accounted for over half of our exports by 1860; tobacco; wheat and flour; sperm oil; cod and mackerel; pork, bacon, and lard; lumber; and naval stores. The exported manufactured articles were chiefly small specialties such as soap, snuff, and nails. Cotton cloth was sent abroad in considerable amounts, mainly to the other Americas, but we continued to import more than we exported. Imports consisted largely of manufactured articles such as cotton, woolen, silk, and linen textiles; iron products, particularly cutlery and rolled bar iron; and china and earthenware. The United States also imported considerable amounts of food, although chiefly things that were not grown at home. Included were currants from the Adriatic; raisins from Spain; nuts from Sicily; figs from Asia Minor; and spices such as cloves, black pepper, cassia, and ginger from the Far East. Tea was consumed in prodigious quantities until coffee superseded it in popular favor in the 1820s; the ordinary coffee came from Central America and Brazil, but special varieties entered from Arabia and the East Indies. Cocoa, sugar, molasses, indigo, and copper were other commodities imported in considerable amounts. Favored wines came from Europe and northern Africa. Altogether American foreign trade was picturesque and profitable, though not the major element of the American economy.

❨ *Atlantic Shipping.* The heyday of the passenger sailing vessel began with the Black Ball Line in 1816, and its fullest flowering came in the 1830s and early 1840s. These so-called packets were regularly scheduled passenger ships that carried freight only incidentally. Packets on the most important New York–Liverpool run were big ships weighing 1,000 tons or more. They were also fast, making the usual eastbound trip in some twenty days, and the westbound voyage, delayed by the prevailing winds, in some thirty-five. The record was set by Ezra Nye in the *Independence* (1836): fourteen and a half days eastbound and twenty days return. The ships were luxurious, with carved woodwork, deep carpets, gleaming mirrors, and plentiful food. They were also boring, for even twenty days were difficult to fill satisfactorily with conversation, reading, writing, and ship concerts, while adverse winds might cause indefinite delays in which the food ran unpleasantly low.

Just as the packet was attaining its greatest perfection it encountered the competition of the steamship, which developed slowly, since a ship in mid-ocean could hardly be floated to the water's edge for major repairs. For Americans the real beginning of the ocean carriers' steam age was 12 April 1838, when the steamer *Sirius* arrived at New York, to be followed the next day by the *Great Western*. Both ships were given tremendous welcomes, featuring banners, parades, fireworks, speeches, and the inevitable and interminable toasts. Two inventions—only novelties during this particular period—gave slight glimpses of the future. The screw propeller, which had been demonstrated by Oliver Evans shortly after 1800, was first used successfully on the *Vandalia* by the Swedish-born inventor John Ericsson.[1] The other innovation was the iron ship, the first practical example of which was built by G. B. Lamar at Savannah (1834); but wide utilization of metal in shipbuilding had to await the production of cheap steel.

Gradually the number of oceanic steamers increased, and even the Federal government got into the act during the 1850s by subsidizing

[1] Ericsson later became famous for his ironclad *Monitor*.

the Collins Line to compete with Great Britain's famous Cunard Line. Thanks in part to a series of appalling disasters to its ships, the Collins Line soon went bankrupt. Despite this failure, by 1860 steamboats were larger, more stable, more dependable, and somewhat faster than most sailing vessels, but they did not monopolize oceanic sailing for many years.

STEAMBOATS ON EASTERN WATERS

Although steam came slowly to the high seas, it quickly permeated American rivers. Early inventors such as John Fitch and Oliver Evans had built practical steamboats, and Robert Fulton successfully demonstrated his ability to the American people. On 17 August 1807 Fulton got up steam on his *Clermont* and, amidst tremendous clankings of machinery and showers of sparks, chugged his way slowly and majestically up the Hudson River from New York to Albany. The thirty hours necessary for the trip were far short of startling, but at least here was a convincing demonstration that a boat powered by steam could counter a river current.

Robert Fulton was not one of the dreamy-eyed inventors who starve in attics. Joining with Robert R. Livingston he obtained a monopoly of steam navigation on the Hudson from the state of New York and similar rights on the Mississippi from Louisiana, thus clamping a headlock on the most important business of the United States. Since funds of the monopoly were scarce, boats appeared but slowly. The first on Western waters was the *New Orleans* (1811), which was built at Pittsburgh and then steamed down the river to engage in local business near New Orleans. The stranglehold of the monopoly was broken by the Supreme Court in the famous case of *Gibbons v. Ogden* (1824).

The *Gibbons v. Ogden* decision opened the way for a vast, competitive expansion of American steamboating, and very soon every navigable stream had its quota of boats. Most important in the East was the traffic on the Hudson River. Here operated such men as "Commodore" Cornelius Vanderbilt and "Uncle" Daniel Drew. Vanderbilt came from Dutch stock and was strong, shrewd, and hard working; in time he entered the business of the Sound and then undertook ocean carrying, particularly to Central America and the Far West. Drew, who started life as a stock drover, was a sanctimonious, hymn-singing reprobate with a whining voice; tobacco juice dribbled down his chin. Such men as he played rough, not only by price cutting, which at one time reduced the New York–Albany fare to 50 cents, but also by stealing passengers. From time to time the owners combined and supported prices, but such agreements soon collapsed. More than once Drew sold out to such a combination in a sort of blackmail deal and then reentered competition under someone else's name.

Traveling on a Hudson River boat was an exciting adventure. At the dock were vast confusion and excitement, with vendors selling everything from oranges and other food to knickknacks and newspapers; reformers distributed tracts telling how to save the world; porters rushed here and there carrying luggage and escorting passengers; competing agents shouted the virtues of their vessels, each of which, if you believed the speaker, was the fastest and most luxurious, and was scheduled to depart practically at once. The boats themselves were impressive, being usually three-deck affairs possibly 150 to 200 feet long. Once on a boat the passenger was awed by the deep rugs, heavy furniture, gleaming mirrors, silk curtains, and oil paintings. The dining salon often seated as many as 300 people at large and varied meals over which the captain presided. For a night trip before 1840, bunks were slung three tiers high on the wall, the blankets being piled on the floor when not in use; later, staterooms were increasingly common. The passenger could buy books and maps, could obtain liquor and other refreshments in the bar, and could even get shaved so that he would be ready for business when he arrived at Albany.

STEAMBOATS ON WESTERN WATERS

West of the Alleghenies steamboating had un-excelled opportunities in the thousands of miles of the Mississippi-Missouri-Ohio system, other navigable streams, and the Great Lakes. Starting on the rivers with the *New Orleans* and on the lakes with the *Walk-in-the-Water* (1818), the steamboat soon dominated the areas in which it could operate. Almost immediately it eliminated the keelboat, the only previous upriver carrier; somewhat more slowly it replaced the flatboat for downriver business.

The Western boat, as compared with the Eastern, had a high-pressure engine that could produce great power and speed. The result was faster passages and lower fares. Whereas the trip from New Orleans to Louisville had taken over sixteen days in 1818, the better boats of the early 1850s covered the same trip in under six days. The Western boat also had an extremely shallow draft to enable it to navigate the typical Western river—the origin of the idea of the unkeeled boat—but this led to arguments over whether a Western boat needed a heavy dew or could operate on a damp plank. By the 1820s the Western boat had assumed its permanent form, even though later boats were larger, faster, and more luxurious. At water level were the machinery and cargo; the fuel was wood, which necessitated frequent stops; the "deck passengers" helped to load as part of their fare. The second deck, and also the third if there were four in all, was devoted to the passengers—sleeping and dining quarters, which in the early years were combined, a ladies' parlor, and a men's sleeping room and bar. The ladies were placed in the stern of the boat to lessen their danger in the event of an explosion of the boilers, which were forward. The top or hurricane deck, later called "the Texas," held the officers' quarters, the steering apparatus, and possibly additional cargo and deck passengers.

The top officer of the steamboat was the captain, who frequently was at least a part owner; he gave the commands, except that he could not interfere with the pilot when the ship was moving, and presided at meals. His right-hand man was the mate. Vitally important was the pilot, whose skilled knowledge was known to command as much as $1,000 a month. In the day before government markings, the pilot had to know 1,000 miles of river by day and by night, in high water and low, and to be aware of the frequent shifts of the channel. Mark Twain later embedded in American literature his personal experiences as a pilot. Also important was the engineer, but since the job was greasy and generally invisible it held small prestige. The crew was casual labor, frequently poorly paid and badly treated, with inferior living quarters.

Travel on a Western steamboat was in many ways pleasant. The trip was generally smooth and relatively fast. The traveler ate and drank copiously and could while away his time with gossip, reading, writing, singing, or cards, although he might be content to watch the ever-changing scenery along the banks. On the other hand, however, there were certain unpleasant circumstances. Everyone rushed hungrily to meals, ate rapidly (often with their knives), dropped scraps of food sloppily, and ended by industriously employing a tooth-pick (possibly an "Arkansas toothpick," or knife) on their probably poor teeth. The bunks, before the general introduction of state-rooms in the forties, were too small. Washing facilities might be no more than one or two dirty basins filled with river water, and a common towel and comb; one New Englander remarked sarcastically that a common tooth-brush was missing only because Westerners did not brush their teeth. Most male cheeks bulged with cuds of tobacco, and the deck soon became slimy with tobacco juice. Drinking was often excessive, sometimes leading to fights, and every man carried at least a bowie knife. Professional gamblers and pickpockets, sometimes given concessions by the owners, infested most boats. Their favorite gathering place was Natchez-under-the-hill until an irate population expelled them and they moved to Vicksburg. Curiously enough, many travelers were still willing to try their "luck," even though luck tended to be only a very small element in any game operated by a gambler. The preference of many women to stay in the women's cabin is understandable.

Not the least of the unpleasant aspects of steamboating were the many accidents, most frequent in the West, but present everywhere. Snags and sand bars caused much trouble, but usually without serious loss of life; getting stuck on a sand bar was a normal and expected part of steamboating. Fires were extremely possible as sparks from the wood fires showered over a wooden boat with cargo stowed carelessly too near the furnace. Particular danger lay in the fact that the steering was controlled by ropes that sometimes burned and made the beaching of the boat impossible. Outstandingly horrible was the burning on Long Island Sound of the steamer *Lexington* on 13 January 1840. The cotton in the cargo caught fire, the tiller ropes burned, and the passengers chose between perishing in the fire and jumping into the freezing water; of a passenger list of 150 only 4 were saved.

Racing, particularly common in the West, was quite dangerous. Each boat was proud of its speed and hated to be passed by a rival. Added speed was obtained by feeding the fires with lard, turpentine, and other combustibles, while a Negro held down the safety valve. The most famous of all these races was after the Civil War, when in 1870 the *Robert E. Lee* and the *Natchez* plowed up the 1,278 miles from New Orleans to St. Louis in three days, eight hours, and fourteen minutes—over 14 miles an hour, including stops. The *Lee* won, but it had been specially prepared for the race, and the *Natchez* was probably the faster boat under normal conditions. A typical racing accident occurred near Natchez in 1837 when the *Ben Sherrod* caught fire, igniting a cargo containing whisky, brandy, and gunpowder. The horror increased when the pursuing boat failed to stop, but cut right through the people who had jumped into the water. The death toll was 175. Worst of all were the frequent boiler explosions. An outstanding case was that of the new, fast *Moselle*, which had just left the dock

at Cincinnati on 26 April 1838 when all four of her boilers exploded practically simultaneously, killing, scalding, or maiming almost all of the passengers. The boat sank in less than fifteen minutes. Over 200 fatalities led to funerals that closed the entire city of Cincinnati. The greatest steamboat disaster of them all occurred during the spring of 1865, when the luxurious river boat *Sultana*, laden with returning prisoners of war, blew up near Memphis. The incredible total of 1,500 were killed in the explosion and ensuing fire—a total, incidentally, equivalent to that which went down with the *Titanic* in 1912.

Some of these steamer accidents were inevitable on the constantly shifting, sand-bar-clogged inland rivers, but many came from poor navigation or sheer negligence. Certainly avoidable were tying down the safety valve; pouring cold water into hot boilers; and allowing the ship to proceed with old and decrepit boilers, improperly stacked cargo, inadequate life preservers, and drunken officers. After an accident a desultory investigation was ordinarily held but passengers could rarely prove the negligence necessary to collect damages. The owners argued that the traveler should select a safe ship, but the average passenger could recognize the danger only after the disaster, when obviously it was too late. The Federal government felt forced to intervene and passed an inspection act in 1839. Each ship was to be licensed only after its equipment had been inspected for safety; an accident caused by negligence brought criminal as well as civil penalties; steam burns were considered prima-facie evidence of negligence. Enforcement of this act left much to be desired at first, but tended to improve.

For many years the steamboat permitted no rivals in the areas of its operations. The peak of its importance came in the 1850s, when such river towns as St. Louis, New Orleans, and Louisville hummed with business, while captains and pilots strutted their streets and crews roistered in the waterfront cafes, saloons, and houses of prostitution. New Orleans actually had more shipping business than New York during some years of the 1830s; and although it did not maintain the pace, it was still one of the top ports of the United States. The Civil War hurt the steamboat business, and in spite of efforts at revival the steamboat ultimately had to admit its failure in the competitive struggle with the railroad.

CANAL BUILDING

In regions where no navigable rivers existed, there might be a stream which was navigable in part or which at least held water sufficient for an artificial river—a canal. During the 1820s and 1830s the United States went canal-mad, every hamlet projecting a spider web of lines with itself as the center; every tavern loafer was able to speak knowingly on such erudite topics as water levels and hydraulic locks. At least 10,000 miles of canals were projected before 1830 and many more later, with talk of a grand canal all the way across the continent. Such excesses are today amusing, but the desire for improved transportation was highly intelligent. Very impressive was the common contention that the horsepower needed to haul a 1-ton load 12 miles a day on an ordinary road could haul 100 times that much twice as far on a canal. Every man, woman, and child in the United States, producer or consumer, expected to benefit by the faster and cheaper movement of persons and things.

The idea of canals was by no means new, even in the United States, but the real start of the canal age came with the building of the Erie Canal, an impressive act of faith by the state of New York, and particularly by its Governor, De Witt Clinton. As a construction project it was at least an early-nineteenth-century equivalent of such later accomplishments as the Panama Canal and Boulder Dam. The first dirt was thrown in central New York at the little village of Rome on 4 July 1817. While the eastern terminus was to be the sizable community of Albany, the western end was the small town of Buffalo, without even a very good harbor; and between these points

lay 363 miles of varying degrees of wilderness. Labor was scarce, leading to heavy dependence on Irishmen who lived and worked under bad conditions. Yankee ingenuity replaced missing labor by special machines to pull down trees, remove stumps, and cut brush and roots. By October, 1825, the opening ceremonies could be held, and a fleet sailed from Buffalo to New York, which was properly decorated for the estimated 30,000 visitors. The impressive inaugural ceremonies were climaxed by the emptying of a keg of Lake Erie water into the Atlantic Ocean, thus symbolizing the wedding of the two bodies of water.

The Erie Canal was not particularly impressive in appearance. Little more than a big ditch, 40 feet wide at the top, 28 feet at the bottom, and 4 feet deep, its cost was around $8 million. And yet the effects of the canal, together with its branches, were almost incalculably great. The cost of the shipment of goods from the Ohio Valley was cut in half and the time by a third. Boats were crowded with travelers, including immigrants, and farm products. New cities grew lustily along the canal. New York City reinforced its position as America's top city.

Canal enthusiasm increased markedly with the completion of the Erie Canal. Of the completed projects several types can be distinguished. Many were short projects designed to avoid river obstructions, and such improvements could be observed from the Saco to the Tennessee. Of outstanding importance were the waterways around the falls of the Ohio River at Louisville (1828), around the falls of the Niagara River (1833), and at Sault Ste. Marie (1855); ordinarily the hotelkeepers, hack drivers, and teamsters of these places were the chief opposition. In many cases the canals were combined with dams and slack-water navigation. Examples were the improvements along the Susquehanna as far north as New York State and similar projects along the Connecticut that permitted navigation as far north as Wells River, Vermont.

A second type of project connected waters that already carried much traffic, such as the Hudson and Delaware, the Schuylkill and Susquehanna, and the Delaware and Susquehanna. The first and last of these produced an inland all-water route from New York to Washington. Most spectacular were the Western canals built to connect the Great Lakes with the Ohio-Mississippi system. Completed between 1830 and 1850 were a Scioto-Muskingum route connecting Portsmouth and Cleveland, a Miami-Maumee route connecting Cincinnati and Toledo, a Wabash-Maumee route connecting Lafayette and Toledo, a Chicago River–Illinois River route that produced the city of Chicago, and a short link at Portage, Wisconsin, to connect the Fox and Wisconsin Rivers. These were magnificent projects in view of the sparse population and little wealth. Indiana alone pledged about a tenth of the entire value of her property to build the Wabash Canal.

A third type of project was designed to connect the various seaboard cities with the Ohio Valley. The merchants of every city from Portland, Maine, to Savannah, Georgia, worried about the dire results—to them—of the construction of the Erie Canal. They dreamed of dozens of more or less fantastic projects to advance their interests, although few even approached success. Both New England and Southern cities found the mountains unsurmountable. Only Philadelphia and Baltimore made significant starts toward real competition with the Erie.

The most elaborate and intriguing of the mountain-crossing projects was the Pennsylvania system, opened in 1834 to connect Philadelphia and Pittsburgh, and then expanded to include branches to Lake Erie and up the Susquehanna. The effort was magnificent, but so costly that the state went bankrupt and defaulted its bond interest for some years after the panic of 1837. The main line of the Pennsylvania system was a most ingenious combination of the latest transportational gadgets. From Philadelphia to Columbia on the Susquehanna was a railroad; the steep grades at each end were conquered by stationary engines that used ropes to raise and lower the cars. From Columbia the route used canal boats along the Susquehanna and Juniata Rivers to the mountains at Hollidaysburg. Between Hollidaysburg and Johnstown were ten inclined planes over the mountains, with additional railroads on the relatively level stretches between the mountains. The ropes that hauled the cars up and down the mountains seemed pretty thin threads of safety to most travelers. From Johnstown to Pittsburgh there was more canal, but the rugged countryside necessitated many impressive aqueducts and tunnels. The route was attractive to travelers seeking novelty, but economically proved slow and costly. Freight and passenger charges were lowered but little. Travelers took five days for the 400 miles, while freight took twice as long. Even the use of sectional canal boats, of which each section could be loaded on a railroad car, helped but little. Ambitious Philadelphia merchants still ground their teeth as they looked toward the north.

Baltimore merchants were as worried as those of Philadelphia, since they realized that the National Road could hardly compete effectively with a good canal. The project finally supported by Baltimore was the Chesapeake and Ohio Canal, which was started with great fanfare on 4 July 1828 by President Adams, who threw the first shovelful of dirt in the presence of some of the Cabinet and most of the diplomatic corps. But troubles harassed the venture. Money came slowly, and only 80 miles of the canal were completed by 1840; Cumberland was reached ten years later, but there the whole venture stopped permanently, with the mountains still ahead. Just as important to Baltimore, the eastern end of the canal followed the Potomac, which meant that Baltimore was only on a branch. Soon the city cooled toward the canal and embraced a much more novel project: a railroad. On the same day that the President was starting the Chesapeake and Ohio Canal, Charles Carroll, the last surviving signer of the Declaration of Independence, was throwing the first dirt for the Baltimore and Ohio Railroad.

The usual canal traffic of the period can be typified by that of the Erie Canal. Freight carriers might be owned either by individuals or companies; they took business as it was offered and tied up at night. Passenger carriers were always company-owned, since more equipment, including changes of horses, was needed for a long, continuous trip. The crews were rough, rowdy, and boisterous, roistering in all the cheap saloons of the canal towns. Regular pitched battles were fought between rival crews to decide, for example, which boat should first use a set of locks.

Canal traffic was above all leisurely, being geared to the walking speed of a horse. In pleasant weather the passenger sat on deck viewing the scenery, reading, writing, chatting, or dozing. His main hazard was the low bridges that might floor him if he stood up at the wrong time. Bad weather brought less pleasure, when upward of 100 passengers were crowded into a boat that seldom measured more than 60 to 70 feet long and 15 feet wide. The passengers might play backgammon or chess, or engage in political disputes. Usually a flute or violin could be produced to lead group singing. Often a minister would seize the opportunity of a captive audience to deliver a sermon. But predominantly the cabin was hot and stuffy, even if one were not bothered by the sprinkling of profanity and tobacco juice.

The average boat had only one general cabin, although there were also quarters for the crew and a galley. At night a curtain separated the ladies from the gentlemen. The berths were hung, three high, from hooks in the walls and apparently had normally the dimensions of 5½ by 2 feet, which must have posed a real problem for a large man. The inadequate and dirty bedclothes were piled in a corner during the day, and at night each man grabbed for himself. When there were more passengers than berths the men drew lots, the unlucky ones ending on the tables or floor. The tables were trestle affairs that were used mainly for meals, at which the captain presided. These accommodations on a fast packet boat, which might average up to 5 miles an hour day and night, cost usually 5 cents a mile, including food. The line boat, carrying both passengers and freight, charged only half as much, while the passenger who furnished his own food could bring his rate down to 1 cent a mile. In

view of prevailing price levels, these prices were not low.

The importance of canals was brief, and before many years people felt surprise at the number of inland towns with "lock" or "port" as part of their names. For much of the country canals were idle during freezing weather. They were located where nature provided water rather than where man wished. They were slower for passengers than stagecoaches, and not enough faster for freight than wagons to permit the shipment of perishables. They could not, of course, compete with rivers when such were available, but what is more important, they were soon not even able to compete effectively with the newest transportational innovation: the railroad.

THE RISE OF THE RAILROAD

The arrival of the railroad took place in the prosperous years before the panic of 1837, at which time the main mechanical problems were overcome, so that with the return of prosperity in the late forties and early fifties railroad expansion came to be awe-inspiring. The earliest railroads were planned only as improved turnpikes, on which horses could pull heavier loads for the same reason that a man can push a wheelbarrow more easily if the wheel rolls over a few boards. Each traveler or farmer or merchant could use his own equipment and pay toll. All the roads would be double-tracked to permit traffic in both directions. This concept was early abandoned as impractical. The first railroads were also conceived only as supplements to water, and not as rivals. They were designed for places where there was no river and where a canal was not feasible. To some extent they might be used when water routes were frozen, or for the amusement of adventurous travelers. Quite typically, the idea of building from New York to Albany or from New York along the Sound toward Boston was not entertained seriously in the early years.

Pioneer railroad lines can be divided into

three general groups. First were the connections between the larger cities, such as between New York and Philadelphia or between Philadelphia and Baltimore. Second were the roads that spread out from a large city like the spokes of a wheel to attract the trade of the back country; a good example was the Boston network. Most impressive, however, were the longer roads by which Eastern cities hoped to tap the business of the growing West, and here Eastern enthusiasm tended to vary inversely with the excellence of canal connections. Boston was particularly hopeful and by 1841 had pushed a railroad to the Hudson opposite Albany. To the sorrow of Boston merchants even the completion of a bridge across the river did not attract great traffic, which persisted stubbornly in going to New York. New York felt somewhat less enthusiasm, but by 1842 a traveler of persistence could ride from Albany to Buffalo by rail, using seven independent lines that made no effort to adjust to each other's track width or train schedules. Of course there was no rail connection between Albany and New York; how could one compete with the Hudson River? As for Pennsylvania, it had been ruined by its canal enthusiasm, so not until the mid-forties did the Pennsylvania Railroad take over the defunct canal enterprise, and not until 1852 could Pittsburgh business move by rail to Philadelphia. Baltimore was extremely enthusiastic about railroads and succeeded in opening the first standard commercial road in 1829, when the Baltimore and Ohio started running excursions a few miles into the country; by 1840 the road had only reached Harpers Ferry. Richmond dreamed, but conquest of the mountains seemed far distant in 1837. Charleston, although it did not succeed in making Western connections, did build the longest American railroad of its day when in 1833 it opened the 136 miles of the South Carolina Railroad to Hamburg, where it hoped to intercept and divert at least part of the traffic usually passing down the Savannah River to Savannah.

The idea of the railroad came from Europe, but Europe had much less difficult and complex problems than America. The United States was a vast country with relatively small amounts of business. The equivalent of a railroad between Albany and Buffalo was difficult to find in contemporary Europe. Moreover, capital was lacking in the United States. Although thousands of people would sign the stock books, most of them failed to make good when assessments were made. The result was that the railroads turned to Federal, state, and local governments for aid in stock subscriptions, land grants, and other favors. Many a town showed considerable foresight by luring a railroad with land for its station and yards.

Technical railroad problems were at first baffling to American amateurs. The story is told that when a Baltimore convention considered the possibility of a railroad, it first authorized such a road and then voted to send a man to Europe to discover the nature of a railroad. Even simple matters like maximum curves and grades, or whether the flanges should be on the inside or the outside of the wheels, produced reams of mathematical computations. Track was a matter for experimentation. Tracks generally were parallel pits filled with crushed rock, on which were placed sleepers and rails. Some builders favored permanence and spiked the rails directly to granite posts; they attained permanence, but practically shook the traveler's internal organs apart. Others liked resilience, even to the extent of placing the entire road on trestles; in time the resiliency turned into collapse, and the trains plunged to the ground. Wilder ideas, which were not put into practice, included a single overhead track from which cars were to be suspended like saddlebags. Track widths varied from 3 to 6 feet, with no uniformity until well after the middle of the century. Originally the rails were made of wood. Then their life was increased by covering them with iron strips, which sometimes came loose, curled up, and drove through the wooden cars with danger of impaling the passengers. Next came the all-iron rail of various designs and weights. Steel was not used until after the Civil War.

Motive power was also a matter of experiment. Horses were used at first, usually to draw the cars, but sometimes to pull them from in-side on a treadmill. Sails were tried, as were winches worked by horses, dogs, or humans. The first locomotives were only upright engines on flatcars and were very inefficient. The "Tom Thumb" was actually outraced by a horse. The locomotive developed rapidly in both weight and power and by 1840 had most of its permanent characteristics, including a steam whistle and a cowcatcher. The wood used for fuel during the first half of the century threw up vast quantities of sparks, so that a passenger sitting beside an open window spent his time beating out small conflagrations in his clothes. Some of the earlier cars were modeled on the stagecoach, but soon the canal-boat idea of a rectangular box was adopted generally. The cars were of wood, with no vestibules, no mod-ern springs, and hand brakes. Windows were seldom opened because of the sparks and soot. Light came from a single oil lamp, while heat was the product of a stove at the end of the car; nearby passengers roasted and others froze, consoled only by hearing the hiss when the tobacco chewers spit on the stove. Sleeping cars appeared before 1840, equipped with bunks, a basin, and a towel. Train crews wore no uniforms because uniforms were considered servile. Frequent acrimonious disputes oc-curred before it was decided that the conductor and not the engineer had the supreme author-ity. All railroads became post roads for mail service in 1833, even though they were often slower than stages. The small-package busi-ness remained a private enterprise; individuals such as W. F. Harnden (Harnden and Com-pany) and Alvin Adams (Adams and Com-pany) continued to carry packages, at first per-sonally and then by hiring special cars.

Early railroad travel was by no means a pleasant experience, being without even the virtue of great speed. Schedules might specify an average of 15 to 20 miles an hour, but sel-dom were maintained, even when the train started on time and did not break down. Peri-odically the cars or the engine slipped off the tracks and had to be lifted back by the pas-sengers; but a machinery failure, a heavy rain, or even excessive numbers of insects on the rails might produce a permanent stop, and a horseman would have to be sent for help. The lack of a proper signal system (the earliest was semaphore) made the search for a missing train difficult. The fare was ordinarily about 5 cents a mile, which certainly was not cheap. The rumbling, swaying, and jolting of the cars, the reeking fumes, the hiss of escaping steam, the hard seats, the lack of ventilation, and other inconveniences impelled one traveler to report, "My journeys on it were by far the most fatiguing of any I undertook in the country." Beyond these annoyances was the accident risk when trains jumped the tracks, collided with others, caught fire, or hit horses or cows.

⟨[*Railroad Connections to the West.* During the 1850s the greatest railroad projects were those connecting Eastern seaboard cities with the metropolitan centers of the Mississippi Valley. Boston was almost inevitably a loser to New York in this competition. Although a Boston to Albany line was completed in the early 1840s, the Hub continued to remain a pensioner, dependent upon the quite ungen-erous lines that made connections farther west. The component parts of the future New York Central Railroad between Albany and Buffalo were also in existence during the 1840s, but not until 1853 did nine roads merge to form that line. The Hudson River Railroad was opened between New York City and East Albany in 1851, but had no physical connection at Al-bany to the West until after the Civil War. The first complete route to Chicago was opened in 1852 by way of the Michigan Cen-tral, and the Lake Shore was completed two years later.

Provisions for the southern tier of counties in New York State were made through the Erie Railroad, which reached Lake Erie in 1851 and three years later was able to send its traffic into Chicago over the Lake Shore. The Erie was state-subsidized,[2] but its triumphant opening excursion, which was honored by Fill-more and his Cabinet, did not give a true taste

---

[2] The cost of construction was $23,580,000, of which $6,000,000 was furnished by the state as a loan that was later transformed into a gift.

of the future. Poorly built, extravagant, mismanaged, it suffered from a route that offered less business than that of its more northerly rival, and also from its 6-foot gauge, which had been specified so that its traffic could not be siphoned off to the cities farther south.

Pennsylvania had practically bankrupted herself to build her ingenious canal system, which almost immediately had demonstrated its complete inadequacy. The Pennsylvania Railroad meant a reversion to private enterprise, and under the able superintendency of J. Edgar Thomson was built rapidly and cheaply, so that from its very start it could pay dividends. It was opened from Philadelphia to Pittsburgh in 1852. Three years later it took over the old canal system for half its original cost and by 1857 was running its trains into Chicago. Farther south the Baltimore and Ohio opened its line to Wheeling in 1852 and within a few years had reached St. Louis.

Southern railroad construction tended to lag behind that of the North. Quite obvious factors were the lesser amount of capital in the South, its smaller cities, its less diversified business, and its totally smaller traffic. Charleston merchants could claim correctly that they were closer to Cincinnati, Louisville, and St. Louis than was New York, but unfortunately there was no direct link by rail between Charleston and any of those cities. By 1860 only one east-west line had been completed—the Western and Atlantic had reached Memphis in 1857. Coming east from Memphis the line split at Chattanooga, a northern section making connections to Richmond, Portsmouth, Washington, and Baltimore, and a southern branch reaching Charleston and Savannah. The route was not very direct, and the Confederacy was to pay dearly for inadequate railroad connections.

As railroads entered the Middle Western cities, Chicago obviously was becoming the metropolis of the future; and from Chicago roads continued to push westward. The Rock Island was the first line to reach (1854) and to bridge (1855) the Mississippi; but by the opening of the Civil War several railroads were on the Iowa plains, and by 1870 they had

reached and crossed the Missouri. A lacework of rails spread over Iowa, Wisconsin, and Minnesota. In Missouri the Hannibal and St. Joseph was completed from the Mississippi to the great bend of the Missouri in 1859, while the Missouri Pacific finished a parallel road between St. Louis and Kansas City in 1865. Still farther south was the Little Rock and Fort Smith.

TRANSPORTATION AND THE FAR WEST

During the pre–Civil War decade American railroad mileage tripled, but this magnificent expansion was far distant from the Pacific Coast, where many transplanted Easterners were avid for news from home. Improved transportation of passengers and freight was desired by all—of course, they were thinking in terms of roads and not of rails. Regular mail deliveries were a government function, but the money thus acquired might be used as a subsidy for regular passenger service. The first feeble efforts to provide mail for the Far West came in 1851, but service was slow and uncertain, with no provision for passengers. Even the proper route for regular service from the Mississippi to the Pacific was somewhat questionable, particularly since the accepted route might very well in time become the path of a railroad. Earlier explorations were supplemented and made more complete by thorough surveys between 1853 and 1855 under the direction of the Secretary of War, Jefferson Davis. The final report favored the southern route, but there was well-founded suspicion that the Secretary had not read the evidence with a completely open mind.

The first regular mail deliveries to the Pacific Coast were provided by the Butterfield Overland Stage Company, which opened a semiweekly service in 1858; the full trip was limited to not over twenty-five days. From the eastern termini of St. Louis and Memphis the paths converged at Fort Smith, Arkansas, and then proceeded by way of El Paso, Yuma, and

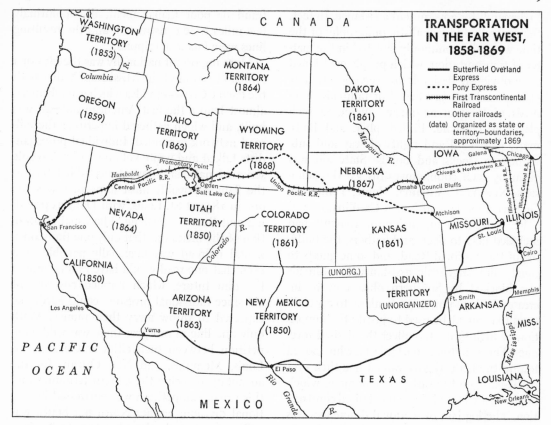

TRANSPORTATION
IN THE FAR WEST,
1858-1869

━━━ Butterfield Overland Express
••••• Pony Express
╫╫╫ First Transcontinental Railroad
┼┼┼┼ Other railroads
(date) Organized as state or territory—boundaries, approximately 1869

Los Angeles to San Francisco, 2,795 miles distant. The undertaking was extremely elaborate, since coaches ran both day and night, which necessitated numerous stations and large reservoirs of men, stock, coaches, food, and equipment. Although a ride on the overland stage was far from a pleasure trip with its jolting, dust, poor food, and lack of elementary sanitary conveniences, at least the time of the trip was cut, and mail was delivered regularly. With the coming of the Civil War the southern route was closed, and Butterfield moved to the central route, from which his stagecoaches were ultimately displaced by the railroad.

Even faster communication came with the Pony Express, which proved more picturesque than permanently important. William H. Russell, of the great freighting firm of Russell, Majors & Waddell, conceived the idea primarily as a means of showing the practicality of the central route and thus attracting a government mail subsidy. Stations were located at 10-mile intervals, and the service was prosecuted by light riders on fast horses. The first riders started their routes in April, 1860, and quite regularly cut the time of Butterfield at least in half; their fastest trip was under eight days. Such service cost $5 a half ounce, compared with the regular postage fee of 3 cents from 1851, and was in reality a telegraph service; its demise was a foregone conclusion when a telegraph line to the Pacific Coast was opened in October, 1861. It demonstrated that the central route could be used the year round; but unfortunately for Russell no mail contract resulted, and the firm of Russell, Majors & Waddell went bankrupt; its assets were acquired in 1862 by Ben Holladay, who in the succeeding years was acknowledged as the stagecoach king of the West.

❐ *The Transcontinental Railroad.* The long-hoped-for building of Western railroads, with their vast distances and inadequate traffic, led to demands for government assistance. In fact, the generally individualistic philosophy of the time was quite commonly violated in the matter of transportation, which people envisioned as so obviously desirable to everyone that any possible aid was justified. For railroads, hundreds of local communities, including such places as Portland, Philadelphia, and Baltimore, gave land and rights of way and subscribed to stocks and bonds. State aid was given by such commonwealths as Massachusetts, New York, Virginia, Maine, Tennessee, Georgia, Florida, and North Carolina.

Federal aid to internal improvements had included help to rivers and harbors, the building of the National Road, and some grants to canals, but large-scale assistance to railroads was blocked by Southern objections to increased Federal power, particularly to expenditures that might be used to justify the imposition of high tariffs to collect the desired revenue. Those railroad enthusiasts who looked toward the Federal government had their eyes particularly on the vast public domain, which might be used to subsidize the desired construction. The log jam of sectional differences was broken in 1850, when Stephen A. Douglas obtained authorization for his Illinois Central Railroad to connect Chicago and New Orleans. Immediately the Illinois Central became America's largest landowner and within six years had sold some 1,300,000 acres at prices of $6 to $25. Possibly more important, the main line of the road was completed by 1860 with the exception of a bridge across the Ohio.

Once the ice was broken, new land grants flowed from the Federal government in an ever-expanding stream. Most important in the fifties were grants to all existing trans-Mississippi states with the exception of Texas, which had retained control of its own public lands and developed its own system of subsidization. These grants were designed to produce state railroad systems, but their effect is doubtful. Several of the states, such as Missouri, Iowa, and California, built a limited number of railroads, but the extent of the encouragement provided by the land grants is questionable. Certainly much of the land was lost through

fraud or poor management, disappointingly few miles were constructed, and the resulting lines were financial cripples.

More important nationally was the idea of a railroad to connect the Mississippi Valley with the Pacific Coast—an idea which was advanced almost before the first American railroad was built, and which gathered impetus as the railroad network expanded. Individual propagandists talked and wrote voluminously. A whole series of national conventions added fuel to the flames; possibly most impressive was the one in 1849 at St. Louis, with Douglas presiding and Benton speaking. The usual assumption of the fifties was that only one transcontinental railroad was financially possible, and even that one road would have profits only in the dim future, which implied government aid since individual investors could hardly be expected to throw away their money. With only one line in prospect there was wild competition between such cities as Chicago, St. Louis, Memphis, and New Orleans for the advantage of being the eastern terminus, and this urban competition was buttressed by sectional division; neither North nor South was willing to concede the advantage to its rival. Even the organization of Western territories necessary for railroad construction required sectional compromises, as in the Kansas-Nebraska Act. Certainly the possibilities of railroad construction were one of the factors that produced governments in all of the Western territories.

Sectional differences prevented any Federal action from favoring a transcontinental road until after Southern secession, and even then the rivalry of Chicago and St. Louis led to the location of the eastern terminus of the line in a relative wilderness, the contrasting pretensions of the two cities being still unresolved. The Union Pacific Act of 1862 actually provided not a single through line, but two connecting roads, the eastern link originating in central Nebraska. The western section was given to the Central Pacific, already in existence in California; the eastern to the new Union Pacific, which technically started on the 100th meridian. Five eastern branches were to spread out like the ribs of a fan, but there was little surprise when the one to Council Bluffs, authorized to be built by the parent company, became part of the main line. The other four were all built on routes differing from those provided by the charter.

Congressional aid to the first transcontinental railroad included the odd-numbered sections of land within ten miles on each side of the road, such building materials as were available on the public domain, and a loan that varied between $16,000 and $48,000 a mile, depending on the nature of the country. Although later critics have contended that the government aid was overly generous, the potential investors of 1862 felt otherwise, with the result that additional bait was offered in 1864—the land grant was doubled and the government loan was reduced to the status of a second mortgage. Even with these concessions construction was slow, and the first 40 miles of the Union Pacific were not accepted by the government until 1866. While war conditions made it difficult to obtain labor and materials, an equally great consideration was the common doubt about whether the venture could show a profit.

The men who built the Union Pacific–Central Pacific were public-spirited but also profit-minded. Their compromise was to charter two construction companies, the Contract and Finance Company for the Central Pacific and the Crédit Mobilier for the Union Pacific. These companies made construction possible by evading the impossible charter provisions that stock must be sold at par and for cash; the construction company bought the stock at par and for cash (check), which immediately was returned to pay the construction contracts; these had been drawn generously enough to take care of the existing market value of the stock. Since profits on the operation of the railroads were extremely dubious, the insiders made their returns on the lucrative construction contracts; the smaller stockholders and the government were the losers. The records of the Contract and Finance Company were providentially destroyed, but those of the Crédit Mobilier became the basis for one of

the most odorous of the post–Civil War scandals.[3]

Construction of the transcontinental Union Pacific–Central Pacific Railroad proceeded rapidly after the Civil War, when additional men, money, and materials became available; particularly rapid progress started in 1867, when the Chicago and Northwestern provided a rail connection to the east. Grading and tracklaying on the Union Pacific were done in 100-mile stretches from east to west, while the Central Pacific started from California. Both railroads employed as laborers many Civil War veterans who were quite competent to seize their guns and deploy into skirmishing lines in case of an Indian attack. The two lines were connected on 10 May 1869 at Promontory Point near Ogden, Utah. A golden spike was driven, engines from both railroads touched noses, and Governor Leland Stanford of California exchanged congratulations with the president of the Union Pacific. The entire ceremony was carried east by telegraph and set off great celebrations in which bells rang and cannon boomed. Decades of aspiration had been climaxed by the spectacular completion of a railroad that made possible all-rail travel from New York to San Francisco. The results, not only in economic terms but also in their effect on the Indians and on white population movements, were bound to be tremendous.

Unfortunately neither the Union Pacific nor the Central Pacific seemed to be able to make money, and thereby came trouble. The Union Pacific was juggled from hand to hand for many years, more for speculation than for efficient operation, and its debt to the government occasioned seemingly endless recriminations. As for the Central Pacific, the original associates sought unsuccessfully for a purchaser and ultimately found their only profits in creating a railroad monopoly in California. Their success was considerable, and the relations between the Central Pacific (later the Southern Pacific) and the California state government came to be one of the less savory episodes in American history. Obviously the connection of government and business provided unpleasant actu-

[3] See pp. 446–447.

alities. The only consolation is the presumption that through Federal aid the first transcontinental railroad was completed perhaps ten years sooner than would have been the case if dependence had been placed entirely on private initiative.

These first great American railroads were in many ways unsatisfactory, but they were greeted with vast popular enthusiasm, which was more credible as a preview of the future than as a commentary on the disappointing present. And the future did not fail their aspirations. When idealists talked of a coast-to-coast railroad during the 1830s, such conversation seemed to contemporaries only slightly less fantastic than a rocket to the moon. In thirty years the dream became reality, and railroads became possibly the most important single factor in creating modern America. Their services in settling the Western plains and in promoting industrialism can hardly be overestimated, while their influence in the outcome of the Civil War was far from negligible. In general, railroads were built by private individuals, with the frequent accompaniment of vast losses due to ignorance, inefficiency, wasteful competition, and downright fraud. Yet out of these confused and often chaotic circumstances somehow emerged the greatest railroad network of the world—a monument to private capitalism working in a relatively unmanaged economy.

CHAPTER 18

Training the New Generation

(1815-1860)

Americans of the first half of the nineteenth century were youthful, boastful, and money-minded, but also highly conscious of their uniqueness and of their high destiny. They felt certain that they had history's finest civilization and they boasted loudly of their presumed superiorities, whether in business or in philosophy, in the arts or in the sciences. Possibly they talked just a shade too loudly, like the small boy trying to conceal a feared inadequacy, but they felt deeply that God had reserved a special providence for Americans. The future was to be the era of American greatness, according to contemporary sources: "All nations are to come under the sway of our principles, but never are they to pass under any yoke." "The day of universal light and liberty is approaching with the certainty of a comet to the sun."

American supremacy rested, according to current ideas, on the twin virtues of democracy and Christianity. Democracy gave to the individual freedom to rule himself and to advance to the limit of his abilities. Christianity—which normally meant Protestantism—was believed to have been directly inspired by God, and to be the source of the highest conceivable morality. The height of the civilization of any other people could be judged by discovering how closely they approached American stand-ards. Every American admitted, of course, that perfection had not as yet been achieved, but most of them felt that its coming was scheduled for the immediate future. Hard work and a few reforms would produce a new Garden of Eden within the generation. Such self-assurance and somewhat bumptious optimism may have sounded naïve and unrealistic to later generations, but they spurred American energy toward accomplishing amazing results.

AMERICAN COURTSHIP

Hope for the future lay above all in the home, where basic moral and religious training for new American citizens was provided. Both boy and girl were given very practical training toward successful marriage. Formal schooling was the smallest part of this background, since book learning other than simple reading, writing, and arithmetic was of limited practical value for the farmer or laborer, or even for the merchant or trader. The average boy expected to become a farmer and learned his trade by practicing it under the eye of his father; no doubt existed that he must be able to build a barn, shoe a horse, and plow a field.

The girl similarly learned housework by helping her mother, so that she early was able to cook, to sew, and to care for small children. Neither boy nor girl had courses in physiology, psychology, or sociology, but life in a large family on a farm stocked with animals had definite educational values. Although current theory held that girls should remain innocent (that is, ignorant) of the "facts of life" before marriage, even though boys sowed their wild oats, actually no farm girl of normal intelligence could have maintained anything like complete ignorance.

Marriage was a pleasant necessity for a boy, but was also a career for a girl. Most of her training, including formal schooling, was directed toward enabling her to catch a husband and to run a home. If she were unmarried by her mid-twenties the rumor circulated that she was a natural spinster, which meant that she had failed in her career. Girls ordinarily married younger than boys, partly because of tradition, but also because the boy either was apprenticed or else owed his services to his father until he came of age. Commonly accepted was the theory of love at first sight between the one boy and the one girl, even though this idea was not taken very seriously by matchmaking friends and relatives. Theoretically the strong, virile man pursued the timid, shrinking woman until he finally overwhelmed her with the ardency of his emotions. Actually the willing girl seldom ran dangerously fast and frequently used all the time-honored feminine wiles to hook her man. Moralists held that courtship should be on a high plane, consisting of long, earnest conversations, particularly on the future of the young couple's souls and on the establishment of a Christian home, with possibly the treasuring of a scented glove or tress of hair. Although the theory was by no means always observed, the rereading of old love letters does invoke the atmosphere of a different world. For example, the ardent abolitionist and feminist Angelina Grimké wrote to her dearly beloved and even better-known abolitionist fiancé Theodore Weld: "I laid awake thinking why it was that my heart panted and reached after you as it does. Why

my Saviour and my God is not enough to *satisfy* me. Am I sinning, am I ungrateful, *am I an* IDOLATOR?"

THE HOME

Ultimately the young couple, if the path of true love ran fairly smoothly, was married. The bride usually preferred a large church wedding, if her family could afford it, and sometimes eliminated the word "obey" from the ceremony. Then came a wedding trip if funds permitted—perhaps to Niagara Falls after 1830—whereupon the bride and groom settled in their new home, inviting their friends to call. This new home was almost always a separate house, although now and then it might be a room in a hotel or tenement. Usually it was built of wood, although a few were stone or brick, while experiments with cement were said to be successful. The richer city family lived typically in a long, narrow, and dark home with living quarters on the first floor, bedrooms on the second, and servants' quarters on the third; Philadelphia houses varied by having the kitchen in the basement, which was really a half story. At the other end of the city scale was the ramshackle and dangerous tenement, unlimited by building restrictions and poorly protected against fire. Farmhouses might vary from the impressive mansion of the Hudson River Valley and the South to the distinctive Western log cabin; usually it was a somewhat nondescript affair, comfortable but not impressive.

Almost all homes lacked the so-called modern conveniences. Heating was traditionally supplied by a fireplace with a reflecting screen to thaw the frost on your back. The Franklin stove was an improvement, even though it did not obviate the need for heavy, long winter underwear. The earliest central heating was a basement fireplace with flues to the various rooms; its maximum success was to avoid freezing the occupants. By 1850 there was a practical furnace, available only to the rich experimenter. Wood was the usual fuel, but coal was increasingly accepted. The water supply for most Americans came from wells, frequently polluted. Philadelphia had the first city water system, and visitors were properly impressed to see housewives with leather hoses washing off their front pavements. The Croton project of New York City came into use in 1842, and other cities followed. Ordinarily untreated river or lake water was pumped through a city system; it contained not only visible impurities, which caused a Chicago visitor to talk about "chowder in his bathtub," but also invisible contamination. Lack of water together with cold houses led many people to restrict their bathing to the warm weather, and consequently a trip in a coach or on a canal boat was a depressing olfactory experience.

Provision for sewage disposal was never adequate. Most houses had outdoor toilets, but even with inside plumbing the absence of a trap and the emptying of sewage into a neighboring stream, frequently near the water supply, was far from healthful. Garbage was seldom collected regularly, but rather was thrown into the streets to be picked over by dogs, cats, hogs, and cows. A user of the streets might wade through manure and garbage, now and then stepping on a dead rat or a sleeping pig. Philadelphia was one of the few cities that cleaned its streets. For lighting, candles were still common, but most homes could afford at least one whale-oil lamp. Gaslights were possible by the 1830s, appearing first on the streets and in theaters and museums. Gradually pipes were laid in the residential streets (tanks had been used earlier), but most people found gas too expensive, inconvenient, and smelly. Cooking was still done over a fireplace in the poorer home, but the more opulent house had the advantage of a cookstove. A refrigerator was the result of the local carpenter's concept of proper insulation. Other refinements possible for the rich were as modern as a dishwashing machine.

House decorations were as ornate as the family could afford, since a money-making civilization showed its wealth by display. While the poorer houses had to be content with paint or whitewash on the walls and mod-est furnishing, the better houses emphasized the elaborate. Wall decorations included French wallpaper in gold, silver, velvet, or satin, oil paintings, etchings, and tapestries, while thick carpets from wall to wall, laid on straw and topped with scatter rugs, covered the floors. The rich curtains might be of satin or damask. The furniture, usually of walnut or some other dark wood, was heavy and elaborately carved. The parlor was the showroom of the house, and the ideal was "studied confusion," with a rich display of mirrors, brass clocks, tables, busts, vases, baskets, boxes, pin cushions, cigar stands, and similar treasures.

Although people generally desired a separate home for each family, the poorest families shared their quarters in squalid tenements, while the richer sometimes sought the luxury of large hotels such as the Astor House in New York or the Tremont House in Boston, which were the nearest equivalents of the modern apartment house. The leading hotel of its day was the Tremont House (1829), with magnificent public rooms, marble mosaic floors, deep carpets, rich curtains, and massive furniture. The dining room could seat 200 people simultaneously. Bedrooms totaled 170, including, quite uniquely, several rooms that were designed for single occupancy. Each room boasted a different lock and was provided with a bowl, pitcher, soap, nailbrush, and toothbrush. The hotel was also proud of eight water closets and eight bathrooms with running water. "Rotunda boys," together with a system of bells and speaking tubes, permitted the guest to find his carriage at the door when he came downstairs. Such luxury was, of course, expensive, costing $2 a day including meals. Other hotels were naturally much less sybaritic; the least luxury was to be found in the rural hostelry, which was a converted home in which customers filled the beds in the order of their arrival. A favored sport was to listen to a "curtain lecture" by the wife of the couple in the next bed.

If the family traveled, it could expect both dirt and vermin. Bedclothes, which might not include sheets, were changed infrequently. Very possibly a single tin basin and soiled towel were the only washing facilities. Meal-time found all the food on the table, and every-one grabbed, undeterred by the landlord at the head of the groaning board. Possibly a girl passed tea and coffee. Eating was fast and messy, many diners persistently using their knives instead of their forks; at the end of the meal the table was strewn with discarded frag-ments of food. Every man then used a tooth-pick, which probably was a sliver of wood or a penknife, but which might be a dainty gold-covered quill. Drinking was frequent and heavy. Most popular was whisky, which sold at possibly 25 to 50 cents a gallon, but a gamut of other liquors was available. Reports had it that the South and West achieved a per capita yearly consumption of 5 gallons. Practically everyone drank, and even a minister might now and then take a drop too much. Tobacco was used in all forms, but mostly for chewing. Spitting boxes were scattered here and there, but the average chewer missed them even when he troubled to make an effort. Many men spat with a careless abandon that might really be dangerous when he was dancing with a partner dressed in a big flounced skirt that swept the floor.

HUSBAND AND WIFE

When the bride and groom settled in their new home, each was filling a place long and care-fully defined by tradition. The husband pre-sumably was the head of the home, the money-maker, and the active partner in politics and commerce. He was expected to control his wife and children and to make all major de-cisions. The wife's sphere was the care of her husband and children in the sanctity of the home. According to the Bible, woman had been created later than man, as a supplement and helpmate; one vigorous feminist con-tended that God had practiced on man and then made woman, but such views were con-sidered practically sacrilegious. Eve, the mother of mankind, was tempted by the ser-pent and fell, whereupon she successfully

tempted Adam. In punishment, God told Eve and her daughters that "thy desire shall be to thy husband, and he shall rule over thee"— an admonition repeated and elaborated by later Biblical writers, particularly St. Paul. Furthermore, women were physically shorter, slighter, and weaker, and, according to con-temporary opinion, further handicapped by sex disabilities and by a brain that was differ-ent in kind and lesser in total ability. Obviously women had been designed to remain in the simple environment of the home.

Religion and nature, said most people, dic-tated the qualities and sphere of woman. She was described as weak, passive, forgiving, moral, sensitive, tidy, clean, placable, humble, meek, delicate, refined, virtuous, benevolent, soft, intuitive, gentle, sensible, and shy. Yield-ing like the willow, she could endure adversity better than the sturdy oak. Being suggestible, she should be careful about reading novels, attending the theater, or going to balls, since thereby she might be seduced into time-wast-ing and even immoral ways of life. Above all she should be pious and modest. Her entire life should be highly religious and moral, while her modesty should be not only of person but also of speech and action, which meant among other things that she should not thrust herself into male occupations. Lydia Sigourney stated the prevailing belief when she asserted that "the sexes are manifestly intended for different spheres, and constructed in conformity to their respective destinations."

The theory of woman's proper sphere did not always coincide with the fact. Certainly not all women were physically weak, as for ex-ample the girl who married at sixteen and did all the housework for a never-ending stepladder of children, or her unmarried sister who worked in a factory or scrubbed floors "from sun to sun." An increasing number of women at-tended college and did satisfactory work, while some of them were even edging successfully into male professions. Many wives tended to be sharp-tongued viragoes rather than the soft and submissive creatures of theory. Sometimes women were not even clean; and vaunted femi-nine modesty had obvious exceptions, such as the wearing of low-cut *décolletage* and the taking of pleasure in waltzing, during which the girl was publicly clasped tightly in the arms of a man who was not her husband. And yet the ideas were still important. Girls tried to look weak and pale by carefully avoiding the sun. They fainted frequently—a ladylike phenomenon aided by poor food, lack of exercise, and tight lacing. They hesitated to go to doctors because of fears for their modesty. By and large they stayed out of higher education and the male occupations, even to the extent of avoiding factories and offices in which they would work beside men, clerking, or even nursing. Authorship was socially acceptable, but women stuck principally to children's stories and other highly moral and didactic literature, to which many signed fictitious names. The normal woman generally accepted the current ideal of her place in the world and tried as best she could to live up to it.

The greatest of all functions of the wife was to nourish and direct her children, for everyone agreed that "our moral and political institutions depend, for their purity and permanence, on that simplicity and singleness of purpose, which are generally imbibed at the mother's knee." Presumably mother had an instinctive knowledge of small children, and often appeared the stereotype of a seated mother surrounded by adoring little ones. Her job was to teach her children, not whether they should vote Whig or Democrat or how they should earn their livings, but the simple and basic religious truths—the value of prayer and church attendance; Sabbath observance; honoring their parents, love, benevolence, charity, kindness, faith, and piety. More practical training, particularly for the older children, was the duty of the father: "The mother holds the reins of the soul; the father sways the domain of the intellect." Differences of opinion existed as to the best methods of child training. Some believed in severity and somberness, with an effort to make the children "see that they are sinners, in guilt and ruin." The more modern trend was to emphasize love and brightness. The results of either approach were not always good. The untrained,

scatterbrained boarding-school miss who became a mother at seventeen had little background for the teaching of deep religious truths, while the harassed mother of ten was more likely to work every waking moment than to gather her children around her knee for instruction. Defects in child training were many, but some contemporary criticisms seem almost incredible: "I am afraid that the next generation . . . will be a poor, weak, inefficient & selfish race, as parents will listen to all their whims & indulge them in sloth & petulance."

Marriage was a sacrament that presumably ended only with the death of one of the partners. Divorce was difficult to obtain, but more important, it was frowned upon by public opinion and was hazardous economically, for neither man nor woman could run a farm satisfactorily alone, while who would take care of the children? But in spite of these pressures, unhappily married people still wanted divorces, and the trend was toward easing divorce laws, even though the process had not gone very far by the middle of the century.

AMERICAN EDUCATION

The family presumably gave its children a certain quota of both moral and practical training, but there were clearly fields in which more formal education was necessary if the country were to be rich and democracy were to be successful. Americans approved of education highly in theory, and one of many orators thundered that education "lies at the basis of the whole social system. No nation, when the majority of the people is well educated, can remain enslaved; no nation, when the great mass is ignorant, can retain its freedom." But such education was not to be the free development of intelligence. It was to inculcate desirable traits such as diligence, self-reliance, honesty, punctuality, morality, and, above all, religious piety and patriotic fervor. Emphasis ought to be placed on the "two great events, towards which the movements of society and the arrangements of Providence have converged, in the ancient and modern worlds respectively:—the introduction of Christianity and the birth of American Democracy."

Seen in the glow of idealism, the reality was extremely drab. Few states even claimed to have the majority of their children in school, and any such claims were of dubious validity. New England insisted that 90 per cent of its children were enrolled in elementary schools during the 1830s, but an actual survey showed only about 10 per cent present on a specific day, while conditions became worse as one went south and west. Furthermore, the schools were ordinarily ineffective, with short, irregular terms and poor teachers. Illiteracy was high in many areas, even though American education was better than that in most other parts of the world. The basic difficulty of the schools was lack of money. Schools of the early nineteenth century were supported almost entirely by the parents, of whom some were poverty-stricken while others saw little advantage in providing more than a minimum of learning, possibly preferring home improvements to further education for their children. In any case, family expenditures for education came at the worst possible time in relation to the finances of the family. Naturally under such conditions people turned to the government for help, even though there were plentiful objections to using tax money in large amounts for the schools. Some felt that such action was an arbitrary leveling of wealth by government fiat, while many, including some of the beneficiaries, feared that money taken for the schools would lessen capital and thus decrease employment. An unexpected hurdle appeared in the stigma of poverty that free education suggested; for many years local governments had provided for needy students, with the result that a self-respecting family hated to admit the necessity of such aid. The growing demand for free education did not include, however, compulsion for children to go to school if their parents did not so desire.

State aid to education continued to grow, but then local schools tried to get the maximum possible aid with the minimum of effort, which necessitated more effective supervision. The first real state school systems appeared in Massachusetts in 1837 and in Connecticut in 1838, led respectively by Horace Mann and Henry Barnard. These outstanding educators actually stressed inspiration more than compulsion and gradually made a deep impression as they edited school journals, spoke, and held teachers' institutes. By the 1850s state-supported and -supervised school systems were common in the North and West and were making some advance in the South. The Western states had the advantage of Federal gifts of land. The most important fight everywhere was for the local school district to have the power of taxation.

❰ *The Elementary School.* American elementary schools were conditioned basically by the lack of funds. Teachers received little more than unskilled day labor, and were paid only when they worked, which in some cases meant less than three months a year. Classes were large, ordinarily having at least thirty to forty students, but possibly a hundred or more. Ages of the students ranged from six to sixteen, and mental ability from moron to genius. When there were not too many big boys, a woman teacher might function at half the pay of a man. A man's wages might be spread over many students by the use of the Lancasterian system, first introduced at New York in 1806, in which the master instructed only a handful of students, who in turn taught their fellows. Low pay for hard work brought little social prestige and attracted mainly the incompetents and failures, such as bankrupt farmers and storekeepers; possibly best were the college students who taught school during their long winter vacations. While here and there were excellent teachers, altogether too many were unable to do more than read and write, and those not very well.

The task of improving teaching was a vicious circle. Better teachers could hardly be attracted without better pay, while better pay was not likely so long as teachers were poor. Men like Mann and Barnard tried to break the circle by improving the morale and training of the teachers; they insisted that teaching was a learned profession—a proposition that did not carry conviction to most Americans. As early as 1823 Samuel Reed Hall had opened at Concord, Vermont, a school designed primarily for the training of teachers, and this idea was gradually copied; most important was the opening of the first American state "normal school" at Lexington, Massachusetts, in 1839. Here prospective teachers not only refreshed their knowledge of the subjects they were to teach, but also studied psychology and teaching methods, and even did practice teaching. As the idea spread through the United States, at least a few Americans were convinced that a teacher needed special training and skills.

The usual elementary school was a one-room shack, possibly 18 feet square, which held thirty or more students with less air per person than a prison. It was located usually on barren and rocky land too poor for farming. Coats were hung on the floor. Toilet facilities were a neighboring cornfield, and there was no doctor, dentist, or gymnasium; organized sports did not exist. Backless seats had the six-year-old swinging his feet in the air and the gawky sixteen-year-old squirming uncomfortably. Rarely were there blackboards, maps, charts, pictures, and books. A piece of slate was used for writing; unruled paper, homemade quills, and ink seemed luxurious. The first great problem of the teacher was to cow the older boys, possibly with his fists or even with a brace of pistols; a woman teacher needed unusual personal dignity. Punishments might include a switching, a ruler on the palm, a book held at arm's length, a dunce's cap, or maybe some more ingenious idea. The newer pedagogical treatises talked of love and kindness, but most masters stuck by the good old birch rod and quoted with approval the Biblical statement about sparing the rod and spoiling the child.

Schoolwork stressed the mastery of the three Rs by feats of memory. Students, often studying aloud in major pandemonium, memorized the alphabet, words to be spelled, rules of grammar and arithmetic, parts of speech, rivers, and state capitals. New ideas were floating around—such as that parsing sentences was not very valuable, that the study of geography should start in the local community, that history should be recounted in the student's own words, that reading might precede learning the alphabet, that spelling and writing might be learned simultaneously—but they were introduced slowly. The masters themselves were poorly educated, read little, and had their hands full with discipline. Parents tended to be conservative, holding that what had been good enough for them was good enough for their children. If teacher inspired the students to catch a mouse to illustrate natural history, or to make their own maps, parents might descend on the school board and the school board on the teacher, to find out the meaning of these newfangled ideas.

Books existed in great variety, since there were no required texts in most schools, and were often inherited generation after generation. Luckily some were so widely used as to be almost universal. Noah Webster's speller was said to have sold fifteen million copies by 1837. Lindley Murray's popular grammar—an eighteenth-century English production—stressed parsing until the child could do it in his sleep. The graded readers of William Holmes McGuffey, published originally from 1836 to 1841, swept the country and probably influenced the United States more than any other book except the Bible; the publishers claimed that 122 million copies were sold in the next century. The Peter Parley geographies of Samuel Griswold Goodrich originated in 1827 and sold seven million in thirty years. They taught geography as the narrative of a small boy, Peter Parley, who visited and described various parts of the world.

Here and there was an "infant school," the predecessor of the modern kindergarten, designed primarily to keep the children of the well-to-do mother from getting underfoot and the children of the working mother out of trouble. Methods were revolutionary, since not even the most rigid disciplinarian could contend that a child of three or four could sit quietly for hours at a time. Efforts were made to capture the child's interest, as by toys, blocks, pictures, and figured wallpaper. Bronson Alcott, the chief prophet of the infant school, insisted that all instruction be unpremeditated, growing out of ordinary conversation. His published "conversations" actually showed a great sense of direction as well as of moral earnestness, but his methods still represented a freshening of the spirit in the educational world. As in so many cases, changed techniques started their progress at the bottom of the educational pyramid.

(*Secondary Education.* Few students advanced beyond the elementary schools. For each 100 students in primary schools in 1840, ten were in secondary schools and one in college. The boy who continued his schooling was generally destined for a profession, most frequently the ministry. Although his preparation for college might be obtained from a tutor, possibly his minister, it usually came from a private academy, which now and then called itself a college. The heart of the secondary curriculum was the classics (Latin, Greek) and mathematics (algebra, geometry), but other subjects included rhetoric, elocution, philosophy, logic, history, botany, and chemistry; there was a notable dearth of modern languages and of most social and laboratory sciences. Learning was entirely by memorization; the teacher asked questions calling for repetition of portions of the text. All life was closely supervised, for the school acted as a substitute for the parents. The military school had an increasing vogue, while for a time there was a manual-labor-school fad, which even spread to the colleges and to a smaller extent to the girls' schools. In the manual-labor school the boy worked three or four hours a day, usually at farming. The work was not designed to obtain educational advantages, but only to permit the poor boy to pay part of his way.

Girls' secondary schools were generally "finishing schools" or seminaries, designed to provide cultural charm and to help the girl catch her man rather than to hold him. The curriculum included such activities as making wax flowers, water colors, tapestry, and fancy needlework, and the final degree might be something like Mistress of Polite Literature.

Personal traits such as neatness, politeness, grace, and modesty were cultivated; and the school kept close control over deportment, Sunday observance, letters home, and similar matters. Here and there were advanced schools such as Emma Willard's Troy Female Seminary and Catherine Beecher's Hartford Female Seminary, in which the girls took approximately the same subjects as were given in boys' preparatory schools, and in which there might be small classes, original compositions, self-government, and even classes graded by ability in which the student could progress at any speed she was able. Most Americans looked askance at these revolutionary ideas, fearing the effect on the presumedly weaker feminine body and intellect. Particular concern was expressed that the "learned female" produced by such a school would be unattractive to men.

The most important development in secondary education was the introduction of the public high school. Although the first such school was the Boston English High School (1821), the idea proved particularly attractive to the West, where it was dominant by the time of the Civil War. The use of the high school was dictated partly by reasons of economy; the district schools, once the older children were removed, could be taught by women. The high school represented a notable expansion of government functions and spending. It afforded opportunity for poor students, helped girls get the same education as boys, and was more sensitive to lower- and middle-class interests, introducing such practical subjects as bookkeeping, surveying, and measurement.

(*The College.* Colleges existed for the favored few, particularly for potential ministers. Amherst, for example, desired to educate "indigent young men of promising talents and hopeful piety . . . with the sole view to the Christian ministry." Most colleges were sponsored by churches, and both faculties and presidents were ordinarily ministers. The lives of the students were closely supervised, unmarried faculty members living in and policing the dormitories. Compulsory chapel started each day at dawn, Sunday church services were unavoidable, and sometimes classes were opened and closed with prayer. This emphasis on religion was by and large not forced on reluctant students, of whom many were God-fearing farmers' sons destined for the ministry, and who of their own accord attended noncompulsory religious services such as mid-week prayer meetings, held spontaneous prayer and self-criticism meetings in each other's rooms, and responded to at least one wave of revivalism in each college generation.

The average college was a small place, heavily weighted with preparatory students. In the 1830s only six colleges claimed to have over 200 collegiate undergraduate students. In order of size these were Yale, Dartmouth, Princeton, University of Virginia, Harvard, and Union. The largest faculty had some thirty members, including the president. Ordinarily the one building of any size was a three- or four-story monstrosity that included both class and dormitory rooms, with practically no equipment in either. The library might contain a couple of hundred volumes and be open only two or three hours a week, the professor in charge doling out books reluctantly. The student could room where he pleased, but was forced to eat at the commons, where he always objected to the food. Two semesters a year were usual; the long vacation was in the winter, and commencement in August. Every day was filled completely for each student, with studying and reciting in alternate hours. The greatest virtue of such a college was its cheapness. In the thirties a fee of $100 normally covered all of a year's expenses except personal clothes and entertainment.

Admission to college was based on an examination showing proficiency in mathematics and the classics, and on a character testimonial from the applicant's minister. The age of entrants was frequently as low as thirteen or fourteen. The curriculum was rigid, each college class studying the same subjects. Latin, Greek, and mathematics were the core, together with a senior course on Evidences of Christianity taught by the president. Some stress was laid on declamation. Less important subjects included chemistry, botany, geology,

mental philosophy, logic, political economy, rhetoric, and the law of nations. Generally there were no modern languages, no laboratory sciences, no social subjects except political economy, and no history, either ancient or modern. These conditions brought objections from the educational radicals. The protests inspired new scientific institutions such as Norwich University and Rensselaer Polytechnic in the early twenties, but their more important effects were on the traditional schools. Here and there appeared a few electives and such new subjects as experimental sciences, romance languages, English literature, and history. The radicals even attacked the classics as lacking utility and being often bad literature filled with scientific errors. This was going too far, and the embattled conservatives struck back. The president of Columbia spoke for the majority when he regretted that "the floods of innovation threaten to destroy the foundations of learning."

College instruction was not of the best, partly because the teachers were overwhelmed by too many and too large classes and had to coach oratory and debate, raise money, police the dormitories, and keep preaching engagements. Large classes in elementary subjects used standard texts; questions merely elicited repetition of sections of the text. Examinations were usually oral. Poor instruction probably was largely responsible for perpetual problems of discipline and for the complete lack of sympathy between faculty and students.

Although students generally were pious, they were also young and vigorous, with a scattering of the ungodly, and with too little recreation. Only a few schools such as Williams had gymnasiums, and there were no organized sports. Musical societies, possibly called Beethoven or Euterpean, provided little relief, while a scholastic organization such as Phi Beta Kappa could hardly be called recreational. Greek-letter societies were growing in spite of official disapproval, but the usual school contained two literary societies, with some such name as Philomathean or Brothers in Unity. These societies had regular rushing and initiation ceremonies, and their main meetings were devoted to reading papers or debating on such subjects as whether wisdom produces happiness, whether the thief is worse than the murderer, and whether pride is necessary to happiness. Because of the lack of extracurricular activities there tended to be outbreaks of drinking, gambling, and fighting—pistols and dirks were not unknown; periodic battles with the town boys were traditional. Practical jokes might be relatively minor affairs, such as causing beds to collapse, stealing the chapel bell, overturning carriages, or bobbing the tails of faculty horses; but at times they developed into real riots, and in more than one case the college buildings were burned.

Colleges had historically existed only for men, even though here and there girls were admitted to classes or girls' schools gave degrees. The first coeducational school was Oberlin, which was forced by financial stringency to admit both women and Negroes. The first Oberlin girls received their BAs in 1841; they reported equality of treatment except that they were not allowed to read their own commencement essays. Many people worried that the girls could not stand the strain of male subjects, but after some initial difficulties they performed classwork satisfactorily. Others feared the girls might become unattractive—or that coeducation might lead to immorality. The Oberlin experience gave no real reason for alarm, but then Oberlin was filled with theological students. All four girls of the first coeducational class married Oberlin men, one quitting school for the purpose. The Oberlin experiment led to an increase of college education for women.

Graduate work before 1860 was rare, being most usual for ministers and less common for lawyers and doctors. One or more theological schools was sponsored by each important religious sect except the Methodist, which placed more emphasis on inspiration. The Congregational school of Andover was the largest and possibly the best, but such institutions as Princeton (Presbyterian), Yale (Congregational), and Lane (Presbyterian) were outstanding. Lane Seminary at Cincinnati,

Ohio, with Lyman Beecher as president, was best known in the West; a secession on the issue of slavery produced Oberlin. The most elaborate curriculum was that of Andover; in three years the college presented in turn Biblical literature and language, theology, and homiletics. A potential lawyer usually read his Coke and Blackstone in a lawyer's office; a popular lawyer drew many students. Tapping Reeve at Litchfield, Connecticut, specialized in legal training and was notable for his early use of the case method. Some colleges had lectures on such matters as torts and crimes, but in any case the prospective lawyer had to pass an oral bar examination, given usually by a committee of local lawyers. Medical training was also given ordinarily through apprenticeship in a practitioner's office; state educational requirements were generally poorly enforced. Probably the best medical school was that of the University of Pennsylvania. The usual course contained (1) theory and practice of medicine, (2) chemistry and materia medica, (3) anatomy and surgery, and (4) obstetrics. Usually there were no clinics and no dissections, and the student might never see a patient or an operation. The professor was paid by student fees, thus profiting by his popularity.

Education in democratic America of the early nineteenth century was in many ways disappointing, and it was to be many years before every boy and girl was to have an elementary education as a matter of right, to say nothing of opportunity to do more advanced work. And yet it was remarkably good in view of the newness of the nation and the state of education elsewhere. Americans could rightfully be proud of their schools and view the future with hope.

SCIENTIFIC PROGRESS

Educational deficiencies retarded but little the development of science, since early in the nineteenth century the two were not closely associated. Americans were quite happy about their scientific achievements. They held that "the present age is emphatically marked with boldness and originality" and looked toward the future with calm assurance. In sober fact, the achievements of Americans were surprisingly large in view of their preoccupation with economic concerns. Of course, the newness of the country in itself brought opportunities. Thousands of persons, in government and in private ventures, explored new areas and reported on their physical structure and wildlife. The collected material needed classification, and here also Americans made important contributions. Asa Gray later received praise from Darwin for his achievements in botany. Constantine S. Rafinesque labored effectively in many fields, even forecasting the doctrine of evolution. Thomas Say worked in conchology and entomology. John James Audubon made a permanent reputation in ornithology, and his bird drawings remain in demand today. John E. Holbrook did fine work in herpetology. A series of state geological surveys, starting in the 1820s, classified the land and mineral resources of the nation. Ocean navigation benefited from the work of Matthew Fontaine Maury, who published his excellent *A New Theoretical and Practical Treatise in Navigation* in 1836. Even the laboratory subjects received attention, as in chemistry and physics. Most eminent of contemporary scientists was Benjamin Silliman, who in 1802 was appointed to the Yale chair (really a settee) of chemistry and natural history. During his long life he was a potent factor in scientific advance, as he taught, gave popular lectures, and edited America's most influential scientific magazine, the *American Journal of Science.*

Scientific advances were generally viewed with approval and pleasure, but sometimes there was trouble as they ran headlong into long-established beliefs, particularly religious beliefs. How could the Mosaic account of the creation and history of the world be interpreted to include geologic finds that indicated the existence of the world for millions of years? How could the ark have contained the almost innumerable species of plants and animals? And what about the Rafinesque theory that forms of life had changed in response to climatic conditions? In fact, some people even speculated that man had evolved from lower orders of animals and had not been created as a complete person. Since most scientists were themselves religious men, they tried as best they could to resolve such conflicts. The saving grace for most people was that they knew so little science that they could scarcely worry about possible conflicts with the Bible. They merely insisted that God was always right, and since He had both made the world and inspired the Bible, there could be no conflict. Any seeming discrepancy would disappear as human knowledge increased.

One obvious field of American scientific interest was that of invention, which fitted well with the materialistic urge of the time. Early inventors such as John Fitch and Oliver Evans had been notably fertile, and soon the list of American inventions was long and impressive, including the cotton gin, Colt revolver, reaper, tidal-power machine (Robert Mills), diving suit, diving bell, submarine (Fulton), "Everpoint pencil," adding machine, typewriter (1829), sewing machine, and solar compass, as well as rubber vulcanization and shorthand systems. The Americans were clearly an ingenious people.

Possibly the most intriguing American scientific developments, in view of both long-run importance and typically American contributions, were in the field of electricity. The advances of the generation before 1860 centered in the work of three men: a college professor, a blacksmith, and a professional artist. The college professor was Joseph Henry, who developed the electromagnet that made possible the transmission of an electrical impulse without decreasing its intensity. The blacksmith was the Vermonter Thomas Davenport, who produced an electric motor (1834) which was completely practical except that the batteries upon which it depended were not adequate sources of power. The artist was Samuel F. B. Morse, to whom is given credit for inventing the telegraph, that nineteenth-century discovery which brought the United States together through almost instantaneous communication.

AMERICAN MEDICINE

The most practical of the sciences—if science is the right word for this period—was medicine. Certainly knowledge in that field was badly needed, for the United States was anything but a healthy country. People worked hard, took little unnecessary exercise, gobbled greasy foods, and were suspicious of night air. The death rate was probably thirty to thirty-five per thousand per year, or about three times the modern rate. Although published lists of deaths and their causes leave many doubts, certainly half of the mortalities were boys and girls under twenty, while a fifth of all deaths came from lung ailments. The typical story of an innocent young girl sinking into a tubercular grave had more than a little basis in fact.

A boy ordinarily learned to be a doctor by an apprenticeship during which he swept the floors, rolled pills, read the few office books, and watched his mentor perform. Possibly he took a couple of courses in medical school, but he performed no dissections and received no clinical experience; rarely he went abroad to Edinburgh or Paris. Most states had ineffective licensing laws requiring an examination by a local committee of doctors. The lack of a license meant that the doctor could not use the law to collect debts, but many practicing physicians apparently were not worried by this disability. The American Medical Association was founded in 1848, but was not important until later. Local medical societies were no great help, since their most usual activity was a dinner in which everyone drank too much, after which possibly a prize was awarded and nonmembers of the charmed circle were denounced as "quacks." Medical literature was large in bulk and small in value. Books were largely of foreign authorship; magazines were of the scissors and paste-pot variety and had a high mortality rate, since doctors seemed no more prompt in paying their bills than were their patients. Medical charges were high, but income low. An office call at $1 was not cheap when it represented a day's work for an unskilled laborer. The average doctor was satisfied with an annual income somewhat smaller than that of a fully employed skilled workman. The result was that most doctors, poorly trained and poorly paid, were not given high social recognition.

The basic trouble with the doctors was that they did not know very much. A fair illustration was the current classification of fevers. Usually they were labeled as continual (not much change), remittent (rising and falling), and intermittent (alternating with chills), but there were other possibilities. "Bilious fever" might include yellow fever, dysentery, typhoid, and septicemia. Malaria might be classified as intermittent, remittent, bilious, congestive, malarial, or typhomalarial. Causation of any fever was a matter of speculation, preference going to the "miasmata" said to be the product of decayed vegetable matter. Alternate explanations included climate, soil, water, or even a comet. Effective quarantine was thus impossible when epidemics such as malaria, scarlet fever, and yellow fever swept the country. The great cholera epidemic of 1832 caused a wholesale exodus from the cities and was said to have produced death rates of 10 to 50 per cent in certain areas. The doctors observed and recorded, but failed to find either the cause or the cure. The president of the Medical Society of New York confessed that "the first and moving cause of this, and all widespread epidemics, is known only to Him, who has established the general laws by which universal nature is governed."

The standard form of treatment for most human ills was first a calming or depressing agent and then a tonic if the patient were still alive. Roughly the same procedure was used for dysentery, tetanus, gastritis, diabetes, cholera, smallpox, insanity, or almost anything else. The calming agent was bloodletting or cathartics. It was suggested that bloodletting, with leeches, cupping, or even cutting a vein or artery, be 10 to 12 ounces at a time, but frequently this amount was exceeded, one doctor reporting the removal of 600 ounces in two months. The cathartic was usually a mercury compound, preferably calomel, which was given in such immense amounts that it literally caused the teeth to come loose. Certainly these measures brought down the fever. Sometimes they also brought the undertaker. If he survived them, the patient was restored with some such tonic as iron, arsenic, quinine, or citrus fruit. The one disease really being conquered was smallpox, since vaccination, an English discovery, was used widely.

One staple of a doctor's practice was obstetrics, although his entrance to this field had come but slowly. Not until 1813 was the lecturer on midwifery given equal standing with the other lecturers at the University of Pennsylvania, and until the middle of the century most births took place at home with a midwife in attendance. The home was safer than a hospital, which was a spreader of disease. The average midwife was dirtier than the doctor, but even the doctor carried infections. An article by Dr. Oliver Wendell Holmes in 1843 contended that much of the sickness of new mothers was carried by the doctors, but protection was still difficult without a knowledge of antiseptics.

Many people went to doctors only as a last resort, and one wonders whether their herbs and incantations and charms were more frequently fatal than the doctors' treatments. Particularly undesirable, however, were the hundreds of patent medicines advertised nationally and sold at almost every store. Popular sellers like Swaim's Panacea and Brandreth's Vegetable Universal Pills claimed to cure everything from a cold in the head to tuberculosis. The herbs that were their main ingredients were probably harmless, but sometimes they contained mercury, arsenic, or other poisons in varying amounts. Bateman's Pectoral Drops, for example, with contents varying between 7½ and 106 grains of opium per pint, probably did their job of quieting the baby all too efficiently.

Americans recognized no inferiority of American medicine, and were particularly pleased to boast of their surgery as practiced by such men as Valentine Mott of New York and John C. Warren of Boston. One medical journal boasted in the 1830s: "The idea of presenting anything new in surgery, at this period, is preposterous." Such claims were amazing in view of the limited knowledge of anatomy, and of the lack of antiseptics and anesthetics. Opening the abdominal cavity, regardless of the technical excellence of the operation, usually resulted in infection and death. The lack of anesthetics not only meant intense pain, which was little alleviated by appeals for trust in the Supreme Goodness, but also produced tight muscles and convulsive jerks that interfered with the operation even when the patient was strapped to the table. Many surgeons were noted as much for the rapidity as for the excellence of their work.

❲ *Medical Progress.* The great tragedy of pain in surgery was that anesthetics had long been known, even if not recognized. Nitrous oxide and ether were both available by 1812, and chloroform by the early 1830s, although morphine was not known until the 1840s. Such drugs as opium, laudanum, nightshade, or even whisky were given orally, but the effects soon wore off. Hypnotism was tried with varying results. The first authentic use of an anesthetic was by Dr. Crawford Long, a frontier Georgia doctor, who in 1842 removed a growth from a friend's neck. More important for the future were the experiments by dentists in Hartford (Horace Wells) and in Boston (W. T. G. Morton) to permit the painless removal of tooth stumps. Ether was first demonstrated in a famous amputation by Dr. Warren in Boston in 1846. In spite of the usual cry of "fraud" raised by many doctors, who talked of undesirable interference with the intentions of God, and in spite of restrictions by men who tried to profit by controlling patents, the use of anesthetics gradually increased.

The introduction of anesthetics was one of the hopeful signs in American medicine. Furthermore, doctors gradually were learning better identification and classification of disease, even though the causes and cures still remained obscure. Doctors also noted the relation of disease to climate, occupations, and even religion and were aware of the close connection between mind and body. Among the real medical contributors was Dr. William

Beaumont, a Yankee army doctor stationed at Mackinac. One day a French Canadian boy at the post received a gunshot wound in his side. He recovered, but there remained an opening through which the stomach was observable. Beaumont used him as a walking laboratory, finding out not only the ordinary processes of digestion, but also the important effects on digestion of emotions such as anger and fear. His work was first-rate, and has been elaborated upon, but not superseded.

There was also improvement in the quality of drugs, which had often been adulterated. The first United States Pharmacopoeia, giving the official standards of purity, was published in 1820 and then revised each ten years. The medical schools placed more emphasis on pharmacy, and soon there came an *American Journal of Pharmacy*. Many new drugs such as codeine, nitrous oxide, silver nitrate, ether, arnica, chlorine, nux vomica, morphine, and strychnine came into use. Rather illuminating was the fact that quinine, the great aid for malaria cases, was sold as a patent medicine in Dr. Sappington's Febrifuge and Ague Pills.

Dentistry obtained its real start as a separate profession somewhere around 1840. Earlier, an aching tooth was yanked by the local doctor or blacksmith. Gradually a few dentists began to appear, using hand tools but being proud of their complete cleaning of cavities before filling them with some such material as gold, iron, or tin. False teeth were at first made of wood, as were Washington's, but then porcelain became usual. At first attached to old stumps, they were never satisfactory, and the dentists developed anesthetics to permit the removal of dead teeth. Real progress came about 1840 with the establishment of the *American Journal of Dental Science*; the first dental school, the Baltimore College of Dental Surgery (1839); and the American Society of Dental Surgeons (1841).

❲ *Medical Retrogression.* The ineffectiveness of regular doctors encouraged the development of irregular practitioners, who could at least make magnificent promises. Faith doctors laid their hands on the patient and blew in

his face. Hydropaths used water internally and externally. Natural Bonesetters manipulated the human frame. But most popular were the various herb doctors, and of these the best known were the Thomsonians. The founder, Samuel Thomson, sickly son of a New Hampshire farmer, had evolved a theory that the life force was an electric fluid which showed itself as heat. Since heat was a friend there should be no bloodletting or mineral medicines. His system of herb medicines and steam baths was sold to subscribers, so that each man could be his own doctor merely by consulting a book and prescribing as specified. Thomson claimed some three million users in 1839, and there were hundreds of societies, infirmaries, and books; some forty magazines; and a yearly national convention. Continual splits and rivalries were perhaps inevitable, and after Thomson's death the various groups united (1845) as the American Eclectic Medicine Society.

Thomsonian medicine represented but one of the protests against excessive bloodletting and drugging. Another such protest came from homeopathy, the creation of a German doctor, Samuel Hahnemann, who died in 1843. His theory was that each disease should be treated by infinitesimal doses of the drug that produced the symptoms of the disease in a well person. He also emphasized proper food, exercise, and diet. Most doctors yelled fraud, and Dr. Oliver Wendell Holmes wrote a book titled *Homeopathy and Its Kindred Delusions*. The idea of proper living habits, stressed by Hahnemann, was the particular domain of Sylvester Graham, a temperance worker. In general Graham avoided meat and stressed fruit and vegetables, which he wanted eaten raw. His name remains to us in the "Graham bread" that he favored. At various places he aroused great enthusiasm or hostility. A Boston mob threatened to lynch him because of a rumor that he was to talk on sex and exhibit nude women—a rumor that proved disappointingly false. The regular doctors followed their usual policy of scoffing at what they called "the science of your own idiosyncrasies."

Possibly the most intriguing medical fad of the period was phrenology, developed by two

European doctors. After years of experimentation they published their results in four bulky and technical volumes (1810 to 1819). Their particular effort was to judge personality traits by physical criteria, and they rejected the common ideas that facial structure and size of the brain were important. They held that general physical characteristics, such as color of hair and eyes, amount of flesh, and type of complexion, made a difference. More important, they maintained that the brain was composed of a bundle of specific functions, such as the senses, acquisitiveness, love of approbation, and benevolence, and that the relative development of each trait could be determined from the outside of the skull. Moreover these traits could be changed with use and disuse, with obviously important implications for such subjects as education and penology.

Phrenology was accepted with enthusiasm by the majority of Americans, including the doctors led by Dr. Charles Caldwell of Transylvania University. Visiting phrenologists were greeted with profound respect. Societies arose all over the land, with their lectures, books, discussions, and casts of heads. Outstanding leaders such as Samuel Gridley Howe, Henry Ward Beecher, Horace Mann, and Clara Barton accepted the ideas. The main objections seemed to come from religious people who felt that God was being pushed aside in favor of a materialistic explanation of human characteristics and actions. In the long run, phrenology was injured most by its friends, who modified and taught it without research, and particularly by practitioners who used it as a sort of fortunetelling device. Possibly naturally, it was linked with other ideas, some of which the phrenologists had earlier discarded, to produce such grotesque results as "phrenopathy" and "magneto-physiognomic-craniology."

A contrasting fad, which Americans greeted with greater reluctance, was hypnotism. Modern interest in hypnotism began in the late eighteenth century with the work of the French faith healer Franz Anton Mesmer, who inspired the common name of mesmerism, or animal magnetism. Most cultured Americans who heard of it—and they included John Quincy Adams, Benjamin Franklin, and Thomas Jefferson—dismissed it as a fraud. American interest increased with the arrival of the lecturer Charles Poyen in the mid-thirties, and soon all America was excited by hypnotic exhibits. Greatest of the American investigators was Phineas Parkhurst Quimby, who paralleled contemporary European discoveries by concluding that all hypnotism was self-induced; but this concept was not generally accepted until much later. Most Americans were of the opinion that hypnotism depended on electricity, which they considered a fluid that passed from doctor to patient. A few doctors used hypnotism for painless operations, while others claimed that it could cure anything from nervousness to cholera. Some said that a magnetized person could peer into a sick man's body and see what was wrong. Others went further and talked of clairvoyance and second sight. A youthful Andrew Jackson Davis hypnotized himself and lectured on such subjects as Swedenborgianism, physiology, languages, geology, astronomy, ethnology, and cosmology; he could translate unknown languages, discover new planets, and diagnose disease. Perhaps the majority of Americans were justified in dismissing the whole affair as a fake, thus throwing out the baby with the bath, but possibly excessive was the contention that the "phenomena are performed by the dark powers of Satan himself." Many years were to pass before Freud used the rejected hypnotism as his first technique in the practice of psychoanalysis. Peculiarly enough, Americans generally rejected the true and useful hypnotism while giving credence to the chimera of phrenology.

CHAPTER 19

Attaining Culture

(1815-1860)

THE FINE ARTS

America of the early nineteenth century was proud of its progress in the arts, even though such pride later became hard to understand. Typical was the field of painting, with its difficulty of obtaining instruction, materials, and a market. Most red-blooded Americans looked a trifle askance at a male artist as not quite a man, and hence the artistic boy usually incurred the hostility of his father as he trained himself, probably by starting on the barn and ending as a portrait painter. The lucky few were able to study in London with Benjamin West until his death in 1820, whereupon the favorite mecca became Rome. Good canvas, oils, and brushes were difficult to obtain. The best market, if a painter wanted to eat, was among retired businessmen—for example, a pork packer who wanted his wife portrayed with her every flounce and jewel. The portrait was essentially the forerunner of the photograph, for even the simple daguerreotype was not available until the 1840s, and every painter produced mainly portraits; Thomas Sully alone did some 2,500.

The artists themselves tended to sneer at portrait painting, but their own preferences were not beyond criticism. They liked "artistic" subjects, which meant Biblical or patriotic scenes stressing such emotions as awe and piety. The few men like Chester Harding, William Mount, and George Caleb Bingham who pictured the scenes of common life are today a welcome relief. However, the artist liked large canvases and splashed gallons of paint on epic religious and patriotic themes. Such "masterpieces" included Benjamin West's "Death on the Pale Horse"; Washington Allston's "Belshazzar's Feast"; Samuel F. B. Morse's "Old House of Representatives"; Rembrandt Peale's "The Court of Death"; and John Trumbull's "The Battle of Bunker Hill" and "The Declaration of Independence." And if a picture gained value through size, why not paint the largest river in the world on the largest canvas in the world? The result was a painting by Henry Lewin (1849) of the Mississippi on a canvas 12 feet high and 1,325 yards long, which was rolled past an enthralled audience.

Two developments of the period ran counter to the ordinary trends. Starting with Thomas Cole in the 1820s there arose the romantic "Hudson River school," which pictured landscapes, although not always in the Hudson River area. The results were usually rather uninteresting brownish productions, and they aroused the scorn of many people who thought it better to look directly at nature than at a picture, but they still represented a hopeful trend. The other development was the use of the nude, which shocked most Americans to the core. The "common-sense" man was certain that only an immoral woman would expose her body to a man and that the viewer would inevitably have improper thoughts. The moral restrictions of the Victorian era tended to limit the use of the nude for many years.

American pictures were difficult to market, partly because few people had the necessary funds, but perhaps more because the wealthy could acquire greater prestige by hanging a foreign master, even if only a copy; the museums were in a similar position. The artists' own societies to train artists and to exhibit and sell paintings were continually rent by fights and schisms. Probably best were the National Academy of Design at New York and the Pennsylvania Academy of the Fine Arts at Philadelphia. A few art unions bought pictures and engravings that were circulated among their members and then divided at the end of the year.

Sculpture was an even less promising art than painting, since the retired businessman was less desirous of a marble statue of his wife than a portrait. Practically the only sculpture before 1830 was of tombstones and shipheads. The first two professionals of any importance were Horatio Greenough and Hiram Powers. Greenough was trained in Italy, and by common belief his chanting cherubs, copied from a Raphael picture, were the first stone group by an American. The United States was sufficiently excited about him to commission a statue of George Washington for the Capitol; the result was an anachronistic seated figure with bare chest, robed in a Roman toga. Powers was a self-taught Westerner who spent the latter part of his life in Rome. His best-known figure was "The Greek Slave," noted more for its slippery and boneless nudity than for its beauty. In fact, the problem of nudity was exceedingly difficult. When Nicholas Biddle sent casts of some Louvre models to the Pennsylvania Academy a tremendous outcry was raised in Philadelphia, and the figures were covered with sheets one day a week to permit the more modest ladies to attend.

The greatest architect of the early nineteenth century was Charles Bulfinch, who left a permanent imprint on the houses, churches, and government buildings of New England; among his works were the capitols at Boston, Hartford, and Augusta. He was for a time in charge of the construction of the national Capitol, and that Capitol was part of the only really planned American city; whether the result of the planning was good has been questioned. Outstanding among the Bulfinch students was Robert Mills, who did many public buildings and monuments, particularly in Washington. His most impressive work was his Washington Monument (1836 to 1884) with its severe and striking simplicity. The original Mills plan called for a colonnade at the base, but luckily the shaft remained bare. Mills also made drawings for the Bunker Hill Monument (1825 to 1843), but they were not used.

The great architectural fad of the period from 1815 to 1860 was the classical revival, for which Jefferson must take much of the praise or blame; he used classical forms in his own home, at the University of Virginia, and in Washington. The revival was reinforced by American sympathy for the Greeks in their struggle for independence, and soon statehouses, churches, banks, and private homes began to look like Greek temples. Ancient forms were copied with great exactness, marble being simulated by flat clapboards, painted brick, stucco, or plaster marked in squares. The appropriateness of a flat-roofed bank with doric columns in New England was more than questionable. The only thing in favor of the classic revival was the even worse Gothic and Italian monstrosities that began to succeed it by the 1840s. Buttresses, vaults, medieval windows, marble floors, and clustered chimneys were certainly more objectionable than the Parthenon substituting for the New York Custom House, while the Italian villas of the popular Andrew Jackson Downing can be praised only because they were surrounded by lawns, shrubbery, and trees.

Furniture tended to become less attractive during the period. Early in the century such designs as Chippendale, Hepplewhite, and Sheraton were common, particularly as they were Americanized in the New York shop of Duncan Phyfe. French influences increased during and after the Napoleonic wars, and furniture became more massive and ornate. People wanted to show off their wealth and assumed that the bigger, heavier, and more elaborately carved the piece of furniture, the more impressive. Generally, the results were depressingly bad.

AMERICAN MUSIC

Americans loved music, although their tastes were usually rather simple. Thousands of girls practiced the piano until they could accompany group singing and entertain their friends with such masterpieces as "Bright Shines the Moon." Untold numbers of boys learned the flute or violin sufficiently to play simple melodies. Everyone loved to sing the old favorites, such as "The Last Rose of Summer," or "Peace within the Grave," and by the 1850s to harmonize on the new, nostalgic Stephen Foster songs of a synthetic South. Because of the inability of many to read music, "singing school" and congregational singing were possible only when the tune and words were "lined out." The usual larger town had at least one good-sized chorus, with possibly a name like the Handel or Beethoven Society, which performed mainly sacred music; Handel's *The Messiah* was given in its entirety as early as 1831. American composers were particularly prolific of hymns, including such favorites as "Stand Up, Stand Up for Jesus," "Just As I Am," and "Rock of Ages." The best known and most influential of American musicians was Lowell Mason of Boston. As a composer, Mason was responsible for such favorites as "Nearer My God to Thee," "My Faith Looks Up to Thee," and "From Greenland's Icy Mountains." As a teacher, he developed methods to be used for large groups, worked effectively with other music teachers, and introduced public-school music at his own expense at Boston in 1834.

Instrumental music was in general not praiseworthy. There was an understandable lack of such instruments as oboe and bassoon, but even ordinary instruments were few in number and poorly played. Reportedly all of New York in the 1830s could not produce enough cellos for the *William Tell* overture, while the first satisfactory string quartet was not organized until the late 1850s. When the New York Philharmonic gave its first concert on 7 December 1842, some of the members were more efficient as ushers than as players. Good soloists, both instrumental and vocal, were usually foreign-born and trained. First of the many top-ranking artists to come to the United States was the violinist Ole Bull, who arrived in 1843, and who drew immense crowds during his two years in America, maybe in part because he was willing to play simple tunes such as "Yankee Doodle." A possible commentary on contemporary taste is the fact that Bull was succeeded in popular favor by a troupe of seven Swiss bell ringers. The greatest splurge of all was made by Jenny Lind, Swedish soprano, who was ballyhooed by P. T. Barnum. When she opened at Castle Garden on 14 September 1850, wearing a virginal white dress and surrounded by a bower of flowers, the audience rose and cheered. Rather disappointingly, Jenny was an awkward and bigoted young lady with a clear voice of little depth and color. The first grand opera was given in New York in 1825 by the company of Manuel García. Practically all opera performers were foreign-born, and apparently their performances were mediocre. The too few actors doubled in various parts, soloists were out of tune, sopranos sang tenor arias, and tenors squeaked in falsetto; the orchestra might have as few as five pieces, with every man for himself; instrumentalists often sat silent through parts they could not play, hoping that the fiddler would keep things going. More important than the inadequacies, however, was the fact that many operas were given, and as far west as New Orleans; over seventy-five different operas were presented in New York before 1840, and a single one, Beethoven's *Fidelio*, was given on fourteen consecutive nights in 1839.

LITERATURE

❰ *Newspapers.* The United States was a comparatively literate nation, and the reading of the average man was the newspaper, which before 1830 ordinarily meant a weekly paper that reprinted copiously from other papers and emphasized domestic and foreign political items. No local parties or fist fights, no sporting page, no advice to the lovelorn, and no strip cartoons alleviated the dull monotony of their pages. A paper like the *Niles' Weekly Register* (Baltimore, 1815) had the main virtue of providing the historian with a statistical storehouse. Now and then a short story, a pungent editorial, or the letter of an irate subscriber brought a rare touch of excitement. Even the advertisements were ordinarily only fine-type listings of articles for sale and remained the same week after week; the only national advertiser who put a punch into his publicity was the patent-medicine manufacturer. The larger cities had daily papers, which were priced exorbitantly.

Newspapers began to change radically in the early thirties. The steam-powered cylinder press reduced costs at a time when Americans were earning more money, and various men saw the possibility of mass markets if prices were reduced and the news made brighter. The new penny paper was designed, not for a Hamilton or Jefferson, but for the average citizen. The New York *Sun*, under Benjamin Day, printed stories of Fanny Kemble and Davy Crockett, of an imaginary trip to the moon, and of the revelations of Maria Monk; it discovered that the exposure of even a spectacularly false story brought additional circulation. The New York *Herald* under James Gordon Bennett stressed personal items, with accounts of parties and of police-court proceedings, and even printed headlines for the editor's own

wedding. The New York *News* introduced the Sunday paper in 1835. The New York *Tribune* under Horace Greeley became the best-known American newspaper, particularly because of its widely distributed weekly edition. All such papers seemed undesirably sensational to the more conservative Americans. In a sense they represented a democratic trend by informing the common man in sprightly fashion of ordinary events. In addition they improved their news coverage and their speed of news gathering, making early use of such means of communication as the telegraph. Their most obvious lacks were cooperative news-gathering agencies and the ability to reproduce photographs.

❰ *Magazines and Gift Books.* Magazines were born and died in bewildering profusion. Over 500 were founded in the first quarter of the century, with not over a fifth of that number in existence during any one year. Typical was the *Southern Rosebud*, which matured as the *Southern Rose*, only to fade to an early grave. The average magazine found difficulty in getting subscribers and then even more difficulty in getting the subscribers to pay. The editor had no funds with which to compensate contributors and often did most of the writing himself. Some of the better-known magazines included the scholarly *North American Review* (Boston, 1815) and *The Knickerbocker Magazine* (New York, 1833); they followed English and Scottish precedent by filling their pages with long and dull articles that theoretically were book reviews. The *Southern Literary Messenger* (Baltimore, 1834), edited for a time by Edgar Allan Poe, was the best of the Southern literary magazines. *Godey's Lady's Book* (Philadelphia, 1830), as edited by Mrs. Sarah J. Hale of "Mary Had a Little Lamb" fame, was the prototype of the modern women's magazines, with departments on such feminine interests as sewing, food, and the care of babies; it was particularly noted for its fashions in hand-colored pictures and for its fabulous monetary success. The *National Police Gazette* (New York, 1845) "exposed" the sins of New York for an exclusively male clientele that apparently did little to remedy the evils. By the 1850s such notable magazines as *Putnam's Magazine,* the *Atlantic Monthly, Leslie's Illustrated Newspaper,* and *Harper's Weekly* came into existence. The last two featured pictures, which necessarily were woodcuts.

Closely allied to magazines were gift books, which were designed as gifts to friends and relatives on such occasions as birthdays and Christmas. Under some such name as *Friendship's Token* or *The Rosebud* the gift book was built around its steel engravings and its lush binding, which might be even silk or velvet. Its tales, poems, and sketches were often signed by well-known authors who were attracted by the good pay and willing to play second fiddle to steel engravings. The more commercially minded author sometimes sent the same contribution to several publications, while the publisher might issue the same gift book under various names—let the purchaser beware.

The prose writings of the gift books and magazines were seldom short stories in the modern sense of the term. More frequently they were sketches or incidents or compressed novels. The few exceptions included the gems of Edgar Allan Poe. Two kinds of sketch appeared most frequently. One was the sentimental incident concerning "a bright and beautiful being, too pure and holy for a sinful world like this." Naturally such a paragon was a young and innocent girl. She fell in love with an equally admirable young man. They touched hands, exchanged vows, and talked of God and Heaven. Then the saintly maiden caught cold, contracted tuberculosis, and went to join the other angels amid scenes of overpowering pathos and piety; whereupon the beloved visited her lonely grave once a week, placing on it a single white rose that he watered with his tears. The other type was the gloomy, macabre, Gothic tale of "the night was dark and stormy" type. A welter of mystery and horror was climaxed at the guillotine or scaffold. Rather remarkably, this kind of material was used by Poe in his masterpieces. Humor generally was scarce and depended heavily on misspelling and dialect. Often there was exaggera-

tion of the type of the Jack Downing letters: "When she yawns, you can see right down to her garters." Most of the humor is today very dead and should be buried.

⟨ Popular Prose Authors. American presses, unsated by the more ephemeral literature, turned out prodigious numbers of books, so that while the bulk of books read in the United States just after the War of 1812 were published in England, the American situation was reversed by the middle of the century. But regardless of the place of publication, a large proportion of the most read authors were European, partly because they were better, but also partly because there was no international copyright, and hence American publishers could appropriate foreign works without the payment of royalties; Charles Dickens's lack of success in obtaining an international copyright law during his trip to the United States probably helped sour him on the American scene. Among the best-selling European authors were Scott, Moore, Dickens, Austen, Hugo, and Dumas; Sir Walter Scott was almost fantastically popular, particularly in the South because of his buttressing of Southern "feudal" stereotypes.

Patriotic Americans protested increasingly at remaining a literary dependency of Europe, while American writers more and more saw the virtues of exploiting uniquely American material, particularly wars and frontier experiences. Washington Irving, the dean of American writers, not only told charming stories of the Hudson Valley, but described Western exploration and fur trade and did the inevitable biography of Washington. James Fenimore Cooper created the heroes and villains of the *Leatherstocking Tales* to the delight of several generations of his countrymen. Other popular writers produced best sellers with American backgrounds. Robert Montgomery Bird romanticized the period of George Rogers Clark in *Nick of the Woods;* John Pendleton Kennedy glorified the patriots of the Revolution in *Horse-Shoe Robinson;* William Gilmore Simms described the Georgia frontier in *Guy Rivers,* and early Indian-white relations in *The*

Yemassee. The list could be expanded to include almost every prominent literary name of the early nineteenth century. Possibly most striking was the beginning of the idealization of the Southern plantation by Kennedy in his *Swallow Barn*, which comprised a series of sketches masquerading as a novel.

Neither the new American authors nor the scenes of their writings were confined to any one part of the country. Traditionally, emphasis has been given to "the flowering of New England," and indeed such names as Hawthorne, Thoreau, Emerson, Whittier, Longfellow, and Holmes are impressive. But other areas had their own reasons for pride. New York boasted such men as Irving, Cooper, and Paulding. The South had its Poe, Bird, Kennedy, and Simms. Even the West could display some literary lights of its own. James Hall and Timothy Flint labored mightily to exploit Western material, and each man edited a magazine in which he favored home productions. Albert Pike's *Prose Sketches*, Augustus B. Longstreet's *Georgia Scenes*, and Joseph G. Baldwin's *The Flush Times of Alabama and Mississippi* were among the better descriptions of Western life.

All American literature was saturated with religious piety and moral earnestness, but this spirit was particularly evident among the New Englanders with their Puritan background. Nathaniel Hawthorne, for example, was inspired to produce penetrating psychological studies that obtained a permanent place in the world's great literature. Whittier was an ardent abolitionist, as were most of his friends, while still another New Englander, Mrs. Harriet Beecher Stowe, wrote the most influential book of its day, *Uncle Tom's Cabin* (1852). Mrs. Stowe also illustrated the increasing feminization of American literature; such names as Susan Warner, Mabel Vaughan, Alice Carey, Lydia Child, Catherine Sedgwick, Sarah Josepha Hale, Fanny Fern, Margaret Fuller, Ann Stephens, Lydia Sigourney, and Gail Hamilton were known to most Americans. In fact, the decade before the Civil War has been characterized in recent times as the "feminine fifties."

Out of New England's preoccupation with religious and moral problems had come the Unitarian revolt, and now the more radical Unitarians went even further in freeing man's personality from past human guilt and in giving him the opportunity for salvation through his own efforts and desires. Outstanding was the brilliant philosopher Ralph Waldo Emerson, who expressed his changed attitude by resigning his ministerial position in the Unitarian Church. Emerson was the moving spirit in establishing a discussion group (1836) called the Transcendental Club, and the term transcendental came to describe the ideas of the club's unusually vocal and literary members. The Transcendentalists represented a democratic force even though their doctrines were almost entirely incomprehensible to the average American. Emerson's own oral effort at definition was: "The Transcendentalist sees everything as an idealist. That is, all events, objects, etc., seen, are images of the consciousness. It is the thought of them only one sees. You shall find God in the unchanged essence of the universe, the air, the waves, the leaf; and in the subjective unfolding of your nature, the determination of the private spirit, everything of religion." A trifle more simply, the Transcendentalists believed that a man's God-given powers could transcend the ordinary human limitations of experience and enter the world of eternal truth. Their members included such outstanding men as Channing, Alcott, Bronson, Parker, and Ripley. Their best-known publication was *The Dial*, edited in the early forties by Margaret Fuller. They experimented (1841) hopefully but not very successfully at Brook Farm in West Roxbury, Massachusetts, with "plain living and high thinking."

American authors at times worked for specific reforms such as abolition, but in general they approved American life and American democracy, so that the exceptions were noteworthy. Henry Thoreau escaped from contemporary life to sing the praises of a semimonastic existence at Walden Pond. Herman Melville hymned the romantic beauty of the South Seas, as in his *Typee*, *Omoo*, and *Moby Dick* (1851). More spectacular, however, were

Cooper's diatribes against American democracy; his point of view so antagonized Americans that for many years they looked askance at his books. Such cases, however, were clearly exceptional.

❨ *Popular Poets.* American poetry was of immense volume but varying value. Some of the most sensitive work was done by Edgar Allan Poe, whose tragic life presumably was the basis and inspiration of his delicate and imaginative poems. The dynamic writings of Walt Whitman reached their full crescendo in *Leaves of Grass* (1855), one of the most powerful expressions of belief in American democracy. But the poetry of Poe and Whitman did not achieve immediate popularity, since people preferred the well-rhymed lines and homely sentiments of such men as Longfellow, Whittier, and Holmes. The overwhelming majority of Americans felt that verse should have lilting meter and jingling rhyme; it should use "poetic" language to describe such "poetic" emotions as patriotism, piety, love, and grief. Tremendous popularity went to the so-called consumptive or graveyard school of poetry, which produced innumerable effusions starting something like:

> Mother! that are weeping
> Away the midnight hour.

The greatest of American poets on the basis of popular appreciation was Mrs. Lydia H. Sigourney, the "sweet singer of Hartford." Although Mrs. Sigourney was uncharacteristically married late in life and proved an overbearing wife and a sharp and not always ethical businesswoman, she filled multitudinous pages of the magazines and gift books with her laments over the deaths of innumerable innocent maidens and pure babies, her thoughts on immortality, and her didactic moralizings. No better comment on popular taste was ever made than when Poe as editor of the *Southern Literary Messenger* placed his beautiful "Israfel" on an inside page so that he could give the place of honor to Mrs. Sigourney's "The Ruler's Faith."

AMERICAN AMUSEMENTS

❨ *The Theater.* Literature was but one of the many ways in which the average American could spend the relatively few hours not devoted to work. Most citizens thought of literature as but one of several amusements. Attending the theater was a diversion of many Americans, even though acting was considered with suspicion by the more proper who felt that entertainers were generally immoral, attracting the worst classes of the community, and that the plays presented were marked by "profaneness, coarseness, indelicacy, low wit." The most concerted protest came from Puritanical New England, and by 1843 the last Boston theater had been transformed into a church. Such criticism had at least a measure of truth. Theaters were usually in the poor parts of town and were patronized by petty criminals and prostitutes. A bar generally did a rushing business. The backless benches of the pit were occupied by the riffraff, who ate, drank, had fist fights, and threw rubbish at the actors or shouted them down, while even the occupants of the boxes might put their feet on the railings. On the other hand, the actors were apparently as moral as average members of the community, while the plays were most frequently those of the English playwrights Shakespeare, Buckstone, and Knowles. Many Americans loved melodrama or spectacles such as *The Silent Witness, or, A Tale of Blood* and *A Fairy Spell*; and some of the theaters were so arranged that the seats of the pit could be removed to accommodate equestrian exhibits. The favorite American playwright was John Howard Payne, whose *Clari, or, The Maid of Milan*, which opened in 1833, included the song "Home, Sweet Home." Several American characters became typed. The stage Indian was either the sly and cruel savage or the noble native, as in Augustus Stone's *Metamora* (1829), played long and successfully by Edwin Forrest. The classic tale of the villainous banker, the charming daughter, the impoverished father, and the simple but heroic country boy was contained in Joseph S. Jones's *The People's Lawyer* (1839). Yankee characters with such names as Hiram Dodge and Deuteronomy Dutiful were well known. A Westerner, such as Colonel Nimrod Wildfire, as played by James Hackett in James K. Paulding's *The Lion of the West* (1831), was easily recognizable. The Negro comic was standardized by Thomas D. ("Daddy" or "Jim Crow") Rice, while the Edwin P. Christy minstrel show came into existence in 1842 with the usual semicircle, Sambo, Bones, white interlocutor, jokes, songs, and dances.

The theatrical performance of the early nineteenth century at least gave the customer a great deal for his money. Ordinarily a three- to five-act tragedy was succeeded by a farce designed to send everyone home happy, while intermissions were filled with songs and dances and other variety acts. The so-called "star system" was in common use; in it, the well-recognized actor or actress toured the country appearing with various local stock companies in standard plays, such as those of Shakespeare. Thereby many Americans were able to see outstanding performers without traveling to the seaboard cities. Undoubtedly the most popular native-born actor was Edwin Forrest, who ordinarily did Shakespearean roles, although he was also interested in native-written plays. His style of acting was robust and vigorous, with much ranting and waving of arms, all of which seemed very attractive in its day.

A long succession of English stars toured America. Among them were Edmund Kean, Charles Kean (his son), Junius Brutus Booth, Charles Mathews, and Tyrone Power. In several cases they were badly treated on the rumor that they had made derogatory remarks about the United States. J. R. Anderson was shouted down in 1831, and rioting resulted, even though Mr. Anderson apologized for his reputed criticisms. The eminent William C. Macready, on a third visit to the United States in 1849, engaged in an acrimonious dispute with Edwin Forrest, who was playing a parallel engagement in New York City. When Macready appeared on the stage, hissing developed

into fist fighting, troops were called, and the resulting Astor Theater riots produced twenty deaths and numerous injuries. Americans obviously took their theater seriously and had definitely anti-English feeling.

The most popular of the feminine stars was the English-born Fanny Kemble, who was descended from a distinguished theatrical family. Coming to America with her father in 1829 she was acclaimed immediately as "the greatest of living actresses," and devoted crowds followed her every step. In time she married a Southerner and retired from the stage. The marriage was not happy, but after she left her husband she was never able to recapture her earlier popularity. The top dancer of the period was Fanny Elssler, who arrived in New York in 1845. Upon her first appearance the pit rose as one man, cheering and waving handkerchiefs. Managers fought for her services, even though the cost of her large company almost ensured a deficit. Prudes bewailed the physical revelations involved in toe dancing, but most Americans were fascinated, while even the intellectuals joined in the applause. The story was told that Ralph Waldo Emerson turned to Margaret Fuller and said, "Margaret, this is poetry," to which Margaret replied, "Waldo, this is religion." Possibly the United States was becoming more sophisticated.

❨ *Other American Amusements.* Americans found their diversions in a number of ways, although many of them felt that amusements must have moral or educational or religious justification lest consciences be troubled. A combination of work and fun, like a house-raising or quilting bee, was justifiable. Politics were necessary, even though they included the fun of speeches, parades, banquets, and heavy drinking. Trappers and explorers such as Jedediah Smith admitted rather self-consciously that they were fascinated in part by the adventure. Even business had its sporting aspects, and celebrations such as the breaking of ground for the Baltimore and Ohio or for the opening of the Erie Canal were not inspired entirely by economic considerations. The observation of Christmas or Thanksgiving had overtones of pleasure, while the dedication of a monument such as that at Bunker Hill had patriotic implications. The greatest single celebration was Independence Day (Fourth of July), with bells, firecrackers, and other noisemakers; a big parade featuring Revolutionary soldiers; a feast with innumerable toasts; and finally a magnificent display of fireworks, made particularly fascinating by the accompanying alcoholic haze.

Travel was exceedingly popular and was considered educational even if it were no more than a walk on Broadway or a picnic at the Elysian Fields of Hoboken. Summer seaside resorts drew large crowds, Newport attracting the wealthy from New York and Boston, Nahant the less affluent from Boston, Rockaway the New Yorkers, and Cape May the Philadelphians. Visitors mostly rocked and ate, but also diverted themselves with cards, balls, and suppers. Sea bathing was a minor occupation, for even though women frequently bathed at isolated beaches and were almost fully clothed, the appearance of a woman in a wet bathing suit raised considerable question about her modesty. The great interior watering places were Saratoga Springs and White Sulphur Springs, both heavily patronized by Southerners avoiding the hot weather and the yellow fever. Saratoga was filled with huge hotels that charged as much as a fantastic $10 a day, American plan. White Sulphur provided individual cottages with maid service, although meals were served in a common dining room. The great goal of Northern travel was Niagara Falls, which inspired reams of panegyrics as visitors stood on the platform at Goat Island, took a steamer to the foot of the falls, or climbed down the stairway and went behind the falls. The richer American could crown his travels by touring Europe and sowing his wild oats in Paris and Rome.

A favorite leisure-time occupation combining education with pleasure was to attend one of the many private museums. For a modest admission fee the entire family could be edified by viewing mammoth bones and Indian relics; human curiosities, such as the Siamese twins; wax figures, such as Washington, Black Hawk, or famous criminals committing their crimes; and even specialty acts of dancing, singing, trained animals, and magicians. Most famous were the Peale museums at Philadelphia, New York, and Baltimore, and Scudder's Museum at New York.

America's greatest showman, Phineas Taylor Barnum, had achieved a national reputation by the middle of the century. A Connecticut Yankee, he had cut his eyeteeth by the shrewd trading necessary in a country store. Gravitating to New York, he presented an ancient Negro woman, Joice Heth, whom he advertised as 161 years old and the nurse of George Washington; Joice recounted appealing anecdotes of "dear little George," but insensitive doctors at her autopsy placed her age at about eighty. The famous dwarf, General Tom Thumb, was under Barnum management, and toured Europe in 1844; he was furnished with an elaborate wardrobe and a pony-drawn coach built to his dimensions. Barnum also brought Jenny Lind to America in 1850, giving her the greatest ballyhoo any singer had ever received. Scudder's Museum was purchased in 1841, and then Peale's was added; a fictitious competition was maintained between them for some years before the two organizations were combined. Barnum's own home, "Iranistan," at Bridgeport, Connecticut, was possibly America's most impressive house, with not only balconies, spires, minarets, and acres of curiosities, but also an elephant to do plowing whenever a train passed.

Museums for art alone were not very attractive unless they contained some specialty such as a mammoth painting or a magic lantern; one might desire to see a machine described as a "catadioptrical phantasmagoria" or to obtain an illusion of motion by peering through a hole at action pictures arranged in rotation and mounted on a round card. The daguerreotype photographic process was brought to the United States in 1839, but involved the use of a copper plate that required a two-minute exposure and hence produced a strained expression on the face of even the most stolid sitter.

The circus was being perfected. Early in the century half a dozen acrobats, clowns, and equestrians had traveled in two or three wagons and had used a canvas wall rather than a tent, but new and bigger ideas were inspired by the arrival from England in 1836 of Cooke's Royal Circus with 130 horsemen and acrobats. By the 1850s America had roughly the modern circus, traveling by rail or boat and being announced by a steam calliope. Among other exhibitions of interest were balloon ascensions and high jumps. An American tradition is Sam Patch, who made his last jump at the 125-foot Genesee Falls in 1829; his death came from alcoholism rather than from the jump.

Outdoor sports tended to be individual rather than team competitions, which in itself is a commentary on the current American character. Furthermore, the role of spectator was not important in most of them. Baseball was just getting its start and had no connection with the Abner Doubleday of legend. Football was no more than the desultory kicking of a ball by college undergraduates. Tennis and golf were known but not played, while basketball had not been invented. Ninepins, tenpins (skittles), bowls, quoits, battledore and shuttlecock, handball (fives), cricket, and archery had their devotees. Water sports were generally on top of the water, as in yachting and boat races; the first swimming school was not opened until 1827, and Americans were poor swimmers. Foot races had some popularity, but there were few gymnasiums, while proper equipment and training were almost totally lacking. Wrestling flourished in the West, with no limit on the accompanying mayhem. Boxers used bare fists; a round ended when one man went down, and possibly 100 or more rounds were needed before the fight ended with the complete insensibility of one

of the contestants. The first real American champion was the 6-foot 3-inch Tom Hyer, who in the forties battered a succession of opponents into unconsciousness. More pleasant were the popular sleighing and skating. Cock fighting was favored in the West, with heavy betting on cocks armed with steel spurs. The greatest of all outdoor sports was horse racing, which might even close Wall Street and Congress. The favorite race was open to all horses and comprised three heats of 4 miles each. In spite of a stop watch (1829) that could time to one-sixtieth of a second, the records still remain a bit uncertain.

Indoor sports were extremely varied. Parties, balls, and teas were obvious possibilities. Billiards became something of a national issue when President Adams installed a table at the White House; women as well as men played. Backgammon, chess, and checkers (draughts) were old sports. Dice games were ancient, but apparently craps was introduced to the United States in about 1840. Card playing had considerable popularity in spite of religious objections. Whist was considered the most scientific game, but euchre, all fours (seven-up), cribbage, twenty-one, and poker had their followers. The professional gambler used all the tricks: marked backs, shaved edges, mirrors, and signals. The most important gambling games, however, used cards only incidentally if at all. Roulette, faro, and chuck-a-luck were the favorites of the gambling houses that lined many city streets. Americans also spent millions each year in all kinds of lotteries, of which many were completely fraudulent. In fact, the prevalence of gambling in all kinds of sports is another characteristic of Americans of the early nineteenth century. All life was a gamble, whether a man started a new business or moved to the West. Gambling was an inherent part of American life, and cards or faro or horse racing were only minor incidents in the search for wealth.

CHAPTER 20

Seeking Perfection

(1815-1860)

THE AMERICAN RELIGION

The United States of the early nineteenth century linked love of country with love of God as the highest of virtues. The Revolutionary period had seen a growth of deism and even of atheism, but this radicalism practically disappeared in the succeeding years. The passenger on a canal boat might have a fellow traveler enquire about the state of his soul. The saloon patron might find the bartender asking about his probable salvation. The mother writing to her son in college, the Lowell girl to her parents, or a man to his beloved might well include admonitions about the love of God. Morning and evening prayers were common in the home, as were long graces at meals. This deep religious sentiment not only was preached from the pulpit, but filled the newspapers and magazines; sinful humanity was reminded perpetually that "the grave will soon be your bed-chamber, the earth will soon be your pillow, and the worm your mother and sister."

Theoretically the United States believed in freedom of conscience, with freedom of religion embedded in the first amendment to the Constitution. Actually, the success of an ag-

nostic or atheist in any kind of profession or business was more than doubtful. A man might be jailed for blasphemy or dismissed from a teaching position because he did not believe in the eternity of future punishment. Mob action sometimes occurred. Even testifying in court was difficult, if not impossible: "If there *really* is such a thing as an atheist we hold it right that his testimony should be rejected, as would that of a person notoriously insane."

The great day of Christians was the Sabbath, which was celebrated very strictly by most Americans. The great majority attended church, even though ministers deplored the stay-at-home attitude of some men, and cities often stopped traffic noises by putting chains across the streets containing churches. Many families barred all unnecessary labor and even ate cold meals. Reading was limited to the Bible and other religious literature. A young lady might have a twinge of conscience if she took a stroll without the proper pious thoughts, wrote to her parents, or read a novel or a letter from her betrothed. "Desecrating" the Sabbath seemed a sign of the potential wife beater, thief, and murderer. But such "profanations" existed, at least according to the more strictly religious citizens. Many people, particularly

Westerners, engaged in drinking and other reveling and patronized stores, saloons, and theaters. In New Orleans, French and Spanish tradition made the day one of social activities, which led godly New Englanders to feel that New Orleans morality was dubious. Newer German immigrants liked to drink beer and listen to music on a Sunday evening. Even native-born Americans liked to travel, such as on a Sunday excursion, while some read the new Sunday newspapers, and businessmen liked their mail on Monday morning, all of which meant Sunday work for many people. One of the hottest arguments of the day was whether railroads should run on Sunday.

An American church might be anything from a cathedral with stained-glass windows and robed choir to a barn from which the cows were temporarily removed. In any case (except the barn) it was used only for religious gatherings, including weddings and funerals. Heating by a single stove was always inadequate, and worshipers frequently brought charcoal embers to avoid chilblains. The pews were usually auctioned upon the opening of the church, and then pew rent was paid. The large church had pews in the back or gallery for the poor people and Negroes, and there was considerable popular demand for "free grace and free seats." The ministers of most faiths were supposed to be well mannered and well educated, but ministerial books advising the pastor not to comb his hair in public, drink too much, or spit tobacco juice on the carpet indicate that the ideal was not always attained. The usual sermon treated some noncontroversial topic such as "Faith," "A Good Wife," or "Devotion." Only occasionally did the minister exercise much power in business or politics, but he had considerable influence on individuals and was at times well paid.

The emotional type of religious meeting was very common, although it seemed to concentrate in particular areas; west central New York State, for example, was called the "burned-over district" because of its susceptibility. The greatest American evangelist was Charles Grandison Finney, who overwhelmed large portions of the nation, including Phila-delphia, New York, and Boston, before settling permanently at Oberlin, Ohio, in 1835. As an intelligent man he realized that conversion was only the beginning of religious experience, but that did not prevent him from using real ingenuity to achieve conversions. It was he who emphasized the protracted meeting, the "anxious seat" for repentant sinners, the "holy band" of converts as assistants, and public prayers by women. The revival stressed the ghastliness of death, the dissolution of the body, and the unmitigated horrors of a physical hell, with much less attention to heaven. When Finney traced with his finger the descent of the sinner from heaven to hell, the finger moving from ceiling to floor, half his auditors would rise unconsciously to see the entrance to the pit. As group hysteria grew, men and women shrieked, jerked convulsively, had visions, and even fainted. Some of the effects were bad and others were not permanent, but many conversions were the real beginnings of useful Christian lives.

DOMINANT PROTESTANTISM

The fact that the United States was overwhelmingly religious did not imply any general uniformity of doctrinal beliefs. Most Americans were Protestant, and the essence of Protestantism was individual Bible reading and conscience. The result was that America became the happy hunting ground for Protestant sects—not only larger groups such as the Methodist, Presbyterian, Baptist, Congregational, and Lutheran, but dozens of smaller sects such as the Moravian, Amish, Restorationist, Bible Christian, Mount Zion, Primitive Christian, New Jerusalem, Seventh-Day Adventist, and "Two-Seeders." Even further, Americans in considerable numbers embraced spiritualism after the "Rochester rappings" of the Fox sisters in 1850. The spiritualists soon were holding national conventions and supporting a magazine of their own, the *Seraphic Advocate*.

The number of independent groups continued to grow—in part from division. The Unitarians increased their divergence from the Congregationalists as the very able William Ellery Channing established the new orthodoxy that man had complete control over his own salvation—an idea intimately related to the transcendental concepts of the time. A younger and even more brilliant Unitarian divine, Theodore Parker, eliminated supernaturalism entirely from his faith. Further splits among the Congregationalists came as liberal sentiment increased, as for example the controversy over whether a child at birth was sinful or only filled with "an unyielding determination to sin." The Presbyterians, who had earlier lost the Cumberland Presbyterians on the issues of emotionalism and an educated clergy, now were involved in a bitter dispute between the New School and the Old School. The liberals established Union Theological Seminary to offset Princeton, but when the conservatives won in 1837 they cast out some 100,000 members who they thought were not truly Presbyterian. The Baptist Church gave unwilling birth to the Campbellites or Disciples of Christ, dedicated to primitive New Testament forms. The Methodists fought over the episcopal tradition, while the Episcopalians had friction between the high- and low-church factions. Even the Quakers of the late 1820s had a seceding group headed by Elias Hicks; the dispute was over the divinity of Christ. By the 1840s both the Methodists and the Baptists had split into Northern and Southern churches over the slavery issue. Clearly Protestantism portrayed no picture of unity and Christian peace—too many dissidents fought too vigorously for their beliefs.

❲ *Various Protestant Religious Communities.* Several of the smaller Protestant groups were particularly interesting, both then and later. The Rappites, headed by George Rapp, revolted from the German Lutheran Church and settled in western Pennsylvania, moving then to Indiana, and ultimately selling their property to Robert Owen before returning to Pennsylvania. Their community organization, backed by religious sanctions, was successful economically; but their practice of celibacy meant the end of their community. Especially noteworthy were the Shakers, founded by an Englishwoman, "Mother" Ann Lee, who, after bearing four children, decided that the marriage relationship was the source of all evil and began preaching celibacy. Mother Lee came to America in 1774; but the Shakers grew slowly, reaching their greatest height from 1840 to 1860, when some 6,000 lived in nineteen communities. The Shakers worked hard, their farms were models of efficiency, and their handicraft articles quickly became valuable. Yet their celibacy aroused ridicule, and their religious dancing more so (hence the name "Shaker" from the prime quality of their dance). Ultimately the celibacy feature was practically fatal, once proselyting ceased. In the 1950s the sect has practically vanished. Among the more spectacular individuals in religious life was Robert Matthews, commonly called Matthias, who rejected denominationalism, cut his hair to resemble pictures of Christ, and roamed the streets of New York speaking to the riffraff. Personally he was very impressive and collected rich "angels" from whom he received money and property. Ultimately Matthias was accused of theft, assault, and murder, and his court appearance marked the practical end of his importance.

Extremely influential was William Miller, a pious New England Baptist, who studied the more abstruse parts of the Bible and came to the conclusion that the end of the world would come on 21 March 1843. Many people accepted his calculations and waited for the day of judgment with mingled fears and hopes. When March 22 appeared as usual, the estimates had to be revised and in time made completely indefinite. Millerites were disappointed and sometimes disillusioned; particularly unhappy were those who had given away property in the prospect of the end of the world.

Among the native communities none was more interesting than that of John Humphrey Noyes at Oneida, New York. Noyes was a shy, awkward, conscientious Vermonter, a graduate of Dartmouth, and a minister. Accepting the views of a little group of "perfectionists" he announced that he had attained perfection, by which he meant purity of heart and not of action. With the followers he attracted, he established a community at Putney, Vermont, where all property (mostly his) was held in common and where there was no marriage; his community was not celibate, however, since Noyes took literally the Biblical injunction to love one another. Conservative Vermont farmers proved difficult to convince and ultimately made impossible the continued existence of the Putney community.

The Vermont troubles inspired in 1848 the removal of the Noyes group to Oneida, New York, where it joined other "perfectionists" who had settled earlier. The first few years saw a desperate struggle for existence, but then, under Noyes's continually more practical leadership, prosperity arrived. An impressive variety of industries was established, highlighted by the production of a very effective and profitable steel trap for the catching of game. Property was held in common. Marriage was a group affair, but the production of children was limited to specially selected young people, and the results were surprisingly good; this example of positive eugenics was given the name "stirpiculture." Such beliefs naturally produced intense outside criticism and attracted a certain number of undesirables, which even the most rigorous examination of candidates did not always exclude. Most notorious was the moody and temperamental Charles Guiteau, who later—and long after his brief stay at Oneida—assassinated President Garfield. But in spite of such exceptions the community existed harmoniously and prosperously for many years under the strong leadership of Noyes.

◖ *The Latter-day Saints.* The greatest in size of the new religions was the Church of Jesus Christ of Latter-day Saints, commonly called Mormon. Founder Joseph Smith was another Vermont boy, although his family moved to New York State when he was quite young. He announced in 1827 that after a vision of the angel Moroni he had dug up golden plates telling of the wanderings of the lost tribes of Israel.

The story told by these plates, as translated through magical spectacles endowed with "the gift and power of God," was of how the wicked Lamanites (Indians) destroyed the good Nephites, of whom Mormon was the last great prophet. Believers in the Smith revelations established a small community at Kirtland, Ohio, near Cleveland; but external and internal troubles, including financial reverses, brought talk of its removal. The new Zion was to be in western Missouri, but Missouri hostility led Smith finally to settle upon Commerce, Illinois, which was renamed Nauvoo. The first Saints arrived there in 1839, and soon the city was the most important in Illinois, hard-working and prosperous. Always central was the big, handsome, intensely active Joseph Smith, a man of great personal strength and magnetism, with an almost incredible versatility.

Illinois residents soon exhibited the same hostility as had those of New York, Ohio, and Missouri—a hostility based on jealousy of Mormon prosperity and political influence, on religious intolerance, and on moral objections, for the doctrine of plural marriage, although never announced officially at Nauvoo, was generally known to exist. Clashes between Mormons and "Gentiles" culminated in the mob killing of Joseph and his brother in 1844. The inevitable Mormon confusion was not ended until Brigham Young became president of the church and decided to move the entire community toward the West. The evacuation began in February, 1846, and was one of the heroic episodes in American history. The faithful left a well-established and prosperous community in the middle of winter with only the possessions they could carry on their wagons and headed for an unknown destination. Ultimately they settled in desert country, where irrigation was needed even for the first crops. Incredible hardships and difficulties were overcome to make Salt Lake City a prosperous community. In government the Mormons formed their own state of Deseret, which became the Territory of Utah by the Compromise of 1850. Statehood was delayed by popular objections to polygamy.

⟦ *The Catholic Minority.* Protestant separatism had one exception in the common hostility of all Protestants to all Roman Catholics. Rumors went the rounds that the Catholics took orders from the Pope, who some day planned to rule the United States, and that the confessional and the convent concealed the wildest of orgies. Alarm increased as Irish Catholics crowded the Eastern cities and German Catholics flooded the Ohio Valley. Protestants proclaimed their desire to save the West from "the Devil, the Pope, and Joe Smith," who apparently were all considered about equally bad. A barrage of anti-Catholic words flowed from the pulpit, the religious press, and itinerant street speakers such as the "Angel Gabriel" (John S. Orr), who drew large crowds in the fifties. Supposed "confessions" crashed the best-seller lists. Rebecca Reed's *Six Months in a Convent* (1835) was the imaginings of an emotionally unstable girl who had attended an Ursuline convent school at Charlestown, Massachusetts. *Awful Disclosures by Maria Monk* were the lascivious dreams of a prostitute with a police record; the really "awful disclosure" was that her ghost writer was a nephew of the president of Yale. The excitement produced by such literature and fanned by men like Lyman Beecher, who should have known better, resulted in mob action at various places against Catholics and their property. The crowning outrage was the burning of the convent that had tried to educate Rebecca Reed; the church was saved only by police action. Even worse, only a few of the mob were ever brought to trial, and they were freed to the plaudits of most of the United States, which continued to boast loudly of American religious freedom.

⟦ *Protestant Proselyting.* Protestants also cooperated in certain religious activities that were generally approved. The American Bible Society (1816) was interdenominational and aimed to put a Bible in every home, free if necessary. The American Tract Society, interdenominational, had dozens of agents to distribute religious tracts, books, and the *Christian Messenger,* all carefully edited to avoid denominational conflicts. The American Sunday School Union became entirely religious and published all kinds of study and lesson helps. It had colored tickets to reward the learning of the Bible, and child prodigies could reel off whole chapters at a time. The American Home Missionary Society (Presbyterian, Congregational, and Dutch Reformed) aided poor churches, customarily by paying part of the ministers' salaries until the churches became stronger. Before 1840 three-quarters of its work was in New England and New York, but then came increasing emphasis on the West. Lyman Beecher expressed the common feeling that if "the West is lost all is lost!"

The most thrilling of the religious efforts at this time was in the field of foreign missions, since somehow the conversion of Chinese seemed more romantic than increasing the fervor of citizens of Vermont or Illinois. Inevitably quoted was the Biblical reference to the world being white for the harvest, and equally inevitable was the assumption that proper efforts would Christianize the world within a generation. The most important single organization was the American Board of Commissioners for Foreign Missions (1810), combining Presbyterian, Congregational, and Dutch Reformed. The first two missionaries went to India in 1812, but decided en route that they should be Baptists. Most of the work of the American Board before 1830 was among the American Indians, but then the emphasis shifted to such places as India, China, Turkey, Persia, and Siam; the largest single establishment was at Hawaii. The missionaries were pious and well-educated, but all too frequently had no knowledge of or sympathy with the culture of the people with whom they were to work, labored too hard, and fought too much with other missionaries. Their original optimism proved unjustified, for conversions came slowly. Of course the American Board was itself but one of the nation's missionary enterprises. In fact there were dozens of other religious organizations of all kinds in the United States, and all testified to the current belief in human perfectibility—American model.

AMERICAN HUMANITARIANISM

In addition to the purely religious movements, there were numerous other reforms that received impetus from religious feeling. In one way, reform was big business, with elaborate and numerous organizations, large yearly budgets, and even interlocking directorates, centering particularly in Lewis and Arthur Tappan, silk importers of New York City. The United States was inspired with widespread reform enthusiasm that might express itself in the advocacy of abolition, temperance, world peace, raising fallen women, or Sunday observance; or in trying to eliminate tobacco, corsets, profanity, or tea and coffee. Most consistent were the Friends of Universal Reform, who advocated just about every change suggested by anyone.

Efforts were made on behalf of almost every type of unfortunate. The poverty-stricken still depended rather heavily on the Lady Bountiful tradition of private aid, with some sentiment that in rich America poverty indicated either a lack of ability and energy or the punishment of God, with which there should be no interference. Many towns gave outdoor aid, which often seemed to evaporate before it reached the intended recipients. Some cities had almshouses, which ordinarily were overcrowded with the poverty-stricken, including the sick and insane, and in which graft eroded the meager city appropriations; theoretically the inmates were provided with work, but actually idleness was the usual rule. Orphans—obviously salvageable material—were given asylums in which the strict discipline suggested prisons, with only here and there more intelligent treatment. The children were provided a little education, some training in farm work or housekeeping, and a dash of play, after which they were apprenticed to farmers and housewives; many ended in prison. An orphan

asylum de luxe was the one established by the will of Stephen Girard in Philadelphia, with the novel provision that no minister could set foot on the grounds. Education for the deaf and dumb was fairly new and followed European methods except that articulation was not taught. The oldest and best institution was the American Asylum, run by Thomas H. Gallaudet at Hartford. As usual the institution was private, tuition for the poor now and then being paid by the state; it took only students under twenty-five, taught them trades and housework, and then placed them. Education of the blind was a complete novelty in the United States when schools were established practically simultaneously in Boston, New York, and Philadelphia in the years 1832 and 1833. Best known was the Boston school of Samuel Gridley Howe, where there occurred the fascinating experiment of first making contact with a blind deaf-mute, Laura Bridgman. By 1841 Laura could hold simple manual conversations. In time she learned to knit and sew, but she never spoke. The work of Howe aroused tremendous enthusiasm throughout the United States.

The feeble-minded and insane had customarily been allowed to roam freely as the butt of village jokes unless they were dangerous, whereupon they were locked in unheated rooms and thrown scraps of food. Some towns paid lump sums to provide for the indigent—a system of many abuses. Others confined them in hospitals, prisons, and almshouses. Most asylums before 1840 were private; the number of state institutions increased rapidly after that year, largely because of the careful and effective work of Dorothea Dix. Most doctors held insanity to be curable, and the usual institution claimed 80 to 90 per cent of cures if the patients were institutionalized early. Such fantastic assertions probably indicate only the lack of proper records. The classifications of cases were varied and incomprehensible, the listed causes were at times almost humorous, and the treatment depended on whether the doctor emphasized mind or body. Early in the century the favored theory was that the insane person had too great a head of steam, which should be lowered by cathartics, emetics, and bleeding. More modern was the "rational" treatment of exercise and games in pleasant surroundings, with hot and cold baths, although many institutions clung to the strait jacket and brutality.

Crime, unfortunately, was widely prevalent in favored America. Attaining wealth with a minimum of sweat produced everything from "rolling" drunks to counterfeiting and horse stealing. Moreover, Americans were vigorously aggressive, whether in gangs such as the Forty Thieves of Baltimore and the Plug-Uglies of New York, which assaulted both each other and passers-by, or in fist fights or affairs of honor. Dueling received increasing criticism, particularly because of such affairs as the Hamilton-Burr fracas, but continued to be widespread in the South and Southwest. Arrests of criminals were probably the exception rather than the rule, and many American judges were almost totally ignorant of the law. The poor man awaiting trial and the petty criminal being punished were ordinarily placed in general rooms of a local jail, without proper sanitation, ventilation, clothing, or work. Early in the century women had generally been segregated, but further improvements were slow in coming.

Major offenders might be hanged in great public ceremonies designed to warn other potential evildoers, but normally they went to state prisons of three types: (1) the old variety, with conglomerate rooms and no work, which largely disappeared by the middle of the century. (2) The "Pennsylvania system" type, which had its origin with the opening in 1829 of the Eastern Penitentiary. Here the usual cell was relatively large (11 feet 9 inches by 7 feet 6 inches) and had an exercise yard attached. The prisoner was completely isolated throughout his stay. After a few days of meditation he was given work as a privilege. The general adoption of this system was retarded by its cost. (3) The "Auburn plan," which was inaugurated in 1816 at Auburn, New York, was used in Sing Sing (1828), and later became almost universal. The prisoner was isolated at night in a small cell (7 feet by 3 feet 6 inches), walked in lockstep to dining room and workshop, and was supposed to observe complete silence at all times.

No prison had even tolerable conditions. The usual situation was inadequate heat, poor sanitation, poor food, graft, high mortality, distinctive clothes, harsh discipline, and almost no recreation, religion, or education. Two reform societies, the Pennsylvania Prison Society and the Boston Prison Discipline Society, were only moderately helpful. The greatest improvement of the period was the increasing segregation of both women and children. The New York House of Refuge was opened for boys in 1825 with private, city, and state funds and was soon followed by other similar institutions. The first school entirely for girls was opened in Massachusetts in 1847.

Possibly the saddest of all the reform movements was that for world peace. The American Peace Society (1828) was the creation of William Ladd, but the best-known peace advocates were "the learned blacksmith" Elihu Burritt, who was reputed to be familiar with a hundred languages, and William Lloyd Garrison, whose thoroughgoing opposition to war ruled out even the honoring of war dead, such as by building monuments. All the usual antiwar arguments were presented, and there was talk of arbitration treaties and a league of nations. The majority of the society approved purely defensive war, whereupon Garrison withdrew and formed his own group. Since opponents to peace were hard to find, the movement tended to lapse into impotence, with not even a quorum at the annual meeting of 1860, and then most members supported the Civil War.

❨ *Temperance and Abolition.* The reform to receive the greatest emotional enthusiasm was temperance, which unquestionably was badly needed by a hard-drinking society in which multitudinous city saloons attracted the vice of their communities. Temperance agitation was of ancient lineage, but national organization was effected when six sermons by Lyman Beecher in 1825 inspired the formation of an

American Society for the Promotion of Temperance (1826). The fighting edge of the reformers was the "Washingtonian movement," by and for reformed drunkards and with a female auxiliary. Every possible type of propaganda was used, including simultaneous annual meetings in the United States and Great Britain from 1833, which must have been quite impressive as massed school children led in the singing of temperance songs. The reformers, being very religious, had some trouble explaining the wine drinking of the Bible, but in general they painted alarming pictures of how a little wine led to stronger drink, with eventual drunkenness, theft, wife beating, and murder. The great internal split was between the temperance and total-abstinence advocates. The end products of the reform were two. The first was individual pledges, including the promises of girls not to accept drinking men as escorts and of employers not to hire liquor users. The second was governmental restriction such as the famous Massachusetts law of 1838 that stipulated a *minimum* purchase of 15 gallons. A number of states provided restrictions on the licensing of saloons, and some permitted local option; but the first state-wide prohibitory law was that of Maine in 1846. The revised Maine law of 1851, adopted on the urging of the well-known prohibitionist Neal Dow, was a model for other states; and by the middle fifties almost half of the states limited or prohibited alcoholic beverages. Except in Maine, the movement collapsed during the Civil War.

The reform that in time proved most important in American history was the abolition of Negro slavery. During the late eighteenth century most Americans had agreed that slavery was undesirable, but then the cotton gin made it profitable, while at the same time Northern extremists such as William Lloyd Garrison became extremely irritating to Southern sensibilities. Southern apologies for slavery turned into positive support until Thomas Dew could write in the 1830s: "I believe it to be the greatest of all the great blessings which a kind Providence has bestowed upon our glorious region." Increasingly Southerners stopped the circulation of antislavery books and pamphlets—in which action, incidentally, they had considerable Northern support. A temperate group like the American Colonization Society (1817), which proposed to free Negroes and send them to Liberia, lost support on all sides.

The most important leaders of the abolition movement were the New York merchants Lewis and Arthur Tappan, while the outstanding field worker was the minister Theodore Weld. These men were essentially moderate and gave priority to a Northern Negro school that would show Negro capabilities and lay the groundwork for ultimate emancipation. The Tappan plans were disarranged by the explosive force of Garrison, and when they formed their New York Anti-Slavery Society (1833) they compromised on the meaningless formula of "immediate emancipation which is gradually accomplished." When the American Anti-Slavery Society was organized later the same year, Arthur Tappan was president and his paper *The Emancipator* was the official publication, but Garrison had to be placated with a minor job and the use of some of his writings. The national society suffered continually from lack of funds, from internal dissension, and from hostility both North and South. Lewis Tappan's home was burned; Garrison was paraded with a halter around his neck; Whittier was pelted with mud; Weld was showered with mud, lampblack, eggs, and stones; and the Reverend Elijah Lovejoy was murdered by an Illinois mob.

The general attitude of the Anti-Slavery Society during the late 1830s was moderate. It stressed such immediate objects as stopping the slave trade and slavery in the territories rather than general abolition. It worked toward strengthening local societies, particularly in the country and small towns. It developed a highly efficient organization for presenting Congress with petitions, of which many were handled by John Quincy Adams. Garrison captured control of the society in 1840, and his radicalism, together with the difficulty of raising money in a period of depression, caused the movement to lose force for some years. Reviving in the late forties, it found increasing support in the North and began to be a power in politics. The Liberty party in 1840 and 1844 had been able to attract very few votes for James G. Birney, but the Free Soil party did better for Van Buren in 1848, and the early fifties saw the birth of the Republican party, through which antislavery sentiment became an important force.

❰ *Women's Rights.* Partly as a consequence of the various reform movements, particularly of the temperance and abolition agitation, came a drive for more rights for women. Active and philanthropically minded women such as Lucretia Mott, Sarah and Angelina Grimké, Elizabeth Cady Stanton, Susan B. Anthony, and Lucy Stone were diligent workers for all sorts of reforms. As long as they remained humble laborers, doing the dull chores and not aspiring to public speaking and office holding, their labors were welcomed. But when they started to do their own speaking they encountered a furious outcry against the immodesty of women appearing before mixed audiences. Hurt feelings led them to look around and find their sisters suffering heavy discrimination in every field of life, with the partial exception of certain types of literature. Their natural reaction was to agitate for more rights and better treatment for women. Their male co-workers generally accepted the desirability of more rights for women, but quite correctly held that feminism would draw new hostility toward temperance and abolition, which they felt were more immediately pressing.

The real start of the modern crusade for rights for women came with a meeting called by Lucretia Mott and Elizabeth Stanton in Seneca Falls in 1848. The main action of the convention was to adopt a women's declaration of independence, which started with "When, in the course of human events" and paralleled the original Declaration except that man took the place of George III. What the feminists wanted first of all was the right of the wife to control her person, earnings, and children. They were also interested, however,

in greater industrial and professional opportunity, and in political rights, including the right to vote. The movement gathered force but slowly in spite of the herculean efforts of its promoters. Only gradually were women's economic and political disabilities lessened and their educational opportunities increased.

UTOPIAN COMMUNITIES

Many Americans were impatient with the slow progress of reform and felt that the shorter road to utopia in social relations was to establish small communities of like-minded persons who would show by their lives the value and effectiveness of the highest ideals. These communities were at times religious in inspiration, and some of these have been discussed earlier, but many of them had little religious motivation, while some opposed traditional religious observances vigorously. Such secular groups insisted that most human ills were produced by faulty living or institutions, and they frequently tried to get away from current capitalism in the direction of socialism or communism. Never were they permanently successful. To some extent they reflected contemporary European utopianism, using the basic concepts and some of the personnel of the European movement. But also they reflected parallel American idealism, and their membership was frequently native-born in large part.

One of the most spectacular of the earlier communities was that of Robert Owen, rich Scots industrialist, who held that human nature was entirely the product of environment and hence could be perfected by ideal living conditions. The proof of the validity of his theories was to come on the banks of the Wabash in Indiana, where in 1825 he established a colony on land purchased from the Rappites. The experiment attracted many able men, but disappointingly small productivity and regimented living soon palled, and dissension became rife. Owen's ideas were a liability, since he opposed private property, organized religion, and the marriage bond—to the horror of most Americans. He also underwrote all losses and in the few years of the community lost most of his private fortune. A friend of his, Frances (Fanny) Wright, toured the United States, supporting radical proposals in politics, religion, and sex to the great embarrassment of most of her friends. Her biggest idea was to buy a few slaves, teach them trades, and then have them pay back their purchase price, whereupon the process would be repeated on an ever larger scale until slavery was ended. She actually started the experiment at Nashoba, near Memphis, but it was very badly managed and soon failed.

The Hopedale Community, near Milford, Massachusetts, was religiously reformist, but compromised with capitalism by organizing a joint-stock company. After a period of success (1841 to 1856) it collapsed. Fruitlands, near Harvard, Massachusetts, was the faddist conception of Bronson Alcott. Its members were so delicately kindhearted that no beast of burden was used, animals were not turned into food, cotton cloth was avoided because it was the product of slave labor, and woolen cloth was eschewed because shearing left the sheep without their coats. The quick collapse of the community came only in time to save the health of the experimenters. At Brook Farm in Massachusetts the Transcendentalists demonstrated how simple living and hand labor could be combined with high thinking. The high thinking turned out to be reasonably satisfactory, even though it was handicapped by the simple living. To have a Hawthorne spend his working hours pitching manure was not an unqualified success, although possibly because land and equipment were both poor.

At any rate the experiment failed. Brook Farm was run along the lines of a Fourierist phalanx —a plan for an ideal society developed by the Frenchman François Fourier and propagandized in the United States by such men as Albert Brisbane and Horace Greeley. Possibly as many as fifty phalanxes were organized in the United States. Their average life was about two years. Another Frenchman, Étienne Cabet, had his own plans for utopia—or Icaria, as he called it. In 1848 he led a group of followers to Texas, but within a year they found their situation impossible and migrated to Nauvoo, which had by then been abandoned by the Mormons. Here again internal dissension brought failure.

The utopian community was certainly the extreme of the reforming spirit of the early nineteenth century, and in many ways merely amusing. But in an important sense such communities were straws that showed the direction of the wind. Men were earnest and optimistic. They were crammed with the highest of ideals and believed firmly that acceptance of their ideals was really possible and would produce something like a perfect world. The ideal world of the future was not some remote possibility, but was to be the creation of tomorrow, or at least the day after tomorrow. Clearly, along the lines of their thinking, America was to lead the world toward perfection. The United States had the highest form of religion and the best type of government, and out of these components would soon come the ideal world for which men's hearts had yearned over the long ages. Rather sadly, the perfectionist spirit declined after 1850. The ideal future faded into the more remote distance as sectional friction darkened the coming days of the Republic.

CHAPTER 21

Westward Expansion

(1815-1860)

POPULATION GROWTH

The United States of the years 1815 to 1860 was a youthfully optimistic nation, aggressively individualistic, certain that the twin advantages of Protestant Christianity and American democracy ensured its future greatness. At home it was expanding vigorously, while abroad it expected that other nations would in time become sufficiently wise to copy American institutions and patterns of thought. The idea of being on the defensive against either outside ideas or outside military force never occurred seriously. Americans were God's chosen people, and He would ensure their triumphant progress.

Expansionist ideas were possible only with a growing population, and the American people were increasing magnificently. The 9,600,000 of 1820 became 23,200,000 by 1850, an increase of over 100 per cent in a single generation; in fact the United States was more than doubling each quarter century. This tremendous upsurge came primarily from the high domestic birth rate. American parents were tremendously fertile, and their children might reasonably be expected to occupy the entire North American continent and then to over-

254

flow into more remote places. Self-confessed possessors of the world's highest culture, what could stop them?

The expected goals of American population growth were not entirely achieved, and certainly the 90 million of 1900 and the 360 million of 1950, which should have come from the doubling during each twenty-five years, were not achieved. The basic explanation is that the birth rate did not remain at the high levels of the early nineteenth century. Apparently the first declines had come early in the century, and then the process accelerated. This falling birth rate was offset in part by a falling death rate. Apparently the life span was increasing throughout the nineteenth century, which meant that greater average ages compensated for the decline in the number of births. One person living to forty was as good statistically as two who died at twenty. Even though the great medical discoveries that conquered so many human diseases came for the most part after the middle of the century, a real start had been made before 1850 in lowering the mortality rate.

Another factor in population growth was immigration, which certainly was increasing, even though the figures are far from certain.

Official records, beginning in 1820, show approximately 308,000 arrivals by 1850. The census of 1850, however, listed the foreign-born at two million, which was almost 10 per cent of the total population, and incredible if the port authorities were accurate. Probably it was the immigration figures that were the more unreliable, which in turn means that any precise statement of proportionate arrivals from each nation cannot be made.

THE IMMIGRANT

The United States seemed a golden land of opportunity to many Europeans. That opportunity was to some extent religious or political, such as for the refugees from the unsuccessful revolutions of 1830 and 1848, but overwhelmingly it was economic. According to common stories the land was incredibly fertile and almost costless, taxes were low, wages of unskilled labor were an impressive dollar a day, and there were no beggars; everyone had fine clothes, magnificent watch chains, and enough money to attend museums and horse races. Here was real opportunity for a poor man to make his fortune.

The poor man desiring to migrate to America was faced with impressive difficulties. He must break lifetime ties of family and friends, with the realization that return was highly unlikely. Even steerage passage might take all his savings, and he necessarily traveled on a small, crowded, uncomfortable, and even dangerous boat; often as many as 10 per cent died of what was called "ship fever." On arrival he was confused by the new language and customs, and was frequently swindled, not only in the boardinghouses and bawdy houses of the port, but also in the purchase of transportation and land. Naturally his opportunities were greater in good than in bad times, and the immigrant flow consequently increased with prosperity, but at any time he might encounter poverty and squalor. On the other hand, however, the majority actually found America a land of great opportunity and lived highly successful lives.

The peoples arriving in the greatest numbers during the period from 1815 to 1860 were the Irish and the Germans. The Irish were the more highly visible because they were glad to escape from farm labor, which had brought them nothing but poverty and hard work, and settle in the cities. Urban centers such as New York, Boston, and Philadelphia developed large slum areas, for the Irish had no proper background for city living. The Irish built railroads, dug sewers, and carried bricks, but seldom entered the skilled trades or tended machines. Their lack of education and of industrial skills, together with a tendency toward boisterousness and pugnaciousness, led native Americans to describe them as the "low Irish." The Germans numbered more well-educated men and women because of the inclusion of political refugees, but many were marked by truculence and crudity as well as the more usually noted traits of cleanliness and industry. While many stayed in the East, a large proportion went West, flooding the area from Cincinnati to St. Louis and then pushing north into Wisconsin, where Milwaukee became a German city. They tended to retain their language, customs, and even dress, and to take their amusements calmly by drinking beer and listening to music. Other lesser groups included English and Scots who disliked home conditions. Jewish synagogues appeared more and more frequently in the cities, for the Jews were city dwellers and tended to enter such businesses as retail merchandising; to some extent they replaced the Connecticut Yankees as peddlers. The Scandinavians began to appear in perceptible numbers by the 1840s, eventually settling largely in such Northwestern areas as Wisconsin, Minnesota, and the Dakotas; they took kindly to farming and were frugal and hard-working. Other groups such as French, Polish, Bohemian, and Italian came in smaller numbers. French-Canadians seeped over the border. A few Chinese arrived with the gold rush. Generally, however, the bulk of immigrants came from northern and western Europe.

The contributions of the immigrants were impressive. Economically, they helped to conquer the West, breaking virgin sod and braving Indians and grasshoppers; they improved American agriculture by introducing more careful and intensive cultivation. They furnished much of the unskilled labor for an expanding America, incidentally pushing many natives into factory work and supervisory jobs; possibly they held down wages, but since labor was sufficiently scarce, the effect was not striking. Some became outstandingly successful, like the Irish-born Alexander T. Stewart, who rose to be the greatest merchant prince of his day. Several of them, like Samuel Slater (textiles), John Roebling (wire rope), and August Belmont (finance), made real technical contributions. In science, men like Priestley, Agassiz, and Audubon were outstanding. In scholarship, Charles Follen, who introduced German to Harvard, and Francis Lieber, political economy expert, illustrated foreign contributions. In politics both Germans and Irish tended to be Democrats until the Republican party attracted most of the Germans; among foreign political contributions were such radical ideas as those of Marx and Proudhon, which were not unmixed blessings. In education the migrants favored government support of free schools. In music, the foreign-born brought both performers and appreciation.

⟪ *Nativist Intolerance.* The immigrants' contributions to their adopted home were many, but the native-born were not always enthusiastic about the new arrivals. Natives felt bitterly about losing jobs to Irish "paddies," regardless of any hypothetical long-run effects. The labor movement was slowed, and wages were at least prevented from rising more rapidly. The foreign-born furnished more than their fair share of defectives, since there were no limitations on who might enter the country. Many immigrants became criminals, even though native Americans committed at least a proportionate number of major crimes. Many reform movements such as temperance and Sabbath observance were retarded. Politically, the immigrant was unfamiliar with democracy and was thought to be influenced unduly by demagogic promises; he took somewhat too kindly to the

formation of city machines. Most exasperating to contemporary Americans was the large increase in the number of Catholics, which included all the Irish and half of the Germans. After all, native Americans were predominantly Protestant.

Native-born resentment brought antiforeign agitation that tended to be heavily anti-Catholic. Street fights and attacks on German social clubs, and even on Catholic schools and church property, were altogether too frequent. Several cities spawned anti-Catholic parties, the New York group electing their mayor in 1837 with the help of the Whigs. Agitation declined when immigration decreased after the panic of 1837, but revived even more strongly by the 1850s. Various groups such as the Supreme Order of the Star-spangled Banner, United Sons of America, and Sons of the Sires united to form the American party, which was designed, in its own words, to protect the United States against the "insidious wiles of foreigners." The party was secret, with the usual grips, passwords, and ritual; and since the members would not talk of their organization, it was commonly called Know-Nothing. After a show of strength in various parts of the Union, the party split over the slavery issue and then died with the depression of 1857. Antiforeign sentiment clearly had considerable support in the United States, even though that strength was not translated into any real limitations of immigration until after 1880.

THE WESTWARD SURGE

Immigration, when added to the native birth rate, created an ever-increasing number of Americans who envisioned opportunity in the great open spaces of the West. Surplus Eastern farmers' sons looked toward the new lands eagerly. Western migration had slowed during the years of the War of 1812, but with the end of the war the floodgates were opened, and the vast movement in the years up to the panic of 1819 became known as the "great migration." Hopeful settlers entered the Ohio Valley in ever greater numbers, but also spread along Lake Erie and occupied the valleys of the Southern rivers (particularly the Mississippi), especially in Louisiana and Missouri. Land was acquired either from earlier residents or from the Federal government under the law of 1800. Not until 1820 did the government recognize the obvious difficulties of the credit system and abolish it, while at the same time reducing the minimum price of public land to $1.25 an acre. The general method of settlement remained much as earlier. The sound of the woodsman's axe was heard from every clearing, the log cabin and homemade furniture remained in general use, crops were simple, and transportation was poor. Southern frontiersmen now and then had a slave or two, usually working beside them in the field, but the great movement of slaves did not come until later. In the older parts of the West, particularly the upper Ohio Valley, manufacturing was developing.

Expanding settlement necessitated territorial and then state governments. Out of the great migration came the states of Indiana (1816), Mississippi (1817), Illinois (1818), Alabama (1819), and Missouri (1821). The delay in the admission of Missouri, for which the necessary legislation had been presented to Congress in 1819, was due to a flare of sectional animosity, based partly on slavery.[1]

After the depression of the early 1820s, movement to the West again started. Land sales boomed to an unprecedented peak of 20 million acres in 1836, only to be stopped by another panic, this one in 1837. The flood of population to the West during this time was inadequately demonstrated by the admission of new states, which included only Arkansas (1836) and Michigan (1837), but retained the equal balance of North and South in the Senate. Some of the new population further filled the Ohio Valley, so that the cities from Pittsburgh to St. Louis grew into important commercial and industrial centers. Toward the north, southern Michigan boomed, while Wisconsin received its first important start. Lead discoveries in the region that included Galena,

[1] See pp. 274–275.

Illinois, and Mineral Point, Wisconsin, helped to draw people to southern Wisconsin. To the south, population flowed into the Gulf states and across the Mississippi into western Louisiana, Texas, and Arkansas. Slaves began to arrive in large numbers; roads were bordered at night with the myriad campfires that marked the slave coffles (chained groups). Some of these slaves were being moved west by their masters, who were taking up new and richer land, while others were being transported by slave dealers who wanted to profit from the richness of Western planters. The center of cotton culture moved beyond the mountains.

The most impressive characteristic of the movement of population was its abrupt halt on the edge of the great Western plains. The years between 1820 and 1860 saw population toeing a line that ran roughly north and south through the great bend of the Missouri River. People accepted as fact the reports of explorers that the vast country to the west was deficient in water and hence unfitted for white agricultural settlement. School geographies called the whole region the Great American Desert, and the Federal government experimented with camels as a means of transportation.

DISPOSING OF THE INDIANS

While a country reputed to be desert intimidated the white farmer, it offered a splendid opportunity to dispose of the Indians. What could be more reasonable—from the white viewpoint—than to move the Eastern Indians, who were an increasing nuisance, to the Western plains? Secretary of War Calhoun stated this policy to Congress in 1823, and President Monroe and his successors put it into effect. As the policy developed it had four main phases: (1) concentration of the Western Indians to make room for the Eastern; (2) removal of the Eastern Indians to the West; (3) more careful control of Indian-white relations, particularly of Indian traders; and (4) the building of army posts to guard the frontier. The line of the supposedly permanent

REMOVAL OF
EASTERN INDIANS,
1830–1840

•••••••• Black Hawk's route,
1832

Indian frontier was that of white settlement, extending to the great bend of the Missouri. The Removal Law of 1830, giving the President power to move the Eastern Indians, authorized him to assure the Eastern tribes "that the United States will forever secure and guarantee to them, and their heirs or successors, the country so exchanged with them." Such solemn guarantees were given in good faith, but events were to shatter the promises within a short generation.

The removal of the Eastern Indians was fa-cilitated by the absence of strong Indian military power, which had generally been broken at an earlier date. North of the Ohio the only real difficulty came with the Sac and Fox, and it was rather a minor incident. The Sac and Fox had agreed to move from northwestern Illinois to Iowa, but were hurried by the advancing white farmers, which made both sides legally wrong. After the Indians had crossed the river, the elderly Black Hawk led a small group back into Illinois (1832) and threw the frontier into an uproar. Troops were gathered, including the young Captain Abraham Lincoln. The Indian braves saw no chance of victory and chanted their death songs as they charged the oncoming whites. When the whites turned and ran the Indians were inspired to a brief bit of successful raiding before they were driven up the Rock and the Fox Rivers, over to the Wisconsin River near the present Madison, Wisconsin, and down that river to the Mississippi. Only 150 of the original 1,000 Indians succeeded in returning home, and Black Hawk himself was taken East to be exhibited—to the disappointment of most of his audiences, since he was elderly and mild in appearance, without even being very red in color. As usual in such cases, the Indians upon their defeat ceded more land.

The removal of the Southern Indians was somewhat more difficult and much more unpleasant. The Five Civilized Tribes occupied possibly 18 million acres in Georgia, Mississippi, and Alabama and were high in the scale of Indian culture; they practiced a settled agriculture, and the Cherokee could boast a regular constitution and a written language. During the late 1820s the discovery of gold in the Indian country produced great enthusiasm among the whites; the Indian land was invaded by prospectors, who were followed by traders, speculators, and settlers. The stories of what happened to the Choctaw, Chickasaw, Cherokee, Creek, and Seminole are depressingly similar. In each case the Indians refused to sell their land, resisting both bribery and intimidation, whereupon the various states placed the Indian lands under white control. Ultimately in each case a removal treaty was achieved by negotiations that were dubious in legality as well as in morality. In the cases of both the Cherokee and the Seminole the regular army had to be used; the result was a ten-year war with the Seminole. In every case the whites invaded the Indian country before the Indians departed, and the Indians ultimately headed west with little more than the clothes on their backs, only to find no preparations for their arrival. They were cheated by white agents and traders and found the plains tribes hostile. The fact that they in time developed satisfactory

civilizations is a tribute to their abilities and to their persistence.

The saddest of all the aspects of the "permanent frontier" was its failure to remain permanent. Within a generation of its establishment, its end was certain, and a new series of treaties brought further Indian concessions, with the elimination of independent Indian nations not far in the future. The return of prosperity during the 1840s brought another tide of westward expansion, which affected the Indians partly by the direct encroachment of white settlement, but also by the increasing number of whites entering Indian country. The states that entered the Union during this general period were Texas (1845), Florida (1845), Iowa (1846), Wisconsin (1848), California (1850), Minnesota (1858), Oregon (1859), and Kansas (1861); practically all the remainder of the West was organized into territories. Most pertinent in relation to the Indians were Iowa, Minnesota, and Kansas, because all of them were in areas that earlier had been assumed to be uninhabitable for white farmers.

THE BOOMING MIDDLE WEST

By the 1850s the agricultural production of the great national staples came to center in the Mississippi Valley, much of it on prairie land that at first had been skirted skeptically but soon proved among the richest in America. The main crops of the area were cattle, sheep, wheat, corn, and hogs—appearing chronologically in that order. Illinois became America's leading agricultural state, emphasizing corn and hogs, and its metropolis Chicago assumed national primacy in meat packing and manufacturing farm machinery. Minnesota hummed throughout the 1850s, and the fertile prairies attracted enough immigrants to transform the meager 6,000 residents of 1850 into a bustling 172,000 ten years later.

The cutting edge of the settled frontier tended to be dominated heavily by land speculators. Nowhere was this situation more apparent than in Kansas. Dozens of the early settlements there were little more than speculative ventures; there were acres of virgin sod, which were advertised in the East by beautiful pictures showing impressively busy cities. Westward-moving farmers frequently bought their land from speculators, either large or small, for practically everyone was a speculator. Although Federal laws through 1840 gave no rights to the man who settled before the land was surveyed, in actual practice his claim was ordinarily respected. Practice became law when the Preemption Act of 1841 authorized the man who had arrived ahead of the survey and who had cultivated the land to buy 160 acres at the minimum price of $1.25 an acre. Legally the public domain was protected by the cultivation provision, by making illegal any preemption if thereby the settler owned over 320 acres, and by an amendment of 1843 that prohibited any man from taking up more than one preemption claim. In actual fact, lax administration made all these provisions easy to evade. Of course the ultimate aim of the Westerners was free land.

OPENING THE FAR WEST

The vast wilderness beyond the great bend of the Missouri gradually became known as it was invaded by people pursuing business, pleasure, or wealth. Government explorers, of whom the first were Lewis and Clark, soon included such outstanding men as Zebulon M. Pike, who surveyed the regions of the upper Mississippi and the Southern plains; Stephen H. Long, who reported extensively on the plains country; Henry R. Schoolcraft, who finally located the source of the Mississippi; and John C. Frémont, whose descriptions of overland routes were later used by travelers as guide books. These government explorers were in many cases greeted in their travels by trappers of the stamp of Jedediah S. Smith and James Ohio Pattie, who were largely responsible for making known the character of the Far Southwest. Money-minded individuals such as Benjamin

L. E. de Bonneville and Nathaniel J. Wyeth had visions of commercial possibilities in the Oregon country. Among others entering the wilderness were invalids seeking health, botanists and other scientists looking for specimens, big-game hunters, Indian painters, missionaries, and dozens of others with motives as varied as human nature.

The earliest wilderness business was the search for furs, particularly beaver. Trappers belonged in general to one of three groups. First were the Indians, who trapped according to their desire for white goods and traded their catches once a year. Second were the employees of the larger fur companies; these men were hired by the year and turned over their entire catches. Third and most picturesque were the independent trappers, often called mountain men. Individualists of the type of the Patties, Kit Carson, Jim Bridger, and Jedediah Smith emerged from the wilderness once a year to trade their furs for the necessities and pleasures of the white man. Their leathery skins and primitive dress made them at times hard to distinguish from the Indians; in fact they frequently lived with native wives and were at times adopted into the Indian tribes. They were bold and reckless men, able to survive the worst hardships the wilderness could produce, and combined uncertain proportions of kindness and cruelty.

Most fur trading was done at the forts scattered throughout the wilderness by the larger companies, but the rendezvous system was in operation between 1828 and 1839; a traders' caravan went west in the spring to a prearranged meeting place, where trading was prosecuted until either the goods or the furs were exhausted, and then the caravan returned east. During the years from 1796 to 1822 the government had its own "factories" for the fur trade, but the system was abandoned primarily because of political pressures brought to bear in behalf of the private companies.

Of the larger fur companies, several, such as the Missouri Fur Company and the Rocky Mountain Fur Company, were rather amorphous groups, with no continuity of corporate existence. The greatest single company was

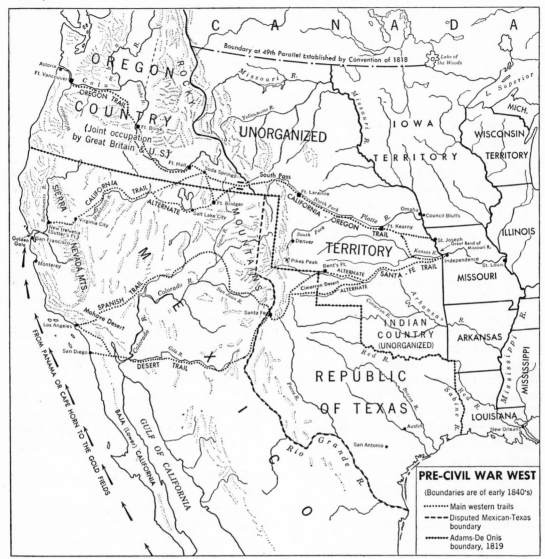

PRE-CIVIL WAR WEST
(Boundaries are of early 1840's)
.... Main western trails
- - - - Disputed Mexican-Texas
boundary
•••••• Adams-De Onis
boundary, 1819

the American Fur Company, owned by John Jacob Astor until the middle 1830s. Astor was inspired by the Louisiana Purchase to project a chain of forts up the Missouri River and down the Columbia. The presumed first link of the chain was Astoria, founded near the mouth of the Columbia by both sea and land parties in 1811; but the War of 1812 brought the abandonment of the fort, and the project was never revived. Astor turned his attention to the Great Lakes, which he soon dominated, and then to the Missouri Valley, where he became the greatest single operator. To the north

in Canada was the Hudson's Bay Company, which combined with its chief rival, the Northwest Company (also Canadian), in 1821. Canadian traders had reached the Pacific Coast (Alexander Mackenzie) in 1793 and dominated the Oregon country after the War of 1812. Chief factor John McLoughlin established himself at Fort Vancouver in 1825 and was able to bar American traders from the country west of the mountains.

The fur trade had both good and bad features in terms of Indian relations. The Indians were delighted to be able to exchange their furs for such useful articles as cloth, guns, ammunition, and hardware, or for such obviously attractive commodities as mirrors, colored beads, and whisky. Trade was ordinarily conducted in one of the many company forts, and these rectangular bastions of pickets or adobe, with their blockhouses at diagonal corners, proved impervious to Indian attack, thus impressing the Indians with white power, and to some extent acting as a deterrent to Indian attack. On the other hand, white trappers and traders were often highhanded and belligerent, with the inevitable results of armed conflicts. The traders quite notoriously charged too high prices for their products and then falsified the books so that the Indian was always in debt— which meant that he felt obligated to return to the same trader the next year. Furthermore, white trappers carried with them the white men's diseases and whisky, both of which proved demoralizing.

A special type of business that crossed the plains in increasing amounts was the traffic to Santa Fe. The markets of the Spanish settlements along the upper Rio Grande had long fascinated Missouri merchants, who actually were closer than those of Mexico City. All trading ventures ended in capture and imprisonment until 1821, which was the year of the successful Mexican revolution, and from that date American trade grew fairly rapidly. The traders left Independence or some nearby town in the early spring, loading their wagons mainly with textiles and hardware. The cautious driver followed the Arkansas River to Bent's Fort in present Colorado and then turned south, but the more aggressive went directly over the Cimarron desert. Arriving at Sante Fe he sold his goods, flirted with the girls, attended fandangos, and ate such exotic foods as chile con carne before returning home ahead of the winter weather. The trade was never tremendous in terms of dollars, but it helped to destroy any possible illusion about either Mexican or Indian power, and the garish accounts of the traders produced a somewhat synthetic golden glow about the handful of .adobe huts that constituted the greater part of Santa Fe.

MANIFEST DESTINY

❲ *Texas*. The American stereotype that the Great Plains was uninhabitable by white farmers led discontented and ambitious agriculturists to look farther afield for opportunity. Edging the southwest perimeter of the United States from Texas to California were lands of varying attractiveness controlled feebly by the Spanish Empire and then after 1821 by the unimpressive new nation of Mexico. On the Northwest Coast lay Oregon, to which we had at least a claim. Although the United States had apparently stopped its expansion with the treaty of 1819, by which we definitely renounced any claim to Texas, ambitious Americans were not long deterred by this fact. Almost before the ink had dried on the treaty, Americans were again on the move.[2]

The fertile Gulf coast of Texas, with its scattering of Spanish settlements and missions, had long attracted the speculative gaze of optimistic Americans. Even before 1800, which meant before the admission of Ohio or the purchase of Louisiana, American filibustering parties were raiding Texas to acquire horses or any other valuables that might be detached. The extent of the connections of these invaders with James Wilkinson was amazing. Philip Nolan, protégé of Wilkinson and friend of Jefferson, entered in 1800, only to be killed and his men imprisoned. Burr probably was headed for Texas, although he never arrived. A son of Wilkinson was a member of the Guitterez-Magee expedition of 1812. Magee had been with Mathews in Florida, and the invading force proclaimed the patriotic intention of freeing Texas from Spanish rule. The 130 men who crossed the border grew to about 2,500 by the time they captured San Antonio; possibly 700 of them were American. Ultimately the invaders were defeated, with a lack of mercy on both sides, and only 93 Americans ultimately escaped. A nephew of Wilkinson, James Long, invaded Texas in 1819 and proclaimed a republic that maintained a precari-

[2] For the diplomacy concerning Texas, Oregon, and California, see chaps. 26 and 27.

ous independence for two years before being defeated. All such expeditions were completely on their own, since the American government gave them no assistance of any kind.

American interest in Texas increased vastly when American farmers began to cross the border. The vanguard was Moses Austin, an ingenious and foot-loose Connecticut Yankee whose hopes of a fortune in Missouri lead had been exploded by the panic of 1819. To the amazement of practically everyone he persuaded the Spanish authorities to give him a grant (1821) on condition that he bring 300 families to Texas. Moses died before he could fulfill his contract, but his work was continued by his son Stephen F. Austin, whose offerings of land soon attracted 5,000 settlers. The successful Mexican revolution of 1821 brought a more liberal land policy for Texas, as power to grant land was given to the state of Coahuila and Texas. Americans by the dozen, including of course Wilkinson, flocked to Mexico to take advantage of the liberality; and starting in 1825 a rapid succession of *empresario* grants, by which the grantees promised to bring settlers, soon made a patchwork of Texas. The Mexicans hoped thereby to increase Texan numbers and wealth, and hence their taxes— a hope that proved ruinous in its realization.

American settlers, lured by attractive *empresario* land advertising, soon began to flow in ever-increasing numbers across the border into Texas. They were estimated as 10,000 in 1827, twice that many in 1830, and 35,000 in 1835. They went as a normal part of the frontier process, originating largely in the nearby American states. They settled mainly in southeastern Texas, where physical conditions were much like those farther east, and where cotton culture was profitable. Theoretically they became loyal Mexicans and good Catholics, but actually neither Mexican army detachments nor priests produced any apparent enthusiasm. Some of them married Mexican girls, thereby attaining larger land grants, but without enhancing their loyalty to Mexico. As usual they were rough, individualistic, and restive; an abortive revolt of 1826–1827 afforded a preview of the reactions of the new settlers

when conditions became distasteful. The successful revolt came in 1836, although nine years then passed before the coming of the expected annexation to the United States.

❡ *Oregon.* Even before Texas became United States territory, restless American settlers were plodding across the 2,000 weary miles to the Pacific Coast. Their first great interest was Oregon, which in the early days was defined as the territory north of California, south of Russian Alaska, and west of the continental divide. The first important American interest resulted from the three-cornered trade that involved New England, the Northwest Coast, and the Far East. Captain Robert Gray entered the Columbia River in 1792, giving the United States an important claim to the entire region. The only practical effort at occupation in the early years was the ill-fated Astor venture; and after the War of 1812 the Hudson's Bay Company, represented in Oregon by John McLoughlin, was able to monopolize the fur trade, even against the tough and aggressive American trappers. Any interest in Oregon was so small that even after the withdrawal of Spain and Russia, a joint occupation agreement seemed satisfactory to Britain and the United States.

American interest in Oregon started to increase in the 1820s when Hall J. Kelley, an almost hysterical New England schoolmaster, began to write and talk of Oregon as practically a modern Garden of Eden. Even though his planned colonization did not materialize and a personal visit was very unhappy, his fervor did not lessen. A second and unusual attractive force appeared in 1831, when four Oregon Indians floated down the Missouri to St. Louis. Their exact intentions are today a trifle uncertain, but religious Americans saw them as the "wise men from the West" asking for Christianity. Before the end of the decade, the Methodists, the Presbyterians and Congregationalists (combined in "the American Board"), and the Roman Catholics had sent missionaries. The Methodists actually worked for the most part with the whites and half-breeds of the Willamette Valley, while the

Presbyterians and Congregationalists lost force with their perpetual bickering; the Catholics made the best showing, but the total mission enterprises were more important in advertising Oregon than in converting Indians. The reputed glories of Oregon attracted restless farmers, who began to make the long trip across the plains to Oregon in 1839, their numbers increasing in the early forties. Several parties were led by missionaries, and when the new arrivals found a government necessary, the plans were made at the Methodist mission. By the mid-forties Oregon was well on its way to being absorbed in the American economy.

❮ *California.* Somewhat less attractive to Americans in the years around 1840 was California, which nominally was Mexican after the revolution of 1821, but which actually had been left pretty much to its own devices. Mexican governors and a handful of poorly equipped troops exercised no more than theoretical control. Whether foreigners such as Americans should be encouraged to settle in California was a question that was answered variously. As a sprinkling of American sailors, trappers, and merchants appeared in California they might find themselves either loaded with land and honors or languishing in prison. Among the early arrivals, two became extremely important. Thomas Larkin settled at Monterey, the capital, in 1832 and became its outstanding merchant; in time he was the first American Consul, the agent of Polk, and a plotter of revolution. John A. Sutter had left Switzerland just ahead of the law and had turned up in California in 1839. He developed a Sacramento Valley estate which he called New Helvetia, and which really constituted an independent principality. An impressive fort guarded the fields, herds, orchards, and vineyards, as well as the luxurious home in which Sutter dispensed lavish hospitality. Sutter even had his own coinage and an Indian army dressed in blue and green uniforms trimmed with red. Sutter was always friendly to Americans, and his fort was the first settlement attained by the American farmers who began to arrive in 1841. He knew personally a good

share of the possibly 700 Americans who had settled in California by 1846.

A growing interest in the Pacific Coast, and the settlement of the Mormons in Utah, led to a yearly increase in the numbers of people crossing the plains. Each spring migrating farmers, fur traders, Sante Fe merchants, and other miscellaneous persons crowded the towns near the great bend of the Missouri waiting for the ground to become firm and the grass green. Faced with the dangers of plains travel, which included not only the Indians but also accidents and sickness, most travelers organized into parties under more or less strict discipline. The traders traveled relatively lightly and rapidly, using horses or mules. Permanent settlers carried more equipment and ordinarily used oxen, which were slow but sure. The mistakes of the settlers soon became visible as the road was littered with jettisoned cargo, and here and there a lonely grave.

The vast majority of early travel across the plains followed the Platte and North Platte Rivers, crossing the mountains through South Pass. Arriving at Soda Springs, southeast of Fort Hall on the Snake River, the Oregon-bound caravans followed the Snake and then cut across to the Columbia, while the California enthusiasts drove southwest to Nevada's Humboldt River and then across the Sierras. Within a few years there were many variations of these general routes, particularly to the west of the Rockies. Unfortunately for the travelers the most hazardous part of the trip came at the end, when men and stock were exhausted and equipment deteriorating. The path from Fort Hall to the Columbia was rocky and perilous, while that to California crossed deserts and high mountain ranges that might be covered with snow if the party had been delayed. The many resulting tragedies included even cannibalism.

THE MINING FRONTIER

American occupation of the Pacific Coast was followed by American acquisition of the desired territory [3] and then by further occupation. But now the trickle of the past became a tremendous flood with the new and inspiring incentive of gold. Despite the fact that the existence of considerable amounts of gold had long been known by the trappers, the gold fever waited upon the discovery in 1848 of free particles of gold in the tailrace of a mill being built for Sutter. When the news returned East, America lost its collective head. Here was uncombined gold that even the average man with no special knowledge and no equipment save hip boots, a pick, and a pan could gather in considerable amounts if he were diligent and lucky. Thousands of Easterners felt the beckoning finger of fate and loaded themselves with hardtack, guide books, and Spanish grammars preparatory to making their fortunes in the West. Many of them organized into co-operative groups, with constitutions and officers, only to discover that their highly moral provisions against swearing, drinking, and gambling were shattered on the way west, while the company itself went to pieces in California under the pressure of economic individualism.

Of the dozens of possible routes to the gold fields, three were most used. The long sea trip around the Horn was attractive in its simplicity, but exasperating in its length. Shorter and fastest of all was the route across Panama, provided that the Argonaut could obtain transportation and survived the hardships and the danger of tropical disease. Various overland routes existed northward from northern Mexico, but by far the most used was the old path along the Platte and through South Pass. By this time most parties went by way of Fort Bridger and Salt Lake City, but there were many alternatives. The gold seekers were frequently ignorant of plains travel and improperly equipped, which explains the new piles of discarded materials and the fresh graves.

The "forty-niner" or later seeker of precious metals did not ordinarily consider himself a permanent settler. He dreamed of the day when he could return home in glory and swagger before his neighbors. Pleasant reveries of

[3] See pp. 320–323, 332–334.

eventual affluence lightened the many hours he stood in the water and strained his back rotating a pan, or those during which he labored mightily to dump gravel into a rough, cleated rocker. Only youth, health, and rosy hopes for the future enabled him to endure the eternal meals of bacon, beans, and saleratus biscuit, his awkward repairs on his crude clothes, and his succession of sicknesses and accidents.

If gold were present at the Sutter mill it must exist elsewhere, and soon the hopeful prospectors were combing every likely part of the West. Mining towns with such picturesque names as Poker Flat and Hell-out-for-noon City mushroomed overnight into prosperous communities, and frequently faded just as rapidly. These primitive communities consisted almost entirely of men, whose amusements were as simple as their work; saloons, gambling halls, and dance halls provided the usual relaxation for evenings and Sundays. For a bigger spree the miner might visit a larger town such as Sacramento, or even the boisterous San Francisco, where the saloons were shinier, the gambling for larger stakes, and the prostitutes younger.

During the 1850s and 1860s, floods of miners inundated prospective boom areas in present Arizona, Nevada, Montana, Oregon, and Idaho in a series of mad rushes that produced the usual uninhibited towns. The greatest single rush of the 1850s was that to Pikes Peak in 1859. Optimistic potential miners flocked across the plains with their wagons lettered "Pikes Peak or Bust!" Unhappily for many of them, the immediately available deposits were rapidly exhausted, and soon returning prairie schooners bore the sign "Busted!" Actually, vast mineral deposits were awaiting later discovery.

The greatest spur to silver mining was the opening of the almost incredibly rich Comstock Lode in Virginia City, Nevada. Mining in that area had first been of the placer variety in a circumstance similar to that of a starving man confining himself to the icing on a cake. With the realization that the quartz rock there was full of silver, a new rush started for Nevada late in 1859. An impressive group of million-aires was spawned when the fabulous "Big Bonanza," a wide vein of almost pure silver, was discovered, although most Nevada miners earned little more than normal daily mining wages. New silver fields were soon opened in Arizona, Idaho, and Montana. From the viewpoint of the typical miner, the greatest drawback to silver mining was the necessity of expensive machinery to extract the metal. Hence the usual discoverer of a silver bonanza tended to sell his claim to a large combination for a pittance.

The never-ending stream of miners changed the face of the Western countryside. In personal terms, some of these men died; some continued to wander in search of the metallic will-o'-the-wisp; some entered such occupations as farming, ranching, storekeeping, or even banditry; some returned home broke; and a few actually made the fortunes that enabled them to build palaces on San Francisco's Nob Hill, loot Europe of its artistic treasures, and sometimes crown their careers with membership in the United States Senate. In social terms, these miners brought about both short- and long-term results. Having outrun the normal processes of law and order they created their own legal codes and enforced them with vigilante committees. Their commonly accepted practices in the holding of mining claims were ultimately embedded into Federal law (1866).

Thousands of vigorous and hardy young miners spread into areas where previously white men had seldom been seen. They had no respect for Indian claims and little for the Indians themselves; frequently they completely demoralized the natives. Western miners helped inspire the government to call a great Indian council in 1851, at which the plains tribes agreed to allow overland travelers unmolested passage and to permit the United States to build forts to guard these migrants. Moreover, the new mining population helped to motivate the organization of territories and states. By 1850 California was a state in the Union, and if the miners' collective voice was not supreme in forming a state government there, at least it was important. When Nevada

became, prematurely, a state during the Civil War, almost its entire population was composed of miners working at or near the Comstock Lode. The Great Plains still remained unorganized Indian country in 1850; but even that early, Oregon, Utah, New Mexico, and Minnesota were territories, each larger than the present states of the same names. The impress of mining on the Far West and of agriculture in the Great Plains produced many more governmental divisions within the next few years. Not only were Minnesota, Oregon, and Kansas new states shortly before the Civil War, but they were soon followed by Nevada (1864) and Nebraska (1867). The remainder of the West was organized into territories, with two main differences from the present: the Dakotas were one territory, and modern Oklahoma was still unorganized Indian country.

The flow of gold from the new mines eliminated the gold-silver ratio, which had remained fairly stable for over half a century, and drove silver out of circulation; silver was so thoroughly eliminated that in time Congress even forgot to provide for its coinage—the "crime of 1873." The discovery of new sources of gold was highly desirable in a period when the number of business transactions was increasing rapidly, because otherwise the fall in prices would have been considerably greater than that which actually came.

The mining rushes, when added to other interests in the Far West, brought increasing pressure on Congress for improved overland transportation, particularly through the use of mail subsidies. Freight was carried slowly and expensively by ox or mule team, controlled respectively by "bullwhacker" or "mule skinner." Mail was carried largely on a basis of charity by anyone going in the general direction of the addressee. The government listened to the pleas for improved mail deliveries even before the first gold rush. Mail service to California by way of Panama was subsidized in 1847, with steamers on both the Atlantic and Pacific sides; the first ship arrived at the Golden Gate just in time for its sailors to desert to the gold fields. Four years later service was provided by way of Nicaragua. Direct overland mail deliveries across the plains originated with a contract (1848) between Independence and Salt Lake City. Connections gradually were made to all important Western communities, even though through service from the Mississippi Valley to the Pacific Coast was not begun by the Butterfield Overland Stage Company until the year 1858.

The jump of settlement across the continent to the Pacific Coast produced immediate and notable changes, but its long-run implications were even more important. Widespread mining booms and the growth of overland business clearly forecast the day when the entire nation would be bound together in a single unit, and when the Indians could no longer control large sections of the continent. Although this process remained far from complete until farmers occupied the Great Plains after the Civil War, the handwriting on the wall was visible.

CHAPTER 22

Nationalistic Politics

(1815-1828)

A ONE-PARTY INTERLUDE

Major American political developments from 1815 to 1850 can be understood only in terms of the contemporary international scene. The wars that were fought in Europe and elsewhere during the nineteenth century were localized. Without widespread conflagrations in which to become involved, Americans found it easier to hoe their own corn and mend their own fences. Foreign affairs of the Republic played a relatively less important role after the Treaty of Ghent than during the preceding quarter century. To be sure, nothing approximating complete isolation was attained, and crises of varying intensity and duration occurred between the United States and foreign nations. Furthermore, the diplomacy of this period was considerably more vital than it was to be from 1873 to 1895. In brief, however, mid-nineteenth-century America was able to devote its tremendous wealth of natural resources and human energy to problems that were essentially domestic.

The people of the United States were able to forget with amazing rapidity the military frustrations and tangled foreign relations that had bedeviled them during the War of 1812. In the years after the second war with Great

Britain, Americans became immersed in their usual political farragoes, development of home manufactures, reconstruction of financial stability, transportational improvements to facilitate Western migration, and recurring conflict between state rights and nationalism.

American party politics were distinctive during this period. At the end of the war the Federalists, who had appeared for a time to be renascent and perhaps destined once again to control the national administration, withered away under blasts from other sections that were outraged at the wartime treason of a few reactionary New Englanders. Halfheartedly the Federalists nominated Rufus King of Massachusetts for the presidency in 1816; he was smothered by the Democratic-Republic candidate, James Monroe. Never again did the Federalists run a presidential ticket, although local machines continued to operate in New England for a few years. Outwardly the United States appeared to have turned into a one-party government during the so-called "Era of Good Feeling" (1816 to 1824). Soon, however, the dominant Democratic-Republicans split asunder in personal factionalism and sectional mistrust, which by 1828 resulted in two recognizably different parties. This later development was eminently natural—the two-party system typifies American politics.

Certainly a cardinal reason for the decline of the Federalist party was that there was no longer much need for it. The policies followed by Presidents Madison and Monroe enabled disheartened conservatives to take a new look at life. By a gradual process, the Jeffersonian party, founded to oppose Hamiltonian Federalism, swung in a 180-degree arc to point unswervingly toward such Hamiltonian principles as protection for manufacturers, Federal assistance to internal improvements, and even a Bank of the United States. By 1816 the philosophy of the Democratic-Republican party was eminently national, and it sounded Federalistic where state rights were concerned.

The only real resistance to this initially imperceptible yet definite trend came from a corporal's guard of old Jeffersonians. John Taylor continued to assail a course of action that extended the sway of the mercantile and manufacturing classes over the administration. John Randolph of Roanoke never ceased hurling his bitter jeremiads in Congress. But these staunch old-timers were left in the lurch to write and orate in vain. While they protested, the circuitous route of the Jeffersonian party toward Hamiltonian principles continued. Both Presidents Madison and Monroe aided this drift. Madison reverted to the conservatism that had characterized his work during the Constitutional Convention as part author of *The Federalist*. Even more complete was the about-face of James Monroe, who as Minister to France had been considered a wild-eyed radical by his enemies. Comfortably established in the White House, Monroe surrounded himself with advisers whose outlook was that of Hamiltonian nationalism. Numbered in this group were John Quincy Adams, William H. Crawford, John C. Calhoun, and especially Henry Clay.

THE AMERICAN SYSTEM

◖ *Henry Clay.* Clay's influence was predominant in both Madison's and Monroe's administrations. This magnetic individual revamped and modernized the Hamiltonian blueprint under the pleasant title of the "American System" and bent his considerable talents toward its successful adoption. Henry Clay was one of the most fascinating American politicians. Dynamic, tremendously appealing in his personality, frank and generous in human relations, even his faults were not abhorrent. Overly garrulous, he drank and gambled probably more than was good for him. His tall, lean figure attracted attention, but his most prominent feature was a large mouth, often stretched to the limit in a wide smile. Clay was no genius; several of his political contemporaries were able to marshal greater intellectual resources. Yet his oratorical ability was high enough to make occasional drivel seem thrilling and important to his audiences.

Nevertheless, all Clay's charm, good fellowship, and patriotism were unable to save him from the dubious distinction of being perhaps the unluckiest American politician. Andrew Jackson stole his Western thunder and blocked most effectively his presidential ambitions. "Harry of the West" seemed always to suffer the fate of being refused nominations when he could have won and being run when election was either hopeless (1832) or at best a toss-up (1844).

Although Clay's personal ambitions were to be thwarted, he was more fortunate in realizing his national economic policy. He worked out a carefully balanced program to give something to almost every major economic group, although more was granted to Eastern manufacturers and Western farmers than to urban laborers. The essence of the American System, as its name suggests, was national; but sectional interests were studiously considered and provided for in detail. Clay's system was a three-legged stool; it stood on a protective tariff, a Bank of the United States, and Federally financed internal improvements.

◖ *The Tariff.* Considerable need had been felt for increased tariff protection immediately after the War of 1812. The amazing growth of the American textile industry started in 1790 when Samuel Slater erected his mill at Pawtucket, Rhode Island; the number of New England factories steadily but slowly increased until commercial restrictions from 1808 to 1815 steered available capital into this industry, and the rate of growth spurted sharply. By the end of the war over 100,000 workers were employed in American textile factories, and domestic cloth had captured most of the American market from British producers; no sooner had peace been signed at Ghent, however, than the Mistress of the Seas (and of the factories) moved to recapture her lost overseas markets and to dispose of her war-accumulated surpluses. With their vast financial resources, British textile-mill owners could afford to take temporary losses on American sales. Furthermore, the British were able to capitalize on the old feeling that imported cloth was better than domestic. By the summer of 1815 English merchant ships appeared off the American coast in considerable numbers and subjected the infant American textile industry to cutthroat competition. Particularly offensive (and effective) was the British policy of "dumping," whereby goods would be sold in America for less than their cost of production and transportation across the Atlantic. This ostensibly ruinous program would be maintained until American competitors went bankrupt. Without competition from United States factories, prices could be handsomely increased under British monopolistic conditions.

This commercial warfare was disastrous for American textiles. Unemployment soared in the wake of closing factories. The harassed American mill owners turned to the government for aid, and the administration harkened to their appeals. Henry Clay reasoned that a healthy domestic economy was impossible without prosperous factories so that the nation might be more self-sufficient in time of war. Under his spur, Congress responded in 1816 with the first protective tariff in American history, previous tariffs having been primarily for revenue.

In view of the positions taken a few years later, the line-up that favored the Tariff of 1816 was composed of strange bedfellows. Naturally Clay's followers, particularly in the Middle West and the East, advocated its adoption. Many Southerners, however, who were destined to become fanatical opponents of protectionism inside of a decade, united behind Clay in 1816. They followed the leadership of John C. Calhoun, at this time an ardent nationalist. Calhoun was sure that the South, the producer of raw cotton, would become a great textile-manufacturing area. Eventually he was vindicated, but not until many years after his death. Another odd attitude was found in New England. Daniel Webster, later champion of the Union and of economic nationalism, opposed the tariff in 1816. At that time Webster spoke for the New England overseas commercial interests who opposed tariffs that might interfere with the carrying trade. By the mid-1820s Webster was representing New England industrialists rather than that section's shippers, and his views on the tariff changed accordingly. In the Tariff of 1816, the final vote saw South Carolina favoring the measure along with the Middle Atlantic states and the West; New England, Georgia, and Louisiana split on the issue; and united opposition centered in Virginia and North Carolina.

The first protective tariff was mild enough in its defense against foreign competition. Duties ranged from 7 to 30 per cent of American valuation. Iron, as well as cotton and woolen textiles, was protected. Special privilege was bestowed upon the harassed New England factories by an absolute ban on imports of cheap cotton cloth from British India. Despite these benevolent provisions, domestic manufacturing interests were not satisfied. The great depression of 1819 soon hit them with shattering impact, and the economic ruin inaugurated by British dumping was completed by this downward movement of the business cycle. Renewed demands for increased protection made sure that the tariff issue would remain a leading national problem.

⟪ *The Bank of the United States.* The second leg of the American System was a Bank of the United States. Again Henry Clay was successful. Support for a charter of a second Bank seems to have been engendered by a common realization that centralized credit must largely control local financing. State banks had multiplied threefold in the five years (1811 to 1816) between the demise of the first and the advent of the second Bank of the United States. An act establishing the Bank passed with full administration support. Modeled on the Hamiltonian institution of 1791, the Bank was capitalized at $35 million; the government would own one-fifth of its stock, and private investors four-fifths. It could engage in ordinary banking practices, was permitted to establish branches throughout the nation, and was to be the depository for Federal revenues. In return for these privileges, the Bank was to pay the government $1,500,000 in three equal installments.

Immediately the Bank made its influence known. Its early management under President William Jones was ruthless and overly aggressive. The Bank speculated wildly, and when the reckoning came during the first months of 1819, it insisted that state banks pay their obligations in specie (coin), which promptly became very scarce. Panic among banking circles resulted, and the policies of the Bank were partially responsible both for bringing on and for intensifying the depression of 1819. Although considerable amelioration in its practices commenced with the administration of Nicholas Biddle in 1819, the Bank had generated enough ill will among many Southerners and Westerners to ensure a continuing opposition upon which Andrew Jackson would later capitalize.

❮ *Internal Improvements.* Federally financed internal improvements formed the third leg of the American System, and only in this field did Clay and the nationalists fail to win a victory. During the War of 1812, American military difficulties had been enhanced by the miserable transportational facilities west of the Appalachians. Furthermore, the back country was tireless in its demands for improved overland and water arteries. Some beginnings had been made in Jefferson's administration several years before the war. In 1808 both the President and his Secretary of the Treasury Albert Gallatin recommended that roads be constructed and that waterways be improved by dredging river channels or digging canals. Deficits in the Treasury that followed the abrupt decline in tariff revenues caused by the Embargo and other trading restrictions never permitted the anticipated surplus for internal improvements to be accumulated, and this ambitious program lapsed.

Yet even before hostilities with Great Britain broke out, the government had managed to start building the Cumberland, or "National," Road, although little could be done until after 1815. An existing road connected Baltimore and Cumberland, Maryland, and the new construction proceeded west through southern Pennsylvania to the Ohio River at Wheeling, in present West Virginia; later it was extended through Ohio and Indiana toward St. Louis. Immediately the National Road became the main artery of overland transportation to the West. Its eastern stretches were comparatively good—with a wide bed featuring stone and gravel construction—but it seriously deteriorated as it progressed. The National Road was to be but one of a vast series of Federally financed internal improvements. The constitutional doubts of the executives, however, abruptly halted the participation of the Federal government and returned the road to the states in which it lay.

Shortly before his second administration ended, James Madison vetoed a bill sponsored by Clay and Calhoun that would have launched a magnified system of Federal internal improvements. The President agreed that such needed to be done, but doubted that the Federal government could act without a constitutional amendment specifically for that purpose. James Monroe echoed the sentiments of his predecessor when he vetoed an act in 1822 that would have applied the payments required from the Bank of the United States to internal improvements. Again constitutional doubts had beset the President.

The need for improved transportation was so pressing, however, that the states had to fill the vacuum left when the Federal government refused to act. The western thrust of the National Road was carried on by the states through which it passed. Considerable improvement in waterways was soon discernible, particularly when the steamboat began to appear on inland rivers. Naturally the success of New York's magnificent Erie Canal impelled a rash of frenetic and overly hasty canal building throughout the nation.[1]

THE SUPREME COURT

The nationalism implicit in the American System received initial impetus from the executive and legislative branches of the Federal government. Yet, according to one school of constitutional thought, opposition by the judiciary could negate the work of the other two. Hence, the position taken by the Supreme Court was vital to the successful continuation of political and economic nationalism. Luckily for Clay and the Madison, Monroe, and Adams administrations, the Court was headed by John Marshall, the noted Virginia Federalist, and he was thoroughly in sympathy with the entire program. Marshall was at the height of his influence from the time of the War of 1812 until well into Andrew Jackson's second term, and he continued his earlier work commenced in the famous cases of *Marbury v. Madison* and *Fletcher v. Peck*.[2] Vital bricks were placed in the wall of Federal judicial supremacy during the postwar period both to abet national supremacy over the states and to maintain the sanctity of contract. Some cases apply to both fields, but discussion shall pertain first to Federal supremacy.

❨ *Bolstering Nationalism.* Since the theory of state rights was the leading opponent of nationalism, Marshall chastised both courts and legislatures of the several states; although in such instances as bankruptcy laws, the right to dam navigable rivers, and permission to tax corporations, the Chief Justice awarded

[1] See pp. 209–211.
[2] See pp. 142–143.

powers to the states that might have been denied. The Court's first nationalistic decision after the War of 1812 was in the case of *Martin v. Hunter's Lessee* (1816). Marshall held that the Federal judiciary could reverse a decision of a state court if the decision was contrary to the Constitution of the United States, as defined by the Supreme Court. Such reasoning was strengthened in *Cohens v. Virginia* (1821). Two brothers, M. J. and P. J. Cohen, sold lottery tickets in Virginia contrary to a law which stated that only Virginia lottery tickets could be sold inside the state. Obviously Virginia had original jurisdiction in this matter, but the question was fought on whether the Supreme Court had appellate jurisdiction under both the Judiciary Act of 1789 and the provision of the Eleventh Amendment about citizens of one state suing those of another. Marshall asserted the Court's right to review the case and, speaking for the majority of the Court, stated clearly his nationalistic philosophy:

. . . the American people are one, and the government which is alone capable of controlling and managing their interests . . . is the government of the Union. It is their government, and in that character they have no other. America has chosen to be . . . a nation; and for all these purposes her government is complete. . . . It can . . . legitimately control all individuals or governments within the American territory. The constitution and laws of a state, so far as they are repugnant to the constitution and laws of the United States, are absolutely void. The states are constituent parts of the United States.

Of particular importance was the case of *McCulloch v. Maryland* (1819). Maryland, disgruntled at the financial activities of the second Bank of the United States, taxed the peculiarly obnoxious Baltimore branch of that institution. When the government appealed to the Federal judiciary, Marshall and his colleagues had to decide on two main issues: whether the act establishing the Bank of the United States was constitutional, and whether the state could tax an agency of the national government. Nationalism colored both decisions. Reiterating that "The government of the

Union, then, is emphatically and truly a government of the people . . . it emanates from them . . . and for their benefit," the Virginia Federalist then applied the traditional "loose interpretation" of the Constitution to the first instance by stating that legislative acts consistent "with the letter and spirit of the Constitution are constitutional." Secondly the Court proclaimed that because the power to tax is the power to annihilate, no state could tax a Federal institution, wholly or in part, for purposes of destruction. Although it was a long time in dying, the theory of sovereign state rights had been dealt a mortal blow.

In the case of *Dartmouth College v. Woodward* (1819), New Hampshire wished to found a state college and thriftily failed to understand why expensive new buildings should be constructed when Dartmouth classrooms were readily available. The state nullified the colonial charter under which Dartmouth had been founded. The college trustees carried the case to the Supreme Court, where John Marshall was visibly affected by the emotional arguments with which Daniel Webster defended his alma mater. In regards to nationalism, Federal authority over a state legislature was again upheld, and the act nullifying the Dartmouth charter was ruled unconstitutional. As shall be seen, this case had even more important repercussions in the battle over sanctity of contracts.

The Court's decision in the case of *Gibbons v. Ogden* (1824) was of far-reaching importance to the expanding commerce and industry of the United States. The New York state legislature had awarded Robert Fulton and Robert Livingston a monopolistic contract to control all steamboat navigation on New York waters and granted them the additional privilege of leasing local rights to others. Under this act, Fulton and Livingston bestowed a lease to Aaron Ogden. Thomas Gibbons, a wealthy New Yorker, decided to test the monopoly's legality and received a Federal license to engage in "coastwise traffic." The New York courts upheld the Fulton-Livingston grant to Ogden, only to have the Supreme Court declare unconstitutional the state law that created the monopoly. The Chief Justice ruled that the Congress had absolute power "over commerce . . . among the several States," and defined "commerce" in the broadest sense as "intercourse," which included navigation and transportation as well as buying and selling. Federal regulatory powers, which became at once so important and so controversial a few decades later, looked back to *Gibbons v. Ogden* for precedents.[3]

(*Protecting Property.* While the Supreme Court was supporting the nationalism of the American System, the innately conservative Chief Justice was vigorously defending certain property rights that he considered threatened by contemporary leveling forces. Three decisions illustrate Marshall's philosophy in this sphere. The pre–War of 1812 decision in *Fletcher v. Peck* ruled that a contract was sacred even when fraudulently obtained. The *Dartmouth College v. Woodward* case (1819) reaffirmed the irrevocability of contracts, when John Marshall argued that a colonial corporation charter was a legal contract and enjoyed constitutional protection under Article I, Section 10, which asserts that "No State shall . . . pass any . . . Law impairing the Obligation of Contracts. . . ." Although perhaps correct in this specific instance, the Chief Justice's decision carried almost frightening implications. Under such reasoning, how could contracts be eliminated when they had become either hopelessly anachronistic or even threatening to the public welfare? The consideration of charters as legal contracts bestowed upon corporations a special type of immunity, and only gradually could they be brought under the control of either the state or the nation.

A final case exemplifying Marshall's economic opinions was in *Craig v. Missouri*

[3] Marshall's successor, Chief Justice Roger Taney, continued the trend toward Federal regulatory powers in *Charles River Bridge v. Warren Bridge* (1837), when he refused to allow a private toll-bridge company in Massachusetts to utilize its state charter to forbid competition. Taney, however, differed sharply with Marshall when, in the same case, he ruled that public welfare must be considered in evaluating the legality of corporation charters as contracts.

(1830), when the Court found that a Missouri law easing strict creditor-debtor relations had violated the constitutional provision against states emitting bills of credit. The West was incensed at this judicial bar against debtor relief.

Without doubt, John Marshall was one of the most important and influential Americans. His love for the nation was deep and strong. He rendered potent assistance to the formation of a truly united country, eventually able to withstand the onslaught of civil war. The private-enterprise system was aided by his economic thinking. Perhaps "independent" describes John Marshall as well as any other word. Whatever he has meant to later generations for good or ill, he acted from the Olympian heights of the Supreme Court, relatively uninfluenced by public opinion. Under his long tutelage the Court gradually assumed tremendous powers. In the hands of patriotic justices (and we have never had a really dangerous or criminal one) this power has never menaced American democracy. In the hands of ruthless jurists, removed from direct popular control, democratic government might have become a travesty.

THE ERA OF GOOD FEELING

While the nationalistic system was being supported by both Congress and the Court, the placid Monroe administrations succeeded those of James Madison. The latter had enjoyed his last year and a half in the White House. Much constructive work was accomplished, and the nation rather quickly forgot the unimpressive figure Madison portrayed when he fled the capital at the time of the British invasion. The Virginia "dynasty" blossomed fully when Monroe was easily elected over the last Federalist nominee in 1816. James Monroe had enjoyed a long and at least partially distinguished career. He had been a Revolutionary officer, a member of Congress under the Articles of Confederation, a Senator from and Governor of Virginia, and

Secretary of both War and State. As an enthusiastic advocate of the French Revolution he had made many friends abroad, although some of his foreign missions were unsuccessful. He became more conservative as the years passed, and he tranquilly acquiesced in the swing to Federalist principles that characterized most of the old Jeffersonian party. Like Madison, Monroe accepted practically all of Clay's nationalistic program with the exception of internal improvements, which he vetoed as unconstitutional.

The Democratic-Republican party—soon to be designated as the National Republican party—was the only nationwide political organization extant after the Federalists declined. Despite arguments over the tariff, the second Bank of the United States, internal improvements, sectional clashes, and individual imbroglios, Monroe's two terms were called the "Era of Good Feeling." So completely had the Federalist organization fallen to pieces that the President was triumphantly reelected in 1820 with literally no opposition. He missed a unanimous vote in the Electoral College only because one member of his own party claimed that George Washington alone was worthy of so signal an honor and threw away his ballot on John Quincy Adams. A political vacuum was created by this temporary one-party system, but it did not last long. As early as the middle of Monroe's second term, personal intraparty differences activated renewed factionalism, leading directly to the resurgent two-party setup.

❐ *Portents of Sectionalism.* If national politics were on the whole calm from 1817 to 1824, there were two major sectional clashes. The first concerned the state of Missouri and was primarily on political rather than on economic or social grounds. In 1820 an equal number of states were slave and free. When Missouri, having fulfilled all necessary requirements, petitioned to enter the Union as a slave state in 1820, many Northerners objected to this prospective termination of equal senatorial representation between the sections. Under the leadership of Henry Clay a compromise was

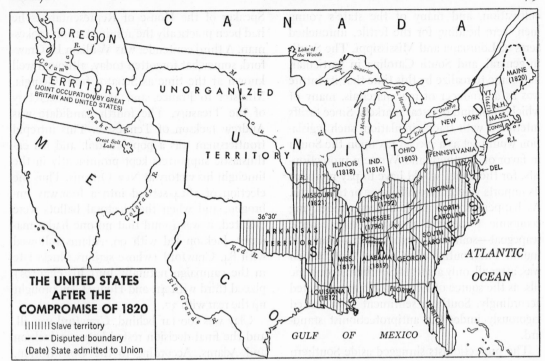

THE UNITED STATES
AFTER THE
COMPROMISE OF 1820

|||||||| Slave territory
---- Disputed boundary
(Date) State admitted to Union

worked out whereby Missouri was admitted as a slave state, Maine was permitted to secede from Massachusetts with the latter's consent and enter as a free state, and the line of 36° 30′ (the southern boundary of Missouri) was extended west to the Mexican border as a demarcation line between slave and free soil, presumably forever. Although tempers had run high, the relative ease with which compromise had been arranged shows that sectional ire had not reached the intensity it would a generation later. America was still able to be logical, reasonable, and intelligent in 1820 about circumstances that would temporarily disrupt the nation in 1860–1861.

The greatest controversy of Monroe's second term was in connection with the tariff, an issue annually becoming more explosive. The Tariff of 1816, which had enjoyed rather general national support with the exception of New England shippers and Virginia agrarians, had failed to satisfy either side. The protectionists, centered in New York, Pennsylvania, and the West, with augmenting support in New England, called for an increased tariff to restrict foreign competition, which was still strong

enough to menace the national economic health. The antiprotectionists, while losing ground yearly in the Northeast, were constantly gaining adherents from south of the Mason-Dixon line. Why had the attitude of the Deep South changed so drastically in less than a decade after 1816?

It should be recalled that Senator Calhoun of South Carolina had enthusiastically joined Henry Clay in pushing through the Tariff of 1816. Calhoun had been confident that a textile industry would surely come to the South. Such, however, had not occurred. The South lacked the capital necessary for manufacturing, and what sectional funds were available tended to go into cotton cultivation rather than industrialism. Furthermore, there was no adequate labor force to work in Southern factories. Slaves were untrained for such tasks, and immigrants tended to stay in the North rather than to compete with slave labor.

To make matters worse for the proud Calhoun, his beloved South Carolina was tumbling into a depression by the mid-1820s. Decades of overly enthusiastic cotton production had rendered large areas unfit for cotton cultivation, and many of the state's young men were heading for the fertile, untouched acres of Louisiana and Mississippi. The South in general, and South Carolina in particular, had come to realize by this time that its future was as a producer of raw materials, many of which must find overseas markets. Since tariffs interfered with trade circulation, such legislation would act as a special tax upon the South in favor of Northern and Western protectionists, for the South would have to pay more for its imports whether from Europe or the North. As happens so often when deep, underlying economic forces are at work, some simple scapegoat—some easy explanation—must be found. The South looked to the tariff, which was, after all, only a part of Southern economic ills, as the source of all its problems and acted accordingly. Southern sentiment soon united vigorously under the antiprotectionist standard.

The protectionists shrugged aside Southern opposition and were able to muster enough strength to pass the Tariff of 1824. Duties were sharply increased on cotton and woolen textiles (up to 33 per cent ad valorem) and to a lesser degree on iron, raw wool, and hemp. Hardly was the ink dry on the Tariff of 1824 when the protectionists were off in full cry for even higher rates. Sullenly Southerners listened to the uproar, and doggedly they fought a rearguard action against the ultraprotectionist policies that they believed responsible for Southern economic ailments. The tariff issue was to explode once more during the next administration.

(*The Election of 1824.* James Monroe had no more than started his second term when the plotting for the contest of 1824 commenced. Already the ostensibly unified administration party was splintering into personal factions, titularly similar, yet actually differing considerably. If the tradition of the Secretary of State succeeding the President who appointed him was to be followed, John Quincy Adams of Massachusetts had the inside track. Yet Henry Clay of Kentucky was popular throughout much of the West, and as Speaker of the House of Representatives he had been practically the administration spokesman. A third contender was William H. Crawford, somewhat forgotten today, although well known at the time as Senator from Georgia, Minister to France, and Monroe's Secretary of the Treasury. The fourth candidate was Andrew Jackson of Tennessee. This intrepid frontiersman was a popular idol, and his enthusiastic supporters kept prominently in the limelight his victory at New Orleans. Thus the election of 1824 settled into a four-way imbroglio; and when the electoral ballots were counted, it was found that no one had a majority. Jackson led with 99, Adams followed with 84, Crawford (whose serious illness late in the campaign naturally hurt his chances) placed third with 41, and Henry Clay brought up the rear with 37.

Clay was too far behind, Crawford was ill, and the final decision rested between Jackson and Adams. According to the Constitution, the House of Representatives must make the selection when no candidate has a majority. Clay's position immediately became pivotal, since he had enough strength to make his choice decisive. After some hesitation, the Kentuckian threw his support to Adams, and the latter was elected. Of course the Jacksonians were beside themselves with rage and promptly leveled the charge that there must have been a "corrupt bargain" whereby Adams would repay his debt to Clay with a political award. This charge appeared vindicated when Clay was appointed Secretary of State. The corrupt-bargain accusation was unfair to both men. Despite some personal animosity, Clay would obviously prefer the strongly nationalistic Adams to Jackson, who was regarded at the time as a state-rights man, and who was, moreover, the Kentuckian's rival for Western popularity. Furthermore, Adams was no man to play politics, and he probably made the appointment because he deemed Clay to be a good man for the State chair. The Jacksonians remained unconvinced and soon influenced the General himself. At first a cheerful loser, with towering indignation Jackson was soon campaigning for 1828.

THE JOHN QUINCY ADAMS ADMINISTRATION

John Quincy Adams had received years of training in public service by the time he became President. Secretary to the American Minister to Russia at the startling age of fourteen, Adams had been a professor of rhetoric at Harvard, a diplomat on several vital foreign missions, Minister to Great Britain and Russia, Senator from Massachusetts, and Secretary of State. The new President was short and fat, with a shrill voice and often a petulant expression. When angry he could be a figure of terrifying intensity as his eyes blazed and an alarming color reddened his bald head. Few Americans have ever been able to match Adams's self-sacrificing patriotism and his incredible diligence and devotion to duty. Yet the President's love of his country was blocked by his own personality traits, which never enabled him to communicate to his fellow citizens his affection for them. Tactless and sarcastic, Adams could make enemies by the manner in which he granted favors. Since he refused to play the political game, his favors were few enough anyway. He would not appoint his followers to governmental positions on political grounds alone, and he did little toward creating an Adams machine. Highly intelligent in political theory and skilled in diplomacy, John Quincy Adams was a rank neophyte in domestic politics—and political astuteness seems to be a necessary ingredient if the President is to enact his policy into law. Perhaps the bitterness of the Jacksonians was intense enough so that Adams must inevitably have had a disappointing administration; but his own political methods, while morally high, helped to ensure his failure.

Adams was an ardent nationalist, and he soon recommended to Congress that it enact an ambitious program for Federally financed internal improvements. This attempt, however, was frustrated in part by the growth of Southern opposition. The South had formerly been in the vanguard of the internal-improvements movement, but by 1825 the most influential thought of that section had concluded that such activities were contrary to Southern interests, since most improvements applied to the West. Without sufficient cotton-state support, the program could not be adopted. The national government was restricted to improving harbors, dredging channels, and awarding land grants; roads and canals remained essentially private, town, county, or state responsibilities.

Especially annoying to national concord was a resurgence of the perennial tariff question. As has been noted, the high-tariff men were not satisfied with the increased rates in 1824, and late in Adams's term they tried again to elevate many duties. Anguished Southerners, aware of the odds against them, gambled on what appeared to be a clever ruse. Cognizant that they might defeat the bill if they could pick up support elsewhere, Southerners looked to New England commercial and even industrial interests. Posing as champions of protection, cotton-state Congressmen amended the tariff bill in order to place high duties on essential New England imports, specifically iron, molasses, and raw wool. The Southern hope was obvious: New England would never accept rigorous levies on its necessary raw materials and would be forced to vote against the whole bill.

Such reasoning, however, proved erroneous. Each year protectionists numerically increased in the Northeast, as industrialism continued to gain at the expense of commerce. With wry faces, most New England Congressmen accepted the entire slate of duties, the unpleasant along with the pleasant. Outraged at their strategic failure, Southerners began referring to the protective measure of 1828 as the "Tariff of Abominations" and started frenzied discussions on how to circumvent this law which they felt was antagonistic toward their sectional prosperity. Finally they decided to await further developments, since the election of 1828 was approaching, and Jackson was thought to be a low-tariff man. For a time it appeared that the tariff controversy had lapsed, but it was the "eye" of the hurricane rather than the end of the storm.

CHAPTER 23

The Jacksonian Era

(1828-1840)

THE ELECTION OF 1828

The election of 1828 unfortunately started the theme of Jacksonian Democracy on a very low note. The contestants of that year were no mystery—it would be General Andrew Jackson against the incumbent President, John Quincy Adams. The latter was dutifully renominated by his conservative followers in the former Democratic-Republican party, called by this time "National Republican." Jackson's followers were referring to themselves as "Democrats," and the modern party which bears that appellation is their direct lineal descendant. In part because of the corrosive memories of four years earlier, the campaign of 1828 was a national disgrace—perhaps the most malodorous in our history, with the possible exception of the Blaine-Cleveland fracas in 1884. Neither Jackson nor Adams can be held personally responsible for the mudslinging, but hotheads on both sides reveled in limitless vituperation.

For a number of reasons, Jackson was peculiarly vulnerable to opposition attack. He had shown a typical frontier love of brawling in his younger days. His duel with Charles Dickinson in Kentucky (1806) was a model of

cold-blooded determination and ferocity.[1] On another occasion the Tennessean engaged in an unrestrained melee with Thomas H. "Bullion" Benton during which Jackson picked up a souvenir—a bullet that stayed in his shoulder for many years.[2] As a military officer Jackson had enforced discipline by executions when he deemed it necessary and had hanged two British subjects after a drumhead court-martial in Florida when that territory was under Spanish jurisdiction. To make matters even worse, there was an irregularity concerning Jackson's marriage to his idolized Rachel. Supposedly her first husband had obtained a divorce, but only after the Jacksons had been married a couple of years did they discover that he had not. The chagrined couple immediately separated until a divorce was obtained and then promptly remarried. But vicious whisperings about Rachel Jackson continued from that time.

[1] In this duel Dickinson fired at the signal and seriously wounded his adversary. Despite his agony, Jackson remained upright and slowly and methodically executed the helpless Dickinson. Jackson carried Dickinson's bullet in his body for the rest of his life. Nineteenth-century surgeons did not dare to operate, for the missile was too close to Jackson's heart.

[2] Benton later became the Jackson administration's leader in the Senate.

278

The supporters of Adams in 1828 found ready ammunition in these circumstances. A handbill, covered with coffins, was widely circulated to give an impression that the General was simply a murderer. A sometimes undercover, sometimes open campaign against Rachel Jackson used every vile innuendo possible. Highly charged propaganda convinced Eastern conservatives that Jackson was no more than an unbridled Western savage who would stride into Washington bringing ruin and rapine to the nation.

An equally unprincipled assault was brought to bear upon John Quincy Adams. The old "corrupt bargain" charge of 1824 was hauled out of the closet and refurbished. The New Englander was falsely accused of spending the public funds for "gambling devices"—in other words, a billiard table that Adams had bought with his own money. The most ridiculous charge leveled against the President was that as Minister to Russia he had sold an American girl to the lust of none other than Tsar Alexander I and, moreover, had maintained a harem of Russian girls for himself. It is safe to say not only that John Quincy Adams was completely guiltless in those particular circumstances, but also that it is extremely unlikely he ever cast a random thought in such directions.

Under this miasma the campaign was waged; and when the final lie had been circulated, Jackson's popularity was too much for his dour opponent. The Tennesseean was elected by 178 to 83 ballots in the Electoral College, having swept New York and Pennsylvania and capturing nearly every vote south and west of the Keystone State. Jackson had been aided by a tremendous outpouring of new voters. Between 1824 and 1828 hundreds of thousands gained the franchise for the first time; only about 350,000 had voted in 1824, but over 1,130,000 cast ballots four years later —an increase of over 300 per cent—and most of the newly franchised supported Jackson. The disappointed Adams stayed for his successor's inauguration and then went home to Massachusetts; but he soon returned to Washington as a member of the House of Representatives, where he served until his death in 1848.

Inauguration Day, 1829, turned out to be one of the strangest in the entire history of the national capital. For some time before, the unwashed thousands had been trekking into the Federal city to see honors accorded to their hero. After Jackson took the presidential oath of office from a dismayed Chief Justice John Marshall, Tennessee backwoodsmen, Baltimore artisans, Southern planters, and avaricious politicians from all over the Union coalesced into a mob. Americans pushed and shoved into the White House reception to get a look at Jackson, to claw and grab at the food, and even more important, to imbibe the alcoholic beverages furnished by the generous victor. Rugs were torn, furniture tipped over, and upholstery ruined by spilled liquor and dirty boots. It is likely that the White House might have been sacked by these delirious enthusiasts had not some genius ordered the punch to be moved outdoors, whereupon the building was soon emptied. Amid such scenes of levity and disorder, the people celebrated the advent of more popular government.

ANDREW JACKSON

Similar to both Jefferson and Lincoln, Andrew Jackson remains one of the more important Presidents of the United States, more for what he symbolized than for what he actually accomplished. Jackson caught the national imagination, and he became the token for democratic movements which, although they had been at work for many years, began to come to the fore during his administrations. "Jacksonian Democracy" is the term applied to the period from 1828 to 1841; its influence was tremendous in politics and hardly less so in the fields of humanitarianism, intellectualism, and the arts. The leveling spirit that bore his name tended to move faster than Jackson. Even so, he was its leader, and to understand Jacksonian Democracy, the character and personality of its titular head must be comprehended.

Jackson was sixty-two when he became President and felt himself to be an old and broken man. He was an impressive figure, immediately recognizable and afterwards seldom forgotten. He was over 6 feet tall and almost painfully thin. A wreath of whitening hair, worn rather long, framed a wrinkled, elongated, mournful face. Jackson's physiognomy, so restrained in repose, could be convulsed by fury as his favorite expletive, "By the E-tarnal!" rolled from his lips. There is considerable evidence, however, that the legend of Jackson's uncontrollable rages is somewhat exaggerated; his anger was often used as a cloak to save him from fruitless discussion with those he knew to be implacable enemies.

Jackson was desperately unhappy, and his emotional state was enough to cause dire foreboding among his followers. Between the time of victory in the election of 1828 and the inauguration in 1829, his wife Rachel had died, and the elation of political achievement was drowned in an ocean of bereavement and loneliness. Bitterness was added to this almost intolerable burden, for Jackson was positive that the slander of his political enemies had quite literally killed his wife. Physical agony vied with mental. The President was racked by splitting headaches, possibly induced by years of tobacco chewing and voracious pipe smoking. Jackson suffered from severe digestive disorders, consumptive coughing spells, and the throbbing aches of old wounds.

Despite this emotional and physical torture, which might have overwhelmed a weaker man, Jackson's compensating resources enabled him to stand firm. Although relatively untrained, his mind was excellent. He was considerably more open to influence than the stereotype of Jacksonian prejudice would admit. He listened carefully to conflicting opinion and then formed his conclusions, although once his course was set, he seldom deviated. Naturally courtly and polite, he could exert a magnetic charm over his associates. It was hard to be neutral about Andrew Jackson. As a strong President he was adored or vilified—he could not be ignored. Certainly the General had some major faults. He could be an implacable enemy, and rare in his personal history are such incidents as when Thomas H. Benton, his old rival from the West, became the Jacksonian leader in the Senate. Although the President's intelligence was high, his ignorance in some fields was lamentable. He was startlingly naïve in general economics, especially finance. His training for executive political leadership was not the best. Yet the relatively uneducated Jackson, nurtured in the violent tradition of the Western frontier and the military camp, seems to have been guided by some vague instinct, some almost unconscious awareness of democratic impulses, and an innate suspicion of forces that menaced the burgeoning national liberalism.

JACKSONIAN DEMOCRACY

Jacksonian Democracy must not be considered a national phenomenon alone, even though a President of the United States was its leader. The national aspects were firmly rooted in state experiences, which indeed both led the way and went further. Influenced by the trans-Appalachian states that had entered the Union prior to 1820, the seaboard states gradually extended the franchise in order to give their citizens the same privileges accorded to Westerners. Steadily the number of states granting relatively universal white manhood suffrage increased. Property qualifications upon balloting were lowered and often wiped out. By the middle of Jackson's two terms, the last New England state abolished its religious restrictions on voting. Disfranchised in part through what we call Jeffersonian Democracy in the early 1800s, the average American enjoyed the ballot a generation later.

Closely allied to this liberalization of the franchise was the national political party, a form of mass democratic expression. Although the term "political party" has been used to describe the Federalist and Democratic-Republican organizations of the 1790s, they were quite unlike modern parties. Political control in the early Republic rested firmly in the hands of a few gentlemen who had the time and the money to dabble in public affairs. Candidates were nominated through the party caucus, in which a handful of leaders over glasses of port or Madeira after dinner would decide upon the list of nominees. The rank and file of the party had little to say about the selection of candidates. By Jackson's time, however, the caucus system was giving way to the national party convention. An organization called the Anti-Mason party, which had a brief flurry of activity thanks to its hostility to the Masonic Order and other secret societies, held a national convention in 1831; soon the two major parties followed this example. Secrecy in politics was lessened, and private deals could be voted out by the party delegates. Political conventions have usually been controlled by a few leaders, but it is harder to ride herd over a convention of hundreds than to manipulate a party caucus in which only a few are concerned.

Another major political development of Jackson's time was the closer adhesion of the state to the national organization. This was nothing novel—one recalls the Jacobin clubs during the 1790s and their alliance with the national Democratic-Republican party. By 1830, however, this process was solidifying around a cement that has been alliteratively called "the pervasive power of public plunder" —awarding Federal jobs to enable the lower-echelon party hacks to eat between elections.

The advent of the "spoils system"—so called from a remark attributed to a Gallic conqueror of ancient Rome: "To the victor belongs the spoils"—was an immediate manifestation of this state-national political-party union. From 1801 to 1825 the almost dynastic arrangement of American executive succession saw each Secretary of State succeed the President who had appointed him. Hence there was never much need for reorganization of the Federal service. Jackson, however, broke this direct line of succession, and many of his ardent supporters demanded that they be rewarded, rather than allow functionaries hostile to the administration to retain their sinecures. "Clean the barnacles from the ship of state" was the way one politico expressed this common sentiment. Convinced that any reasonably intelligent American could handle post-office or other departmental jobs, Jackson acceded to these demands, and many civil servants were discharged and their places taken by Jacksonians. Actually the removals were by no means wholesale; about one-third of the Federal posts were vacated by Adams men and filled by administration supporters. Nevertheless, Jackson must assume considerable responsibility for inaugurating a system that steadily worsened until it became a national scandal after the Civil War.

Quite obviously the advent of recognizable modern political parties with their national conventions, state machines allied with central organizations, and use of governmental jobs for selfish political advantage resulted in a lowering of Federal standards. Unquestionably there was more corruption in politics during and after Jackson's time than before. A certain coarsening process was at work, which may be the price paid for increased democracy. As the old saw has it, "Omelets can't be made without breaking eggs," and few today would favor a reversion to the purer but more regal and more gentlemanly rule of a few upper-class individuals. After all, democracy means political mass participation, and where mass action occurs, it is often accompanied by a leveling in manners and even morals.

The victory in 1828 had been won by the "Democratic party," composed of strange bedfellows. Southerners, Westerners, and many urban elements from the East had lined up behind the impressive figure of the Tennessee General. Southerners who hated high tariffs and felt little affection for Federally financed internal improvements supported Jackson under the somewhat mistaken conviction that he was a state-rights man and would check the burgeoning nationalism that had characterized the previous administrations. Western enthusiasts voted for "Old Hickory," convinced that he would ameliorate certain of their sectional grievances, such as the lack of adequate transportation and the presence of Indians on lands coveted by white men. Most inland citizens were apprehensive about the fiscal power of the Bank of the United States, hopeful for an inflated currency, but divided on the tariff question.

The third sectional bloc in Andrew Jackson's Democratic party came from the East, especially from the seaboard cities. Its members split on the tariff (usually dependent on whether a local industry was protected) and on internal improvements. Many in this group feared the growing power of the industrialists and resented the latter's special privileges leading to monopolistic control granted to them by national, state, or city governments. Especially interesting was their attitude on the monetary question, and in this arena they clashed with their supposed allies, the Western farmers. The latter hoped to lighten their debt burden by easy credit and by the issuing of larger amounts of paper money so that prices would rise. The Eastern urbanites were opposed to higher prices on the commodities that they had to buy and supported a "hard-money" or "specie" standard. At first remaining in uneasy alliance with their Western adversaries, the Eastern anti-inflationists grew more restive and active in the early and middle 1830s, reaching a climax of influence during Martin Van Buren's administration, 1837 to 1841.

Local machines representing these hard-money interests were found in Massachusetts under the historian George Bancroft and in Pennsylvania under James Buchanan. The most influential of the seaboard Democratic groups was in New York City, and it bore the rather striking name of "Locofoco." [3] As the reform element in Tammany Hall, the Democratic organization of New York City, the Locofocos were headed by William Leggett, prominent antimonopolist, and William Cullen Bryant, the eminent poet and editor of the New York *Evening Post*. They received considerable assistance from the beautiful, intelligent, and erratic Fanny Wright, who supported most contemporary reform movements. Gradually this wing of the Democracy began to exert more influence, and its culminating

triumph was achieved in 1836 when Jackson issued his Specie Circular, which ordered payments in hard money for public lands. Continuing to hold sway under Van Buren, the Locofoco elements stayed loyal to the Democratic party after many of the Western Jacksonians deserted to join the Whigs in 1840.

CABINET TROUBLES

Andrew Jackson had to manage this three-horse team from the executive chariot, and a difficult chore it was. Before any specific action could be taken, an imbroglio in the Cabinet threatened administrative prestige. John C. Calhoun of South Carolina had supported Jackson and in return had been accorded the vice-presidential nomination and was expected to succeed Jackson after a single term. Friends of Calhoun filled the Cabinet, with the exception of Secretary of War John Eaton and Secretary of State Martin Van Buren. Leader of the upstate New York Democracy, Van Buren was the son of a tavern keeper in Kinderhook on the Hudson River. From such modest beginnings Van Buren had risen to political eminence in the Empire State. Suave, intelligent, likable, and devious, Van Buren has been characterized as "rowing to his objectives with muffled oars." This "Little Magician" hoped to be President, and he shrewdly recognized that Calhoun's influence over Jackson must be removed. Luckily for Van Buren, events played into his hands through a silly controversy called the Eaton Affair.

Andrew Jackson had appointed an old crony, Major John Eaton, as Secretary of War. Both Jackson and Eaton had known Peggy O'Neill, a pretty and vivacious girl, whose father owned a Washington inn where the two Tennesseeans had lived. Peggy had been married to a dissolute purser in the Navy and while he was away on cruises carried on a flirtation with Major Eaton. After her husband's death, she married the Major. Early in his administration Jackson saw with surprise and growing resentment that the Cabinet ladies, acting on the ex-

---

[3] This arresting nomenclature came through the use of "locofoco" matches to hold a meeting when opponents had turned out the lights.

ample of Mrs. Calhoun, who was shocked by Peggy's reputation, snubbed Mrs. Eaton at official receptions and refused to admit her into their homes. The President liked Peggy and he well remembered the false and cruel vituperation that he felt had killed his wife. He resolved to do something about it. The height of his intervention occurred in what must have been the most peculiar Cabinet meeting in American history. Andrew Jackson assured his Cabinet that Mrs. Eaton was "as chaste as a virgin," but even this presidential guarantee could not melt the social frost overhanging Washington. Incensed, Jackson stopped meeting with his official advisers. The only Cabinet officer to make political capital from the whole ridiculous situation was Martin Van Buren, a widower who could afford to be pleasant and attentive to Mrs. Eaton. After all, the Secretary of State did not have to explain such conduct to an irate spouse.

In lieu of the usual advisory meetings, an informal group known as the "kitchen cabinet" (they regularly met in the White House kitchen, where Jackson could seek counsel given through clouds of tobacco smoke) began to assume considerable influence. Van Buren and Eaton represented the official Cabinet, but most members were newspapermen and politicians, among them Francis Preston Blair, eldest of the famous triumvirate of father and two sons who contributed significantly to the Republican victory in 1860; Duff Green, publisher of the *Congressional Globe*; Amos Kendall of Kentucky, whose ill-health formed a bond with the President; and the important New England Democrat Isaac Hill, soon to be Senator from New Hampshire. Considerable headshaking among the anti-Jacksonians followed when the existence of this semiofficial group became known.

While the kitchen cabinet was attending to business that could not be conducted so long as the President would not meet with his regular aides, new evidence added to Jackson's growing wrath against John C. Calhoun. He learned that the South Carolinian, while Secretary of War in Monroe's Cabinet, had wished to censure Jackson for the invasion of Span-

ish Florida. For over a decade Jackson had been under the impression that Calhoun had defended him against William H. Crawford and John Quincy Adams. The President wrote Calhoun for a denial, the latter equivocated, and Jackson broke with him completely. Acting on a sly suggestion from Van Buren that a mass resignation of the whole Cabinet would save political embarrassment, Jackson forced all to do so.

The new Cabinet was strengthened by the addition of such men as Edward Livingston of New York as Secretary of State, Lewis Cass of Michigan, Secretary of War, and as Attorney General Roger B. Taney, later Secretary of the Treasury and Chief Justice of the Supreme Court, who delivered the famous decision in the case of *Dred Scott v. Sanford* (1857). Van Buren was rewarded for his faithful services by appointment as Minister to Great Britain. He left for London only to find that the vote for confirmation in the Senate had ended in a tie and Vice-President Calhoun had the sour satisfaction of casting the decisive vote against his New York antagonist. "It will kill him, sir, kill him dead; he will never kick, sir, never kick!" was Calhoun's estimation of his deed. "Bullion" Benton struck a sounder note when he observed that Calhoun may have ruined a diplomat but had elected a Vice-President. True enough, Jackson considered Van Buren a self-sacrificing martyr. "The Fox of Kinderhook" became Vice-President in 1833 and four years later Jackson's successor in the White House.

WESTERN PROBLEMS

([*Internal Improvements*. While these devious social and political movements operated in the background, the Jackson administration started. The West received a rude shock on the question of Federally financed internal improvements. The midlands had assumed that its Western President would favor an expanded program for transportation. Congress had passed a measure to connect the Cumberland Road to the South along a route proceeding from the Ohio River to Maysville, Kentucky, and thence to Florence, Alabama. This proposed extension, the Maysville Road, lay entirely inside the state of Kentucky; Jackson vetoed the bill, describing the Maysville extension as a state road and asserting that Federal financing would be clearly unconstitutional. Although admitting that he favored a constitutional amendment empowering the Federal government to take such action, he concluded that his real duty was not to enhance the public debt but to reduce it. The Maysville Road veto definitely established the Democratic party policy of insisting that intrastate improvements must depend on state or local action.

❡ *Indian Troubles.* If many Westerners were shaken by this executive intervention, they were heartened by the President's position in regard to the Indians, although to modern eyes it is perhaps the worst blot on the Jacksonian escutcheon. "Old Hickory" had a typical frontier detestation of the Indians as "red vermin," and he illustrated this opinion in some direct action. When the Sac and Fox tribes attempted to repossess some land in Illinois, Jackson sent Federal troops to crush them. In Florida the unruly Seminole were harassed in a prolonged if desultory war, defeated, and the survivors forced to flee deep into the swampy jungles of the Everglades. Choctaw, Chickasaw, and Creek were likewise forced from ancestral lands in the South and sent beyond the Mississippi.

Unfair treatment of the Indians is perhaps most evident in the case of the Cherokee, who appealed to the United States Supreme Court. After first refusing to accept jurisdiction (*Cherokee Nation v. Georgia,* 1831) John Marshall, speaking for the majority as usual, upheld the rights of the Indians to their lands in the case of *Worcester v. Georgia* (1832). Even the highest tribunal could not save the Cherokee from enforced exile, however, as Jackson refused to execute the decision. White settlers poured onto their lands, and the Cherokee were pushed far across the Mississippi.

❡ *Land Policy.* Another recurring Western problem concerned Federal land policy. The transmontane regions were loud in their demands for a price reduction on unclaimed Federal lands and the right of a squatter to have first claim ("preemption") on the tracts that he occupied. Although neither of these hopes was realized during the Jacksonian period, they were constantly before Western eyes, arousing Western enthusiasm. If not much progress could be recorded, at least the West objected to regression, and this danger appeared near when a motion in Congress aroused the midlands. New England had long watched with disapproval the draining of her farm population to more fertile Western acres, and if this exodus from the Northeast could not be halted, it might be delayed. Acting on such reasoning, Senator Samuel Foot of Connecticut offered a bill in 1829 stipulating that new public lands be temporarily withdrawn from sale. Administration leader Senator Thomas H. Benton replied with considerable asperity for the West and accused New England of selfish political maneuvering. Ever alert to sectional opportunity, South Carolina rushed to Benton's side in the person of the handsome and fluent Senator Robert Y. Hayne, who called for a Southern-Western alliance against the more commercial and industrial Northeast.

Hayne's challenge was immediately accepted by Daniel Webster of Massachusetts. With his short, powerful body and huge head, Webster was a leonine figure. Straight, coal-black hair, a beetling brow, flashing dark eyes, and a grim mastifflike expression about the mouth commanded him international as well as American attention. On a later visit abroad he was the man of the hour to British society, evidently in part because many Englishmen assumed that he was the famous author of Webster's *Dictionary.* There seems considerable veracity in the remark concerning the "immortal Daniel" that "no man could be as great as he looked." He often equivocated in politics; his vote could be influenced by selfish interests; and although a marvelous orator on occasion, he could be pompous or ponderous either through the alcohol to which he was overly prone or through a lack of preparation. The most heroic action of his life—his advocacy of the Compromise of 1850—brought him under a hail of abuse that might better have greeted his purchased allegiance to the Bank of the United States.

In his two replies to Hayne, however, Webster was the epitome of the great orator. Speaking for hours at a stretch before packed Senate galleries, he brilliantly defended the name of Massachusetts, pointed to that commonwealth's contributions to the national welfare, and finally assailed the growing spirit of sectionalism that was coming into flower under the tutelage of John C. Calhoun and other Southern extremists. Webster finished with his stirring peroration, "Liberty and Union, now and forever, one and inseparable!" The menacing combination of the South and the West was broken before it could be formed, and the Foot Resolution was forgotten in the national excitement attending this thrilling debate. But sectionalism was not routed—not even by the hammering forensics of a Daniel Webster.

JOHN C. CALHOUN

The early years of Jackson's first term continued to be affected by a quarrel between the President and John C. Calhoun, the skilled and intelligent champion of South Carolina. While remarkably handsome as a young man, Calhoun's appearance during his last two decades was startling. White hair sprouted in a thatch over a stern and ravaged face. Brooding eyes and a skin of ashen pallor helped to create a melancholic and saturnine impression. In manners Calhoun could be the soul of chivalrous politeness, but also he could be arrogant and disdainful toward those he felt to be his social and intellectual inferiors. His moral standards were lofty, and his colossal integrity untouchable. Perhaps the most brilliant mentality of his political generation, Calhoun's incisive mind and implacable logic were highly adept at stripping away nonessentials. These natural gifts might have made John C. Cal-

houn a great President, but his status in American history remains debatable. With all his undeniable talents, Calhoun's narrow legalistic approach and his inability to compromise left him a hermit in national politics. His influence on the nation he loved so well for so long was, in the last analysis, unfortunate. Perhaps he loved his state too much.

During his early career Calhoun was a leading nationalist, ardently supporting the War of 1812 and enthusiastically abetting economic nationalism during the Era of Good Feeling. He had been an able Secretary of War under Monroe, an influential Senator, the Vice-President under Andrew Jackson, and until Van Buren's machinations ruined him, the presidential heir apparent. Calhoun's political vendetta with Andrew Jackson led him to resign his vice-presidential post, and in 1832 South Carolina sent him back to the Senate. Even before the break with Jackson, Calhoun had completely reversed his former nationalism to become the fountainhead for Carolina "home rule." Calhoun was deeply concerned to see that South Carolina was progressing so slowly and concluded that economic nationalism, especially the tariff, was the root of his state's ailing health. He feared the ruthless impositions of the despotic majority upon the minority, and his able mind searched for a method by which his state could escape from this paradoxical tyranny in the democratic process.

Calhoun's anxiety was reasonable. Democracies have always faced a stern and basic difficulty concerning the status of minorities. If the majority rules, what rights are retained by the minority? Is not, perhaps, the rule of the majority the most intolerable of all, since it is so difficult to change? Calhoun immersed himself in such questions, expressing his solution in *The South Carolina Exposition*, which he later expanded into the famous *Disquisition on Government*. The Carolinian argued that in the American political system minority rights could be protected by the doctrine of nullification, whereby a state could declare national acts that were detrimental to its local interests "void and of no effect" inside its boundaries.

Although he maintained in principle that the states were absolutely sovereign, Calhoun realized that a single state must not have a final veto. Therefore he admitted that nullification could be limited, but that only the several states, not the Federal government, could enforce compliance to national law. By a process akin to amending the Constitution, three-quarters of the states would have to vote against the nullifying state; once this had been done, the latter would have to repeal its ordinance of nullification. By 1830 Calhoun was voicing sectional sentiments that had previously found expression in the Virginia and Kentucky Resolutions and in the pronouncements of the Essex Junto extremists during the War of 1812.

The position of the President on the questions of state sovereignty and nullification was central. Supporters of Calhoun's doctrines hoped that the ostensibly state-rights Jackson would give them his blessing. An opportunity arose in 1830 when "Old Hickory" and his party leaders attended the Jefferson birthday dinner. The honor of proposing the first toast fell to the President. Amid a breathless silence, Jackson, grim-faced and implacable, turned pointedly toward Calhoun, transfixed him with a steady glare, and slowly said, "Our Federal Union! It must be preserved." Terrible as was the occasion, Calhoun had the mental resources to meet it. He responded with the toast, "Our Union, next to our liberty the most dear. May we all remember that it can only be preserved by respecting the rights of the states and distributing equally the benefits and burdens of the Union." The cards had been exchanged; how would go the duel?

TARIFF AND NULLIFICATION

While philosophical jousts were being conducted, actions in more prosaic fields were taking place. South Carolina had never ceased opposing the Tariff of Abominations (1828), and late in the President's first administration the antitariff forces were able to bring about some reduction. Jackson had been quite non-committal on the whole question; perhaps he did not understand it very well. With no opposition from the White House, the Tariff of 1832 lowered the rates of 1828 on some items. Might one assume that elated South Carolinians celebrated their victory with hosannahs of delight in relief from "arbitrary taxation"? Far from it; the reduction in the new tariff was very little, and protectionism appeared to be riveted upon the country once and for all.

Storms of protest rose higher than ever in the Palmetto State, although many Carolina unionists denied the Calhounian doctrine of nullification. These nationalists, however, were defeated in a special election; and in November, 1832, a convention called for that purpose declared the Tariffs of 1828 and 1832 "null, void, and no law" inside the state limits; no Federal tariff duties could be collected after 1 February 1833. The nation watched President Andrew Jackson. Although his Jefferson-dinner toast had discouraged state rightists, had he not upheld the state of Georgia against the Supreme Court? The sectionalists should have reread his Maysville Road veto more carefully, for that expressed the executive sentiments.

With the inflexible determination that characterized the Tennessean when his opinion had solidified, Jackson left no doubt where he stood in regard to South Carolina's action. He issued a proclamation asserting that nullification was ". . . *incompatible with the existence of the Union, contradicted expressly by the letter of the Constitution, unauthorized by its spirit, inconsistent with every principle on which it was founded and destructive of the great object for which it was formed.*" Near his conclusion the President warned Calhoun and his followers, "The laws of the United States must be executed . . . my duty is emphatically pronounced in the Constitution."

Jackson's words were soon backed by deeds. He reinforced the Federal forts near Charleston, announced that additional troops might be sent South, and sponsored a "force bill" in Congress, according disciplinary powers to the President. The crisis atmosphere deepened, and many Americans feared that dissolution of the Union was forthcoming. Actually both sides were in a position to welcome compromise. While the North rallied around Jackson, Calhoun soon perceived that South Carolina was receiving little encouragement from sister slave states. On the other hand, Jackson hoped to avoid coercion if conciliation could work as well. Behind the bombastic utterances of extremists in both camps, agreement was soon reached. Clay, as usual, led the compromisers, and a new tariff bill raced through the House and Senate; Jackson signed it on the same day that he approved the force bill. This Tariff of 1833 specified that all duties higher than 20 per cent would be scaled down to that figure in ten annual graduated reductions.

The South Carolina convention that had nullified the tariff laws reconvened with its economic objections partially satisfied and solemnly repealed the ordinance of nullification. To show that the delegates yielded not a whit on the philosophical question of state rights, however, with equal solemnity the force act was declared null and void. Since the Federal government had no desire to utilize coercive measures on a meaningless issue, nothing was done in retaliation for the latter nullification. Thus both camps raised pennants of victory. Jacksonians could argue that the laws of the nation were being enforced and that South Carolina had surrendered when it repealed tariff nullification. Carolinians could point with pride to their stout resistance, which had compelled tariff reduction. Although the compromise was eminently satisfactory, sectionalism as a problem remained unsolved and would repeatedly disturb national tranquillity, although secession rather than nullification was to become the weapon of the militant South.

JACKSON AND THE BANK OF THE UNITED STATES

It was not alone the tariff controversy that moiled national surfaces; tempers edged even higher during the running fight concerning the recharter of the Bank of the United States, al-

though the division was more on class than sectional economic lines. The history of the second Bank had been spotty. Managed with a reckless disregard for economic common sense or national welfare during its first three years, the Bank had been reformed under new management in 1819 and continued to improve under Nicholas Biddle, a prominent Philadelphian who was president of the institution from 1823 to 1836. Prudent investments, high dividend rates to its stockholders, and considerable service to the government through its fiscal activities tended to make the Bank hailed in conservative upper-class Eastern circles. Not so in the South and West, however. Farmers wishing easy credit were dismayed at the stiff collateral requirements for loans maintained by the central Bank office in Philadelphia—policies reflected both in its branches throughout the country and in local banks. There was the usual rural feeling that centralized banking operated for the wealthy rather than for the poor. The Bank was equally unpopular among Eastern workingmen, but for a diametrically opposite reason. Laborers disliked the paper currency issued by the Bank and the correspondingly higher prices. Whatever the divergent reasons, the poorer classes, both East and West, tended to oppose the Bank. Many still agreed with the sentiments voiced in 1819 by Senator Thomas H. Benton who had roared, "All the flourishing cities of the West are mortgaged to this money power. . . . They are in the jaws of the Monster. A lump of butter in the mouth of a dog—one gulp, one swallow, and all is gone!"

Opposition to the Bank found its champion in Andrew Jackson. What relatively little historical reading the President had done convinced him that high finance was dangerous. Moreover he was incensed that the Bank had opposed his candidacy in 1828 and refused jobs and loans to Jackson men. For a year or two during his first term he remained silent on the subject, and advocates of the Bank made a grave miscalculation. Erroneously positive that the Bank was so popular that Jackson would have to fall into line, Nicholas Biddle's supporters decided to force the issue. This group was concentrated in the National Republican party, soon to adopt officially the name "Whig," and its candidate Henry Clay needed a good platform from which he could fight Jackson in 1832. Bank supporters brought forth a bill, early in election year, to recharter the Bank, although the original charter still had over three years to run. The bill was steered through Congress by narrow majorities and sent to the President for signature.

Jackson returned the bill with a veto so blistering that Nicholas Biddle complained, "It has all the fury of a chained panther biting the bars of his cage. It is really a manifesto of anarchy. . . ." To be sure, Jackson's economic arguments were none too impressive. After objecting to both the number of foreigners who owned Bank stock and the overly extensive power enjoyed by the institution, the President leveled his guns on the class issue:

Many of our rich men have not been content with equal protection and equal benefits, but have besought us to make them richer by act of Congress . . . . [But] we can at least take a stand against all new grants of monopolies and exclusive privileges, against any prostitution of our Government to the advancement of the few at the expense of the many. . .

Irate at the executive rebuff, the Bank forces threw themselves into the campaign of 1832 with abandon. They spent vast sums (for that day) by hiring orators, subsidizing newspapers, and plastering the nation with handbills (among them copies of Jackson's veto) opposing the President. The Bank used its financial power to reward its friends and to punish its enemies; on occasion supporters of Jackson found notes suddenly presented for repayment.

The brilliant Henry Clay stormed about the country answering the speeches of Jacksonian men. Daniel Webster worked hard; he had been economically influenced by Nicholas Biddle. In one instance "Black Daniel" wrote to the president of the Bank that his "retainer" had not been "renewed or *refreshed*" and that prompt action had better be forthcoming if his efforts were to be continued. While the elec-

tion struggle thundered over the nation, one of the greatest Americans did nothing. Calhoun, the Achilles of South Carolina, sulked in his tent, calling maledictions upon both sides. Under his leadership, South Carolina threw away her electoral votes on an obscure candidate. Withdrawals of sectionalists and the fulminations of Bank supporters went for naught. Jackson's political science was as masterful as his economics was dubious. He romped to an easy success, overwhelmed Clay by 219 to 47 electoral votes, and scored gains over 1828 even in New England.

No man or institution crossed the regal Andrew with impunity. Shortly after his second term commenced, he chastised the Bank of the United States by withdrawing Federal funds. To accomplish this he had to shuffle his Cabinet, sending Edward Livingston to France so that his Secretary of the Treasury (known to be opposed to the withdrawal of Federal money from the Bank) could be kicked upstairs to the State Department. His first appointee to the Treasury chair procrastinated so much that Jackson fired him and moved Roger Taney into the vacancy. With a more unified Cabinet behind him, Jackson removed the national funds during the summer of 1833 and deposited them in many state banks, which promptly became known as "pet banks." This system continued until the Independent Treasury was established under Van Buren in 1840.

The Bank supporters exploded with even greater wrath over the withdrawal of Federal funds than they had on the question of the recharter. There is little reason to doubt that Nicholas Biddle, by suddenly calling in loans, precipitated a business panic, hoping that hard times would compel the government to surrender. Jackson grimly refused to budge. Finally protests from the business interests, hardpressed by the credit log jam, forced Biddle to reverse his policies. This he did to such an extent that a flood of paper money increased prices and eased credit. A wild boom was encouraged and continued for three years. Land sales doubled and redoubled, state vied with state on internal improvements, and the heady flush of confidence filled speculators "on the make" with superb optimism.

Eventually the President interfered. Jackson had always been partisan to metallic currency, and by 1836 he was listening sympathetically to the appeals of his Eastern hard-money supporters, who became insistent that the inflation be brought under control since its impact was devastating upon city laborers. The President obliged when he issued his famous Specie Circular, which ordered that all payments for public lands must be in coin. The West was soon drained of hard money by Eastern creditors. This caused something of a chain reaction, for land speculation had been a leading factor in the boom of the 1830s. The tightened requirements for land and the immediate decline in land sales rapidly spread in an ever-widening whirlpool. A dash of ice water had been tossed on the merry flames of easy credit and wild speculation. The Specie Circular was directly, if only partially, responsible for bringing on the panic and depression of 1837.

To Americans living in the days of multi-billion-dollar deficits in governmental spending, it is rather surprising to see that, late in Jackson's second term (shortly before the depression), the United States had wiped out its debt and found itself with a somewhat embarrassing surplus. Income from tariffs and land sales caused this unusual development. Amusingly enough, no one knew what to do with the surplus. After considerable debate it was divided among the states according to their representation in Congress. Some states used their share for education, some for internal improvements, and one divided it upon a per capita basis. The advent of the depression of 1837 wiped out surpluses of any kind, and the nation soon reverted to its typical position of deficiency in Federal revenues.

THE JACKSONIAN SUCCESSION

The phrase Jacksonian Democracy applies not only to the General's two administrations but also to the single term of his successor, Martin Van Buren. "The Fox of Kinderhook" had played his cards with magnificent skill since 1829, and he raked in the presidential stakes. In effect, Jackson simply dictated Van Buren's selection to the compliant Democratic party. By this time the opposition was known officially as the Whig party. The derivation of the name is interesting. His enemies were used to snarling that Jackson was in reality "Of Veto Memory King Andrew I," and a widely circulated cartoon showed a robed, crowned, and sceptered Jackson trampling on the Constitution. Because their party opposed the "King," Jackson's opponents adopted the eighteenth-century British political appellation of "Whig," the party that supposedly fought royal prerogatives in England.

The American Whig party lasted only about a generation, for it was inchoate in organization and divided in policy. Sometimes all factions could unite—as in 1840—and then it was a powerful party. Similar to the contemporary Democrats, but in contrast to the later sectional Republicans, Whig strength was both above and below the Mason-Dixon line. Unluckiest of major American political parties, the Whigs elected two Presidents during their short history, and both of them died in office. The slavery controversy of the 1850s split the Whig party irrevocably, the vast majority of its Southern adherents becoming Democrats and most Northern Whigs drifting into the Republican ranks.

Fearful that they could not defeat Van Buren with a single candidate and a normal campaign, the Whigs tried a novel experiment in the election of 1836. They nominated several "favorite sons" from different states, hoping that they would pick up enough scattered support to deny Van Buren an electoral majority and throw the choice to the House of Representatives. Their attempt was unsuccessful, however. Comfortably wrapped in the Jacksonian mantle, Van Buren enjoyed an easy victory in the Electoral College. The inauguration was a combined Jackson–Van Buren triumph. Satisfied that he left his policies in able hands, the General returned to his beautiful Tennessee home called "The Hermitage," where he lived in retirement, sallying forth occasionally to instruct his successors, until he died in 1845.

Opinion of the merit of Andrew Jackson has remained divided after his death as it was during his life, although most modern historians, in contrast to those a half century ago, consider him to have been one of the great American Presidents. Jackson was a strong Chief Executive who looked upon his function in the American government as one of leadership as well as administration. Many Presidents have meekly followed Congress, but Jackson, like Lincoln, both Roosevelts, and Wilson, asserted more vigorously the executive prerogatives. There was much to condemn in Andrew Jackson. He could be vindictive, naïve, and ruthless. He allowed personal animosities to influence his stand on impersonal legislation. On specific matters he could often be wrong. Yet his vigor, his enthusiasm, his sensitiveness to the people's desires, and the protection he afforded to average Americans against the special privilege of the time have earned him more admiration and love than most Presidents have enjoyed. His service toward the creation of a more democratic America has made Andrew Jackson a part of the national memory.

❬ The Van Buren Administration. As did Calvin Coolidge in 1929, Jackson left the White House just before an economic storm broke, and the tempest's fury raged around the head of Martin Van Buren. The calamitous depression of 1837 fell like judgment day on the expanding American economy. Van Buren was blamed for it; human nature seems to have a tendency to indict those temporarily in power for economic ills brought on by perhaps two decades of improvident growth. During the 1820s and the 1830s a wild boom had continued, broken occasionally by short downward revisions, but in general continuing upward in an inflationary spiral. States rivaled one another in ambitious and often foolhardy internal improvements. In emulation of New York's Erie Canal, it seemed as if there was hardly a rivulet in the nation that was not being dredged, widened, or extended into a canal. Land speculation was rife throughout the West, and sales were concluded not so much for purposes of settlement or development as to resell later at a higher price. Industrialism in the Northeast grew rapidly—too rapidly. Crop failures in the middle 1830s coincided with a financial panic in Europe at the same time. Furthermore, for several years there had been continual meddling with the national financial and credit system.

In its fight against Jackson, the Bank had created a largely artificial panic; and when recovery came, the inflation resulting from the flood of paper money based on Federal funds pouring into the pet banks led to a dizzy advance. In addition to these basic economic factors, the sudden shock of Jackson's Specie Circular, which stiffened credit requirements, brought on a psychological wave of panic selling and plunged the nation headlong into depression.

Times were hard until well into the early 1840s. From a high of 25 million acres in 1837, land sales plummeted to a bare 1 million in 1841. State after state defaulted on bonds sold to finance chimerical adventures. Estimates of the percentage of textile factories that had to close ran as high as nine-tenths. Thousands of artisans were thrown out of work in the cities. Agricultural commodity prices collapsed; the decline of cotton from 18 to 8 cents a pound prostrated the South. Unaware of any governmental obligation to protect its citizens from the effects of their own economic misdeeds, the Van Buren administration wrung its hands and did nothing. Private charity was about the only form of relief. Practically all that Van Buren could suggest was financial reorganization in the form of an Independent Treasury as a depository for Federal revenues, rather than utilization of either a Bank of the United States or state banks. After prolonged debate, the Treasury measure passed in 1840. Within a year the Whigs repealed it, but when the Democrats returned to power under James K. Polk the Independent Treasury system was restored and this time lasted for half a century.

In many ways Van Buren did a good job. His devotion to the principles of Jacksonian Democracy was obvious; through his close affiliation with the more radical Eastern Locofoco elements, the President added new leaven to Jacksonianism. In the Texas question and in disputes between Great Britain and New York State, Van Buren showed intelligence, restraint, patience, and common sense. If national economic collapse had not shadowed his administration, Van Buren's place among the better Presidents would be assured. But the contrast between the brilliant prosperity of Jackson and, although the fault was not his own, the depression under Van Buren afflicted the Democrats with an almost intolerable political burden that tended to throw into reverse the advance of Jacksonian Democracy.

CHAPTER 24

Whig versus Democrat

(1840-1850)

THE ELECTION OF 1840

The party battles of the 1840s were sure to be breathlessly exciting; the Whigs and the Democrats were in relative equipoise during most of the decade, and a handful of votes in such pivotal states as New York or Pennsylvania could swing an election either way. In 1840, however, Whig auspices were excellent. The Democrats felt compelled to renominate Van Buren, even though the shadow of national economic depression darkened the hopes of the "Fox of Kinderhook." Confident of victory, the jubilant Whigs gathered in convention. Henry Clay was their party leader, and he deserved the nomination, but his enemies inside the organization convinced most of the delegates that Clay could not win without a military reputation to titillate the electorate. In his place the Whigs nominated for the presidency William Henry Harrison, Indian fighter at Tippecanoe exactly twenty-nine years before,[1] and awarded the vice-presidential choice to John Tyler, an anti-Jackson Demo-

crat. Harrison was an upright and patriotic gentleman, although characterized by no unusual brilliance or intelligence. His advisers told him to go home to Ohio and keep his mouth shut, and he found it easy to accede. The Whigs were undecided for a time how to organize their campaign, but their dilemma was solved for them when a Democratic editorial sneered that Harrison was so undistinguished that he would be content with a pension of $2,000 a year, a log cabin, and an abundance of hard cider. Immediately the Whigs had found their platform.

The Harrison party banned discussion of important issues; the Bank and the tariff were to remain in limbo. All Whig energies were devoted toward proving to the masses that "Tippecanoe" Harrison was a simple backwoodsman, no better than any other American. The truth was that Harrison belonged to one of the finest old Virginia families, and instead of living in a log cabin, he resided in a beautiful and spacious house from which broad lawns spread down to the Ohio River. The Whigs portrayed Van Buren as a gilded aristocrat wallowing in "opulent luxury" at the public expense. The

[1] Losing the Whig nomination to Harrison was almost more than the impulsive Clay could stand. He snapped, "My friends are not worth the powder and shot it would take to kill them! . . . I am . . . always run . . . when sure to be defeated, and now

betrayed for a nomination when I, or anyone, would be sure of an election."

President's origins were solidly plebeian—his father had been an innkeeper. It was amusing and yet disheartening to see the Whigs, spokesmen for the upper economic groups, pose as the champions of leveling democracy, beating the Jacksonians at their own game.

The Whigs released a political hurricane. All over the nation Harrison rallies met in the ruddy glare of flambeaux while wagons were rolled into position, complete with log cabin, "buckeye" bench, chained raccoon, and barrels of hard cider. Soon the stirring refrains of "Van, Van's a used-up man!" and "To guide our ship, we'll try old Tip!" would echo from well-lubricated throats. Whig orators stumped the countryside; Whig editors wrote with contagious and enthusiastic confidence. When the Democrats tried to discuss vital problems, they would be answered with the ringing slogan, "Tippecanoe and Tyler Too!" In one of the most ludicrous elections in American history, Van Buren was practically shouted out of office, and Harrison swept to an impressive electoral triumph, although the popular vote was close.

THE HARRISON-TYLER ADMINISTRATION

Inauguration Day, 1841, was cold and rainy. The aged General Harrison—he was 69—stood around in the dank weather so long reading his inaugural address and listening to the importunities of job-hungry Whig politicos that he caught a cold that, turning into pneumonia, killed him a month later. It was the first time that a President had died while in office, and the dismayed Whigs watched their vice-presidential candidate, John Tyler of Virginia, elevated to the White House. Tyler had never cloaked his political opinions. Although he felt a personal animosity for Andrew Jackson, on most issues Tyler was a confirmed Democrat who favored a relatively low tariff, detested the Bank of the United States, and was ardently desirous of expanding American territory into the West. He had been nominated

for the second slot on the Whig ticket in the expectation that he might capture some support from anti–Van Buren Democrats. Perhaps he did, but the Whigs paid an extravagant price for it.

Henry Clay was still the Whig chieftain, and there was some hope that he and the new President could cooperate. At first all went well; Tyler was perfectly amenable to a preemption bill that allowed squatters on government lands to have initial opportunity to purchase 160 acres at $1.25 per acre. This harmony proved illusory, however. The battle was joined when Clay sponsored a bill to charter a third Bank of the United States, incorporated in the District of Columbia and able to found branches throughout the Union wherever the state permitted. Tyler vetoed the measure. The resourceful Whigs tried to allay the President's constitutional doubts and fears of a financial monopoly by a second bill, curtailing the establishment of branches, and changing the name "Bank" to "fiscal corporation." Unimpressed, Tyler vetoed this one too. Led by Clay the disgruntled Whigs resigned en masse from the Cabinet [2] and read Tyler out of the party—they called the President "His Accidency" thereafter. Tyler surrounded himself with old friends from Virginia and spent a pleasant term featuring family picnics along the Potomac.

An important by-product of the split between Tyler and the Whigs was John C. Calhoun's *rapprochement* with the Democratic party. Ever since 1832 Calhoun had wandered in the political wilderness, hurling anathemas upon Whig and Democrat alike. Following the death of Secretary of State Abel P. Upshur of Virginia, killed by an exploding cannon while visiting a warship, Calhoun accepted Tyler's request to fill the State vacancy. In effect, the South Carolinian rejoined the Democratic party, since Tyler could no longer be considered a Whig. Calhoun's appointment is an important landmark in the southward drift of the

[2] For a time Daniel Webster continued to be Tyler's Secretary of State until he had concluded his negotiations with the Briton Lord Ashburton in 1842. Then Webster joined his fellow Whigs outside the administration.

Democratic party, which gradually changed from its liberal Jacksonian position in the 1830s to that of a mouthpiece for the Southern extremists in the late 1850s.

THE ELECTION OF 1844

Obviously the Whigs would never stomach President Tyler for renomination, and the Democrats did not want him either, so both parties looked for new candidates in 1844. It was Clay's turn for the Whigs, and he received an easy nomination. Van Buren supporters formed a majority at the Democratic convention, but many Southerners were suspicious— with reason—that the "Little Magician" was becoming imbued with an antislavery virus. The situation was further complicated when Van Buren and Clay made a gentleman's agreement to sidestep the explosive question of Texas annexation, a decision that lost the nomination for Van Buren and perhaps the election for Clay. Led by Robert J. Walker of Mississippi, Van Buren's party enemies quietly moved among the Democratic delegates implying that the New Yorker's candidacy was hopeless because he could not attract expansionistic enthusiasts. Their strategy paid rich dividends. A "dark-horse" (unexpected) candidate, James K. Polk of Tennessee, received the nomination; and the expansionists were able to write into the Democratic platform a plank calling for—masterful language—"the reoccupation of Oregon and the reannexation of Texas." With his typical ill fortune Clay lost New York by a few votes, and Polk was elected.[3]

THE POLK ADMINISTRATION

James K. Polk has risen steadily in the estimation of American historians during the past

half century. While cold in personal deportment and totally lacking in the dynamic magnetism that Americans appear to love in their politicos, Polk was aggressive, determined, intelligent, and successful. If a dark horse at the convention, he was a well-known American. A native Tennesseean, he became Jackson's protégé in that state, serving as Governor. He had been a prominent and able Speaker of the House of Representatives, serving as Jackson's administration leader there. Polk carried into the White House his lifelong pattern of unrelenting labor, and he almost toiled the clock around during his single term; he seems to have killed himself by overwork. Not the least noteworthy of his labors was his diary, which has given historians a reasonably complete recall of a President's hopes and aspirations. This dogged and industrious Executive knew precisely what he wanted and methodically set about accomplishing his ends.

Polk detested the idea of a Bank of the United States, and in 1846 he engineered the reestablishment of the Independent Treasury, which would act as the Federal depository. This system had first been introduced by Van Buren, but the Whigs had thrown it out in 1841. Once reinstated, the Independent Treasury remained, with some modifications made during the Civil War, until it was superseded by the Glass-Owen Federal Reserve Act in 1913. Another accomplishment of the Polk administration was to lower the tariff. The Walker Tariff of 1846 slashed the rates that the Whigs had increased in 1842 to a rough approximation of those in the Compromise Tariff of 1833. Low duties were maintained until higher schedules returned with the Republican-sponsored Morrill Tariff (1861). A measure that earned the President considerable opposition in the West was his veto of a "rivers and harbors" internal-improvement bill. Polk had the usual Executive constitutional doubts.

Although detailed discussion of the important diplomatic events that occurred under Polk must await more extensive treatment later,[4] they deserve some mention here, since

[3] The antislavery Liberty party ran a candidate who seems to have garnered enough potential Clay votes to have aided significantly Polk's thin triumph in New York.

[4] See Chaps. 26 and 27.

they were inextricably woven with the domestic issues. Polk wished to annex Texas, Oregon, and considerable portions of Mexican territory. Only in Texas was his plan defeated— and this by only three days; President Tyler just beat him to it (1 March 1845). In Oregon a predecessor's rapid action could not cheat Polk of his triumph. Great Britain and the United States compromised that vast Northwest territory by extending the Canadian-American boundary of 1818 along the 49th parallel to the Pacific. Polk's action in arbitrating Oregon while all of Texas had been taken inflamed the Middle West, which was already upset by his veto of the rivers and harbors bill. A common feeling west of the Appalachians and north of the Ohio River considered that the Democrats were bent on satisfying Southern slave owners rather than Northern farmers.

Polk's administration was featured by a remarkably successful war with Mexico, 1846 to 1848. General Zachary Taylor conquered part of northeastern Mexico; Stephen Kearny, John Charles Frémont, and others brought California first independence and then annexation; and Winfield Scott marched his army overland from coastal Vera Cruz, through the mountains, and on to capture Mexico City, bringing an end to the war. By the Treaty of Guadalupe-Hidalgo (1848) the United States annexed the territory west of the Rockies, south of Oregon, and north of a line roughly established by the lower Rio Grande and Gila Rivers. For these losses, Mexico received about $18 million. James K. Polk was a land-hungry man, and he dined sumptuously.

THE ELECTION OF 1848

The campaign of 1848 was destined to be heated, for the Mexican War had been as much political as military, and both sides used the contest for partisan advantage. Polk had pledged himself to serve only a single term, and he kept his word. The Democrats nominated Lewis Cass of Michigan, a prominent

Jacksonian who had held important Cabinet positions. Cass was not opposed to the penetration of slavery into new territory and thus was acceptable to Southern Democrats. The Whigs again turned to a military hero, this time General Zachary Taylor, who had defeated the Mexicans at Buena Vista. Taylor, "Old Rough and Ready," was relatively uneducated and almost entirely nonpolitical. Although he owned a Louisiana sugar plantation and many slaves, he was no apologist for slavery. Taylor, the Southerner, had fallen under the influence of Senator William H. Seward of New York, an opponent of African bondage; and the General spoke for the North, while Cass the Michigander echoed Southern sentiments.

As in 1844, a third party held a pivotal position in some Northern states. The Liberty party had been revamped under the name of the Free Soil party. Attracting many of the radical New York Democrats called "Barnburners," [5] the Free Soilers nominated Martin Van Buren, who ran surprisingly well. He received some 300,000 votes, and his party elected thirteen members to the House of Representatives and two Senators. Both Whigs and Democrats suffered from the activities of the Free Soil party, but with the defection of the Democratic Barnburners in New York, Cass was hurt more than Taylor. New York went Whig by a small majority, enabling that party to score its second and final national triumph.

SLAVERY: NORTHERN OPINION

Even before the election of 1848 sectional shadows were darkening national skies. During the Mexican War a mischievous proposal in Congress intensified the augmenting hostility between the North and South. In 1846 an army-appropriation bill was being debated in

[5] Their opponents, the more conservative "Hunker" element in New York Democracy, claimed that the antislavery supporters were like the Dutchman who burned his barn to get rid of the rats—i.e., they were willing to sever the Union to get rid of slavery.

the House of Representatives when David Wilmot, an antislave Pennsylvanian, arose to offer the "Wilmot Proviso," which stipulated that any territory gained from the Mexican War must forever be free soil. Proponents of this measure offered it as an amendment to almost every bill during that session of Congress, and two young Illinois Congressmen had opportunity to vote on the proviso over forty times, Stephen A. Douglas voting against the proposal and Abraham Lincoln supporting it on every occasion. The Wilmot Proviso was never enacted, but it aided mightily in fanning the flames of sectional animosity.

By the late 1840s circumstances had evolved in such a manner as to furnish additional ammunition to those arguing that two nations were coming into being. Throughout the nation politics was in ferment over the slavery problem, although there was no complete victory for any particular shade of opinion. Despite the attempts of both Northern and Southern radicals to promote sectional hostility, a majority of Americans still looked to compromise.

There were three main factions among Northerners on the slavery issue. The first and largest was divided among itself, ranging in opinion from those who rivaled Mississippi planters in negrophobia to others who thoroughly disliked the institution of slavery. All of this first group, however, were united in their determination that they would not risk severing the Union on the antislavery issue. A second wing took the stand that while there was no right to interfere in the domestic institutions of states, slavery should not be permitted to expand, but must be confined to the states where it already existed. The third group was the small abolitionist minority, which remained repugnant to the typical Northerner, who resisted both the inflammatory doctrines of the Garrisonians and the somewhat milder offerings of the Tappan brothers, Theodore Weld, and the Grimké sisters. It must again be emphasized that the abolitionists of both varieties remained small minorities during the entire pre–Civil War period. In mid-century

most Northerners were willing to arbitrate on the slavery question.

SLAVERY: SOUTHERN OPINION

More immoderate was Southern feeling about slavery, although even here the forces of compromise also formed a majority in 1850. The Southern radical minority was, nevertheless, more powerful than the corresponding extremists in the North. Unable or unwilling to recognize that most Northerners were opposed to interference with slavery where it existed, many in the South lumped together the mildest critic of that institution with the abolitionist as uncompromising enemies of the Southern way of life. By 1850 there had been a half century's hardening of sectional attitude below the Mason-Dixon line on the question of slavery. Late in the eighteenth century such liberal Southerners as George Washington and Thomas Jefferson took the lead in condemning slavery, although they always voiced a doubt about what system might replace it. Many early abolition societies centered in the upper South. Early in the nineteenth century, however, a combination of economic, social, and psychological changes impelled Southern opinion to retreat to a more reactionary position. The South of 1850 was a far cry from the section that had bred the glorious philosophy of Virginia liberalism as expressed in the Declaration of Independence.

The economic shift in the South was extremely important in creating a different intellectual climate. In the late 1700s Southern economy languished under slavery; the necessity of supporting the bondsman during his unproductive years of childhood and old age, in addition to the high death rate among slaves, impelled many Southerners to cry for relief. The invention of the cotton gin and the ensuing expansion into virgin Western territory wrought a revolution in plantation economics, especially in the Gulf states. For a time slavery helped the South to prosper. The speedy ginning process enabled the cotton states to meet the skyrocketing demands of textile mills in both New and old England. Handsome profits could be realized raising cotton in unspoiled territory, such as in the Mississippi Delta area during the 1820s. Eventually the supply of new cotton lands in the Southwest began to run short; and many plantations, caught between a lesser yield from overworked acres and rapidly increasing prices for field hands, could return little if any profit. Nevertheless, the old idea of Southern prosperity through slavery continued to mold opinion in that section. Another contributing factor was the feeling that conditions were so rigorous in growing cotton and particularly sugar that white men could not stand the brutal physical labor involved.

If economic reasons were potent in forming a Southern frame of reference toward slavery, equally important were social and psychological aspects. Slavery was more than an economic system for providing a labor force; it was also a pattern for race relationships. Bad as it was, slavery did establish a settled way of life between the white master and the Negro slave. It was in general a cruel, immoral, and inefficient method—but nonetheless a method—of civilizing and Christianizing the Negroes, many of whom had been smuggled into the South directly from the jungles of Africa. One must sympathize with the abolitionist when he insisted that slavery was a terrible moral and social wrong; that man's ownership of man is entirely contrary to the democratic and liberal tradition. At the same time one must agree with the Southerner when he declared during the mid–nineteenth century that the Negro was not ready for freedom—that immediate emancipation was impossible without the most violent social repercussions.

The race-relationship problem was never considered by the abolitionist. He demanded only immediate and total emancipation, and he never attempted to furnish any adequate substitute for the institution during the years when the ex-slave must be trained for citizenship. More moderate Northern opinion was much fairer about recognizing the difficulties involved in sudden freedom for the bondsmen. Occasionally a halfhearted suggestion would be heard that freed Negroes be given an area somewhere in the West for themselves, akin to Indian reservations, but little attention was paid to this. More support attended a proposal that the slaves be bought by private philanthropy, freed, and sent back to Africa. Several objections were forthcoming here. For one thing, the Negro had become Americanized and had little desire to return to his ancestral home. For another, the one attempt of the American Colonization Society was not very successful. Several thousand former slaves were sent to Liberia in West Africa during the 1820s, but they tended to rivet slavery on the natives. Finally, it was difficult to garner the necessary cash for such an expensive undertaking. It was this final aspect that blocked the best and most obvious solution to the whole vexatious dilemma: to follow the lead of Great Britain and emancipate the slaves, as was done in the British West Indies during the 1830s, by vast appropriations from the national treasury to the planters. Slavery was too well entrenched on the American mainland and our nation was too economy-minded to travel this sensible course, although oceans of blood and money might thereby have been saved.

Augmenting the difficulties mentioned above was the position of the free Negro, both North and South. All over the Union his status was almost intolerable, perhaps worse than in slavery. Hated and feared by the poor whites, the ex-slave was discriminated against everywhere. Economically he was forced to take the worst jobs at the poorest pay. Socially he was denied access to theaters, restaurants, hotels, and even general public transportation. He became the scapegoat for the economic ills of Northern laborers, and anti-Negro feeling was as grotesque and ugly in the packed slums of New York as in the piney woods of upland Georgia. In the South the free Negro was in danger of being shanghaied into slavery, and he had little legal recourse to prove his independent status. The social problem of race relationship is never very simple, and to many nineteenth-century Southerners it must have seemed that any change in the position of the slave was fraught with the most awful prospects of chaos and bloodshed.

Arising from both the economic and social factors was a reaction that was almost psychotic. Many Southerners lived in districts where the white inhabitants were decidedly outnumbered by their Negro thralls. Fear of slave uprisings lived constantly with Southern whites, and there were instances of recent memory to feed their panic. The revolution of the Haitian Negroes during the 1790s had never been forgotten in the South. This dread that American slaves might emulate their Caribbean cousins was intensified when a Virginian slave named Nat Turner organized an insurrection that killed over fifty white men, women, and children before it could be checked and the ringleaders executed (1831). A thrill of terror coursed through the South. Coincidentally, a trickle of abolitionist propaganda began to appear in the cotton states. Hotheads like William Lloyd Garrison were perfectly willing to advocate that the slaves should alter their unfortunate way of life by doing violence to their masters. Under the influence of these twin stimuli, the panic atmosphere in the South reached almost insane proportions among some. It became literally dangerous for an individual to question the institution of slavery and its concurrent social controls over the Negroes.

《 *The Southern Defense.* With its sectional attitude tempered by economic prosperity, real or spurious; with no readily available social alternative to replace the institution; and beset by an unreasoning terror psychosis, the South was forced to move from its former position of apologizing for slavery toward actively promoting Negro bondage as a positive good for both master and slave. Planters turned for consolation and inspiration to two famous sources. In the Bible the word "servant" means slave, and in the United States Constitution slavery is clearly recognized although not mentioned by name. African bondage was thus adorned in the finest religious and

political garb. Soon a more positive assertion of the bountiful aspects of the master and slave relationship began to be heard. Chancellor William Harper of Virginia; Professor Thomas R. Dew of William and Mary College; George Fitzhugh, prominent lawyer and author; and Carolina fire-eater Edmund Ruffin were among the many to proclaim boldly that slavery was natural, economical, and morally good. Southerners launched a vigorous counterattack against their Northern foes, leveling accusing fingers at Northern exploitation of helpless industrial workers, who had no security in childhood, illness, or old age, as typifying a worse kind of slavery than that characteristic of the South. The more unrestrained the abolitionist attacks, the more frenzied became the answering claim about the physical, moral, and philosophical excellence of the slave system to which the Southerner found himself riveted.

During the 1830s Gulf-state defiance of the Northern antislavery movement took congressional action. Abolitionist petitions poured into Congress in such numbers that Southern Representatives passed a "gag resolution" automatically tabling such controversial tracts. This aroused ex-President John Quincy Adams, regularly sent to the House by his Massachusetts constituents ever since his retirement from the White House. Adams objected to the gag resolution not because of sympathy for Garrisonian principles, but to oppose an infraction of the constitutional right of petition. Session after session, the alarming old man, his bald head glinting under the gaslights, thundered his defiance at the proslavery Representatives. Gradually he gained support, until in 1844 the obnoxious legislation was repealed, much to the anger of the South. At about the same time as the gag resolution had been introduced, Southern Congressmen interfered with the delivery of the Federal mails. In 1835 the Postmaster General announced that Southern postmasters might refuse to deliver any abolitionist literature that they considered "incendiary." In the face of angry Northern protest, this heavy-handed operation was soon repealed, but many cotton-state postmasters continued to discard antislavery material until after the Civil War. Indeed, Southern public opinion practically compelled them to do so.

The embattled South was rising to defend its maligned way of life, and looked upon the Wilmot Proviso during the Mexican War as a deliberate affront. Although the Proviso had been defeated, faint mutterings of secession began to be heard. Additional Southern alarm was engendered by the rapid growth of Northern parties pledged to arrest the extension of slavery into new territories. The Liberty party of 1840 and 1844 attracted relatively few ballots; four years later the Free Soil party polled over 300,000 votes. The South determined that if slavery was to be contained, if citizens of the cotton states could not move freely into lands won through common endeavor, they would leave the Union. With conditions at this point of tension, a new tempest blew from the West. California was ready to petition for admittance into the United States as a free state.

CALIFORNIA AND THE SECTIONAL CLASH

Gross and ugly as were some of its manifestations, California had enjoyed a population boom unprecedented in American history. As a northern borderland of Spain's hemispheric empire, California had dozed in its well-advertised sunshine while the rancher, the friar, and the soldier made little impression on the sprawling domain. Inconsequential results followed an exchange of Mexican for Spanish rule. Racked by internal disorders, Mexico could do little to halt a small influx of Americans who either deserted from ships or trekked overland across the Sierra Nevadas into the great central valley. A few hundred Americans were outnumbered by about 6,000 Mexicans when the Mexican War broke out, but the United States conquered California easily. After a short interim of independence under the "Golden Bear Republic," California was annexed, along with Utah and New Mexico territories, by the Treaty of Guadalupe-Hidalgo in 1848.

The sectional crisis of 1850 might have been delayed for a time had not gold been discovered near Sacramento, California, early in 1848. Details of the gold rush are covered elsewhere; here we are primarily concerned with political repercussions rather than with economic or social alterations.[6] Over the Oregon-California trail, around Cape Horn by clipper ship, or by a three-legged voyage to Panama, an overland trip through the noxious isthmian jungles, and a Pacific journey to San Francisco, thousands poured into "El Dorado" seeking the precious metal or offering services to miners. Europe, Asia, and Australia, as well as the United States, were represented in the gold fields, and a population growth that might have taken decades was accomplished in two years. By 1850 California had all the requirements necessary, and its 80,000 people were agitating for admission as a free state.

If California's petition was the prime instigating factor in the mid-century crisis, other problems had been building pressure for years and were near the exploding point. A territorial government had to be established for the country between Texas and California. The precise boundaries of Texas and the disposition of the Texan state debt awaited decision. Northern Representatives called for a cessation of slave auctions in Washington, D.C., having found it highly disconcerting to be interrupted in the midst of an antislave oration by the cries of the slave auctioneer floating in through the open windows of the Capitol. Southern slave owners were adamant in their determination that stronger legislation was needed to stop slaves from escaping into the North and to recover those fugitives already resting in havens beyond the slave states. The issue of California statehood was superimposed upon these other conflicts, some of which had festered for years.

If the slavery question formed the underlying ground swell to sectional dispute, specific crisis was caused by the general question of the expansion of slavery into the new territories. Several schools of thought were recognizable

[6] See pp. 264–265.

by 1850. The Wilmot Proviso adherents wished to close any expansion of the evil institution forever. Southern fire-eaters maintained that slaves were property, property was clearly protected by the Constitution, the Constitution was the law of any lands under United States dominion, and therefore slavery could could go anywhere except into a state that was recognized to have the right to outlaw slavery if it wished. But only a state could do this, Southerners argued, certainly not a territory. More moderate opinion both North and South hoped to extend the 36°30′ line of the Missouri Compromise westward to the Pacific: free soil above, slave below. Unfortunately this would divide California. A new group, especially strong in the West, supported the democratic viewpoint later promoted by Stephen A. Douglas. This was "popular" or "squatter sovereignty," in which the people of the territory would decide for themselves, before statehood, whether to enter the Union as a free or a slave state.

Radical abolitionists in the North and fire-eating "ultras" in the South had a fine time roiling the unsettled national waters, but without question most Americans at mid-century ardently hoped that some governmental action could ease the almost unbearable strains rending the national fabric. Important questions were asked. In this grave emergency would statesmen of dispassionate intellect and enlightened patriotism rise above the narrow partisanship that was so rampant? How could these divergent opinions be satisfied? Congress devoted itself to this epochal task during the session of 1849–1850.

CONGRESSIONAL FIREWORKS

In personnel it was one of the most impressive Congresses in American history that settled down to work during the gloom of December, 1849. Prominent were such rising lights as Jefferson Davis of Mississippi, fresh from his brilliant military career under Zachary Taylor; Stephen A. Douglas, the "Little Giant" from

Illinois; handsome, brilliant, and arrogant Salmon P. Chase, staunch antislave Ohioan; and the sensitive and intelligent William H. Seward of New York, prominent adviser of President Taylor. If Senate galleries commented in excited whispers about these recently elected members, even greater attention was focused on the great triumvirate, making its final appearance on the national platform: Henry Clay, Daniel Webster, and John C. Calhoun were being starred in their farewell roles.

At first it appeared that all the senatorial talent would be wasted as the House of Representatives split in a sectional wrangle about the election of a Speaker. For three solid weeks the deadlock between Robert Winthrop of Massachusetts and Howell Cobb of Georgia continued. Tempers flared, unseemly brawls broke out on the floor of Congress, and members showed up armed with pistols before Cobb was finally elected and business commenced. While the House was altercating and balloting, a group of influential Senators quietly worked on an "omnibus bill" that might compromise outstanding sectional differences. Stephen A. Douglas did most of the work, but it was decided that the honor of presentation should go to Henry Clay, the "Great Compromiser," whose constituents in Kentucky had recently returned him to the Senate after an eight-year absence.

Late in January, 1850, Clay arose in the Senate to present an over-all plan to placate the embittered North and South. With his abundant natural magnetism Clay pleaded for the adoption of statehood for California; territorial status, with slavery not mentioned, for New Mexico and Utah; the abolition of the slave trade in the District of Columbia (although slavery itself could not be outlawed without the consent of the people of Maryland and the Federal District and without paying compensation to the slave owners); a strict fugitive-slave law and a pronouncement that the national government could not interfere with the slave trade between states; and finally the settlement of Texan boundaries and debts. Clay begged his compatriots to adopt a give-and-take attitude; to utilize cool, considered judgment; and thus to keep the Union intact.

The great debate thundered in earnest. Opposition was both able and impressive. So ill that he could not stand erect (he died within a month) Calhoun's implacable eyes burned into his audience as he sat listening to his words being read by a Senator from Virginia. Calhoun opposed the compromise. Ominously he called upon the North to cease its warfare against the South and its institutions and to allow Southerners an equal share in developing the new Western territories. Effective opposition was heard from the North as well when William H. Seward addressed the Senate. Voice of the antislave Whigs, Seward admitted that under the Constitution slavery could not legally be excluded from the territories, but he made a reference that was to haunt him for the next decade and very likely to become the chief reason he was never President of the United States. He stated that there was a "higher law" than the Constitution that would eradicate slavery from the nation.

Daniel Webster occupied a pivotal position. His home state of Massachusetts was a hotbed of abolition, especially among the intellectuals of the Boston and Concord literary schools. Although he recognized what would be in store for him, Webster immolated himself for his ideal of the Union. In his "seventh-of-March speech" he refurbished Clay's arguments and called upon the North to accept the fugitive-slave bill, to which there was the greatest opposition. With undeniable truth he asserted that the nature of the climate and topography of the arid prairies, the high plateaus, and the rugged mountains of the Far West would bar slavery forever. Therefore why risk disunion on theoretical questions that would be settled by nature? When his oration was published in the newspapers, the abolitionists exploded with denouncements. "Ichabod," "Benedict Arnold," and "Judas Iscariot" were among the obloquies hurled at him. The noted poet, John Greenleaf Whittier, wrote:

> All else is gone; from those great eyes
>   The Soul has fled:
> When faith is lost, when honor flies,
>   The Man is dead!

Webster shook before these onslaughts, but grimly continued to work for the omnibus bill. His final public appearance saw the most heroic act of his life.

As Congress echoed with speeches both soothingly conciliatory and fiercely partisan, trouble loomed from the White House. President Zachary Taylor, a Louisiana sugar planter, had been persuaded by Seward that the only real issue was the admittance of California as a free state. Taylor refused to support some other provisions of the omnibus bill, and his attitude was obviously leaning toward a veto. Certainly the sectional extremists in Congress had enough power to block any two-thirds vote to override an executive prohibition. Passage hopes improved when the President became ill and died during July, 1850, and Millard Fillmore, a relatively obscure New York politician who had been given the second position on the Whig ticket to achieve a pleasant sectional balance, was elevated to the presidency. Convinced that only compromise could save the Union, Fillmore favored passage.

THE COMPROMISE OF 1850

Motivated by the combined efforts of the national administration, old giants Clay and Webster, and newer luminaries such as Stephen A. Douglas, the five separate measures that are called collectively the omnibus bill squeaked through both Houses and were signed by President Fillmore. Although there was considerable shifting of votes on each of the five parts contained in the Compromise of 1850, enough support was garnered for all. Both sections could point to individual successes, but in general the North came off slightly better. California was admitted as a free state. The slave *trade* (not slavery itself) was banned in the District of Columbia, thus protecting the sensibilities of Northern Congressmen. The one clear triumph of the South was the inclusion of an extremely severe Fugitive Slave Act. Important in themselves rather than representative of any particular sectional

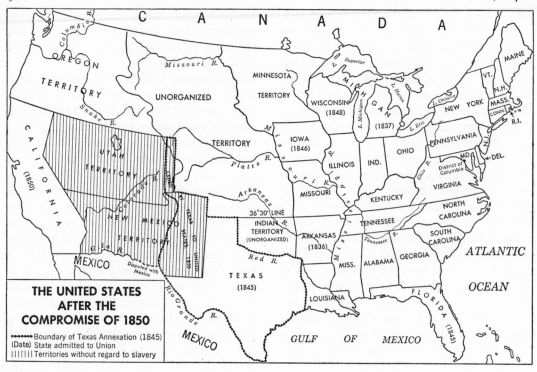

THE UNITED STATES
AFTER THE
COMPROMISE OF 1850

●●●●●●Boundary of Texas Annexation (1845)
(Date) State admitted to Union
||||||| Territories without regard to slavery

victory were the granting of territorial status for New Mexico and Utah (each considerably larger in area than the present states) with no mention of slavery, and the reduction in the size of Texas (the land between the present western boundary of that state and the Rio Grande River going to the United States) in return for national assumption of the Texan state debt amounting to roughly $10 million. While partisans on both sides shouted objections, most Americans rejoiced at the passage of the Compromise of 1850.

With the advantage of hindsight we can see that adoption of the omnibus bill was imperative to maintain the Union. Ever higher had risen the flames of Southern secessionism. In 1849 a call had gone out for the convocation of a Southern conference at Nashville, Tennessee, during the next year. While the debates over the compromise raged in Washington, the delegates at Nashville talked about secession, but decided to await the final outcome of national efforts to conciliate. The meetings reconvened during November, 1850, after the omnibus bill

had become law. Its personnel was even more radical than before, and after assailing the omnibus bill the delegates called for elections to an official Southern Congress that might take the South from the Union. During the winter of 1850–1851 elections were held all over the cotton states. Although there were close contests in Mississippi and South Carolina, twin strongholds of Southern nationalism, the advocates of conciliation and unionism were victorious everywhere.

In view of the white-hot tempers into which many Southerners had been whipped, it is extremely likely that secession would have come in 1850 if some of the ardor of the "ultras" had not been dampened by the adoption of a strict Fugitive Slave Law. Considering that it took a relatively much stronger North four years, hundreds of thousands of casualties, and billions of dollars to win the Civil War in the early 1860s, the task might have been impossible a decade earlier. The ten years from 1851 to 1861 were characterized by unprecedented Northern growth in population, wealth, and industry. Annually during the 1850s the gap widened between the sections, and the desperate South fell ever more behind. Apparently the Compromise of 1850 failed, for it did not avert sectional strife and all its attending horrors. But the Compromise did gain time—precious time. Americans in a unified nation today owe a heavy debt to the supporters of conciliation a century ago. In the last analysis they saved the United States.

CHAPTER 25

A More Nationalistic Diplomacy

(1815-1842)

POST-NAPOLEONIC REACTION

Although American domestic matters significantly overshadowed foreign affairs during the era that followed the War of 1812, diplomatic problems remained sufficiently pressing to perturb American citizens and threaten the peace of the Republic. Danger of entanglements abroad might have been greatly pronounced had not the historical nineteenth century been characterized by relative peace throughout the world.[1] For almost a century no general world conflict clouded international horizons. From the time when French imperial legions were defeated at Waterloo, the great powers lived in relative amity until the field-gray armies of the German Empire swarmed across the Belgian frontier during the summer of 1914. To be sure, wars were fought during this period: the Crimean War of 1854–1855; the Franco-Austrian War of 1859; the American Civil War; the Wars of German Unification, 1864 to 1871; the Russo-Japanese War of 1904–1905; and a whole series of revolutions in Europe and Latin America, imperialistic bushwhacking ex-

peditions, and periodic strife in the Balkans. These conflicts did not spread, however, and the world wars that had disturbed international tranquillity from 1689 to 1815 were not duplicated during the nineteenth century.

In all likelihood, this situation was extremely lucky for the young American Republic. There has been a tendency throughout the national history to become involved in world conflicts. The record seems clear: of the eight international wars that raged from 1689 to 1945, the American people entered every one, four as a colony of Great Britain and four (1776, 1812, 1917, 1941) as an independent nation. The fortunate lack of opportunity to become embroiled in European or Asiatic quarrels for almost a century enabled the United States to grow in numbers and in strength, in agriculture and in industry, in learning and in civilization, until powerful enough to play a leading role on the international stage.

Events dictated a century of world peace, but American farmers and city folk were neither seers nor mediums; they were unblessed with foresight. As they surveyed world vistas shortly after the conclusion of the second war with Great Britain, the situation seemed fraught with menace for the United States. America was out of step with the rest of the

[1] Many historians use the term "nineteenth century" in reference to the period between the end of the Napoleonic Wars in 1815 and the outbreak of World War I in 1914 rather than to the arbitrary dates, 1800 to 1900.

world. Europe had celebrated the downfall of Bonaparte with a headlong dive into reaction, and this global environment did not lead to attitudes of easy complacency for the citizens of a liberal republic. Abroad, the age of Metternich had dawned.

Once Napoleon had been exiled to the bleak Atlantic outpost of St. Helena, Europeans could relax from the travails of military endeavor, settle down to peaceful pursuits, and attempt to reweave their torn economic and social fibers, lacerated by a quarter century of revolutionary impact and strife. If postwar adjustment was difficult for the United States, which had fought a partial war for three years, the European situation was far worse. Dynasties of 1,000 years' tenure had been overthrown, social castes reveling in centuries of privilege had been rudely ousted, and hundreds of thousands of war dead and wounded attested to the military efficacy of the "nation in arms," which had been a leading by-product of the nationalism born in revolutionary France. In little more than two decades Europe had changed drastically and unalterably.

Even the most unsophisticated modern observer of mankind's past can see that the French Revolution and the subsequent extension of its teachings by Napoleonic armies marked a new day over the world. A dynamic Europe could not suddenly become static; the *ancien régime* was dead—eradicated by novel forces and movements overwhelming in their impact on continental institutions. Yet with obstinate and dogged tenacity, the energies of European statesmen after 1815 were devoted to wiping out the memory of one of the most portentous twenty-five years in European history; toward accomplishing a traumatic reaction of forgetfulness among the peoples of Western civilization. The attempt eventually failed, but its temporary success was surprising, and for several years the United States had to inhabit a world in which reaction appeared triumphant.

❨ *The Congress of Vienna.* Among the gold and glitter that attended the balls, parties, and concerts of the Congress of Vienna in 1815,

European diplomacy set about to resurrect the prerevolutionary Continent. Under the watchful tutelage of the Austrian Prince von Metternich, ably assisted by the mystical and enigmatic Tsar Alexander I of Russia; the slippery French turncoat Talleyrand, cleverly salvaging from the ruins of defeat considerable advantage for his nation; and the staunch British conservatives, the Duke of Wellington and Lord Castlereagh, the Congress of Vienna hammered out the philosophical framework that would dominate Europe. Across card tables, in quiet whispers during the performance of a Mozart sonata, or in casual conversations during intermissions at a ball, the diplomats of 1815 attempted to checkmate by astute movements of kings, queens, and bishops the new forces of nationalism and liberalism that they abhorred. Three standards motivated their decisions: legitimacy, compensation, and reaction.

By legitimacy the diplomats meant the right of the legal dynasty to return to power. All over Europe prodigal sons and daughters trekked back to their ancestral capitals. Corpulent, lethargic old Louis XVIII was seated once more on the throne of France; and corrupt Bourbon monarchs, ready to settle old scores with their more liberal subjects, again wielded scepters in Spain and southern Italy. The House of Orange was reestablished in the Netherlands, and that of Savoy in northwestern Italy and the island of Sardinia. Dozens of German princes crept back from exile.

By compensation they meant that one favor deserved another. If a victorious member of the coalition that had defeated Napoleon gave up land, it expected some compensation. Austria surrendered part of the Netherlands (Belgium) to the Dutch and was compensated by the acquisition of Lombardy-Venetia in northeastern Italy. Sweden's ruler, the former French Marshal Bernadotte, whose alliance with France's enemies saved his throne, ceded Finland to Russia, but annexed Norway. Even defeated France, although stripped of most of its conquests, was permitted to retain some territory along its eastern frontier. Reaction became the political climate of Metternich's

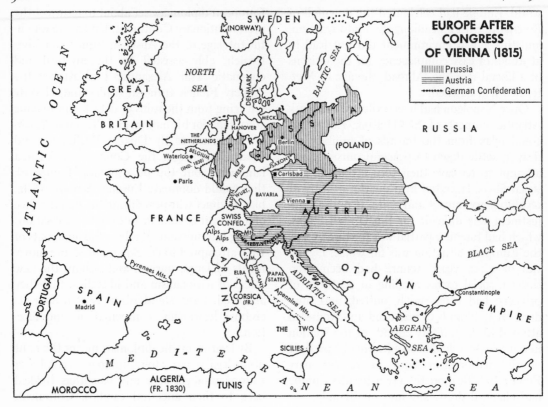

Europe. Liberty and nationalism had been at least the handmaidens of the French Revolution, but post-Waterloo statesmen were determined to erase them from the world. Restoration of conservative monarchs largely took care of liberalism and any incipient democracy. The deliberate parceling of national groups to foreign control illustrated the contemporary hatred for the principle of national self-determination. Polish aspirations for an independent state were crushed as Austria, Prussia, and especially Russia wiped off the map Bonaparte's resurrected Poland, which he had called the "Grand Duchy of Warsaw." Belgian hopes were disregarded, and the southern Netherlands were handed over to the Dutch, alien in religion, language, and economic interests. Liberal desires for a united Italy were dashed as white-clad Austrian troops took over the northeastern portions of the peninsula and remained on call for reactionary dynasties throughout Italy. Spaniards who wished for a more liberal government suffered under the combined malice, cruelty, and stupidity of the miserable King Ferdinand.

《 *The Quadruple Alliance.* To maintain this reconstructed Europe, diplomatic action was instrumental. The victorious powers whose united endeavor had exiled the imperial Corsican continued their coalition after 1815 in the form of a Quadruple Alliance between Great Britain, Austria, Prussia, and Russia. Before five years had passed, however, Great Britain reverted to her traditional isolation, and defeated France celebrated her readmission into polite European society by filling Britain's place. The Quadruple Alliance was no paper organization; it acted with considerable energy and effectiveness. When Italian societies worked in secrecy for the unification of their country, Austrians filtered down the ridges of the Apennines to crush them. When German university students agitated for increased political liberalism and intellectual freedom, Metternich and the German princes retaliated with the "Carlsbad Decrees," riveting an iron censorship on liberty to speak, write, and teach. When Spaniards rose against their intolerable monarch, French troops marched across the Pyrenees to reinstate him in Madrid.

A word of caution should be given concerning the terminology of this period. The phrase "Holy Alliance" is often used to describe the coalition of the reactionary powers. The Holy Alliance was the creation of Alexander I, and this amorphous league really existed only in the murky mentality of the "Tsar and Autocrat of all the Russias." It had something to do with "Christian morality" and considerably more with ultraconservative social philosophy. Metternich of Austria and the King of Prussia humored the Tsar by ostensibly joining this foggy alliance; but no one, not even Alexander himself, really understood it very well. The important fact is that when Americans spoke of the Holy Alliance during the 1820s, they really were referring to the Quadruple Alliance. The former was mystical nonsense; the latter's armed forces were standing threats to liberalism and nationalism all over Europe. Would this menace be extended to the New World? The Monroe administration had to live with great monarchical powers that looked upon the United States with mingled contempt, derision, and fear. Although the eight years between 1817 and 1825 have been designated the Era of Good Feeling, the term was as inaccurate in the foreign as in the domestic field. Only Anglo-American relations were particularly amicable, for the air had been somewhat cleared by the postwar settlements (the Rush-Bagot understanding of 1817 and the Convention of 1818) that partially demilitarized the Canadian-American frontier and set up the Canadian-American boundary along the 49th parallel. Otherwise, however, the President and his advisers had to grapple with some thorny international problems. Above and beyond the menace emanating from Metternich's Europe, attention had to be focused on the lax and inefficient Spanish administration of Florida, and consideration given to the status of the new Latin American republics, which had elevated national standards in place of Spain's red and gold banner.

THE FLORIDA ACCESSION

Any American intervention in Florida was sure to cause criticism abroad, for it would be in sharp contrast to the current European belief in legitimacy—Florida was Spain's colony and should stay in that category. Yet affairs along the Spanish-American border in the Southeast had become intolerable. In addition to the geographical position of Florida, which largely controlled the sea lanes to and from the mouth of the Mississippi, the weary Castilians could not police their own territory. Spanish rule over the peninsula of citrus and sunshine had always been somewhat weak, and the hammerings taken by Madrid during the long wars between 1792 and 1815 had further sapped its administrative energies. Laws could be enforced in the vicinity of St. Marks, Pensacola, and St. Augustine, but most of Florida was terrorized by refractory Indians and runaway slaves, often leagued together. The proximity of a foreign colony harassed Georgia planters, whose slaves had an easy escape route across the frontier, sometimes returning with Indian allies to settle old scores. After 1815 these mixed Negro-Indian depredations increased. Since Spain was manifestly unable to protect American territory from such attacks, the Monroe administration ordered General Andrew Jackson to chastise the marauders.

"Vigorous" would describe Jackson's Florida campaign. He burst across the Florida border like a bombshell in 1818. Within a few weeks he occupied every Spanish stronghold save St. Augustine, whipped the Indians, deposed the Spanish governor and installed an American in his stead, applied the laws of the United States to Spanish territory, and tried and executed two British subjects for inciting the Indians. Exultantly the Tennesseean communicated

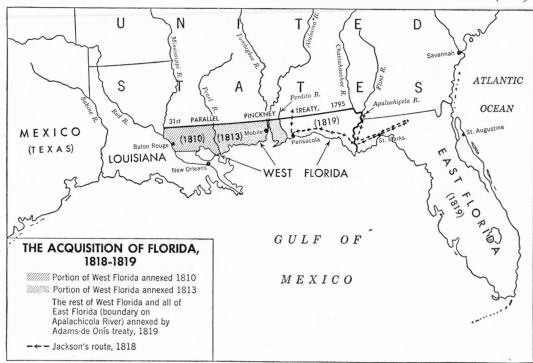

THE ACQUISITION OF FLORIDA,
1818-1819

///// Portion of West Florida annexed 1810

░░░░ Portion of West Florida annexed 1813

The rest of West Florida and all of
East Florida (boundary on
Apalachicola River) annexed by
Adams-de Onís treaty, 1819

–←– Jackson's route, 1818

the news of these extravagant accomplishments to the dazed administration in Washington. The Cabinet met in special sessions. Echoes of wrath arising from the execution of the two Britons drifted across the Atlantic from London. Secretary of War John C. Calhoun was sufficiently disturbed by Jackson's cavalier behavior to recommend that the General be reprimanded. At this juncture, however, John Quincy Adams intervened to defend the man who was to become his implacable enemy.

It was through no sentiments of affection for Jackson that Adams behaved as he did. It so happened that Jackson's Florida campaign both reinforced and coincided with what Adams had been telling the Spanish Minister to the United States. Long before Jackson's intrusion into a neighbor's lands, the United States and Spain had bickered over their boundary in West Florida (the United States had seized portions of West Florida in 1810 and 1813). In addition rival claims to Texas had to be considered, and a correct boundary drawn between Spanish and American territory from Louisiana to the Pacific Northwest. Rather than apologizing to Spain for Jackson's

invasion of East Florida, Adams boldly used the episode as a lever to pry the whole colony from the Castilians.

Adams charged that Jackson's punitive mission proved beyond question that Spain could not administer her dominion to the south, and the New Englander suggested to Don Luis de Onís, Spanish Minister to Washington, that Spain had two choices: she could administer and control Florida so that attacks emanating from that quarter into American territory would cease, or she could cede the whole area to the United States. The Secretary of State pointed out that the first alternative was clearly impossible, so only the second was practicable. Following considerable discussion and many months of Spanish procrastination (Madrid hoped that Great Britain might intervene), accord was finally reached in 1819, although Spain did not ratify the treaty until 1821.

Under the terms of the Adams–De Onís Treaty the United States did not "purchase" Florida—the remaining part of West Florida and all of East Florida was acquired in return for assuming "not more than $5,000,000" in claims owed by Spain to American citizens. A

**LATIN AMERICAN STATES
DURING THE 1820's**

Most boundaries are tentative

definite boundary was slashed across the continent whereby Spain gave up her tenuous assertion to Oregon and the United States renounced a vague right to Texas. The Adams–De Onís agreement represents a surprising diplomatic surrender by Madrid. Although there was obviously little way in which Spain could have stopped the American encroachments into Florida, the Iberian was used to employing even more dilatory tactics to delay the inevitable. Perhaps the disheartened Spaniards who were losing most of the hemisphere by revolution were glad to get at least something for Florida.

EUROPE AND THE AMERICAS

The Florida drama was being played before a backdrop of Latin-American insurrections. Influenced by many years of Spanish hegemony, which had oscillated between studied neglect and oppressive control, and aware of the turmoil overseas, the more liberal Latin Americans had taken advantage of the motherland's difficulty during the Napoleonic invasion of the Iberian peninsula to elevate revolutionary standards. Local governments (juntas) were set up from Mexico City to Buenos Aires. When the Bourbon Ferdinand refused to grant colonial demands for far-reaching reforms, the Spanish American dependencies began declaring their independence. These new republics appealed to the United States for recognition, but the Monroe administration delayed the usual American practice of recognizing *de facto* governments (those which actually hold power) until the delicate negotiations over Florida had been concluded. Once this had been done, however, the southern republics were recognized, most of them during the middle 1820s, despite agonized Spanish wails that we had promised not to do so. The allegation from Madrid was incorrect; the United States had given no such pledge.

The altered status of Florida, and more particularly the revolutions against Spain in Latin America, were observed with marked distaste across the Atlantic. Rebellions against anointed sovereigns were anathemas to Metternich and his colleagues. There seemed to exist a possibility that the Quadruple Alliance might attempt to restore "legitimacy" in the New as it had in the Old World. Monroe and Adams nervously watched European developments. They had to face the possibility that the four reactionary powers actually might send troops to fight in the jungles and on the mountains of Latin America to restore his rebel colonies to the King of Spain. We now know that such talk was verbiage; the Duc de Polignac's Memorandum to Great Britain (1823) specifically disavowed any French intention to intervene in Latin America. Although John Quincy Adams suspected that no foreign intervention was imminent, preparations had to be made against any eventualities.

Not only did the constant interventions of the Quadruple Alliance in Europe alarm the American administration, but one of the reactionary powers had taken action in the Western Hemisphere. In 1821, by ukase (decree) of Tsar Alexander I, Russia asserted dominion over the land south of Alaska down to the 51st parallel (on the coastline of present British Columbia) and ordered foreign ships from adjacent waters. The ukase of 1821 caused little concern among Americans, since the extreme Northwest was too distant for worry. Yet Russian activity alarmed Monroe's advisers and was an important factor in forming the mental attitudes that led to the Monroe Doctrine. In 1824 Russia withdrew to the 54°40′ line, which marks the modern southernmost thrust of Alaska.

While the ukase of the Tsar was still in effect, however, Great Britain communicated to the United States a most interesting suggestion: joint Anglo-American action. After withdrawing from the Quadruple Alliance in order to pursue an independent course, the British had been scrutinizing with cold suspicion the behavior of their erstwhile associates. Especially did London dislike the conversations overheard in the various Quadruple chancellories concerning the possibility of intervention in Latin America to restore Spanish rule. Was this because the noble heart of Britannia ached in sympathy with the nationalistic aspirations of downtrodden and oppressed Latin Americans? Hardly; contemporary English leaders could rival Metternich himself in their violent repugnance toward any social change. Wellington, the Iron Duke, was adamantly opposed to even the most necessary and overdue British reforms.

It was rather a question of hardheaded economics that prompted Great Britain to take the initiative against its former colleagues. Once the republics in Central and South America had been proclaimed, they were no longer subject to the extremely restrictive Spanish colonial trade laws. As independent states they welcomed English merchandise, and a profitable relationship had been quickly established. Any reconquest by or for Spain would terminate this pleasant association, and British commerce would again be barred from lucrative markets. Recognizing that the United

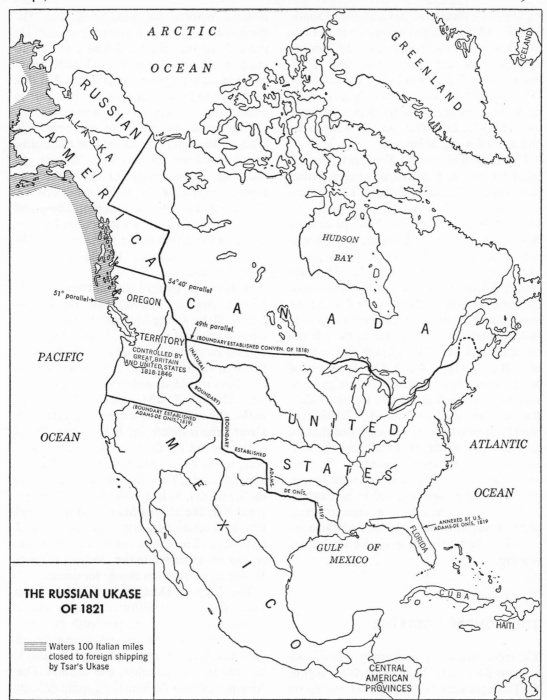

ARCTIC OCEAN

GREENLAND

ICELAND

RUSSIAN AMERICA

ALASKA

51° parallel

54°40' parallel

OREGON

49th parallel

(BOUNDARY ESTABLISHED CONVEN. OF 1818)

TERRITORY
CONTROLLED BY
GREAT BRITAIN
AND UNITED STATES
1818-1846

(NATURAL

BOUNDARY)

(BOUNDARY ESTABLISHED
ADAMS-DE ONÍS, 1819)

(BOUNDARY

ESTABLISHED

ADAMS-

DE ONÍS,

1819)

PACIFIC

OCEAN

CANADA

HUDSON
BAY

UNITED
STATES

MEXICO

GULF   OF
MEXICO

FLORIDA

ANNEXED BY U.S.
ADAMS-DE ONÍS, 1819

ATLANTIC

OCEAN

CUBA

HAÏTI

CENTRAL
AMERICAN
PROVINCES

**THE RUSSIAN UKASE
OF 1821**

Waters 100 Italian miles
closed to foreign shipping
by Tsar's Ukase

States was fearful of foreign invasion of Latin America, and had in fact regularly suggested to London that joint undertakings to protect the hemisphere be commenced, Foreign Secretary Lord Canning saw his opportunity.

The gist of Canning's suggestion was that Great Britain and the United States should issue a joint proclamation guaranteeing the independence of the Latin-American republics, and that both nations disavow any territorial ambitions for themselves in Central and South America. Despite its former messages to London along much the same course, the Monroe administration was confronted with a dilemma. Great Britain would be a powerful ally —but would it be too powerful? Was it really in the interests of the United States to sign a pact with John Bull? Did America want to accept a self-denying ordinance?

The mild and courtly President Monroe asked for advice. From their Virginia retirement the aged founding fathers, Thomas Jefferson and James Madison, recommended joint action with Great Britain. Other prominent Americans had similar thoughts, and there is some evidence that Monroe was ready to go along; but contrary counsel was offered by John Quincy Adams, and eventually the opinions of the dogmatic New Englander prevailed. Adams asserted that any joint undertaking with Great Britain would make it appear as though the United States were "a cock-boat in the wake of a British man-of-war." The Secretary of State was sure that the danger of foreign intervention in Latin America was no more likely than that the Andean peak of "Chimborazo would sink into the sea." He suggested that we take unilateral action, confident that the British would have to support us anyway. Furthermore, the United States did not want to sign a self-denying pledge in regard to hemisphere territory. Florida had recently been annexed, and to many Americans Mexico and Cuba appeared to be legitimate fields for further expansion.

THE MONROE DOCTRINE

The culmination of John Quincy Adams's advice was the famous Monroe Doctrine, part of the President's annual message to Congress on 2 December 1823. The diplomatic portions of the message are contained in two widely separated sections. In the first, Monroe stated that the Americas were "henceforth not to be considered as subjects for future colonization by any European power. . . ." After considerable

material devoted to domestic matters, the President returned to the foreign sphere. He pointed out that the Latin-American nations enjoyed the recognition of the United States and warned the Quadruple Alliance that "we should consider any attempt on their part to extend their system to any portion of this hemisphere as dangerous to our peace and safety," although he promised that the United States would not interfere with "existing colonies or dependencies of any European power." Next came the rather condescending pledge not to interfere in European affairs, and Monroe concluded with a reiteration that European intervention in the Americas would be considered a signal act of hostility against the United States.

It should be recalled that in comparison to France, Austria, Prussia, and Russia, the United States during Monroe's terms was powerless, weak, and impotent. With a tiny army and an inconsequential navy, such American assertion of hemispheric control was considered both ridiculous and insolent in the ministries of Europe. The Monroe Doctrine received noticeably augmented respect, however, once Great Britain quietly let it be known that if a crisis ensued, the thousand ships of the Royal Navy would be likely to back up Mr. Monroe's announcement. That put quite a different light on the matter. While both chagrined and enraged that the United States had taken such unilateral action on a course he had initiated, Canning had no choice but to comply, for the sentiments expressed in the Doctrine followed British aspirations too closely for denial.

The Monroe Doctrine has been a living force in American history. To some extent, Americans had acted independently ever since the American Revolution, and to any nationals such assertions of freedom and power tend to be popular. Nevertheless, the Monroe Doctrine has grown into something quite different from its original nature. Initially a pronouncement by a President concerning issues peculiar to his own administration, the Doctrine was received with cordial if not with delirious enthusiasm by the American people. It was largely forgotten, however, for almost two decades until James K. Polk triumphantly dragged it from hiding to offer as an apologia for his expansive territorial ambitions in Oregon. Admitted to be government policy by most Americans during the 1840s, the Monroe Doctrine became largely a Democratic-party plank during the next decade, opposed by many Whigs and Republicans who considered it a cloak to mantle Southern conspirators avid for new slave lands. The Mexican crisis of 1863 to 1867 [2] saw the Monroe Doctrine come of age to be almost universally considered a cardinal point of American foreign policy, although it was still long in the future before the European powers officially recognized it. Eventually the Doctrine held almost sacred implications for the typical American.

THE DIPLOMACY OF ADAMS AND JACKSON

After the activity that saw boundary settlements with Great Britain and Spain, the annexation of Florida, and the publication of the Monroe Doctrine, American diplomacy entered a relatively quiescent period. During the administrations of John Quincy Adams, Andrew Jackson, and Martin Van Buren, the foreign relations of the United States were less hectic than during the eventful years of the Napoleonic Wars and European reconstruction or the later American territorial aggrandizement of the 1840s. Several diplomatic events between 1825 and 1841 merit discussion, however.

John Quincy Adams had been in diplomacy during much of his political life, and it is surprising that his foreign policy while President was relatively sterile in accomplishment. Abroad he was perpetually frustrated by the intelligent and unfriendly British diplomat George Canning (in 1827 Adams noted in his diary with prim satisfaction that Canning had died). At home the President's political mal-

adroitness and the undying enmity of the Jacksonians made unified action in the foreign field impossible. American failure to participate in the Pan-American Congress in 1826 typifies Adams's Latin-American ineptitude.[3] The President hoped to sign a commercial treaty with Great Britain so that the United States might enjoy the tropical riches of the British West Indies. Highhandedly Adams asserted that this trade was a natural American right rather than a privilege accorded by a friendly neighbor. Coldly the British rebuffed his clumsy overtures.

To Adams's mortification, his foe Andrew Jackson, exhibiting a startling amount of restraint and charm, succeeded precisely where his predecessor had failed. Jackson politely requested the British to grant such a treaty, and in 1830 relatively unrestricted Caribbean trade was opened to American shippers. The arrogant and proud Andrew was more in character when he clashed with the French over the question of unpaid debts owed by that nation to the United States. These debts were in the usual form of claims of American citizens against France, most of them dating from the time when Napoleon had illegally confiscated American vessels. For two decades France had promised to pay and had done nothing to fulfill its pledges. In 1830 the Bourbon monarchy was ousted by revolution, and the new Orleanist dynasty under King Louis Philippe acceded to power in Paris. The new French government expressed a willingness to settle accounts with the United States, and in 1831 a treaty to that effect was ratified. But the French Chambers refused to appropriate the necessary funds. Jackson had sent his former Secretary of State, Edward Livingston, to apply extra pressure, but still no francs were forthcoming.

In 1834 Jacksonian patience, stretched taut by Gallic procrastination, snapped. In his annual message to Congress, the General castigated the French and asked Congress to pass legislation permitting him to seize French property in the United States. The French

---

[2] The Hapsburg Maximilian was installed as Emperor of Mexico by Napoleon III of France. See pp. 421–422 for further details.

[3] Two delegates were sent; one died en route and the other arrived too late.

were enraged by Jackson's arbitrary behavior, and a minor war panic followed when Paris broke off diplomatic negotiations. Although the French Chambers finally got around to appropriating the first payments, the impasse was maintained when Paris loftily announced that no money would be sent to the United States until Jackson had apologized. The doughty Tennesseean reacted with the choleric assertion that he would never do so. Late in 1836, however, Jackson relented enough in his annual message to Congress to aver that he had no intention "to menace or insult" the French, although he followed this disarming statement with a stout denial that he had apologized at all: ". . . the honor of my country shall never be stained by an apology from me for the statement of truth and the performance of duty. . . ." This policy of acknowledging fault with one side of the mouth while denying it with the other was sufficient. The French stated that their honor had been satisfied, and the claims were eventually paid. Diplomatic relations were soon restored, and the whole affair, which brought little credit to either side, was quickly forgotten. Jackson's dilemma over Texas shall be discussed later.[4]

CANADIAN TROUBLES

The next President, Martin Van Buren, had scarcely eased himself into the executive chair before he was faced with diplomatic difficulties. For many years some Canadians had been restive under British domination, and their enthusiasm for more complete "home rule" was channeled into outright rebellion in 1837. American popular opinion, especially along the northern frontier, strongly sympathized with the Canadian rebels, since many citizens of the United States thought that such policy would lead inevitably to the incorporation of Canada into the Union. When British and loyalist troops easily defeated the insurrectionists, many of the latter fled to New York sanctuary and continued fighting from American bases.

4 See p. 325.

A rebel force seized an island in the Niagara River above the Falls, and the *Caroline*, a small American ship, was used to ferry men and matériel to the rebels. After its first trip, the *Caroline* was attacked by a British detachment, which, after killing an American named Amos Durfee, set fire to the ship and cut it loose to run aground above the great cataract.

Upstate New York flew into a rage when the news of this "dark deed in the night" was circulated. Hundreds rushed to offer their services to the cause of Canadian independence, and war between the United States and Great Britain might have followed had not President Van Buren worked tirelessly for peace. He sent the resplendent figure of the gargantuan General Winfield Scott to upstate New York, and this intervention helped to allay bellicose tempers, although a ground swell of discontent still ran. Although the Canadian Revolution was pretty well over by the end of 1837, American effort in its behalf did not cease. A secret society called "Hunter's Lodges" enrolled thousands of Americans and pledged to oust Great Britain from the American continent forever. The border remained in turmoil.

Just when it appeared that the Anglo-American crisis was finally evaporating, it was suddenly intensified by the arrest in Utica, New York, of Alexander McLeod, a British subject, charged with the murder of Amos Durfee on the *Caroline*. Great Britain sternly notified Washington that any injustice to McLeod would be deemed a cause for war. Van Buren found his hands legally tied—not only was the case political dynamite in foreign affairs, but he could do nothing official about it. On such matters as the killing of one of its citizens, a state has complete jurisdiction, and the national government has no right to interfere. Van Buren could only work behind the scenes, hoping desperately that McLeod would be acquitted. Luckily the prosecution at the trial had no clear proof, and McLeod was found not guilty. Even if the latter had been convicted and sentenced to death, the Governor of New York probably would have pardoned him. The McLeod case stands as a prime example of the restrictions placed upon the national government and the power accorded to the states even when foreign affairs are involved.

THE WEBSTER-ASHBURTON TREATY

The accession of the Harrison-Tyler administration in 1841 found relations with Great Britain still unpleasantly controversial, despite relaxation along the New York–Ontario border. For decades a vexatious disagreement over the precise boundary of the northeastern United States and the Canadian province of New Brunswick had smoldered. Of lesser importance, but still disturbing the harmony of Anglo-American relations, were such instances as the precise delineation of the frontier at the northern tip of Lake Champlain, British action in regard to the mutinous cargo of the slave ship *Creole*, the need for an extradition treaty between the United States and Canada, English reluctance to apologize for the *Caroline* affair, American failure to participate wholeheartedly in enforcing the ban on the African slave trade, and the perennial question of Oregon. For several years the course of British foreign policy had been directed by the aggressive Lord Palmerston, and under such leadership little could be done to lessen the friction. In 1841 a more conciliatory government assumed control in London and soon evinced a desire to settle disturbed relations with the United States.

This amicable disposition was shown by the appointment of Alexander Baring, Lord Ashburton, as special envoy to Washington. Ashburton had been friendly enough in his attitude toward Americans to marry a Philadelphia heiress, and negotiation was possible with the cultured, courtly, and humorous Ashburton. As Secretary of State, Daniel Webster represented the American side, and this New Englander had recently returned from basking in the warmth of British recognition. An air of cooperative friendship marked the discussions that were carried on in 1842.

⟨ The Northeastern Boundary. The most important decision reached by Webster and Ashburton concerned the Maine–New Brunswick boundary. As described in the Treaty of Paris (1783), which ended the American Revolution, the border was impossibly inexact. Landmarks were described that were either completely ambiguous or even nonexistent. For

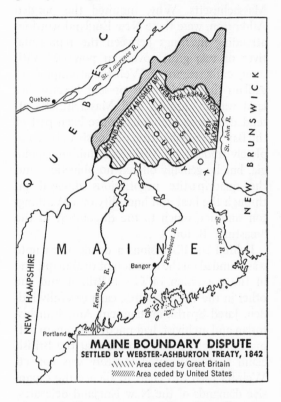

MAINE BOUNDARY DISPUTE
SETTLED BY WEBSTER-ASHBURTON TREATY, 1842
\\\\\\ Area ceded by Great Britain
///////// Area ceded by United States

almost half a century neither Canadian nor American paid very much attention to the 12,000-square-mile area in dispute, but during the 1830s lumberjacks from both Canada and the United States trickled into Aroostook County forests. The rival nationals clashed in what has been called the "Lumberjacks'" or Aroostook War in 1838, and although some skulls were cracked, no lives were lost. Sullen resentment did not die down, however, and there was always the danger that the controversy might suddenly be intensified. Not only control over woodlands was concerned. The British were extremely eager to get at least a portion of the disputed territory so that a military road could be cut through the wilderness between Quebec and Halifax without a lengthy detour around American territory.

To make matters even more difficult, the Webster-Ashburton negotiations could not be restricted to the arbiters of the United States and Great Britain alone. Representatives from two other powers were present in the persons of gentlemen from the states of Maine and Massachusetts. Why, inquired the puzzled Ashburton, were these New England worthies attending meetings between the representatives of two great sovereign powers? With some embarrassment Webster attempted to explain that Maine was present because her land was in dispute, and Massachusetts attended because Maine had once been part of the Bay State. Ashburton obviously never completely understood Webster's dubious apologia, but he genially offered no objection, and the quadripartite negotiations dragged on through the heat and humidity of a Washington summer, much to the discomfort of the "roasting" Briton.

Behind the discussions a comic-opera note was sounded on the question of rival maps, one in the possession of Great Britain and the other in the United States, each carefully hidden. Jared Sparks, an eminent American historian and archivist, had uncovered a map dating from 1783 which showed that the British claim to the disputed territory was correct. Webster used this chart to silence the expansive demands of the New England delegates, convincing them that they had better compromise or they might lose everything. Coincidentally the British government (although Lord Ashburton did not know of its existence until later) had a map strongly supporting the American contention. This was later utilized to calm British discontent over what the opposition called a surrender to the Americans. When the negotiations were finally concluded and compromise reached, cartological secrets were still guarded.

The northeastern boundary was arbitrated, the United States receiving some 7,000 of the 12,000 square miles in dispute. Although their share was smaller most Britons and Canadians were relatively satisfied, since their military

road to the Atlantic could be constructed. Maine and Massachusetts each received $150,000 from the United States to assuage their loss, and this stipulation was written into the treaty with Great Britain. Ashburton was highly dubious about the inclusion of matters pertaining to the Federal government and its component parts, but agreed in the interest of compromise. Later research has shown that the American contention was the more nearly correct, and we should have received almost all of the disputed territory, but neither Webster nor Ashburton had that information available. Certainly Anglo-American concord was worth 5,000 square miles of tangled woodland.

❨ *Other Agreements.* Once the chief source of contention had been arbitrated, the negotiators made more rapid progress with the others. The United States gained a small tract that rectified the frontier at the northern reach of New York's Lake Champlain. Partial settlement of the *Creole* controversy was achieved,[5] although no final adjudication could be accomplished until 1853, when the American owners of the slaves received about $110,000. A new extradition treaty was written with Canada whereby certain criminals of both nations could be more easily returned home for punishment. A partial apology was received for the *Caroline* sinking.

A final controversy involved the slave trade, and this question had to be most tactfully handled, thanks to its American domestic implications. The repulsive traffic in human flesh between West Africa and the Americas had been outlawed by international agreement (1808), and police action undertaken. While somewhat lax at first, the Royal Navy intensified its patrolling after 1833, when Great Britain emancipated slaves throughout the Empire. If stopped by a British frigate, however, many slavers would run up an American

[5] The *Creole*, a domestic American slaver, was carrying a cargo between Virginia and Louisiana when her slaves mutinied, murdered an officer, and landed at British Bermuda. The murderers were hanged, but since they had touched free soil the rest of the slaves were freed. The American owners demanded compensation.

flag, and the United States was adamant in refusing the right of search in time of peace. Webster and Ashburton managed to reach an accord stating that American and British warships should patrol together so that the United States frigate could search American ships. A specified tonnage of American men-of-war was to be maintained for this dual surveillance. Despite these promises the opposition of Southern Congressmen made American participation in this worthy cause somewhat less than satisfactory until the Civil War.

Although the negotiations of 1842 left something to be desired on both sides (Oregon, for example, was sidestepped), the conversations between the British special envoy and the American Secretary of State were conducted in a spirit of amity and geniality. Both nations gave something and received something. Later Anglo-American discussions could refer back to the Webster-Ashburton negotiations as establishing precedents for conciliatory solution of outstanding disputes between the two great Anglo-Saxon nations.

CHAPTER 26

Manifest Destiny

(1842-1846)

WESTWARD IMPULSES

The early 1840s witnessed the rapid development of the proannexationist fever called "Manifest Destiny." For many years some Americans had been referring to their country as one peculiarly endowed with a divine mission by its Creator to occupy the entire western portion of the North American continent and perhaps eventually the whole hemisphere. This viewpoint had its roots in the distant American past. Even in colonial times some Americans were asserting that they possessed virtues indigenous to life on this side of the Atlantic. Once independence had been won, such sentiments became more common. Patriotic utterances, extravagant claims to inherent virtues, and derogatory expressions concerning the institutions and manners of other peoples applied to early-nineteenth-century America as to most adolescent nations. During the 1840s this long-standing feeling became something of a mania.

The expansion of American population tended to produce an overflow into areas outside United States jurisdiction, but Americans seemed little concerned about the color of the flag flying over lands that they coveted. Even

after the purchase of Louisiana Territory had increased the national domain by millions of acres, aggressive Americans continued to overflow the western and southern boundaries. President Franklin Pierce in his inaugural address hardly needed to admonish his fellow citizens that they should "not be controlled by any timid forebodings of evil from expansion." No such forebodings had entered their minds.

Americans were expansionistic, but they were also highly moral and religious, which meant that they felt the necessity to justify their expansion on some basis other than the simple desire for wealth that new lands might satisfy. The easiest rationalization was the contention that the United States had valid legal titles by exploration, by settlement, or by purchase; in no case, however, would the expansionist grant Indian claims on such grounds. Sometimes, as with Oregon, American claims had validity. Sometimes, as with West Florida, they were very doubtful; and at other times, as with Texas, they were demonstrably erroneous. Now and then national assertion of occupational rights was fantastic, as when we talked about "our well-founded claim" to Oregon (when practically no Americans lived north of the Columbia River) being based on contiguity and "greatly strengthened . . . by the rapid advance of our population."

If exploration and occupation were the first point of the expansionistic philosophy, a second considered the westward surge to be an inevitable natural right based on God's law and God's desire. The idea of natural rights was particularly strong during the late eighteenth century. A good example of this applied to the control of the mouth of the Mississippi; it seemed to Americans to be in accord with divine purpose that the outlet of the great river should be controlled by those who navigated its waters. The same argument had obvious application to the whole continent, including portions held by Canada and Mexico, but also could be used overseas, even as far as Hawaii and the Philippines. Perhaps an extreme was reached when William H. Seward announced in 1859 that, concerning Cuba, "every rock and every grain of sand in the island were drifted and washed out from American soil"— evidently the territory of the United States had moved a little toward the south.

A third justification for American expansion was the belief that Americans would cultivate the land, as Thomas H. Benton said, "according to the intentions of the CREATOR" and bring advanced national institutions, especially the Protestant religion, to the benighted natives. Obviously this doctrine was tailor-made for the Indian, but it was not restricted to him; even the most advanced European civilization was held to be inferior to the American. President Jackson talked of "extending the area of freedom," and at the time of the Mexican War, members of Congress felt that we should "be recreant to our noble mission" if we did not expand our territory when we were militarily able to do so.

A fourth plank in the expansionistic platform stressed self-defense. No matter what the circumstances that pertained to neighboring territories, nearby portions of the United States could claim that possession of neighboring tracts was imperative for national safety. Toward the south, Cuba, Mexico, and other Caribbean lands were held necessary to establish control of the Gulf area. To the west we had to have the Pacific Coast, then Hawaii, and perhaps other islands of the Pacific. A fifth argument, little used until the late nineteenth century, was that as a global power we must exercise our influence for world leadership toward the perfect ends we had in mind.

Although the origins of Manifest Destiny can be traced back for generations, that philosophy reached its triumphant maturity during the 1840s in quarrels with Great Britain over Oregon, over the question of Texas annexation, and in the recurring difficulties with Mexico. The term Manifest Destiny appears to have been popularized by John L. O'Sullivan, editor of the New York *Democratic Review*. In commenting on the Oregon controversy with Great Britain, he stated that the distant Northwest must be American because it is our duty ". . . by the right of our manifest destiny to overspread and to possess the whole of the continent which Providence has given us for the development of the great experiment of liberty and federated self-government entrusted to us." Even earlier O'Sullivan had envisaged that America's ". . . floor shall be a hemisphere—its roof the star-studded heavens, and its congregation a Union . . . of happy millions . . . governed by God's natural and moral law of equality." O'Sullivan's corollary was obvious: God wills that the American people must sweep to the Pacific, and woe betide the Spaniard, Russian, Englishman, Mexican, or Indian who stands in the path of divinely inspired juggernaut. Manifest Destiny, according to its advocates, became considerably more than any temporary expansionism of an administration in Washington; it was the deep moral and religious responsibility of a whole people.

A more sophisticated and cynical age may smile at the naïve enthusiasm of O'Sullivan and his contemporaries. At first glance it might appear to be hypocrisy, but the American of that time truly and sincerely believed that his way of life was so superior to any other that God ordained him to bring the blessings of liberty, civilization, and progress to somnolent, barbaric, or decadent peoples. Manifest Destiny was adopted by most Americans during the 1840s, and it particularly influenced the Tyler and Polk administrations. The energy it generated swept over part of Oregon Territory, over Texas, and over the northern and northwestern stretches of Mexico, until by 1853 a third of a nation had been added since 1845.

THE UNITED STATES, GREAT BRITAIN, AND OREGON

❰ *Early Development.* The Oregon controversy illustrated the first important adaptation of Manifest Destiny. There should be no cause for wonder that dispute arose concerning Oregon, for an imperial tract was at stake. The disputed area was, of course, far larger than the present state of Oregon. It totaled some 500,000 square miles, which extended north and south from the border of Russian Alaska to the utmost limits of Mexican California and east and west from the continental divide in Montana and Wyoming to the foggy waters of the Pacific. The ocean teemed with fish; the fertile and well-watered land was covered with some of the finest timber in the world. Mineral and agricultural resources of unknown richness awaited exploitation.

Originally four nations—Spain, Russia, Great Britain, and the United States—eyed Oregon with interest. The first explorations were conducted by Spaniards, but by the late eighteenth century the Iberian was too weak to develop this initial advantage; Spain had to cede its monopolistic rights to Great Britain in the Nootka Convention (1790). In the Adams–De Onís Treaty of 1819, the United States took over what was left of Spain's Oregon title. The Tsar's ukase of 1821 illustrated the high-water mark of Russian interest in Oregon, for soon the Russians retreated to Alaska, abandoning their claims to the south. With Spaniard and Russian withdrawn, Briton and American could settle down to a binational dispute.

Both Great Britain and the United States had claims of remarkable similarity. Each asserted its right to Oregon by discovery, exploration, and occupation. If Britain could point to the eighteenth-century voyages of Captains James Cook and George Vancouver, the United States could refer to the discovery of the Columbia River by Captain Robert Gray. When the English brought up the explorations of Hudson's Bay Company factors and trappers, the Americans could retaliate by mention of the wandering mountain men and other employees of the American and Rocky Mountain Fur Companies. In addition, the United States stressed the government-directed explorations of Lewis and Clark, whose expedition journeyed all the way to the Pacific from 1804 to 1806. Both nations were hard pressed to explain "occupation" very readily, since for years fur trappers, traders, and missionaries made up about all the white population of the territory.

❰ *Joint Occupation.* It will be remembered that Great Britain and the United States had delayed final disposition of the Oregon country when they established a joint ten-year occupation in the Convention of 1818. In 1827 this joint government was extended indefinitely, subject to termination by either side on twelve months' notification. It was all to American advantage to procrastinate on Oregon, for the early development of the area was essentially British. The American Fur Company of John Jacob Astor was a weak and struggling organization in comparison to the mighty Hudson's Bay Company, which had created the equivalent of a private empire in Oregon.[1] Even as late as the middle 1830s only a handful of Americans lived anywhere in the half-million square miles. Under the benevolent dictatorship of the Hudson's Bay Company factor in Oregon, Dr. John McLoughlin, the British were the *de facto* rulers of the Northwest until 1840.

Yet Americans were never completely ab-

[1] Recent research has shown that actually the stockholders of the British Northwest Fur Company bought out Hudson's Bay in 1821, but they retained the more popular name.

sent. Easy-living mountain men searched for beaver and otter on the fringes of the territory. An infrequent exploration party would pass through en route to the mouth of the Columbia. Methodist, Presbyterian, and Roman Catholic missions were established on occasion to convert the Indian. The influence of the missionaries was potent. They usually farmed as well as preached, and the letters of such a man as Marcus Whitman to fellow religionists in the Middle West enthusiastically described the fertile soil in the Oregon valleys. Nevertheless, for years American husbandmen were uninterested in the Pacific Northwest. There was still plenty of available land in the Mississippi Valley, and improving transportation was bringing Eastern markets closer. It was considered unnecessary to undertake the hazards of a journey through 2,000 miles of prairies, mountains, and deserts to reach a territory that might become British soil.

By 1840 this negative attitude began to change. Much of the best land in the Middle West was already preempted, and explorers reported that the Oregon trip, although difficult, was by no means impossible. Fervor for Oregon began to be noticeable among farmers of the upper Middle West; a few started, others followed, and by 1843–1844 hundreds began making the gradual ascent of the South Pass through the Rockies, following the Snake River until it met the Columbia, and after proceeding along the banks of the latter, turning south near the Pacific to the rich Willamette country. By 1845 some 5,000 Americans lived in Oregon, almost all south of the Columbia River. By this time they outnumbered the British, and they began clamoring for annexation to the United States.

❮ *The Oregon Compromise.* At this juncture, diplomatic negotiations were becoming heated. Although a surprising number of Americans were apathetic about the distant Northwest, others, influenced by the theory of Manifest Destiny or by the more mundane desire for rich agricultural fields, were calling for the annexation of all the disputed territory. The British never expected the whole of Ore-

gon; they admitted that the land south of the Columbia must go to the United States. But they were stubborn in their insistence that the land north of the great river was theirs, and particularly did they stress that the western two-thirds of the present state of Washington and all of Vancouver Island must remain part of the empire. The main British objection to the natural policy of extending the 49th parallel (established in 1818 as the boundary between the United States and British Canada) all the way to the Pacific was that Vancouver Island would be divided. Earlier American offers to arbitrate along the present boundary were repeatedly turned down by the British.

The Oregon controversy came to a head during the election of 1844. The Democratic platform of that year combined the desires of Manifest Destiny expansionists (both proslave Southerners and Free Soil Northerners) by advocating "the reoccupation of Oregon and the reannexation of Texas." During the campaign such slogans as "All of Oregon or none!" and "Fifty-four forty or fight!" (the 54th parallel is the southern boundary of Alaska) began to ring throughout the nation. Bombastic utterances called upon the government to refuse any compromise with the English and to seize the whole territory, which would have included about half of modern British Columbia. At the same time Southerners were shouting for the annexation of Texas.

Even though the narrow victory of the Democrat James K. Polk over his Whig antagonist Henry Clay was no lucid mandate for expansion, both President Tyler and President-elect Polk acted as if it were. Motivated by this erroneous, if potent, reasoning, Tyler engineered the admission of Texas into the Union. The Polk administration looked toward the Northwest. In his inaugural address the new President coolly asserted the right of the United States to all of Oregon, although this was something of a bluff on Polk's part. While the cheers of the annexationists still echoed about him, Polk quietly offered to arbitrate the Oregon question with Great Britain along the 49th parallel. Lord Pakenham, the British Minister, showed diplomatic ineptitude by re-

OREGON SETTLEMENT, 1846

‑ ‑ ‑ Boundary of Oregon Territory, jointly occupied by Great Britain and United States, 1818‑1846

///// Area in particular dispute

—— Boundary established by Oregon Compromise, 1846 (Modern states inserted)

jecting immediately Polk's suggestion without communicating its terms to his government. Evidently the knotty Vancouver Island question was basic in Pakenham's refusal.

Polk bided his time after this rebuff until he sent his annual message to Congress in December, 1845. Aggressively the President reasserted the American claim all the way to the 54th parallel. Even more provocative was his resurrection of the largely forgotten Monroe Doctrine and his application of it to the Oregon controversy. Polk stated that it was the proper time "to reiterate and reaffirm the principle avowed by Mr. Monroe and to state by cordial

concurrence in its wisdom and sound policy . . . no future European colony or dominion shall with our consent be planted or established on any part of the North American Continent. . . ." Although the Doctrine was not yet elevated to a holy status, Polk had started it on the way. The final unpleasant surprise for the British contained in the annual message of 1845 was the presidential announcement that joint occupation of the territory would be terminated at the end of the next year.

London was able to see in the harsh words of the American administration that the

United States was determined to get Oregon at least to the 49th parallel. Luckily for peace, internal conditions in both nations at the time worked against war, despite the bellicose and jingoistic alarums from both sides of the Atlantic. American Southerners, satiated temporarily with the vast acquisition of Texas, were disinterested in a war with Great Britain over the Far Northwest. Furthermore, war with Mexico was looming ahead in the near future, and the Polk administration considered one enemy at a time sufficient. Despite all the noise and tumult of the election, only in the Middle West were any important segments of the American people willing to fight over Oregon.

Conditions leading to pacification existed in Great Britain as well. An important economic battle was being waged in the home islands at this time. Agitation for repeal of the protective tariffs on grain imports (the "Corn Laws") heightened friction between the landowners and the industrialists who favored free trade. A terrible potato famine was decimating the Irish. Anti-imperialists were unusually active. Politics were in flux, and neither the Conservatives (the old Tories) nor the Liberals (the former Whigs) had strength enough to furnish true national leadership. In the last analysis, Oregon was a long way off, the British Empire already sprawled all over the world, and most Englishmen simply did not consider Oregon worth a war with their best customer.

With conciliation in the air, compromise was not long delayed. In order to sound out senatorial opinion first, in mid-summer, 1846, Polk sent to the Senate the Oregon Treaty before he signed it. Despite the stubborn fight against ratification led by Senator Edward A. Hannigan of Indiana, the Senate voted to accept. Polk signed the treaty with Great Britain, and the latter soon ratified the pact settling the Oregon controversy. The area was divided along the 49th parallel, although an exception was made in Britain's favor by extending the line southward so that all Vancouver Island could remain under the Queen's rule. The United States enjoyed somewhat the better of the bargain. South of the Columbia River there could be no question as to title—5,000

lusty American farmers had made the Willamette Valley an agricultural marvel. But in the wedge north and west of the Columbia, any American claim on the basis of occupancy was a trifle tenuous—precisely eight Americans lived north of the Columbia River in 1846. Occupation was not the reason why the western two-thirds of the present state of Washington is American; that pleasant result came about through diplomatic negotiation. There are similarities between the Oregon discussions and those between Webster and Ashburton. In the former, Great Britain gave in a trifle; in the latter, the United States. Both were sensible, intelligent, and civilized decisions that avoided a war, repugnant to the interests of both nations.

THE ANNEXATION OF TEXAS

⟨ *American Penetration.* Although the entrance of Texas into the Union antedated by more than a year the Oregon Compromise, discussion of it has been withheld until this point, for the Texan Revolution, independence, and annexation are inextricably woven into the background of the Mexican War. The sprawling and ill-defined province of Texas was a vague extremity of Spain's North American domains. When Mexico tore down the Castilian banner and proclaimed independence, Texas was included as part of the new country. Neither Spaniard nor Mexican ever made much attempt to settle Texas; its distance from Mexico City ensured relative isolation for the northern borderlands. It was not until the middle 1820s that the Texan population began to increase, and these new settlers came not from Mexico, but wandered across the Sabine River from American Louisiana.

The United States had long cast covetous glances toward the Southwest. A tenuous claim to the territory had been specifically denied so that the acquisition of Florida could be facilitated in the Adams–De Onís Treaty of 1819. Even as early as that year, however, some grumbling emanated from the South that

Texas was worth more than Florida. Once he was President, John Quincy Adams attempted to rectify his renunciation of Texas by purchasing the territory. He sent Joel R. Poinsett, a prominent South Carolinian, to Mexico City in an attempt to persuade the Mexicans to sell Texas. The somewhat ingenious argument forwarded by Poinsett to the dumfounded Mexicans was that they should be delighted to rid themselves of their northeastern lands, since a reduction in their nation's size would make Mexico City closer to the center of the country. The Mexicans were not exactly enamored of this suggestion and countered with a proposal that the United States might like to cede Louisiana to Mexico. With opinion so divergent, Poinsett was recalled during the next administration and returned home with little to show for his Mexican adventures save the American introduction of the flamboyant red flower that bears his name (poinsettia).

Andrew Jackson was interested in Southwestern expansion, and he too tried negotiation. After Poinsett had been recalled, "Old Hickory" sent the flashy and devious Anthony Butler to Mexico City. Butler was instructed to discuss the possibilities of buying not only Texas, but all the land west to the Pacific, and the Mexicans could fill in a blank check as far as price was concerned. The political situation in Mexico, however, was so explosive that no government could have lasted a day if any such sale of Mexican land had been consummated. Realizing that he was doing little, Butler wrote to Jackson that he had better forward a half-million dollars so that the necessary Mexican officials could be bribed. Jackson wrote on the envelope containing this rather immoral suggestion, "A. Butler. What a Scamp!" Scamp or not, Butler was not recalled until the outbreak of the Texan Revolution in 1836. While the American government was trying to buy Texas, American citizens were settling the extensive reaches of the Lone Star country and making it American territory by natural occupation.

By the mid-1830s about 30,000 Americans lived in Texas. The story of their coming from the United States in response to the enthusiastic invitation of the Mexican government is curious. While Mexico shrank with abhorrence from any diplomatic overtures to purchase its northeastern province, paradoxically it was embarking on the policy of welcoming American migrants and in so doing, losing Texas. Under an early deed, Moses Austin, a peripatetic Connecticut Yankee, was awarded an immense tract of Texan land, and his son Stephen established a colony at the city that now bears the family name. A small but steady flow of Americans settled on the fertile lands of east Texas and started raising cotton with slave labor. The American outpost in Texas grew slowly during the 1820s, despite Mexican offers of practically free land while the United States insisted on $1.25 an acre. Adjacent areas in the United States were populated more rapidly than was Texas during these early years, although radically increased numbers came across the Sabine River from Louisiana after 1830.

⟨ *The Texas Revolution.* Stephen Austin tried to live in accordance with Mexican laws, but many of his more rambunctious fellow citizens refused to follow his example. The first American settlers in Texas contained some extreme individualists, some so individualistic that they had fled to avoid hanging. To such hardened persons, Mexican rule was laughable. All migrants to Texas were supposed to become Roman Catholics, but this provision tended to be honored in the breach. Continual bickering between Mexico City and the tiny Texas establishments was intensified when Mexico outlawed slavery and the Texans refused to comply. The Mexican government changed with chameleonlike rapidity, and the Texan tended to feel amused contempt for it. Mexico watched with distress the refractory attitudes of its new citizens and in 1830 attempted to halt further immigration from the United States, but this similarly was ignored. Conditions seemed to be ameliorated when General Antonio López de Santa Anna, presumably a republican reformer, seized control of the Mexican government with the cordial best wishes of the Texans. This "Napoleon of the West" soon evinced his dictatorial ambitions, however, and he reinforced his garrisons beyond the Rio Grande, attempting to bring the province under direct control. The reaction in Texas was swift; local committees akin to Revolutionary Minute Men raised the pennant of rebellion and proclaimed their independence in 1836.

A Texan army was rapidly recruited under the command of General Samuel Houston. This able officer and politician was a native Tennesseean and had been Jackson's protégé in his home state, serving as Representative and Senator from, and Governor of, Tennessee. Houston appeared to be headed for great heights in national politics—perhaps even the Presidency—when calamity suddenly afflicted him. Houston married the young daughter of a prominent and wealthy family, but almost immediately after the wedding she left him and returned home. While Tennessee neighbors whispered, Houston went all to pieces, headed south down the Mississippi, and finally wandered west to live with the Indians. His habits during this exile were summed up by his Indian nickname, "Big Drunk." Houston regained his composure and, after an eastern visit to see President Jackson, traveled to Texas, where his ability was recognized by his appointment as military leader. He had his work cut out, for the Mexican dictator was hurrying north with an army.

A preview of what might be expected from Santa Anna was given at the mission house called the Alamo at San Antonio and at the small town of Goliad, where the Mexicans annihilated two Texan forces almost to the man. Reportedly shouting the slogan "Exterminate to the Sabine," the Mexicans pressed to the north, when disaster struck Santa Anna. While enjoying a pleasant siesta at San Jacinto (April, 1836), the Mexican army of 1,500 was hit by Houston's force of scarcely half that size, and the Latin antagonists were completely routed. Santa Anna was taken prisoner, and Houston had great difficulty in stopping a spontaneous "necktie party" which was gathering to honor the Mexican with a hempen noose. Houston kept Santa Anna alive so that he could compel

him to sign a treaty, although after this had been done, the Mexican protested, with truth, that it had his forced signature. Diplomatic negotiations made little difference; San Jacinto was decisive. What little opportunity the Mexicans might have had was made even more difficult by considerable man-power and matériel assistance to Texan rebels from the United States. Mexico was never again able to invade Texas in force, although border raids were common.

⟨ *The Lone Star Republic.* A new state had come into being: the independent Texan Republic, sometimes called the "Lone Star Republic" after its flag. A government and constitution modeled upon those of the United States were established, and Sam Houston became the first President. With impressive unanimity Texans wished to join the United States, and they communicated their desire to Washington. Andrew Jackson might have been expected to welcome the admission of Texas, especially under his old friend Houston, but the President hesitated. The issue was laden with political nitroglycerin, and Jackson did not even recognize the new republic until near the end of his administration. Undaunted, the Texans made renewed overtures to the next President, Martin Van Buren. Again they were rebuffed; Van Buren feared that Texan annexation would mean war with Mexico. The latter nation steadfastly refused to recognize Texas and had not forgotten the unneutral volunteers and supplies sent from the United States to Texas during the revolution. Furthermore, Van Buren was under the influence of Northern Free Soil men, who viewed the entire Texas question as a "slavery plot" to bring that vast Southwestern domain into the Union so that new slave states could be carved from it.

This second snub both bewildered and hurt the Texans. There was some shift in sentiment away from annexation, and Texas began devoting its explosive energies to the hazardous course of independence. Under Presidents Houston and the mellifluously named Mirabeau Buonaparte Lamar, Texas strove to ad-

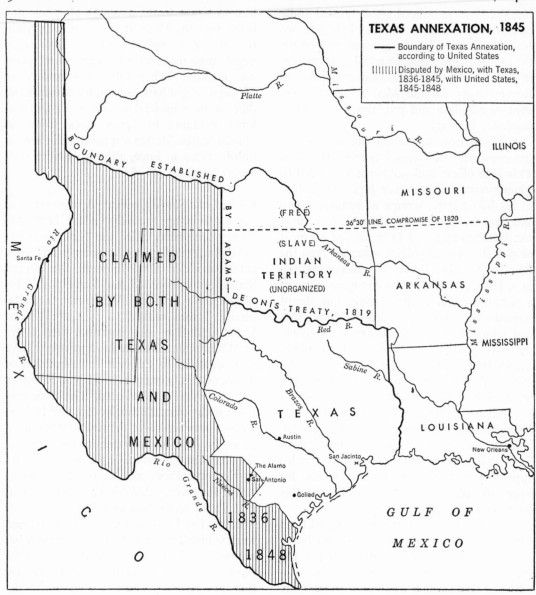

TEXAS ANNEXATION, 1845

— Boundary of Texas Annexation, according to United States

|||||||| Disputed by Mexico, with Texas, 1836-1845, with United States, 1845-1848

minister its vast territory, achieve recognition from the great powers, promote overseas trade and commerce, erect a strong and solvent government, increase the size and efficiency of the Texan army and navy, and above all maintain its precarious independence against Mexico. Even with the hurt resentment caused by the brusque rejection of the United States, most Texans continued to cherish the hope that some day they would be part of the American Union, although others urged that their real

destiny lay as a buffer state between the United States and Mexico. Menaced by Mexico and harassed by financial difficulties, the new republic struggled into the 1840s.

Initially Great Britain showed remarkably little interest in the Lone Star nation, but after a few years increased attention from London was discernible. Britain became enamored of the economic possibilities in a great cotton-producing area outside the tariff walls of the United States. Not only would American

Southern planters have to compete with those in Texas, and thus lower the prices paid for British cotton imports, but also pressure from Southerners might force the United States to abandon protection and become a free-trade area. Despite these attractive dreams, British hands were partially tied by a moral repugnance toward the slavery that existed in Texas. London communicated a strong hint that abolition of slavery was practically a condition for full British approval and perhaps even protection against both Mexico and the United States.

President Tyler, sympathetic toward Texan annexation, was worried about these evidences of British interest. Abel P. Upshur, who had become Secretary of State after Webster's resignation, had questioned the British about their intentions south of the Rio Grande. London replied with polite circumventions, and the controversy was enhanced by John C. Calhoun, who succeeded Upshur after the latter's untimely death. The eminent South Carolinian expressed surprise that Great Britain would bring up the slavery question in regard to Texas and warned that the United States might annex her southwestern neighbor because of this unwarranted intervention from across the Atlantic. Calhoun then proceeded to admonish the British about emancipation and went on to proclaim the benevolent glories of African bondage in America.

(*Annexation At Last.* Following this somewhat gauche display, Calhoun and Tyler brought a treaty to annex Texas before the Senate in 1844; the President hoped that he would get the necessary two-thirds majority in the upper house. He did get a two-thirds vote, but unfortunately for Tyler's expansionistic aspirations, it was *against* annexation. Some Senators had voted nay through fear of war with Mexico, others because of constitutional scruples, and still others because of the controversial slavery issue. Both supporters and opponents of Texas annexation settled back to listen for the voice of the people to be expressed in the election of 1844. The Democrat Polk was running on a platform calling for the reoccupation of Oregon and the reannexation of Texas, while Clay, the Whig nominee, maintained a studied vagueness in regard to Southwestern expansion.

When the Democratic slate squeaked through to victory, lame-duck President John Tyler assumed that the people had truly spoken, and he persuaded the House and Senate to annex the Texan Republic by joint resolution (which needed only a simple majority rather than the two-thirds necessary for a treaty). This was done on 1 March 1845 just before the new administration was to be inaugurated. Tyler's action was speedy enough to forestall belated British efforts to aid Texan independence through London's pressure on Mexico to recognize her lost province as a free nation.[2] This might have been followed by official British protection to the Lone Star Republic. But despite these foreign machinations, enough Texans wished to join their compatriots to the north so that ratification soon followed, and the independent Lone Star Republic became part of the United States.

[2] Mexico had already ratified a treaty whereby Texan independence would be recognized in return for a Texan pledge that it would not join any other nation.

CHAPTER 27

The Mexican War

(1846-1848)

BACKGROUND TO CONFLICT

When the news reached Mexico City that the lost province of Texas had been annexed by the United States, the populace reacted sharply. Mexico immediately recalled her minister to Washington and completely severed diplomatic relations. This rupture was most inopportune, for there were serious controversies extant between the two nations that needed adjudication, and the question of Texas annexation had been superimposed upon the heavy burdens already straining the relations between the unfriendly neighbors. The turbulence of Mexican domestic politics had created disorders in which American citizens had been killed and American property destroyed. The Mexican government had promised to pay claims amounting to some $2 million, but practically continuous revolutions had forced Mexico to default on these obligations as well as others. By the middle 1840s President Polk was angrily insisting on immediate payment.

Another difficulty was created by the continuing interest of the President in acquiring additional Mexican territory, and Polk's attitude was deeply resented in Mexico City. The

slender, intense, and toil-burdened Tennesseean was eying the Far West with avarice. Not only would occupation of the lands west of the Rio Grande be a natural extension of America's surge to the Pacific, but it might check the activity of British and French agents in California who were calling upon their respective governments to evince greater interest along the Pacific Coast. If such developments in California occurred, a necessary application of the Monroe Doctrine would immediately involve the United States. Finally a dispute arose over whether the Nueces River or the more southerly Rio Grande formed the boundary between Texas and Mexico. American insistence on the Rio Grande was incorrect; the Nueces had marked the limits of the province of Texas.

James K. Polk was a most determined and tenacious individual. He knew what he wanted and was determined to get it, but naturally he hoped to accomplish his ends by peaceful means. Receiving vague assurances that the Herrera government would receive an American "commissioner," the President appointed the slippery and artful John C. Slidell of Louisiana as "envoy extraordinary and minister plenipotentiary" to Mexico City. Slidell was instructed to assume payment of the claims in return for Mexican recognition of the Rio Grande as the correct southern and western boundary of Texas. Furthermore, he was to offer $5 million for the New Mexico country and $25 million for California.

The terms that Slidell was to offer leaked out in the capital, and Mexicans exploded in denunciation of any negotiations with the American envoy. The shaky Herrera government was menaced by a military cabal under General Paredes, avowedly hostile to the United States. Herrera knew that his political career was finished if he even met Slidell. Therefore he fell back upon a technicality, saying that he would be willing to confer with a "commissioner" to discuss claims, but not with a "minister plenipotentiary" to discuss anything else. Even this could not save Herrera; the Paredes revolt was successful; and Slidell, recognizing that agreement with the General was impossible, returned to the United States during the spring of 1846. Diplomacy had failed utterly.

At the same time that Slidell was being snubbed in Mexico City, Polk was providing himself with an alternate policy against the likelihood of collapsing negotiations. The President utilized the presence in Mexican territory of the youthful army officer John Charles Frémont, who was on his third expedition to the Far West. In addition, Polk dispatched a naval squadron to the Pacific Coast. Even more bellicose action was soon to come. When he heard that Slidell had not been received, the President took the incendiary action of ordering General Zachary Taylor into the disputed area between the Nueces and the Rio Grande Rivers. Tension mounted higher during the early spring of 1846, especially after Slidell had narrated the account of his Mexican tribulations into Polk's sympathetic ear. The President's determination was matched in Mexico City. The Paredes government sincerely believed that a victorious war with the United States would solidify the discordant elements in Mexico and ensure the new regime's stability.

As the weeks dragged by and Washington received no news from Taylor on the Rio Grande, Polk grew more restive. Finally he could stand it no longer, and on 9 May 1846 he summoned the Cabinet to discuss the advisability of requesting a congressional declaration of war against Mexico on the grounds of unpaid claims and insulting behavior toward Slidell. All agreed on war, but two Cabinet members wished to delay until an overt act of aggression by the Mexicans would bring into the conflict a more united America. The administration finally decided to wait.

By a surprising coincidence, that very evening dispatches arrived from General Taylor, stating that on 25 April his troops had been attacked by the Mexicans and some Americans were killed. Cabinet reservations had been fully met, and Mr. Polk had a war on his hands. On 11 May the President appealed to Congress for a declaration of war on the grounds that "Mexico . . . has passed the boundary of the United States, has invaded our territory and shed American blood upon the American soil." Congress on the next day followed the executive request and, after voting the war resolution by comfortable majorities, appropriated funds for an army and supplies.

The Mexican War (1846 to 1848) was a dual responsibility of both Mexico and the United States. For a long time Polk was held to be the villain of the melodrama. Historians, particularly those who viewed Manifest Destiny as a rationalization of the "slavocracy's" aggression, looked upon Polk as a despicable and outrageous bully who, after picking a quarrel with a helpless neighbor, coldly despoiled the weaker adversary of rich lands. There is certainly some truth in this stereotype. Polk's over-all attitude was not placatory, and he deserves censure for sending an army into disputed territory.

It should be remembered, however, that Mexico refused any negotiation at all. The Mexican contention that the annexation of Texas was a manifestly unfriendly act had no foundation. It must be granted that American activity during the Texas Revolution in 1836 had broken international law when American citizens contributed supplies and money as well as volunteers to Mexico's rebels. But our national behavior on the annexation of Texas in 1845 was above reproach. For almost a decade the independent Lone Star Republic had maintained its independence against a much larger Mexico, enjoyed the recognition of all the great powers, and as a sovereign nation could do as it wished. Furthermore, any perusal of Mexican official correspondence or newspapers during the middle 1840s shows that Mexico was eager for war. The Mexicans were confident that their soldiers, annealed through constant revolutionary activity, could whip the tiny Indian-fighting United States army. Both nations were trigger-tempered, and responsibility must be divided between Mexico City and Washington.

THE MEXICAN CAMPAIGN

❮ *Taylor and Buena Vista.* The initial enthusiasm with which the United States entered the war partially evaporated, despite the practically uniform success enjoyed by American arms. Most Northern Whigs and many Northern Democrats soon considered that the war was being fought in behalf of Southern interests to benefit the expansion of slavery. Protest meetings were held in Northern cities, some editorial opinion became practically pro-Mexican, and one Northern paper offered a prayer that "the hordes under Taylor and Scott be swept into the next world." In Congress this feeling was illustrated by an obscure young Illinois Representative named Abraham Lincoln who needled Polk with his "Spot Resolution," which cast grave doubts upon the President's veracity in his official explanation of the reasons for the outbreak of hostilities. Increasing Whig opposition called for peace, and the administration eventually had to listen.

As usual in the wars of nineteenth-century America, the minuscule professional army was engulfed by swarms of ardent volunteers as volatile in enthusiasm as they were untrained in warfare. Gradually they were hammered into the semblance of an army. The Mexican

War was chiefly inspired by Southern *élan;* naturally, most volunteers came from neighboring states rather than from the distant North, although the Upper Middle West manifested considerable enthusiasm. Any military shortcomings of the American forces were not too important; Mexican conditions were worse. The inevitable dissensions that split Mexican politics were duplicated in her armies, and they sometimes showed little will to fight.

There were three main American campaigns during the two-year course of the war. General Zachary Taylor conquered some of northeastern Mexico, but the Polk administration stranded him among the arid plateaus there. Several individuals, notably Stephen W. Kearny, contributed to the conquest of New Mexico, Arizona, and California. The decisive final blow was struck at the heart of Mexico when General Winfield Scott marched from Vera Cruz to capture Mexico City, thus ending the war.

It will be recalled that it was a Mexican attack on Taylor's army that started the fighting. Defeating the Mexicans in several minor engagements along the border, Taylor plunged southwest and advanced on the city of Monterrey, which fell in September, 1846. Taylor, however, had allowed an entire Mexican army to evacuate the city. Temporarily laying aside his sword for a pen, the American General in northeastern Mexico castigated the Polk administration in an article appearing in the New York *Express* for failing to support him adequately. This peculiar behavior further infuriated Polk, who was watching with small delight the creation of a military hero who might (as he did) become the Whig presidential candidate in 1848.

Taylor's displeasure at the government in Washington was further enhanced by the sudden appearance of an old enemy, General Antonio López de Santa Anna. This kaleidoscopic individual was in and out of power in Mexico so often that a revolving door might have been put in the Mexican Capitol for his exclusive use. Exiled after his crushing defeat by the Texans in 1836, only two years later Santa Anna had returned to defend Vera Cruz when

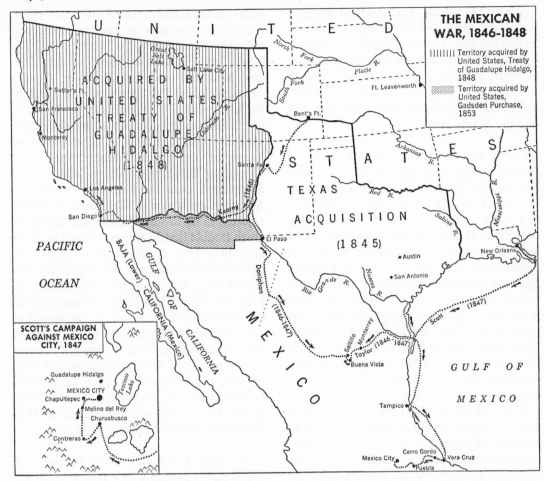

THE MEXICAN
WAR, 1846-1848

||||||| Territory acquired by
United States, Treaty
of Guadalupe Hidalgo,
1848

////// Territory acquired by
United States,
Gadsden Purchase,
1853

SCOTT'S CAMPAIGN
AGAINST MEXICO
CITY, 1847

a French squadron bombarded the city to punish the Mexicans for their inability to repay Gallic bondholders.[1] Even a heroic wound could not save Santa Anna from a future loss of power, and when the war with the United States broke out he was living in Cuban exile. Polk allowed himself to be hoodwinked by the wily Latin. Santa Anna promised that if he were permitted to return to Mexico, he would end the war on terms advantageous to the United States. Hoping that some advantage might accrue, Polk swallowed these dubious assurances and ordered the blockading squadron to allow the Mexican safe passage. Santa Anna landed in Mexico, marched to the capital

[1] In the bombardment of Vera Cruz Santa Anna lost a leg, which was later interred in a special mausoleum built for that purpose in Mexico City.

in triumph, announced his determination to defeat the Americans, and moved against Taylor with a large army.

Taylor had done little since his siege of Monterrey because no reinforcements had arrived, and his army was plagued by disease. Nevertheless, he advanced south to meet the Mexicans at Buena Vista late in February, 1847. Outnumbered almost three to one, the Americans had an extremely close call. Taylor's tactics were miserable, but he was saved by the fighting ability of his soldiers and by the personal efficiency of such officers as Jefferson Davis, Colonel of the Mississippi Rifles; Braxton Bragg, future Confederate General; and George H. Thomas, the Union "Rock of Chickamauga" in 1863. After heavy fighting extending over two days, Santa Anna's army was forced to retreat. Taylor settled down at the nearby town of Saltillo, but was able to accomplish little for the remainder of the war —Polk's hostility toward him became ever more pronounced. Military action spread to other quarters, but "Old Rough and Ready" had gained a reputation that would put him into the White House.

◖ *Kearny and California.*   One of the better American officers during the Mexican War was Stephen W. Kearny. At the outbreak of hostilities he was in Missouri with a small force of 1,700, resoundingly entitled "The Army of the West." Ordered to proceed to Santa Fe in New Mexico and thence to California, Kearny headed southwest. His "army" was a motley aggregation of hard-bitten regular soldiers; untrained farm boys; a brigade of devout Mormons whom Brigham Young had sent to earn some needed cash for the development of Utah; and a group of "engineers" directly from Germany, who filled the air with Teutonic wails and curses as they struggled across the endless reaches of the Far West.

Somehow the level-headed Kearny molded these divergent elements into a reasonable facsimile of a military organization and proceeded to capture Santa Fe without a battle in mid-August, 1846. After proclaiming New Mexico to be part of the United States, Kearny dispatched Colonel Alexander Doniphan with most of the army in a vast southward semicircle to join Taylor in northeastern Mexico. Despite the hazards of the inhospitable terrain, roving bands of Mexicans, and the ever-present danger from Indian attack, Doniphan accomplished his mission with conspicuous success and reached Saltillo in the early spring of 1847.

Meanwhile Kearny started west with the remainder of his forces. After a grueling three-month march through the arid Southwest during the autumn of 1846, Kearny reached California only to face new problems. Here American success had been almost too complete. It seemed as if practically everyone in the area was conquering the El Dorado of the West for the United States. Sailors from the naval squadron had captured the coastal cities. A group of American settlers had proclaimed an independent nation, the "Golden Bear Republic," even before they knew that the Mexican War had commenced. John Charles Frémont, in the Far West at the outbreak of the war, assumed command of the American forces and engaged in desultory skirmishes with Mexican Californians. The arrival of Kearny further complicated the picture.

Ignoring the fact that Kearny held a direct commission from the President to establish American authority in California, Frémont objected to his loss of influence and caused so much trouble that Kearny was forced to arrest him. In a later court-martial Frémont, the glamorous "Pathfinder of the West," was dismissed from the army for insubordination. Polk soon offered him a new commission, but Frémont refused to accept it. He served as Senator from California a short time later and emerged in 1856 as the first Republican presidential candidate. Kearny quietly administered his sunset empire until his return to the East. California became part of the United States by the Treaty of Guadalupe-Hidalgo in 1848 and a state of the Union two years later.

◖ *Scott and Mexico City.*   The decisive campaign against Mexico City was slow to get under way. Finally Polk, completely disgusted with Taylor, stripped the latter of most of his troops, gathered new detachments, and turned the total over to the command of General Winfield Scott, a hero of the War of 1812. Scott was an immense person, 6 feet 4 inches in height and memorable in girth. The General's love for finery was reflected in the gaudy color and trappings of his uniforms, which earned for him the derisive nickname of "Old Fuss and Feathers." For all his harmless vanity, Scott was one of the finest American generals, and his campaign against Mexico City was both intelligently planned and skillfully executed.

Assembling first at New Orleans, Scott's army was transported down the coast of Mexico, and in March, 1847, the Americans successfully attacked the port city of Vera Cruz, natural gateway to the interior. The portly General led his army of almost 11,000 men west through the jagged vistas of the mountains along the old route traversed by the soldiers of Cortes over three centuries before. Santa Anna, back in the capital after his defeat at Buena Vista, showed remarkable inertia in failing to fortify several positions along the road where Scott would have had to pay a heavy price for further advance. Not until the pass of Cerro Gordo had been reached did the Mexicans put up a fight (17–18 April 1847). The Americans were victorious and pushed on to the city of Puebla, where the army rested. Following abortive peace feelers to the Mexicans, the advance continued in August.

When Scott's army tramped down into the great central valley of Mexico in which the capital is located, sharp fighting ensued. Ably assisted by such future military luminaries as Robert E. Lee, Ulysses S. Grant, and George B. McClellan, Scott defeated the Mexicans at Contreras, Churubusco, and Molino del Rey late in August and early in September. On 13 September 1847 the decisive engagement of the campaign was joined when a dramatic American charge up the heights of Chapultepec won the day.[2] Mexico City surrendered within twenty-four hours.

Even while the fighting proceeded, the United States had made repeated attempts to negotiate a peace; but the still hopeful Mexicans refused. Realizing that Scott's invasion of south central Mexico might bring a sudden end to hostilities, Polk decided that it would be wise to have a personal representative on hand. Therefore he dispatched a strange emissary to accompany Scott from Vera Cruz to Mexico City. Rather than some resplendent politician accoutered in the full panoply of a "minister plenipotentiary," Polk sent the insignificant Nicholas Trist, chief clerk in the

State Department. Probably Polk wished a man so unimportant that he could be thrown to the wolves of outraged popular opinion if anything went wrong. Of course Scott was highly suspicious of Trist, and the two men forthwith embarked on a puerile quarrel complete with angry communications (those of Trist being remarkably lengthy, since Polk's personal representative considered thirty-odd pages a short note) until they patched up their difficulties and combined to frustrate the President wherever possible.

THE TREATY OF GUADALUPE-HIDALGO

As soon as the Mexicans surrendered, Scott and Trist started peering about in search of a Mexican government that could sign a treaty of peace with the United States. While the quest continued, in Washington the President had come to the conclusion that Trist was assuming too much responsibility, and he summarily recalled him. Trist refused to come home. Communicating a few random thoughts in a terse note to Polk (precisely sixty-five pages in length) as to why he could not and would not be fired, Trist remained and finally signed the Treaty of Guadalupe-Hidalgo with a temporary Mexican government. Polk was beside himself with fury, and in his diary he angrily castigated this "impudent and unqualified scoundrel" for refusing to be dismissed. Yet the situation had evolved so that the choleric President had no choice but to swallow his chagrin and accept the work of his discredited representative.

The altered circumstances that made Polk support Trist's treaty were essentially twofold. Whig opposition to the war was reaching dangerous proportions, and there appeared to be considerable likelihood that Congress might refuse to appropriate the funds necessary to prolong the war. In addition, a menacing ground swell was arising in the ranks of the ultraexpansionists of the Manifest Destiny school. These extremists were calling for the

---

[2] The Battle of Chapultepec is remembered in Mexican history as the "Slaughter of the Innocents." Cadets of the Mexican Military Academy, most of them in their early teens, were placed in the front-line defenses and were practically wiped out. Although Mexican historians have decried such American brutality, mere children should never have been ordered into battle.

total annexation of Mexico all the way to Central America. Polk was an ardent expansionist himself, and he had come to want more territory than called for in his original instructions to Trist, yet he perceived the folly of attempting to incorporate into the Union some seven million unruly and bellicose people of different language, religion, and national background. If the President did not accept Trist's Mexican treaty, the augmented territorial ambitions of some Americans might not be contained. Therefore Polk had to approve it, although his unfortunate envoy was later persecuted with vengeful malice.[3]

One would think that even the most land-hungry American would have been satisfied with the Treaty of Guadalupe-Hidalgo. By it Mexico lost two-fifths of its total area—if the earlier loss of Texas is included, one-half. The present states of California, Nevada, and Utah, in addition to all of Arizona north of the Gila River, half of New Mexico, and smaller portions of Colorado and Wyoming, were added to the Union. The American claim to the Rio Grande as the southwestern boundary of Texas was confirmed. As a sop to the vanquished, the United States paid Mexico $15 million for the territory acquired and assumed about $3 million in claims owed to American citizens by Mexico. Although the United States had obviously won a great victory, the Mexican government could at least point to the money as compensation. The Treaty of Guadalupe-Hidalgo was ratified by the American Senate in March, 1848.

❨ *The Gadsden Purchase.* Only five years elapsed before the final American nibble at Mexico took place. Agitation for a southern transcontinental railroad operated in behalf of the accession of the land south of the Gila River in what is now Arizona and New Mexico. President Franklin Pierce sent James Gadsden as a special envoy to Mexico City in 1853 to buy the necessary tract. After lengthy negotiation, the Gadsden Purchase was accomplished,

whereby the United States paid $10 million for the extreme Southwest.[4] Gadsden was not able to acquire title to the area around the mouth of the Colorado River, and thus the entire Gulf of California remained Mexican.

MANIFEST DESTINY AND SECTIONALISM

Although the expansionism called Manifest Destiny had existed practically from the beginnings of American history, it came to a violent focus during the 1840s and into the early 1850s. Little more than a decade encompasses its crest, but it was as intensive as it was short. From 1842 to 1853, particularly concentrated between 1845 and 1848, the United States gained disputed land along its northeastern boundary; the tremendous Texan Republic; much of Oregon Territory; and all the extensive tracts north of present Mexico, south of Oregon, and west of Texas. Behind diplomatic maneuvering and martial activity ran the strong tide of population pressure. Americans were driving toward the West, and woe betide those who stood in the way—Indian, Mexican, and even Briton were elbowed aside in this ruthless sunset thrust. A third of a nation was added, and the present limits of the continental United States drawn.

During the 1840s the young Eagle screamed in triumph; and well did Americans, giddy with the headstrong enthusiasm of their national adolescence, eagerly look toward a future that might find the United States stretching from the polar wastes of Arctic Canada to the reeking jungles of Darien on the Central American Isthmus. For the next ten years, Southern Democrats would gaze with avaricious longing at Cuba, the rest of Mexico, and Central America. The vision of annexing Canada would die hard in the North, and traces of it would be evident as late as the twentieth cen-

---

[3] It was long after the Civil War before Trist was reimbursed by Congress for his expenses in Mexico City, which he had paid from his own pocket.

[4] The United States was also given the right of transit across the Isthmus of Tehuantepec where Mexico is narrowest, a possible but not probable site of a canal from the Atlantic to the Pacific.

tury. But never again would the United States duplicate its expansion of the 1840s. Manifest Destiny was to be immolated in the leaping flames of sectionalism. It was not beyond the limits of possibility that both Cuba and Canada would enter the Union during the 1850s, but the attempts of either the North or the South were to be blocked by the other. The Compromise of 1850 appeared to have settled sectional matters, and if it had been maintained, another wave of acquisition cloaked in divine righteousness could have evolved. The Compromise failed during the early 1850s, however, and the likelihood of further external growth surrendered to the onset of internal cleavage.

CHAPTER 28

The Diplomacy of Sectionalism

(1848-1860)

LIBERAL ENTHUSIASMS

If the circumstances of American foreign policy during the 1850s were somewhat less critical than during the early years of the Republic or during modern times, they were still important. In this sphere, as in the domestic, forces both national and sectional commingled. In some instances, particularly in mutual dislike of European monarchism and in joint efforts to develop trade with the Far East, the two sections acted with common purpose. In others, expansionistic in the main, sectionalism deeply influenced final decisions; neither the North nor the South was willing to allow the other new territorial acquisitions that might tip the scales in the slavery controversy.

Considering the United States as the first major republic, it was natural that American popular opinion should have supported the widespread European revolutions of 1848. Liberal uprisings occurred throughout most of that continent, and for several months it appeared that democracy and nationalism would sweep triumphantly from the Pyrenees to the Russian border. Back swung the pendulum, however, and the extravagant hopes of 1848 seemed dead by the next year. Disappointment

336

thus imbued Americans with even more pronounced sentiments of hostility toward the conservative and despotic monarchies of the Old World. Playing upon this theme, Secretary of State Daniel Webster earned domestic plaudits by insulting the Hapsburg monarchy in his reply to an Austrian protest against American sympathy for the Hungarian revolt. Webster haughtily compared the Hapsburg domains to "a patch on the earth's surface" in relation to the size of the United States. This gauche and sophomoric attitude so typical of the age was echoed by James Buchanan, Minister to Great Britain, who appeared at a royal ball clad in conventional black evening clothes —he wore a sword so that he would not be mistaken for a servant—instead of the usual full diplomatic regalia. Luckily Queen Victoria was more amused than outraged, and ebullient Americans toasted Buchanan for his refusal to array himself in the "trappings of flunkies."

Traditionally sympathetic to the underdog, Americans welcomed defeated European liberals, extending a hospitable refuge to Irish rebels, German *émigrés*, and refugees from all the Central European states. Especially theatrical was the reception accorded to Louis Kossuth, hero of the abortive Hungarian uprising of 1848. During most of 1851 citizens of the United States competed among themselves to arrange testimonial banquets, benefit performances, and lavish parties for the "Illustrious Magyar." So costly were the entertainments that expenses ate up all the money which was supposed to further Hungarian independence. Poor Kossuth finally sailed for Europe with little but memories to show for his social successes; Americans had turned against him once it became clear that Kossuth wished something close to United States intervention in continental matters.

THE ANGLO-AMERICAN CLASH IN CANADA

With antimonarchical sentiments in full cry, naturally the traditionally unfriendly relations between Great Britain and the United States would have little opportunity to improve during the early 1850s. To most Americans, Great Britain remained the eternal enemy, and, as was true for another seventy-five years, school children throughout the United States read in their primers sanguinary accounts of hardhearted redcoats, and their elders were fed a steady diet of "perfidious Albion" in many of their newspapers. Fully cognizant of ancient wrongs, tens of thousands of Irish were landing in New York and Boston, aching to "twist the Lion's tail," and native politicians were often delighted to accommodate them. It was approaching high noon for the British Empire. Flushed with a realization of their tremendous accomplishments, English diplomats, officers, authors, and manufacturers tended to view other nationalities with supercilious contempt. As first cousins, Americans found the whiplash of British condescension especially maddening.

The national dislike of England was heightened by clashes in several arenas. Once again in the news was the perennial fishing controversy. Ever since the end of the American Revolution, and particularly since the Treaty of Ghent in 1815, periodic diplomatic ex-

changes were necessary to clarify the complicated question of American fishing rights in Canadian waters. By 1853 Canadians were attempting to limit these privileges through an "illiberal interpretation" of the Convention of 1818, pertaining to Americans landing to buy bait and supplies, or to salt or dry their catch. Resistance was offered by Yankee fishermen, and outright warfare on the rolling green swells of the Grand Banks appeared imminent.

❡ *The Reciprocity Treaty of 1854.* Another Canadian matter needing adjustment concerned the economic difficulties that operated against British North America. The repeal of the Corn Laws [1] had removed tariff protection from Canadians and forced them to compete in a free-trade empire. Since American tariffs continued, Canadian exports to the United States were severely cut. Caught in this economic vise, an increasing number of Canadians were agitating for annexation to the Union so that American tariffs could protect them. The Queen's government naturally had no desire to lose Canada, and it saw an avenue of possible compromise by which American fishing rights might be bartered for reduced tariffs on Canadian exports to the United States.

As special negotiator to the United States in 1854, London appointed the suave and sophisticated Lord Elgin. Even though he personally disliked Americans either individually or en masse, Elgin scored a diplomatic triumph, partly through paying little attention to moral scruples. Certainly Elgin bought up some Canadian legislators and probably some Americans too. Although representatives from the Canadian Maritime Provinces had been noisy in their denunciation of expanded American fishing rights, a magical silence soon fell. Many Representatives and Senators were spokesmen for rural areas that opposed Canadian participation in American food markets. Elgin hur-

[1] The Corn Laws were akin to protective tariffs on grains (in England "corn" referred to all grains, especially wheat) that had been imposed to aid British agricultural interests. Since tariffs usually bring on retaliatory tariffs, British industrial groups wished free trade. Repeal of the Corn Laws during the 1840s marked a great victory for the manufacturers.

dled this roadblock, not only by financial favors liberally bestowed, but also by giving parties so lavish that the treaty was said to have been "floated through on champagne." Elgin's secretary later explained such behavior with the cynical query, "If you have got to deal with hogs, what are you to do?"

The Reciprocity Treaty of 1854 gave American fishermen practically unlimited rights in northern waters, and Canadians were awarded the less important privilege of fishing along the American coast as far south as Chesapeake Bay. Tariffs between Canada and the United States, notably on foodstuffs, were almost abolished. This agreement was to be soon broken, but at the time it gave convincing testimony to the persuasive powers of Lord Elgin—and his pocketbook.

THE ANGLO-AMERICAN CLASH IN THE CARIBBEAN

A perplexing dispute between the two nations in the Caribbean and Central America was even harder to solve. During most of the nineteenth century Great Britain refused to recognize the Monroe Doctrine and its concomitant of special American rights in the Western Hemisphere. Not until the turn of the century would Britain surrender control of the Caribbean to the United States. Prior to that time, a British naval squadron based at the West Indian island of Jamaica offered a standing threat to American political and economic aspirations throughout the Caribbean periphery. Furthermore, Great Britain had quickly and permanently won commercial supremacy in South America.

Although the United States could offer little effective opposition below Panama, Central America was another story. In the humid lands between Mexico and South America, both Anglo-Saxon nations had established interests. For many years British lumbermen had lived at Belize (British Honduras), and although that area did not become a Crown Colony un-

til 1862, English influence was predominant there. In the Panama environs the United States had taken the lead through the Treaty of 1846 with New Granada (Colombia), in which America promised to protect the right of transit across the New Granadan province of Panama, presumably against any British aggression.

The discovery of gold in California roiled Anglo-American relations and made Central America even more vital to both countries. The fastest way to the gold fields from either Europe or the Atlantic Coast of the United States was to sail for Central America, traverse the Isthmus of Panama, and reembark for California on the Pacific side. Both nations hostilely jockeyed for position there. Complicating the issue further was the discussion of an isthmian canal from the Atlantic to the Pacific. Obviously possession of such a strategic waterway would be a most valuable asset for either Britain or the United States. An isthmian canal was possible at three points. The shortest and most direct was at Panama; a second could bisect Nicaragua, utilizing a lake and two rivers; and the third might cross the Isthmus of Tehuantepec, where Mexico narrows to its minimum width. In Tehuantepec the United States already had a prior claim, because of the Gadsden Purchase of 1853. The Panama Railroad furnished yet another American assertion to special rights in Central America. In 1855 an American company succeeded in constructing a railroad through the dense and matted jungles of Panama at a terrific cost in money and lives.

With the United States preeminent in Panama to the south and to a much lesser extent in Tehuantepec to the north, and with Great Britain entrenched at Honduras, Nicaragua, the middle area became the ground of contention. During the 1840s the British moved on both Nicaraguan coasts. An English naval officer, acting on his own initiative, seized control of the Pacific Gulf of Fonseca, although London disavowed this act. But on the eastern coast the British were adamant in their refusal to leave. A protectorate over the

CENTRAL AMERICA DURING
THE 1850s

////// British colonies or protectorates

Mosquito Indians had been erected there, and despite American objections the Union Jack seemed nailed to the Nicaraguan mast.

《 *The Clayton-Bulwer Treaty.* As was usual when Anglo-American relations reached a breaking point, diplomacy hastened to the rescue. In the year 1849 Sir Henry Bulwer (brother of the famous author of *The Last Days of Pompeii*) was sent to America to negotiate with John M. Clayton, President Taylor's Secretary of State. After protracted deliberations, the Clayton-Bulwer Treaty was signed (1850). This proved to be one of the most unpopular agreements ever contracted

by the United States; only after intermittent attempts covering the next half century was America able to wriggle out from under its encumbrances. The Clayton-Bulwer provisions stipulated that both nations promised that the construction of any canal through the Central American Isthmus would be mutually undertaken by the signatories, and that neither would ever fortify it. Even worse to many Americans was one of the few self-denying ordinances in our national history, when both the United States and Great Britain pledged to annex no territory in the Caribbean environs. The language utilized in the latter provision was deliberately ambiguous, especially in regard to Britain's Mosquito protectorate. London argued that it had agreed in the Clayton-Bulwer Treaty to annex no *more* territory, but that the Mosquito protectorate was already part of its empire. Washington maintained that Britain was breaking the pact's terms by its refusal to clear out of southeastern Nicaragua.

For the next several years peril continued to exist that war might break out over the continued British occupation of the sublimely unappetizing Mosquito coast. After local disorders in 1854, an American naval squadron bombarded the British-held village of Greytown in Nicaragua, and perhaps only the outbreak of the Crimean War between Britain and Russia stopped the former from taking retaliatory measures. Equally disturbing to international harmony was an American soldier of fortune named William Walker, the "Grey-eyed Man of Destiny," who led several filibustering expeditions into Nicaragua and actually became dictator of that strife-torn land. Britain viewed Walker as an agent of the American government working for the annexation of Nicaragua by the United States. Although he was awarded considerable early support by Manifest Destiny Southerners, Walker soon lost American favor by acts of obvious self-aggrandizement; and when he was finally shot by a Nicaraguan firing squad, Washington mourned him as little as did London.

Later in the decade pressure from the business interests of both nations helped to allay the mutual hostility. The old argument about the folly of warring upon one's best customer again became prominent. Especially vocal were the manufacturers of Great Britain, and the international situation played into their hands. Hardly was the Crimean War smoke disappearing when Emperor Napoleon III appeared to be threatening the *status quo*. Under these circumstances Great Britain decided that possession of the Mosquito coast was not worth the continuing enmity of the United States. In 1859 Britain signed a treaty with Nicaragua, officially withdrawing from its protectorate. Soon President Buchanan was able to announce that outstanding difficulties with Great

Britain had been solved. It seemed as if relations between the two nations were to enter a period of cloudless skies, but the outbreak of the Civil War was destined to plunge the Anglo-Saxon countries again to the brink of combat.

THE UNITED STATES, SPAIN, AND CUBA

A nagging difficulty in foreign relations applied to the Spanish island of Cuba. It was here that the most obstinate and concerted efforts of American expansionists during the 1850s were focused. Yet a significant difference existed between this expansionism and that of less than a decade before. The 1840s were much more national; the 1850s were chiefly Southern-inspired. The more intelligent supporters of slavery were aware of the hardening Northern attitude toward a Southern thrust into the continental West. Furthermore, many Southerners were becoming positive that geography formed an insuperable barrier in that direction. Also, Southern annexationists were resentful that their section did not appear to have shared equally in the spoils of the Mexican War. Hence Southerners tended to look across the Gulf of Mexico toward Cuba, the "Pearl of the Antilles." There, they reasoned, was a land natural for slavery. Its soil was fertile, its climate hot, and its polyglot population had much Negro blood. Tropical products—tobacco, sugar, and cotton—would thrive under the "blessings of slavery." In addition the planter, haunted by the fear of slave rebellion, wished stability to come to the island so that Cuban revolution would not be emulated on Southern plantations.

Americans have often formed secret societies to abet almost every cause in which they believed, and the Southern annexationists were no exception. An organization called the Knights of the Golden Circle was established. Showing the usual mystical ritualism and elaborate nomenclature typical of such societies, the K.G.C. worked to bring all lands inside the "Great Circle" [2] under American dominion and recruited thousands of members for this purpose. The sectional motif of the Knights of the Golden Circle was clear; it was composed almost solely of Southerners or Southern sympathizers, and eventually it became a leading anti–Civil War "Copperhead" agency in the North.

Expansionist hopes for Cuba were thwarted by two major elements: the opposition of the North and the implacable determination of Spain not to lose her most valued American possession. In the first instance, Northerners who fought so doggedly to stem slavery's penetration onto the plains of Kansas were not likely to applaud slavery's extension anywhere else. Many above the Mason-Dixon line asked themselves whether forcing thousands of new slaves to groan under the overseer's lash was worth conflict with Spain, and perhaps with Great Britain and France as well. Again and again, despite the efforts of the pro-Southern Pierce and Buchanan administrations, Northern hostility or, at best, indifference frustrated attempts to procure Cuba and perhaps the entire Caribbean. Indeed, this sectional aspect was probably decisive. A Manifest Destiny that had ripped from Mexico its northern provinces only a few years before might well have shown no respect for Spanish sensibilities over Cuba if the American Union were not approaching its temporary dissolution.

The second primary factor protecting Cuba from annexation by the United States was the international picture. The Spanish monarchy was only a feeble shadow of its sixteenth-century might, but it was still a major European government and by no means completely impotent. Keenly aware of their colossal loss of territory, power, and prestige since 1800, the proud Castilians were determined to retain Cuba. Even if a Spanish government had wished to sell that island to the United States, it is extremely unlikely that Spanish popular

opinion would have tolerated it, and rebellion would have been a probable outcome. In addition, if the United States seized Cuba, Great Britain and France might object most vehemently, even to the point of war.

❨ *Annexation Attempts.* Nevertheless, the United States continued the intensive interest in Cuba that has typified our national diplomacy almost from the beginning. The island's geographical position dominated not only the Caribbean, but also the American Gulf coast, and possession of this strategic spot by a strong and aggressive foreign power would be intolerable to American security. During the period before the great surge of Manifest Destiny, American efforts had been aimed at opposing British and French machinations in Cuba, since we preferred the island to remain Spanish rather than to fall into stronger hands. As late as 1843 the United States sent to Madrid an absolute guarantee of military and naval aid if another power attacked Cuba.

The contagious verve and *élan* of Manifest Destiny expansion, however, altered this hands-off attitude; and starting in the late 1840s the United States began trying to get Cuba for itself. The insatiable James K. Polk, not content with his impressive haul from the Mexican War, approached Spain with an offer of $100 million for the West Indian colony. The reaction in Madrid was so instantaneously antagonistic that negotiations were abruptly terminated. Other avenues had to be taken.

When the United States appeared unable to possess Cuba by diplomacy the filibuster stepped forward. The middle years of the nineteenth century were tailor-made for these private soldiers of fortune, and Latin America furnished its share of opportunity. A Venezuelan named Narciso López was one of the more prominent filibusters. He interested himself in the cause of Cuban freedom, convincing others that the masses on the island were panting for liberation from Spanish misrule. López aroused considerable American enthusiasm in New Orleans and Key West, which became the twin centers of intrigue against Spanish Cuba. Rash young Southerners, imbued with both idealis-

---

[2] A rough circle is formed if a line is drawn following the Gulf coast of the United States from Florida to Texas, on down the Mexican shore, turning north at the Yucatán Peninsula, and thence back to Florida. Naturally the Caribbean islands inside the circle were included.

tic fervor and more prosaic hopes for profit, enlisted under López's filibustering banner. Three times López tried to seize Cuba between 1849 and 1851, and in the culminating fiasco the infuriated Spaniards publicly executed López and fifty American followers in the square at Havana. The reaction to the news in New Orleans was swift; the Spanish consulate in that city was sacked, and a crisis was immediately forthcoming. Actually the Spaniards had a much better case than did the United States, since the López expeditions were manned, financed, outfitted, and dispatched from American soil in flagrant disregard for neutrality. The United States was clearly responsible for the actions of its citizens and apologized to Spain. The Iberian Queen magnanimously liberated many Americans still imprisoned for their participation in the third López attack on Cuba.

❧ *Bungling Diplomacy: The Aix-la-Chapelle Dispatch.* With the death of the filibuster, the diplomat (to use the term loosely) again came forth. The Pierce administration, Southern-influenced and expansionist-minded, was eager to annex Cuba and to allay by foreign adventure the surging sectionalism that was dividing the nation. If Pierce had any real hope of persuading Spain to sell Cuba, it would be hard to picture a worse appointment than that of Pierre Soulé as Minister to Spain. Soulé, expatriate Frenchman and resident of Louisiana, was an implacable foe of monarchism and a vehement supporter of Cuban annexation by the United States; he soon made himself *persona non grata* in Madrid.[3] While the American Minister was licking his social wounds in Spain, news from Cuba appeared to grant him an opportunity for revenge. The *Black Warrior*, an American ship, was seized by the Spanish authorities in Havana on a technicality,

and bellicose Americans demanded redress for this grievance. Secretary of State William L. Marcy of New York instructed Soulé to demand both apologies and an indemnity for the *Black Warrior* outrage. The rattlebrained Soulé exceeded his instructions by adding a couple of personal embellishments in the form of a forty-eight-hour ultimatum and a demand that those responsible in Havana be dismissed. The Spanish government completely ignored Soulé, dealt directly with the owners of the confiscated ship, and returned it, leaving the disgruntled American envoy to brood over another rebuff.

If Soulé was the diplomatic marplot during his first few months in Spain, he became the scapegoat for the Pierce administration through his connection with the famous—or infamous—Aix-la-Chapelle Dispatch ("Ostend Manifesto"). Although it is difficult to feel much sympathy for as bumptious and empty-headed an individual as Pierre Soulé, he unjustly received the full brunt of international censure for a course of action started by Secretary of State Marcy. During 1854 Marcy instructed Soulé to offer Spain as much as $130 million for Cuba; and if the arrangement could not be made, the American Minister was to do all in his power "to detach" the island from Spain. Shortly afterward Soulé was sent to Belgium to confer with James Buchanan, Minister to Great Britain, and John Y. Mason, Minister to France, on how to obtain Cuba. The trio was to notify the administration of their conclusions.

After initial sessions at Ostend the three Americans moved to Aix-la-Chapelle, where they signed the dispatch erroneously called the Ostend Manifesto. Embodying some of the more amazing examples of bullying and aggressive diplomacy, the Aix-la-Chapelle Dispatch stated:

. . . Cuba is as necessary to the North American republic as any of its present members. . . . Its immediate acquisition by our government is of paramount importance. . . . Should Spain reject [our offer] . . . then, by every law, human and divine, we shall be justified in wresting it from Spain. . . .

---

[3] While attending a party at the home of the Marquis de Turgot, French Minister to Spain, Soulé objected to another guest's slurring reference to the low-cut front of Mrs. Soulé's gown. After acrimonious discussion, the American challenged De Turgot to a duel and, shooting him in the leg, crippled the Frenchman for life. Understandably this bravura did little to enhance Soulé's popularity in Madrid.

When this remarkable communication was published, many Northern newspapers, opposed to slavery expansion, roared their denunciations. So great was the noise that the cowardly Secretary of State Marcy remained publicly silent about his instructions that Soulé should "detach" Cuba, allowing popular opinion to think that Soulé and the other two at Aix-la-Chapelle were responsible for the whole idea of "wresting" the island from Spain. Not until many years later did research uncover the role played by William L. Marcy.

As the sectional flames leaped higher, the possibility of annexing Cuba lessened. The North became more determined that slavery must be contained externally and internally. The somewhat introverted turn that national attentions were to take after the Civil War was being forecast during this time. Many Northerners were deeply concerned about the transcontinental railroad and internal progress; they feared that efforts devoted to Caribbean or other expansion for slaveholders might be at the expense of Western farmers and the issue of free homesteads. This common feeling was given crude, vulgar, but expressive voice during a debate on the annexation of Cuba late in the 1850s, when Senator Benjamin F. Wade of Ohio snarled, "Shall we give niggers to the niggerless or land to the landless?" The South could not undertake foreign conquest alone, and Cuba was destined to stay Spanish until almost the end of the nineteenth century. Yet all through his term, President Buchanan forlornly chanted his endless song of Cuba, as he tried to divert national attention from the domestic crisis. As late as 1860 both factions of the Democratic party carried planks calling for annexation of Cuba.

THE UNITED STATES AND THE FAR EAST

《 *China.* The expansionistic tendencies toward Cuba illustrate the sectional aspects of American diplomacy during the 1850s; the more national aspects are shown by the in-

trusion of the United States into the Far East. Both North and South tended to act together in Asiatic considerations. Naturally the North, as the great commercial area of the Union, would be interested in expanding American markets in Asia, for its ships would carry most of the cargoes, and its factories would provide most of the goods. As a producer of raw materials, the South showed lively determination

THE FAR EAST DURING THE 1850s

to increase its exports of cotton and tobacco. Furthermore, the dynamic Protestantism of mid-century America saw an unparalleled opportunity to spread the gospel if converts could be found among the almost countless millions in Asia.

As early as 1784 intrepid Yankee seafarers had nudged ajar what was eventually to become the "Open Door" in China. The years that followed developed a closely regulated but highly lucrative trade between America and China. Although never more than a small percentage of our European commerce, the old China trade has retained a well-merited glamour and luster. American economic relations with the Far East received impetus during the 1840s and 1850s, following the construction of the greatest sailing ships ever built: the magnificent clippers. Not only characterized by a beauty that was almost breath-taking, these ships were also extremely practical vessels, and despite their slender silhouettes they were fine cargo carriers. Such was the speed of the clippers that they captured much oceanic trade from Great Britain.

Although profiting from imports of Chinese silks and tea, the United States chafed at the commercial restrictions imposed by the Manchu Emperor on trade with "foreign devils." Only the port of Canton was open to European and American shipping, and Western merchants dreamed of the increased rewards that they could garner if more Chinese ports were opened. Luckily the United States did not have to breach Chinese commercial walls itself; Great Britain accomplished that task in the so-called Opium War (1839 to 1842). Ostensibly for the purpose of maintaining exports of British Indian opium to China, this rather sordid struggle was probably as much to open China to Western economic penetration as to rivet the use of narcotics on unfortunate Orientals. To share in the commercial opportunities that British guns had made available, the United States sent the talented and erudite Caleb Cushing of Massachusetts to the Far East in 1843. Cushing's mission was a brilliant success, and in a treaty signed at the temple of Wanghia in Portuguese Macao (1844) China granted to the United States considerably expanded commercial privileges, as well as the right of extraterritoriality.[4]

During the 1850s the United States was content to follow in the footsteps of the European powers in China, rather than try to forge an independent policy. After new concessions had been wrested by Britain and France, America would demand the same privileges under "the most favored nation agreement," in which if one shares, all share. When China was being ripped to pieces during the frightful Taiping Rebellion (1850 to 1864), which has been estimated to have killed some twenty million

[4] Extraterritoriality is the right of a nation to maintain courts for its own nationals in a foreign country. Under the Treaty of Wanghia, an American who was charged with a crime in China would be tried by an American court, even though no similar permission was granted to Chinese citizens in America. Naturally the Chinese looked upon extraterritoriality as an insult. Both Great Britain and the United States renounced this right, but not for about a century (1943).

Chinese, Britain and France took advantage of the unhappy empire's difficulties and warred against it. Sporadic military and naval action between 1858 and 1860 culminated in the sacking of Peking, the Manchu capital, and the European allies dictated peace terms through which new trade advantages were granted. Without bloodshed the United States soon won the same rights. Evidence of the friendship that has typified Sino-American relations until the mid-twentieth century was the amicable reception extended to Anson Burlingame, American Minister to China during and after the Civil War. So highly did the Manchu government regard Burlingame that he was appointed to head a Chinese mission abroad. In 1868 China and the United States signed the Burlingame Treaty, which facilitated the migration of Chinese "coolie" labor to California.

❨ *Japan.* More directly American than the penetration of China was the opening—or more properly the coming out—of Japan. That complex and interesting nation had originally welcomed European advent during the sixteenth century, and a vigorous trade was carried on with the Spaniards, the Portuguese, and the Dutch. Deciding that their civilization was menaced by Western customs, and disgusted by the overzealous proselyting of Catholic and Protestant missionaries, the Japanese withdrew into complete isolation early in the seventeenth century. For the next 250 years Japan remained frigidly aloof from the rest of the world. Its citizens were forbidden to leave the home islands, shipwrecked foreign sailors were apt to end up as sideshow attractions in Japanese circuses, and the only window outside was through the southern port of Nagasaki, where severely curtailed trade with the Dutch was conducted.

The American government was desirous of commercial relations with Nippon, and at the very least wished American ships to be allowed to pick up provisions, fuel, and water. Naturally we wished also to save our sailors from torture or death if their ships ran aground on the uncharted coasts of Japan. With both Northern and Southern support, a naval expedition was outfitted under the command of Commodore Matthew Perry, brother of the victor at Lake Erie in 1813. Perry's small squadron sailed for Japan in 1853 and during July boldly dropped anchor in Tokyo Harbor. The rattled Japanese tried to persuade Perry to leave for Nagasaki, but with mingled threats and promises the American stood his ground until he was sure that the Nipponese were sufficiently impressed. At that point Perry sailed for China after promising to return next year. While he was gone, the Japanese debated among themselves their future policy, and they finally decided to welcome Perry, lest he take exception to the lack of Tokyo hospitality by knocking down the city.

The Americans were received in a markedly more friendly manner upon their return in 1854, and after considerable banqueting—and immediate Japanese acceptance of Western whisky—the Treaty of Kanagawa was signed. The fanfare was more impressive than the treaty itself. No commercial articles were included, and only restricted watering and provisioning privileges were extended. At best, Japan had taken only a shaky first step toward world participation.

If the accomplishments of Matthew Perry have been a trifle overemphasized, those of Townsend Harris, the first American Consul General to Japan, have been somewhat overlooked. The Japanese wished no foreign diplomats in their nation, and they ostracized Harris. Yet his conciliatory attitude and painstaking efforts were rewarded with a real commercial treaty (1858), which opened additional ports to American trade and extended some semblance of extraterritoriality. In 1860 a Japanese mission was sent to the United States, arousing considerable curiosity, and Americans flocked to gape at the Oriental visitors. After the Civil War farsighted diplomats such as Robert Pruyn continued to improve relations between the two nations. Many Japanese students were sent to American universities, and Japanese industry began to look across the Pacific for instruction in manufacturing, which was so important a part of Japan's amazingly rapid westernization, one of the most important of the happenings of the nineteenth century.

Intervention in the Far East during the 1850s evinced a manifestation of American foreign policy that would return late in the century. There was a different American outlook on Asia than on Europe. Most Americans viewed with horror diplomatic involvement with Europe, but many were willing to play power politics in Asia, not only alone, but also in concert with the European powers that they feared so much. Despite the fact that Asiatic trade was much less than that with Europe, Americans acted vigorously beyond the Pacific but veered away from the other side of the Atlantic. Perhaps we were cognizant of greater potential danger from strong European countries, but had little fear of the weaker Asiatic nations. To be sure, American involvement in the Far East was spasmodic at this time, and never characterized by anything like full participation there, but the theme was at least partial intervention rather than isolation.

American foreign policy during the decisive decade of the 1850s was essentially an interesting sidelight to the great sectional struggle. While Americans were delighting in studied insults to European monarchies, welcoming the bedraggled refugees of 1848, discussing Canadian fisheries and American tariffs, watching with apprehension British moves in Central America, reading with either pleasure or rage the latest news about Cuba, or studying the strange mores of exotic Asiatic peoples, it was always with an eye toward the dominant internal problems. The sectional quarrel was about to go beyond words.

CHAPTER 29

The Clouds Gather

(1850-1854)

MID-CENTURY UNIFYING FORCES

The decade introduced by the Compromise of 1850 was to be one of the most portentous in American history. It opened on a clear note of hope that sectionalism had been sufficiently allayed so that it could no longer menace the national unity. It closed with the specter of fraternal strife at hand. During the ten years before Abraham Lincoln was elected President in 1860, forces seen only dimly during the earlier years began to assume enhanced significance. While Americans threw new miles of gleaming railroad track between cities, broke untouched acres with the plow, tinkered with labor-saving machinery in home workshops, furrowed the seas with graceful clipper ships, roamed across the grassy midlands in prairie schooners, proudly surveyed the green and white of new cotton fields, and engaged in myriad other activities typical of the flowering economy, two powerful and paradoxical currents were fast flowing. One was unifying; the other was divisive. On the one hand the United States was forging a stronger Union. On the other the nation was splitting along the Mason-Dixon line. Both tides ran simultaneously, and the continuation of the American

346

Union hung in the balance. By 1861 the divisive factors were to eke out a victory, although the battle had been fierce and the margin of the divisive over the unifying forces was slight. But it was enough.

An obvious question might be asked: how could the United States be welding a nation stronger than ever before during a decade that was to conclude with the secession of South Carolina and the lowering clouds of civil war? The answer appears to lie in the fact that the United States was becoming more national in transportation, communication, and business markets than ever before. The most important transportational development was the growth of the American railroad system. The 1850s witnessed a tremendous expansion. At the beginning of the decade there were only some 9,000 miles of track in use; ten years later 30,000 miles crisscrossed the nation. Consolidated systems (trunk lines) between the Atlantic seaboard and the Mississippi Valley drew the East and the Middle West together. Pushing ever westward, the railroad leaped the Mississippi in the 1850s and by 1860 had reached St. Joseph, Missouri, gateway to the Far West. While most construction was to the north of the slave states, the cotton kingdom was by no means overlooked. Considerable Southern expansion occurred, and the most significant link between Dixie and the Middle West was the Illinois Central Railroad, which thrust through Illinois, into Kentucky, and thence toward the Gulf.

Other fields of transportation were active in binding together isolated sections into more national unity. Coastal commerce boomed, and the oceanic steamship made steady if slow inroads into the hegemony of sailing craft. During the decade all Americans could thrill to the glorious clipper ships, pride of the merchant marine. The impressive inland steamboat traffic, several decades old by this time, was faced by railroad competition. Yet the 1850s noted a high-water mark of steamboat travel on the Mississippi and its tributaries. Despite canals and east-west railroads, mountains of Western produce continued to stream south to New Orleans. Transportation was better, faster, and cheaper than previously; and the United States was well under way toward the creation of a national system.

During the same years, equal progress was recorded in the field of communications. Telegraph wires spread across almost all the nation, and practically instantaneous communication between its far-flung sections became a reality. The Federal post office improved its services after the introduction of the postage stamp, and private express companies attained new efficiency. Communication in ideas became easier. With more adequate transportational facilities and constant technological innovations, newspaper readership increased, and such a paper as Horace Greeley's New York *Tribune* could exert its pervasive influence over 1,000 miles and become the political Bible of the Wisconsin farmer as well as the Connecticut husbandman. A Southern poet such as Edgar Allan Poe could be assured of an augmented Northern audience through the greater distributing efficiency of the great New York, Boston, and Philadelphia publishing houses. Between 1850 and 1860 such cultural fields as art, music, and drama became more national.

Localism declined and Americanization advanced in the arena of business enterprise. Restricted markets gave way to country-wide selling areas. Northern manufacturers found customers throughout the Middle West and even in the Gulf states. McCormick reapers, Seth Thomas clocks, and Colt revolvers were American household words rather than evidences of local pride in nearby industry. Some might ask at this point: did the development of a manufacturing North and to a lesser degree the West make inevitable a conflict with the agricultural South? In the main the answer would appear to be negative. Often the most healthful economies see a national dovetailing of industrial and agricultural areas; the former supplying manufactured goods in exchange for the raw materials of the latter. Furthermore, although it is true that industrialism was taking unprecedented strides in the North during the 1850s, the triumph it was to win after the Civil War was, at this time, premature. The clear-cut supremacy gained by the business philosophy that permeated most American institutions in the postwar years had not yet been achieved. Certainly the West and most of the North rivaled the South as bastions of an agricultural way of life. Economically there were many reasons why the North and the South should have been able to live together in mutual prosperity and amity. The basic attitudes of hatred that were to culminate in war were based largely on other grounds.

Works discussing the decade of the 1850s must describe at considerable length the divisive factors in the America of that time; thus perhaps the reader gains a false impression that disunion and civil war were absolutely inevitable. This philosophy was expressed by William H. Seward when he averred that there was an "irrepressible conflict" between the North and the South. Yet it should be emphasized strongly that civil war *might* have been avoided. What could have saved the day? Stronger leadership from the Pierce and Buchanan administrations? The organization of Southern unionist sentiment to equal secessionist pressures? Slightly more determined efforts at compromise? It is, of course, impossible to say, but perhaps little more than any one of these could have enabled the United

States to avoid one of the greatest calamities in its history. Although statistics are lacking, there seems every reason to believe that throughout the fateful decade leading to Fort Sumter a majority of Americans continued to love the Union and hate sectionalism.

After all, Americans above and below the Mason-Dixon line had a common sense of identification arising from experiences apart from the Old World. Both sections nurtured a like tradition that could be traced back before the Magna Charta abroad and to earliest colonial times on this side of the Atlantic. Education, religion, manners, and morals showed more similarities, North and South, than differences. Together the sections had fought three wars. Side by side, Northerner and Southerner had advanced to the West, fought the Indians and killed the animals, and brought to the savage wilderness the crude and raw but dynamic and thrilling process of Americanism. Although the sorry story of disunion must occupy the next pages, it should be remembered that it was a *nation* which was being rent asunder, not the clash of two hopelessly divided semiautonomous sections.

❨ *Unionist Victory: The Election of 1852.* As the thoughtful American surveyed the national scene during the two years that followed the Compromise of 1850, he might take heart that sectionalism had been allayed and that the worst of the crisis was over. As the months passed, both North and South appeared to have accepted the settlement; and this pleasant aspect was mirrored in national election results. President Millard Fillmore quietly served the remainder of his term and gracefully retired to the semioblivion from which destiny had called him. Both parties looked for new candidates in 1852.

The Democrats found exactly what they were looking for in Franklin Pierce of New Hampshire, a prominent "Doughface"—a Northerner with Southern principles. Pierce had made a slow, steady, dignified, and relatively unblemished trip up the political escalator, gaining additional notice from martial experience during the Mexican War. The Democratic platform included a straightforward pledge to complete acceptance of the Compromise of 1850.

The Whigs were in a less fortunate position. The fiery arguments of two years before had divided their ranks rather more than their adversary's; too many Southern Whigs could not forget that Northerners of their party had taken the lead in extreme hostility toward the South. Hence their platform, while supporting the Compromise, did so with greater equivocation than had the Democratic. Furthermore, they had more difficulty in finding a candidate acceptable to both sectional wings. Finally they agreed upon Winfield Scott, hopeful that his soldierly fame could win for them in 1852 as handily as military reputations had done in 1840 and 1848.

For all his ability, however, Scott was a little too pompous for the electorate, and his nickname of "Old Fuss and Feathers" was not likely to arouse the populace as had the more vigorous appellations of "Old Tip" and "Old Rough and Ready." During the campaign many Southern Whigs worked for Pierce, the Democrat, and the latter won an easy victory, carrying all but four states. This debacle was fateful for the Whig party; never again did it run a presidential candidate.

MID-CENTURY DIVISIVE FORCES

With a friendly administration heading comfortable congressional majorities, the Compromise appeared to face serene skies, but this apparent political tranquillity was essentially a surface phenomenon. The distant rumblings of sectionalism were getting louder, even while most Americans rejoiced that both Northern and Southern extremists had been put to flight. Actually, the Compromise carried within itself its own nemesis. So emotionally charged had been the debates that the slavery controversy had been brought forcibly before the nation, and it proved almost impossible to ignore. Many Northerners had perused the printed speeches of Salmon P. Chase and William H. Seward, finding themselves believing every word. Many Southerners had nodded assent to the rhetoric of Robert Toombs or John C. Calhoun when they accused the Free Soilers of waging deadly war against Southern institutions. The bitterness of the controversy had electrified the rather diffident nation into an awareness of a grave political and moral problem. Neutrality was becoming more difficult.

Even as early as 1852 portents ominous for the future might be discerned by pessimists. Political dissolution of the Union had been forecast by the schisms in the American churches. The great evangelical Protestant sects had divided on the moral issue of slavery; the Presbyterians in 1838, the Methodists in 1844, and the Baptists a year later. These denominational chasms that were sunk along the Mason-Dixon line tended to widen steadily. Additional sectional hatred was brewed by the publication in 1852 of one of the most influential novels ever written. Harriet Beecher Stowe had completed *Uncle Tom's Cabin* although, as she put it, "God wrote it." Characterized by a naïveté, bias, and saccharine sentimentality that would ensure few readers today, Mrs. Stowe found myriad contemporaries ready to laugh or cry over the tribulations of Little Eva, Topsy, or kindly old Uncle Tom, and equally prepared to experience a deep revulsion against the cruelties of the sadistic Simon Legree. *Uncle Tom's Cabin* sold by the hundreds of thousands both here and abroad. Another great audience was reached when the novel appeared in dramatic form; the Northerners flocked to local theaters to watch enthralled as Eliza fled across the ice with savage bloodhounds in pursuit. Many Northerners were profoundly impressed by this indictment of slavery; most Southerners turned from it in disgust to cry that it was a base slander of a gracious way of life that Mrs. Stowe could not or would not understand.

Even more threatening to national unity was the fact that many Northerners were refusing to obey the stipulations of the Fugitive Slave Act, the only real Southern victory in the Compromise of 1850. One of the most arbitrary pieces of legislation ever to pass an American Congress, the act was harsh enough to ensure opposition to enforcement. Under its rigorous provisions, Southerners were permitted to go anywhere in the country in search of escaped slaves. If the refugee were discovered, the owner could call upon law officers for assistance, and even bystanders could be pressed into service to aid in the chase. Obstruction to the recovery of a slave by his master was heavily punished by fine and imprisonment. There was little way in which the accused fugitive could legally protect himself from false charges, for his testimony could not be heard in court—the word of the ostensible owner was enough. True to its promise, the Federal government tried to enforce the legislation; and a torrent of opposition emanated from many Northern localities.

Soon the streets of Northern cities began to be the scenes of pitiful tableaux as a Negro who might have escaped from a Carolina plantation years before was hunted by improvised posses. Citizens of Schenectady or Boston who might have viewed slavery calmly as distasteful but nothing to get upset about felt a compelling hatred for the institution when a terrified fugitive might be dragged from a nearby alley. Sometimes violent opponents of slavery attacked Federal marshals while the latter were performing their duties and, wresting the fugitive from them, spirited him away to lasting freedom in Canada.

A notable instance of public disorder under a case emanating from enforcement of the Fugitive Slave Act occurred in Boston during May, 1854. A recently escaped slave named Anthony Burns was apprehended and detained in jail. A mob of abolitionist sympathizers tried to storm the prison to free Burns, but the attempt failed. So menacing was the temper of many Bostonians that Massachusetts state troops, a civilian posse, and detachments from both the United States Artillery and Marine Corps had to escort the fugitive along black-draped streets through a dense crowd of many thousands who booed and hissed as Burns was rowed to a waiting ship and returned to Virginian bondage. It was estimated that it cost the United States government approximately

$100,000 to return this single escaped slave. The publicity attending this arrest further widened the sectional gulf, and even more Northerners echoed the sentiments of the sage of Concord, Ralph Waldo Emerson, when he commented about the Fugitive Slave Act: "This filthy enactment was made in the nineteenth century, by people who could read and write. I will not obey it, by God!"

Northern resentment at this arbitrary legislation led to renewed activity of the Underground Railroad. This organization had been formed during the 1830s to aid the escape of slaves into the North. Traveling by night and hiding out by day, the fugitive would be escorted from the home of one abolitionist sympathizer to another until he was free from pursuit. Penalties for assisting an escapee had been drastically increased by the Fugitive Slave Act of 1850. Consequently, operation of the Underground Railroad became decidedly more dangerous, for now the slave would have to reach Canada before he could be secure. Yet dauntless men continued this work until well into the Civil War. Although Southern newspapers were full of furious editorials against the activity of this undercover organization, only a relatively tiny percentage of slaves ever escaped. According to the Federal census of 1860, a mere 803 of some 3,500,000 Southern slaves fled to freedom during that year. To the inflamed imagination of Dixie, however, it seemed that many thousands were being lost annually.

RAILROADS, POLITICS, AND SLAVERY

If moral agitation were running stronger during the early and middle 1850s, the sectional truce was shattered in 1854 more by economic than by ethical motives. The rupture came over railroad legislation rather than through any direct sectional action pertaining to slavery. From the very moment when California joined the Union, the vision of a transcontinental railroad began to be discussed in concrete rather than abstract terms. Naturally the question of the western route to be followed was sectionally important, since future political alliance with the Far West might depend on whether the railroad connected California with the North or the South. Geographically, four general routes were considered: the most northerly would extend from Minnesota through the Dakota country, Montana, and Oregon Territory to a terminus on Puget Sound; a second would strike west from Chicago through Iowa, Nebraska, Wyoming, and thence to San Francisco; a third would progress from St. Louis through Kansas and eventually to the Golden Gate; and the most southerly would proceed from Texas, through New Mexico and Arizona, and into Southern California, reaching the Pacific at or near Los Angeles.

Quite naturally the expansive energies of Southern politicians operated in behalf of the fourth route. The cotton states enjoyed a tremendous initial advantage because the Compromise of 1850 had given territorial status to all American land between Texas and California, while the area to the north was still unorganized. The last obstacle to the Southern route appeared to evaporate in 1853 when the Gadsden Purchase acquired from Mexico the land south of the Gila River, the natural avenue through the Southwest. Jefferson Davis of Mississippi, Secretary of War in Pierce's Cabinet, was especially prominent in preparing the way for the transcontinental railroad along the Gila.

❨ *Stephen A. Douglas.* Northerners watched the development of Southern railroad plans with small delight. Notably perturbed was the able, flamboyant, and aggressive Stephen A. Douglas, idol of the Illinois Democracy. Although a native Vermonter, Douglas moved to Illinois as a young man and soon identified himself with the turbulent egalitarianism of the frontier. He became a highly successful lawyer, more through his dynamic personality and oratorical ability than from arduously acquired legal knowledge. Politics was his lifeblood, and where his public career was concerned he seldom allowed moral niceties to restrain his action. Douglas was neither evil nor hypocritical; he was merely impervious to vague ethical considerations that seemed to him unimportant. Yet his belief in democracy was a living force. Elected to the Senate in 1846, Douglas was obviously a coming man. He was deeply involved in economic matters, rendering great service to his state when he engineered congressional approval of widespread land grants to the states for railroad construction. His own Illinois Central Railroad had proved a bonanza both for Douglas and for Illinois.

As head of the Senate Committee on Territories, the barrel-chested Douglas saw that he must block the Southern-sponsored railroad along the Gila if his home town of Chicago was to be the eastern terminus of the transcontinental artery. Yet the Southern route was all territorially organized, and the Northern route had no chance until the unincorporated tracts between Iowa and Utah became territories. Furthermore, the United States would have no land to grant to railroad entrepreneurs unless territorial governments were provided. Douglas resolved to rectify this condition, and his senatorial post gave him opportunity to do so.

THE KANSAS-NEBRASKA ACT

When the Senator from Illinois plotted his future course in the territorial question, he was assisted by local politics in Missouri. The venerable Thomas H. ("Bullion") Benton, former Jacksonian leader, was attempting to regain his seat in the Senate. Benton advocated territorial organization of the West, but insisted that the 36°30′ line of the Missouri Compromise be extended. Since Kansas and Nebraska lay north of this line, both would become free-soil areas. Benton's opponent, the proslavery David Atchison, agreed on the need for territorial government, but wished no restrictions to be placed upon slavery. Douglas disliked slavery, but he regarded that issue as morally unimportant in this instance, for he

steadfastly believed that climate and topography would create free soil on the Western plains. He accepted Atchison's thesis.

The essence of the Kansas-Nebraska bill that Douglas advocated was "popular," or "squatter," sovereignty, which stipulated that when the area had sufficient population to become a United States territory its people would decide among themselves by majority vote whether or not they wanted slavery. But Douglas was not content to stop here, and his final step was disastrous. He realized that the South must have some compensation before it would agree to territorial status for Kansas and Nebraska. The "Little Giant" therefore decided to add to his legislation a specific repeal of the Missouri Compromise and its 36°30′ boundary line between slave and free soil.

For many years most historians assumed that Douglas deliberately introduced the Missouri Compromise repeal in order to court Southern sympathy for his presidential aspirations. In addition it was thought that Southerners cooperated with Douglas in writing the bill. After all, the Kansas-Nebraska bill would allow the people of the territories to have slavery if they wished and potentially opened to Southern penetration lands that had been considered closed to slavery for a generation. Upon closer examination, however, these reasons do not appear to have been the primary motivations for the Kansas-Nebraska legislation. Douglas the railroad promoter and Northern Democratic politician seems predominant over Douglas the Southern conspirator and presidential hopeful. Popular sovereignty was a watchword among the unruly Democrats of the upper Middle West, and Douglas was iterating a doctrine long popular when he extended it to the Western plains. In addition, Douglas truly believed in the democratic viewpoint that the people of an area should solve for themselves problems that applied to their locality. Finally the "plot" theory of Douglas's advocacy of Kansas-Nebraska popular sovereignty is weakened by the fact that there is no evidence that Southerners worked with him in drawing up the Kansas-Nebraska

THE WESTERN UNITED STATES
AFTER PASSAGE OF
KANSAS-NEBRASKA ACT, 1854

||||||| Area north of 36°30′ line opened to slavery
by Kansas-Nebraska Act

••••••• 36°30′ line established between free and
slave territory by Compromise of 1820

——— Boundaries of Kansas-Nebraska territories

bill. Indeed, contemporary sources suggest that the bill came as a distinct surprise to Southern Congressmen. There was no *immediate* response from below the Mason-Dixon line. The Southern attitude initially appears to have been composed of hesitation, doubt, and equivocation until Northern attacks on the measure compelled the slavery advocates to pick up their cudgels in defense of the Kansas-Nebraska bill.

After all, thousands of intelligent Southerners recognized the obvious geographical truth that slavery was unlikely to thrive in prairie country, more suitable for wheat and corn than for cotton and sugar. These perspicacious

Southerners feared that their section was fighting a battle already lost and that their energies would be dissipated upon the rolling plains of the West—energies that might better be conserved for Caribbean and Mexican expansion into lands which by nature were well adapted to the intensive and semitropical cultivation that was natural for slavery. Half-heartedly and reluctantly the South straggled into position beside Douglas, although such support noticeably increased as Northern attacks upon the legislation grew more unrestrained. In the long run the Kansas-Nebraska bill was useless for the South.

Despite his stirring and abiding faith in the

democratic expression of popular will that is indigenous to popular sovereignty, Douglas made a tremendous miscalculation when he sponsored it. He underestimated the moral fervor that antislavery propaganda had generated. To Douglas the question of territorial organization was essentially political and economic; to thousands of his fellow Northerners this legislation was moral treason that filled them with consternation and horror. If the South slowly accepted Douglas's reasoning, a majority in the North quickly condemned it as a dastardly betrayal of Northern interests and a crass surrender to Southern aggression. Throughout the North and the West mass meetings convened, inflammatory petitions circulated, and vitriolic editorials were written. Even Douglas admitted that he could have traveled from "Boston to Chicago by the light of his burning effigies."

President Franklin Pierce was persuaded by the uneasy alliance of Northwestern Douglasites and Southerners that the Kansas-Nebraska bill would bring badly needed popularity and prestige to his administration, and the wavering President was converted. With the obstinacy that sometimes characterizes a weak individual once his mental sails are set, Pierce threw his full support behind the measure, by threats and pleadings compelling many reluctant Northern Democrats into line. Congress split sectionally rather than politically over the Kansas-Nebraska bill. Some Northern Democrats opposed this legislation, and Northern Whigs were against it almost to a man; both Southern Whigs and Democrats felt obliged to support it. The Kansas-Nebraska bill passed both houses of Congress after debates that featured startling partisanship.[1] This act was to furnish an abundance of trouble, and its effects revolutionized party politics, which in turn furthered rampant sectionalism.

[1] In one exchange between Senator Wade of Ohio and Senator Badger of North Carolina, the latter queried, "You mean that when I go to settle in Nebraska, I can't take my old black mammy with me?" "We haven't the slightest objection to your taking your old black mammy to Nebraska," Wade shot back, "What we object to is selling her when you get her there!"

POLITICS IN FERMENT

The Kansas-Nebraska Act hit with devastating impact the fragile political balance, toppled the relative equipoise between Whigs and Democrats, and in so doing almost immediately wrecked the former and eventually the latter. The tottering Whig organization, already suffering from its defeat in 1852, received a blow from which it could never recover. So intense had been the opposition of their Northern fellow Whigs to the Kansas-Nebraska Act that most Southerners reluctantly but inevitably gravitated into the Democratic ranks. The Democrats became in the main the spokesmen for the Southern plantocracy. In the North, however, all was confusion, and the political landscape was littered with party debris.

An epochal year in American political history was 1854, for perhaps never before or since have there been so many recognizable factions and parties. Mention has been made of the major parties and their internal factions. In addition, there were smaller political organizations. One was the Free Soil party, which had polled such an impressive total in 1848; although its votes had fallen off during the 1852 national referendum on the Compromise, it was still an important factor. Another party supported the principles of Neal Dow, reform Mayor of Portland, who brought to Maine the first state-wide prohibition of intoxicating beverages. The zealous prohibitionists were called "Maine Law men," and they attracted considerable support from Northern reformers, who seem to have held a balance of power in some states. Even more productive in the political record of 1854 was the emergence of two new national parties, the first only a temporary aberration, but the second destined to rule the nation for most of the next century.

❮ *The Native American Party.* The first organization was the Native American party, an excrescence somewhat akin to European fascism. Its basic philosophy was one of religious and especially racial intolerance. Many

Americans of the "old stock" were disquieted by the unprecedented numbers of foreigners who had migrated to the United States during the 1840s and 1850s. Chiefly Irish and Germans, these immigrants faced the usual antipathy from the older settlers. Discriminated against on all sides, the Irishman and the German faced serious problems. The lowest paid and dirtiest manual-labor jobs went to him, and landlords were reluctant to grant decent accommodations at reasonable rents. While many of the Germans headed for rural life, thousands of them stayed in Eastern or Middle Western cities, where they joined the mass of the Irish in teeming slums that were far worse than any in the United States today. The immigrant of the mid-century found only one practicable method of self-protection, and that lay in the power of his ballot. Party leaders in the cities were by no means averse to political support from the underprivileged, and urban machines traded rapid and easy naturalization for a vote at election time. Many Americans watched the rise of the urban political machines and blamed the immigrant.

Superimposed upon the economic and political hostility toward these new Americans was a wave of anti-Catholicism. Almost all the Irish and many of the Germans were Catholics, and the predominantly Protestant America of that time reacted against the supposed menace from Rome. Lies widely believed maintained that every Catholic church had an arsenal in the basement and that the "Papists" awaited only a sign from the Vatican to conquer the United States. The ugly intolerance was channeled into political activity by the formation of the Native American party in the early 1850s. Its popular appellation was Know-Nothing, since a member was supposed to answer in that way if asked about the party. A secret organization somewhat along the line of the later Ku Klux Klan, the Native American party maintained an elaborate oath and a complicated ritual. Officially anti-immigrant and anti-Catholic, the Know-Nothings pledged to vote for no "foreigner" or Catholic. Cynical politicians anticipated that this suppuration would be permanent, and Native

American organizations rapidly arose all over the Union. Their success in 1854 was startling, and much of the Northeast went Native American. Fortunately the party proved unable to cope with the rising sectionalism that was tearing to pieces more admirable political organizations. If it went "up like a rocket" in 1854, it was "down like a stick" in 1855, when a more fair-minded and tolerant attitude took over. Yet the party continued for a few more years and carried the state of Maryland for ex-President Millard Fillmore in the election of 1856.

❨ *The Republican Party.*   When Free Soilers, Maine Law men, and Native Americans were added to the factions battling for control inside the Whig and Democratic camps, politics above the Mason-Dixon line were in a fine state of confusion. It was natural that some attempt to bind together these discordant elements should be made. Most members of the smaller parties and many in the major organizations found that they had one thing in common—they were against the Kansas-Nebraska Act and its possible extension of slavery into the territories. Spontaneous meetings were held throughout the free states during 1854 in efforts to channel differing opinion into political action. Assemblies at Ripon, Wisconsin, and Jackson, Michigan, were among the first to convene, and at the latter meeting the old Jeffersonian term "Republican" was used. Late in the year the new party was well under way —converts were streaming in to join. Nevertheless, the new organization was admittedly sectional and could hope for no Southern support.

The Republicans did not err in stating a violently antislavery thesis, for they had other weapons in their arsenal. Advocacy of a higher tariff wooed the manufacturers. The Western farmer harkened to Republican promises of a Homestead Act that would open the governmental lands to settlers and offer free farms to the homesteader. Proponents of internal improvements listened eagerly to party pledges for a new rivers and harbors bill and for the rapid construction of a transcontinental railroad. When these practical planks were added to the moral fervor generated on the issue of slavery extension, an impressive combination of Republican crusading enthusiasm and rugged common sense gave bright promise of future political success.

Americans of the 1850s were politics-ridden; more so than ever before or since. While the generalizations "Whig," "Democrat," "Native American," and "Republican" must be used, it should be realized that these supposedly cohesive organizations were closer to temporary combinations of independent state machines during Federal elections rather than truly national parties. Politics was the great American sport. Not only were national elections held every two years, but state and local elections were going on almost continually. Indeed, only the mid-summer and mid-winter months were free from political imbroglios. In addition to the many national organizations, each of the states had two, three, or even more recognized political factions. With so many parties, politicians, and elections, the American people were kept in a constant state of political frenzy, and their emotions never had time to cool. When the politicians found themselves in difficulty they could always seek escape in arrant sectionalism. Both Northern and Southern politicos reveled in sensational charges against the other section and granted little opportunity for judicious reasoning or attitudes of compromise. The emotionalism whipped up during elections played no small part in the formulation of uncompromising attitudes that made sectional settlement even more difficult.

CHAPTER 30

Approaching Dissolution

(1854-1860)

THE KANSAS CIVIL WAR

While politicians were inflaming Northerners and Southerners, even more divisive action was taking place on the grassy hills and flat plains of the West. During 1854–1855 civil war broke out in Kansas. The principle behind Douglas's Kansas-Nebraska Act was popular, or squatter, sovereignty, by which the will of its inhabitants, as decided by democratic action, would determine the status of slavery in the territory. Therefore it became a matter of essential importance which section actually peopled Kansas and Nebraska. Even more vital than any sectional aspect was the inevitable surge of the American westward movement. Settlers were ready to enter the disputed area, and on both sides land hunger was a sharper motivating agency for intrusion than any philosophical pangs emanating from the slavery question.

Yet if sectionalism was not the key to "why" Kansas and Nebraska were settled, it was important in deciding "how." Concerning Nebraska there was little dispute; it was tacitly assumed that Free Soil Iowans would win out. But Kansas, lying due west of the slave state of Missouri, was another matter. Missourians, hemmed in by free soil to the north and east, feared that their institution could not continue

to exist if antislavery men closed in on the third side. Yet many Northerners were adamant that slavery must be continued to its present bounds. Therefore, into unhappy Kansas came both sides spoiling for a fight, each determined to "save" the territory from the other.

Proslavery Missourians pushed into the abutting area in eastern Kansas, while others who stayed home tried to interfere with Northern migrants along the Missouri River. Additional thousands from that slave state would trek into Kansas on election days to cast quick ballots before going home. Even with distance operating against them, the Free Soilers waged a manful fight that eventually succeeded. New Englanders formed armed bands, financed by the abolitionist Emigrant Aid Society, and joined Middle Westerners attracted by the lure of inexpensive land. Carrying "Beecher's Bibles," [1] the antislavery men tilled their farms on watch for Missouri "border ruffians."

Outright warfare on the Western prairies

---

[1] Beecher's Bibles were rifles sent to Kansas in packing cases stamped "Bibles." They were named after the eminent abolitionist minister in Brooklyn, Henry Ward Beecher, who gained considerable notoriety through his feat, in somewhat dubious taste, of dramatizing the evils of slavery by the auction of a beautiful mulatto girl from his pulpit.

356

UNORGANIZED TERRITORY

MINNESOTA TERRITORY

WISCONSIN

MICHIGAN

L. Michigan

Jackson

NEBRASKA TERRITORY

I O W A

Chicago

Omaha Council Bluffs

Platte R. Ft. Kearny

Mississippi R.

St. Joseph

ILLINOIS

INDIANA

KANSAS

Kansas City Westport Lawrence

Topeka Lecompton Lawrence

Kansas R.

Arkansas R.

Independence

St. Louis

Pottawatomie Creek

Osage R.

M I S S O U R I

KENTUCKY

Ohio R.

TERRITORY

**MISSOURI-KANSAS AREA,
1854-1855**

|||||||| Slave territory

Kansas-Nebraska territories
open to slavery, 1854

T E N N E S S E E

A R K A N S A S

Arkansas R.

Mississippi R.

Tennessee R.

MISSISSIPPI

ALABAMA

was not long delayed. Isolated murders were committed throughout eastern Kansas, and on one occasion a mob of Missourians sacked Lawrence, the Free Soil stronghold. An individual who was to play a spectacular role in American history first achieved prominence in Kansas during 1855. An ardent abolitionist named John Brown, aided by his sons, perpetrated a massacre on Pottawatomie Creek when five proslavery settlers were hauled out of bed and butchered with sabers. Driven underground for a time, John Brown would emerge four years later at Harpers Ferry, Virginia.

These disorders were only a few of the many arising from the Kansas-Nebraska Act, and they filled the Pierce administration with dismay. As usual, the President vacillated between the undeniable fact that Free Soilers

were peopling Kansas and his natural predilection toward the South. Faced with this dilemma, rather than take any arbitrary action, Pierce was content to drift and to appoint new governors to the territory. Only after many months of continuing disorders did the President dispatch Federal troops to strife-torn Kansas. While army bayonets enforced a temporary quiescence, national attention turned to politics, for in that arena the eventual fate of Kansas might be decided.

THE ELECTION OF 1856

The climate of election year was made more torrid by as sorry an example of vicious partisanship as ever disgraced the American Congress. In 1854 Massachusetts had sent to the

Senate the handsome, intelligent, arrogant, humorless, and abolition-tainted Charles Sumner, epitome of the best and the worst of the Boston "Brahmin" aristocracy. In one of the most acidulous speeches in the national annals, Sumner addressed the Senate on the subject of "The Crime in Kansas," during which he gratuitously insulted the venerable if somewhat senile Pierce Butler, senior Senator from South Carolina. A young relative of Butler named Preston Brooks was a Representative from the Palmetto State, and he decided to avenge his kinsman. The next day while Sumner was busy at his desk on the floor of the Senate, Brooks strode up to him and proceeded to belabor Sumner over the head with a cane until the weapon was shivered by the force of the blows. Sumner was driven to the floor, his head badly lacerated, and his back severely wrenched. Some Southern Senators watched the attack without interfering. Assailed in the Northern press as "Bully" Brooks, the South Carolinian resigned from the House, returned home, and was triumphantly reelected while cotton-state admirers sent him scores of new canes.

Under such conditions of animosity the national conventions gathered. The high-spirited Republicans were snowballing in strength and viewed themselves as the party of the future. A platform was adopted that roundly castigated "those twin relics of barbarism, polygamy and slavery."[2] The convention soon nominated John Charles Frémont, "Pathfinder of the West," who had been one of the multiconquerors of California. The fading Know-Nothings selected ex-President Millard Fillmore as their candidate. The Democrats were still the majority party, although sadly riven by Northern and Southern extremists. Both wings managed to combine behind James Buchanan, longtime Pennsylvania political wheelhorse, who had fortunately been absent as Minister to Great Britain during the Kansas controversy and who, unlike most politicians of the time, had kept his mouth shut.

[2] Polygamy referred to the Latter-day Saint policy of multiple marriages, which was highly unpopular with more orthodox Americans of that day.

The election was close; Frémont and his beautiful wife, Jessie Benton Frémont, daughter of old "Bullion," waged a strong campaign. The smashing Republican September triumph in Maine cast a shadow of terror over the Democratic ranks. The decisive battle was in Pennsylvania, and by flooding that state with money the Democrats managed to win. Their campaign against the sectionalism of the Republicans had persuaded a majority of the nation that the election of Frémont would mean an automatic dissolution of the Union. Although beaten, the dynamic Republicans had come close to success after an existence of only two years, and they could view the future with boundless optimism.

THE BUCHANAN ADMINISTRATION

Most Americans were glad to see the end of the craven Pierce administration, and they welcomed the new President. James Buchanan was in his middle sixties, a bachelor, and a prosperous gentleman farmer from fertile Lancaster County in southern Pennsylvania. He was tall, rather heavy-set, and reasonably prepossessing in appearance. His political record was as full in length and variety of service as it was unspectacular in actual accomplishment. Buchanan had been, at various times, Representative and Senator from Pennsylvania, Minister to Russia and Great Britain, and Secretary of State. Despite his political successes, the President was full of self-doubt and hid his anxieties behind an austere and formal outward front. In normal times he might have enjoyed a minor triumph as President, for he was an indefatigable worker, but the political tornadoes that buffeted him shattered his spirit. He had the same unfortunate weakness and indecision that characterized Franklin Pierce, and when impaled on a dilemma Buchanan would find refuge in sullen personal vindictiveness. Again, similar to Pierce, "Old Buck" was subservient to pressure from the Deep South, and the leaders of his Cabinet were Southern members Howell Cobb of Georgia, John B.

Floyd of Virginia, and Jacob Thompson of Mississippi.

❡ *The Dred Scott Case.*   Two days after Buchanan had been inaugurated, the country was aroused by the Supreme Court's decision in the case of *Dred Scott v. Sanford.* The old Jacksonian enthusiast Roger B. Taney presided over a Court that was decidedly Southern and Democratic in sympathy; only two Justices could be deemed to hold Republican opinions toward slavery. The facts in the case were clear enough. A slave named Dred Scott had been taken by his master, an army officer, from slave soil in Missouri to Illinois and later to Minnesota Territory. After his master's death Scott was returned to bondage in Missouri. Some abolitionists saw a test case in the episode and sued in his name, maintaining that residence on free land had made Scott a free man. After some time the case finally reached the Supreme Court.

With Buchanan's acquiescence, Chief Justice Taney resolved to go beyond the instance of the slave Dred Scott to decide the question of slavery in the territories once and for all. He knew that the two Northern dissenters on the bench, Justices Curtis and McLean, planned to write their opinions on the subject, and the Chief Justice wanted to beat them to the punch. In a quavering voice so faint as to be almost inaudible to the silent crowd jammed into the tiny Supreme Court chambers, Taney read his far-reaching decision. He made short work of the case at hand. *Dred Scott v. Sanford* would not be heard at all since Scott was a slave—an item of property—and not a citizen. Only a citizen was permitted to bring a case before the national judiciary. Not content to restrict himself to this simple declaration, Taney plunged ahead to clarify his stand on the legal status of slavery in the territories by announcing what he would have decided if he had allowed the case to come before the Court. The Chief Justice maintained that any citizen of the United States had a right to take his property into any Federal territories. Congress could say nothing against any particular type of property, and therefore the congressional ban against slavery north of the 36°30′ line of the Compromise of 1820 was contrary to the Constitution and hence was null and void. Six other Justices read opinions that were at least not contrary to Taney's arguments, although Curtis and McLean filed the vigorous dissents expected of them. The Dred Scott decision upheld completely the ultra-Southern opinion on slavery in the territories.

While many in the South celebrated the pronouncement of Taney and averred that the issue was now permanently settled, a considerable group of Northerners agreed with Horace Greeley when he wrote in the *Tribune* that the Court's decision was worth no more than "any pro-slavery stump speech" and that the verdict must not be allowed to stand. Actually there was much truth in the Republican opposition. Taney was on very shaky legal grounds when he denied national citizenship to freed slaves despite the fact that they had been permitted to become citizens of several states. When Taney declared outlaw congressional controls in the national territories over slavery, which had been utilized for a half century, it was an assertion of judicial power so sweeping that it might have made a John Marshall gasp. The reputation of Roger B. Taney has been unfortunately blackened through his close association with the Dred Scott case. His earlier services in Jackson's Cabinet as well as his decision while Chief Justice in *Charles River Bridge v. Warren Bridge*, which denied special privilege, have been largely forgotten because of his partisanship during the final days of his great career.

❡ *The Douglas-Buchanan Split.*   While the echoes of the constitutional crisis still reverberated, Buchanan was forced to look west toward Kansas, where, if disorders there were only sporadic, the uneasy truce was near the breaking point. President Pierce had appointed several governors to Kansas during the Kansas civil war, but they had proved unequal to the task. Buchanan managed to persuade Robert J. Walker of Mississippi, ardent expansionist, Secretary of the Treasury under Polk, and author of the 1846 tariff measure that bears his name, to accept the difficult task of administering "Bleeding Kansas." Despite his Southern antecedents, which might have impelled him toward partisanship, Walker made a brilliant record. When dishonest means were used to disfranchise many Free Soil voters, Walker refused to tolerate the trickery, and he was abruptly recalled by Buchanan. To the antislavery forces in the North it appeared that the President was determined to make Kansas slave territory, despite the obvious fact that the Free Soil population was larger. In fact, by 1857 Kansas had all the population requirements for statehood. But whether free or slave was still to be determined.

Northern suspicion of the President became a certainty when the administration threw its support behind the notorious Lecompton Constitution. Written in the Kansas town of Lecompton, this constitution was a major fraud. It legalized slavery in the territory, but allowed a vote to be taken on whether slavery should be contained at its present status or opened for additional numbers of bondsmen. Fully aware that whichever way they voted, slavery could not lose, the Free-Soil advocates stayed away from the polls by the thousands, and the proslave minority voted in the Lecompton Constitution. The Southern-influenced Buchanan administration accepted this constitution as the basis on which Kansas was to become a state and, despite its fraudulent aspects, made its support an administration measure.

Watching these machinations darkly from the side lines was Stephen A. Douglas, author of the Kansas-Nebraska Act. Whatever his political manipulations, Douglas was eminently sincere in his support of the theory of popular sovereignty. He could not gainsay the fact that the Lecompton Constitution was a glaring violation of that doctrine. Douglas could restrain himself no longer. Snapping "By God, sir, I made Mr. James Buchanan, and by God, sir, I will unmake him," he openly broke with the administration and traversed the nation, bitterly attacking the President's Kansas policy. The vengeful Buchanan promptly struck back, hoping to ruin Douglas by withdrawing Federal patronage from him and by firing his sup-

porters wholesale from government jobs. The Illinois Democracy stayed loyal to its leader, however. The effects of the Douglas-Buchanan split were widespread, and it forecast the deep chasm that would divide Northern and Southern Democrats in 1860, for when the "Little Giant" denounced the ultra-Southern view, thousands from the slave states vowed that they would never accept him as President. Meanwhile Kansas was forced to struggle along under its territorial government until it was able to enter the Union as a free state in 1861.

❨ *The Depression of 1857.* While tempers raged high over the Kansas controversy, sectional relations were affected by an extremely severe depression that fell upon the national economy during 1857. The underlying cause was, as usual, overspeculation. If the depression of 1837 had been fueled by wild gambling on land and internal improvements, the economic calamity of two decades later seems to have been brought on largely by speculation in railroads. So important was a railroad that a municipality or a state would do almost anything to facilitate its construction. Fraudulent stock issues were tolerated, land was given away, and little or no taxation was promised. A rash of new lines was built, while existing short lines were being amalgamated into new combinations. Oceans of additional railroad securities inundated the markets, and a naïve optimism shoved prices ever higher. When panic psychology took over, most of the railroads went into receivership, those of real value as well as the more visionary.

The depression had other causes. The termination of the Crimean War on the Continent lessened the demand for American foodstuffs abroad, and soon Russian and Central European grain was again in vigorous competition with American wheat in the world markets; prices rapidly collapsed. General overoptimism in business was followed by equally unreasonable pessimism. Major financial houses toppled, and credit rigorously contracted. Hard times across the Atlantic made it difficult for Europeans to hold onto their American securities. While recovery was much faster than in most other major depressions, the panic and crash of 1857 severely jolted Northern economy as factories closed and long lines of unemployed formed outside agencies of private charity.

To the delight of the advocates of slavery, the South largely escaped the economic debacle. Naturally there was some hardship, but cotton prices stayed firm, which to the Southerner seemed additional proof that his way of life was superior to that of the North. This conclusion was incorrect, but nevertheless it was widely believed at the time; and Southern independence received new support from those who proclaimed that their only economic hardships were due to subservience to Northern industrialism, which had proven itself ruinous. A like hardening of attitude became evident among some, but by no means all, Northern businessmen. While the commercial interests tended to retain a conciliatory attitude toward Dixie in fear of a loss of Southern markets, many manufacturers concluded that the low-tariff policy had wrecked their economy and they must no longer allow Southerners to control the government. This opinion was probably as incorrect as the Southern, but a slow drift of former conservatives to the Republican ranks picked up speed.

THE LINCOLN-DOUGLAS DEBATES

The increased power of the sectional Republican party was shown in the mid-term elections of 1858. In general the Republicans were triumphant, and many a Democratic stronghold in the free states fell to their determined assault. The new party could jubilantly mark four years of steady and unprecedented political progress. Many of the disheartened Northern Democrats began to wonder if their continued alliance to the ultraslavery supporters was not proving to be political suicide.

One of the few Republican defeats of 1858 took place in Illinois, but there the Democratic victory was pyrrhic. Stephen A. Douglas was up for reelection in that year. Although both

ardent Southerner and the sullen Buchanan looked upon him with hatred, Douglas' strong fight for popular sovereignty had further endeared him to the Illinois Democracy. Yet the Republicans found a powerful candidate in the Springfield lawyer Abraham Lincoln, who had served a term as Whig Congressman. It is difficult to imagine two more evenly matched opponents. Douglas was a true spellbinder with an instinctive flair for dramatic timing in his oratory. Although Lincoln lacked some of the incandescent qualities of the "Little Giant," the former's homely charm, seriousness, and intelligence made him a worthy antagonist.

Lincoln and Douglas agreed to meet in a series of debates held throughout Illinois during the summer and fall of 1858. Tremendous excitement attended these orations, not only in the Middle West, but throughout the nation, for most of the great Eastern papers had correspondents on hand. Douglas hammered away at the theme that the Republicans were sectional extremists, while Lincoln tried to make clear the distinction between those like himself who wished to restrict slavery to its present confines and those ultraabolitionists who wished to exterminate it everywhere. During their debate at Freeport, Lincoln asked Douglas a loaded question. How, he inquired, can the people of a territory, using the doctrine of popular sovereignty, outlaw slavery when the Supreme Court had decreed in the Dred Scott case that as property slaves could be taken into any territory of the United States?

Douglas was placed on a dreadful spot. If he denounced Taney's decision and declared that the Court was wrong, conservatives, particularly in the South, would have nothing to do with him. Yet he could not deny popular sovereignty and hope to retain the support of the Middle Western Democrats. His final answer was masterful. He asserted that Taney's decision was actually of no importance, since the people of a territory, if opposed to slavery, could make that institution impossible by the simple feat of refusing to pass local ordinances protecting slavery. The Illinois Democracy was satisfied with this answer, and in an extremely close contest the Douglas men won a majority in the state legislature and returned their hero to the Senate. Yet Southerners saw in Douglas's equivocation a real menace to their property, and determination to oppose his candidacy in 1860 was solidified. Abraham Lincoln, although defeated, had won national attention through his strong fight against so impressive an opponent.

JOHN BROWN'S RAID

By 1859 the Union-loving American could tally the dreary score of sectional rancour and see that the existence of the American nation was in gravest peril. Obstruction to the Fugitive Slave Act, continued operation of the Underground Railroad to Canada, the publication of *Uncle Tom's Cabin*, the Kansas-Nebraska legislation, the Brooks-Sumner imbroglio, civil war in Kansas, the rise of a great Northern sectional party, the Dred Scott decision, the Lecompton fraud, sectional depression, and the awkward position of Northern Democrats as personified by Stephen A. Douglas were milestones along the road to Fort Sumter. Yet the greatest single item of cleavage was still to come.

John Brown had returned to the East after his massacres in Kansas to further his grandiose plans for eradicating slavery forever. He met with abolitionist leaders in Boston and New York to receive financial assistance, although fortunately for them his benefactors did not enquire too closely about how the funds were to be used. John Brown's plans were arranged; he would start a slave insurrection in Virginia and fan its flames throughout the South. Brown was a true fanatic; if not actually insane, at least he had pronounced psychopathic tendencies. He had a logic-tight fixation on the slavery question and would not be restrained from striking against it, for he believed he was following God's orders. More specifically, Brown would travel to Harpers Ferry, seize the city, call upon the slaves from the surrounding countryside to join him, arm them, and then lead his constantly augmenting Negro armies

throughout the cotton states. His plot was hopelessly visionary, and no man with full mental powers would have attempted it.

When all was set, Brown and a handful of white followers, among them his three sons, descended from the hills upon the Virginia railroad city. The "conquest" of Harpers Ferry was easy after some fighting and the death of several defenders, but the slaves remained inert to an appeal to revolt. Retreating to a railroad roundhouse, Brown grimly awaited the inevitable. Virginia militia and United States troops (under Colonel Robert E. Lee) were rushed to the city, and following a brief but sharp engagement Brown was wounded and forced to surrender. He was rapidly arraigned, tried, convicted, and hanged for treason to the state of Virginia.

The Southern reaction to John Brown's raid was instantaneous and practically unanimous. Every fear of slave insurrection that had haunted Southern dreams for thirty years had been vindicated. In the mind of the typical Southerner, radical abolition and its political wing of Republicanism were obviously responsible for the outrage. The planter and his minions looked upon John Brown as the insane tool of the higher-law philosophy of a William H. Seward [3] or the unrelenting and fanatical hostility of a William Lloyd Garrison. Thousands below the Mason-Dixon line alleged that John Brown had shown that their very lives would be in danger if the Republicans ever took over the national administration.

Whatever their political convictions, most Northerners at first looked with abhorrence upon Brown's murders. Quickly the Republicans denied any complicity in the actions of the fanatic. Yet a noisy minority of extreme abolitionists hailed Brown as a modern saint, and no less a personage than Ralph Waldo Emerson claimed that by his death in such a cause, Brown had made the gallows as glorious as the cross. Southerners were aghast when they read such sentiments approving slave re-

[3] Seward had referred to a "higher law" than the Constitution, holding slavery to be wrong. The statement may have cost him the presidential nomination in 1860.

bellion and murder. Many Northerners who were originally appalled by Brown's savagery began to modify their opinions when they saw the frenzied reaction from the South and the vengeful attitude of Virginia in bringing about Brown's execution so rapidly.

THE CLEAVAGE WIDENS

The 1859–1860 session of Congress was disgraced by an almost complete breakdown of the national legislative machinery, so bitter were the sectional hatreds. A book was an instigating factor. In 1857 a North Carolinian named Hinton R. Helper, speaking for the Southern poor white, wrote an economic tract called *The Impending Crisis of the South, and How to Meet It*. By juggling statistics as he wished, Helper pointed straight to slavery as the focal point of his section's economic grievances and called for the South to rid herself of the institution that was ruining half the nation. Naturally the planters were apoplectic with rage at Helper; and when the Republican party circulated excerpts from *The Impending Crisis* during 1859, this fury was directed at the Republicans, and Southern determination to oppose men from that party was heightened. In the scowling brows, snarling retorts, and hate-filled eyes of American Congressmen, the sorry state of the Union could be read.

By election year, 1860, the dreary march of events toward secession and civil war was approaching a climax. Crisis after crisis had inflamed sectional passions. Despite the continued progress in forging a more national transportation system and business economy, and despite the development of an American literature and drama, the divisive forces in mid-century society were approaching their temporary victory. Love of the Union was concentrated more in the North than in the South, but even in the former section many people were restive. Some Northerners were alienated by the Buchanan administration's cowering before Southern pressure, the refusal of the President to sign a homestead bill bestowing free land on actual settlers, or the Executive unwillingness to pour Federal resources into internal improvements. Others were distressed by the low-tariff program, which, they felt, ruined Northern manufacturers. Greater than any other single factor in making the North implacable toward compromise was the adamant determination of Free Soil men that slavery must be contained to its present boundaries. They concluded that until the Republican party headed the national government there was constant peril that slave territory might suddenly spread into Mexico, Central America, or the Caribbean. Perhaps unforeseen slavery expansion into the West might rivet that institution forever on the North American continent. Yet the Northerner had no reason to break the national ties. Annually his section pulled away both in numerical superiority and in material strength. Time was on his side, and if he held unflinchingly, eventual victory was inevitable.

To the determined Southerner no such pleasant future was discernible. The Dixie sectionalist felt that his very way of life was threatened. It seemed to him that a crass and money-mad North was determined to ruin him economically through high tariffs and exorbitant charges for transportation, credit, and services; to tear down the barriers between the races; and to abandon his women and children to slave rape and murder. All these dire forebodings might come to pass if the Federal government were administered by an "abolitionist." The Southern "fire-eater" had been emotionally whipped into such a state that he was unwilling to attempt to differentiate between an Abraham Lincoln, who hated slavery and was firm in his opposition to its extension, but who was equally adamant that there was no right to interfere with the domestic institutions of a state, and on the other hand, a John Brown, who was perfectly willing to soak the South in blood if he could eradicate the institution that he detested. To the Southerner all who were not wholeheartedly with him must be hateful enemies.

To be sure, there was a large minority in the South and an even larger group in the North who hurled maledictions at their own sectional extremists and labored mightily for harmony and accord until the outbreak of war, and some even after hostilities had commenced. But, as so often happens, the relatively unimpassioned majority could be led or driven, outmaneuvered, and defeated by organized and more ardent minorities. By 1860 the Southern fanatics were shouting that they would never accept an antislavery Northerner as President, be he Democrat or Republican, and that they would shatter the Union before bowing to such a fate. The skeins of the national fabric were strained to the breaking point.

CHAPTER 31

The Union Cracks

(1860-1861)

THE ELECTION OF 1860

The American people anticipated with suspenseful excitement the election of 1860, for it would obviously be pivotal. The sectional Republican party was only six years old, but it had grown into a political giant, merging some of its original emancipation fervor into a more practical program. The Democrats were still the largest national party, but the abrasions of the past few years had torn its fibers internally, and it was near dismemberment. A surprisingly large number of Americans, chiefly old time Whigs and Know-Nothings, wandered in the political wilderness apart from both major parties. Growls of defiance constantly welled from the cotton states, and a steady rataplan of threats promised that immediate secession would follow a "Black Republican" sectional victory. Yet Northerners had listened to the "wolf cry" of secession so long that many assumed it was mere psychological warfare.

National attention turned toward Charleston, South Carolina, for it was in this seething core of disunionism and Southern rights that the Democratic convention met during April, 1860. Northern Democrats were almost solidly for Stephen A. Douglas, and they formed a

majority among the delegates. A majority was insufficient, however, for until 1936 a Democratic candidate needed two-thirds support before he could be nominated. Southern extremists under the able leadership of William L. Yancey of Alabama would not accept Douglas and his "pernicious" doctrine of popular sovereignty. After several days of continuous wrangling, some delegations from the slave states walked out, forcing the convention to disband since an insufficient number remained to select a candidate or to write a platform. A few weeks later Northern delegates met at Baltimore and nominated Douglas on a platform of acceptance of the Supreme Court's stand on slavery. Southern Democrats met at Richmond, nominated John C. Breckinridge of Kentucky, and called for Federal protection of slavery in the territories. The one truly national political organization in the United States had split wide open, and frantic attempts to heal the lesion failed.

Shortly after the Democrats had disbanded at Charleston, the Republicans met in Chicago; naturally the news from South Carolina was an elixir to their spirits. The Republican conclave was destined to become one of the most exciting in political history. Although the

365

THE ELECTION OF 1860

( )   Electoral vote
————   Lincoln-Republican (180)
⣿⣿⣿   Douglas-Northern Democratic (12)
|||||||| Breckinridge-Southern Democratic (72)
/////   Bell-Constitution-Union (39)
▭   Territories not voting

Republicans could count on no support from the slave states, they sniffed victory in the air, and their nomination was a coveted prize. Certainly there was no dearth of candidates. Prominent aspirants were the antislavery champions William H. Seward of New York and Salmon P. Chase of Ohio. The venal and shady Simon Cameron had the weighty Pennsylvania delegation behind him. More conservative support went to a border-state politician, Edward Bates of Missouri. Most of the raucous Western element lined up behind Abraham Lincoln of Illinois. It was soon evident that the main battle was to be between Seward and Lincoln. The urbane New Yorker had a greater national reputation and considerably more political experience than did the Springfield lawyer, but his advocacy of the extreme antislavery position and his use of such unfortunate phrases as "the irrepressible conflict" and "a higher law" chilled conservative support and created a notable handicap. Lincoln had earned country-wide recognition through his debates with Douglas in 1858, and even more accolades by a successful speech at the Cooper Union in New York during the following year.

Even with his Western support, reflected in the clamorous enthusiasm of the galleries at the Chicago "Wigwam" where the convention was held, Lincoln still might have lost if his campaign managers, sometimes without his knowledge, had not made deal after deal with the supporters of other hopefuls. Their wire-pulling was enough to make Lincoln the Republican standard-bearer. Perhaps it is illustrative of the above point that Seward, Chase, Cameron, and Bates all joined Lincoln's Cabinet. The Republican platform was masterful. After reaffirming its faith in the Declaration of Independence, attacking "disunionism," and iterating eternal opposition to the spread of slavery into new territories, the platform pledged no interference "in the domestic institution [slavery]" of a state. More pragmatic demands called for a transcontinental railroad, a Homestead Act, and higher protective tariffs.

With a sectional Republican party and two sectional factions in the Democratic camp, Union-loving conservatives, especially in the border slave states, had to look elsewhere. This vacuum had been filled by a new organization called the Constitutional Union party, composed in the main of both Northern and Southern Whigs and Know-Nothings. Standing on "the Constitution of the Country, the Union of the States, and the enforcement of the laws," the Constitutional Unionists nominated John C. Bell of Tennessee. Thus four candidates appealed to the electorate in 1860: Lincoln for the Republicans, Douglas for the Northern Democrats, Breckinridge for the Southern Democrats, and Bell for the Constitutional Unionists.

The contest was hot with acrimony and bitterness. Republican partisans formed marching societies called "Lincoln Wide-awakes" and held parades in the Northern cities. Southerners countered with "Breckinridge Minute Men." The contest settled down to a struggle in the North between Lincoln and Douglas and in the South between Breckinridge and Bell. Douglas flailed away at the main Republican weakness, that the victory of Lincoln would dissolve the Union. The Northern Democrat toiled effectively and diligently, but he could never catch Lincoln. The South was aflame with Bell and Breckinridge rallies, the former stressing conservative love of the Union and the latter propounding sentiments of Southern nationalism.

With tension almost unbearable, the November results rolled in. Abraham Lincoln had won a sweeping electoral victory, 180 to 72 for Breckinridge, 39 for Bell, and only 12 for Douglas (all 9 from Missouri and 3 of New Jersey's 7). A breakdown of the popular votes shows quite a different story, however, and furnishes some evidence as to public opinion on the eve of war.

	Free states	Slave states *	Total
Lincoln	1,840,022	26,430	1,866,452
Douglas	1,212,432	164,525	1,376,957
Breckinridge	279,728	570,053	849,781
Bell	72,905	515,974	588,879

* The eight so-called "border" slave states are, of course, included.

These statistics reveal some interesting facts. Lincoln's vote was practically nonexistent in the slave states, even in such a border state as his native Kentucky. Breckinridge did rela-

tively much better in the free states than did Lincoln in the South. Bell waged an amazingly strong fight in the slave states, where he came close to matching Breckinridge's total, despite the latter's advantage of many local Democratic machines to help him. Lincoln, the most sectional candidate, was a minority choice. In fact, no *defeated* major party presidential candidate until 1904 polled as small a percentage of popular votes as did Lincoln in winning the campaign of 1860. Incidentally, these figures form an indictment of the Electoral College system; Lincoln's 1,866,452 popular votes were worth 180 electoral votes, but Douglas's 1,376,-957 were only worth 12.

SECESSION OF THE LOWER SOUTH

To the shock of many Northerners who had assumed that the threats from the Lower South were only windy emanations, the implacable South Carolinians almost immediately called for a special convention to take their state out of the Union. On 20 December 1860 this convention unanimously declared that ". . . the union now existing between South Carolina and other States under the name of the United States of America is hereby dissolved." During the following month, Mississippi, Florida, Alabama, Georgia, and Louisiana seceded, and in February the imperial domain of Texas followed. The coastal areas on the Atlantic from North Carolina to Key West and along the Gulf Coast to the Mexican border had left the United States.

Yet only South Carolina enjoyed unanimity in the special secession conventions. In all the other seceding states there was a strong minority that opposed the fire-eaters who wished to emulate the Palmetto State. Especially in Georgia were the antisecessionists strong, and under Alexander H. Stephens (who became Vice-President of the Confederate States) they doggedly fought until the last moment. Staunch old Sam Houston bellowed opinions echoing his nationalistic heritage from Jacksonian Democracy in a losing fight against the

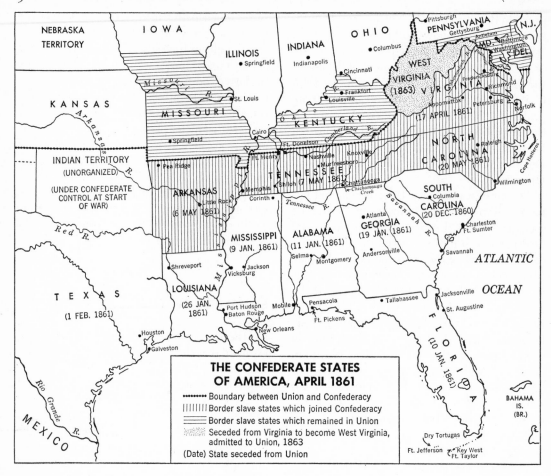

THE CONFEDERATE STATES
OF AMERICA, APRIL 1861

········· Boundary between Union and Confederacy
||||||| Border slave states which joined Confederacy
▬▬▬ Border slave states which remained in Union
░░░ Seceded from Virginia to become West Virginia,
     admitted to Union, 1863
(Date) State seceded from Union

divisive forces in Texas. Even in South Carolina James Pettigru eloquently upheld American nationalism. The unionists of the South argued that their sectional problems could best be solved by remaining inside the United States. They warned that exclusion from the West and the impossibility of recovering fugitive slaves would be only part of the price paid for Southern independence. Despite their entreaties, these loyalists were unable to prevail against the contagious enthusiasm aroused by cotton-state nationalism.

Union strength was concentrated in the Upper South, and it is significant that only South Carolina and the Gulf states seceded before the firing on Fort Sumter (12 April 1861). Seven slave states left the Union prior to the outbreak of hostilities, but eight lagged behind until Lincoln called for volunteers to crush the

"rebellion." Within a short time Virginia, North Carolina, Tennessee, and Arkansas joined the Confederacy, their majorities convinced that "coercion" of sovereign states was unconstitutional. Although rife with supporters of Jefferson Davis, the northernmost tier of slave states—Delaware, Maryland, Kentucky, and Missouri—stayed loyal. In the latter instances Southern unionism and prompt Federal action prevailed.

The prosecessionists of the South believed that their grievances against the North were so deep and that their minority status was so fixed that there was no future for them in the United States. Implanted in Southern political thought was the conviction that, through choice, sovereign states had joined the Union. In so doing, they had not divested themselves of sovereignty, and by their own choice they could withdraw. Such was the constitutional right of secession, nurtured by some eighteenth-century Virginia agrarians and brought into flower by John C. Calhoun and his later followers. Most Southern unionists agreed with this philosophical viewpoint, but based their opposition to secession on expediency rather than legality.

The constitutional side, however, has often been overrated. Perhaps "Southern nationalism" gives a clearer picture of contemporary sentiment than does "State rights." Southerners who had noticed immigration pouring into the North, increasing the number of free states, concluded that since the Republican party would not allow either new states or territories to be opened to slavery their section would be relegated to a perpetual status of inferiority. Soon, they feared, the Republicans would be strong enough, protests to the contrary notwithstanding, to move against slavery and the whole system of race relationship in the cotton states. Yet if Southerners boldly declared their independence, they could see the glorious vision of a great slave-holding republic, "the last foray of aristocracy," perhaps encompassing within its borders Mexico and the West Indies, and assured prosperity through freedom from "money-grubbing Yankees." Although Americans today would conclude that the secessionists were wrong, they had a strong legal case and moved in the finest traditions of the right of a people to self-determination. If they were wrong, they were magnificently wrong. Modern Americans from Maine and Oregon as well as from Virginia and Texas can look back with pride upon the accomplishments of both secessionist and unionist in the South on the eve of the Civil War.

Early in February, 1861, delegates from the seceded states met at Montgomery, Alabama, and formed the Confederate States of America. Jefferson Davis of Mississippi was elected President and the Georgia unionist Alexander H. Stephens became Vice-President. A constitution was written embodying many features of its United States counterpart. There were some conspicuous Confederate exceptions, however. One provided that the President could have only a single six-year term. Another gave the Executive power to veto individual items in an appropriations bill rather than having to kill the whole measure. Other stipulations permitted citizens to take slaves everywhere in the national domains, compelled new territory to protect slavery, and forbade admittance of states without two-thirds support in both houses. Southern agrarian thinking was illustrated by specific barriers against protective tariffs, industrial bounties, and internal improvements.

NORTHERN CURRENTS

While the new government was establishing itself at Montgomery, what of the North? As the dire news of the secession of the Lower South filled their newspapers, Northern citizens divided among themselves on how to deal with the frightening crisis. We can only surmise, but probably opinion fell into these recognizable categories. There was a surprisingly large number of Northerners who sympathized with the South. Confederate apologists, many of whom became Peace Democrats or "Copperheads" during the war, were scattered all over the North, but tended to be congregated in the large cities and in the Middle Western areas close to the slave states, especially in the lower tier of counties in Ohio, Indiana, and Illinois, which had been settled primarily by Southern overflow.

At the other pole of Northern opinion stood the left-wing "Radical" Republicans, many of them abolitionists, who hated the South so much that they welcomed the dissolution of the Union. Their sentiments were temporarily publicized by Horace Greeley's New York Tribune, which recommended that "the erring sisters" be allowed "to go in peace." Both the abolitionist Republicans and the Peace Democrats formed minorities inside their own parties; the mass of Northern citizenry, Democratic and Republican alike, looked with abhorrence on secession no matter how they felt about slavery; and if the Federal flag was fired upon, they would fight.

Divergent opinion convulsed both the North and the South, but the most complete chaos of mixed sentiments and emotions afflicted the border slave states. Caught between a love for the Union and equal affection for the state, the Upper South wavered back and forth and, as has been seen, finally split, four going to the Confederacy and four staying in the United States. Yet whichever way their state decided, thousands supported the opposition; there were Confederate regiments of Kentuckians and Missourians. Even families were divided, and it was not unusual for brother to fight brother in the deepest and ugliest application of civil war. One thing seems abundantly clear concerning the border states— while many of their citizens would rally around Lincoln to save the Union, they would never war against the South in a battle for the emancipation of slaves.

CONCILIATORY ATTEMPTS

While distrait Americans searched for help and guidance, none was forthcoming from the lame-duck Buchanan administration. Although Lincoln had been elected in November, 1860, he could not take over the reins of government until the following March, a hiatus of four full months. In the interim about all Buchanan could do was to announce firmly that secession was obviously unlawful, but he stated with equal vigor that he could do nothing about it, since states could not be coerced. He made only a halting gesture of resistance to rebellion. In January, 1861, the President sent the *Star of the West*, an unarmed merchant ship, to the Federal Fort Sumter in Charleston Harbor, but Confederate guns drove it away. After that, in poor health and with shattered nerves, the aged President wandered around the White House, praying and weeping.

Conciliation had saved the United States in 1850, so it was natural for the strong unionist opinion both North and South to turn once more toward attempted amicable settlement. This course was inaugurated by Senator John

J. Crittenden of Kentucky. This venerable successor to Henry Clay brought before Congress, two days prior to the secession of South Carolina, a series of placatory measures called collectively the "Crittenden Compromise." His proposals were weighted heavily in favor of the South. Crittenden called for reestablishment of the old 36°30′ line between free and slave territory, both at that time and "hereafter acquired"; [1] a ban against congressional anti-slavery legislation pertaining to Federal districts inside slave states; no congressional barriers against the internal slave trade; availability of Treasury funds to compensate the owners of escaped slaves; and repeal of the Northern "personal-liberty laws," which had interfered with the recovery of fugitives. Sops to the North were a relaxation in the stringency of the Fugitive Slave Act of 1850 and the thorough suppression of the African slave trade.

A congressional committee was making some progress toward the adoption of the Crittenden Compromise, but the hostility of the President-elect threw sand in the gears. Lincoln notified his fellow Republicans on the committee that he would be unwilling to countenance *any* extension of slave territory. In a later missive to William H. Seward, Lincoln clarified his position: ". . . on the territorial question—that is, the question of extending slavery under the national auspices,— I am inflexible. I am for no compromise which assists or permits the extension of the institution on soil owned by the nation." Yet Lincoln would go all the way on enforcement of the Fugitive Slave Act and protection of slavery in the states where it already existed. In fact, Lincoln promised that he would support an "unamendable amendment" to the Constitution that would forever maintain the institution of slavery in the slave states. He was to repeat this assurance in his first inaugural address.

Solidified by their leader's opposition, the Republicans in the Senate were able to defeat the Crittenden Compromise. Similar discus-

[1] This provision for the future was especially repugnant to Republicans, who feared that it might spur Southern expansion into Mexico or the Caribbean.

sions in the House of Representatives fared no better. Virginia made the last real attempt to avert the coming war. At its invitation, delegates from many of the states still in the Union met under the chairmanship of ex-President John Tyler and recommended that the Missouri Compromise line of 1820 be reintroduced, and that new territory be added to the United States only by majorities of both free- and slave-state Senators. The Virginian attempt came too late, however. The Union was already broken, and events had moved too precipitantly to be recalled.

During the last days of the lame-duck Buchanan administration, the problem of the disposal of Federal territory inside the confines of the seceded states was ever in the public eye. The Union government offered little resistance to Confederate encroachments, and by the early spring of 1861 only four Federal forts remained independent of Confederate control. There was little question about two of them. Fort Taylor at Key West and Fort Jefferson in the Dry Tortugas could only be taken by strong naval forces, and the Confederacy did not have this strength. Fort Pickens at Pensacola and Fort Sumter in Charleston Harbor, however, were vulnerable to land batteries. National attention was directed to the latter, for it stood as a symbol of Union strength and authority in full view of the fiery South Carolina secessionists. Even the timid Buchanan could see that some semblance of Federal authority must be maintained, even if only for prestige, so he rebuffed efforts of the Confederate authorities to gain possession of the two citadels and even sent the *Star of the West* on its halfhearted attempt to supply Fort Sumter. The final disposition of the problem was forced to await the new administration.

Buchanan's term ended in an atmosphere of despair and panic. Public opinion was as confused as the President's, and it appeared that the constitutional experiment of federated government was irrevocably lost. Some indication of the national perplexity and flux can be seen in a recommendation made to the City Council by Mayor Fernando E. Wood of New York early in 1861. Wood called for the secession of New York City from the Union and its establishment as a free municipality, trading with both the Union and the Confederacy. Naturally this bizarre proposal was defeated, but that it could be even seriously entertained is indicative of contemporary conditions. Gotham was perhaps the most panic-stricken and appeasement-ridden of the Northern cities. This attitude was fostered by many New York businessmen, terrified at the loss of Southern markets and prospective default on Southern debts, and by thousands of city laborers filled with dread that freed slaves would enter into competition with them for manual labor jobs.

LINCOLN TAKES OVER

Any balm for the shattered national morale that might have been applied by the President-elect was sadly lacking. Abraham Lincoln stayed home in Springfield, Illinois, for three months, saying very little, and that of dubious efficacy. In February he left his home state and proceeded slowly toward Washington for his inauguration. His speeches en route made little impression. National perturbation about his qualities of leadership was not allayed when detectives warned that a plot existed to assassinate him as he passed through Baltimore, and Lincoln was persuaded to by-pass the Maryland metropolis and slip into Washington incognito.

Inauguration Day, 1861, was cheerless and tense. Some confidence in the new President was restored by his address, in which, after reiterating that he had neither the power nor the desire to interfere with slavery in the states where it existed and that he would approve an "irrevocable" amendment perpetuating that institution, he concluded:

In your hands, my dissatisfied fellow-countrymen, and not in mine is the momentous issue of civil war. The government will not assail you. You can have no conflict without being yourselves the aggressors. You have no oath registered in heaven to destroy the government, while I have the most solemn one to "preserve, protect, and defend" it.

Despite Lincoln's beautifully expressed address, the situation called for more than ringing prose. Political exigencies interfered with the formulation of an effective policy, and while the crisis between the United and the Confederate States wavered in the balance, Lincoln was forced to waste precious hours meditating on such weighty matters as the postmastership in some obscure Wisconsin hamlet. For several weeks there seemed little noticeable difference between Lincoln and Buchanan in so far as leadership was concerned. The situation in regard to the border states was so tense that the administration dared not recall the dispersed Union navy for possible blockade duty, or even take adequate defensive measures for Washington, D.C., which would be completely cut off if Virginia and Maryland seceded. During the troubled days when dilatory measures seemed advisable, Lincoln mused upon what should be done about Forts Pickens and Sumter.

❨ *Seward's "Thoughts."* Secretary of State William H. Seward watched with displeasure the drift of affairs and what seemed to him the disastrous inertia of the inexperienced President. As head of the State Department, Seward considered the possibility of utilizing the threatening foreign situation to force a decision. Especially menacing were France and Spain. Napoleon III was in the process of organizing a coalition to cast in troubled Mexican waters, and at the invitation of the internally stricken Santo Domingo, Spain was about to take that West Indian nation back into its empire. Great Britain in Canada and Russia in Alaska were always potential troublemakers. Seward concluded that a sharp crisis in foreign affairs might serve to avert an American civil war.

On 1 April 1861 (a significant date?) Seward submitted to Lincoln a paper entitled, "Some Thoughts for the President's Consideration." In this strange missive the Secretary of State called for the North to make sudden demands on France and Spain and to a lesser degree on Great Britain and Russia for "satisfactory explanations," and if these powers re-

fused to answer, immediately to declare war on at least the first two. Presumably Seward thought that the South would scurry back into the Union to defend the Stars and Stripes. As Southern hopes for independence were primarily based on European recognition and, in case of war, material aid, Seward's plan was obviously demented. The document concluded with an assurance that if Lincoln were unable or unwilling to direct "energetic prosecution" of whatever policies were decided upon, the Secretary of State would undertake to assume such responsibility.

Historians have long pondered about this aberration of one known to be a sensible and hardheaded politician. Majority opinion among scholars still leans to the theory of Seward's temporary folly, but perhaps a note of caution should be inserted. There is at least a possibility that it was part of a masterful bluff that Seward was pulling, not on Lincoln, but on the European nations. He had deliberately let it be noised around continental chancelleries that as Secretary of State he would follow a most aggressive course. If his "Thoughts" to Lincoln became known they would reinforce the feeling in Europe that the powers would have to lean over backward to avoid offense, since a madman headed the foreign office of the United States.

Other portions of Seward's communication to the President were sound enough. He advocated that the basis of controversy between the Union and the Confederacy be changed from an issue of abolition against slavery to one of union against disunion, a course already promulgated by the President. Although Seward recommended that Fort Sumter be abandoned, he stated that he would "maintain" every other "fort and possession in the South." Whatever the New Yorker's motives, Lincoln handled the affair perfectly. He gently reminded Seward that as President he would have to direct policy, yet he did so with such good will that his Secretary of State could not feel rebuffed. After a somewhat inauspicious commencement, Seward conducted the foreign policy of the United States with assurance and marked ability for the rest of the war.

OUTBREAK OF THE CIVIL WAR

Weeks of brooding over the disposition of the Union fortresses inside the seceded states were finally resolved by Lincoln's decision to reinforce and resupply their garrisons. Relief expeditions were dispatched to both Pickens and Sumter, despite the objections of some Cabinet members. Fort Pickens was successfully supplied and remained in Union hands throughout the war. The results at Charleston were quite different. When the Confederate government realized that a relief expedition was under way, it ordered General Pierre Beauregard, commanding the shore batteries at the South Carolina city, to drive off the supply ships. The pugnacious Beauregard did more than that; he called upon the Union Commandant at the fort, Major Robert Anderson, to surrender. Anderson refused to comply, and early on the morning of 12 April 1861 Confederate guns opened on the Federal fortress.[2] The relief ships were driven away, and after resistance of a day and a half with no casualties on either side Anderson surrendered Fort Sumter. The American Civil War, perhaps the greatest tragedy in the nation's history, was under way.

❨ *The Tragedy of the Civil War.* From the vantage point of almost a century, it is obvious that the Civil War was folly. The actual fact remains that by 1861 the Union was indissoluble. Consider what a Southern victory would have meant. Two frightened and suspicious republics would have been destined to live under conditions of either open hostility or uneasy neutrality, certainly for many years, so great were the grounds of contention between them. What would two separate republics do about the Mississippi River; would the Confederacy have been willing to allow free transit for Northern ships to the Gulf of Mexico? What would become of the Western territories? Would Northerners, so implacable in their resistance to an extension of slavery into

[2] The honor of firing the first shot was given to the aged secessionist, Edmund Ruffin.

new lands by their own Southern fellow nationals, be more amenable to intrusion by the citizens of a foreign state? How would the Federal lands, arsenals, forts, navy, and treasury be divided?

Other grave questions had to be asked. Would the Monroe Doctrine continue to bar European intervention into the Western Hemisphere, or would avaricious powers eagerly seize the opportunity to play the Confederate against the United States and amass rich possessions in so doing? What of the minorities in the border states, no matter which way they went? What would have happened to national transportation and markets? Could Southern Americans really forget what Lincoln expressed so beautifully in his inaugural address: "The mystic chords of memory, stretching from every battle-field and patriot grave to every living heart and hearthstone all over this broad land"?

Furthermore, the secessionists were misled in using the accession of Lincoln and the Republicans as the reason for which the cotton states must leave the Union. For at least well into the discernible future, the new administration could offer no real threat to the South. There were Republican majorities in Congress, but they were so slight that they could not have pushed through punitive measures against the institution of slavery. The fifteen slave states were more than enough to block any Constitutional amendment contrary to their sectional interests. In addition the Supreme Court had shown its Southern sympathy. Confederate supporters before and during the Civil War were also incorrect when they accused Lincoln of being a gross "baboon" of the worst ultraabolitionist cast. Not so: Lincoln and the majority of his party had little antagonism toward slavery in the states where it existed; they were so far from the extreme Garrisonian abolitionists that the latter were openly disgusted with the President's opposition to emancipation. Yet the time for reason, judgment, and sober evaluation had gone by, and fervent emotionalism had riveted a hold upon too many Americans to allow counsels of mediation to prevail.

CHAPTER 32

Blue versus Gray

(1861-1865)

THE RIVAL POWERS

Americans in the middle of the twentieth century find it difficult to understand how the exuberant citizens of the new Confederate States of America hoped to win the Civil War. The material odds against them were titanic. Almost 22,000,000 persons remained in the Union, against some 9,000,000 in the states that seceded; and of the latter number, approximately 3,500,000 were Negro slaves. The United States had about a four-to-one advantage over the Confederacy in potential soldiers —white males between fifteen and forty years of age. The Union preponderance over the new Southern nation was almost nine to one industrially, six to one in industrial workers, two to one in railroad mileage, and three to one in monetary reserves, not counting the potential output of the Nevada, Colorado, and California gold and silver mines. The United States retained the vast majority of arsenals and munitions plants. It possessed practically all the merchant marine and could easily import materials lacking to the Northern war effort. The Navy stayed loyal and was available to blockade the Southern coastline. The United States was an established government

374

and enjoyed the recognition of all the nations.

Despite this awesome cataloguing of Northern strength, however, the South was confident of victory; and indeed it took four solid years of one of history's greatest wars before the gamble for sectional independence had been lost. The Confederate States of America had some advantages too. Perhaps the greatest Southern asset was that to achieve victory it did not have to *win* the war. Anything less than an overwhelming Northern triumph meant success for the South and the establishment of Confederate independence. At no time from 1861 to 1865 did Southerners aspire to conquer the North; that was so manifestly impossible that even the most visionary secessionist dared not anticipate such a conclusion. It was unnecessary, anyway. All the Confederate armies would have to do was to fend off Union attacks, perhaps destroy the Northern will to win by large-scale raids into Union territory, and wait until discouragement and war weariness brought most Northerners to a conclusion that the South was unconquerable. Any ensuing peace would grant Southern independence as a foregone conclusion.

Furthermore, Confederates realized that they were battling in a great tradition. With no

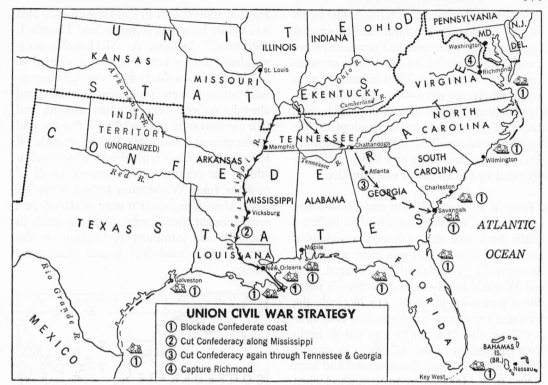

UNION CIVIL WAR STRATEGY
1. Blockade Confederate coast
2. Cut Confederacy along Mississippi
3. Cut Confederacy again through Tennessee & Georgia
4. Capture Richmond

war of conquest to be waged, they were called upon to defend home, family, and way of life. They could fight along interior lines of transportation and communication, allowing the stronger foe to waste his resources and drain his enthusiasm. Even if defeated time after time, Southern armies could retreat and fight, retreat again and fight again, over a thousand localities of a vast interior, strengthened and abetted by familiar scenes and by thorough topographical knowledge. When, Southern orators shouted, have a free people, especially Anglo-Saxons, ever been crushed in a struggle for self-determination and independence?

There were other Confederate advantages. The Southerners, poor white as well as wealthy planter, lived a more outdoor life, rode horseback and hunted more often than did his Northern counterpart. The military tradition was bred deep in Southern blood, and the plantation owner considered it a high privilege for his son to attend West Point or Annapolis and to continue serving in the armed forces, while many Northern parents tended to direct their offspring into the more economically lucrative fields of transportation and industry. Confederate leadership was better than the Union during most of the war, and the Southern soldier usually showed to slightly better advantage. From 1861 to 1865 Northern casualties were to be higher than Southern, and in most engagements where equal numbers fought, the Confederate army was victorious. Not until defeatism and desertion sapped Southern energies already weakened by the hammering of more rather than superior troops and better matériel of war did the hard-pressed citizens of the Confederacy bitterly acquiesce to ruin and degradation.

Despite the imminence of hostilities neither side was prepared for any war, let alone a long one. Hordes of eager aspirants for martial glory were filled with a pitifully naïve confidence that there would be a battle or two and then either "Johnny Reb" or "Damn Yank" would scurry home whipped. Not wanting to miss the fun, thousands swamped the military entrepôts, and these unsophisticated recruits had to be fed, clothed, armed, and trained. The hand-ful of West Pointers was inundated by a locust swarm of politicians who had persuaded com-pliant state authorities to grant them commis-sions. Some of these "political brigadiers" were worth whole regiments—to the other side. Careful planning was almost impossible, and desperate officers were forced to adopt rule-of-thumb procedures. Behind the lines, profiteers descended on Richmond and Washington, in-toxicated by the aroma of easy plunder.

❨ *Rival War Aims.* Union and Confederate war aims differed considerably. The bellicose South from the start planned a defensive struggle. Union strategy was more ambitious. As originally promulgated by the aged Gen-eral Winfield Scott—soon to retire—it jelled into a four-point program: (1) blockade the Southern coastline; (2) divide the Confeder-acy along the Mississippi; (3) cut it again through Georgia to the Atlantic; (4) capture Richmond (the Confederate capital had been moved from Montgomery to Richmond when Virginia joined the Confederate States). The first three were wise and statesmanlike deci-sions, and they eventually won the war; but on the grounds of military expediency, far too much Union energy was dissipated on abortive campaigns against Richmond. Here economic and especially political motives superseded the military. Although Richmond was the chief headquarters of Confederate munition manu-factures, Northern hopes turned toward taking the city as the symbol of disunion and the heart of the rebellion.

THE FIRST MAJOR CLASH: BULL RUN

Especially vocal was the Northern press as it thumped its tom-toms in the foolish slogan, "On to Richmond!" This pressure became so great that despite the fact that his men were still untrained, Union General Irvin McDowell was ordered to proceed toward the Confed-erate capital with an army of about 35,000 men. General Pierre Beauregard, victor at Fort

Sumter, moved into defensive positions, ably assisted by Joseph E. Johnston and Thomas J. "Stonewall" Jackson. As McDowell's army wandered deeper into Virginia, it seemed to be about half a military force and half the an-nual outing of some prominent marching and chowder society. Men, muskets, wagons, and gun caissons were festooned with flowers, and undisciplined soldiers felt free to straggle off to cool themselves with drinks of water. To add to the confusion, an immense horde of civilians from Washington tagged along be-hind. Many Congressmen were in attendance; some brought their families and were ready to celebrate the imminent destruction of the "rebels" with roast-chicken and champagne picnics.

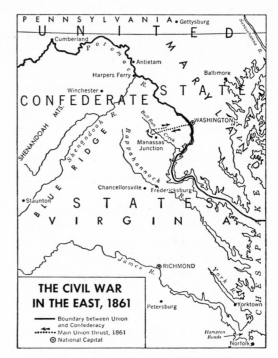

THE CIVIL WAR IN THE EAST, 1861

—— Boundary between Union and Confederacy
······ Main Union thrust, 1861
⊙ National Capital

As the midsummer sun beat down, the Union and Confederate forces clashed at the small stream called Bull Run near the village of Manassas Junction (21 July 1861). Mc-Dowell's tactics were sound enough, and his untrained men were giving a good account of themselves. The Confederates were on the verge of rout when the cry, "Rally behind the Virginians! Look! There's Jackson standing like a stone wall!" heartened the wavering Southern levies—and gave to Jackson his eternal nickname. A smashing flank attack on overextended Federal lines caused a recoil that was followed by a sudden panic in the Northern ranks. Back toward Washington scrambled a heterogeneous mass of soldiers, officers, and civilians (some Congressmen had to abandon their picnic hampers in the sudden flight). In effect, the Northern capital was left defenseless against Confederate occupation. But the Southern troops were almost as demoralized by victory as their antagonists by defeat. Alcoholic celebrations and casual desertions removed any possibility of following up the Confederate success. The North grimly realized that the Civil War was to be an arduous and tortuous journey and settled down to business. In the long-range view, First Bull Run perhaps harmed the South even more than the North.

ACTION IN THE WEST, 1861–1863

Following this initial battle, the Eastern or Virginian front quieted down for many months. Throughout most of the Civil War, the sectional pattern of military developments tended toward Union victory in the West and defeat in the East. Although many of the really spectacular clashes were fought in the few score miles between southern Pennsylvania and central Virginia, and these captured most of the popular attention, it was beyond the Appalachians in Tennessee and along the Mississippi that the Confederacy was stricken. During the first two years almost the only

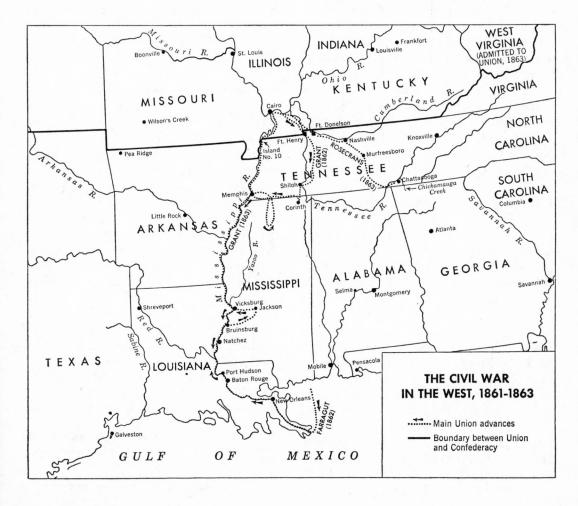

THE CIVIL WAR
IN THE WEST, 1861-1863

┅┅┅ Main Union advances

───── Boundary between Union
         and Confederacy

major Union successes were achieved in that quarter.

Before the general Union strategy of opening the Mississippi and driving through Tennessee toward northern Alabama and Georgia could come into fruition, the western flank had to be secured in Missouri. Here the ability and energy of two men served well the Union cause. Francis Preston Blair, Jr., of the famous Maryland triumvirate of father and two sons, and General Nathaniel Lyon of the regular army acted with energetic dispatch. When Lincoln called upon the state governors for volunteers to put down the rebellion, Governor Claiborne Jackson of Missouri characterized the directive as, "revolutionary, inhuman, and diabolical." He tried to organize his state for the Confederacy, but Blair and Lyon moved too fast for him. They seized arsenals and rapidly equipped thousands of Union supporters. At Booneville during June, 1861, Lyon defeated the Confederates and cleared pro-secessionist elements from central Missouri. Despite Lyon's defeat and death at Wilson's Creek only a few months later, the final Union victory that saved Missouri was won by General Samuel R. Curtis at Pea Ridge in northern Arkansas early in May, 1862. There was considerable bushwhacking and foraging throughout the war, however, in the Missouri section.

⟨ *Ulysses S. Grant.* Tennessee was a harder nut to crack. Union generalship was equal to the task, especially after the advent of Ulysses S. Grant, most successful of the Northern commanders. Grant was a short, stocky, round-shouldered, laconic individual who had made a dismal failure of his life until the Civil War broke out. A native of Ohio, he had been an undistinguished cadet at West Point, had fought gallantly but without much recognition during the Mexican War, suffered through the dreary boredom of garrison duty, and resigned from the army rather than face a court-martial for drunkenness. He failed at farming and failed at business, and when the war broke out Grant was a $12.50-a-week clerk in his brothers' leathergoods store in Galena, Illinois. In 1861, however, with thousands of recruits to be trained, anyone with a military background was desperately needed. West Pointer Grant became a lieutenant colonel and was soon promoted to brigadier general.

Ulysses S. Grant was no flaming meteor of martial brilliance, but he accomplished what generals are supposed to do—he won battles. He could fight; in fact he seems to have had a constitutional inability to retreat once he was under way, and if checked he doggedly took his (and his men's) punishment and kept moving ahead. Grant was well trained to begin with, and he learned more as he went along. He accepted both advice and responsibility without protest. He was able to comprehend broad strategy without sacrificing an awareness of tactical problems. His relations with the Navy were excellent, and he was always willing to coordinate his activities with that arm. Unsentimental, phlegmatic, and practical rather than dashing and flamboyant, Grant could not emulate McClellan's popularity with his own soldiers. Grant would accept too heavy casualties to become a great hero to his men, but in so doing he aided tremendously in winning the war.

However, several months passed before Grant had a chance to show his wares. Meanwhile, John Charles Frémont was in partial command in the West, and he acted as if he were President and Abraham Lincoln were some governmental clerk. Frémont ostentatiously ignored orders and on his own initiative freed the slaves in Missouri, despite the fact that emancipation was temporarily contrary to administration policy. Out went John Charles Frémont. The plodding and unoriginal General Henry W. Halleck was soon made commander in the trans-Appalachian sector.[1] He was jealous of Grant, but finally allowed the latter to display his abilities in a strike toward Tennessee.

⟨ *Clearing the Mississippi River.* A glance at a map will show that access to western Tennes-

---

[1] It is strange that a general who showed as little talent as Halleck was awarded such high positions. After his Western command he was made Chief of Staff.

see and indeed to the whole central Upper South fans out from a focal point along three rivers that run roughly parallel for about 100 miles. The Cumberland, the Tennessee, and the Mississippi were each defended by a major fortification. The Mississippi was guarded by Island No. 10 (the tenth island down that river from where the Ohio enters), the Tennessee by Fort Henry, and the Cumberland by Fort Donelson. During February, 1862, Grant, in conjunction with naval forces, advanced against Fort Henry. A flotilla of gunboats under the direction of Flag Officer (equivalent to Rear Admiral) Andrew H. Foote captured Fort Henry just before Grant's army arrived, although the Confederate garrison was able to withdraw to Fort Donelson. Grant stolidly pushed on toward the latter and besieged it. When the Southerners tried to break out of the trap they were thrown back. Finally the Confederate commander, General Simon B. Buckner, had to ask for surrender terms, and Grant's answer made him the darling of victory-starved Northerners: "No terms except an unconditional and immediate surrender can be accepted. I propose to move immediately upon your works." The fall of Fort Donelson abandoned most of western Tennessee to the Union and temporarily rolled back the Confederates almost into northern Mississippi and Alabama.

The Southerners retreated under the command of General Albert S. Johnston, with Grant hot on their trail. The taciturn Northerner became careless; it almost wrote finis to his brilliantly inaugurated career. Early in April Johnston suddenly counterattacked at Shiloh (Pittsburg Landing). During the first day the Union troops were almost driven into the Tennessee River, but rapid Federal reinforcements on the morrow saved Grant's army. The wounded General Johnston and 25,000 others killed, wounded, or captured on both sides bore witness to the ferocity of the action at Shiloh. The Confederates, now under General Pierre Beauregard, drifted back to Corinth, Mississippi, and set up a defense line running northeast to Chattanooga, Tennessee.

Meanwhile, stirring developments had been occurring along "Old Man River." Early in April Admiral David Farragut led a Union fleet in a dramatic sweep from the mouth of the Mississippi toward New Orleans, stormed past its defenses, and with surprising ease captured the greatest Confederate city, which remained in Union hands during the rest of the war.[2] Farragut's gunboats proceeded slowly up the river as far as Port Hudson, Louisiana. At about the same time a combined land and river operation attacked the Confederate positions on Island No. 10, forcing their surrender. By the end of 1862, the westernmost portion of the Confederacy, called the Trans-Mississippi Department (Louisiana, Arkansas, and Texas), was connected to the rest of the South for only a few score miles between the river cities of Port Hudson and Vicksburg, Mississippi.

Vicksburg was by far the strongest Confederate position remaining on the Mississippi. After resting his troops during the latter part of 1862, Grant advanced against that stronghold during the late winter of 1863. Vicksburg lay on a vast bend of the Mississippi near the mouth of the Yazoo River, and the surrounding countryside was a maze of semicleared brush and myriad creeks and rivulets. Grant's campaign against the city (April–July, 1863) was a marvel of army coordination with naval gunboats and mortar barges. Deciding that a frontal attack was impossible, Grant marched his command of 43,000 south of Vicksburg; crossed the river at Bruinsburg; hammered his way east to Jackson, the capital of Mississippi, in a series of battles; and looped back to the west to close on Vicksburg from the rear. Union gunboats played an accompaniment of steady bombardment. A six weeks' siege followed until 3 July, when General John C. Pemberton was forced to surrender the city and al-

[2] Union soldiers under General Benjamin F. Butler occupied the city on 1 May. Annoyed at the ill-concealed scorn of the New Orleans women toward his troops, the commandant won his appellation of "Beast Butler" when he issued his "Order 28," which stated, "When any female shall by mere gesture or movement insult or show contempt for any officers or soldiers of the United States, she shall be regarded and held liable to be treated as a woman about town plying her avocation"—i.e., jailed as a prostitute. The reaction in the South can be imagined.

NEV.
(1864)

UTAH
TERRITORY
(1850)

Colorado R.

COLORADO
TERRITORY
(1861)   Bent's Ft.

Ft. Kearny

NEBRASKA TERR.   (1854)

St. Joseph

Lawrence *Kansas R.*

Kansas City   Missouri R.

St. Louis

ILLINOIS

KANSAS
(1861)

Arkansas R.

MISSOURI

Baxter Springs

Cairo

ARIZONA
TERRITORY
(1863)

Santa Fe

NEW MEXICO
TERRITORY
(1850)

Gila R.

Apache Canyon

El Paso

UNORGANIZED

INDIAN TERRITORY
(UNORGANIZED)
(UNDER CONFEDERATE
CONTROL AT START
OF WAR)

ARKANSAS
Little Rock

Memphis

T R A N S

Red R.

M I S S I S S I P P I

TEXAS

D E P A R T M E N T

Austin

Houston

San Antonio

Galveston

MISSISSI

Vicksburg

LOUISIANA

Port Hudson
Baton Rouge

New Orleans

GULF OF CALIFORNIA

M E X I C O

Rio Grande R.

TRANS-MISSISSIPPI
DEPARTMENT
~~~~~~~~~~

(Dates) Refer to admission
of state or territory
to United States

GULF   OF

MEXICO

most 30,000 troops. The fall of Vicksburg happened simultaneously with the great Union victory at Gettysburg, Pennsylvania (1 to 3 July), to make celebrations of the Fourth unusually festive for the North. A few days later, Union General Nathaniel P. Banks proceeded north from New Orleans and seized Port Hudson. The Mississippi River had been opened completely, and the Confederacy severed along its vertebrate column.

The Trans-Mississippi Department played a minor role in the war after 1863, although considerable guerrilla activity continued to harass Missouri and Kansas.[3] Moreover, there was an important campaign in Louisiana. The rather inept General Banks was ordered to clear the Confederates from the Red River Valley, which remained the chief avenue of communication and supply to the Confederate

Far West.[4] In 1864 the Southern General Edmund Kirby-Smith repulsed Banks, retaining control of western Louisiana until the very end of the war. Indeed, Kirby-Smith was the last Confederate general to surrender a large force.

ACTION IN VIRGINIA, 1862–1863

(McClellan. While Missouri and Kentucky were being saved for the Union, western Tennessee conquered, the Mississippi cleared, and the Confederate West largely isolated, no such pleasant outcomes were discernible in the Eastern theater of operations. Here defeat attended the Stars and Stripes. Following the

[3] Among the very few bona fide massacres of non-combatants in the Civil War were two perpetrated by Confederate irregulars under the notorious William C. Quantrill. Lawrence, Kansas, and Baxter Springs, Missouri, were sacked during 1863.

[4] Even the Far West had a spirited engagement during 1862. Confederate hopes of success in New Mexico were frustrated when General Henry H. Sibley's force suffered so many casualties while winning a battle at Apache Cañon (Glorietta Pass) that Confederate abandonment of the Southwest became mandatory.

Northern disaster at First Bull Run, little occurred in the Virginia sector while both sides trained new levies. The main Union force in the East was called the Army of the Potomac, and General George Brinton McClellan was soon appointed to its command. A brilliant West Pointer, McClellan had earned plaudits in the Mexican War, but later resigned his commission to enter business. In sharp contrast to Grant, McClellan succeeded in his civilian endeavors, and when the war broke out he was president of the Ohio and Mississippi Railroad.

Small, compact, reddish-haired, and dark-eyed, McClellan won a few skirmishes in Kentucky and western Virginia early in the war, receiving accolades from the Northern public that were disproportionate to the services he rendered. Still young, it is not surprising that success went to his head; McClellan's letters to his doting wife show him to have been a most conceited individual. He became highly intolerant of criticism and even advice—his treatment of President Lincoln was sometimes disgraceful.[5] Yet McClellan was as able an administrator and organizer as ever whipped raw recruits into a polished military machine. On his advent, the Army of the Potomac was still in chaos; after six months under "Little Mac's" direction it was perhaps the strongest army in the world.

McClellan's talents were impressive, but as a general he was lacking in dash, verve, initiative, and possibly courage. Controversy still exists among military historians about a final evaluation of his ability, but the modern consensus seems to be that he failed because he was unwilling to take a chance. Every great general throughout history has had to assume calculated risks, for seldom can victory be unconditionally guaranteed. McClellan could fight well defensively, but when he was to attack, even if he had a two-to-one superiority over Lee, he would procrastinate while beseeching Lincoln for reinforcements; he would either avoid battle altogether or, if he did fight and win, fail to follow up his initial advantage. Furthermore, McClellan suffered the additional liability of being the chief object of Radical Republican hostility. McClellan was a Democrat, and he made no attempt to hide his opposition to the emancipation of the slaves. With thousands of Massachusetts sol-

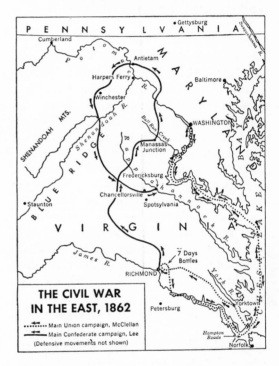

THE CIVIL WAR
IN THE EAST, 1862

······· Main Union campaign, McClellan
━┿━ Main Confederate campaign, Lee
(Defensive movements not shown)

diers under his command, McClellan unfortunately compared that commonwealth to South Carolina as twin extremes that should both be chastised. Lincoln for a time stood between McClellan and his political enemies but finally gave in to Radical pressure and fired him on two separate occasions.

For many months during the late fall and early winter of 1861–1862, McClellan dawdled so much that the daily newspaper phrase, "All quiet on the Potomac," was a bitter Northern joke. Lincoln became restive enough to ask that if General McClellan was not planning to use his army, might the President "*borrow*

[5] In one instance, Lincoln called at McClellan's house while the latter was out, waited for him in the parlor, and was left sitting there while the General came in and went upstairs to bed. It is typical of the President that later he mildly stated that he would hold General McClellan's horse if that could bring victory.

it?" Finally he ordered McClellan to proceed against Richmond, and during February, 1862, the advance got under way. Rather than fight through the miles of matted woods and overgrown country between the two capitals, McClellan decided on a flanking attack. Enjoying control of the waterways, he transported about 100,000 men down Chesapeake Bay to the Virginian peninsula between the James and York Rivers east of Richmond, landed, captured Yorktown, and marched overland toward the Confederate capital.

《 *Lee and Jackson.* Midway in the campaign General Robert E. Lee was placed in command of Richmond's defenses. Lee remains the great hero of the Confederacy and one of the finest Americans. Scion of the aristocratic Virginia family whose imprint had been deep on America for many generations, he embodied all that was noble in the tradition of the old South. Handsome, tall, dignified, cordial, and intelligent, Lee was the idol of most Southerners, although his personal aloofness made familiarity difficult. As were most of the great Civil War generals, Lee was a West Pointer, had served with distinction in the Mexican War, and had continued his martial career during the decade prior to the attack on Fort Sumter.

Such was Robert E. Lee's reputation that Chief of Staff Winfield Scott offered him command of the Union forces before the secession of Virginia, but the offer had to be refused. Lee hated slavery (he had emancipated the few slaves whom he inherited) and loved the Union, but when Virginia joined the Confederacy he felt obliged to follow his family and his friends. One of the great generals in history, he was at his best in skillfully keeping off balance a superior enemy. When served by brilliant assistants, Lee was almost unbeatable, but the loss of such luminaries as Stonewall Jackson and Jeb Stuart made the Lee of 1863 to 1865 not quite the master he had been earlier. Perhaps the Virginian's chief military fault was an inability to enforce ruthlessly his decisions upon insubordinate or unwilling underlings. It is highly unlikely that either Grant

or Sherman would have allowed such conduct as Augustus W. Longstreet's at Gettysburg to escape condemnation. It is typical of Lee that he accepted responsibility in that instance, when perhaps a more immediate compliance to direct orders by Longstreet might have saved the day.

During 1862 Lee was a thunderbolt, however. He had only some 60,000 men in his Army of Northern Virginia, and he was confronted by McClellan with 100,000 coming from the southeast, and menaced by McDowell with 40,000 to the north. At first McClellan's advance seemed irresistible. His juggernaut crunched ahead, pushing back the Confederates; and at one point Union outposts drew within five miles of Richmond, with a clear view of that city's church spires. Not for almost three years were the Union armies to be again that close.

It was during McClellan's advance that Thomas J. "Stonewall" Jackson started his meteoric career. The early months of 1862 were dark with disappointment for the Confederacy. Union forces were sweeping through western Tennessee, New Orleans had fallen, and it appeared that Richmond's end was near. Southern spirits received an injection of adrenalin from the news that Stonewall was loose in the Shenandoah Valley. Jackson was beyond question one of the finest American soldiers. He had been a professor of military science at the Virginia Military Institute, and he appears to have taught himself as well as his students. A taciturn Calvinist, Jackson was no prototype of the Southern gentleman. Tall, lean, angular-featured, and brown-bearded, the humorless, rather dour Jackson was a stern but just disciplinarian, close to a religious fanatic, and above all a fighter. The daring and mobility of his campaigns became practically legendary, and it seemed that if Jackson's "foot cavalry" were to drop out of sight, it might appear in the vicinity of Portland, Maine. Stonewall was Lee's right hand, and their collaboration was highly successful.

Jackson never exceeded the brilliance of his 1862 Shenandoah Valley campaign. Lee ordered him to take what pressure he could off besieged Richmond by keeping McDowell and other Union generals busy in the Shenandoah west of Washington. This fertile valley runs for about 200 miles between the Blue Ridge and the Shenandoah Mountains, and Jackson knew it like the palm of his hand. He had only 16,000 troops facing a total of 60,000 under three Union generals. Late in May Jackson struck. In two weeks he marched 175 miles; routed over 10,000 soldiers under the Massachusetts politician General Banks; feinted McDowell repeatedly out of position, helping to keep him from joining McClellan at Richmond; destroyed Union stores throughout the valley—and accomplished all this with a loss of only 600 men. He then eluded his baffled enemies and marched to join Lee.

By this time McClellan was close to the Confederate capital, and Lee hoped to catch the Army of the Potomac in a trap. The Southerner attacked in the Seven Days' Battle (26 June to 2 July 1862), but after bitter fighting Lee's subordinates were unable to bring off a pincer movement, permitting McClellan to withdraw in good order. The Northern general had inflicted heavier casualties than his own troops had suffered, his army was still intact, and he wished to try again; but the Radical Republican pressure on Lincoln to get rid of him became too strong to be denied. Lincoln fired McClellan, appointed General John Pope in his stead, and pulled the Army of the Potomac back toward Washington. The failure of the Peninsular Campaign was not all McClellan's fault; President Lincoln and Secretary of War Stanton must share in the blame.

❬ *Lee's First Invasion of the North.* General Pope had earned something of a reputation in the West. He pompously announced to his men that "he was used to seeing the backs of the enemy." He marched south toward Richmond, and at Bull Run, field of disaster for the North, it happened again. Working in perfect unison, Jackson and Longstreet showed General Pope some Confederate faces and inflicted a terrible defeat on him that sent the Northern Army back toward Washington. Gloom again settled over the Union.

Almost immediately after the Southern victory at Second Bull Run, Lee decided on a bold stroke—an invasion of the North. His aim was not to conquer Northern territory; it was rather a large-scale raid. In September, 1862, Lee's army crossed the Potomac and swung into Maryland. Confederate hopes that the citizens of this slave state would rise at the sight of the Stars and Bars were doomed to frustration, and the stirring refrains of "Maryland! My Maryland!" were heard seldom thereafter around Confederate campfires.

Pope was succeeded by McClellan, who Lincoln felt could meet the emergency. As the gray-clad Southerners moved through Maryland, McClellan and the Army of the Potomac hustled alongside, keeping themselves between Lee and such Union cities as Washington and Baltimore, giving ground to avoid letting the Confederates through to the east, much the way that a good defensive end in football will drift back a few yards to keep the play inside. By incredible luck some of McClellan's men captured Lee's "Order 191," which contained Confederate battle plans, forcing the Virginian to improvise new tactics at the last moment.

❬ *Antietam.* The inevitable clash came at Antietam Creek (Sharpsburg) on 16 and 17 September between almost 80,000 Federals and 40,000 Confederates. Frontal Union attacks along the whole line made the first day of battle perhaps the bloodiest of the entire war.[6] By the second evening McClellan had won a technical victory in the sense that Lee was forced to retreat across the Potomac into Virginia. But Antietam was not a complete triumph; the Union commander had made no attempt to follow up his gains with enough energy to capture Lee and his entire army. Despite the fact that Antietam must be classified as a military draw, it had impressive diplomatic and political results. Shortly after the

[6] The savagery of the fighting on 16 September is illustrated by what happened to Confederate General John Gordon of Georgia, who was wounded five separate times on that day—twice in the leg, once in the arm, once in the shoulder, and finally through the face.

withdrawal of Lee to the south, the British government decided not to recognize Confederate independence and was never again so close. Antietam also gave Lincoln the courage to issue his Emancipation Proclamation.

❲ *Union Defeats.* Distrait at McClellan's continued inertia, Lincoln fired him for the second and final time. The General soon resigned his commission and returned to civilian life, emerging in 1864 as the Democratic presidential candidate against Lincoln. His succes-

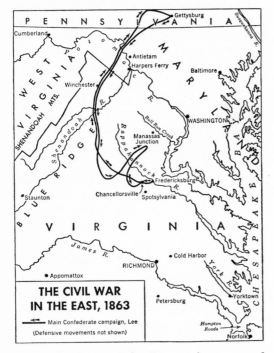

THE CIVIL WAR IN THE EAST, 1863

⟵▬▬ Main Confederate campaign, Lee
(Defensive movements not shown)

sor to the Army of the Potomac's command was General Ambrose E. Burnside, whose dramatic facial foliage was to merit him a type of minor immortality through the noun "sideburns." Poor Burnside did not want the command, protesting that he was unfit for the task, and his autoanalysis was mercilessly accurate. His army trudged down the carmine trails toward Richmond with the usual results. At Fredericksburg, Virginia (13 December 1862), Burnside ordered a suicidal frontal attack on Lee's strongly defended positions, and 12,000 Federal and 6,000 Confederate casualties paid for the Union general's errors in judgment. Out went Ambrose E. Burnside.

The next replacement was little better. Wearily Lincoln gave the command to General Joseph "Fighting Joe" Hooker. While his men appeared to like him better than they had Burnside, "Fighting Joe" built hopes too high with remarks of doubtful modesty: "My plans are perfect. May God have mercy on General Lee for I will have none." During May, 1863, Hooker sent 130,000 troops against Lee at Chancellorsville, Virginia. When all seemed going well for the Northerners, Jackson's "foot cavalry" came boiling out of the woods on the Union flank, rolled it up, and sent the Army of the Potomac headlong into another defeat. The careworn Lincoln paced the White House crying, "My God! My God! What will the country say? What *will* the country say?" Southern enthusiasm over this signal victory was stemmed, however, by the tragic news that a Confederate sentry had mistaken Jackson for a Union officer and shot him. While Jackson was prostrated from this wound, pneumonia set in, killing the great Stonewall. The Southern war effort was never again quite so efficient without Jackson's daring, coolness, and initiative.

❲ *Lee's Second Invasion of the North: Gettysburg.* Robert E. Lee immediately seized the opportunity opened by the Union defeat at Chancellorsville. He started his second and final invasion of the North. Crossing into Maryland with 75,000 veterans, Lee headed for Harrisburg, Pennsylvania, planning diversionary raids on Baltimore, Washington, and perhaps Philadelphia. General George Gordon Meade had been appointed to the Army of the Potomac command, and he retreated northward. By chance the two armies clashed at the small Pennsylvania hamlet of Gettysburg. Here for three days (1 to 3 July 1863) was fought the greatest single engagement ever waged in the Western Hemisphere. For the first two days the tide swung back and forth between 100,000 Union soldiers and 75,000 Confederates, and Lee still had hopes of victory until he erred on the fateful third day.

Meade's troops were firmly ensconced on both his flanks, and Lee gambled on a frontal attack against the Union center. General George Pickett of Longstreet's Corps was ordered to lead his Virginians and General James J. Pettigrew's North Carolinians against Cemetery Ridge, a full mile away. After an artillery barrage, the field-gray lines of Pickett's 15,000 men started their long march toward destruction. The guns quieted, a hush came over both armies, and when Pickett's charge came, it was magnificent. Only a few Confederates, however, managed to reach the crest of the ridge before being killed or captured. Pickett's men fell back shattered, almost three-quarters of them dead or wounded. On the next day Lee's retreat started. General Meade had fought a gallant and successful battle, but at this crisis he failed, allowing Lee to escape. The Potomac was in flood; Lincoln begged the Union commander to strike instantly to trap the Southern host at the river's bank, but Meade claimed that his men were too tired for further action. If Meade was correct, Lincoln did not think so. Eventually he fired him and brought in Ulysses S. Grant in an attempt to achieve final victory in the Eastern theater.

ACTION IN THE WEST, 1863–1865

《 *Chattanooga and Chickamauga.* Grant had experienced some trying moments in the West after the capture of Vicksburg and the opening of the Mississippi. The next item on the Union agenda there was to strike at south central Tennessee and thence toward Georgia, with the eventual destination of the important Confederate railroad junction of Atlanta. Grant sent General William S. Rosecrans to attack the vital central Tennessee sector, and at Murfreesboro (31 December 1862 to 3 January 1863) Rosecrans met a Confederate army under the impressively named General Braxton Bragg. Murfreesboro was almost as dogged and bitter an engagement as Shiloh. Although Rosecrans claimed victory, the battle was a draw. The Union forces advanced again, despite a diversionary raid by the ebullient Confederate cavalry officer John H. Morgan, who

swept through Kentucky, Indiana, and West Virginia, striking deep into northern Ohio before being captured. The outmaneuvered and outnumbered Bragg was pushed out of the important Tennessee city of Chattanooga, and it seemed that a tremendous Federal victory was near. The overconfident Rosecrans charged ahead too rapidly, Bragg was reinforced by General Longstreet's command, and the Union troops stumbled into a trap at Chickamauga, near Chattanooga (18 to 20 September 1863). The Northerners wavered and fell back; a complete rout might have ensued had not General George H. Thomas's men refused to budge, gaining for their commander his nickname, the "Rock of Chickamauga."

The defeat was sobering enough, however, to cause Grant to hasten reinforcements toward beleaguered Chattanooga. Grant was ably assisted by "Fighting Joe" Hooker, William T. Sherman, and the indefatigable Thomas, who never lost a battle during the whole war. Meanwhile the Confederates had occupied the parallel commanding heights of Lookout Mountain and Missionary Ridge south of the city, and unless they could be dislodged, Chattanooga was in dire peril. The "Battle in the Clouds" (24–25 November 1863) saw 2,400-foot Lookout Mountain fall to Hooker's men, and on the following day Thomas's intrepid soldiers stormed precipitous Missionary Ridge on which the Southern forces were massed.[7] The defeated Bragg was forced to retreat toward Atlanta, and Grant had won additional accolades. When he was called to the East, William T. Sherman was appointed to succeed him in the West.

《 *Sherman and Thomas.* The controversial Sherman was well qualified to assume his high command. In the prime of life, Sherman was tall and straight, slender, and sharp-featured, with heavy wrinkles around his eyes and mouth. Mentally he was keen; perhaps more than any other Civil War officer he understood war in its modern total sense, and he acted

[7] Neither Grant nor Thomas gave the order to scale Missionary Ridge. The troops appear to have done so on their own initiative.

THE CIVIL WAR
IN THE WEST, 1863-1865

····■···· Union advances
(Rosecrans, Grant,
and Sherman)

◄━━━ Confederate advances

Inset of Chattanooga area

CHATTANOOGA AREA,
SEPTEMBER—NOVEMBER, 1863

accordingly. He comprehended that the military and the civilian population work together to form a war effort and that campaigns must not be restricted to action against only armies. Exceptionally able in the smaller tactical sphere, Sherman was a master strategist, and he was willing to assume breath-taking risks, if the potential advantage merited such gambles. Sherman's devastating marches through Georgia and the Carolinas were the vital lunges that destroyed much of the Southern will to resist. Sherman could afford to say "War is hell"—he proved it.

After resting his battle-weary forces for several months, Sherman advanced toward Atlanta during the spring of 1864. He was ably opposed by General Joseph E. Johnston, who had succeeded the discredited Bragg, but Sherman inched ahead through the extremely difficult country north and west of Atlanta. President Jefferson Davis became impatient with Johnston's tactics of retreat and delay and superseded him with the brave but rash General John B. Hood. The latter fought Sherman but was brushed aside, enabling the Union army to enter Atlanta (2 September). This Union success had important political repercussions, for it helped considerably to restore public confidence in Lincoln's handling of the war effort.

Hood decided upon a tactical ruse to lure Sherman away from further penetration of

Georgia, and the Confederate hurried north into Tennessee, hoping to invade Kentucky and perhaps even Ohio. By all the military textbooks, Sherman should have followed Hood to protect his menaced lines of communication and supply. Instead, the Northerner coolly ordered General George Thomas to handle the enemy and started with his own command toward the southeast. Sherman's confidence in his subordinate was entirely justified. The Confederates were initially checked at Franklin, Tennessee, and the final debacle came late in November. Outnumbering Hood's weary soldiers about two to one, Thomas practically annihilated them near Nashville. The 40,000 Confederates who had marched into Tennessee were almost obliterated as a fighting force; only a few thousand made their escape. Nashville was perhaps the worst single defeat suffered by either side during the entire conflict.

❨ *Disemboweling the South.* Hood's advance to the north had left Georgia practically defenseless in front of the implacable Sherman. After burning Atlanta to mark his farewell,[8] he struck into the heart of Georgia with 62,000 men. Without supply lines to Union bases, the army had to live off the land—and the land was rich. "Marching through Georgia" was an autumn outing, since nothing could oppose the Union advance. Sherman ordered complete destruction of everything valuable to the Southern war effort. Detachments fanned out for 30 miles on both sides of the column to burn, destroy, or seize. Roads and bridges were ruined; manufacturing establishments burned; steel rails pried up, heated, and wrapped around trees; and cotton gins wrecked. Foragers called "bummers," some working for the army and some on their own, scoured the Southern countryside for livestock and other

[8] Sherman's philosophy can be seen in his reply to appeals from the citizens of Atlanta that he spare the city: "We don't want your Negroes, or your horses, or your lands, or anything you have, but we do want and will have a just obedience to the laws of the United States. That we will have, and if it involves the destruction of your improvements, we cannot help it."

foodstuffs. There was much destruction of private property and considerable looting, or as it is sometimes euphemistically called, "collecting souvenirs." It should be emphasized, however, that Sherman kept his men under iron discipline, and the devastation of Confederate property was balanced by the respect shown for the persons of Confederate citizens. There were no cases of murder or rape. In comparison to the utter horror that modern war visits upon civilians, Sherman's army behaved remarkably well. Yet nineteenth-century Americans were not used to such total property ruin, and the Union General's reputation suffered accordingly.

The triumphal advance through Georgia lasted about a month, ending when Sherman occupied the blockaded seaport of Savannah, which was taken close enough to the holiday season to enable the general to notify Lincoln, "I beg to present you as a Christmas gift the city of Savannah, with one hundred fifty heavy guns and plenty of ammunition. Also about twenty-five thousand bales of cotton." After resting his men a few weeks, Sherman was on his way again. He rolled into South Carolina, and the havoc wrought in that unhappy state surpassed that in Georgia. To Northern troops, South Carolina was responsible for the whole war, and they looked upon it with cold hatred. When Sherman's men approached Columbia, the state capital, they sang, "Hail Columbia, happy land. If I don't burn you, I'll be damned." Although the General did not order that it be done, most of the city was consumed in flames. Sherman's invasion of the Carolina back country necessitated the relinquishment of Charleston, which had withstood years of naval siege. The sorry plight of Georgians was duplicated and extended in the Carolinas. As the war came to an end, Sherman, outnumbering the ragged and fatigued forces opposing him under Joseph E. Johnston, was already in North Carolina, closing fast on Virginia. In about five months, Sherman's army had marched over 700 miles, destroyed property valued at $100 million in Georgia alone, captured several important cities, looted scores of towns, and in effect eviscerated the South. Never before or since has any American area been devastated to the extent that Georgia and the Carolinas suffered under William Tecumseh Sherman.

ACTION IN VIRGINIA, 1864–1865

([*Stalemate.*   While the Confederacy was being prostrated in the West, it was doing better in the East. Even the great prestige and the military ability of Ulysses S. Grant seemed un-

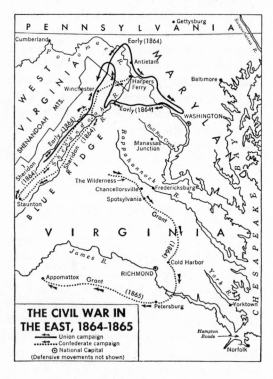

THE CIVIL WAR IN THE EAST, 1864-1865
➤—➤ Union campaign
•••➤•••➤ Confederate campaign
⊙ National Capital
(Defensive movements not shown)

equal to the task in Virginia, and for several months his record against Lee was little better than those of McClellan, Pope, Burnside, Hooker, and Meade. Refusing a desk job, Grant assumed personal command of the Army of the Potomac, and typically he decided upon a frontal advance against Richmond, his primary objective being the destruction of Lee's Army of northern Virginia rather than the capture of the capital. Grant shifted into high dur-

ing May, 1864. His soldiers were forced to fight their way through a scrubby underbrush area known with descriptive accuracy as "the Wilderness." Lee artfully utilized his inferior numbers with magnificent effect, and the battered Federals were unable to break through. Grinding slowly south, Grant tried again at Spotsylvania Courthouse, where a portion of the line was called with merciless accuracy the "Bloody Angle," but was once more hurled back. The ferocity of the fighting there was described by Grant's aide-de-camp, Horace Porter:

It was chiefly a savage hand-to-hand fight across the breastworks. Rank after rank was riddled by shot and shell and bayonet-thrusts, and finally sank, a mass of torn and mutilated corpses; then fresh troops rushed madly forward to replace the dead, and so the murderous work went on. Guns were run up close to the parapet, and double charges of canister played their part in the bloody work. The fence-rails and logs in the breastworks were shattered into splinters, and trees over a foot and a half in diameter were cut completely in two by the incessant musketry fire. . . . We had not only shot down an army, but also a forest.

Stemmed from the north, Grant swung to the southeast with Lee following in order to keep his forces between the Union army and Richmond. Grant had grimly announced, "I propose to fight it out on this line if it takes all summer," but the engagement at Cold Harbor a few miles east of Richmond (1–3 July 1864) was too much. Again the ensanguined ranks of the Army of the Potomac were repulsed with some 10,000 men killed and wounded. Grant was forced to make new plans, for the public outcry at his lengthy casualty lists was rising to dangerous proportions. Many Northerners failed to see that the Union could afford to take punishment; the North had a never-ending source of replacements, while the battered Confederates, even though their losses were only about half those of Grant, were being bled white. To add to Union discouragement during that terrible July, Washington was threatened for a time by General Jubal A. Early's daring raid.

❪ *Appomattox Courthouse.* During the summer and fall of 1864 Grant swung his troops south of the James River and advanced on Richmond from the southeast, in a maneuver somewhat similar to McClellan's Peninsular Campaign of 1862. The railroad center of Petersburg formed the chief defensive position protecting the Confederate capital's underbelly. Grant wound his tentacles around both Petersburg and Richmond; the slow, dreary, agonizing constriction of a protracted siege followed. Lee had long been able to use the Shenandoah for diversive attacks to relieve pressure on Richmond, so Grant ordered General Philip Sheridan to oust Confederate forces from that valley. Sheridan fell on the Shenandoah like a pile driver, scattered the opposition, and proceeded to show that Sherman was not the only Union commandant to understand the place of devastation in warfare. The Shenandoah was turned from a fertile paradise into a smoking wasteland, terminating the war there.

By the spring of 1865 the future was discernible to all but the most unregenerate Southern nationalists. The Confederacy had been smitten in the West, and in the East Grant was slowly tightening his hangman's noose around Richmond and Petersburg. Desertion and war weariness were taking a dreadful toll in the Southern armies. Late in March, as Sherman neared from the south, Sheridan hurried to the Richmond environs and overwhelmed a Confederate force at Five Forks, enabling Grant to end his nine-month siege by starting the pay-off attack (1 April). The Army of the Potomac broke through Lee's thin defenses, forcing the great Virginian to abandon Petersburg. Without the latter, Richmond was indefensible and had to be abandoned amid scenes of arson and looting. Lee retreated to the southwest with Grant close on his heels. By the end of the first week in April, Lee had barely 30,000 tattered, worn, and hungry troops to face Grant's well-armed, well-clothed, and well-fed 100,000 in the Army of the Potomac. Furthermore, Sherman's 60,000 were on the way.

The inevitable end came at Appomattox Courthouse, Virginia, on 9 April 1865, when Robert E. Lee surrendered the Army of Northern Virginia. The negotiations between the handsome Southerner, resplendent in his new gray uniform, and the shabby, stumpy Grant, clad in his usual private's garb with general's shoulder straps, were marked by gratitude and dignity on Lee's part, and by the unassuming generosity of the victor. In accepting Lee's surrender, Grant magnanimously allowed Confederate officers to retain their side arms and permitted Southern soldiers to keep their horses and mules: "They will be needed for spring plowing," as he put it. Two weeks later Joseph E. Johnston surrendered to Sherman, and the last major Confederate force, that commanded by General E. Kirby-Smith in the Trans-Mississippi Department, gave up late in May. Perhaps a suicide in South Carolina best symbolized the end of the most sustained and widespread struggle in the history of the Western Hemisphere. Veteran secessionist Edmund Ruffin, who had been given the honor of firing the first shot against Fort Sumter to start the war, heard of the Confederacy's surrender and put a bullet through his head.

CHAPTER 33

On the Seas and Across the Seas

(1861-1865)

NORTHERN SEA POWER

Although the military preponderance of the North was obviously the cardinal factor in achieving victory, the Civil War stands as a conspicuous example of the efficacy of sea power. The Union merchant marine was a keystone in the arch of success. With oceanic shipping firmly in hand, any basic needs of the Northern war effort could easily be found in Europe. Indeed, Northern troops were almost entirely armed with imported European weapons at first. During the initial fourteen months of the war, only about 30,000 of a total 750,000 muskets and rifles issued to Union soldiers were supplied by American manufacturers. The colossal agricultural surpluses of Northern farms could be transported abroad to procure essential foreign credits. Possession of the merchant marine gave the North an initial advantage that the South, blockaded and cut off from imports except for what squeezed through the Union naval lines, could never match.

The Union navy was even more important. While some individual officers followed their native states into secession, the mass of the fleet's personnel stayed with the Union. Fol-

lowing the firing on Fort Sumter, one of Lincoln's first acts was to announce a blockade of the Southern coastline all the way from Maryland to the Mexican border, even though use of a "paper blockade"—one without actual power to enforce—was contrary to the traditional American position. At first there were fewer than fifty ships in the United States Navy, but the number of men-of-war steadily increased until the North had over 600 by the end of the war. Easily penetrable in 1861, the influence of the blockade was soon felt, and between 1862 and 1863 it strengthened its efficiency so that slow economic strangulation drained away Confederate vitality.[1]

In addition, the striking power and military effectiveness of the Union armies were considerably increased by naval coordination. Especially in the Western campaigns was the water arm impressive, and such triumphs as the captures of Forts Henry and Donelson, Island No. 10, and Vicksburg were either entirely naval operations or at least would have been immeasurably more difficult had not gunboats and mortar barges been available to soften the defenses. Although railroads were important,

[1] For the Southern aspects of the blockade, see p. 405.

much transportation was still by water, and the natural avenues of invasion into the South were by way of such rivers as the Cumberland, the Tennessee, and the Mississippi. Union control of the inland as well as the oceanic waters was a prime factor in eventual victory. President Lincoln paid the navy a graceful compliment when he stated, "Nor must Uncle Sam's web-feet be forgotten . . . not only on the deep sea, the broad bay, and the rapid river, but also up the narrow muddy bayou and wherever the ground was a little damp, they have been and made their tracks."

Along the Atlantic and Gulf coastlines, Union victory was helped and the task of blockading lightened by independent naval operations that picked off, one by one, the leading Confederate ports. Perhaps the most famous action was Admiral David Farragut's epic capture of Mobile, Alabama, during the summer of 1864. This intrepid officer had himself lashed to the mast so that he could better direct the operations. Reputedly shouting, "Damn the torpedoes! Full speed ahead!" Farragut led his ships through the gauntlet of heavy fire from the shore batteries and took the city. Norfolk, Virginia, Roanoke Island, North Carolina, and especially New Orleans also fell to the Union navy. Early in 1865 a sixty-ship armada captured Wilmington, North Carolina, last major entrepôt for Confederate blockade runners.

SOUTHERN SEA POWER

Faced with overwhelming sea odds, the Confederacy could not hope to match the naval strength of the powerful antagonist and considering the circumstances was reasonably successful in finding substitutes, although the most spectacular Confederate experiments, those with submarines, failed. Confederate submarines were excellent as underwater craft —that was the trouble. They submerged far too easily and tended to stay down indefinitely. One ill-fated submarine, the C.S.S. *Huntsley*, foundered *five* separate times, usually drown-ing the whole crew on each occasion. At least on the fifth dive she was able to take a Union blockading ship with her.

Far more important was a revolution in naval warfare dramatized by the spirited clash between two armored vessels, the C.S.S. *Merrimac* (technically the *Virginia*) and the U.S.S. *Monitor*. These ships were no innovations; ironclads had been built for all the major European naval powers, but the engagement at Hampton Roads, Virginia, during March, 1862, made it obvious that the day of the wooden warship was over. Shortly after the secession of Virginia the Union naval base at Norfolk had to be hastily abandoned, and the old frigate *Merrimac* was burned. The Confederates raised the hulk, cut down the superstructure, armed and armored it, and equipped the bow with a metal ram. Her engines were pitifully slow, but even with this handicap the *Merrimac* soon made her presence obvious. While General McClellan's Army of the Potomac was engaged in the Peninsular Campaign, Union sea communications and indeed the whole blockade were menaced by this Southern ironclad ram.

On 8 March 1862 the *Merrimac* crawled at 5 knots (her top speed) toward the blockading Union squadron, destroyed or drove aground three warships, and withdrew to finish the job on the morrow. The next day a strange sight greeted the *Merrimac*'s crew. During the winter of 1861–1862 the Swedish-born inventor John Ericsson had built the famous *Monitor* for the North. Remarkably unseaworthy (the ship went down with all hands off Cape Hatteras a few months later) the craft's eerie appearance made obvious her nicknames of "a cheese box on a raft" and "a tin can on a shingle." An armored deck rising barely above the water line carried a revolving two-gun turret containing the crew inside. She had been rushed to Hampton Roads and arrived just in time to save the Union wooden blockaders. The two exotic vessels joined combat and hammered away at point-blank range, but neither was able to harm the other. This drawn combat actually can be classified as a Northern victory, for the baffled *Merrimac* never came out again and was soon burned to avoid capture. Other Confederate ironclad rams were built, but they never again played a decisive role in military or naval action.

The acme of the Confederacy's ability to strike back on the water was attained with the construction of the famous oceanic raiders, the *Sumter,* the *Florida,* the *Shenandoah,* and the *Alabama.* These were the most renowned of some eighteen cruiser raiders that flew the Stars and Bars from the South Atlantic to the Bering Sea. Most raiders were Confederate-armed and commanded, but British-built and partially British-manned. The *Shenandoah* caused havoc near the end of the war, and after the war was over (although she was not cognizant of that fact) smashed the Northern whaling fleet in the Bering Sea. The most successful commerce destroyer was the *Alabama,* built as "Ship 290" at the Laird yards in Scotland. Under the command of Captain Raphael Semmes, former Union naval officer, the *Alabama* cruised all over the world for about two years, sank a blockading ship of the Union navy, destroyed scores of Yankee merchantmen, and made her name a terror in Northern ports before finally being battered to pieces off Cherbourg, France, by the stronger U.S.S. *Kearsarge.* Her spectacular career subsequently touched off delicate and dangerous negotiations between Great Britain and the United States.[2]

Tremendous damage was done to the American merchant marine by these Southern raiders. They destroyed over 250 ships, and their depredations form a landmark in the decline of the American carrying trade. Oceanic insurance rates went up almost 1,000 per cent during the war. Hundreds of Northern ships were sold to foreign nationals so that they would not be attacked by Confederate cruisers. The total losses in this field might have been considerably higher if the Confederacy had been able to do much privateering. The Union blockade kept prizes from being brought into

Southern harbors, and the failure of the Richmond government to win recognition of independence from the great powers closed most European ports. Even so, a handful of privateers took some sixty Union vessels.

THE DIPLOMATIC SITUATION

The irrepressible combination of Northern military, naval, and, as shall be seen, industrial supremacy finally overpowered the South and destroyed the Confederate will to resist. Nevertheless there was one sphere in which all the Northern preponderance might have been brought to naught. This was in foreign affairs, and here the South had its greatest chance and lost perhaps the most vital battle. If the Union navy was much more potent than the Confederate, European sea power was vastly stronger than either. Northern industrial production was impressive; the output of European factories could have swamped it. All that the Confederacy needed, Europe had. Continental intervention was the clearest and most obvious path to Southern victory and independence; naturally the Richmond administration made every effort to procure assistance from across the Atlantic.

Of particular consequence was the attitude of the two European leaders, France and Great Britain. The warmest friend of the new Southern Republic was Napoleon III, Emperor of France. The crafty and double-dealing Bonaparte did everything in his power to help the Confederacy, not through love for the Southern way of life, but because he was preparing to (and soon did) invade Mexico to establish a satellite French Empire there. He welcomed the prospect of two rival American nations that would be too concerned with each other to offer much resistance to Gallic adventures south of the Rio Grande. Therefore Confederate success was furthered by Napoleon III. On several occasions he tried to grant recognition to the Confederacy, French shipyards worked for Jefferson Davis, and a Paris banking house floated a Confederate loan. But

[2] For the diplomatic aspects of these Confederate raiders, see pp. 395–396. The final settlement of the controversy between Great Britain and the United States is discussed on pp. 425–426.

Bonaparte dared no unilateral action; he was forced by France's international position to work in unison with his neighbor across the English Channel, and despite his personal preferences for recognition of Southern independence he never chanced a lone course.

The pivotal nation was Great Britain, for Paris had to follow in London's footsteps. Ostensibly one might imagine that the United States had little to fear on that score; on the eve of the Civil War relations with Great Britain were more friendly than for three-quarters of a century before. Central American controversy and vexatious boundary disputes had been settled. Tariff reciprocity between Canada and the United States had proved highly beneficial to British North America. Yet the advent of the Civil War brought new crises between Britain and the North, some of them so serious that war or peace, Union victory or defeat, wavered in delicate equilibrium.

Both the Union and the Confederacy had some trumps to play for British support. The North had a recognized government. It enjoyed a strong moral argument through the initial attitude of the triumphant Republican party toward slavery, for Great Britain had emancipated slaves throughout the empire and would respond to a Northern proclamation that the Civil War was being fought for freedom and liberty. The United States had long been Britain's best customer, and an immediate flood of war orders tightened these economic cords, giving impetus to English industrial prosperity. A series of bad years for British agriculture necessitated heavy imports of Northern grains, which reached such proportions that farsighted Northerners averred, "Old King Cotton's dead and buried; brave young Corn is King!" Finally, some influential segments of English society had a natural affinity for the United States. The mass of British industrial laborers were joined by liberal intellectuals such as John Bright, Richard Cobden, and John Stuart Mill in favoritism toward the North.

Yet the Confederacy had some staunch friends in Great Britain. The English nobility, much more effective and powerful politically a century ago than today, looked upon the Southern planters as aristocratic kinsmen. If some economic ties were strong with the North, for years Southern cotton had been the leading British import, and some four-fifths of Britain's vast cotton-textile industry was dependent on Gulf-state supply. Many Englishmen sympathized with Southern nationalism, believing that an Anglo-Saxon people had the right to establish an independent government. At first the persuasive Northern moral appeal had to be discarded. Pressing domestic issues made the Lincoln administration unable to utilize the emancipation argument. Pro-Southern Englishmen were quick to point out that there was no slavery or antislavery involved— had not Lincoln constantly asserted that it was a war to save the Union, not a struggle to liberate the Negro? Finally, a few British imperialists were charmed by the possibilities that might be opened for British expansion in the Americas when two hostile nations might neutralize one another.

A primary Confederate misconception applied to Great Britain. Almost to a man, Southerners were confident that London would soon intervene to smash the Northern blockade. "King Cotton" was the imaginary potentate who was supposed to accomplish this feat. Southerners assumed that once cotton exports to England were stopped, unemployment, distress, and famine would finally culminate in rioting throughout the midland textile areas, forcing the Queen's government to intervene in behalf of the Confederacy in order to renew cotton supplies. Operating in this frame of reference, the Davis administration made one of its most colossal and far-reaching errors. In 1861 the South resolved to help the Union blockade do its work. A Confederate embargo on cotton exports was declared, and hundreds of thousands of bales were either confiscated or destroyed to create a cotton shortage that would immediately precipitate an English depression and speed intervention. As a result, most of the enormous cotton crop of 1861 never went abroad. There is every reason to believe that the Northern blockade was so loose and ineffectual during the first months of the war that about all 1861 cotton could have reached Great Britain and France. With the foreign credits received, the Confederacy could have bought firearms, ammunition, clothing, paper, medicines, and other vitally needed or soon to be nonexistent commodities. The South placed its bet on cotton futures and woefully lost.

The economic truth was quite contrary to that believed by ardent Southerners. Rather than a sudden shortage of cotton, there was an actual surplus in Great Britain, almost a two years' supply. Until 1863 the British and to a lesser degree the French textile industries continued to operate. The politically influential British cotton-textile manufacturers enjoyed two years of unprecedented prosperity, since prices skyrocketed and their cotton supply on hand multiplied in value many times. The British laborer, eventually prostrated by the depression after 1862–1863, did not have the franchise until 1867, and during the war years he could give no direct political expression to his discontent. When the economic pinch did come it was partially alleviated by some Southern cotton that came through the blockade as well as by new supplies from Egypt and India. Relief was sent to the stricken English industrial areas by the Union, and that helped too. Northern hearts were warmed during the middle of the war when the depression-ridden workmen of Manchester, England, sent to President Lincoln expressions of confidence that his cause was just. Lincoln replied with his usual knack for saying the correct and tactful thing.

UNION CRISES WITH GREAT BRITAIN

These long-range results described above did not have an immediate effect, and until the end of 1863 continued embroilments between the United States and Great Britain delighted Southerners. The first Anglo-American crisis was a tempest over nothing. Soon after the start of the war, Lincoln announced the existence of the rebellion, called for volunteers, and proclaimed a blockade of the South. Less than a month later, Great Britain recognized the "belligerent status" of the Confederacy. This was not recognition that the Confederate States of America was an independent nation; that was never accorded by London, although it was very close during the summer of 1862. If Confederate independence had been bestowed, very likely the Union would have declared war on Great Britain. Recognition of a state of belligerency is quite another matter; all that meant was that London took official cognizance that a war was being fought; if this had not been done, British shippers could not have acknowledged the legality of the blockade. Nevertheless a wave of convulsive fury swept the North, for the proclamation did give the Confederacy such belligerent rights as the construction of commerce raiders. London was amazed at the depth of Union reaction to what seemed an obvious and neutral course. Britain made partial amends by forbidding either side to bring privateers' captures into her ports. This severely curtailed Confederate privateering both by helping much Northern commerce to escape capture and by depriving the South of potentially valuable credits through the sale of prizes in England.

❨ *The Trent Affair.* Any furor over recognition of Confederate belligerency was a pale shadow of the explosion detonated on both sides of the Atlantic by the *Trent*'s seizure by a Union warship. During the autumn of 1861 Jefferson Davis sent to Europe two diplomats, John Slidell to France and James M. Mason (not the John Y. Mason who signed the Aix-la-Chapelle Dispatch in 1854) to Great Britain. Slipping through the Union blockade to Cuba, the Southern envoys reembarked for Europe on the British steamer *Trent*, presumably secure under the protection of the Union Jack. Acting completely on his own initiative, Captain Charles Wilkes of the U.S.S. *San Jacinto* forced the *Trent* to lie to, boarded her, and removed Mason and Slidell. The North rang with delighted shouts of approval, but Great Britain was seized with collective rage. It was perhaps a strange attitude for the United States to maintain, for presumably that nation had fought in 1812 for the very principle violated by Wilkes: freedom of neutrals from seizure on the high seas. The Union captain should not have taken the two Southern diplomats, and his action was closely related to the odious practice of impressment. Legally he could have brought the ship into port for "search," but there was no right to remove individual passengers.

So serious was the crisis between the two nations that both prepared for sudden hostilities; British reinforcements were hastened to Canada. Diplomatic protest over the *Trent* affair was arbitrary and peremptory; that it was not even more bellicose was due to the intervention of Prince Albert, consort to Queen Victoria, who, although practically on his death bed, toned down the original wording so that it was not a cause for war. Lincoln was placed in an embarrassing situation. Wilkes's impetuosity was so popular with the mass of Northern citizens that to disavow his action might be ruinous politically. Yet the Union was in the wrong, and Lincoln knew it. Eventually he and Secretary of State Seward collaborated on a masterful answer to Great Britain's protest, which, although it released the two Confederates (who proceeded to Europe), politely complimented the British on finally acceding to the American argument against the right of seizure. The storm then died down, although tempers remained dangerously high.

(*Britain Almost Recognizes the Confederacy*. The aim of President Lincoln's foreign policy was, of course, the exact converse to that of the Confederacy. The Union had to make sure that Great Britain would not recognize Confederate independence. Military action was the real determining factor, and Union battle successes were directly contributory to the eventual decision of Great Britain to refuse recognition. Yet it was very close during the summer of 1862. No friends of the North were Lord Palmerston, the Prime Minister who had long been the voice of mid-century British imperialism, and Earl Russell, the Foreign Secretary.

The latter was considered at the time more amenable to Northern sentiments, but later research has conclusively demonstrated that Russell if anything was even more hostile toward the Union than the supposedly implacable Palmerston.

It should be recalled that the spring of 1862 featured Northern defeat. The failure of McClellan's Peninsular Campaign and Pope's dreadful thumping at Second Bull Run were followed by Lee's first invasion of the Union. Simultaneously Palmerston and Russell were discussing the advisability of recognizing the Confederate States of America. Although the entire British Cabinet was in favor of such a move, it was prudently decided to await news of Lee's Maryland campaign. The British anticipated a Confederate victory, but instead dispatches told of the tremendous battle of Antietam and Lee's consequent retreat into Virginia. Five days later Lincoln announced his Emancipation Proclamation, and the North at last was able to utilize the highly effective moral argument that the war was to free the slaves as well as to save the Union. Never again were the British so close to official recognition of the Confederacy.

(*Britain's Oceanic Responsibility*. The final crisis between Great Britain and the United States during the years from 1861 to 1865 concerned the British-built Confederate raiders and rams. Several cruisers were constructed in British shipyards for the South. Charles Francis Adams, able American Minister to London and third generation of the famous Massachusetts family, vociferously protested about these vessels. In particular he objected to the construction of "Ship 290" at the Laird yards in Scotland as an unneutral act. Finally harkening to Adams's strictures, the British government moved leisurely to halt the transfer of "290" to the Confederacy. So dilatory was London's action, however, that the ship had time to slip away. She sailed to the Azores, picked up guns and supplies, and as the C.S.S. *Alabama* proceeded to festoon the bottom of the seas with Yankee merchantmen. Although Great Britain had not technically been proved guilty, Adams regularly presented damage claims for the *Alabama*'s victims. A sudden sobering reflection that a precedent dangerous to Great Britain's future interests was being established caused the Queen's government to seize in 1863 the *Alexandria*, a new raider being built for the Confederacy.

The final exigency concerned the Laird rams, two powerful ironclads that could have smashed into splinters any ships of the Union navy through either gunfire or ramming. Charles Francis Adams increased the tempo of his importunities and threats as the two rams neared completion under the watchful eyes of the Laird brothers. On 5 September 1863 Adams delivered to Earl Russell the equivalent of an ultimatum when he notified the Foreign Secretary that if the rams sailed under the Stars and Bars, "It would be superfluous in me to point out to your Lordship that this is war." Actually Adams's note was unnecessary; two days prior to its delivery Russell had secretly ordered that the rams be seized. One French ram was built and delivered to the Confederacy, but it arrived too late in the war to see service. The Laird-rams controversy was the last major crisis, and relations between Great Britain and the United States were conspicuously more friendly during the last two years of the war when it became increasingly evident that the South could not win.

As nations usually do, Great Britain pursued a selfish policy during the American Civil War. It was not in her interest to help the South achieve independence. The Confederacy would have to do that unaided. Once it became reasonably obvious that the South was unconquerable, then the coveted recognition would have been extended. If more Southern victories had been won, especially at Antietam, history might have been far different. Britain would not lift a finger, however, in a failing cause, even when, in the paroxysms of defeat early in 1865, the South offered to emancipate her slaves in return for British recognition.

Britain had military reasons for its reluctance to aid the Confederacy, in addition to the economic fact that it is unwise to war against one's best customer. Although the Royal Navy was much stronger than even the greatly augmented Union fleet and probably could have smashed the blockade and flattened Northern coastal cities, the price paid would have been exorbitant. The scattered British merchant marine, bastion of the national economy, would have been easy prey for American commerce raiders and privateers. Even though reinforcements had been sent to British North America, crack Northern armies could have invaded Canada and might have been able to conquer it. There were simply not enough compensating factors to overcome the obviously negative results for Great Britain that Anglo-American conflict would bring.

The international situation restrained the Queen's government as well. Although France usually acted as an ally, relations with Russia were conspicuously unfriendly.[3] The Crimean War had been over for less than a decade, and continuing imperialistic clashes made the likelihood of war between the Lion and the "Bear That Walks Like a Man" ever present. Here lies the main reason, perhaps, why Britain admitted culpability and eventually (1872) paid heavy damages for the Union losses suffered from the *Alabama*. If Great Britain helped to establish the precedent that a neutral could build commerce raiders for a belligerent and allow them to sail from neutral ports, Britain's supremacy of the sea would be in dire peril. English dreams became nightmares in which a future war with Russia might feature myriad American-built "Alabamaskis" and "Shenandoahovs" sliding out from American harbors under the double-eagle flag of the Romanovs to prey upon British merchantmen.

In the last analysis, the normal wartime relations between the Anglo-Saxon nations were reversed temporarily between 1861 and 1865. Usually Britain has been the dominant sea

[3] Russia was the only great power that appeared amicably disposed toward the Union. During 1863 twin Russian flotillas visited New York and San Francisco; many grateful Northerners hailed the Russians for this supposedly friendly gesture. Actually the Tsar expected war with Great Britain almost momentarily and wanted his fleet on the high seas, prepared to raid British commerce, rather than have it bottled up in the Baltic by a Royal Navy blockade.

power and the United States the leading neutral carrier (1793 to 1802, 1803 to 1812, 1914 to 1917, 1939 to 1941). It was the other way around during the Civil War, and Britain knew it. Therefore she hesitated to take any temporary advantage that might come to roost in future conflicts. It was well for the Union that London realized what issues were involved, for British intervention was the one manifest avenue by which Southern independence could have been gained and the Union permanently severed.

CHAPTER 34

Behind the Gray Lines

(1861-1865)

THE DAVIS ADMINISTRATION

While the military, naval, and diplomatic tides of the Civil War surged to and fro, Southern life had to cope with traditional ways as well as with new trails hewn out by martial exigencies. The Confederate States of America found this twofold task extremely difficult. Not only did the beleaguered citizens of the new Southern republic have to defend themselves against the more numerous and the more powerful adversary, but ordinary civilian problems were further complicated by the arduous necessities of feeding, clothing, arming, and training the army. An untried government had to wrestle with these difficulties, and it was a burdensome and onerous chore, lightened somewhat by Confederate administrators experienced in United States government positions.

Emulating the Union, the Confederacy bestowed considerable authority and responsibility upon its Chief Executive, and these powers were amplified by the war emergencies. Therefore the character, personality, and ability of Jefferson Davis, the first and only President of the Confederacy, became highly important. Although in many ways a great man, Davis was unable to serve his people with the consum-

398

mate skill demonstrated by Abraham Lincoln, his Union counterpart. Davis was a native Kentuckian—born only a few miles from Lincoln's birthplace—but while still a boy moved to Mississippi, where his elder brother Joseph had earned a fortune planting cotton. Young Jefferson Davis grew up in considerable luxury. A West Point graduate, he made an outstanding record as Colonel of the Mississippi Rifles during the Mexican War. In addition to his army career, Davis had been a planter, a lawyer, a Senator from Mississippi, and Secretary of War in Pierce's Cabinet. He was of ordinary stature, slender and handsome, with chiseled aquiline features. He was the finest type of Southern gentleman, the embodiment of honor and incorruptibility. His intelligence was high, and his will strong and indomitable. Usually he was courteous in personal relations.

Unfortunately his faults matched his impressive virtues. The President's health was poor, and chronic indigestion made him testy and irritable. His wife reported that he would return home, after a day spent directing the Confederate war effort, "a mass of throbbing nerves." Davis was overconfident and intolerant of criticism. As an administrator he felt that he must attend to everything himself; especially in his dealings with the War Department did he squander valuable hours upon minutia. Davis's considerable abilities in the military sphere gave him an excuse to meddle in strategic and even tactical direction, much to the despair of his generals. The President's fondest hope had been to command the Southern armies, and the top civilian job was little consolation. Davis played favorites among the Confederate generals, and his admiration for Braxton Bragg remains as puzzling as his distrust of Joseph E. Johnston. He seems to have been jealous of Robert E. Lee. The Confederate Executive was no politician, and he made no effort to form a "Davis party." Unwilling or unable to stir up much enthusiasm for his administration, he found it difficult to manage the war effort. Political squabbles between the President and both Congress and the state governors testify to Davis's inability to play the political game, and the South suffered as a result.

If Jefferson Davis was wanting in some respects, Vice-President Alexander H. Stephens was worse. A prominent planter and politician, Stephens had served as Senator from Georgia before the war. He had made no attempt to conceal his dislike for secession and openly fought to keep Georgia in the Union, although he reluctantly followed his state when it seceded. In an effort to pick up support from the former unionist element in the South, Stephens was elected Vice-President. His appearance was arresting. Stephens was a tiny, thin, beardless, wrinkled man who looked like a caricature of a dissipated adolescent. Although disturbed psychologically, he had a fine mind and considerable erudition. "Little Alex," however, could never submerge his strict state-rights convictions—he had opposed secession on the ground of expediency rather than illegality—for the better welfare of the whole Southern nation. Stephens constantly interfered with President Davis's conduct of the war. Long before the end, Stephens left Richmond and retired to his Georgia home, from which he constantly sniped at his superior. In a letter to a personal friend he characterized Davis as "weak and vacillating, timid, peevish,

obstinate . . . he is aiming at absolute power" —which seems a strange way to describe a potential dictator. The Confederacy received little assistance from its Vice-President.

Strangely enough at first thought, the most vocal and uncompromising secessionists were seldom rewarded with high governmental posts in the nation that they had been so instrumental in creating. Such fire-eaters as Lawrence M. Keitt, Robert Barnwell Rhett, and William L. Yancey were given either minor jobs or none at all. Robert Toombs was Secretary of State for a few months, but resigned after quarreling with Davis. Naturally these extremists were outraged when a unionist like Stephens was made Vice-President. Evidently Davis recognized that the ultrasecessionist talents so valuable in shattering the Union were not the best qualities for building a new nation. Many of the President's political troubles came from these disgusted and irate fire-eaters.

Men of varying talents held Confederate Cabinet positions, but all had a primary task in getting along with the irascible President and learning to tolerate his pettifogging interference. Jobs in Jefferson Davis's Cabinet were no sinecures. During the short life of the Confederacy there were four Secretaries of State, five Attorneys General, and six Secretaries of War. Cabinet officials worthy of mention were Judah P. Benjamin, corpulent, affable, and perspicacious, who held three separate positions, although his greatest fame came as Secretary of State; Christopher G. Memminger, Secretary of the Treasury during most of the war, serving as well as could be expected in view of the fearsome odds that he faced; and Stephen R. Mallory, an excellent Secretary of the Navy, although he suffered under the direction of the more military minded Davis, who paid relatively little attention to maritime affairs.

THE CONFEDERATE OPPOSITION

A popular misconception has stressed the unanimity of opinion and effort of the Civil War South, forming a stereotype of a whole section rushing as one man into battle with the hated Yankee and after heroic and total resistance finally being beaten to its knees by the stronger enemy. Naturally there is considerable truth in this ideal; hundreds of thousands in the Confederacy fought, worked, and suffered for homeland and way of life with an unselfish devotion. Certainly Southern women earned lasting renown for their courageous acceptance of extra tasks. Usually the Southern armies fought hard and well. Nevertheless, a leading reason for the defeat of the South was the extent of disagreement and dissension that rotted away the Confederate military and civilian *élan* until collapse came in 1865. Partially the South was crushed by Northern military and industrial preponderance; partially it committed suicide.

For thirty years prior to the outbreak of the war Southern orators had fulminated about state rights. Many never forgot these sentiments and applied them as easily to Jefferson Davis and their own Richmond government as they had to the menace implicit in Lincoln and the "Black Republicans." President Davis had the clear-cut and farsighted vision to perceive that some centralization must come and that state rights and local home rule were luxuries that the searing cauldron of war must temporarily engulf, but many of his fellow sectionals could not follow his argument.

By the end of 1862 a powerful opposition to Davis and his administration existed throughout the South, although it was stronger in the older coastal areas and in the mountains than it was in the Southwest, where Southern nationalism predominated over state rights. South Carolinians, proud of their heritage, particularly fought against Richmond centralization. Influential newspapers such as the Richmond *Examiner* and the Charleston *Mercury* subjected Davis's policies to searching scrutiny and usually blasted them with abandon. Although professing the loftiest motives of disinterested patriotism, this internal opposition was belligerent and powerful enough to hamper seriously the Confederate war effort.

There were three main areas of conflict between President Davis and his domestic opposition: conscription, the lifting of habeas corpus, and the powers of the state governors. It was only natural that resistance to the draft should develop. To most mid-century Americans, conscription was redolent of the foulest European tyranny, and opposition to forced military service was as much in the American tradition as spontaneous protest against arbitrary taxation. "Unconstitutional," "despotic," "malevolent," and "dictatorial" were only a few of the adjectives hurled at the Richmond government for inaugurating conscription, and the immoderate and open fight against it undoubtedly contributed to the failure of the Southern draft.

The privilege of the writ of habeas corpus, whereby the accused must know the nature of the charges against him and a reasonably prompt date must be set for trial, has long been a revered democratic right. Without such protection for individuals, arbitrary arrest is made easy for tyrants. Yet it has been admitted that some personal liberties must temporarily be curtailed in the interest of popular safety during public emergency. Early in 1862 President Davis asked the Confederate Congress for permission to suspend habeas corpus and to impose martial law in areas either menaced by the advance of Union armies or infested by unusually treasonous activities. This would mean that possible deserters or persons of doubtful loyalty might be held for further investigation. Twice the Confederacy lifted habeas corpus, first from February, 1862, to February, 1863, and second from February to August, 1864. Once more Davis's opponents professed to see the darkest manifestations of despotism, and late in the war they were powerful enough to frustrate renewed attempts to reinstitute the ban.

Jefferson Davis had a most difficult time with a few of the state governors, some of whom appeared to feel that Lincoln was far less a threat to their state than the sensitive and high-strung Confederate President. Among others, Governor Zebulon B. Vance of North Carolina was a nettle in the Confederate garden, but by far the worst was Governor Joseph E. Brown of Georgia. This worthy opposed almost every act designed to strengthen the Southern war potential and thereby to achieve victory. Brown was not a traitor; he was rather a narrow-minded and mistaken partisan, but his influence was most harmful. Not content with attacking conscription so heatedly that many of his constituents refused to pay any attention to it, Brown retained the impressive number of 8,000 in state jobs so that they would be draft-exempt. This back-country governor also exploded with rage at the suspension of habeas corpus.

The main clash between Georgia and the Confederacy came in the sphere of state-troops control. Governor Brown maintained that his Georgians should stay home to defend their state. When Sherman moved toward Atlanta in 1864 Brown immediately demanded heavy reinforcements from Davis, warning the President that if they were not forthcoming he would call upon all Georgians fighting in Lee's army to "return to their own state and within their own limits to rally round her glorious flag." There was no way in which Davis could comply, hence there is little cause to wonder why Sherman was able to march through Brown's domains with almost no opposition.

After Davis lost control of Congress in 1863, the growth of the opposition became speedy and catastrophic.[1] Old unionists who never believed in secession joined hands with those who were fearful that Davis meant to establish a military dictatorship. The effect of this combination's impressive propaganda was to augment desertions from the army, flaunt economic restrictions, break down the will to resist the enemy, and, in the last analysis, to be worth many thousands of Union soldiers in bringing about the defeat of the Confederacy.

[1] The degree of hostility to the Davis administration is exemplified by the fact that throughout the four years of the Civil War, the President vetoed thirty-eight bills and the Confederate Congress passed thirty-seven of them over his veto.

SOUTHERN MAN POWER AND MONEY

Supplying men for the army was perhaps the most essential task of the Confederate government. As in the Union, the first news of Fort Sumter brought wild excitement and a rush of men to the colors; they came so fast in 1861 that not all could be used. Volunteering was heavy throughout the first year, but began to slacken at about the same time that many of the original twelve months' enlistments were expiring. A bounty act could accomplish little, and during the spring of 1862 Davis was forced to sponsor the first conscription bill in American history.

Under the terms of this draft, as passed by the Confederate Congress, men between the ages of eighteen and thirty-five (later seventeen and fifty) were subject to call. The exemptions were generous to start with and were later amplified. Physical and mental disability were not the only reasons for exemption. Draft-deferred were such occupations as Confederate and state governmental service, teaching, mail carrying, ferrying, railroad labor, textile-factory work, and ownership of twenty or more slaves —the latter savagely resented by many less affluent Southerners. Furthermore, the principle of substitution plagued the Confederacy as well as the Union. A conscripted individual could either persuade or indeed purchase another to take his place. The states offered bounties to stimulate enlistments, and many individuals took advantage of these payments. Men would sign up with a regiment, collect a bounty, desert as soon as possible, and in another regiment again go through the same procedure. Confederate conscription was not a success. Relatively few soldiers were garnered by this method, and its effect upon popular morale was deleterious. Many of the more unionist Southern mountain areas were so hostile to the draft that the government dared not attempt to enforce compliance.

Generally speaking, a larger proportion of men of military age served in the South than in the North, although the exact number of Confederate soldiers is impossible to determine because accurate statistics are nonexistent. Some 1,300,000 were on army lists, but many names were repeated. Perhaps something approximating a million would be a fair estimate. The Confederate forces were plagued by desertion, and the increase in those absent without leave during the last two years of the war was an important factor in the Southern collapse. Late in 1864 it was reported that over 100,000 had deserted, although not all were motivated by selfishness or cowardice. The financially impotent Southern republic was unable to take adequate care of soldiers' families. There were many cases of actual hardship, and numerous desertions must have been in response to appeals from home.

In finance the Confederacy failed to an even greater extent, although it is difficult to understand how it could have been ameliorated, since the problems in the financial field were insoluble. When the war started the South had only a few hundred thousands of dollars on hand, including some cash seized from confiscated Federal mints. The Confederacy used all the time-honored measures of a war government in financial difficulty—increased taxation, bond sales, foreign loans, and fiat money.

The taxation story was dismal, for there was not enough cash in the South to make it worthwhile. The central government was practically ignored when it taxed the states. Excise levies on such commodities as tobacco, liquor, salt, and other goods brought in little. Something of value was received when a tax paid in the form of goods was imposed, but the two chief Southern assets, land and slaves, were not included. No levy on incomes was possible; and as the months passed, money in circulation drained away, except for paper. Taxation sources almost completely dried up; during the war the Confederacy received about 1 *per cent* of its total income from taxation.

The same insufficiency of circulating cash made Southern bond sales fail. Some improvement came when bonds were made redeemable in commodities, but no widespread success was possible. Little assistance came from abroad.

Some Confederate bonds were sold in England, and an ambitious campaign was carried on in France during 1863, but it made little difference. During the last two years of the Civil War, foreign investors were too chary of Confederate prospects to risk their money on Southern bonds that would obviously be defaulted after a losing war.

Printing paper money was the only method remaining, and it was utilized very widely. Confederate paper was backed only by a promise to redeem two years following any conclusion of peace with the United States. During the war about $1 billion in fiat money was printed and circulated by Jefferson Davis's government. Confederate dollars were never on a par with Union gold dollars, and they fluctuated wildly with the success or failure of Southern arms, for all knew that this currency would become worthless if the South lost. By 1864 Confederate paper had depreciated to about 30 to 1 with gold, and by the spring of 1865 it was practically valueless. Naturally a giddy inflation commenced, profiteers found easy gleanings, and the morale of Richmond clerks on $1,000 a year or, even worse, of Confederate privates at $16 a month can be imagined. After the war the Confederate debt was wiped out, and even today Confederate currency is worth little more than the commodity upon which it is printed.

CONFEDERATE WAR INDUSTRY

The Civil War meant that the basically agricultural Southern people had to industrialize at least to some degree. At the commencement of hostilities the noted Tredegar Iron Works at Richmond was the only heavy-ordnance plant throughout the seceded states. Yet an impressive job was accomplished industrially, especially in arming the troops. Union arsenals were seized in 1861, and some 200,000 muskets and rifles were amassed by this action. Perhaps 300,000 private firearms were owned by individual Southerners, and some of these became available for the army. Approximately 600,000 came through the blockade. As Confederate victories were won, many Union firearms were captured. Southern domestic production soared from such establishments as the main arsenal at Richmond and a new plant at Selma, Alabama. Tredegar expanded handsomely to become the scientific testing laboratory for new inventions and contained among its sprawling works machine shops, forges, and sawmills that kept 2,500 men busy. Almost a score of new munitions factories were founded during the war. Certainly much credit for Confederate achievement in this field must go to General Josiah Gorgas, head of the Ordnance Department. Under Gorgas's direction the Southern soldier was adequately armed throughout the entire conflict, a remarkable accomplishment for a nonindustrial people.

The Richmond government helped new manufactories get started by assuming half the construction costs, provided that they were erected for war production. Originally a 75 per cent profit was allowed on war contracts, but this was later reduced to 33⅓ per cent. The Confederate authorities worried about procuring war necessities and achieved some successes and some failures. A potential shortage in gunpowder was averted by the utilization of new sulfur deposits and the rapid increase of nitrogen output. Production of textiles scored some gains. Certain commodities, however, remained constantly scarce. Paper and ink were always difficult to obtain; pins and needles became practically family heirlooms. A tragic scarcity in medicines and opiates could never be adequately met—the effects upon Confederate soldiers facing amputations without anesthetics can be imagined. Lubricants were in short supply. Petroleum resources could never be developed, whale oil was cut off by the blockade, and such desperately contrived substitutes as cotton oil and peanut oil could not meet the demand. Perhaps the scream of ungreased axles sounded the Confederate requiem.

Naturally the shortage of specie, the flood of paper money, and the augmented needs of a war economy resulted in a dizzy upward spiral of Southern prices, with wages falling steadily

behind. In 1863 a dejected soldier wrote home that the price of liquor in Richmond was so high that "it would cost about fifty dollars to get tight here." By the middle of 1864 the price structure went insane, and such collector's items as a $350 ham and a $1,200 barrel of flour were the subjects of heated and dismayed conversations among Southern housewives. Efforts of the Confederate government failed to halt the inflation. An "Impressment Act" (1863) allowed Richmond to regulate prices, in addition to seizing commodities, and did bring some temporary relief, although eventually it fell far short of its goal; any good it accomplished was at the cost of tremendous popular ill will.[2]

VARIED ASPECTS OF THE SOUTHERN HOME FRONT

Hardship and privation might not have been so difficult for Southerners to bear had Confederate life mirrored greater equality of sacrifice, but such was not accomplished. There was widespread speculation, and many Southerners amassed great wealth from their fellow countrymen's misery by monopolistic hoarding of needed foodstuffs and other goods. A common sight in Southern ports during the conflict was the flashily dressed individual who owned a blockade runner, often parlaying a small investment into a fortune on one successful voyage. Certainly the South as a whole was afflicted by the war's impact far more heavily than the North, and the unequal effects engendered considerable resentment among the poverty-stricken who watched others living in riotous luxury.

Vital to any nation at war as well as in peace is the food supply, and here a good job was done by the wartime South. In general the Confederacy was well fed, and the relatively few instances of malnutrition—there was an occasional food riot in Richmond and other

[2] Perhaps a half-billion dollars was owed to private citizens by the Confederacy for goods seized during the war. This debt was, of course, never paid.

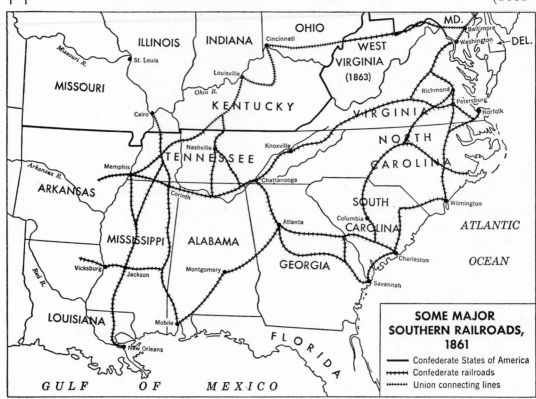

SOME MAJOR
SOUTHERN RAILROADS,
1861
—— Confederate States of America
+++++ Confederate railroads
++++++ Union connecting lines

cities—were caused by faulty transportation or exorbitant prices rather than by any actual shortage in food. Many of the Dixie farmers trudged off to war, but the slaves tended to stay loyal, and Southern women assumed many backbreaking agricultural tasks. Wheat, corn, and vegetable output remained sufficient for soldier and civilian.

This success was in part due to a curtailment of other farming production. Early in the war the cultivation of both cotton and tobacco was drastically reduced. From a high of 4,500,000 bales in 1861, cotton production tumbled to a scant 300,000 in 1865. Some 2,500,000 bales were destroyed during the war, most of them by plantation owners in response to government directives. This restricted cotton output naturally caused a price boom in that commodity in Europe and the North; on the New York market the price leaped from 13 cents a pound in 1861 to $1.90 in 1865. Toward the end of the struggle shrewd Northern traders connived with unscrupulous Union officers to

make fortunes by seizing contraband cotton that legally belonged to the United States.

Southern transportation was a constant headache from 1861 to 1865. Nothing like a complete sectional railroad system had been built before the firing on Fort Sumter, and there were few trunk lines anywhere below the Mason-Dixon line. The main east-west route of the Confederate railroad network went from Richmond to Chattanooga, proceeding then to Memphis on the Mississippi. The capital was connected to Charleston through Wilmington, North Carolina. A third railroad ran from Savannah to Atlanta, connecting with the main western line at Chattanooga. A fourth joined Charleston and Atlanta. Most Southern lines, however, were short branches connecting one city to another nearby, or the interior to the nearest port. Many cities might have two lines entering from opposite directions, but often they remained unconnected through the center of town, largely because of local carrying interests who wished to haul passengers and freight between the two terminals. There were no effective railroad connections from the main portion of the Confederacy beyond the Mississippi.

Few aspects of Southern life suffered more from the Civil War than did Confederate railroading. The South lacked almost completely the means to produce rolling stock or tracks, and one railroad usually had to be repaired by ripping up another. Union generals understood this grave enemy weakness and destroyed railroads whenever possible. Sherman's devastation in Georgia and the Carolinas applied to this means of transportation and was an important factor in winning the war. By 1865 railroading in the South was almost a thing of the past. There could be little substitution from other means of transportation. River travel was hampered by a growing scarcity of ships and increasing Union control of the major inland waterways. Horse-and-wagon transport was compelled to remain the lifeline of the Confederacy.

The Union blockade was a positive force in bringing on Southern defeat, and hardly an aspect of life in the South escaped its pervasive results. Tissue-thin in 1861, the Northern "blockade" steadily strengthened as time passed. The Confederates struck back with some privateering, the oceanic depredations of the famous commerce raiders, and particularly blockade-running. The last was carried on throughout the four years, although it ceased major operations after the fall of Wilmington, North Carolina, in January, 1865. In addition to that Carolina city, other home ports of the blockade-runners were originally Charleston, Savannah, Mobile, New Orleans, and Galveston. Gradually they were either isolated (Galveston), blockaded (Charleston and Savannah), or captured (New Orleans and Mobile). Nevertheless, almost every inlet along the Southern coast remained a potential haven for blockade-runners.

Ships engaged in this dangerous but profitable enterprise were owned by the Confederate government, by the Southern states, and by private persons, both Southern and foreign.

A relatively small percentage of goods even attempted to enter the Confederacy directly from Europe. Continental exports tended to go to Cuba, Bermuda, or Nassau in the Bahamas. Sleek, fast, shallow-drafted, and gray-painted blockade-runners would slide into some Caribbean harbor, pick up their cargoes, and silently depart. Although the Northern blockade relentlessly increased its efficiency, literally thousands of passages sneaked through the Union lines; and one intrepid steamer, the *Hattie*, made it sixty times. As Stephen Vincent Benét, author of the great Civil War epic *John Brown's Body*, so graphically expressed it:

For the coasts are staked with a Union net
But the dark fish slip through the meshes yet,
Shadows sliding without a light,
Through the dark of the moon, in the dead of
    night,
Carrying powder, carrying cloth,
Hoops for the belle and guns for the fighter,
Guncotton, opium, bombs and tea.
Fashionplates, quinine and history.
For Charleston's corked with a Northern fleet
And the Bayou City lies at the feet
Of a damn-the-torpedoes commodore;
The net draws tighter and ever tighter,
But the fish dart past till the end of the war,
From Wilmington to the Rio Grande,
And the sandy Bahamas are Dixie Land.

The Southern labor supply caused much concern. Although the idea of the "Confederacy in Arms" has been exaggerated, a greater proportion of whites was withdrawn from the labor pools in the South than in the North. Women, the aged, and children toiled to fill the need, but it was primarily slave labor that enabled the South to continue to fight so long. The slave population stayed loyal, and most Negroes quietly tilled their fields, even on plantations where only women watched over them. Despite sectional fears for more than a generation that slave rebellion was imminent, there was remarkably little trouble with the Negroes. Not only was most army labor done by slaves, but late in the war there was talk of forming Negro fighting regiments in the Confederate army; the Union had already used such units both for service and for combat. In a last spasm to achieve European recognition of Confederate independence, freedom from slavery was in effect offered to Negro soldiers, but it was too late to accomplish anything. If slave rebellion was unknown, however, desertions from the farm were not. Many Negroes ran away, particularly after the Emancipation Proclamation, and thousands usually tagged along after invading Northern armies, causing anguished concern among Union quartermasters who had to feed them. Yet despite the runaways, the basic loyalty of the slave population helped the South to fight on through the four bitter years.

Notwithstanding the heroic efforts of some citizens, the South lost the Civil War, and in so doing was ruined for many decades. Invaded, conquered, and humiliated, the South watched the obliteration of its whole way of life. Without compensation, the Thirteenth Amendment expunged some $2 billion in assets when it freed the slaves, although this cannot be considered total loss since the Negro population remained as a labor force. In the prostrate South, devastated as no part of the United States has ever been before or since, the task of reconstruction, almost hopeless to begin with, was made worse by the victory of fanaticism in the North. But that is a later story.

CHAPTER 35

Behind the Blue Lines

(1861-1865)

ABRAHAM LINCOLN

From 1861 to 1865 the North had a much easier time than did the South, although most of the same baffling dilemmas that plagued Confederate civilians harried those above the Mason-Dixon line. Luckily for the Union, it was served with conspicuous ability by its Chief Executive. If there is anything to the theory that democracy carries within itself the saving grace of somehow finding the right man for the right time, the character and personality of Abraham Lincoln would seem to offer proof. Many biographers have started lives of Lincoln with a chip on their shoulder: no man could be that impressive—I must write the truth about him—he must be "debunked." Yet again and again the originally hostile author has found that his researches only confirm the popular impression; Lincoln was a man of destiny.

Nevertheless, the appearance of this shambling Illinois lawyer and politician was in drastic contrast to the stereotype of the great popular leader. Lincoln's towering 6-foot 4-inch stature and powerful frame did not lend themselves to dignity and grace; any such impression was ruined by his slouching posture and his clothing, which looked like a rumpled bed.

He was homely, definitely so, yet at the same time his ugliness had fascination. From Lincoln's head sprouted stiff, unruly, black hair, which was graying toward the end of his life. He had a high brow, prominent ears, a swarthy complexion, and a strong chin, the latter smooth-shaven as late as his election to the presidency, but bearded at the time of his inauguration in the hirsute vogue that swept nineteenth-century American males. His hands and feet were large and ungainly enough to cause him embarrassment. His eyes were deep and gray, often with a pensive, melancholic expression.

Although never trained by much formal education, Abraham Lincoln's intelligence was impressive, and his literary talent amazing— as long as the English language is read, such sublimities of thought and felicities of expression as his Gettysburg Address and his Second Inaugural Address will never die. Lincoln was deeply humane, and the necessity of issuing orders that often resulted in the deaths of thousands of his fellow citizens caused him spiritual agony. Despite his inflexibility on basic moral issues, he was quite without pride, and the President's willingness to turn the other cheek was a source of somewhat irritated wonder to his more hot-tempered associates.

Lincoln was not a happy man, despite his love of badinage and humor. He was always telling stories, but there is a great deal of evidence that he used this method to escape from the broody melancholia that was often with him. He was haunted by feelings of insecurity and often tortured by doubts. During some of the most tense days of the Civil War, the President was almost heartbroken by the death of a son. His marriage was occasionally a purgatory. Yet there was certainly another side to his home life; the much-maligned Mary Todd Lincoln really loved him, and if her extravagance, temper tantrums, and lack of tact often drove him to the edge of desperation, she may have forced some degree of greatness upon the easygoing, slovenly, and relatively unambitious Lincoln.

All in all, the Civil War President was a most complex and complicated individual, although the varied aspects of his personality and character were just right for the troubled times. His love of the common people and the democratic philosophy was abiding and instinctive. Lincoln was a strange but extremely effective popular leader. He could stand firm for principle, and he would not budge on bedrock issues such as no extension of slavery and the preservation of the Union; but his tolerance and wisdom, his ability to grow, and his peculiarly democratic virtues were instrumental in guiding the Union to victory. He could flatter and cajole, capitalize on the self-interest of one and utilize a patriotic appeal to another, and keep by his side divergent groups and contrary individuals necessary for the task at hand. Above and over all else, Lincoln dramatized for the average American the meaning of the amorphous democratic philosophy with his "government of the people, by the people, and for the people." Perhaps this is the chief reason why Abraham Lincoln has remained our most beloved President.

THE LINCOLN CABINET

All the Chief Executive's tolerance, humor, and persuasiveness were needed to keep his War Cabinet together, for it was a most heterogeneous group. The suave, brilliant, and devious Secretary of State William H. Seward assumed at first that he would become the acting Prime Minister of the administration. Yet Lincoln quickly turned the contemptuous attitude evinced by the small, vivacious, parrot-beaked New Yorker into complete loyalty, and the Lincoln-Seward partnership became a most valuable Union asset. The Secretary of the Treasury was the vainglorious, opinionated, and sly Salmon Portland Chase of Ohio. All during his Cabinet tenure, Chase considered it a grotesque misfortune for the Union that fate had chosen the ungainly Middle Westerner to be President when he himself could have done so much better. To be sure, Chase was a fairly effective Secretary of the Treasury, but politically he was dynamite, being the favorite of the Radical Republicans. Modern historians have found it difficult to forgive Chase's conniving with Lincoln's enemies in the Republican party in order to gain for himself the nomination in 1864. Chase resigned from the Cabinet after this abortive attempt, and was kicked upstairs to become Chief Justice of the Supreme Court.

The shady Simon Cameron, first Secretary of War in Lincoln's administration, remained at that post long enough to enrich his friends with army contracts and to solidify his Pennsylvania machine firmly in power before the President was able to get rid of him, still early in the war. Cameron was succeeded by Edwin M. Stanton, small, thickset, bespectacled, and heavily bearded. This former Democrat was industrious, able, and magnetic, but also irascible, impetuous, quarrelsome, and heavy-handed. Lincoln's easygoing manner infuriated the Secretary of War. Stanton would rush into a Cabinet meeting with important dispatches from some such place as Pea Ridge and have to sit writhing on the edge of his chair while the President maundered on about old days riding circuit in Sangamon County, Illinois, or read aloud from the "humorous" works of Artemus Ward or Petroleum V. Nasby. Sometimes Stanton was extremely rude to his superior, but Lincoln gently offered no demurrer.[1] New vigor and efficiency had come to the War Department under Edwin M. Stanton, so Lincoln put aside any personal feelings.

An equally grim old mastiff watched over the Union navy. Gideon Welles's preparation for his navy post had been a trifle tenuous; he served as postmaster and later as an editor in Hartford, Connecticut. He was an admirable administrator, however, and miraculously enough the stern-faced, white-bearded Welles was the only man in the Cabinet who right from the start recognized the ability of the untrained President and did not think that he could do a better job. Welles was relatively quiet in Cabinet sessions, but his alert mind saw everything that went on, and he promptly wrote his impressions in his *Diary*, which remains one of the best records of the Civil War. His remarks about some of his colleagues were devastating. He always clashed with Chase, whom he despised, and originally with Seward, whom he accused with reason of meddling with maritime matters.[2] Edward Bates, Montgomery Blair, and Caleb B. Smith were less important members of Lincoln's Cabinet.

MANNING THE UNION ARMIES

The Union government had the primary responsibility of furnishing the men to "crush the rebellion." The North was even more unprepared for a long war than the somewhat more bellicose South. At first martial zeal was unrestrained in the free states. When the tidings of Fort Sumter resounded throughout the North, myriad recruits jammed into the enlistment offices. Even Lincoln illustrated the typical Northern unreadiness for a four-year holocaust; his call of April, 1861, was for only three-month volunteers. The icy shock of First

Bull Run did away with such woolen-headed opinion, and men were summoned for three-year enlistments. At no time during the Civil War was there a real shortage of Union troops, although the quality of some of them left much to be desired.

The majority of Union as well as Confederate soldiers were volunteers. Naturalized Irishmen, Germans, and other recent Americans joined the native-born in Northern regiments. Many foreigners, both expatriate soldiers of fortune or citizens of European countries, came either to fight or to observe. McClellan's headquarters was famous for the number of continental noblemen in attendance upon the "Union Napoleon."

The Northern armies were composed of many politics-ridden regiments recruited by the states. The usual process might go something like this: some politician would decide to earn a little publicity through patriotism and announce the formation of a regiment, calling for enlistments. He would receive a commission from the state as Colonel, the other officers would be appointed by the state or elected by the men, and an advertising campaign would seek to woo volunteers. Many of these political worthies were extremely poor officers, but gradually the worst of them were weeded out through death or resignation.

All through the war both the Federal government and the several states paid bounties to encourage enlistments, often as much as several hundred dollars per volunteer. In fact the Union spent some $300 million in bounties during the Civil War, and the states probably exceeded this staggering figure. The same type of person in the North as in the South jumped bounties in order to reenlist and re-collect. The price of bounties kept climbing as original enthusiasm ebbed away, and the Southern example of conscription soon had to be followed. At first the draft was applied to the states through a quota system, but still not sufficient progress was recorded. In 1863 Federal conscription was introduced and proved to be even a more resounding failure than its Confederate counterpart. If the state was unable to meet its quota (and previous volunteering was taken

---

[1] Someone told Lincoln that Stanton had stated that he was a fool. The President only smiled and said, "Then I expect I must be one, for he is almost always right, and generally says what he means."

[2] Early in the war Seward apologized for such behavior, admitting that he had interfered with Welles's Navy Department. The intrepid Gideon caustically noted in his *Diary*, "To this I cordially assented."

into consideration), a national draft would call as many men as needed to fill the lack. Physical and occupational exemptions were allowed, and the bounty system was continued. The most unfortunate provisions were that a man conscripted could go to the draft office with a substitute and be exempted for the whole war, or if he paid $300, be exempted from any one draft call. The real philosophy behind the Union conscription was to raise revenues and to keep the price of substitutes at a reasonable level, but naturally this could not be publicized.

The $300 exemption was the cause for the charge, "Rich man's war, poor man's fight." To the wealthy speculator such a sum was perhaps the cost of entertaining a few friends at Delmonico's famous New York restaurant, but to the city laborer at $1.50 to $2 a day it might as well have been $3 million. There was tremendous Northern popular resistance to the draft; the southern tier of counties in Ohio, Indiana, and Illinois were ablaze with resentment; and disorders afflicted Boston, Troy, and Albany; but it was in the nation's metropolis that the most serious outbreak occurred.

Without taking any adequate precautions and without officially notifying the city and state authorities, the Federal draft went into effect in New York City on 11 July 1863.[3] Two days later a frenzied mob, composed chiefly of Irish laborers, sacked the draft office, looted private homes, lynched eighteen Negroes and left them dangling from street posts, burned the Colored Orphan Asylum, attacked the New York *Times* and *Tribune* buildings, and fought pitched battles with policemen and soldiers. Not until 16 July was order restored. Although estimates of the total casualties have often been ridiculously exaggerated, probably something like seventy to eighty deaths and hundreds of broken heads marked this greatest urban insurrection in the nation's history. A few weeks later, with heavy reinforcements patrolling the streets, the conscription was carried out in New York City.

[3] The city was temporarily depleted of troops since detachments had been hurried to Pennsylvania to fight at Gettysburg.

Compared to the Confederate host, the Union army was well-armed, well-clothed, and well-fed. Yet perhaps 200,000 were absent without leave from the Federal army at one time or another. As in the South no adequate support was accorded to soldiers' dependents, and presumably many deserters went home for that reason. The modern American soldier would be aghast at conditions under which the Civil War troops served. The plight of Union soldiers was somewhat mitigated by the Sanitary Commission, an organization of private citizens, which looked after the health, well-being, and recreation of the Northern troops. As its name suggests, the commission's personnel was vigilant in examining the sanitary conditions in the army camps. Although not an employee, Clara Barton, the famous nurse and later director of the American Red Cross, worked in close conjunction with the Sanitary Commission. Even with such devoted assistance, food, medical care, and opportunities for amusement were far less readily available to the Civil War "Boy in Blue" than to the modern "GI."

NORTHERN FINANCES

Union finances wrote a far more successful story than did the Confederate monetary system. No wonder; the North had retained the Treasury and most of the mints, and the large amount of gold and silver on hand was steadily augmented by the production of Western mines.[4] As an established government, the Union had little difficulty in selling bonds to pay for armaments in the European nations. The effervescent prosperity put more money into circulation than ever before, and some of this trickled into the government's coffers. Yet war's capacious maw swallowed so much matériel that new sources of revenue had to be uncovered. Increased tariff schedules, elevated

[4] Although Nevada had an insufficient population for statehood, it was admitted into the Union in 1864, partly because of the Comstock Lode's fabulous silver production, and partly to gain a needed state vote for the ratification of the Thirteenth Amendment.

excise and income taxes, and personal loans to the nation in the form of bond purchases all played essential roles.

Following their party platform of 1860, the Republicans passed the Morrill Tariff (1861), vigorously increasing the tariff duties, which had been reasonably low since 1846. Tariffs continued to rise during the war and returned many millions to the government. Heavy excises were placed upon most commodities, although as usual mild vices such as tobacco and alcohol were taxed the heaviest. In 1863 the first American income tax became law, and levies finally went up to 10 per cent on the highest incomes. Such a tax was later held unconstitutional, and not until 1913 did the Sixteenth Amendment allow the government to tap again this lucrative source of revenue. Nevertheless, returns from tariffs, excise levies, and income taxes remained disappointingly low.

A more successful story was written in selling government bonds. Two chief markets for the purchase of bonds are banks and "persons" (either individuals or corporations). Early in the war sales were not going well; the bankers complained that they were not allowed sufficient return on their investments, and the public remained apathetic to buying appeals. Secretary of the Treasury Salmon P. Chase soon allowed banks to purchase bonds below par, and in 1863 he sponsored the passage of the National Bank Act whereby banks were permitted to issue paper currency up to 90 per cent of the value of government bonds owned.[5] Chase also commissioned the eminent Philadelphia financier Jay Cooke to float the first of the modern bond drives. Cooke was handsomely compensated, and he fell to with a will. Speeches, pamphlets, and advertisements appealed to the patriotism of Northern citizens, and inside of a year Cooke had disposed of $400 million to Northern citizens.

All these efforts were unable to keep the United States out of fiscal difficulties, and

[5] Not until the passage of the Glass-Owens Act of 1913 (Federal Reserve) was the somewhat inelastic currency under the National Bank Act of 1863 superseded.

deficit spending became common, although it never reached the astronomic heights achieved in the Confederacy. During the war some $450 million in paper "greenbacks" was issued by the United States, and these were backed only by the promise of the government to redeem them someday. This much additional circulating medium naturally increased prices and was important in brewing considerable inflation, but again, not to the same extent as in the South. The value of greenbacks was never at par with gold dollars, and they fluctuated in accordance with the success of the Union armies, dipping as low as $100 in paper for $39 in gold at one time. Many years later (1879) the greenbacks were redeemed at 100 cents on the dollar. Despite increased revenues from tariffs, excises, and income taxes, the United States was about $2 billion in debt by 1865, excluding the total Confederate debt, which was never assumed.

UNION INDUSTRIAL AND AGRICULTURAL GROWTH

The Civil War brought to the North a mushroom and scattered, but nonetheless impressive, industrial growth. At first the dire forebodings of the conservative businessmen who had warned that secession would mean Northern economic collapse seemed to come true. The sudden impact of lost cotton-state markets, the repudiation of debts owed by Southerners, the closing of the Mississippi River to Western commerce, and the general uncertainty made 1861 so bleak that more business houses closed during that year than during panic-swept 1857. Unemployment struck Northern urban laborers, land values slumped, and stocks crashed. The panic was of short duration, however. By early 1862 the realization of the immensity of the forthcoming war effort and its unprecedented industrial requirements brought back prosperity's glow. Speculation became rife; railroad, oil, and most manufacturing stocks spurted upward sharply. Unemployment declined, and there was a rush to establish new businesses.

Naturally armaments led the way. Although relatively better off than the Southern antagonist, the Union had no adequate munitions industry until military necessity applied the goad to production. During the first year of the war most matériel had to come from overseas, although by the middle of 1862 the Union was approaching self-sufficiency in this realm. Through the procurement of government contracts, new firearm manufactories were founded and old ones improved. Government arsenals accomplished miracles of production for that time; the one at Springfield, Massachusetts, had an output of 1,000 rifles a day by the end of the war. An ever-augmented flood of muskets, pistols, and heavy ordnance furnished the wherewithal for victory.

The war boom was not restricted to armaments. Most industrial production soared. New iron ranges were speedily developed in the Lake Superior region, and iron output during the war went up more than 20 per cent. Coal production doubled, and bituminous as well as anthracite began to be more widely utilized for industrial purposes. Perhaps the greatest Cinderella story was in petroleum. The first wells were sunk late in the 1850s at Titusville, Pennsylvania, and a gusher spouted there in 1859. Natural rock oil came just in time, for the war severely restricted the use of whale oil. So much petroleum was used for both illumination and lubrication that the number of barrels produced in 1864 was six times that of 1860.

Augmented demands for uniforms stimulated the woolen industry, which doubled its output in three years. The boom in wool was accompanied by a revolution in men's clothing. Largely because of the improved sewing machine and other technological innovations, ready-made suits rather than the more expensive hand-tailored clothing became common, and the methods used to furnish hundreds of thousands of uniforms were easily duplicated for civilian markets. Wartime whisky distilling and sugar refining established new records. Shoe factories hummed under the stimulus of army orders.

The Civil War years saw both an increase and a consolidation in the Northern railroad system, although its progress was somewhat slower than had been the case during the 1850s. In 1861 the North was far superior to the South in miles of track and numbers of rolling stock, and this disparity steadily increased. While the Southern railroads were being captured and destroyed, or merely wearing out, the Union lines expanded and improved. A new railroad was opened running from New York State on Lake Erie to Cincinnati, and another was opened from the Atlantic Coast to the West. Consolidation with smaller and weaker lines strengthened both the Pennsylvania and the Chicago and Northwestern systems. More double-tracking, greater use of the standard gauge, new locomotives and cars, and better terminals were vital in transporting men and matériel to fighting front or civilian center. During the war the first transcontinental railroad was commenced, although its completion belongs to a later period.

In general the war years were kind to the Northern farmer. Not only did new demands for his foodstuffs come from the army, but simultaneously some poor European crops necessitated large-scale utilization of Northern grain. From 1861 to 1865 American agricultural exports valued at a third of a billion dollars were shipped overseas. Luckily the weather was good in the Middle West during the war years. Inflated currency and augmented demands caused an exhilarating rise in farm-commodity prices. Less pleasant for the countryside population was the labor shortage. Many of the younger farmers went off to war; and even with wages for agricultural laborers at the then unheard-of figure of $2 a day, help was still hard to get. The lack was partly filled by women's work in the fields, partly through immigrant toil (by 1864 immigration was again under way in considerable numbers), and partly by increased use of agricultural machinery. Factories producing harvesters, reapers, and binders enjoyed banner years.

Several acts passed by Congress were of epochal importance to the Northern (and eventually the Southern) farmer. In 1862 the government acceded to the demands of many agricultural groups when the famed Homestead Act was written into law. Under its terms a farmer could procure from the government a quarter-section amounting to 160 acres, which became permanently his after five years of residence. The Morrill Land Grant Act of the same year allotted to each state as many times 30,000 acres of the public domain as the total number of the state's electoral votes. The proceeds from subsequent sale were to be used to establish a college of "agriculture and mechanic arts." Also in the same vital year, a Federal Commission of Agriculture was established. The real effect of these three acts, however, belongs to the postwar period.

While generally agriculture and industry prospered during the conflict, there were some significant exceptions. If wool skyrocketed, cotton textiles slumped as the source of supply from the South gradually dried up, and many thousands were forced to find work elsewhere. The merchant marine took a battering from Confederate raiders, and the Civil War marks the beginning of a long period of commercial decline. All was not loss, nevertheless, since most ships were sold to foreign concerns and the proceeds invested in new domestic enterprise. After 1865 New Bedford and Nantucket no longer saw great whaling days. Worst of all was the effect of inflation. Northern prices never went berserk to the degree of those in the South, but the cost of living sharply increased. The usual effect was felt by those unfortunate enough to be on fixed salaries or pensions. Although wages were elevated they lagged well behind prices, and there is little question but that real wages fell abruptly between 1861 and 1865. Realization of this caused much urban discontent and unrest.

With so much money floating around, many corralled impressive fortunes through overly favorable contracts, speculative enterprises, and in some instances outright graft. Particularly were the contracts awarded by the War Department under Simon Cameron in 1861 a national scandal. Not only were prices charged to the government exorbitant, but even worse, the quality of many commodities bought for the army was disastrously low.

Sand was mixed with sugar, leather approximated cardboard, grains made up much "coffee," arms previously condemned as useless or even unsafe were resold, and so inferior was the composition of woolen wastes into a material called "shoddy" from which uniforms were made that the very word has become an adjective meaning cheap, worthless, and sleazy. Many Northerners secretly traded with the Confederacy, either overland in the Middle West or at sea by owning and operating blockade-runners. Some army officers and crooked businessmen cheated the nation out of proceeds from confiscated cotton near the end of the war. It should be emphasized, however, that these borderline criminals were a minority, and most businessmen supplied the government with commodities of good quality at a fair price.

The effect of the over-all Northern prosperity was to bring about much conspicuous consumption. More puritanical Northern contemporaries were outraged by the waste and luxury flaunted by the "shoddy aristocracy." In all the Northern cities the shops were ablaze with the finest European imports. Theatrical entertainment enjoyed halcyon days. Sharp speculators, fraudulent contractors, and dishonest politicians along with their feminine counterparts crowded the well-known restaurants. The suddenly affluent displayed their prosperity with ostentatious clothing, glittering jewels, and magnificent carriages. Whether the war increased drinking, prostitution, and general sexual license is hard to ascertain, but the letters, diaries, editorials, and sermons of the time furnish some evidence that such happened.

UNION POLITICAL OPPOSITION

The Civil War led to no political hiatus in the Union. The initial wave of enthusiasm for the North that followed the bombardment of Fort Sumter temporarily resulted in something akin to sectional political unity; and although this soon began to splinter, some manifestations continued throughout the war. Of course Lincoln had been elected as a Republican, but the decision that the Northern theme should be the maintenance of Union rather than the eradication of slavery led to a temporary end to the Republican party. The administration altered its name to the National Union party, naturally heavily Republican in personnel, and called upon "loyal" Democrats to rally behind Lincoln and his prosecution of the war.

❡ *The Copperheads.* In response to the National Union appeal, the Democratic party split into three recognizable major segments. Most Democrats stayed in their old party, eagerly attacking the Lincoln administration's policies, although they remained basically loyal to the Union and to the subjugation of the "rebellion." A numerically small wing harkened to Lincoln's call, and these so-called War Democrats joined the administration, giving credence to the claim that the National Union party was a truly coalition organization. The third bloc of the Northern Democrats bitterly opposed the prosecution of the war. Ranging in opinion from those manifesting an innate pacifism that reacted against war per se to the other pole of extreme Southern sympathizers, many of whom were outright traitors, these "Peace Democrats" or "Copperheads" [6] constantly urged adoption of a negotiated peace and recognition of Confederate independence. The Copperhead membership was organized into several secret societies whose activities tended to overlap. The first was the Knights of the Golden Circle, which had been vocal in advocacy of slave-state expansion into Mexico and the Caribbean during the 1850s. Most of its members drifted into a later organization called the Order of American Knights and after 1863 into another known as the Sons of Liberty.

The Copperheads were surprisingly strong, numbering in the hundred thousands. The precise aggregate is unusually difficult to ascertain, for after the war many tried to cover any

[6] The name was ostensibly merited through the wearing or showing of a copper coin, but certainly most of their opponents considered the Copperheads to be human varieties of the venomous reptile.

evidence of anti-Union feeling from 1861 to 1865, such sentiments having become decidedly unpopular. Centered in the lower Middle West and in New York City, the Copperheads were able to hamper seriously the conduct of the war. They stirred up resistance to the draft, especially in New York during the great Draft Riots of July, 1863. Lincoln and the unionists were perpetually raked in the editorial pages of such newspapers as the Chicago *Times* and the New York *Daily News*. The most ambitious Copperhead effort culminated in a plot to seize Chicago with the help of Confederate prisoners of war during the Democratic convention of 1864. Lack of nerve and prompt countermeasures caused the cabal to fail. Also abortive was an attempt to set New York afire by simultaneous arson in the leading hotels of the city. It was the result of Copperhead intrigue that killed President Lincoln.

The amount of disloyal conversation and writing permitted of the Copperheads during the Civil War astounds modern Americans used to total war and relatively unanimous opinion on basic issues. Although occasionally a newspaper felt the lash of official chastisement, the Copperhead press was permitted great license. The leading Eastern antiwar newspaper, the New York *Daily News*, was allowed to publish many editorials similar to the following:

Let not the perfidious Administration invoke the sacred names of the Union and the Constitution in the hope of cheating fools into the support of the unholy war which it has begun. . . . What then, in this dreadful emergency should Northern citizens do? . . . no sympathy or support should be given the Administration. . . . He is no Democrat who will enter the army or volunteer to aid this diabolical policy of Civil War. . . . The wealthy will not supply means . . . and the poor man has the same right to refuse his services in the unholy struggle. Without the support of the Northern Democracy the Administration cannot prolong the war it has so wickedly begun. It will be baffled . . . disgraced, defeated, and accursed.

Furthermore, the North (as well as the South) was plagued by a lack of press censorship, and even the loyal papers regularly printed the most meticulous details of troop movements, as well as general commentary on over-all strategy. Robert E. Lee regularly perused the columns of the New York *Herald*, and on more than one instance gleaned information that his Confederate spies had been unable to discover.

(*Constitutional Disputes.* To those today who have heard constantly of Lincoln's greatness, it is surprising that so many of his Northern contemporaries feared and detested the "Great Emancipator" and heatedly objected to his prosecution of the war. This group had some powerful arguments on their side, too, for sometimes Lincoln did act contrary to the Constitution. In 1861–1862 the administration temporarily cracked down on disloyal sentiments, and although its action seems remarkably forbearing rather than despotic to modern eyes, some 13,000 were arrested during the war for fomenting resistance to conscription, criticizing the government too vehemently, or trafficking with the enemy.

Particularly in two areas did Lincoln circumvent the Constitution and defy the pronouncements of the courts. The first of these was over suspension of the right of habeas corpus. As in the South, many in the North vigorously opposed the relinquishment of such a fundamental right. In order to keep Maryland in the Union, by Executive order in 1861 Lincoln had hundreds of Southern sympathizers tossed into Federal prisons without charge, although most of them were soon released after taking an oath of loyalty to the United States. John Merryman, one of those arrested, appealed to Chief Justice of the Supreme Court Roger Taney to grant a writ of habeas corpus so that he might have a speedy trial. Taney obliged, but the prison commandant refused to honor it, stating that such writs had been suspended by the President. In *Ex parte Merryman*, Taney then declared that the writ could be removed only by Congress, not by the President. To hurdle Taney's roadblock, Congress passed the Habeas Corpus Act (1863), giving Lincoln the power to suspend the writ.

A second field of contention was over the trial of civilians by military courts. To be sure, the final decision was not forthcoming until after the war, but Lincoln appears to have been acting on illegal grounds during the conflict. A famous case arising from the civilian-military jurisdictional dilemma concerned Clement L. Vallandigham, Representative from Ohio. This prominent Copperhead disregarded an order by Union General Ambrose E. Burnside and was tried by a military court-martial, found guilty, and sentenced to prison, but Lincoln decided to exile him to the Confederacy. The Southerners did not want him and permitted Vallandigham to proceed to Bermuda and thence to Canada, from which he ran for Governor of Ohio but was soundly beaten.[7] Lambdin B. Milligan, another Peace Democrat, was arrested under the Habeas Corpus Act on the grounds of fomenting rebellion and was swiftly convicted by a military court. In 1866 the Supreme Court held in *Ex parte Milligan* that there was no right to try civilians in military courts when civilian tribunals were in existence. Certainly this decision cast grave doubts upon the legality of many acts passed during and especially after the Civil War. Basic to the whole dispute was the almost insoluble issue of the precise delineation of the President's wartime powers, and every American conflict has seen controversy on that point.

(*The Radical Republicans.* If Lincoln was beset from the one side by the Peace Democrats, the Radical Republicans, the ultra antislavery wing of his own party, attacked from the other. Such prominent Congressmen as Charles Sumner of Massachusetts, Benjamin Franklin Wade of Ohio, Henry Winter Davis of Maryland, and Thaddeus Stevens of Pennsylvania considered the President a weakling and a coward for his initial refusal to make freeing the slaves the leading issue of the war. Obsessed by the moral wrong involved, these partisans were unable to comprehend Lincoln's broader and more subtle policy of waiting until the proper psychological moment be-

[7] The famous sketch, *The Man without a Country* by Edward Everett Hale, was based on this case.

fore making the war to save the Union also a struggle to emancipate the bondsmen.

The Radical Republicans constantly quarreled with Lincoln, and their pressure steadily intensified. Early in the war they were loud in denouncing the President for rebuking the erratic General John Charles Frémont for inaugurating emancipation in Missouri on his own initiative. Starting with the appointment of a Joint Committee on the Conduct of the War (December, 1861), Radical Congressmen snooped about and interfered with military matters, selecting such officers as Generals George B. McClellan and Fitz-John Porter as objects of their unrelenting hostility, while praising Frémont, "Beast" Butler, and "Fighting Joe" Hooker as paragons of military virtue. The committeemen seem to have been motivated more by how the particular officer felt about slavery rather than by how effective he was in the field. Even the publication of the Emancipation Proclamation in September, 1862, cleared the air only momentarily, and soon the Radical pack was again in full cry on the slavery question.

Even more heated was the executive-legislative clash on future treatment of the Confederacy after the war was over. Spurning the President's plan for eventual leniency toward the South, Congress passed in 1864 the Wade-Davis bill, which foreshadowed some of the paths along which the later Reconstruction would run, but Lincoln killed it with a pocket veto. The Radicals reacted angrily to this, plotted to nominate another in Lincoln's stead until convinced that such action would be politically ruinous, and rapped the President's knuckles in the Wade-Davis Manifesto, which challenged Lincoln by asserting that "the authority of Congress is paramount . . . and if he [Lincoln] wishes our support, he must confine himself to executive duties . . . and leave political reconstruction to Congress." There is every reason to believe that had Lincoln not attended Ford's Theater on the fateful evening of 14 April 1865, he would have been subjected to the same vituperation and abuse that fell upon his luckless successor, Andrew Johnson.

THE EMANCIPATION PROCLAMATION

Actually the Radicals should not have been so suspicious of Lincoln on the emancipation issue. Both were traveling in the same direction; only their velocities differed. Although Lincoln's hatred for slavery was real, his political intelligence recognized that immediate emancipation in 1861 would probably have lost the border slave states, thousands of Northern Democrats in the army, and perhaps the war itself. Lincoln had to delay, to wait, to bide his time until the proper moment. All through 1861 he hymned on the tune of unionism and soft-pedaled the slavery question. As late as the summer of 1862 he replied in the negative to Horace Greeley's fervent New York *Tribune* editorial, "The Prayer of Twenty Millions," calling for freedom for the bondsmen. The President stated:

My paramount object in this struggle *is* to save the Union, and *not* either to save or destroy slavery. If I could save the Union without freeing *any* slave, I would do it; and if I could do it by freeing some and leaving others alone, I would also do that. . . . I have here stated my purpose according to my view of *official* duty, and I intend no modification of my oft-expressed *personal* wish that all men, everywhere, could be free.

For a time Lincoln mused upon the possibility of compensated emancipation for the slaves in the Union border areas, but there was little enthusiasm for it either in Congress or in the border states, and the project soon lapsed. Finally Lincoln decided that the political advantages of liberation overshadowed the obvious disadvantages, and he resolved to free at least some of the slaves. Emancipation would stir up support among the Radical Republicans, and it would have attraction for Europeans. Perhaps the progress of the war and the consequent rise in feelings of hatred against the enemy would keep the antiemancipationists quiet. At any rate Lincoln decided that it was worth the gamble. The President discussed the matter with his Cabinet during the summer of 1862, and although some were favor-

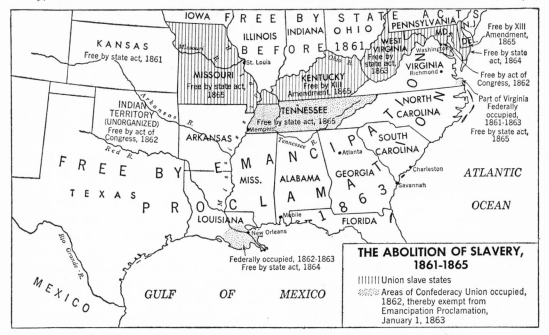

THE ABOLITION OF SLAVERY,
1861-1865

||||||| Union slave states

Areas of Confederacy Union occupied,
1862, thereby exempt from
Emancipation Proclamation,
January 1, 1863

able, it was agreed that a proclamation must not be published until Lee's first invasion of the North had been checked or it might appear to be the last despairing wail of a defeated nation. McClellan's victory at Antietam was more of a draw than a smashing triumph, but it was sufficient for political purposes.

On 22 September 1862 the Emancipation Proclamation was issued. It was a peculiar document. It stated that on 1 January 1863 all slaves in states "in rebellion against the United States shall be then, thenceforward, and forever free." Possibly Lincoln hoped that this might impel some states to return to the Union so that they could keep their slaves, but such an eventuality was recognized as extremely remote. The act had the strange result of freeing not a single slave in areas where they *could* be liberated and it freed all the slaves where they *could not* be emancipated. The border slave states were not unaffected, and even Confederate districts controlled by Union troops before 1863, such as the city and environs of New Orleans, were untouched by the proclamation. However, as Northern armies widened their occupancy of the Confederate States after 1 January, the Emancipation Proclamation became potent. Yet to be precise it

was the Thirteenth Amendment to the Constitution that freed all the slaves, everywhere in the United States.

THE REELECTION OF LINCOLN

The immediate political consequences of Lincoln's antislavery policy were disastrous. The autumnal congressional plebiscites of 1862 reflected deep hostility to emancipation and general dissatisfaction with the administration's conduct of the war. The National Union party of Republicans and War Democrats narrowly escaped a debacle; only New England and scattered state support saved it, for the Democrats captured New York, New Jersey, Pennsylvania, Ohio, Indiana, Illinois, and Wisconsin. Union victories at Gettysburg and Vicksburg during 1863 enabled the administration to make a mild comeback, but unionists looked toward the presidential election of 1864 with trepidation.

National unionist gloom was heightened during the spring and summer of that year by the staggering Northern losses at the Wilderness, Spotsylvania Courthouse, and Cold Harbor. The confident Democrats gathered for their convention in Chicago with the Copperheads unusually strong. A peace plank was written into the platform, assailing the administration for "four years of misrule by a sectional, fanatical, and corrupt party" which had carried "our country to the verge of ruin," and calling for a negotiated peace with the Confederacy. The Democrats then proceeded to nominate General George B. McClellan, former commander of the Army of the Potomac, only to see their candidate accomplish the weird feat of accepting the Democratic nomination while denouncing its peace platform. The Copperheads were beside themselves with fury at this "treachery," and the most extreme pro-Southerners spent the months before election cursing both McClellan and Lincoln with equal fervor. Inside the National Union party, the Radicals tried to bypass Lincoln, but their attempts to nominate one of their own—Salmon P. Chase, for instance—failed, and Lincoln was permitted to run for a second term.

So dismal were the National Union prospects for the autumn election that during the summer Lincoln asked his Cabinet members to sign their names to the back of a sheet of paper. After the victory had been won, he read to them what they had signed: ". . . it seems exceedingly probable that this administration will not be re-elected. Then it will be my duty to cooperate with the President-Elect as to save the Union between election and inauguration." Military successes shortly after the signing of this melancholy communication had saved the President, especially Sherman's capture of Atlanta and Admiral Farragut's dashing success at Mobile. Although the popular vote was extremely close (Lincoln took New York by only 7,000 ballots) the President won an overwhelming electoral victory, 212 to 21 for McClellan. Lincoln's accession to a second term was heightened by his sensitive and beautiful Second Inaugural Address, which concluded:

With malice toward none, with charity for all, with firmness in the right as God gives us to see the right, let us strive on to finish the work we are in, to bind up the nation's wounds, to care for him who shall have borne the battle and for his widow and his orphan, to do all which may achieve and cherish a just and lasting peace among ourselves and with all nations.

A little more than a month after inauguration and only five days after Lee's surrender at Appomattox, President and Mrs. Lincoln decided to attend Ford's Theater in Washington. The presentation on that dire 14 April was *Our American Cousin*, a popular farce featuring a stock character of nineteenth-century American drama, the arrogant, stupid, and foppish English nobleman. While the President chuckled from the Executive box, and a sentry supposed to guard the street door wandered down to a saloon for a beer, John Wilkes Booth, Copperhead scion of the eminent theatrical family, stole upstairs, pushed aside the curtain, leaned in, placed a small pistol almost against Lincoln's head, and fired. As the President slumped over, Booth leaped from the box down onto the stage, catching and breaking his leg on an American flag—how symbolic —and managed to make a temporary escape before a posse soon cornered him in Virginia and killed him. Lincoln was not the only Northern leader marked for slaughter on that night. A second assassin entered Secretary of State Seward's bedroom, knifed him, and slashed Seward's son almost fatally when the latter rushed in to protect his father. A third conspirator was supposed to kill Ulysses S. Grant; he jumped on the side of the General's carriage, only to flee before the impassive and steady glare of the victor at Appomattox.

Lincoln was carried across the street from the theater into a private home and placed upon a bed. He lived throughout the night but died early the next morning without regaining consciousness. His black-draped funeral train crept across the nation from Washington back to Springfield, Illinois, and silent crowds marked its somber passage with tears that were real and unashamed.

THE CIVIL WAR: CONCLUSIONS

The assassination of the President wrote a tragic epilogue to the American Civil War, perhaps the greatest single calamity in the nation's history. Three major conflicts—the Civil War and World Wars I and II—have been fought by the United States during the last century. Of these, the Civil War alone killed and mutilated only American citizens, devastated only American landscapes, and destroyed only American property. Some may point out that World Wars I and II were on a much wider scale, and their casualties were far higher. True, but their effect upon the American people and land was far less centralized or implacable than the Civil War, waged, as Winston Churchill said, "to the last desperate inch." Tremendous as have been the twentieth-century blood baths, their influence upon the United States has varied. Soldiers and their families suffered, but the civilian economy thrived. In the two global conflicts, Europe, Asia, and Africa were partially laid waste; the Western Hemisphere remained inviolate. American casualties in the Civil War were about four times greater than in World War I, and roughly equal to those of World War II. But in comparison to the latter, it was a much smaller population that fought the Civil War; the close to a million casualties from 1861 to 1865 represent 1 of 31; in World War II they were only 1 of 145. In the latter contest there was national harmony for the most part and a common sense of elation in the hard-won triumph; the Civil War left almost half the nation ruined and hate-filled.

The effect of the four-year holocaust during the 1860s was direct and sustained. It has often been referred to as creating modern industrial America, and there is some truth in this allegation. Nevertheless, industrialism was well under way previously and would have come inevitably. To be sure, the Union remained intact, and the moral wrong that was slavery expunged. But what was the war's effect on the generation that fought it, and on later generations?

Not only were approximately 275,000 killed, the vast majority being young men in their prime, but the physical and psychological scars upon the almost 700,000 wounded and prisoners festered for years. Who can calculate exactly the effect upon individuals who were incarcerated in such dreadful Confederate prisons as Andersonville and Libby, or at the Northern "Devil's Island" at Elmira, where the basic miseries of prison life were made almost unbearable by the polar blasts of an upstate New York winter? How deep were the mental wounds of those who underwent amputations at the front, often without anesthetics, or rotted away in crowded, filthy, reeking, germ-ridden hospitals? Nor did the military alone suffer. Who can gauge the emotional impact upon women who waited month after month and then year after year for men who never came back from the war? These shattered wives and mothers were without even the bitter assurance that husband or son was dead, for there were many thousands of "unknown soldiers" in unmarked graves.

The war left a sizable number of Northerners with a heritage of animosity toward the defeated foe, and the next few years were to see the ugly harvesting of hate, during what has been called with a lack of precision "Reconstruction." It was worse in the South, much worse, for there the losses of wealth, social position, and loved ones were made doubly intolerable by the added legacy of blasted illusions and sacrifice in vain for a losing cause.

The Civil War was unavoidable once secession came, for the Union was indissoluble. Unquestionably the war contained some national benefits. Unrestrained sectionalism had been dealt a mortal wound. Almost four million Negro Americans faced a brighter future. The United States was destined to throb with industrial vigor, and technological improvements would revolutionize the American way of life. Millions of Europeans would find better conditions on this side of the Atlantic. New horizons beckoned in education, literature, the arts, and recreation. But was it because of, or in spite of, the Civil War? To keep the nation intact, Americans paid a fearful price from 1861 to 1865. Was it too high?

CHAPTER 36

Reconstruction Diplomacy

(1865-1877)

PROTECTING THE MONROE DOCTRINE

To a greater extent than ever during the years that followed the conclusion of the Civil War, the United States turned its back on foreign affairs to concentrate upon domestic issues. Naturally this could be no "turtle-in-the-shell" withdrawal, for close commercial ties with Europe made such action impossible. Nevertheless, American isolation was considerable. For one thing, Europe lived in peace for a generation and more after the conclusion of Bismarck's Wars of German Unification (1864 to 1871), and thus Americans could avoid entanglements when there were no general wars to invite incidents.

Furthermore, the great American thrust to the West was under way to a more concerted extent than formerly, and the burgeoning American economy was adjusting, amalgamating, and developing. Too many vistas were opening at home to make foreign escapades very popular. This introverted process was, however, gradual. It was not until the middle 1870s and 1880s that what has been called the "nadir of American diplomacy" was reached. During the first seven years that followed Appomattox (1865 to 1872) much happened of

interest and importance in the field of international relations, despite some degree of American public apathy.

As part of its ponderous legacy, the Civil War left difficulties with other nations, since American internal strife had created something of a diplomatic vacuum in the Western Hemisphere. Spain, harkening to the appeals of some citizens of the rebellion-ravished island republic of Santo Domingo, had taken that Caribbean nation back into the Castilian Empire (1861). Peace refused to come to Santo Domingo, however, and local disturbances continued to harass the Spaniards, discouraging their attempts to gain popularity. Menaced by growls from the victorious Union, Madrid withdrew from Santo Domingo in 1865.

❮ *France and Mexico.* Considerably more dangerous to American security and world peace were the steps paced off by the devious French Emperor Napoleon III. This Bonaparte had proved himself no friend of the Union during the Civil War, and his hostile attitude climaxed in his Mexican adventure (1861 to 1867). Mexico had continued to suffer from periodic revolutions during the 1850s. Shortly before the outbreak of the American Civil War, a somewhat more liberal Mexican faction had elected to the presidency a full-blooded Indian named Benito Juárez, who proceeded to inaugurate some needed reforms. The more conservative opposition, composed mainly of large landowners, high army officers, and certain prelates of the Mexican church, appealed to Napoleon III to restore law and order. The French potentate was willing to accept the call, and his pretext was furnished when the Juárez government, unable to meet its obligations to foreign bondholders, announced a two-year suspension of payments. Playing his usual undercover game, the French Emperor persuaded Great Britain and Spain to join France in a tripartite naval expedition and force Mexico to honor its financial requirements to the citizens of the three European monarchies by bombarding the Mexican coast. Late in 1861 a naval expedition captured Vera Cruz, the leading Mexican port. By this time the British and the Spaniards were able to perceive that Napoleon III planned an actual conquest of Mexico and, unwilling to underwrite this venture, withdrew. A French army marched to Mexico City, drove Juárez into the north, and established quasi-control over the resentful Mexican populace. Obviously Napoleon planned to create a French puppet state in an American country.

Even before his military intervention had taken place, Napoleon III had made contact with Maximilian von Hapsburg, brother of the Austrian Emperor. Maximilian was renowned for an amiable disposition, a lovely young wife, magnificent blond whiskers, and a fine marine aquarium on the Adriatic. Apart from his family connections, his other qualifications for high executive position were a trifle tenuous, but Napoleon offered to install the Austrian as Emperor of Mexico. The youthful Hapsburg first announced that he would not don the imperial diadem unless the Mexican people wanted him, but a rigged poll in Mexico and the pleadings of his ambitious wife, Carlota, finally impelled him to accept—a decision that would ultimately cost him his life. In 1864 Maximilian signed with Napoleon III the Convention of Miramar, in which the French Emperor promised continuing military assistance

in return for economic exploitation of Mexico. During the same year Maximilian and Carlota sailed to Mexico. Conditions were still in flux throughout the new Hapsburg Empire. For two years the French army had chased President Juárez all over central and northern Mexico, and although the Gallic invaders were able to control the strip between Vera Cruz and Mexico City, most of the nation elsewhere remained in turmoil.

Meanwhile, what of American opinion? Obviously the United States had to proceed with extreme caution. The Union was having quite enough trouble with gentlemen named Jefferson Davis, Robert E. Lee, and several hundred thousand more without adding the armed might of the second military power of Europe. Hence, Lincoln and Seward initially could take no direct measures against the French in Mexico—a circumstance in direct violation of the Monroe Doctrine—but had to wait until victory over the South had been achieved. Nevertheless, the United States made clear its opposition to Napoleonic imperialism in the Western Hemisphere when the House of Representatives voted unanimously (109 to 0) that ". . . it does not accord with the policy of the United States to acknowledge any monarchical Government . . . in America under the auspices of any European power." When the Civil War finally ended, 50,000 battle-hardened Union soldiers under General Philip Sheridan were rushed to the Rio Grande, and Secretary of State Seward was able to accelerate the vigor of his protests to Paris about French intervention in Mexico. Yet he did not attempt to go too far, recognizing that the proud French might fight rather than accept humiliation. In place of angry notes stressing violation of the Monroe Doctrine, Seward exerted on France a soft but steady pressure, much as a bored host appears to be patting on the back an unwelcome guest while actually pushing him toward the door.

Concurrently with heightened American ability to object, Napoleon III was reaching the gloomy conclusion that his Mexican sands had just about run out. Many of his subjects who opposed the political and educational power of the church in France were assailing a policy of assisting the church in Mexico. Juárez and his guerrillas seemed unconquerable, French casualties and expenses were running much higher than had originally been anticipated, and to a lesser degree the menacing rise of Prussia along France's northeastern frontier may have worried the Emperor. During the spring of 1866, despite his promises at Miramar two years before, Napoleon III resolved to withdraw French forces from Mexico and abandon Maximilian to his fate.

The loss of French military power was a deathblow to Hapsburg rule in the Americas. With magnificent courage and utter folly, the Austrian insisted on remaining at his post. His distrait wife, realizing that only hostility could be expected from the Mexican populace, sped to Europe and pleaded her husband's case before both Napoleon III and the Pope. The former would and the latter could do nothing. Juárez swept back into power and captured Maximilian. The gallant fool was shot by a Mexican firing squad, despite general international requests to Juárez that he be spared. In an unhappy culmination to a dreadful sequence, Carlota went mad with shock and grief after receiving the news of her husband's execution. She lived until 1927, finally dying at the end of sixty years' insanity.

Napoleon III's Mexican venture was full of dramatic happenings and human tragedy, but its real importance concerns the Monroe Doctrine. From the time that the Virginian President first promulgated his doctrine in 1823, the French invasion of Mexico stands as its chief challenge. Although American pressure does not seem to have been decisive in this instance, never again would a European power try so nakedly and boldly to establish a colony in the Western Hemisphere as did Napoleon III in Mexico during the middle 1860s.

SEWARD'S IMPERIALISM

After the Civil War, William H. Seward divided his time between doing what he could to hasten the collapse of the Hapsburg Empire in Mexico and nurturing his own expansionistic schemes. He covetously scrutinized neighboring territory, ever alert to opportunity. While a Whig and a Republican during the 1850s, Seward had opposed Democratic expansionism, but after 1865 he exhibited a land hunger equal to that of James K. Polk, even if he were unable to feast so abundantly as the latter. Seward's efforts were largely frustrated by America's postwar disinterest in foreign adventure, but that was not the fault of the Secretary of State. A major reason for Seward's aggressive foreign policy was his desire to relieve some of the Radical Republican pressure against President Andrew Johnson by gaining prestige for the tottering administration through annexation of Caribbean or Pacific territory.

Seward was willing to accept almost anything anywhere. He tried to obtain a naval base in Santo Domingo, but failed. He warmly advocated purchasing the Danish West Indies (the Virgin Islands), and found that the Scandinavian owner was eager to sell. A speedy agreement on price was reached; the Danish parliament accepted the terms, but the American Senate turned them down. Many Senators felt that the price of $7,500,000 was too much —this was $300,000 more than Alaska cost— and that there was little sense in annexing West Indian Negroes when the Southern freedman remained such a problem. Yet another failure of the Secretary of State was recorded when his overtures to annex Hawaii collapsed. Empty Midway in the Pacific marked the only insular accession accomplished by the expansive New Yorker.

❨ *The Purchase of Alaska.* Seward's major success was in Alaska, and even here his victory was touch and go. For many years Alaska had been a Russian possession. During the eighteenth century, the Tsar's power had leaped from Siberia across the Bering Strait to plant the Romanov double-eagle standard on North American soil. Early in the next century the Russian empire builder Alexander Baranov established Russian rule in Alaska and planted trading posts down the Pacific Coast almost as far as San Francisco. Russian energies lapsed after Baranov's death, and the tiny settlements lay in somnolence. Continually during the middle nineteenth century, war between Russia and Great Britain remained a strong possibility, and the Russians feared that the Queen's navy could easily conquer Russian America. The Tsar decided that Alaska must be sold to the United States rather than be allowed to go for nothing. In 1867 Alexander II notified his Minister to Washington, Baron Edouard de Stoeckl to see if he could get as much as $5 million for Alaska.

The astute Stoeckl did better than that. According to his story he casually dropped a hint or two, and the avid Seward was at his side. Naturally Stoeckl was pleased when Seward offered him $7,200,000 for the territory. So eager was the Secretary of State that he concluded terms of the exchange at four o'clock in the morning in a session that had begun at midnight. Seward had the foresight to procure the support of Charles Sumner, powerful head of the Senate Committee on Foreign Relations, and under the latter's direction the annexation treaty was rushed through the Senate before anyone really understood what was happening. Soon the public awoke, and a storm of ridicule and resentment raged around Seward. "Walrussia," "Seward's Folly," and "Johnson's Polar Bear Garden" were only a few of the derisive phrases hurled at the administration for a purchase that many found foolish. Those farsighted Americans who had some inkling of the wealth of fish and fur, to say nothing of the potential mineral resources, of Alaska appeared to be overwhelmed. Although the Senate had approved, the House had to appropriate the necessary funds, and there such a result seemed initially unlikely. Deeply discouraged, Stoeckl later confessed that he suggested to the Tsar that Russia offer Alaska to the United States for nothing and thus shame us into paying the agreed price. Alexander quickly vetoed the idea; he was fearful it might be immediately accepted. Actually the situation was not as dark as it seemed to the Russian Minister. The influence of Sumner, the clever manipulations of Seward, the

strong likelihood that Stoeckl bribed some Congressmen, and the potent heritage of friendship that Americans felt for Russian gestures of amity during the war were enough to swing the balance for annexation. The House passed the necessary appropriation by a heavy majority. The purchase of Alaska was one of the great American diplomatic achievements, since the annual catch of salmon alone far exceeds the total price originally paid.

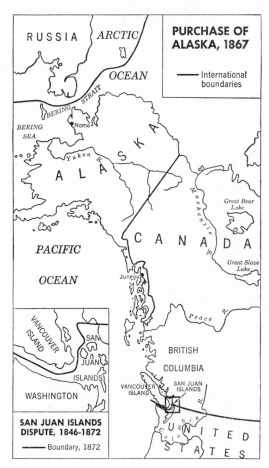

GRANT'S CARIBBEAN POLICY

When the untutored and disappointing Ulysses S. Grant became President, his administrations were saved from total failure only by accomplishments in the foreign field. Even so, little credit can go to the President. He considered diplomatic assignments as he did civil

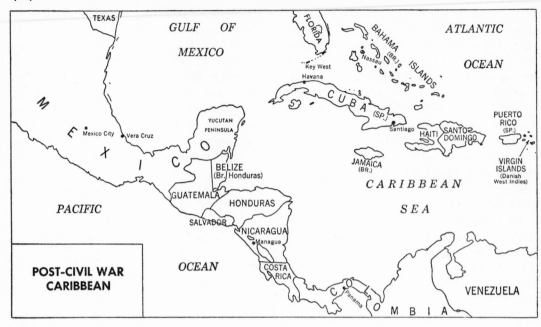

POST-CIVIL WAR CARIBBEAN

—they were to go to good friends or political henchmen. The incompetent Elihu B. Washburn was appointed Secretary of State.[1] Other examples of the General's lack of perception in furnishing diplomatic personnel were the commissions to both General Robert C. Schenck and a nephew of Benjamin Butler. The former was appointed Minister to Great Britain, and although he may have ennobled English life through the introduction of draw poker to the British aristocracy, he helped America's reputation not at all when he allowed his name to be used in connection with fraudulent mining stock that was sold to credulous Englishmen. Butler's nephew topped an impressive career of drunken bellicosity while Consul in Cairo with the purchase of dancing girls.

Unfortunately, Grant showed his usual narrowness in the diplomatic field. It was not the General who engineered a successful foreign policy, but rather the happy accident that he appointed Hamilton Fish of New York to succeed Washburn as Secretary of State. This cultured, sagacious, and urbane individual threaded his way through extremely precarious negotiations with consummate ability, even though only part of his energies could be

[1] See p. 424.

devoted to any task at hand. Fish had to expend much effort in warding off Grant's clumsy interventions into situations about which he knew and understood little.

The eyes of the Secretary of State were opened almost immediately, for soon Grant directed his basilisk stare at the island of Cuba. There a rebellion against Spanish misrule had broken out late in 1868, and although Cuban disorders had been almost continuous for many years, this uprising was on a much larger scale than before. American citizens were molested, and American property was destroyed. The Cuban insurgents were able to develop strong American sympathy for their cause by accusing the Spaniards of atrocities. During 1869–1870 Grant fell prey to these sentiments and decided to recognize the belligerency of the Cubans; if this had been done war with Spain was a likelihood. There is every reason to believe that the much stronger United States could have won such a war, but the nation had enough problems at home, and its army and navy had been quite thoroughly demobilized. Furthermore, it would have been almost impossible to conduct the delicate *Alabama* claims discussions with the British under war conditions. For these reasons Fish threw himself solidly against Grant and the war party. He finally managed to divert the General's attention with other matters, ending Grant's meddling in Cuban affairs.[2] The rebellion in Cuba gradually drained away, relative order being restored in 1878.

One method utilized by Fish to take the President's mind from Cuba was to allow him a full head of steam on his plan to annex Santo Domingo, only recently freed once more from Spain, but finding the course of independence rough and rocky. Some island politicians wished amalgamation with the United States, and many American army officers and businessmen applauded the idea. Although his Secretary of State was cognizant of his plans, Grant took most of his Cabinet by surprise when he casually showed them a treaty to annex the island. His plan failed when he was unable to swing Senator Charles Sumner to his side in the Santo Domingan matter. Indeed, the opposition of the Senate's Chairman of the Foreign Relations Committee was enough to kill annexation. A puerile quarrel soon followed between the furious Grant and the supercilious Sumner; the President was observed silently shaking his fist at Sumner's house while passing.[3] The vengeful Grant punished his adversary by stripping his Senate committee post from him.

HAMILTON FISH AND THE ALABAMA CLAIMS

Although comic opera in nature, the Santo Domingan episode had an important repercussion. Because of it, Sumner, the nation's lead-

ing advocate of enmity to Great Britain, was forced out of a position from which he could have seriously embarrassed the approaching negotiations between Washington and London. In addition, Sumner's close personal friend and fellow Anglophobe, John Lothrop Motley, noted historian and Minister to Great Britain, was discharged. Grant was delighted to get rid of Motley since he disliked him for parting his hair in the middle, a coiffure highly repugnant to the eminent soldier. On such bases were Grant's decisions formed.

The greatest accomplishment of Hamilton Fish was his outstandingly successful settlement of major disputes with Great Britain. At first the outlook was bleak. If the English tended to be conciliatory, American public opinion retained its traditional hostility toward the overseas cousin. Many Northerners were unable to forget British sympathy for the Confederacy. Irish-Americans continued to look upon the English as their everlasting enemies.[4] Other Americans hoped to annex Canada to the United States. Especially virulent was Northern hatred of Britain for the latter's construction of the *Alabama* and other Confederate raiders.

Senator Charles Sumner capitalized on such feelings when he angrily attacked the British (1869) for prolonging the Civil War by two full years by constructing the *Alabama*. Sumner went on to particularize the damage claims that should be forthcoming. It was not difficult, he thought. The total cost of the four years of Civil War was $4 billion, and Great Britain was responsible for half—i.e., $2 billion. Also to be paid were direct and indirect claims that would total another $125 million; according to Sumner's arithmetic, $15 million were for direct damages by the *Alabama*, and $110 million both for loss of American ships to foreign registry and for higher insurance. He concluded that "everybody can make the calculation," and his supporters began talk-

---

[2] Grant finally issued a proclamation of neutrality in 1870. He even remained quiescent three years later when the Spaniards seized the ostensibly American ship *Virginius*, which was supplying the rebels, and summarily executed fifty-three of those on board. Later Spain paid an indemnity, and the crisis lapsed after it was found that the *Virginius* had no right to claim American registry.

[3] One of the better remarks attributed to Grant happened at this time. When someone reputedly told him that Senator Sumner did not believe in the Bible, Grant snorted, "No, he did not write it."

[4] The Fenian movement, which worked for Irish independence, was active at this time. Convinced that Great Britain could be defeated by attacks on Canada, twice (1866, 1870) Fenian armies attempted to conquer British North America, although of course they failed.

ing about receiving Canada in lieu of the $2,125,000,000. Lesser points of conflict between Great Britain and the United States concerned the perennial question of American fishing rights off Canada and Newfoundland, general claims on both sides arising from the war, and possession of the disputed San Juan Islands in Puget Sound, east of Vancouver Island (see map on p. 423).

After Sumner's dismissal from his vital senatorial post, Hamilton Fish was able to proceed unhampered. Britain, fearful of precedents that the *Alabama* set for her own maritime safety if commerce raiders could be built by neutrals, was ready to make amends. A distinguished group of Americans, Canadians, and British met at the nation's capital and drew up the Treaty of Washington (1871). American fishermen were granted extended fishing rights in Canadian waters. In return, the disappointed Canadians were permitted the dubious privilege to fish American coastal areas and were allowed a sum of money to equalize their bad bargain, an amount eventually set at the rather high figure of $5,500,000. British claims of about $2 million were permitted, and American claims disavowed. The San Juan Islands were to be arbitrated by the German Emperor, who awarded them to the United States in 1872. Most epochal was the settlement of the *Alabama* claims. Great Britain apologized for her construction, admitted full responsibility, and agreed to pay damages set by an arbitration board.

The five-man arbitration tribunal, composed of an Italian, a Swiss, and a Brazilian in addition to American and British members, met at Geneva, Switzerland, during 1871–1872. Immediately an impasse was reached when American public opinion and political exigencies caused Hamilton Fish to present the preposterous claim of $2 billion at 7 per cent interest retroactive for two years. A sudden war scare followed as choleric English-

men insisted that the total cost of a victorious war with the United States would be only a fraction of so vast a sum. Happily the tribunal was able to wriggle out on a technicality, and Fish, having assuaged the American extremists, was glad to settle for a more reasonable figure. The final outcome was that Great Britain paid $15,500,000 for the *Alabama* depredations.

Considerable resentment and enthusiasm were discernible on both sides of the Atlantic when the arbitration decision was published. Jingoes in Great Britain protested that the Lion had truckled under to the Yankee upstarts and that the payment was too much. Bellicose Americans were dismayed when they realized that the total sums awarded to Canada for fishing rights and to England for general claims whittled the actual amount received down to approximately $8 million. In general, however, a majority in both nations recognized that this was a much cheaper way than through military action. The Treaty of Washington and the Geneva Tribunal could have established an influential precedent, for two great powers had agreed to arbitrate a matter extremely serious to both. How much happier the course of future history would have been if this fortunate solution had erected a lasting precedent.

The rather decrepit postwar administrations were saved from general ineffectiveness by their conduct of foreign affairs. Especially in Grant's case was the contrast to domestic policy noteworthy. The relinquishment of France's empire in Mexico, the annexation of Alaska, the successful avoidance of hostilities with Spain, and the fortunate arbitration of controversies with Great Britain mark the last important episodes for several years in American diplomatic history. Internal affairs had moved to captivate the American interest to a larger extent than before or since. The nation was entering its most isolationist period.

CHAPTER 37

Executive Reconstruction

(1865-1866)

POSTWAR CONDITIONS

Perhaps the guns were silent; perhaps most of the bloodshed had ceased; but the Civil War died away slowly, its thunder rumbling and muttering over the postwar generation, with some of its echoes dimly heard even today. The somewhat inexact word Reconstruction is usually applied to describe American conditions, especially in the South, between Appomattox and the final withdrawal of Federal troops from the states of the former Confederacy in 1877. Certainly true reconstruction was not accomplished during this period; that came after rather than before 1877.

❬ *The North.* A dazzling contrast was exhibited by the North and South during the months immediately after the surrender of the Confederate armed forces. Despite memories of war's horrors and the aching loss of slain loved ones, to the victory-flushed North the conflict had been something of a vast regenerative agency; the towering experience of that generation. The cardinal facts were that the North had won, the Union had once more been hammered together, and the slaves had been freed. Relatively simple needs motivated

the victor's thoughts and actions. The victorious Union army now had to be demobilized, war output reconverted to meet civilian demands, and a stern watch maintained lest the triumph be lost during the peace that followed. The crude, vulgar, pushing, and acquisitive but also effervescent, farsighted, ambitious, and courageous Northern postwar society had won more than a military conflict. Even if the final success had not quite yet been accomplished, the old struggles over tariffs, the disposal of public lands, and governmental aid to private enterprise could be tallied on the Northern score sheet as well as the more obvious salvation of the Union and the destruction of Negro bondage. The future horizons were shining.

❬ *The South.* How different was the prostrate South. As the bone-tired and discouraged Confederate veteran plodded homeward during the weeks that followed Lee's surrender, he moved through a violated land amid an aura of paralyzed inertia and hopelessness. On all sides were ruined buildings, ravaged fields, smashed fences, brush-grown farms, torn-up railroads, abandoned houses, collapsed bridges, fire-leveled ginning works—a wilderness of devastation. Everywhere were quiet, apathetic, stunned men and women. A mountain of work was necessary, but any Southern energies beyond the quest for the most basic necessities seemed absent during the summer of 1865.

Conditions were even worse in the cities or more properly what was left of the cities. Conflagrations had gutted Richmond, Atlanta, Columbia, and others. Charleston, a prewar center of grace and culture, was mourned by a Southerner: "Grim, black, crumbling chimneys, bending and broken walls, shapeless piles of former splendor, are the silent sentinels of both glory and ruin." A Northern reporter said of Columbia, the capital of South Carolina:

. . . Two thirds of the buildings in the place were burned, including, without exception, everything in the business portion. Not a store, office, or shop escaped; and for the distance of three fourths of a mile on each of twelve streets there was not a building left. . . . Every public building was destroyed, except the new and unfinished state-house. . . .

The countryside similarly offered scenes of devastation. Charred plantation houses stood bleakly in weed-choked acres throughout the more ravaged Southern districts. Gristmill dams were ruined, and water wheels had been broken. The rice plantations of Louisiana were in miserable condition, and their complex systems of irrigated fields had reverted to swampy underbrush. Levees along the Mississippi had caved in through neglect, and rich delta lands were inundated each spring. Southern agriculture was marked by worn-out or broken equipment, scarce supplies of fertilizer and seeds, and slain or runaway livestock. War-bred negligence and military havoc had been superimposed upon fields that had been too often improvidently mined rather than farmed. In many areas the Negro labor force had fled or, if available, either refused to work or found that the planter had no money to pay wages.

Land values had shrunk to ridiculous levels. Acres formerly selling for many dollars were almost given away, and many other tracts either were abandoned or changed hands through forced sales because of tax delin-

quency. The shortage of currency caused a veritable social revolution, for the destitute Southerner found it almost impossible to provide for even the barest essentials, and many ancestral homes were forfeited. Confederate generals sometimes went hungry. On at least one occasion men and women snatched up the grain that was spilled while horses were being fed. It was said of one South Carolina plantation: "The slaves are gone. The family is gone. A single scion of the house remains, and he peddles tea by the pound and molasses by the quart, on a corner of the old homestead, to the former slaves of the family, and thereby earns his living." For Southerners about the only escape from grinding poverty other than emigration, was through cooperation with Northern enemies who flocked to the South, and this would be at the expense of self-respect and neighbors' friendship.

Southern railroad transportation, never very efficient even before the war, had practically collapsed. Wherever the armies had marched and fought, connections had been severed and cities isolated; remaining lines were in sorry decrepitude. Depots had been burned, roadbeds allowed to deteriorate, locomotives and rolling stock had become scarce and dilapidated, ties rotted, and steel rails had sprung. Many of the more important bridges were down. During war's aftermath, the miserable railroads that remained operating in the South were forced to charge passenger fares ranging between 6 and 11 cents per mile, and high freight rates continued to depress Southern industrialism. Many steamboats had been wrecked or destroyed during the conflict, and those which remained had to pick their precarious way along rivers lacking buoys, marked channels, and adequate wharves. The roads of the South were abominable. Transportation remained one of the most urgent Southern problems.

In finance and industry Southerners were afflicted with a lack of circulating money, which mitigated against recovery. The abolition of hundreds of millions of dollars worth of Confederate paper currency, the eradication of slave assets, and the tendency of Northern investors to drain the South of resources hurt as well; hence industrialism could not develop very rapidly.

The labor problem was pressing. Deaths during the war had removed vast numbers who might have helped the South to a speedier recovery. Hordes of wounded veterans were totally incapacitated, and many of the ostensibly unharmed were psychologically incapable of working at the prosaic tasks of reconstruction. The poor whites, especially in the mountain sections, remained in thrall to the debilitating effects of hookworm and a dull, vitamin-lacking diet. Large numbers of the former upper classes, despite the occasional heroic efforts of individuals, were untrained for manual labor. At first not much assistance was forthcoming from the ex-slaves. Often the Negro freedmen considered that liberation from slavery meant liberation from toil, and they often joined an exodus that depopulated some sections, flocking to the cities where food, excitement, and recreation were more readily available.

THE PROBLEM OF THE FREEDMAN

The question of the Negro freedman remained a Southern issue of a gravity equal to if not greater than that of the Negro slave. Slavery was dead, but the old race-relationship matter was very much alive. For the freedman, slavery had been a poor teacher of industry, thrift, or self-reliance. The abilities that the Negro has so abundantly demonstrated in modern times had been forced to lie dormant under slavery. Uneducated, untrained, and unreliable, the Negro freedman of the immediate postwar era was a lamb loose among the wolves. If the Thirteenth Amendment had liberated him from forced toil and the overseer's lash, it had no less freed him from the protection and care of his master. Now the freedman was forced to provide for himself and his family. Often he was unable to do so, and starvation would have been widespread had not the Freedman's Bureau and the Union

Army distributed millions of rations. The impact of disease became more acute. On the prewar plantation, the master's wife had usually acted as a physician for the slaves, but following liberation, the ex-slave tended to rush to the cities where, living in squalid slums, epidemics ran riot. The social and economic disorders attending the aftermath of the Civil War were enhanced by the intrusion of partisan politics over the bewildered freedman.

The South must bear considerable responsibility for the vindictive Northern attitude that developed over the Negro question. The evidence seems to show that the great mass of Southern white men accepted as inevitable the status of the Negro as a freedman. Many, however, assumed that the only real change would be economic; toil without recompense would change to a wage relationship. The white Southerner was often unwilling to accept any alteration in the race-relationship factor and insisted on retaining many of the controls that had characterized prewar slavery.

Most of these controls were embodied in the so-called "Black Codes," which were instituted by the Southern states as soon as possible. While there were local differences, certain elementary similarities established a common pattern. Usually the freedman had to sign a yearly contract with a plantation owner, and if the former broke it, he would forfeit any wages due. In some states, if the Negro ran away while under contract, he could be captured and returned to his employer. Negroes under eighteen were usually apprenticed to planters, and the latter were permitted to inflict moderate corporal punishment. "Vagrants" (Negroes not employed) were subject to arrest, trial, and conviction, whereupon they would be sentenced to a term of hard labor— on a neighboring plantation. Legal testimony by freedmen was severely curtailed, the right to bear arms was forbidden, and sometimes curfew laws were established. While Southerners held that the Black Codes were necessary to curb Negro abuses, many in the North cried that slavery was being reinstituted. The unfortunate celerity with which the Southern states passed these codes was unquestionably instrumental in bringing swift retribution from the conquerors.

NORTHERN POSTWAR OPINION: THE MODERATE POSITION

Years of war, particularly civil war, inevitably leave a permeating heritage of hate, which, however, affects individuals with differing intensity. Many in the North were obsessed with an implacable enmity toward the defeated antagonist and lived under a shadow of fear that the victory would be thrown away by excessive leniency. The Northern population was subjected to bombardment by politicians who saw in postwar hatred a lasting source of forensic ammunition; by clergymen who seemed to have forgotten some of the Biblical tenets about gentleness and mercy; and by newspaper editors, early-day sensationalists, who fed their readers a never-ending pap of lurid Southern atrocity stories.

Yet many Northerners, perhaps a majority, felt that the war was over and that the shattered nation had best reunite as quickly as possible. The typical Union soldier seems to have been characterized by less animosity toward the foe than the usual civilian. Grant, Sherman, Hancock, and others hastened to express their hope that the war wounds would be rapidly healed, although some of them changed their minds in the years that followed.

Unfortunately for the cause of American reconstruction, the complacent and friendly elements in the North were soon captured and directed by the faction composed of fanatical extremists.

❨ *Andrew Johnson.* Although not cognizant of the fact at first, the South was fortunate when Abraham Lincoln was succeeded by Andrew Johnson. "Tennessee Andy" was a Southerner himself, born and raised in the mountains of Carolina and Tennessee. From a poverty-stricken and opportunity-lacking boyhood, Johnson rose to political prominence,

driven by a burning ambition.[1] Throwing himself into the hurly-burly of Tennessee politics, Johnson soon became the raucous voice of the eastern Tennessee mountaineers and the mortal enemy of the planters from the western part of that state. For twenty years Johnson steadily progressed in politics, becoming governor; and when the Southern states began seceding, he was a Senator from Tennessee. During the grim winter of 1861 Southern Senators individually delivered their farewell addresses and withdrew, until only one seat from the seceded states was left occupied. Despite the defection of Tennessee, Andrew Johnson stayed loyal to the Union, reproving the rebels as desiring to destroy Southern freedom. Johnson's devotion was rewarded by an appointment as war Governor of Tennessee, and he labored diligently to restore to the Union his battle-torn state. When Lincoln and his cohorts decided that a loyal Southerner would help the National Union ticket in the election of 1864, Johnson became the vice-presidential nominee and eventual successor to the martyrized Lincoln.

Johnson was a stocky individual with pleasant features and a relatively attractive personality. He was intelligent and usually courteous toward others, and he was a powerful, if unrestrained, author and orator. Perhaps his greatest weaknesses were his flaring temper, which sometimes led to a loss of self-control, and an occasional lack of tact and discretion. His language was often abusive. He believed that the Southern planter had ruined the mountain whites, and he never tired of expressing his hatred forcibly and violently. When he stated near the end of the war, "Treason must be made infamous and traitors must be impoverished," the Northern Radicals naturally concluded that here was one of their own. Senator Ben Wade openly rejoiced that John Wilkes Booth had removed Lincoln's moderate influences and that a policy of vengeance under Johnson could now proceed unhampered. The Radicals erred in their estimation

[1] Until he married a school teacher who instructed him while he worked as a tailor, Johnson was practically illiterate.

RECONSTRUCTION, 1865-1877

——— Boundaries of military districts established by Reconstruction Act, 1867

Dates of military control withdrawn are when ordered, although sometimes troops were sent back later

of Andrew Johnson, however. Once the war had removed the Southern planter as an economic and social factor, Johnson's implacable attitude toward the defeated section immediately softened, for he had no desire to punish the poor Southerners. He entertained serious doubts about the advisability of Negro suffrage, unless it be extended to a few of the more literate freedmen. Soon the Radicals were dumfounded to see that Johnson was planning to continue Lincoln's policy of moderation toward the ex-Confederacy.

❮ *Presidential Reconstruction.* Lincoln's basic point on reconstruction had been his "10 per cent plan," whereby the seceded state was once more restored to full constitutional privileges when 10 per cent of the qualified voters at the time of secession took an oath of allegiance to the United States. Although he never stipulated the exact percentage, Johnson continued relatively unchanged his predecessor's

program. Both Presidents insisted that the Southern states had never really left the Union, since secession was constitutionally impossible; the Confederate states had been rather in a condition of "suspension," and the task of the postwar Federal government was to remove this "suspended status" quickly and smoothly.

Although generally following Lincoln's policies, Johnson added one embellishment. Lincoln had disfranchised top-rank Confederate military and naval officers, as well as holders of important positions in the Confederate government. To these, Johnson added those who owned property worth more than $20,000. This was about the only vindictive item on the Johnsonian agenda.[2] Otherwise his generosity

[2] There was some persecution of individual Confederates. Several were executed or imprisoned for the assassination of Lincoln by the hysterical action of a quasi-legal military court-martial, although at least two were probably innocent. Captain Henry C. Wirz, a Swiss immigrant, was hanged for alleged atrocities committed on Union soldiers at Andersonville Prison,

was almost breath-taking. He accepted the unionist governments set up by Lincoln for Virginia, Tennessee, Arkansas, and Louisiana. For each remaining state he appointed a native citizen as governor, who was to call a constitutional convention for his state. Ordinances of secession were to be repealed, the Thirteenth Amendment abolishing slavery ratified, and the repudiation of the Confederate debt legalized, but otherwise almost complete freedom of action was permitted.

Congress was not in session for many months during 1865, and the President was able to proceed about as he wished in regard to Reconstruction. According to Johnson, by December, 1865, all but two of the former Confederate states were back in the Union, and it was these reconstructed state governments that enacted the Black Codes. Furthermore, they elected many prominent ex-Confederates to high position in both the state and the nation. The fury of the Radicals was boundless when along with others of the same ilk, Alexander Stephens, Vice-President of the Confederate States of America, showed up in Washington to be seated as a Senator from Georgia to serve in the government that he had spent four years in trying to destroy. The Radical faction threw down an arrant challenge to Johnson when it refused to seat these Congressmen from the presidentially reconstructed states, thus publicly breaking with the administration.

NORTHERN POSTWAR OPINION: THE RADICAL POSITION

It was no cause for surprise that the Radicals would refuse to countenance Andrew Johnson's leniency. As early as the middle of the Civil War the Radical program had been formulated, and it was powerful enough to clash with Lincoln. Even a politician of Lincoln's

consummate ability could do no more than to check rather than halt the Radical juggernaut. There seems little reason to doubt that Lincoln's course during the immediate postwar years might have been as hostilely received as Johnson's. The only question seems to be whether the tact and acumen of the martyred President would have been able to slow down the Radical onslaught that overwhelmed the Tennesseean.

❲ *The Radical Leaders.* Certainly the Radicals had effective personnel directing their attacks. Thaddeus Stevens of Pennsylvania became practically the dictator of the House of Representatives. Aged, ill, quarrelsome, and bitter, Stevens was a memorable spectacle. His impressive height, bowed by age at the time of his greatest influence, his limping gait, and his expressive features either fascinated or repelled. An ashen pallor, piercing eyes, lantern jaw, protruding lower lip, furrowed brow, strong nose, and deeply etched lines around the mouth combined to make him appear a throwback to the most implacable seventeenth-century Massachusetts Bay Puritan divines, even if his private life did not show much clerical restraint.

Stevens had been first an Anti-Mason, later a Whig, and finally a Republican. His belief in democratic equality was abiding, and his confirmed anti-Masonic and fiery abolitionist positions had early marked him as a man to watch. Stevens's thrilling fight for the establishment of a free public-school system in Pennsylvania was perhaps the most meritorious of his life. Stevens could hate and hate well; there was nothing of the hypocrite in him. He fiercely advocated Negro equality, and unlike many of his fellow Radicals he liked the Negro personally. He believed with every particle of his body and brain that the wealthy Southerner in attempting to destroy the Union had fought against democracy itself. Such philosophical conclusions were not mitigated when Confederate raiders burned his iron foundry in southern Pennsylvania.

Except in hatred for the defeated "rebels," the Radical leader in the Senate was almost

---

although conditions there appear to have been beyond the commandant's control. Jefferson Davis was imprisoned, for a time in irons, and although soon released was never enfranchised. Many prominent Confederates, among them Secretary of State Judah P. Benjamin, fled abroad.

the antithesis of Stevens. Charles Sumner of
Massachusetts was regally tall, handsome, erudite, and cultured through association with
both Boston Brahmins and European aristocrats. Yet Sumner's fanaticism and intolerance rivaled anyone's; he was lacking in
breadth, warmth, and humor, in short, in most
of the attributes that make a person loved.
His mental processes were illustrated when,
during a debate, an opponent claimed that
Sumner forgot the other side of the argument.
The Brahmin stormed, "There is no other
side!" In the next echelon behind these two
chiefs came such Radicals as coarse, vigorous,
and ruthless Benjamin F. Wade; fat, wheezing,
oily Benjamin ("Beast") Butler of New Orleans fame; the untutored and intemperate Zachariah Chandler of Michigan; and on a somewhat higher level, John ("Black Jack") Logan
of Illinois, idol of the Union veteran; the
effective, dynamic, and relentless Oliver P.
Morton of Indiana; and the elegant, massive,
and sarcastic Roscoe Conkling of New York.
Others in this faction were Edwin M. Stanton, who continued as Secretary of War in
Johnson's as he had in Lincoln's Cabinet;
George W. Julian of Indiana; and George
Boutwell of Massachusetts. Ulysses S. Grant
was a somewhat later convert.

(*Radical Philosophy.* The philosophy of the
Radicals was based on fear—fear that the
Southerners might light the torch of rebellion
again, fear that the Negro might once more
be plunged into slavery, and fear that the Republican party might be ousted from the national political control that they felt it richly
deserved to retain. The Radical fear of rebellion was mistaken. The evidence is abundant
that the mass of white Southerners accepted,
if reluctantly and grudgingly, the fact that the
war had been irretrievably lost. The dominant
faction was incorrect in the second category
as well, although it is not surprising that the
Radicals saw in the Black Codes the recurring
pattern of slavery. Yet modern scholars can
see that some controls were necessary to bring
the ill-prepared Negro across the bridge between slavery and freedom. As to the issue of

retaining their political control, these left-
wing Republicans were right. Events soon
proved that an immediate continuation of their
tenure must rely on the freedmen's votes, and
without them the natural alliance of the white
Southerner and the conservative Northern
Democrat would hurl the Radicals from governmental authority.

The faction headed by Stevens and Sumner
was fortunate in being able to capitalize on
war hatred, fanning these flames into a forest
fire through effective, powerful, and unrelenting propaganda, which continued until late in
the century. Over the Northern countryside
traveled the Radical orators; into Northern
homes came the Radical press. Little effort was
made to be subtle, and sledge-hammer tactics
appeared to accomplish all that was necessary.
With some cynicism, the Radical appeal to
war prejudices and hatreds was called "waving
the bloody shirt"—a process that attempted to
tie the Democratic party as closely as possible
to treason. Oliver P. Morton snarled:

Every unregenerate rebel . . . calls himself a
Democrat. Every bounty jumper, every deserter,
every sneak who ran away from the draft. . . .
Every man . . . who murdered Union prisoners
. . . who contrived hellish schemes to introduce
into Northern cities the wasting pestilence of
yellow fever, calls himself a Democrat . . . every
one who shoots down Negroes in the streets . . .
and murders women and children by the light of
their flaming dwellings, calls himself a Democrat.
. . . In short, the Democratic party may be described as a common sewer and loathsome re-
ceptacle, into which is emptied every element of
treason North and South, and every element of
inhumanity and barbarism which has dishonored
the age.

Massachusetts Senator George Hoar was quite
honest about the political issues involved when
he asserted that the Republican party was composed of ". . . the best elements in our national life . . . the survivors and children of
men who put down the rebellion and abolished slavery, saved the Union and paid
the debt. . . ."

Therefore it became necessary, according to
the Radical philosophy, to disfranchise the

Southern white, whom they knew to be an implacable enemy, and to grant the ballot to the Negro freedman whose vote could be controlled. Thaddeus Stevens told Congress during 1867:

If impartial suffrage is excluded in the rebel States then every one of them is sure to send a solid rebel representative delegation to Congress, and cast a solid rebel electoral vote. They, with their kindred Copperheads of the North, would always elect the President and control Congress. . . . I am for Negro suffrage in every rebel state. If it be just, it should not be denied; if it be necessary, it should be adopted; if it is a punishment to traitors, they deserve it.

Spearheaded by Stevens and Sumner, the Radicals moved against Johnson and his entire policy of moderation toward the South. Refusing to seat the Congressmen elected by Johnson's reconstructed governments in the former Confederacy, the Radicals formed a heavy majority on the Joint Committee on Reconstruction—which would write the epochal Fourteenth Amendment to the Constitution—and made clear their determination that they, not the President, would dictate the terms for full Southern readmittance into the Union.

❨ *The Fourteenth Amendment.* It was not long before the Radicals turned from defense to offense. Two important measures were passed by both Houses and eventually steamrollered over Johnson's vetoes. The first was an expanded Freedman's Bureau bill, which was to strengthen and extend the original act passed during March, 1865. To some degree it was a Northern relief and rehabilitation program to care for, feed, and protect both the Negro freedmen and destitute "loyal refugees" (white). The Bureau was under the over-all direction of the War Department and the Union army. The second Freedman's Bureau bill added little to what was original in the first, but rather intensified the powers of that organization. In short, the two Freedman's Bureau bills made the Negro practically a ward of the Federal government, rather than abandoning him to the states and their "Black Codes." These measures made certain that

military rule and governmental "paternalism" would continue in force throughout the defeated South. Johnson vetoed the second bill. He protested that he shared with Congress concern over the destitute freedman, but sharply stated that military rule, army courts, and legislation applying to parts of the United States still unrepresented in Congress were contrary to the Constitution. At first the Radicals were unable to muster enough votes to override the veto, but a short time later the second Freedman's Bureau bill was enacted in a slightly amended form, since a two-thirds vote was obtained partly through parliamentary trickery.

Even before their final victory on the Freedman's Bureau, the Radicals were able to push through a second major item of legislation. This was a civil-rights bill, which became the precursor of the Fourteenth Amendment. This measure made the freedmen citizens of the United States with equal civil and judicial rights to the white inhabitants and stipulated terms of punishment for anyone interfering with the freedman's privileges. Johnson vetoed this act as unconstitutional, but the Radicals were able to ride triumphantly over his objections.

While the President and Congress argued and bickered, the Joint Committee on Reconstruction plowed through masses of evidence, most of it biased, and wrote the Fourteenth Amendment to the Constitution. Acceptance of its terms became necessary before a former Confederate state could reenter the Union. Certainly this amendment was one of the most far-reaching items of legislation in the nation's history. Its first section iterated the gist of the Civil Rights Act when it declared, "All persons born or naturalized in the United States . . . are citizens of the United States and of the state in which they reside." Next follows the pregnant sentence that has become the heart of the amendment: "No State shall make or enforce any law which shall abridge the privileges or immunities of citizens of the United States; nor shall any State deprive any *person* of life, liberty, or property, *without due process of law.* . . ." [3]

[3] Italics added.

Certainly there is every reason to believe that at least the majority of the Radical Congressmen who wrote the amendment considered that this section applied to the freedman and inserted these restrictions on possible state legislation that might harm the Negro. Nevertheless, most cases before the Federal courts arising from the Fourteenth Amendment have pertained to corporations as "legal persons" protected especially from state regulations that the judiciary considered to be "discriminatory" or contrary to "due process of law."

Section 2 of the amendment obviated the three-fifths "compromise" of the Constitutional Convention of 1787 by inserting the stipulation that "respective numbers" be counted for both taxation and representation. Since Negroes were to be counted equally with whites, the question of freedman suffrage became intensified, for the Southern states would now have five-fifths representation. Interestingly enough, there was no direct compulsion on the states to allow the Negro to vote. The provision was carried that the state's representation would be reduced proportionately to the number disqualified, unless the vote was refused for "participation in rebellion, or other crime."

Section 3 wrote into the Constitution the disfranchisement of leading Confederates and the refusal to allow them to hold office in the United States or any state if they had "taken an oath . . . to support the Constitution of the United States" and then engaged in "insurrection or rebellion." Section 4 guaranteed the validity of the Union debt and forbade payment of the Confederate debt or any "claim for the loss or emancipation of any slave." The final section was the usual permission to Congress to pass appropriate legislation to carry out the provisions of the amendment.

THE CONGRESSIONAL ELECTIONS OF 1866

As the Radicals feared, the Southern states might be able to defeat the Fourteenth Amend-

ment, and if it was to be passed at all the whole character of the Southern state governments would have to be drastically altered; but in 1866 the Radicals did not have enough power to accomplish this. A temporary calm befell the political arena as the pivotal congressional elections of that year drew near. This was the showdown for both President Johnson and his antagonists. To help candidates favorable to his policy of moderation, Johnson embarked on his famous "swing around the circle," a series of speaking engagements from Washington to Chicago and back to the capital by way of Pittsburgh. The Radicals were ready for him, and they packed his audiences with hecklers. The President took personal issue with some of them from the rostrum and made something of a fool of himself.

Johnson's position was further weakened by the oceans of personal abuse that flowed around him, as well as some unlucky occurrences. The Radicals charged that the President was personally immoral, probably insane, and an inveterate drunkard.[4] During the summer two terrible race riots, one in Memphis and the other in New Orleans, proved useful to the President's enemies, who accused Johnson's policies of inciting the disorders. Radical looms wove new threads into the "bloody shirt." In the autumn elections Johnson's supporters, Democrats and conservative Republicans alike, went down to a crashing defeat. What little the President had formerly been able to do to check the Radicals was now over; the elated extremists had a clear two-thirds majority in Congress. A generation of embittered Southerners would mark the result of this fanatical triumph.

---

[4] There was one instance that gave credence to this charge. Johnson was ill on the day of his vice-presidential inauguration in 1865, but Lincoln begged him to go through with the ceremonies. To fortify himself for the ordeal, Johnson imbibed brandy too assiduously, which, in his weakened condition, went to his head. He delivered an incoherent harangue that made his intoxication obvious to his partly horrified and partly amused audience. Actually, abundant evidence shows Johnson to have been an extremely temperate individual.

CHAPTER 38

The Radical Juggernaut

(1866-1869)

THE VINDICTIVE TRIUMPH

As soon as Congress met after the election of 1866, the Radicals swung into the saddle and broke into full gallop. Act after act was passed, with the result that, almost two years after the termination of hostilities, the bandages were ripped from the nation's partially healed wounds. Electoral votes from the seceded states were declared void until Congress should declare otherwise. The date upon which the new Congress met was set back from December to the previous March to mitigate against a long, presidentially dominated interim. In essence, Johnson's powers as Commander in Chief of the armed forces were stripped from him, and army control given to General Grant.[1] The rights of the Supreme Court to interfere with Reconstruction acts was somewhat curtailed. The Tenure of Office Act limited the President's power to dismiss his own appointees from Cabinet and other positions—if an Executive appointee needed congressional approval to be hired, the act held that he needed congressional permission to be fired.

[1] At first sympathetic toward both the defeated South and the Executive policy of leniency, by 1867 Grant had gone over to the Radicals; political advantage seems to have been the chief motivating factor.

The most drastic of all the Radical legislation pertained directly to the ten seceded states that had belonged to the former Confederacy.[2] This law was officially entitled "An Act to provide for the more efficient government of the Rebel States," but is more commonly called the Reconstruction Act (2 March 1867). It passed Congress, was vetoed by Johnson, and was promptly repassed over his objections. The Reconstruction Act was one of the most influential and momentous pieces of legislation ever to pass an American Congress. The basic point was that existing governments in the ten states of the former Confederacy were swept away, and in their place five "military districts" were established, each under the control of a Union Major General, abetted by the Federal army.[3] If the commanding officer so willed, civil courts could be replaced by military tribunals. The general in charge was to register all qualified voters, including Negroes and excluding those

[2] Tennessee, under Radical auspices, was back in the Union by this time. The quality of its governor, "Parson" William G. Brownlow, can be judged from his reference to President Andrew Johnson as "that dead dog in the White House."

[3] Virginia formed the first district; the Carolinas, the second; Georgia, Florida, and Alabama, the third; Mississippi and Arkansas, the fourth; and Louisiana and Texas, the fifth.

disfranchised for Confederate service. A convention was to be called that would have to write a state constitution guaranteeing both Negro suffrage and acceptance of the Fourteenth Amendment. Once the latter was adopted by three-fourths of all the states, then and only then would any reconstructed state be removed from army rule and permitted to reenter the Union. To make sure that former Confederates would neither control the new state governments nor direct national affairs, each new Senator and Representative would have to take an "iron-clad oath" that he had never voluntarily aided the Confederacy. The effects of this important act on the South will be noted later.[4]

THE IMPEACHMENT OF PRESIDENT JOHNSON

The final major plank in the Radical floor plan was to get rid of Andrew Johnson. The "Vindictives" had hoped that the President would fly off the handle and commit some illegal indiscretion. Avoiding this snare, Johnson, although he vetoed almost every Radical measure, faithfully executed the provisions of each once it became law. The Radicals finally decided that they might have a case in the President's action against a member of his Cabinet. Edwin M. Stanton, Lincoln's able but choleric Secretary of War, occupied the same position under Johnson. Although he had long since enlisted with the Radicals, Stanton unscrupulously retained his War portfolio and acted as a spy, reporting to the enemy chieftains details of the President's political strategy as revealed in Cabinet councils. Johnson's patience seemed eternal, but he finally acted when he procured Grant's promise to replace Stanton. Johnson fired the latter, and Grant officially took over; but the General reneged on his pledge when Stanton refused to leave, and Grant openly joined the Stevens-Sumner faction. Johnson then tried to oust Stanton in favor of General Lorenzo Thomas, but Stan-

[4] See pp. 439–441.

ton barricaded himself in the War Department and refused to budge. This effort to rid himself of a faithless subordinate brought Johnson under attack for breaking the Tenure of Office Act, even though Lincoln had appointed Stanton.

The Radicals were confident that they could impeach and convict their enemy. There was little problem in the House of Representatives. Bitter old Thad Stevens, deathbed ill, marshaled his forces and easily procured the impeachment. Under the Constitution the trial must be held in the Senate, and a provocative situation immediately developed. There was no Vice-President (Johnson had been in that capacity when Lincoln was murdered), and if Johnson were convicted the president pro tempore of the Senate (a Senator temporarily elected to be presiding officer) would move into the Executive mansion. This post was held by "Bluff Ben" Wade of Ohio, one of the most thorough and zealous of the Radicals. Although his ballot obviously would be swayed by personal ambition, Wade remained in his senatorial seat to cast a "guilty" vote. Indeed, so sure was Wade of his pleasant future that he went around selecting a Cabinet. This situation probably worked to Johnson's advantage, for the prospect of Benjamin Wade in the White House was repugnant to many.

Yet initially there seemed little hope for Andrew Johnson. Only twelve Democrats sat in the Senate, and seven Republicans had to be persuaded to break with their party if the necessary nineteen votes (one-third plus one) for acquittal were to be obtained. Nevertheless, several factors aided the President. Chief Justice Salmon P. Chase of the Supreme Court was presiding officer at the trial and proved to be surprisingly impartial, although classified as one of the foremost Radicals. Johnson's legal talent was far superior to that of his foes, and the President earned favorable comment by his aloof and dignified restraint, which was in sharp contrast to the venomous attitudes displayed by his opponents.

Actually the trial was mainly on the basis of partisan politics rather than on any juridical issues. The Radicals were hopeful as the first voting commenced on 16 May 1868. Only seven of their party were doubtful, but before packed and breathless galleries amid painful tension, one by one all seven voted for acquittal. By the narrowest margin of one vote President Andrew Johnson was declared not guilty on the first article of the impeachment. A ten-day adjournment ensued before the second balloting, and during this interim the frantic Radicals concentrated their fire upon the unfortunate Senator Edmund G. Ross of Kansas, supposedly the most irresolute of the seven. Republican voters in his state were ordered to bombard Ross with telegrams, but the Senator stayed firm.[5] On the second and final vote Johnson was again saved by one ballot, thus ending the attempt to remove him. The seven Republicans who voted with the President paid a heavy price for their independent disregard of party orders. The public careers of all were hopelessly blasted, since their party leaders never forgave that which was looked upon as political treason in Radical circles.

THE ELECTION OF 1868

Andrew Johnson was still President of the United States for almost a year after his acquittal, but during this time he was little more than a figurehead, so thoroughly had his powers been whittled away. He was largely forgotten as Americans watched the preliminaries for the election of 1868. The Radical Republicans were now potent enough to place one of their own in nomination. Chief Justice Salmon P. Chase ardently sought that honor, but his impartiality during Johnson's trial made him an anathema to the Radicals. The convention was easily stampeded to Ulysses S. Grant, by this time thoroughly under "Vindictive" auspices. Prior to 1867 Grant showed no interest in politics beyond a slight preference for the Democrats—he had voted for Buchanan in 1856 and supported Douglas in 1860. During the postwar era, however, he perceived in his foggy way that his destiny lay with the Radicals.

[5] One dispatch to Ross read, "Kansas repudiates you as she does all perjurers and skunks."

The Democrats had no such easy choice. They had considered Grant for a while, but the General had been captured by the opposition. Some supported Johnson, but party leaders were convinced that the incumbent President would be overwhelmed at the polls. Senator George H. Pendleton of Ohio had a sizable following; and the ever-hopeful Salmon P. Chase, having failed to procure the Republican nomination, shopped around among the Democrats, but his disqualifications were obvious. After twenty-odd ballots, the convention nominated Horatio Seymour of New York, largely forgotten today, but a well-known politician in his own day. Seymour had had a long career in the New York Democratic party and had been one of the wartime governors of the Empire State. Although a loyal Northerner, Seymour had severely criticized Lincoln's conscription policy, and during the terrible New York City draft riots of 1863 he had made the mistake of addressing a crowd as "My friends."

In the campaign the Republicans harped upon the theme of Seymour the Copperhead and admonished Northerners that his election would mean the return of slavery to the South. Naturally Seymour was an outspoken opponent of the "Vindictive" program for the former Confederacy, preaching doctrines of amity and brotherhood toward the erstwhile enemy. While there were some minor issues, it was the Radical treatment of the conquered South that furnished most of the election pyrotechnics.

When the 1868 results were known, at first glance it appeared that General Grant had won an easy triumph, scoring 214 to 80 in the Electoral College and roughly 3,000,000 to 2,700,000 in the popular referendum. But as the Radicals conned the election statistics in detail, a significant truth dawned upon them: it was primarily Grant's 700,000 Negro votes from the congressionally reconstructed states that elected him—Seymour had won an actual majority of the national white ballots. Reconstruction in the South had won the Republican victory, and Radicals became doubly convinced that these supposedly temporary state governments must be fostered as long as possible. Negro suffrage had to be maintained by the Grant administration—the alternative was political defeat.

MILITARY RECONSTRUCTION

While these political jousts were occupying much national attention, the Reconstruction governments were getting under way in the South. The Reconstruction Act of March, 1867, had placed all the previously Confederate states save Tennessee under United States army rule. The local reaction to these military regimes was determined in part by the character and degree of fanaticism exhibited by the Union major general in charge, although army control is seldom very popular with civilians. Some of these generals (John M. Schofield and Winfield S. Hancock, for instance) stirred up little opposition in their districts, but others (Philip H. Sheridan and Daniel E. Sickles) were Radical enough to merit the enthusiastic dislike of their southern subjects.

Under the terms of the Reconstruction Act, local control could not return to a militarily ruled state until it had written and adopted a constitution guaranteeing Negro suffrage and ratifying the Fourteenth Amendment. Furthermore, the Fourteenth Amendment had to be part of the Constitution before any readmittances would be allowed. The latter point was arbitrarily settled by Congress during July, 1868, when the Fourteenth Amendment was declared in force. Since Radical destiny was closely entwined with Negro suffrage, the Fifteenth Amendment was soon offered to the states. Ratified 30 March 1870, it stated, "The right of citizens of the United States to vote shall not be denied or abridged by the United States or by any State on account of race, color, or previous condition of servitude." Thus was the Negro, freed by the Thirteenth Amendment and made a citizen by the Fourteenth, granted the franchise in the Fifteenth. Despite its brave words, the Fifteenth Amendment has been disappointing. Through such dodges as white "grandfather clauses," poll taxes, and "literacy tests," the meaning of the amendment has been circumvented. Many American citizens have had their constitutional privilege to vote denied on the actual grounds of race and color.

Perhaps methods more directly practical than Constitutional additions to help the Southern Negro during Reconstruction were used by two potent organizations, the Freedman's Bureau and the Union League clubs. The former had been instituted by two acts of Congress (1865, 1866) and was responsible for feeding, protecting, overseeing, and finding employment for ex-slaves. Sweeping judicial powers were accorded to the Freedman's Bureau, and its agents were diligent in punishing those who interfered with Negro rights. This was one reason why the Bureau was so unpopular with white Southerners. Another was the manner in which the Bureau financed its operations. Although its head, General Oliver O. Howard, was a high-minded and devoted public servant, many of his underlings took advantage of corrupt opportunities to cheat and rob Southerners. Despite its obvious defects, however, without the Bureau's ministrations it is hard to see how the Negro masses could have been supported during the early years of Reconstruction.

The second powerful Northern-sponsored organization in the South was the Union, or "Loyal," League, which existed for the primary purpose of garnering the Negro's vote for the Republican party. Union League clubs—secret societies—were formed throughout the South, and the freedman was subjected to a barrage of propaganda and political pressure. Union League teachings stressed that unless the Negro voted Radical, slavery would be reintroduced. The Negroes were herded to the polls during elections, and their ballots were marked for the national Republican organization or for the local Radical Republican machine. All sorts of mendacious promises were given to the gullible freedman, ranging from the usual pledge of "40 acres and a mule" to such asininity as a machine to pump out the "black blood" and replace it with "white." The leading Radical failure to assist the freedman was in the economic sphere. If finding farms for the ex-slave had been worked on as diligently as high-pressuring him into voting Republican, the lot of the former bondsman might have been easier in the grim years ahead. The conclusion seems obvious: the Radicals were not disinterested friends of the Negro—instead they were concerned with using him for their own selfish political advantage.

CARPETBAG RECONSTRUCTION

Under the watchful direction of the Union army, the Freedman's Bureau, and the Union League clubs, the South was made over between 1867 and 1877. Gradually state after state wrote constitutions guaranteeing Negro suffrage and ratifying the necessary constitutional amendments. According to the Reconstruction Act, once this had been done, local self-government could return to the former Confederate state, thereby ending military rule. By the end of 1870 eight of the eleven seceded states had formed independent governments. Yet these governments were of a type never seen in the United States before or since. The mass of the white electorate had been disfranchised, and the vote was given to the Negro. This was especially galling to white Southerners, not only because many of them considered the freedman unqualified to cast his vote wisely, but also because most of the Northern states refused to allow Negro suffrage at home while insisting upon such procedure in the South.

During the time of these Reconstruction governments there was a veritable invasion of Dixie by Northerners, some of them so destitute that they were able to carry all their possessions in small satchels made from strips of carpeting; hence the name "carpetbagger." They were joined by renegade Southerners called "scalawags," and this combination upheld the Radical philosophy during the years that followed. In most of the Southern states,

white carpetbaggers and scalawags, backed by the votes of the untrained and uneducated freedmen, ran the governments. Political organization was solidly based on Negro ballots, and many of that race served as members of state legislatures, although few were awarded higher positions.

To most Americans the character of the Reconstruction regimes is a familiar story. They wallowed in a mire of graft, corruption, and inefficiency. State after state piled up debts far larger than four years of terrible war and two years of halfhearted "reconstruction" had been able to accomplish. The average cost of each annual session of the Louisiana carpetbag legislature rose ten times over former levels. Monopolistic charters were granted to corporations under suspicious circumstances, vast sums were realized through questionably legal state lotteries, and private corruption enjoyed halcyon days. Many of the Radical governors amassed fortunes on salaries of a few thousand dollars a year. Southern resources worth millions were tapped by watered stocks and valueless bond issues. Land taxes were so drastically increased—in Mississippi they went up 1,400 per cent—that forced-tax-sale notices filled Southern newspapers. State legislatures appropriated money for food, liquor, and frivolous luxuries for individual members.[6] The disfranchised Southern whites looked on with drawn and bitter faces, powerless to stop the saturnalia of corruption. A political and economic orgy was taking place.

Perhaps it was impossible to avoid governments of this type during that period. Corruption was certainly not indigenous to the postwar South. Everywhere in the United States during the late 1860s and early 1870s urban and state machines indulged in truly epic peculation—the Tweed Ring in New York, for instance—and no Southern carpetbag organization could match them. The ill-trained Negro freedman, intoxicated by his first breaths of liberty, was not responsible. In the last analysis,

[6] In South Carolina, the legislature voted to reimburse its popular carpetbag speaker for the sum of $1,500, which he had lost on a horse race the day before.

most of the evils that besmirched Reconstruction governments in the South were symptomatic of moral conditions throughout the nation. It was rather the fact that Southern conditions were imposed by a hated victor many months after the war was over that caused much of the implacable resentment among Southern white men.

Indeed, the positive good accomplished by these primarily bad governments must not be forgotten. In comparison to slavery, the former bondsman was considerably better off than before the war. For the first time a free public-school system came to the South. Poor as it admittedly was, it was better than nothing. If tax costs were invariably too high and corrupt inefficiency typical, roads were built, bridges repaired, rivers dredged, buildings constructed, and charters awarded to new railroads. Although exorbitant, taxes were assessed more equally than before. Local government and the courts were overhauled. Temporarily, democracy and egalitarianism made some real progress. Many of the gains scored under carpet-bag control were erased when "Bourbon Reactionaries" captured the state governments from the Radicals and proceeded to organize the "Solid South," with Negro disfranchisement a basic policy.

THE SOUTH STRIKES BACK

Slowly, during the Reconstruction years, the Southern states managed to oust their carpet-bag rulers and restore local self-government. By 1874 only South Carolina, Florida, and Louisiana lacked home rule. There were many reasons for this Southern white resurgence. As time passed Northern war hatred cooled, and many Northerners lost interest in continually chastising a fallen adversary. The carpetbaggers tended to fall into factional disputes, and usually their divided strength was insufficient to retain power. Finally, the drift toward local self-government was possibly enhanced by direct Southern action, which quite early in Reconstruction began to use terroristic methods against the white carpetbagger and his Negro henchman.

Southern secret societies working toward eradication of "foreign" rule became widespread. Occult organizations arose throughout the ex-Confederacy, dedicated to white supremacy and the restoration of Southern rule. The Knights of the White Camellia, the Native Sons of the South, the White Brotherhood, and others attracted some attention. By far the largest and most powerful, however, was the Ku Klux Klan (evidently from the Greek word *kyclos* meaning "circle"), which was formed between 1866 and 1868, with the respectable Confederate cavalry General Nathan Bedford Forrest as its leader.[7] There were aspects both amusing and frightening about the Ku Klux Klan. It specialized in ridiculous mumbo jumbo. The area dominated by the Klan was called the "Invisible Empire," and its members were headed by a Grand Wizard, served by such underlings as Grand Dragons, Hydras, Genii, and Furies. Members were called Ghouls. The usual costume of the reconstruction Klansman was a red robe (white sheets were used later) and a high, conical hat covered with cabalistic markings.

Terror was the weapon utilized against carpetbaggers and Negroes. Especially effective were attempts to play upon the superstition of the illiterate freedman. A favorite trick of the Klansman was to conceal a water bag under his robe, make a midnight call upon a Negro, demand a bucket of water, turn aside to pour the contents into the hidden bag, and grimly announce, "That's the best drink I've had since I was killed at Pittsburg Landing (Shiloh)." Sometimes a detachable head was removed and offered to the terror-stricken freedman. In relations with its white enemies, the Klan usually dispatched lugubrious warnings headed by such esoterica as "Windy Cave —Doleful Hour." The mildest salutation was

[7] It should be recognized that there were two separate Ku Klux Klans. The first is referred to above. The second (1915) was organized as a money-making venture, reaching its height during the 1920s. The later Klan was anti-Semitic, anti-Catholic, and anti-foreign-born, in addition to maintaining its earlier hostility to the Negro.

"Damn your soul"; and Klan communications generally carried threats—for example, unless the recipient immediately left the area, ". . . you . . . will be led out by the Klan and learnt to stretch hemp."

Although at first the Klan carried on quasi-legal "court" proceedings against its white and black foes, physical terror became increasingly common. Beatings, tar and featherings, ear croppings, and even outright murder were made part of the Klan pattern of operation. Criminals began to scrawl "K.K.K." at the scene of their crime so that no official investigation would commence. So extreme did some elements become that General Forrest officially disbanded the organization in 1869, but many local "dens" continued to exist. During 1871 the irate Federal government struck back with three "force bills," one of them aimed directly at the Klan, affixing heavy penalties for "conspiracy." Grant promptly sent Union troops into nine South Carolina counties where the Klan had been unusually active, the writ of habeas corpus was suspended, and a round-up of Klansmen was started. Eventually eighty-two persons were either fined or imprisoned, or both, and the Klan was virtually destroyed by the end of 1871.

THE SUPREME COURT
AND RECONSTRUCTION

Such action as the restriction of constitutional court privileges again brought legalistic aspects to the fore. One might well ask, what was the Supreme Court, traditional watchdog of in-dividual rights under the Constitution, doing while the implacable Radicals inflicted military rule upon states of the Union? Certainly Andrew Johnson, with almost monotonous regularity, had voiced his doubts about their constitutionality as he vetoed Radical measure after measure, only to see the "Vindictive" majority override his objections. Theoretically the Court tended to uphold the President; in practice it stood aside silently and allowed the Radicals to proceed unhampered.

The judiciary's decisions in *Ex parte Milligan* and *Ex parte McCardle* [8] clearly expressed the opinion that military courts were illegal when civil tribunals were available, yet in the Reconstruction Act the Radicals were able to impose military court-martials almost everywhere in the former Confederacy and removed such issues from the national Court's control by parliamentary trickery. In *Texas v. White* (1869) Chief Justice Salmon P. Chase, speaking for the majority, upheld the Lincoln-Johnson theory that the seceded states were never out of the Union. Nevertheless, the Radicals continued to treat the Southern states as conquered provinces. In several decisions during the 1870s the Court interpreted the meaning of the Fourteenth and Fifteenth Amendments to apply to state political action against the Negro but not to social rights. Yet the Radical governments continued to discriminate against the white Southerner in favor of the freedman. Congress had temporarily ripped up the Constitution, but the Court did nothing. It was perhaps the depth of judicial prestige in the nation's history.

[8] See p. 415.

CHAPTER 39

The Age of Grant

(1869-1877)

ULYSSES S. GRANT

While action and counteraction convulsed the South, and the Radicals by refusing to admit that the war was over made the word reconstruction seem paradoxical, the stormy Johnson administration was succeeded by those of Ulysses S. Grant. There was much reason to hope that the renowned soldier would make an excellent President. To hundreds of thousands in the North he was almost a sacred figure; had he not won where so many had lost? Others had helped, but his leadership had been decisive and he remained the great Northern hero of the Civil War. Outstanding during his military career from 1861 to 1865 had been his solid dependability, his courage during a temporarily adverse situation, his modest self-assurance, his lack of histrionics, his ability to adapt himself to new conditions, and his willingness to accept and profit from advice. Many of his fellow citizens saw in the stocky, clear-headed Grant of the war years an individual who seemed to have all the attributes necessary to organize a successful government that would gain in efficiency and direction what it might lack in glamour and dynamic forensics. Yet the Grant administrations were tawdry failures.

There seems an almost uncanny dichotomy between Grant the soldier and Grant the President. Some might say that his failure in civilian direction was due to his military background, but sometimes officers have proved capable civilian administrators. Rather than growing through the broadening effects of age and experience, Grant appeared to lose ground even in the qualities that had made him an excellent general. He seems to have been mentally unfit for the presidency. When subordinates would come to him with a problem for solution, Grant would sit in silence, drawing on his Havana cigar as the minutes dragged by. He would evade and procrastinate, never coming to grips with an issue.

Even worse was his attitude toward his position of grave responsibility. Grant seems to have looked upon the Executive chair as a soft, upholstered sofa bestowed upon him by grateful Americans for his brilliant war record rather than as a stiff, hard-backed seat of responsibility. He administered the government for a few close friends rather than for all the people; indeed "cronyism" was a scandal from 1869 to 1877. He had a blind spot in evaluating others. Crass spoilsmen such as Jay Gould were able to hoodwink the naïve soldier and con-

443

vince him that material favors were accorded through personal liking rather than as covert bribes. If individuals were personally acceptable to Grant, that was all that was necessary. He allowed actual criminals to escape merited chastisement through a distressing inability to tell right from wrong. Personally honest himself (although he accepted lavish gifts), Grant allowed his administration to become synonymous with corruption.

The President's personal relations were often conducted on a petty and vindictive basis. He sometimes appointed reformers who were promptly dismissed once they began to clean up some of the graft. Grant's squabble with Senator Charles Sumner was conducted on such a ridiculous level that it seemed more like an imbroglio during a grammar-school recess than any high-minded difference of opinion between two eminent statesmen. The President seemed to get more vindictive and politics-ridden as he grew older. By the early 1870s, the magnanimous victor at Appomattox had changed into a spiteful persecutor of the South.

❰ *The Cabinet.* Grant's first official action, the appointment of his Cabinet, filled the nation with wonder and astonishment. Nominated to the post of Secretary of State was Elihu Washburne of Illinois, completely and totally unfit for the job on the grounds of interest, intelligence, and training. Indeed, Grant admitted that Washburne's appointment was a plum in reward for the latter's congressional backing during the war, although the Secretary would resign almost immediately to accept the position as Minister to France.[1] By chance the President replaced Washburne with Hamilton Fish of New York, who became one of the most successful Secretaries of State in American history and won for the Grant administration what few plaudits it deserved. The War portfolio went to General John Rawlins, Grant's aide-de-camp during the war, who was

succeeded after his death by several others, among them the corrupt William W. Belknap. The confused and naïve President tried to appoint Alexander T. Stewart, a prominent New York merchant, to the Treasury position, despite a law of Congress which stipulated that no one engaged in trade or commerce can accept that assignment. The narrow Radical George Boutwell of Massachusetts was little improvement. A wealthy Pennsylvania invalid named Adolph E. Borie became Secretary of the Navy. Borie had contributed generously to the Republican campaign fund in 1868, but there seemed no other reason for his appointment, since he did not ask for the job and it came as a surprise to him.

Tribute should be accorded to some able, honest, and efficient public officials in Grant's Cabinet. In addition to Hamilton Fish, other luminaries were Rockwood Hoar of Massachusetts, Attorney General; and two Secretaries of the Interior, Jacob D. Cox of Ohio and Benjamin H. Bristow of Kentucky. Significantly, almost every one of the honest and incorruptible officials either was forced out by Grant's open dislike for reformers or else resigned in disgust. Kaleidoscopic changes typified Grant's Cabinet during both administrations.

POLITICAL CORRUPTION: STATE AND CITY MACHINES

Operating behind the awesome military prestige of the General-President and instrumental to the success of the national party were the mighty Republican state machines, each under the direction of a political boss, usually a United States Senator. These organizations were cemented to the national party by political patronage in the form of Federal governmental jobs that the state politicos could distribute to their faithful party hacks. Public "civil" service became a laughable misnomer, and the amount of corruption in such cesspools as the New York City Customs House made responsible government a farce. Major Republican machines able to produce party

[1] Rumor had it that Washburne asked for the French assignment rather than the more important British post because his English was too abominable for London, whereas he could use an interpreter in Paris.

majorities for most elections were headed by Benjamin Butler in Massachusetts, Zachariah Chandler in Michigan, Roscoe Conkling in New York, Don Cameron in Pennsylvania, and "Black Jack" Logan in Illinois.

Before narrating the details of Grant's turbulent domestic maneuvers a point must be reiterated that was made in connection with the Reconstruction governments in the South. Corruption was the order of the day in state and local rule as well as in the national arena. Politics became a stench in the public nostrils during the decades immediately following the Civil War. It might well be argued that the slimy pinnacle was reached in municipal government. Corrupt machines thrived in such cities as Chicago, St. Louis, Philadelphia (where the "Gas Ring" was a potent ally of the Cameron state organization), and even the nation's capital. "Boss" Shepherd ran the debt of Washington, D.C., up to $17 million, and without any reasonable doubt part of that sum was for graft to the Shepherd organization. Grant let the extent of his displeasure be shown by appointing Shepherd Chairman of the Board of Public Works.

❰ *The Tweed Ring.* Conditions in New York were the most intolerable of all. Tammany Hall, the venerable Gotham Democratic machine, was firmly in the grasp of the prodigiously fat William Marcy Tweed, whose "ring" was all-powerful in the city. Perhaps never have urban peculations reached such impressive statures—the precise amount stolen by Tweed and his associates is impossible to determine, but estimates run from $30 million to $200 million. Accepting no city political office himself, Tweed remained in the background (or as much in the background as his 300 pounds would permit) and worked behind such fronts as the dapper Mayor A. Oakey Hall, Peter B. Sweeney, and the nefarious Richard B. "Slippery Dick" Connolly. All businessmen desiring city contracts had to do business with the ring.[2] The New York City Court House was

estimated to cost a few hundred thousand dollars. When Tweed was finally forced to relinquish his stranglehold on city finances, that building was still incomplete, and New York had already been charged $12 million.

Corruption of so epic a scope eventually attracted attention, and attacks were launched against the ring by *The New York Times*; Thomas Nast, the acidulous cartoonist of *Harper's Magazine*; and a prominent New York Democratic lawyer, Samuel B. Tilden, the latter somewhat belatedly. Despite the frantic efforts of Tweed to bribe his way out of trouble (Nast was offered a half-million dollars to focus his cartoons on other subjects), the books kept by the ring were seized, and the organization collapsed. Tweed fled to Europe, only to be extradited and returned to New York, where he died in jail. Others received stiff penitentiary sentences. Unfortunately, reform was of short duration in the national metropolis—within a few years Tammany Hall was again back in power.

BUSINESS AND NATIONAL POLITICS

❰ *The Gold Corner.* General business morality during the 1870s showed little improvement in comparison to political ethics. This was the era of the "robber barons," and while such individuals as Jay Gould, James Fisk, and Daniel Drew were more successful and more predatory than most, their ethics were typical of many of their contemporaries. Jay Gould was a destroyer rather than a creator. Though modern times may look askance at the tactics of a Rockefeller or a Carnegie while driving competitors into bankruptcy, at least they contributed significantly toward the growth of industrial America. Rather than constructing a great business, Gould hoped to wreck prosperous establishments so that he could buy them

---

[2] In typical operation under the Tweed Ring, if a plasterer were to bill the city for $5,000 the ring would insist that the bill be changed to $55,000—

$50,000 for Tweed and his colleagues. New York City was assessed for ordinary wire coat hangers at $5 apiece. The amount spent for carpeting was estimated to have been enough "to cover the City Park three times."

cheaply, drive up their value, and sell out at a handsome profit. He even purchased the famous New York *World* in order to print false stories about the financial condition of companies that he wished to control.

Jim Fisk, Yankee huckster, was a huge Falstaffian person whose vulgarity reached almost heroic proportions. Dressed in an admiral's uniform—he owned the Fall River Steamboat Line—Fisk was a traffic-stopping spectacle as he wheeled about New York in a magnificent equipage, usually accompanied by one or more of the girls from his private opera house. His moral caliber can be judged by his jaunty observation, "I worship in the Synagogue of the Libertines." When one of his most vicious coups failed, he laughed it off with the comment, "Nothing is lost save honor." "Uncle Dan'l" Drew was a canting old hypocrite who spent the Sabbath singing hymns, and on at least one occasion he defrauded his own pastor and fellow parishioners with watered stock.[3]

Two of this infamous trio were able to work on the gullible and unsuspecting President Grant. Gould and Fisk decided to "corner gold," but they needed help from the government. At that time gold was a commodity that could be bought and sold on the open market in the same manner as wheat, corn, or steel. Yet it was also a standard of value and a medium of exchange, hence many businessmen contracted debts that had to be paid in gold. Gould and Fisk concluded that they could secretly buy up available gold supplies, thus creating an artificial shortage, drive the price sky-high, and clear fortunes. There was danger, however, that the government might release Treasury gold in the emergency, thus smashing their corner.

Therefore Gould directed his attentions to Grant, working through the ministrations of Grant's brother-in-law; after being introduced to the President he lavished gifts upon the un-

suspecting Grant and his wife. The unsophisticated General thought that such presents were simple expressions of affection and admiration from Gould, and he credulously suspected nothing when Gould dropped hints that it would be ruinous to the national prosperity if Treasury gold were released in the near future. As usual, Grant did not commit himself; he probably did not realize what was happening.

Now that the only obstacle to their plan was presumably breached, Gould and Fisk proceeded to purchase vast amounts of gold. On "Black Friday" (24 September 1869) the partners let the word slip out that if gold was necessary, Gould and Fisk were the only ones who could supply it. A wild panic immediately occurred as businessmen faced with gold obligations frantically bid against one another. Gold skyrocketed, but most other stocks crashed. Finally prodded into action by his Secretary of the Treasury, Grant ordered the release of government gold. Gould received advanced word from his White House source of information, and it is typical of some business ethics of the time that he silently unloaded his gold supply without saying a word to his partner. Fisk, although caught short and stripped of a fortune, was not angry with Gould. He thought it was a good joke on himself.

¶ *Crédit Mobilier.* Business and local political corruption was matched by disclosures of financial immorality in the national government. Although the actual peculations had occurred before Grant came into office, the Crédit Mobilier scandal cast a baleful light on men close to the President. Crédit Mobilier was a construction company formed to procure the contract to build the Union Pacific Railroad, the eastern portion of the transcontinental line. By an interesting coincidence, the boards of directors of both the Crédit Mobilier Construction Company and the Union Pacific Railroad were composed of the same persons. Without competitive bidding, the directors of the Union Pacific awarded lucrative contracts to the directors of Crédit Mobilier (them-

---

[3] "Watered stock" is used for corporation securities not based on solid assets; the term is attributed to Drew. Starting as a drover, "Uncle Dan'l" was paid so much per pound for his cattle. On the way to market he would feed salt to his stock and then let them consume gallons of water, which increased both their weight and Drew's profits.

selves) and by assessing unreasonably high construction costs defrauded of millions of dollars both the government, which paid bounties for railroad construction, and small investors who purchased stock.

Crédit Mobilier securities were offered to important Senators and Representatives to quell possible embarrassing congressional questions. Most intolerable to the public was the revelation that this stock did not have to be purchased in advance; payment could be made from future dividends, which were guaranteed to be generous. This promise was not exaggerated, for Crédit Mobilier cleared 348 per cent profit in one year. When these shady transactions became public, political careers were ruined for such prominent individuals as Schuyler Colfax, Vice-President of the United States; Representatives Oakes Ames and James Brooks; and New Hampshire's Senator James W. Patterson. Others narrowly escaped a like fate, among them James A. Garfield, future President of the United States, who had to do some fast talking before exonerating himself. Additional major scandals that tainted the Grant administrations occurred during the General's second term and will be discussed in proper chronological sequence.

GRANT'S FIRST-TERM LEGISLATION

Little constructive legislation was passed during Grant's first administration. There were some insignificant tariff reductions. Civil service, which was ever becoming more malodorous, remained unreformed, even though Grant appointed a commission under George William Curtis to "cleanse the Augean stables" of political partisanship, which was making responsible public positions mere gifts for spoilsmen's disposal. Curtis worked hard, but Grant gave him no support, and the reformer finally resigned in disgust. Government jobs became more openly corrupt than ever.

It was during Grant's tenure in the White House that Reconstruction government sank to new lows in the South. Despite the readmit-

tance into the Union and the concomitant restoration of home rule in Virginia, Mississippi, and Texas, the other states of the former Confederacy languished under Radical maladministration. Grant seemed to have an unerring faculty for selecting the worst Reconstruction governments to support with Federal soldiers. It was during his terms that the Force Acts placed part of South Carolina under martial law and removed thousands of persons from the protection afforded by civil courts. The Vindictive program remained potent.

Grant was perplexed by the monetary problem. That is not surprising, for it was extremely complicated, and the General was more untutored in finance than in most other topics. Several controversies raged over the eventual disposal of the Civil War greenbacks. This fiat money had been based only on the promise of the government that eventually the bills would be redeemed. How and in what form redemption would take place had been left for future decision. During the war the greenbacks had fluctuated in value, although never on a par with gold dollars.

A primary question was whether the purchasers of United States war bonds, which had been bought with "cheap" greenbacks, should be paid off in greenbacks or in gold. Business interests, reflected in the stand of the Republican party, clamored for payment of the bonds in "coin," which they interpreted as gold. Andrew Johnson and most of the Democrats advocated the Pendleton, or "Ohio," plan, whereby the bonds purchased in greenbacks would be paid in greenbacks and thus would continue the war inflation. In 1869 the Republicans were able to push through payment of the bonds in gold, and the bondholders of course realized a handsome profit.

A second controversy concerned the greenback itself. Should this paper dollar be brought to parity with the gold dollar? Should the greenbacks remain in circulation or should they be withdrawn, with deflation as a probable result? Farmers and other debtor groups who hated a scarce dollar and low prices objected to parity with gold and were particularly vehement in advocating more, rather than fewer, greenbacks. Eventually something of a compromise was reached whereby the greenbacks were brought to equality with the gold dollar and made redeemable in gold (1879). They were not withdrawn from circulation, however, and $346,681,016 remained outstanding. Yet no new issues were permitted, and the farmers had to turn to other means to expand the national currency.

The monetary question was further complicated by the strange action of the Supreme Court. In the case of *Hepburn v. Griswold* (1870), Chief Justice Salmon P. Chase concurred with the majority (5 to 3) that the action of Civil War Secretary of the Treasury Salmon P. Chase in issuing greenbacks had been unconstitutional. This almost incredible decision would have resulted in chaos had it been permitted to stand. Vacancies on the Supreme Court existed, however, and the quick appointment of two new justices who favored making greenbacks legal tender soon reversed *Hepburn v. Griswold*.

THE ELECTION OF 1872

With the South still partly carpetbag-governed, with little reform legislation to flourish, and with official corruption either proved or at least widely suspected, the Republican party looked toward the election of 1872 with trepidation. Worse was still to come, for their ranks were soon split with dissension. An influential wing, sickened by the low moral fiber of the administration, seceded from the party to form the Liberal Republican party. Eminent Republicans enlisted under the Liberal banner, among them Lyman Trumbull, former abolitionist war horse; Carl Schurz, spokesman for the powerful Middle Western Germans; Charles Francis Adams, distinguished son of John Quincy Adams, railroad president, and able Minister to Great Britain during the Civil War; Supreme Court Chief Justice Salmon P. Chase; and two prominent editors, Edwin L. Godkin of the influential weekly newspaper the *Nation* and Horace Greeley of the New York *Tribune*.

With hopes high, the Liberal Republicans met in convention, excoriated the Grant regime, and after some backing and starting passed over Charles Francis Adams and Salmon P. Chase to nominate Horace Greeley, eccentric editor of the New York *Tribune*. It was a strange selection. Greeley was brilliant, industrious, and honest. Yet during the thirty-odd years that he had directed editorial policy for one of the great national newspapers, he had shown himself to be erratic, impetuous, undependable, and naïve. He had supported at times such enthusiasms as spiritualism, food faddism, and utopian socialism, and even worse, he had said some kind things about free love. Greeley's appearance was such that he was an easy target for caricatures. Nearsighted, ingenuous, baby-blue eyes peered benignly from behind thick spectacles. His round head and plump face, the latter fringed by a corona of thin white whiskers, made him look like a pallid sunflower.

On the relatively few issues, such as high protective tariffs, from which Greeley had never deviated, he had maintained positions contrary to those supported by the Democratic party. Any possibility of his election to the presidency was contingent upon Democratic support, and it would be hard to imagine a man to whom the Democrats could turn with less fervor than to the *Tribune's* editor, who as both a Whig and a Republican had seldom stopped his vigorous onslaughts against the Democratic party. Yet the latter had no other choice and reluctantly followed the Liberal Republican leadership.

The Republicans easily renominated Grant and his still impressive military record. Every Civil War battle was refought, fresh gore was spattered on the "bloody shirt," the spoilsmen and their henchmen trotted into the front lines, and the great Republican state machines started rounding up the votes. A vicious attack whirled around the spinning head of poor Greeley. The cartoons of Thomas Nast were so cruel that the bewildered editor complained that he never knew whether he was running "for the Presidency or the penitentiary." To add to his burdens, Greeley's wife died during the campaign. Despite his frantic activities, which included a host of speaking engagements during which he insisted that the breach between the North and the South be healed and that they should "clasp hands across the bloody chasm," Greeley's position was hopeless.

Aided by the Union veteran vote, the Negro vote from the South, and the business vote (the industrialists contributed generously to the Republican campaign fund), Greeley was inundated in a startling defeat. Grant rolled up a popular majority of 3,600,000 to 2,800,000 and won in the Electoral College, 262 to 66. Greeley carried only the border states of Maryland, Kentucky, Tennessee, and Missouri and two reconstructed Southern states, Georgia and Texas. Worn out by his strenuous campaign, bedaubed by the political mud that had been hurled at him, and prostrated by the death of his wife, Greeley went insane and died only a month after election.

SECOND-TERM SCANDALS

So it was to be a second administration for Ulysses S. Grant. Hardly was the new term under way when scandal after scandal broke upon the nation. Many of them emanated from the White House, although again it must be noted that Grant was not personally responsible. Congress reflected the tenor of the day when Benjamin Butler engineered the "salary grab." In this legislation, the salaries of the President, Senators, and Representatives were doubled. There was little objection to this; such increases were long overdue. Public outcry became heated, however, when the increases were made retroactive for two years so that each individual concerned received a handout of several thousand dollars. Indignation over this mean advantage was sharply registered during the congressional elections of 1874, when many suddenly affluent incumbents were swept from public office.

Far worse were two instances emanating from the Treasury. Rumors of widespread peculations in that department had circulated for years, but not until Benjamin H. Bristow became Secretary of the Treasury were the facts brought to light. The first disclosure concerned the "Sanborn contracts." The Treasury had granted contracts to one John A. Sanborn of Massachusetts to collect unpaid taxes. Sanborn recovered some bona fide obligations to the government, but in addition he used his privileges to blackmail respectable businessmen by threatening lawsuits to collect fraudulent tax claims. He amassed $427,000 through these tactics, keeping the rather impressive fraction of one-half for himself, or more properly for the political machine of Benjamin Butler. William A. Richardson, who had succeeded George Boutwell as Secretary of the Treasury, was forced to resign for having permitted the Sanborn contracts.

The "Whisky Ring" brought scandal right into the White House. The indefatigable Bristow presented evidence to Grant that certain Treasury officials had connived with crooked distillers to defraud the government of millions of dollars owed on the whisky excise tax. At first Grant seemed sympathetic to the investigation when he snapped, "Let no guilty man escape." But the President lost all interest in the proceedings once the trail led straight to a personal friend, John McDonald of Missouri [4] and even worse, to General Orville E. Babcock, Grant's private secretary. The President went so far as to intervene in Babcock's trial and enabled him to escape on a technicality, although Babcock promptly resigned. Bristow was treated so coldly in Cabinet sessions that he too soon tendered his resignation.

Hard on the heels of these disclosures came the Belknap scandal. William W. Belknap, to whom Grant felt a personal obligation, had been appointed Secretary of War. Soon Washington buzzed with surmise on how the Secretary and his extravagant wife could entertain so lavishly on his government salary. Eventually this financial legerdemain was explained. At that time Indian affairs were under the control of the War Department, and the Secretary

---

[4] Instead of being punished, McDonald was later appointed by Grant to the post of supervisor of internal revenue.

was permitted to lease contracts for feeding reservation Indians. Although these jobs were paid a pittance, the opportunity for graft was almost unlimited; Belknap had been paid almost $25,000 for one such appointment. When the story broke, the House impeached Belknap unanimously, but the Secretary fled to Grant, who accepted his resignation just before the Senate was to vote on his impeachment charge. A Senate majority condemned Belknap, but the necessary two-thirds vote was lacking, since many Senators felt that once he had resigned, the Secretary of War had moved beyond their jurisdiction. If the President had refused to accept such a suspiciously hasty resignation, no doubt Belknap would have received his deserved punishment. In all these scandals, however, about all the accused had to do was to assure Grant that the "reformers" were trying to chastise the President through "persecuting his friends," and the General would condone rather than condemn.

During these scandal-beset times, Southern conditions were slowly changing. Over Grant's two terms, most of the former Confederate states were able to oust their carpetbag governments and restore white sovereignty. The passage of time lessened war animosities; the ballots of thousands of new voters to whom the Civil War was partly legendary, the removal of disfranchisement from prominent ex-Confederates, the tendency of the carpetbag organizations to fall into internal dissension, and the burgeoning opinion in the North that racial equality had been premature in the South all aided in the restoration of home rule. Nevertheless, as late as the autumn of 1876 Louisiana, Florida, and South Carolina were still under carpetbag rule, a factor that would seriously influence the disputed election in 1876.

THE DEPRESSION OF 1873

As if scandals in high places and the continuation of Southern disorder were not sufficient to plague Ulysses S. Grant, a major depression

afflicted the nation during the 1870s. As usual, the causes were numerous. Furthermore, the depression was not restricted to the United States alone, but was truly world-wide; the typical economic disturbances that follow wars seem to have occurred. Not only did the American Civil War convulse natural economic factors, but there were the Crimean War, the Franco-Austrian War, and the three Wars of German Unification to add to the distress. All the great industrial nations suffered, and America's griefs were heightened by the forced sale of American securities by depression-ridden European investors. Inside the United States a tremendous expansion in industry and transportation had boomed—perhaps too much. An ocean of new securities poured onto the markets faster than purchasers could be found. Especially devastating was the amount of extralegal business activities, whereby such speculators as Jay Gould had ruined many prosperous enterprises. Government costs had soared through the amount of graft on the local, state, and national level.

Often depressions need a catalytic agent to change the psychological aura from one of confidence to one of panic. This was furnished when the nation learned with horrified disbelief that the Philadelphia banking house of Jay Cooke and Company had closed its doors in 1873. Cooke had been a fabulously successful financier of the Civil War, and presumably his acumen made investments with him unusually safe. Yet Cooke had gone overboard on railroad securities and was forced into bankruptcy. The panic immediately spread, and stocks plummeted to such an extent that the New York Stock Exchange closed its doors. The nation had received a shock severe enough to turn the panic into a full-fledged depression. Bad times extended from 1873 until almost the end of the decade; discouragingly the depression tended to worsen each year. During the panic year of 1873, 5,000 business establishments toppled into bankruptcy, 8,000 in 1875, and over 10,000 in 1878. Lowered wages, extensive unemployment, individual hardship, labor violence, monetary chaos, collapsed prices, and oppressive uncertainty continued to distress the United States until gradually recovery came during 1879–1880.

THE DISPUTED ELECTION OF 1876

As in 1872, the Republicans awaited the contest of 1876 with little ardor. The outraged people had swept the Democrats to victory in the mid-term contests in 1874, and obviously nothing had happened during the last two years to restore confidence in the Republican administration. Nevertheless, the Republican convention featured some confident oratory. The magnetic James G. Blaine of Maine, rising star of the GOP, was placed in nomination by the noted religious agnostic, Colonel Robert G. Ingersoll, as:

. . . the man who has torn from the face of treason the tongue of slander . . . the man who has snatched the mask of Democracy from the hideous face of the rebellion. . . . Like an armed warrior, like a *plumed knight*, James G. Blaine marched down the halls of the American Congress and threw his shining lance full and fair against the brazen foreheads of the defamers of his country and the maligners of his honor.

Despite this impassioned oratory, the majority of the Republican delegates felt that the recently uncovered facts of Blaine's speculation in the Little Rock and Fort Smith Railroad was too much of a handicap when the party already was shadowed by corruption.[5] Blaine was shelved for later use, and unenthusiastically the nomination was bestowed upon Rutherford B. Hayes, reform Governor of Ohio. The Republicans were attempting to convince the electorate that they were turning a new leaf.

The confident Democrats had little difficulty in selecting Samuel J. Tilden as their standard-bearer. Tilden was a small, nervous, dark-complexioned hypochondriac who had been an extremely successful railroad-corporation lawyer. He had been a lifelong Democrat, gaining a reputation as a reformer through his

[5] For more complete discussion of Blaine's railroad transactions, see Vol. II.

attacks on the Tweed Ring, although his enemies were quick to point out that he entered the fray only after it had been won by the exertions of others. As Governor of New York, Tilden had vigorously prosecuted a "Canal Ring" that was defrauding the state. Wrapped in the mantle of reform, Tilden appeared likely to win.

When election results in 1876 became known, the fondest Democratic hopes seemed realized. New York and other pivotal states tumbled into the Tilden column, and he promptly amassed 184 electoral votes; since 185 was a majority in the Electoral College, he needed to garner only one more. The popular majority was strongly for the Democrat. The Republican campaign chairman, Zachariah Chandler of Michigan, went to bed drunk and despondent on election night, and many of the Republican papers conceded victory to Tilden. But alert editors on the pro-Hayes *New York Times* noticed that there were twenty electoral votes in dispute, and since Hayes had 165 he could become President if he made a clean sweep. The awakened Chandler dispatched telegrams to the Republican organizations in Louisiana, Florida, and South Carolina: "Can you hold your state?" This touched off the worst controversy in American political history, and not until 2 March 1877, two days before the inauguration of the new administration, did the nation know for sure who was to be the next President.

It was a most complicated situation. Of the twenty disputed electoral votes, one was from Oregon and concerned a technicality. The state was obviously Republican. Difficulty was concentrated in the nineteen electoral votes from the three Southern states of South Carolina, Florida, and Louisiana. There both sides had engaged in an orgy of illegality. The Republican carpetbag regimes had thrown out thousands of Democratic votes (in Louisiana a 9,000 Democratic majority was changed to a 4,000-vote deficit by the simple procedure of discarding 13,000 ballots). By threats and intimidation, Southern white Democrats kept thousands of Negro Republicans from the polls. Democrats and Republicans sent in

THE ELECTION OF 1876

( )   Electoral votes
     Hayes-Republican (165)
/// Tilden-Democrat (184)
     Disputed-Republican by Compromise
     of 1877 (20)
     Territories not voting

sharply differing election returns from the three states. Which should be selected?

The Constitution gave little assistance. The pertinent section reads, "The President of the Senate shall, in the presence of the Senate and the House of Representatives, open the certificates, and the votes shall then be counted." But which votes would be counted, Democratic or Republican? If the House of Representatives made the selection, as it constitutionally does when no candidate has an electoral majority, Tilden would win, for the Democrats had a majority in the lower house. Democrats would not countenance senatorial selection, for they were a minority there. After months of threats and counterthreats, frenzied debate, and high passion on both sides, a compromise solution was finally worked out and passed by act of Congress.

A commission of fifteen was selected, composed of five from the House, five from the Senate, and five from the Supreme Court. The Republican Senate furnished three of their own party and two from the other. The Democratic House sent three Democrats and two Republicans. Supposedly Supreme Court justices

have no political affiliations, but this sophistry was overlooked, and two with Democratic backgrounds were matched by two Republicans. The other vote, and undoubtedly the deciding one, was given to Justice David Davis, an Illinois Liberal Republican. Poor Davis was writhing on the griddle, for he would individually elect a President of the United States. He was granted an avenue of escape, which he instantly accepted, when the Illinois legislature offered him a senatorial seat recently vacated by death. The deciding position was then given to Associate Justice Joseph P. Bradley. Bradley, who at first appeared to lean toward Tilden, had an eleventh-hour change of heart and sided with the Republicans; on every one of the disputed ballots, the Republicans won by 8 to 7. The commission declared that Rutherford B. Hayes had captured each of the twenty votes in doubt, earning a 185 to 184 decision in the Electoral College, and would be inaugurated President of the United States.

Beyond question, this was the most dubious presidential election in American annals. A clear majority of the American people had favored Tilden, and the method of counting the electoral votes was, at best, highly irregular. Outraged Democrats openly threatened rebellion, and a new civil war loomed as a distinct possibility.

THE COMPROMISE OF 1877

Conflict was avoided, however, for several reasons. Samuel J. Tilden deserves considerable credit for allaying the bellicose sentiments of his supporters. He had patriotism enough to place the welfare of his country above his personal ambition; furthermore he was timid and pacifistic by nature. Tilden threw his influence for conciliation and peaceful acceptance of Hayes. More important, a tacit deal seems to have been made by Southern Democrats and some Republicans. The usual interpretation of the "Compromise of 1877" has been that there was a simple exchange whereby Southern Democrats would acquiesce to the inauguration of Hayes in return for a pledge to remove Federal troops from the last of the former Confederate states, allowing the restoration of home rule throughout the entire South. Recent research has shown that this traditional viewpoint is too narrow. To be sure, there was a split between Southern and Northern Democrats, the former tacitly agreeing to the Republican presidential triumph. Yet by the spring of 1877 the question of Union soldiers in the South was something of a dead letter; the last of the Reconstruction governments were collapsing in utter disintegration; and Grant, together with other leading Republicans, had privately admitted that it was impossible to keep troops in the South much longer. Southerners, however, did wish a guarantee to this effect, and so the restoration of home rule was an issue in the compromise.

Often overlooked were Southern demands for a place in Hayes's Cabinet (an ex-Confederate was soon appointed as Postmaster General) and especially the cry that national financial support should go to Southern internal improvements. Dixie hopes in this direction were focused on the anticipated construction of the Texas and Pacific Railroad, which would strike to southern California through Texas, New Mexico, and Arizona. Eventually the railroad was built with much the same type of Federal assistance that had been given to the Union Pacific and the Central Pacific Railroads. Despite the impassioned opposition of the Northern Democrats, the Republican–Southern Democratic coalition was able to bring about the Compromise of 1877 and permit the election and inauguration of Rutherford B. Hayes. With the inevitable withdrawal of the last Federal military detachments from the South during the next summer, home rule became universal throughout the South. The sectional solidarity that has seen the South almost always in the Democratic camp in national elections became a fact, although factional disputes between the conservative "Bourbon" planters and the "wool-hat boys" (the poor whites) caused considerable turmoil for years.

Despite its somewhat unfair termination, the disputed election of 1876 did more than write finis to the sordid story of Reconstruction, which finally dragged its weary twelve-year course to an end. The election illustrated that the American people were politically mature enough to settle peaceably a situation that would probably have been attended by violence almost anywhere else in the world. Compromise had finally worked, as it had in 1820, 1833, and 1850, but whereas these former settlements had proved illusory and temporary, that of 1877 was destined to be permanent. With the most virulent forms of sectionalism and political controversy left behind, Americans could view the future with considerable optimism, for to a large degree they had come of age.

Readings

The literature of American history is almost infinite in amount and variety. The most any reading list can hope to accomplish is to indicate the more important works, and even here there will be differences of opinion. Below are listed first some of the more useful general works which touch most of the chapters of the book and for which further references will not be made. Then follow readings arranged by chapters of the text. Groups of books are arranged alphabetically according to authors, except that biographies are arranged alphabetically according to the subjects. Titles have been contracted wherever it was possible to do so without confusion. Contemporary accounts have been included only when unusually valuable, and an effort has been made to exclude narratives that are primarily antiquarian. Certain older books have been omitted as unavailable in most libraries. Many of the books are useful for more than one chapter, but the longer citation is given only once.

GENERAL HISTORIES. Those by individual authors include C. A. and M. R. Beard, *Rise of American Civilization* (4 vols., 1927–1942); E. Channing, *History of the United States* (6 vols., 1905–1925), to 1865; J. B. McMaster, *History of the People of the United States* (8 vols., 1883–1913) and *History of the People of the United States during Lincoln's Administration* (1927), to 1865; J. F. Rhodes, *History of the United States* (9 vols., 1909–1928), 1850 to 1909. Older works by E. M. Avery, George Bancroft, Richard Hildreth, E. P. Oberholtzer, James Schouler, N. S. Shaler, H. von Holst, and Justin Winsor are seldom used today. Somewhat more limited are such books as R. H. Gabriel, *Course of American Democratic Thought*

(1940) on various types of American thinking from 1815; and G. Myers, *History of American Idealism* (1925).

Cooperative histories include notably A. B. Hart (ed.), *The American Nation* (28 vols., 1904–1918), heavily political; A. Johnson and A. Nevins (eds.), *Chronicles of America* (56 vols., 1918–1951), short and generally well written; A. M. Schlesinger and D. R. Fox (eds.), *History of American Life* (13 vols., 1927–1948), emphasizing the social, economic, and intellectual aspects of American history. Individual volumes of these series will be cited under specific chapters. Primarily devoted to pictures are J. T. Adams (ed.), *Album of American History* (4 vols., 1944–1948); R. P. Butterfield, *The American Past* (1947); M. B. Davidson, *Life in America* (2 vols., 1951); R. H. Gabriel (ed.), *The Pageant of America* (15 vols., 1925–1929); A. Rogers (comp.), *American Procession* (1933).

Collections of contemporary material include M. Berger, *British Travellers* (1943), 1836 to 1860; H. S. Commager (ed.), *America in Perspective* (1947), travels, *Documents of American History* (1949), political; H. S. Commager and A. Nevins (eds.), *Heritage of America* (1949); L. M. Hacker and H. S. Zahler, *Shaping the American Tradition* (2 vols., 1947); O. Handlin (ed.), *This Was America* (1949), travels; A. B. Hart (ed.), *American History Told by Contemporaries* (5 vols., 1897–1929); W. McDonald, *Documentary Source Book* (1926), 1606 to 1926; J. L. Mesick, *English Traveler* (1922), 1785 to 1922; F. Monaghan, *French Travelers* (1933), 1765 to 1832; A. Nevins, *America through British Eyes* (1948), *British Travellers* (1923); W. Thorp, M. E. Curti, and C. Baker (eds.), *American Issues* (2 vols., 1941); W. S. Tryon (ed.), *Mirror for Americans* (3 vols., 1952), travels 1790 to 1870. S. J. Buck, *Travel and Description, 1765–1865* (1914) is a bibliography.

The best collection of biographies is A. Johnson and D. Malone, *Dictionary of American Biography* (21 vols., 1928 to 1944). Less valuable is *Appleton's Cyclopedia of American Biography* (1886–1922).

The relation of geography to history is presented by I. Bowman, *The New World* (1928); R. H. Brown, *Historical Geography* (1948); H. R. Muelder and D. M. Delo, *Years of This Land* (1943); E. C. Semple, *American History and Its Geographic Conditions* (1933); R. B. Vance, *Human Geography of South* (1932). The most impressive historical atlas is C. O. Paullin, *Atlas of Historical Geography* (1932), but useful are such smaller works as J. T. Adams, *Atlas of American History* (1943); D. R. Fox, *Harpers Atlas* (1920); A. B. Hart and H. E. Bolton, *American History Atlas* (1930); C. L. and E. H. Lord, *Historical Atlas* (1953).

Dictionaries of American history include J. T. Adams and R. V. Coleman (eds.), *Dictionary of American History* (6 vols., 1940); M. Martin and L. Gelber, *New Dictionary of American History* (1952); R. B. Morris, *Encyclopedia of American History* (1953). Also useful is E. A. R. Seligman and A. Johnson (eds.), *Encyclopedia of the Social Sciences* (15 vols., 1930–1935).

The student of historiography will profit from M. Kraus, *Writing of American History* (1953); a larger field is covered by H. E. Barnes, *History of Historical Writing* (1937). L. Gottschalk, *Understanding History* (1950) describes historical method, while A. Nevins, *Gateway to History* (1938) and L. M. Salmon, *The Newspaper and the Historian* (1923) discuss some of the problems of the historian. The best guide for the researcher is H. P. Beers, *Bibliographies in American History* (1942). Extremely useful are W. H.

Allison and others, *Guide to Historical Literature* (1931); G. G. Griffin, *Writings on American History* (34 vols., 1908–1952); J. N. Larned (ed.), *Literature of American History* (1902). Periodicals have been indexed in *Poole's Index* (1893), and more recently in *Reader's Guide* (1901–). Federal documents are indexed in J. G. Ames, *Comprehensive Index* (2 vols., 1905); B. P. Poore, *Descriptive Catalogue* (1885); *Tables and Annotated Index* (1902); and more recently in a single volume for each session of Congress. Among the more notable collections of government documents are *American State Papers, Foreign Relations 1789–1828* (6 vols., 1832–1861); *Diplomatic Correspondence of the United States, 1783–1789* (7 vols., 1833–1834); R. J. Bartlett (ed.), *Record of American Diplomacy* (1947); S. F. Bemis and G. G. Griffin, *Guide to Diplomatic History* (1935), a bibliography; C. E. Carter (ed.), *Territorial Papers of the United States* (12 vols., 1934–1945); L. M. Goodrich and M. J. Carroll, *Documents on American Foreign Relations* (1945); C. E. Hill, *Leading American Treaties* (1922); W. M. Malloy, *Treaties . . . 1776–1937* (4 vols., 1910–1937); J. B. Moore, *International Arbitrations* (6 vols., 1898), *Digest of International Law* (8 vols., 1906); F. N. Thorpe, *Federal and State Constitutions* (7 vols., 1909).

Historical magazines embracing all American history are the *American Historical Review* (1895–) and the *Mississippi Valley Historical Review* (1915–). Most states have historical societies that publish periodicals, and in addition there are many other special journals such as *Agricultural History* (1927–), *American Economic Review* (1911–), *Annals of the American Academy of Political and Social Science* (1890–), *Catholic Historical Review* (1913–), *Journal of Economic History* (1941–), *Journal of Negro History* (1916–), *Journal of Southern History* (1935–), *New England Quarterly* (1928–), *Pacific Historical Review* (1932–), *Political Science Quarterly* (1886–).

CHAPTER 1. NEW WORLDS FOR THE TAKING

EUROPEAN BACKGROUND. E. P. Cheney, *Dawn of a New Era* (1936), to 1453, *European Background* (1904), very good; H. Pirenne, *Medieval Europe* (1936), *Medieval Cities* (1925), fine scholarship; G. C. Sellery and A. C. Krey, *Medieval Foundations* (1929), to 1660; C. Stephenson, *Medieval History* (1935), to 1600.

GENERAL COLONIAL HISTORIES. C. M. Andrews, *Colonial Period* (4 vols., 1934–1938), to 1770; C. L. Becker, *Beginnings of American People* (1915), brief, through Revolution; O. P. Chitwood, *Colonial America* (1931), text; E. B. Greene, *Foundations of American National-*

ity (1922); M. W. Jernegan, *American Colonies* (1929), well organized, to 1750; C. P. Nettles, *Roots of American Civilization* (1938), excellent; M. Savelle, *Foundations of American Civilization* (1942), text through Constitution; L. B. Wright, *Atlantic Frontier* (1947), much nonpolitical.

AMERICA OF RED MAN. GEOGRAPHY. E. Huntington, *Red Man's Continent* (1919); J. R. Smith, *North America* (1942). INDIANS. J. Collier, *Indians of Americas* (1947), generalized; W. C. Macleod, *American Indian Frontier* (1928); D. McNickle, *They Came Here First* (1949), interesting; A. H. Mallery, *Lost*

America (1951), before 1000; P. Radin, *Story of Indian* (1927), all Americas; F. W. Seymour, *Story of Red Man* (1929), popular; C. Wissler, *Indians of United States* (1940), anthropology.

EXPLORATION. GENERAL. W. C. Abbott, *Expansion of Europe* (1938), to 1789; J. Bakeless, *Eyes of Discovery* (1950), clear; J. B. Brebner, *Explorers of North America, 1492–1806* (1933), scholarly; B. de Voto, *Course of Empire* (1952), through Lewis and Clark; J. E. Gillespie, *History of Geographical Discovery, 1400–1800* (1933), short and simple. SPECIFIC COUNTRIES. NORSE. H. Hermannsson, *Problem of Wineland* (1936), brief; F. J. Pohl, *Lost Discovery* (1952), careful. PORTUGUESE. H. V. Livermore, *Portugal* (1947), factual; S. E. Morison, *Portuguese Voyages to America* (1940), informative; E. Prestage, *Portuguese Pioneers* (1933). SPANISH. M. Bishop, *Odyssey of De Vaca* (1933), popular; H. E. Bolton, *Spanish Borderlands* (1921), Southwest, *Coronado* (1949), *Rim of Christendom* (1936), Kino; E. G. Bourne, *Spain in America* (1904), good; A. G. Day, *Coronado's Quest* (1940), easy reading; T. Maynard, *De Soto* (1930); S. E. Morison, *Admiral of the Ocean Sea* (2 vols., 1942), final word on Columbus; H. I. Priestley, *Coming of the White Man* (1929), also French, Dutch, Swedes; I. B. Richardson, *Spanish Conquerors* (1919);

R. K. Wyllys, *Pioneer Padre* (1935), popular on Kino. DUTCH. L. Powys, *Henry Hudson* (1927). FRENCH. H. P. Biggar, *Voyages of Jacques Cartier* (1924); M. Bishop, *Champlain* (1948); C. W. Dahlinger, *Marquis Duquesne* (1932); J. Delanglez, *Louis Jolliet* (1948); F. Gaither, *Fatal River* (1931), La Salle; A. C. Laut, *Cadillac* (1931), popular; S. Leacock, *Mariner of St. Malo* (1914), Cartier; W. B. Munro, *Crusaders of New France* (1918), includes ways of life; G. L. Nute, *Caesars of the Wilderness* (1943), Radisson and others; F. Parkman, *La Salle* (2 vols., 1879), *Pioneers of France* (1865); F. B. Steck, *Jolliet-Marquette Expedition* (1927); C. Wittke, *History of Canada* (1941). ENGLISH. E. F. Benson, *Sir Francis Drake* (1927), reads well; D. B. Chidsey, *Sir Walter Raleigh* (1931), *Sir Humphrey Gilbert* (1932); F. T. McCann, *English Discovery of America* (1952), scholarly, to 1585; W. McFee, *Sir Martin Frobisher* (1928), useful; D. B. Quinn, *Sir Humphrey Gilbert* (2 vols., 1940), *Raleigh* (1947), scholarly; H. L. Rowland and G. B. Manhart, *English Commerce and Exploration* (1924), reign of Elizabeth; E. G. R. Taylor (ed.), *Original Writings of the Two Richard Hakluyts* (2 vols., 1935); H. R. Wagner, *Sir Francis Drake's Voyage around the World* (1926); J. A. Williamson, *Voyages of John and Sebastian Cabot* (1937), *Age of Drake* (1938), scholarly.

CHAPTER 2. **COLONIZATION AND IMPERIAL CONFLICT**

GENERAL. C. M. Andrews, *Colonial Folkways* (1921), largely social; G. L. Beer, *Origins of British Colonial System* (1908), 1578 to 1600; W. L. Dorn, *Competition for Empire, 1740–1763* (1940); L. H. Gipson, *British Empire before American Revolution*, 7 vols. to date, (1936–), monumental; A. D. Innis, *Expansion of England under Stuarts* (1932); J. M. Morse, *American Beginnings* (1952), contemporary accounts; A. P. Newton, *European Nations in West Indies* (1933), to 1688; H. L. Osgood, *American Colonies in Seventeenth Century* (3 vols., 1904–1907), largely political; L. J. Ragatz, *Fall of Planter Class in Caribbean* (1928), detailed; J. A. Williamson, *Caribbee Islands* (1926). See also Chap. 1 (General Colonial Histories, and Exploration, French).

SOUTHERN COLONIES. M. P. Andrews, *History of Maryland* (1929), *Virginia* (1937), not easy reading; V. F. Barnes, *Dominion of New England* (1923), Andrus; J. E. Calloway, *Early Settlement of Georgia* (1948); V. E. Chatelain, *Defense of Spanish Florida* (1941), monograph; R. V. Coleman, *First Frontier* (1948), *Liberty and Property* (1951), careful on Virginia settlements; R. S. Cotterill, *Old South* (1936), good to Civil War; E. M. Coulter, *Short History of Georgia* (1947), very good; V. W. Crane, *Southern*

Frontier (1929), 1670 to 1732; W. F. Craven, *Southern Colonies in Seventeenth Century* (1949); C. Eaton, *History of Old South* (1949), excellent; A. A. Ettinger, *James Edward Oglethorpe* (1936); J. G. Fletcher, *John Smith* (1928), readable; A. Henderson, *North Carolina* (5 vols., 1941); W. B. Hesseltine, *South in American History* (1943); C. Johnson, *British West Florida* (1943), monograph; C. L. Mowat, *East Florida as British Province* (1943), monograph; A. B. Saye, *New Viewpoints in Georgia History* (1943), good on settlement; F. B. Simkins, *History of South* (1953); B. Smith, *Captain John Smith* (1953); D. D. Wallace, *South Carolina* (4 vols., 1934–1935); T. J. Wertenbaker, *First Americans* (1927), Virginia, *Old South* (1942), *Patrician and Plebeian in Virginia* (1910), *Planters of Colonial Virginia* (1922), *Torchbearer of the Revolution* (1940), Bacon's rebellion, *Virginia under the Stuarts* (1914); G. E. Williams, *Behold Virginia* (1951) gives the seamier side of the seventeenth century.

NEW ENGLAND. J. T. Adams, *Founding of New England* (1921), critical of Puritans, *Revolutionary New England* (1923); R. H. Akagi, *Town Proprietors of New England Colonies* (1924); C. M. Andrews, *Beginnings of Connecticut* (1934), to 1662, *Fathers of*

New England (1921), very good; E. A. Bailey, *Radicalism in Connecticut* (1920), just before Revolution; V. F. Barnes, *Dominion of New England* (1923), Andros; I. M. Calder, *New Haven Colony* (1934), good monograph; L. C. Hatch (ed.), *Maine* (3 vols., 1919); R. G. Lounsbury, *British Fishery at Newfoundland* (1934), 1634 to 1763; S. E. Morison, *Builders of Bay Colony* (1930), biographical; T. J. Wertenbaker, *Puritan Oligarchy* (1947); G. F. Willison, *Saints and Strangers* (1945), Puritans.

MIDDLE COLONIES. C. A. Barker, *Background of Revolution in Maryland* (1940); W. W. Comfort, *William Penn* (1944); W. F. Dunaway, *History of Pennsylvania* (1948), good; S. G. Fisher, *Making of Pennsylvania* (1932); A. C. Flick (ed.), *History of New York* (10 vols., 1933–1937), very good; G. T. Hunt,

Wars of the Iroquois (1940), scholarly; D. L. Kemmerer, *Path to Freedom* (1940), New Jersey in eighteenth century; S. G. Nissenson, *Patroon's Domain* (1937), detailed; A. Pound and R. E. Day, *Johnson of the Mohawks* (1930), scholarly; C. Ward, *Dutch and Swedes on the Delaware* (1930), seventeenth century; T. J. Wertenbaker, *Founding of American Civilization: Middle Colonies* (1938).

FRENCH. W. B. Munro, *Seigneurs of Old Canada* (1914), simple account; F. Parkman, *Count Frontenac* (1877), *Half-century of Conflict* (2 vols., 1892), *Montcalm and Wolfe* (2 vols., 1884); M. Savelle, *History of Canadian Boundary* (1940), 1749 to 1763; R. G. Thwaites, *France in America* (1905); G. M. Wrong, *Rise and Fall of New France* (2 vols., 1928), scholarly. See also Chap. 1.

CHAPTER 3. EMPIRE CLEAVAGE

GENERAL COLONIAL HISTORIES. See Chap. 2.

PRECEDENTS OF REVOLUTION. J. T. Adams, *Provincial Society* (1927), reads well; R. G. Albion, *Forests and Sea Power* (1926), excellent; C. M. Andrews, *Colonial Background of American Revolution* (1931), *Boston Merchants and Non-importation* (1917); A. H. Basye, *Lords Commissioners of Trade* (1923), monograph; C. L. Becker, *Eve of the Revolution* (1921); R. P. Bieber, *Lords of Trade* (1919), late seventeenth century; W. A. Brown, *Empire or Independence* (1941), efforts at reconciliation; C. Day, *History of Commerce* (1938), good on mercantilism; O. M. Dickerson, *Navigation Acts* (1951); E. B. Greene, *Revolutionary Generation* (1943); L. A. Harper, *English Navigation Laws* (1937), scholarly; E. F. Heckscher, *Mercantilism* (2 vols., 1935), complete; L. W. Labaree, *Royal Government in America* (1930), excellent; J. C. Miller, *Origins of American Revolution* (1943), excellent; H. L. Osgood, *American Colonies in Eighteenth Century* (4 vols., 1924–1925); L. B. Packard, *Commercial Revolution* (1927), clear; H. Robinson, *British Empire* (1936); C. Rossiter, *Seedtime of the Republic* (1953); A. M. Schlesinger, *Colonial Merchants and American Revolution* (1918), 1763 to 1776; C. H. van Tyne, *Causes of War of Independence* (1922), authoritative; G. A. Washburne, *Imperial Control of Justice* (1923). For individual colonies, see Chap. 2.

WEST. C. W. Alvord, *Illinois Country* (1920), *Mississippi Valley in British Politics* (2 vols., 1917);

N. M. Belting, *Kaskaskia* (1948), excellent; J. B. Brebner, *North Atlantic Triangle* (1945); A. L. Burt, *Old Province of Quebec* (1933), scholarly; A. B. Darling, *Our Rising Empire* (1940); L. P. Kellogg, *British Regime in Wisconsin* (1935), *French Regime in Wisconsin* (1925); C. H. Metzger, *Quebec Act* (1936); N. V. Russell, *British Regime in Michigan* (1939), to 1796.

DECLARATION OF INDEPENDENCE. C. L. Becker, *Declaration of Independence* (1922), good; M. M. and H. F. Carlton, *Declaration of Independence* (1926), easy reading; E. Dumbauld, *Declaration of Independence* (1950), explains phrase by phrase.

BIOGRAPHIES. ADAMS, S. R. V. Harlow, *Samuel Adams* (1923); J. C. Miller, *Sam Adams* (1936), very good. ADAMS, J. See Chap. 10. CARROLL. E. H. Smith, *Charles Carroll of Carrollton* (1942), good. FRANKLIN. C. L. Becker, *Benjamin Franklin* (1946); V. W. Crane, *Benjamin Franklin* (1936), source of ideas; B. Fay, *Franklin* (1929); A. H. Smyth (ed.), *Writings of Franklin* (10 vols., 1907); C. C. van Doren, *Benjamin Franklin* (1938); C. C. van Doren and others, *Meet Dr. Franklin* (1943). HANCOCK. H. S. Allan, *John Hancock* (1948). HENRY. J. Axelrad, *Patrick Henry* (1947). JEFFERSON. See Chap. 11. PAINE. M. A. Best, *Thomas Paine* (1927); W. E. Woodward, *Tom Paine* (1945). PENDLETON. D. J. Mays, *Edmund Pendleton* (1952), Virginia Republican.

CHAPTER 4. **THE AMERICAN REVOLUTION**

GENERAL. J. R. Alden, *American Revolution* (1954), largely military; P. Davidson, *Propaganda and American Revolution* (1941); J. F. Jameson, *American Revolution as Social Movement* (1940); J. C. Miller, *Triumph of Freedom* (1948), excellent; C. E. Russell, *Haym Solomon* (1930), finance; G. O. Trevelyan, *American Revolution* (6 vols., 1899–1914), English author; C. H. van Tyne, *War of Independence* (1929); C. Ward, *War of the Revolution* (2 vols., 1952), first rate. See also Brown, Egerton, Greene, Chap. 3.

WAR ON LAND. J. R. Alden, *General Gage* (1948), *General Charles Lee* (1951); T. S. Anderson, *Command of the Howe Brothers* (1936); A. H. Bill, *Valley Forge* (1952), excellent, *Campaign of Princeton* (1948), readable; W. H. Blumenthal, *Women Camp Followers* (1952), trifle dull; T. Bodley, *West in Revolutionary War* (1938); A. Bowman, *Morale of American Army* (1943); T. A. Boyd, *Light-horse Harry Lee* (1931), good; M. Decker, *Benedict Arnold* (1932), reads well; R. M. Dorson (ed.), *American Rebels* (1953), narratives of participants; E. Forbes, *Paul Revere* (1942), interesting; J. W. Fortescue, *British Army*, vols. 8, 9, 10 (1919–1920); W. A. Ganoe, *History of United States Army* (1942); L. Gottschalk, *Lafayette* (3 vols., 1935–1942), American connections; M. Haiman, *Kosciuszko* (1943); C. S. Hall, *Benjamin Tallmadge* (1943), secret service; F. J. Hudleston, *Gentleman Johnny Burgoyne* (1927); J. A. James, *George Rogers Clark* (1928); V. L. Johnson, *American Commissariat* (1941), supplies; L. Montross, *Rag, Tag and Bobtail* (1952), excellent; H. Nickerson, *Turning Point of Revolution* (1928), good on Burgoyne; F. Palmer, *Clark of the Ohio* (1929); J. M. Palmer, *General von Steuben* (1937); S. W. Patterson, *Horatio Gates* (1941); O. L. Spaulding, *United States Army* (1937); W. S. Stryker, *Battle of Monmouth* (1927); C. C. van Doren, *Secret History of American Revolution* (1941), conspiracies, mainly Arnold; W. M. Wallace, *Appeal to Arms* (1951), straightforward; H. E. Wildes, *Anthony Wayne* (1941).

NAVAL. C. S. Alden and A. Westcott, *United States Navy* (1943); W. M. James, *British Navy in Adversity* (1926); G. W. Johnson, *The First Captain* (1947), readable on John Paul Jones; D. W. Knox, *United States Navy* (1948); A. A. Lawrence, *Storm over Savannah* (1951), good on siege; L. Lincoln, *John Paul Jones* (1943); C. H. Metcalf, *United States Marine Corps* (1939), scholarly and readable; F. Pratt, *American Navy* (1938), episodical; H. and M. Sprout, *Rise of Naval Power* (1939), policy, not fleet.

LOYALISTS. A. G. Bradley, *United Empire Loyalists* (1932); L. H. Gipson, *Jared Ingersoll* (1920); J. A. Thompson, *Count Rumford* (1935), easy reading; C. H. van Tyne, *Loyalists in American Revolution* (1902).

CONTINENTAL CONGRESS. R. H. Barry, *Mr. Rutledge* (1942); J. P. Boyd, *Anglo-American Unity* (1941), Galloway plan; E. C. Burnett, *Continental Congress* (1941), scholarly, (ed.) *Letters of Members* (8 vols., 1921–1928); W. C. Ford and G. Hunt (eds.), *Journals of Continental Congress* (34 vols., 1904–1937); C. L. Meigs, *The Violent Men* (1950), not distinguished; L. Montross, *The Reluctant Rebels* (1950), mostly personal; J. B. Sanders, *Executive Departments* (1935), *Presidency* (1936), detailed; D. D. Wallace, *Henry Laurens* (1915); E. Young, *Forgotten Patriot* (1950), Robert Morris.

FOREIGN. GENERAL DIPLOMATIC HISTORIES. T. A. Bailey, *Diplomatic History* (1950), pungent; S. F. Bemis, *Diplomatic History* (1950), factual; J. H. Latané and D. W. Wainhouse, *American Foreign Policy* (1940); D. Perkins, *American Foreign Policy* (1948). SPECIFIC. S. F. Bemis, *Diplomacy of American Revolution* (1935); S. Bonsal, *When the French Were Here* (1945); E. S. Corwin, *French Policy and American Alliance* (1916), definitive; G. Lemaître, *Beaumarchais* (1949); G. M. Wrong, *Canada and American Revolution* (1935), English view.

STATES. W. C. Abbott, *New York in Revolution* (1929); P. A. Crowl, *Maryland during and after Revolution* (1943), monograph; H. J. Eckenrode, *Revolution in Virginia* (1916); F. H. Hart, *Valley of Virginia* (1942); M. B. Jones, *Vermont in the Making* (1939), 1750 to 1777; L. Lundin, *Cockpit of Revolution* (1940), New Jersey; M. B. Macmillan, *War Governors of Revolution* (1943); E. Newton, *Vermont Story* (1949); J. Pell, *Ethan Allen* (1929), vivid; R. J. Purcell, *Connecticut in Transition* (1918), to 1818; C. M. Thompson, *Independent Vermont* (1942), detailed; R. F. Upton, *Revolutionary New Hampshire* (1936); F. F. van de Water, *Reluctant Republic* (1941), 1724 to 1791, Vermont; S. C. Williams, *Tennessee during Revolutionary War* (1944); C. Williamson, *Vermont in Quandary* (1949).

BIOGRAPHIES. FRANKLIN AND OTHERS. See Chap. 3. JEFFERSON. See Chap. 11. WASHINGTON AND JOHN ADAMS. See Chap. 10.

CHAPTER 5. **TOWARD A NATIONAL GOVERNMENT**

STATE GOVERNMENTS. A. Nevins, *American States during and after Revolution* (1924); F. J. Turner, *Significance of Sections* (1932). See also individual states, Chaps. 2, 4.

CONTINENTAL CONGRESS. See Chap. 4. SPANISH. See Chap. 9. INDIANS. See Chap. 9. VERMONT. See Chap. 4.

CONFEDERATION. D. Aaron (ed.), *America in Crisis* (1952), chapter on Shays' Rebellion; R. L. Brunhouse, *Counter-revolution in Pennsylvania* (1942), conservative reaction; T. C. Cochran, *New York in Confederation* (1932), economic; L. B. Dunbar, *"Monarchical" Tendencies* (1922); M. Farrand, *Fathers of the Constitution* (1921); J. Fiske, *Critical Period* (1898), outdated, but Fiske gave name to period; E. B. Greene,

Revolutionary Generation (1943); M. Jensen, *The New Nation* (1950), important, *Articles of Confederation* (1940), largely nonpolitical; F. J. Klingberg, *Morning of America* (1941); L. Montross, *Reluctant Rebels* (1950); F. R. Mullaly, *Massachusetts Insurrection* (1947), monograph; E. W. Spaulding, *New York in Critical Period* (1932); D. Wecter, *When Johnny Comes Marching Home* (1944).

LAND DISPOSAL. T. P. Abernethy, *Western Lands and the Revolution* (1937); B. H. Hubbard, *Public Land Policies* (1924); R. M. Robbins, *Our Landed Heritage* (1942), best; A. M. Sakolski, *Great American Land Bubble* (1932), speculation; P. J. Treat, *National Land System* (1910), 1785 to 1820.

CHAPTER 6. **THE CONSTITUTION**

GENERAL. FORMATION. C. A. Beard, *Economic Interpretation of the Constitution* (1913), famous study, *Supreme Court and Constitution* (1912), mostly convention; M. Farrand, *Framing of the Constitution* (1913), *Fathers of Constitution* (1921); E. B. Greene, *Revolutionary Generation* (1943); H. Lyon, *The Constitution* (1936), popular; L. Montross, see Chap. 5; A. T. Prescott, *Drafting the Constitution* (1941), from Madison notes; R. L. Schuyler, *Constitution* (1923), formation; C. van Doren, *Great Rehearsal* (1948), scholarly.

RATIFICATION. C. A. Beard, *Economic Origins of Jeffersonian Democracy* (1915); E. M. Earle (ed.), *The Federalist* (1937); H. Hill, *George Mason* (1938), opponent; C. E. Miner, *Ratification by New York* (1921); E. W. Spaulding, *George Clinton* (1938), opponent; L. I. Trenholme, *Ratification in North Carolina* (1932).

JAY. See Chap. 10. MADISON. See Chap. 14. MARSHALL. See Chap. 11.

CONSTITUTIONAL HISTORIES. W. E. Binkley, *Powers of President* (1937); E. S. Corwin, *Doctrine of Judicial Review* (1914), essays, *The President* (1940); C. G. Haines, *Role of Supreme Court* (1944), 1789 to 1835, anti-Federalist; H. C. Hockett, *Constitutional History* (2 vols., 1939), factual; R. H. Jackson, *Struggle for Judicial Supremacy* (1941); A. H. Kelly and W. A. Harbison, *American Constitution* (1948); A. C. McLaughlin, *Constitutional History* (1935); G. F. Milton, *Presidential Powers* (1944); C. B. Swisher, *American Constitutional Development* (1943), good; C. Warren, *Supreme Court* (3 vols., 1937), standard authority.

CHAPTER 7. **CONTINUING ECONOMIC COLONIALISM**

IMMIGRATION. GENERAL. L. Adamic, *Nation of Nations* (1945), arranged by groups; M. R. Davie, *World Immigration* (1936), good perspective; O. Handlin, *The Uprooted* (1951), from standpoint of immigrant; M. L. Hansen, *Atlantic Migration* (1940), good; S. P. Orth, *Our Foreigners* (1920); G. M. Stephenson, *American Immigration* (1926), from 1820; C. Wittke, *We Who Built America* (1939), by groups. SPECIFIC

GROUPS. D. Cunz, *Maryland Germans* (1948); A. B. Faust, *German Element* (2 vols., 1909), standard; P. S. Foner, *Jews in American History* (1945), to 1865; H. J. Ford, *Scotch-Irish in America* (1915), good; M. Glasgow, *Scotch-Irish* (1936); M. L. Hansen and J. B. Brebner, *Mingling of Canadian and American Peoples* (1940), scholarly; A. H. Hirsch, *Huguenots of Colonial South Carolina* (1928); J. R. Marcus,

Early American Jewry (1951), excellent—to 1794; A. Mulder, *Americans from Holland* (1947); M. J. O'Brien, *Hidden Phase of American History* (1919), colonial Irish; F. F. Shrader, *Germans in Making of America* (1924), to about 1860; R. Wood (ed.), *Pennsylvania Germans* (1942), good.

ECONOMIC HISTORIES. J. A. Barnes, *Wealth of American People* (1949), social view; E. L. Bogart and D. L. Kemmerer, *Economic History* (1947); J. R. Craf, *Economic Development* (1952); J. Dorfman, *Economic Mind* (3 vols., 1946–1949), economic thought; H. U. Faulkner, *American Economic History* (1949); E. C. Kirkland, *History of American Economic Life* (1951), excellent; B. and L. P. Mitchell, *American Economic History* (1947); F. A. Shannon, *America's Economic Growth* (1951), incisive; G. Soule, *Economic Forces* (1952); H. F. Williamson (ed.), *Growth of American Economy* (1951), detailed; C. W. Wright, *Economic History* (1949).

AGRICULTURE. P. W. Bidwell and J. A. Falconer, *Agriculture in Northern United States* (1925), detailed; E. L. Bogart, *Economic History of Agriculture* (1923); J. E. Brooks, *The Mighty Leaf* (1952), tobacco; W. H. Clark, *Farms and Farmers* (1945), simple and readable; A. O. Craven, *Soil Exhaustion in Virginia and Maryland* (1926); E. J. Dies, *Titans of the Soil* (1949), farming leaders; L. C. Gray, *Agriculture in Southern United States* (2 vols., 1933), detailed; A. B. Hulbert, *Soil* (1930), influence on history; J. C. Robert, *Story of Tobacco* (1949); J. Schafer, *Social History of Agriculture* (1936), good; J. C. Sitterman, *Sugar Country* (1953).

MANUFACTURING. F. J. Allen, *Shoe Industry* (1916); G. and D. Bathe, *Oliver Evans* (1935), inventor; R. Burlingame, *March of the Iron Men* (1938), inventions, including agriculture; V. S. Clark, *History of Manufactures* (3 vols., 1929), uneven; A. H. Cole, *Wool Manufacture* (2 vols., 1926); F. E. Coyne, *Cooperage Industry* (1940); J. S. Davis, *American Corporations* (2 vols., 1917), New Jersey plans of Hamilton (see also lives of Hamilton in Chap. 10); W. Kaempffert, *History of American Inventions* (2 vols., 1924); J. Mirsky and A. Nevins, *World of Eli Whitney* (1952); J. Storck and W. D. Teague, *Flour for Man's Bread* (1952), milling; H. Thompson, *Age of Invention* (1921); R. M. Tryon, *Household Manu-*

factures (1917); standard—to 1860; A. D. Turnbull, *John Stevens* (1928), inventor.

LABOR. GENERAL. F. T. Carlton, *Organized Labor in American History* (1920); M. R. Clark and S. F. Simon, *Labor Movement* (1938), simple; J. R. Commons and others, *History of Labour* (4 vols., 1918–1935), *Documentary History* (10 vols., 1910–1917), vast information; F. R. Dulles, *Labor in American History* (1949), popular; P. S. Foner, *Labor Movement* (1947), Marxist; H. Harris, *American Labor* (1939), fine on unions. SPECIAL. C. Bridenbaugh, *Colonial Craftsman* (1950); M. W. Jernegan, *Laboring Classes in Colonial America* (1931); R. B. Morris, *Government and Labor in Early America* (1946), exhaustive; A. E. Smith, *Colonists in Bondage* (1947), white servitude and convicts. NEGRO. H. Aptheker, *To Be Free* (1948); B. G. Brawley, *Social History of American Negro* (1921); J. H. Franklin, *From Slavery to Freedom* (1947), excellent; R. Ottley, *Black Odyssey* (1948), popularized Negro history; J. S. Redding, *They Came in Chains* (1950), history; C. G. Woodson, *Negro in Our History* (1941).

TRANSPORTATION AND TRADE. L. D. Baldwin, *Keelboat Age on Western Waters* (1941), first rate; W. T. Baxter, *House of Hancock* (1945), to 1775; T. A. Boyd, *Poor John Fitch* (1935), good on steamboat; S. Dunbar, *History of Travel* (4 vols., 1915); R. A. East, *Business Enterprise in Revolutionary Era* (1938), scholarly; J. T. Flexner, *Steamboats Come True* (1944), early experiments; S. E. Foreman, *Rise of American Commerce* (1927); J. H. Frederick, *Development of Commerce* (1932); V. D. Harrington, *New York Merchant* (1935), on eve of Revolution; E. R. Johnson and others, *Domestic and Foreign Commerce* (1915), detailed; B. H. Meyer and others, *History of Transportation* (1948), detailed; S. E. Morison, *Maritime History of Massachusetts* (1921); W. B. Parsons, *Robert Fulton* (1922); L. Sellers, *Charleston Business on Eve of Revolution* (1934); F. B. Toller, *Meeting House and Counting House* (1948), Quaker merchants; E. M. Turner, *James Rumsey* (1930), steamboat; R. Wright, *Hawkers and Walkers* (1927), peddlers. For China trade, see Chap. 17.

FINANCE. D. R. Dewey, *Financial History* (1936); C. P. Nettles, *Money Supply of American Colonies* (1934); H. White, *Money and Banking* (1935).

CHAPTER 8. PRODUCING AN AMERICAN CULTURE

GENERAL. M. E. Curti, *Growth of American Thought* (1951), excellent, *Roots of American Loyalty* (1946), first rate; M. Kraus, *American Culture on Eve of Revolution* (1928), monograph, *The Atlantic Civilization* (1949), European-American contacts; J. A. Krout and

D. R. Fox, *Completion of Independence* (1944), general history; P. Miller, *New England Mind* (1953); S. E. Morison, *Puritan Pronaos* (1936), seventeenth-century mind; R. B. Perry, *Puritanism and Democracy* (1944), interpretation; M. Savelle, *Seeds of Liberty*

(1948), development of American loyalty; D. Wecter, *Saga of American Society* (1937), interesting; H. Wish, *Society and Thought in Early America* (1950), social history.

FAMILY AND WOMEN. M. S. Benson, *Women in Eighteenth Century* (1935), scholarly; A. W. Calhoun, *History of American Family* (3 vols., 1917–1919); E. A. Dexter, *Colonial Women of Affairs* (1924); S. Ditzion, *Marriage, Morals and Sex* (1953); G. F. Dow, *Everyday Life* (1935), Massachusetts; E. M. Earle's various books on colonial life are old but good; W. Goodsell, *History of the Family* (1915); W. C. Langdon, *Everyday Things* (1937), popular; G. Markun, *Mrs. Grundy* (1930), morals; E. McClellan, *History of American Costume* (1937), many pictures; E. S. Morgan, *Puritan Family* (1944), *Virginians at Home* (1952), colonial; A. Train, Jr., *Story of Everyday Things* (1941).

AMUSEMENTS. F. R. Dulles, *America Learns to Play* (1940), interesting; J. Holliman, *American Sports* (1931); J. A. Krout, *Annals of American Sport* (1929), many pictures; H. Manchester, *Four Centuries of Sport* (1931).

CITIES. F. P. Bowes, *Early Charleston* (1942); C. Bridenbaugh, *Cities in the Wilderness* (1938), excellent; C. and J. Bridenbaugh, *Rebels and Gentlemen* (1942), Philadelphia; H. C. Brown, *Story of Old New York* (1934); H. D. Eberlein and C. V. D. Hubbard, *Portrait of a Colonial City* (1939), Philadelphia; F. Monaghan and M. Lowenthal, *This Was New York* (1943), in 1789; S. I. Pomerantz, *New York, 1783–1803* (1938); T. J. Wertenbaker, *Golden Age of Colonial Culture* (1942), largely on cities.

EDUCATION. H. K. Beale, *Freedom of Teaching* (1941), historical; W. C. Bronson, *Brown University* (1914); E. P. Cheney, *University of Pennsylvania* (1940); L. M. Crosbie, *Phillips Exeter* (1923); E. P. Cubberly, *Public Education* (1919), long standard; C. E. Cunningham, *Timothy Dwight* (1942), Yale; M. E. Curti, *Social Ideals of American Educators* (1935), selected men; W. H. S. Demarest, *Rutgers* (1924); E. W. Knight, *Education in United States* (1941), text; P. Monroe, *Public School System* (1940), history; S. E. Morison, *Founding of Harvard* (1935), *Three Centuries of Harvard* (1936); J. K. Morse, *Jedidiah Morse* (1939); E. Oviatt, *Beginnings of Yale* (1916); L. B. Richardson, *Dartmouth* (2 vols., 1932); C. F. Thwing, *Higher Education* (1906), long standard; H. R. Warfel, *Noah Webster* (1936); T. J. Wertenbaker, *Princeton* (1946); T. Woody, *Women's Education* (2 vols., 1929), scholarly.

LITERATURE. C. Angoff, *Literary History* (2 vols., 1931), to 1815; R. Blankenship, *American Literature* (1931), clear; P. H. Boynton, *Literature and American Life* (1936); H. P. Brown, *Sentimental Novel* (1940), scholarly—to 1860; V. L. Calverton, *Liberation of American Literature* (1932), good on split from Eng-

land; D. L. Clark, *Charles Brockden Brown* (1952); J. D. Hart, *Popular Book* (1950), best sellers; I. H. Herron, *Small Town in American Literature* (1939); L. Howard, *Connecticut Wits* (1943), scholarly; H. M. Jones, *Ideas in America* (1944), interpretative essays; E. E. Leisy, *Historical Novel* (1950); F. L. Mott, *Golden Multitudes* (1947), best sellers; V. L. Parrington, *Main Currents in American Thought* (3 vols., 1927–1930), well written; F. L. Pattee, *First Century of American Literature* (1935), good, to 1870; A. H. Quinn (ed.), *Literature of American People* (1951), exhaustive; R. E. Spiller and others, *Literary History* (1953); W. F. Taylor, *History of American Letters* (1936); E. Wagenknecht, *Cavalcade of American Novel* (1952), detailed.

MAGAZINES. F. L. Mott, *American Magazines* (3 vols., 1930–1938); F. L. Pattee, *American Short Story* (1923); L. N. Richardson, *Early American Magazines* (1931), to 1789; A. de V. Tassin, *Magazine in America* (1916), readable; J. P. Wood, *Magazines in United States* (1949).

NEWSPAPERS. W. G. Bleyer, *History of American Journalism* (1927); M. W. Hamilton, *Country Printer* (1936), New York State; R. W. Jones, *Journalism* (1947), compendious; S. Kobre, *Colonial Newspaper* (1944); A. M. Lee, *Daily Newspaper* (1937), heavy; F. L. Mott, *American Journalism* (1941), fine; A. Nevins, *Evening Post* (1922).

THEATER. O. S. Coad, *William Dunlap* (1917); G. Hughes, *American Theater* (1951); M. G. Mayorga, *American Drama* (1932), monographic; L. Morris, *Curtain Time* (1953); M. J. Moses, *American Dramatist* (1925); A. H. Quinn, *American Drama* (1923), to 1860.

ART. V. Barker, *American Painting* (1950); W. Born, *Landscape Painting* (1948); P. Boswell, Jr., *American Painting* (1939), excellent; C. Bridenbaugh, *Peter Harrison* (1949), early architect; H. J. Cahill and A. H. Barr, Jr., *Art in America* (1935), largely architecture; J. T. Flexner, *American Painting* (1947), colonial, *America's Old Masters* (1939); H. C. Forman, *Architecture of Old South* (1948), technical; S. Isham and R. Cortissoz, *American Painting* (1936), well written; O. W. Larkin, *Art and Life* (1949), best on all arts; H. Major, *Domestic Architecture* (1926); J. H. Morgan, *Gilbert Stuart* (1939); L. Mumford, *Sticks and Stones* (1924), architecture and society; E. Neuhaus, *American Art* (1931); R. Pratt, *Early American Homes* (1949), to 1812; E. P. Richardson, *Way of Western Art* (1939), relations to Europe; C. C. Sellers, *Charles Willson Peale* (2 vols., 1947), detailed; L. Taft, *American Sculpture* (1925); T. E. Tallmadge, *Architecture* (1927); T. T. Waterman, *Dwellings of Colonial America* (1950), good pictures; W. T. Whitley, *Gilbert Stuart* (1932).

MUSIC. L. C. Elston, *American Music* (1925); J. T.

Howard, *Our American Music* (1931), best; G. Vernon, *Yankee Doodle Doo* (1927), popular music to 1860.

SCIENCE. D. Aaron (ed.), *America in Crisis* (1952), chapter on yellow fever; E. S. Dana and others, *Century of Science* (1918), heavy; J. C. Ford, *David Rittenhouse* (1946), astronomer; M. B. Gordon, *Aesculapius Comes to Colonies* (1949), very good; C. R. Hall, *Samuel Latham Mitchell* (1934); U. P. Hedrick, *Horticulture* (1950), to 1860; T. Hornberger, *Scientific Thought in American Colleges* (1945), to 1800; B. Jaffe, *Men of Science* (1944); G. P. Merrill, *American Geology* (1924), ponderous; F. R. Packard, *History of Medicine* (2 vols., 1931), annalistic; J. H. Powell, *Bring Out Your Dead* (1949), yellow fever; A. D. Rodgers III, *American Botany* (1944); H. B. Shafer, *American Medical Profession* (1936), monograph, to 1850; R. H. Shryock, *Development of Modern Medicine* (1947), excellent; H. E. Sigerist, *American Medicine* (1934), in social setting; D. J. Struik, *Yankee Science* (1948), New England.

RELIGION. GENERAL. A. D. Belden, *George Whitefield* (1930); V. Fern, *American Church* (1952), handbook of Protestant sects; W. M. Gewehr, *Great Awakening in Virginia* (1930); E. B. Greene, *Religion and the State* (1941), mostly period of Revolution; E. F. Humphrey, *Nationalism and Religion* (1924), exhaustive, 1774 to 1789; G. A. Koch, *Republican Religion* (1933), cult of reason; G. C. Loud, *Evangelized America* (1928), revivals; H. M. Morais, *Deism* (1934), eighteenth century; H. K. Rowe, *History of Religions* (1924), good; A. P. Stokes, *Church and State* (3 vols., 1950), fine scholarship; W. W. Sweet, *American Churches* (1948), essays, *Religion in American Culture* (1952), *Religion in Colonial America* (1942), *Revivalism* (1944), *Story of Religions* (1930). DENOMINATIONS. H. Asbury, *Bishop Asbury* (1927), Methodist; G. G. Atkins and F. L. Fagley, *American Congregationalism* (1942); R. P. and L. Boas, *Cotton Mather* (1928); S. H. Brockunier, *Roger Williams* (1940), very good; E. C. Chorley, *American Episcopal Church* (1946); E. Curtis, *Anne Hutchinson* (1930); R. M. Jones, *Later Periods of Quakerism* (2 vols., 1921), world story; H. E. Luccock, *Methodism* (1926), popular; W. W. Manross, *American Episcopal Church* (1935); T. Maynard, *American Catholicism* (1941); P. Miller, *Jonathan Edwards* (1949), *Orthodoxy in Massachusetts* (1933), 1630 to 1650; K. B. Murdock, *Increase Mather* (1925); A. H. Newman, *Baptist Churches* (1915); T. Roemer, *Catholic Church* (1950); C. H. Smith, *Story of Mennonites* (1941), good; M. L. Starkey, *Devil in Massachusetts* (1950), Salem witch trials; W. W. Sweet, *Methodism* (1933); R. E. Thompson, *Presbyterian Churches* (1907); L. J. Trinterud, *Colonial Presbyterianism* (1949).

REFORM MOVEMENTS. A. Deutsch, *Mentally Ill* (1946); O. W. Elsbree, *Rise of Missionary Spirit* (1928), 1790 to 1815; C. B. Goodykoontz, *Home Missions* (1939); O. F. Lewis, *Development of American Prisons* (1922), 1776 to 1845; B. McKelvey, *American Prisons* (1936); E. W. Rice, *Sunday School Movement* (1917); G. M. Stephenson, *Puritan Heritage* (1952). For abolition, see Chap. 20.

CHAPTER 9. BEYOND THE APPALACHIANS

GENERAL. R. A. Billington, *Westward Expansion* (1949), includes colonial; D. E. Clark, *West in American History* (1937); L. R. Hafen and C. C. Rister, *Western America* (1941), factual; W. N. Nash, *Virgin Land* (1950), interpretative; R. E. Riegel, *America Moves West* (1947), reads well; R. L. Rusk, *Literature of Middle Western Frontier* (2 vols., 1925); H. R. Shurtleff, *Log Cabin Myth* (1939); F. J. Turner, *Frontier in American History* (1920), includes famous essay, *Early Writings* (1938); W. P. Webb, *The Great Frontier* (1952), expands Turner thesis.

LAND DISPOSAL. K. P. Bailey, *Ohio Company* (1939), 1748 to 1792; J. S. Davis, *American Corporations* (2 vols., 1917), Duer and Scioto; P. D. Evans, *Holland Land Company* (1926), Buffalo area; W. G. Lester, *Transylvania Colony* (1935); G. E. Lewis, *Indiana Company* (1941), 1763 to 1798; L. Shaw, *Early Land Companies* (1939). See also Chap. 5.

SOUTHWEST. T. P. Abernethy, *Frontier to Plantation in Tennessee* (1932), to 1860; D. T. Clark, *History of Kentucky* (1937); C. C. Cleveland, *Great Revival in West* (1916); F. G. Davenport, *Ante-bellum Kentucky* (1943); D. Davidson, *The Tennessee* (2 vols., 1946); E. Dick, *Dixie Frontier* (1948), readable; C. S. Driver, *George Sevier* (1932); S. J. Folmsbee, *Sectionalism in Tennessee* (1939), to 1845; A. Henderson, *Conquest of Old Southwest* (1920), to 1790; C. L. Skinner, *Pioneers of Old Southwest* (1921), to 1860; S. E. White, *Daniel Boone* (1922), simple; S. C. Williams, *Lost State of Franklin* (1924), detailed.

NORTHWEST. B. W. Bond, Jr., *Civilization of Old Northwest* (1934), 1788 to 1812, stresses political; S. J. and E. H. Buck, *Civilization in Western Pennsylvania* (1939); R. C. Downes, *Frontier Ohio* (1935), scholarly, 1788 to 1803; W. Havighurst, *Land of Promise* (1946), all phases to 1850; A. L.

Kohlmeier, *Old Northwest* (1938), mostly political; J. M. Miller, *Genesis of Western Culture* (1938), upper Ohio valley, 1800 to 1825; E. H. Roseboom and F. P. Weisenburger, *History of Ohio* (1934), very good; L. D. Stilwell, *Migration from Vermont* (1937), excellent; F. E. Wilson, *Arthur St. Clair* (1944); C. Wittke (ed.), *History of Ohio* (6 vols., 1941–1944), excellent; J. E. Wright and D. S. Corbett, *Pioneer Life in Western Pennsylvania* (1940).

SPANISH. T. P. Abernethy, *Burr Conspiracy* (1954); H. Alexander, *Aaron Burr* (1937); C. M. Burson, *Don Esteban Miro* (1942); J. W. Caughey, *Bernardo de Galvez* (1934), very good; T. R. Hay and M. R. Werner, *James Wilkinson* (1941), reads well; J. R. Jacobs, *Tarnished Warrior* (1938), Wilkinson; G. W. McGinty, *History of Louisiana* (1949); N. Schachner, *Aaron Burr* (1937), defense; A. P. Whitaker, *Mississippi Question* (1934), 1795 to 1803, scholarly, *Spanish American Frontier* (1927), 1783 to 1795; J.

Wilkinson, *Wilkinson* (1935), defense. For Louisiana Purchase, see Chap. 13; for Jay and Pinckney treaties, Chap. 10.

INDIANS. J. W. Caughey, *McGillivray of the Creeks* (1938); R. C. Downes, *Council Fires on Upper Ohio* (1940), to 1795; H. A. Innis, *Fur Trade in Canada* (1930), scholarly; W. H. Mohr, *Federal Indian Relations* (1933), monograph, 1774 to 1788; J. M. Oskison, *Tecumseh* (1938); C. L. Skinner, *Beaver, Kings and Cabins* (1933), good on fur trade; W. E. Stevens, *Northwest Fur Trade* (1928), excellent monograph, 1767 to 1800. For general descriptions, see Chap. 1 (America of Red Man). HARRISON. See Chap. 24. JACKSON. See Chap. 23. WAYNE. See Chap. 4.

TRANSPORTATION. A. B. Hulbert, *Waterways of Western Expansion* (1903), *Braddock's Road* (1903); R. L. Kincaid, *Wilderness Road* (1947). See also Baldwin, Dunbar, Flexner, Hulbert, Meyer, Chap. 7.

CHAPTER 10. THE FEDERALIST SHIP OF STATE

GENERAL POLITICAL. H. Agar, *Price of Union* (1950), the presidency; W. E. Binkley, *American Political Parties* (1943), interpretative; C. A. M. Ewing, *Presidential Elections* (1940), statistical from 1860; B. Furman, *White House Profiles* (1951); R. G. Gettell, *American Political Thought* (1928), really politics; G. H. Haynes, *Senate of United States* (2 vols., 1938), detailed; R. Hofstadter, *American Political Tradition* (1948), biographical; S. Lorant, *The Presidency* (1951), pictures; W. O. Lynch, *Fifty Years of Party Warfare* (1931), 1789 to 1837; C. E. Merriam, *History of Political Theories* (1920), good; H. D. Milhollen, *Presidents on Parade* (1948), pictures; E. E. Robinson, *Evolution of Political Parties* (1924); E. Stanwood, *History of Presidency* (1928), elections; M. O. Whitton, *Our First Ladies* (1948), to 1865.

FEDERALISTS. J. T. Adams, *New England in Republic* (1926); L. D. Baldwin, *Whiskey Rebels* (1939); J. S. Bassett, *Federalist System* (1906); H. J. Ford, *Washington and His Colleagues* (1918); J. Hart, *Presidency in Action, 1789* (1948), very detailed; J. R. Jacobs, *Beginnings of United States Army* (1947), 1783 to 1812; F. J. Klingberg, *Morning of America* (1941), good; E. P. Link, *Democratic-Republican Societies* (1942), pushing democracy; E. S. Maclay (ed.), *Journal of William Maclay* (1928), Senator; J. C. Miller, *Crisis in Freedom*

(1951), Alien and Sedition Acts; B. M. Rich, *Presidents and Civil Disorder* (1941), includes whisky rebellion; N. Schachner, *Founding Fathers* (1954); L. D. White, *The Federalists* (1948), administrative history. For Jay and Pinckney treaties, see Chap. 12.

BIOGRAPHIES. ADAMS. C. F. Adams (ed.), *Works of John Adams* (10 vols., 1850–1856); J. T. Adams, *Adams Family* (1930); C. D. Bowen, *John Adams* (1950), slightly fictionalized; G. Chinard, *Honest John Adams* (1933); J. Whitney, *Abigail Adams* (1947). GALLATIN. H. Adams, *Albert Gallatin* (1943). HAMILTON. C. Bowers, *Jefferson and Hamilton* (1925), favors Jefferson; D. Loth, *Alexander Hamilton* (1939); N. Schachner, *Alexander Hamilton* (1946). JAY. F. Monaghan, *John Jay* (1935). JEFFERSON. See Chap. 11. MADISON. See Chap. 14. MONROE. See Chap. 22. WASHINGTON. F. R. Bellamy, *Private Life of Washington* (1951), good; B. Fay, *George Washington* (1931); J. C. Fitzpatrick, *George Washington* (1933); D. S. Freeman, *George Washington* (6 vols., 1948–1954), excellent; R. Hughes, *George Washington* (3 vols., 1926–1930), emphasizes human qualities; C. P. Nettles, *George Washington* (1951); L. M. Sears, *George Washington* (1932); N. W. Stephenson and W. H. Dunn, *George Washington* (2 vols., 1940); H. Swiggett, *The Great Man* (1953).

CHAPTER 11. **THE REVOLUTION OF 1800**

DOMESTIC EVENTS. C. A. Beard, *Economic Origins of Jeffersonian Democracy* (1915); C. Bowers, *Jefferson in Power* (1936), defense; C. R. Brown, "*Essex Junto*" (1915), monograph; E. Channing, *Jeffersonian System* (1906); A. Johnson, *Jefferson and His Colleagues* (1921); L. White, *The Jeffersonians* (1951), administrative history; C. M. Wiltse, *Jeffersonian Tradition* (1935). See also Chap. 10 (General Political).

BIOGRAPHIES. ADAMS. See Chap. 10. HAMILTON. See Chap. 10. JEFFERSON. D. J. Boorstin, *Lost World of Thomas Jefferson* (1948), his philosophy; C. G. Bowers, *The Young Jefferson* (1945), entertaining; J. P. Boyd (ed.), *Thomas Jefferson Papers* (7 vols., 1950–1953), these and later volumes will replace old collection of P. L. Ford; G. Chinard, *Thomas Jefferson* (1929); M. Kimball, *Jefferson* (3 vols., 1943–1950), carry story to 1789; A. Koch, *Philosophy of Jefferson* (1943), *Jefferson and Madison* (1950); D. Malone, *Jefferson and His Times* (2 vols., 1948–1951), other volumes in preparation; B. Mayo (ed.), *Jefferson Himself* (1942), life in own words; S. K. Padover, *Jefferson* (1942), best one-volume life; C. P. Patterson, *Constitutional Principles* (1953); N. Schachner, *Thomas Jefferson* (2 vols., 1951). MARSHALL. A. J. Beveridge, *Life of John Marshall* (4 vols., 1916–1919); E. S. Corwin, *John Marshall* (1919); D. Loth, *John Marshall* (1949); B. W. Palmer, *Marshall and Taney* (1939). RANDOLPH. H. J. Eckenrode, *The Randolphs* (1946); R. Kirk, *Randolph of Roanoke* (1951).

CHAPTER 12. **FEDERALIST FOREIGN POLICY**

GENERAL. S. F. Bemis (ed.), *American Secretaries of State* (10 vols., 1927–1929); A. B. Darling, *Our Rising Empire* (1940); W. S. Holt, *Treaties Defeated by Senate* (1933); G. H. Stuart, *Department of State* (1949). See also Chaps. 4, 10.

SPECIFIC. G. W. Allen, *Naval War with France* (1909); S. F. Bemis, *Jay's Treaty* (1923), *Pinckney's Treaty* (1926); A. L. Burt, *United States, Great Britain and British North America* (1940), 1783 to 1812; A. C. Clauder, *American Commerce* (1932), effects of French troubles; B. Fay, *Revolutionary Spirit* (1927), attitude toward France; C. S. Hyneman, *First American Neutrality* (1934); E. W. McInnis, *Unguarded Frontier* (1942), Canada; W. R. Manning, *Nootka Sound Controversy* (1904); R. B. Mowat, *Diplomatic Relations of Great Britain and United States* (1925). SPANISH. See Chap. 9. WASHINGTON. See Chap. 10. ADAMS. See Chap. 10.

CHAPTER 13. **JEFFERSON'S FOREIGN POLICY**

GENERAL AND EUROPEAN. E. F. Heckscher, *Continental System* (1922); W. W. Jennings, *American Embargo* (1921); F. E. Melvin, *Napoleon's Navigation System* (1919); L. M. Sears, *Jefferson and the Embargo* (1927). See also Chap. 4 (Foreign, General Diplomatic Histories); Bowers, Channing, Johnson, Chap. 11; Burt, Darling, Chap. 12. For Adams, see Chap. 10; for Jefferson, Chap. 11; for Madison, Chap. 14; for Monroe, Chap. 22.

NORTH AFRICA. C. S. Alden, *Lawrence Kearny* (1936); G. W. Allen, *Navy and Barbary Corsairs* (1905); R. W. Irwin, *Diplomatic Relations between United States and Barbary Pirates* (1931); C. L. Lewis, *Romantic Decatur* (1937); L. B. Wright and J. H. Macleod, *First Americans in North Africa* (1945).

LOUISIANA PURCHASE. W. B. Hatcher, *Edward Livingston* (1940); E. W. Lyon, *Louisiana in French Diplomacy* (1934); J. A. Robertson, *Louisiana under Spain, France and the United States* (2 vols., 1911).

LEWIS AND CLARK. J. Bakeless, *Lewis and Clark* (1947); B. de Voto (ed.), *Journals* (1953); E. W. Gilbert, *Exploration of Western America* (1933), 1800 to 1850; E. Hueston, *Star of the West* (1935), journalistic; J. Mirsky, *Westward Crossings* (1946), only fair; A. P. Nasatir, *Before Lewis and Clark* (1952), upper Missouri; M. S. Wade, *Mackenzie of Canada* (1927), preceded Lewis and Clark. See also general Western histories, Chap. 9; Bakeless, Brebner, De Voto, Chap. 1.

WEST FLORIDA. I. J. Cox, *West Florida Controversy* (1918), C. N. Howard, *British Development of West Florida* (1947), 1763–1769.

CHAPTER 14. "MR. MADISON'S WAR"

GENERAL. J. W. Pratt, *Expansionists of 1812* (1925); see general accounts, Chap. 13.

BIOGRAPHIES. CALHOUN. M. L. Coit, *John C. Calhoun* (1950), excellent; A. Styron, *Cast-iron Man* (1935); C. M. Wiltse, *John C. Calhoun* (1944). CLAY. B. Mayo, *Henry Clay* (1937); G. G. van Deusen, *Henry Clay* (1937). MADISON. I. Brant, *James Madison* (4 vols., 1941–1953); E. M. Burns, *James Madison* (1938); S. K. Padover, *The Complete Madison* (1953); A. E. Smith, *James Madison* (1937).

WAR OF 1812. H. Adams, *War of 1812* (1944), pertinent parts of his seven-volume work; R. G. Albion and J. B. Pope, *Sea Lanes in Wartime* (1942); F. F.

Beirne, *War of 1812* (1949), reads well; C. J. Dutton, *Oliver Hazard Perry* (1935), not good; H. Hatcher, *Lake Erie* (1945); H. Keenleyside, *Canada and the United States* (1952); E. McInnis, *Canada* (1947); E. S. Maclay, *American Privateers* (1924); S. E. Morison, *Harrison Gray Otis* (2 vols., 1913), Hartford convention; R. D. Paine, *Fight for a Free Sea* (1920); A. Pound, *Lake Ontario* (1945); F. Pratt, *Preble's Boys* (1950), naval war; F. A. Updyke, *Diplomacy of War of 1812* (1915); C. Wittke, *Canada* (1941); J. F. Zimmerman, *Impressment of American Seamen* (1925). For histories of navy, see Chap. 4 (Naval). J. Q. ADAMS. See Chap. 22. JACKSON. See Chap. 23. HARRISON. See Chap. 24.

CHAPTER 15. THE AMERICAN FARM

GENERAL. C. R. Fish, *Rise of Common Man* (1937) and R. E. Riegel, *Young America* (1949) cover agriculture among other topics. G. W. Pierson, *Tocqueville and Beaumont* (1938) tells of two travelers; others well known in the period include F. E. Trollope, Harriet Martineau, Frederika Bremer, Basil Hall, J. S. Buckingham, F. A. Kemble, and William Cobbett. See also Chap. 7 (Economic Histories, and Agriculture).

SPECIFIC. H. Christman, *Tin Horns and Calico* (1945), New York antirent agitation; A. O. Craven, *Edmund Ruffin* (1932), Southern agricultural editor; A. L. Demaree, *Agricultural Press* (1941); D. M. Ellis, *Landlords and Farmers* (1946), New York antirent agitation; D. Giles, *Singing Valleys* (1940), corn; W. T. Hutchinson, *Cyrus Hall McCormick* (2 vols., 1930–1935), good on reaper; W. C. Neely, *Agricultural Fair* (1935); E. P. Prentice, *American Dairy Cattle* (1942); J. C. Robert, *Tobacco Kingdom* (1938); L. Rogin, *Farm Machinery* (1931), good on plow and wheat machinery; J. C. Sitterson, *Sugar Country* (1953); H. F. Wilson, *Hill Country of Northern New England* (1936); G. R. Wood, *Lumbering in Maine* (1935).

SOUTH. J. S. Bassett, *Southern Plantation Overseer* (1925); J. T. Carpenter, *South as Conscious Minority* (1930); C. S. Davis, *Cotton Kingdom in Alabama* (1939), exhaustive; W. E. Dodd, *Cotton Kingdom*

(1919), about 1850; J. H. Easterby, *South Carolina Rice Factor* (1945); C. Eaton, *Freedom of Thought in Old South* (1940); F. P. Gaines, *Southern Plantation* (1924), rise of a tradition; S. McIlwaine, *Southern Poor White* (1939); F. L. Owsley, *Plain Folk of Old South* (1949); R. W. Shugg, *Origins of Class Struggle in Louisiana* (1939); F. B. Simkins, *South Old and New* (1947); C. S. Sydnor, *Development of Social Sectionalism* (1948). See also Cotterill, Eaton, Hesseltine, Simkins, Chap. 2.

NEGRO. H. Aptheker, *Slave Revolts* (1943), scholarly; F. Bancroft, *Slave-trading* (1931); J. C. Carroll, *Slave Insurrections* (1938); J. W. Coleman, Jr., *Slavery Times in Kentucky* (1940); A. H. Fauset, *Sojourner Truth* (1938); R. B. Flanders, *Plantation Slavery in Georgia* (1933), good monograph; J. H. Franklin, *Free Negro in North Carolina* (1943); L. P. Jackson, *Free Negro Labor in Virginia* (1942); U. B. Phillips, *American Negro Slavery* (1918), *Life and Labor in Old South* (1929); W. D. Postell, *Health of Slaves* (1951); J. B. Sellers, *Slavery in Alabama* (1950), monograph; W. H. Stephenson, *Isaac Franklin* (1938), slave trader; C. S. Sydnor, *Slavery in Mississippi* (1933); R. H. Taylor, *Slave Holding in North Carolina* (1926); C. G. Woodson, *Mind of the Negro* (1926), letters, *Century of Negro Migration* (1918). For general Negro histories, see Chap. 7 (Labor, Negro); for abolition movement, Chap. 20 (Reform Movements).

CHAPTER 16. INFANT MANUFACTURES

GENERAL. W. W. Belcher, *Economic Rivalry between St. Louis and Chicago* (1947), 1850 to 1880; T. C. Cochran and W. Miller, *Age of Enterprise* (1942); L. Hartz, *Economic Policy and Democratic Thought* (1948), denies importance of laissez-faire theory; E. W. Martin, *Standard of Living in 1860* (1942); W. Miller, *Men in Business* (1952), early nineteenth century; M. Minnegerode, *Certain Rich Men* (1927), reads well; K. W. Rowe, *Mathew Carey* (1933); G. W. Smith, *Henry C. Carey* (1951), economist; W. B. Smith and A. H. Cole, *Fluctuations in American Business* (1935), scholarly; F. W. Taussig, *Tariff History* (1931); G. W. van Vleck, *Panic of 1857* (1942). See also Chap. 7; Fish, Riegel, Chap. 15 (General).

MANUFACTURING. K. Bruce, *Virginia Iron Industry* (1930), good; A. H. Cole, *American Carpet Manufacture* (1941); C. M. Green, *Holyoke, Massachusetts* (1939); F. Greenslet, *Lowells and Their Seven Worlds* (1946); H. Josephson, *Mill Girls and Magnates* (1949), Lowell; M. MacLaren, *Electrical Industry* (1943); B. Mitchell, *Cotton Mills in South* (1921), *William Gregg* (1928), Southern mill owner; A. C. Regli, *Rubber's Goodyear* (1941); J. Rohan, *Yankee Arms Maker* (1935), Colt; V. Shalkman,

Economic History of a Factory Town (1935), excellent on Chicopee; C. F. Ware, *Early New England Cotton Manufacture* (1931); R. F. Wolf, *India Rubber Man* (1939), simple on Goodyear. See also Chap. 7.

FINANCE. R. C. H. Catterall, *Second Bank of United States* (1903), standard; J. E. Hedges, *Commercial Banking* (1938), to 1863; L. H. Jenks, *Migration of British Capital* (1927), to 1875; M. G. Madeleine, *Monetary and Banking Theories* (1943), Jacksonian period; H. E. Miller, *Banking Theories* (1927), to 1860; A. Nevins, *Bank of New York* (1934); W. B. Smith, *Economic Aspects of Second Bank* (1953).

TRADE. L. E. Atherton, *Pioneer Merchant in Mid-America* (1939), *Southern Country Store* (1949); F. M. Jones, *Middlemen in Domestic Trade* (1937), 1800 to 1860; J. W. Livingood, *Philadelphia-Baltimore Trade Rivalry* (1947); K. W. Porter, *Jacksons and Lees* (2 vols., 1937), Boston merchants; H. E. Wildes, *Lonely Midas* (1943), Girard.

LABOR. See Chap. 7. L. Adamic, *Dynamite* (1931), violence in labor movement; S. P. Orth, *Armies of Labor* (1919); N. J. Ware, *Industrial Worker, 1840-1860* (1924).

CHAPTER 17. A SHRINKING UNITED STATES

GENERAL. C. H. Ambler, *Transportation in Ohio Valley* (1932), detailed; A. F. Harlow, *Old Wires and New Waves* (1936), telegraph; H. Hatcher, *The Great Lakes* (1944); A. B. Hulbert, *Paths of Inland Commerce* (1920); W. J. Lane, *Indian Trail to Iron Horse* (1939), New Jersey; G. R. Taylor, *Transportation Revolution* (1951), 1815 to 1866, excellent; R. L. Thompson, *Wiring a Continent* (1947), scholarly on telegraph. For Morse, see Chap. 19. See also Chap. 7; Fish, Riegel, Chap. 15 (General).

ROADS. A. Chapman, *Pony Express* (1932); R. P. and M. B. Conkling, *Butterfield Overland Mail* (3 vols., 1947), very detailed; J. A. Durrengerger, *Turnpikes* (1931), Middle Atlantic states; H. D. Fowler, *Camels to California* (1950); J. V. Frederick, *Ben Holladay* (1940), 1862 to 1866; D. Gardiner, *West of the River* (1941), trails and transportation; L. R. Hafen, *Overland Mail* (1926), scholarly; A. F. Harlow, *Old Post Bags* (1928); E. Hungerford, *Wells Fargo* (1949), to 1869; P. D. Jordan, *National Road* (1948), excellent; W. E. Rich, *History of Post Office* (1924), to 1829; R. W. and M. L. Settle, *Empire on Wheels* (1949), Majors, Russell, and Waddell.

OCEAN. R. G. Albion, *New York Port* (1939), 1815 to 1860, *Square Riggers on Schedule* (1938), packets; F. L. Benns, *Struggle for West Indies Trade* (1923); N. S. Buck, *Anglo-American Trade* (1925), 1800 to 1850; H. E. Chapelle, *American Sailing Ships* (1935), somewhat technical; J. B. Connolly, *Canton Captain* (1942); C. C. Cutler, *Greyhounds of the Seas* (1930), clippers; F. R. Dulles, *China and America* (1946), *Old China Trade* (1930); D. M. Henderson, *Yankee Ships in China Seas* (1946), reads well; E. P. Hohman, *American Whaleman* (1928), mostly 1830 to 1850; H. C. Kittredge, *Shipmasters of Cape Cod* (1935); R. A. Rydell, *Cape Horn to Pacific* (1952), trade around Horn; H. Sinclair, *Port of New Orleans* (1942); E. A. Stackpole, *Sea Hunters* (1953), whalers.

RIVERS. W. Andrews, *Vanderbilt Legend* (1941); F. E. Dayton, *Steamboat Days* (1925); F. L. Dorsey, *Master of Mississippi* (1941), Shreve—some errors; G. L. Eskew, *Pageant of the Packets* (1929), superficial; L. C. Hunter, *Steamboats on Western Rivers* (1949), definitive; W. J. Lane, *Commodore Vanderbilt* (1942); W. J. Peterson, *Steamboating on Upper*

Mississippi (1937); H. and E. Quick, *Mississippi Steamboatin'* (1926), readable; B. White, *Daniel Drew* (1910). See also Chap. 7.

CANALS. D. Bobbe, *De Witt Clinton* (1933), Erie Canal; E. L. Bogart, *Internal Improvements in Ohio* (1924), scholarly; W. F. Dunaway, *James River and Kanawha Company* (1922), monograph; A. F. Harlow, *Old Towpaths* (1926), reads well; E. D. Le Roy, *Delaware and Hudson Canal* (1950); J. W. Putnam, *Illinois and Michigan Canal* (1918); C. Roberts, *Middlesex Canal* (1938), good monograph; W. S. Sanderlin, *Chesapeake and Ohio Canal* (1946), monograph.

RAILROADS. G. L. Albright, *Official Exploration for Pacific Railroads* (1921); F. B. C. Bradlee, *Boston and Maine* (1921); G. H. Burgess and M. C. Kennedy, *Pennsylvania Railroad* (1949); G. T. Clark, *Leland Stanford* (1931); C. J. Corliss, *Main Line of Mid-America* (1950), Illinois Central; S. M. Derrick,

South Carolina Railroad (1930); P. Gates, *Illinois Central and Colonization* (1934), scholarly; A. F. Harlow, *Old Waybills* (1934), express companies, *Steelways of New England* (1946); S. H. Holbrook, *Story of American Railroads* (1947); E. Hungerford, *Baltimore and Ohio* (2 vols., 1928), *Men and Iron* (1938), New York Central, *Men of Erie* (1946); E. C. Kirkland, *Men, Cities, and Transportation* (2 vols., 1948), excellent on New England; L. O. Leonard and J. T. Johnson, *Railroad to the Sea* (1939), readable on Union Pacific; O. Lewis, *The Big Four* (1938), Central Pacific; J. Moody, *The Railroad Builders* (1919), general; J. R. Perkins, *Trails, Rails, and War* (1929), Union Pacific; R. E. Riegel, *Story of Western Railroads* (1926), trans-Mississippi; R. R. Russell, *Communication with Pacific Coast as Issue* (1948), to 1864; M. D. Stevers, *Steel Rails* (1933), popular; J. G. van Deusen, *Ante-bellum Southern Commercial Conventions* (1926); N. C. Wilson and F. J. Taylor, *Southern Pacific* (1952).

CHAPTER 18. **TRAINING THE NEW GENERATION**

GENERAL. G. Adams and E. Hutter, *Mad Forties* (1924), odds and ends; H. C. Brown, *Brownstone Fronts* (1935), delightful on New York; M. Minnegerode, *Fabulous Forties* (1924), colorful; A. Nevins and M. H. Thomas (ed.), *Diary of George Templeton Strong* (4 vols., 1952), New York life. See also Curti, Chap. 8 (General); Fish, Riegel, Chap. 15 (General).

FAMILY. H. Asbury, *Gangs of New York* (1928); E. H. Cady, *The Gentleman in America* (1949); A. L. Kuhn, *Mother's Role in Childhood Education* (1947), 1830 to 1860; A. M. Schlesinger, *Learning How to Behave* (1946), etiquette; H. B. Woodward, *Bold Women* (1953), unusual women. See also Chap. 8.

EDUCATION. R. P. Baker, *Chapter in Education* (1924), Rensselaer; E. L. Bolzau, *Almira Hart Lincoln Phelps* (1936); P. A. Bruce, *University of Virginia* (5 vols., 1920–1922); E. M. Coulter, *College Life in Old South* (1928); L. A. Cremin, *American Common School* (1951), 1815 to 1850; C. W. Dabney, *Education in South* (2 vols., 1936); J. H. Denison, *Mark Hopkins* (1935); E. Earnest, *Academic Procession* (1953), reads well; S. H. Fisher, *Litchfield Law School* (1933); R. S. Fletcher, *Oberlin College* (2 vols., 1943); F. Freidel, *Francis Lieber* (1948), South Carolina College; C. M. Fuess, *Amherst* (1935); A. Godbold, *Church College of Old South* (1944), detailed; M. E. Harveson, *Catherine Esther Beecher* (1932); F. J. Hosford, *Father Shepherd's Magna Charta* (1937), Oberlin; S. L. Jackson, *Strug-*

gle for Free Schools (1941), New England and New York; E. M. McCallister, *Amos Eaton* (1942), Rensselaer; H. C. Minnich, *William Holmes McGuffey* (1936); H. K. Rowe, *Andover Theological Seminary* (1933); O. Shepard, *Pedlar's Progress* (1937), Bronson Alcott; B. C. Steiner, *Henry Barnard* (1919); R. J. Storr, *Graduate Education* (1953); L. H. Tharp, *Until Victory* (1953), Horace Mann; R. E. Thursfield, *Henry Barnard's American Journal* (1945).

SCIENCE. J. S. Chambers, *Conquest of Cholera* (1938); T. Coulson, *Joseph Henry* (1950); E. Earnest, *John and William Bartram* (1940); N. B. Fagin, *William Bartram* (1933), botany; D. Fleming, *John William Draper and Religion of Science* (1950); J. T. Flexner, *Doctors on Horseback* (1937), very good; H. W. Haggard, *Devils, Drugs and Doctors* (1929), medicine; S. Harris, *Women's Surgeon* (1950), J. M. Sims; A. G. Harvey, *Douglas of the Fir* (1947), gave name to Douglas fir; W. B. Hendrickson, *David Dale Owen* (1943), geology; F. H. Herrick, *Audubon* (2 vols., 1917); F. Landon, *Lake Huron* (1944), account of Beaumont; C. L. Lewis, *Matthew Fontaine Maury* (1927), mapping of ocean; J. S. Myer, *William Beaumont* (1912); W. F. Norwood, *Medical Education* (1944), to 1860; H. R. Raper, *Man against Pain* (1945); V. Robinson, *Victory over Pain* (1946), anesthetics; A. D. Rodgers III, *John Torrey* (1942), botany; W. M. and M. S. C. Smallwood, *Natural History* (1941); F. L. Taylor, *Crawford W. Long* (1928). See also Chap. 8.

CHAPTER 19. ATTAINING CULTURE

GENERAL. See Chap. 18.

ART. R. Crouse, *Mr. Currier and Mr. Ives* (1930); H. M. P. Gallagher, *Robert Mills* (1935); A. T. Gardner, *Yankee Stonecutters* (1945), 1800 to 1850—good; T. Hamlin, *Greek Revival Architecture* (1944); O. W. Larkin, *Samuel F. B. Morse* (1954); C. Mabee, *Samuel F. B. Morse* (1943); J. H. Morgan, *Gilbert Stuart and Pupils* (1939); H. T. Peters, *Currier & Ives* (2 vols., 1929). See also Chap. 8.

MUSIC. C. Brink, *Harps in the Wind* (1947), Hutchinson family, singers; J. Erskine, *Philharmonic-symphony Society* (1943); I. Goldberg, *Tin Pan Alley* (1930), popular music; J. T. Howard, *Stephen Foster* (1934); G. S. Jackson, *Early Songs of Uncle Sam* (1933), popular songs; P. D. Jordan, *Singin' Yankees* (1946), Hutchinsons; J. Mattfield, *Hundred Years of Opera* (1927); A. L. Rich, *Lowell Mason* (1946); O. G. Sonneck, *Early Opera* (1915); E. Wagenknecht, *Jenny Lind* (1931); R. Walters, *Stephen Foster* (1936). See also Chap. 8.

THEATER. R. H. Ball, *Amazing Career of Sir Giles Overreach* (1939), biography of stage character; D. Bobbe, *Fanny Kemble* (1931); L. S. Driver, *Fanny Kemble* (1933); C. E. Foust, *Robert Montgomery Bird* (1919); P. Graham, *Showboats* (1951), scholarly, reads well; R. D. James, *Old Drury of Philadelphia* (1932); J. S. Kendall, *Golden Age of New Orleans Theater* (1952); M. J. Moses, *Fabulous Forrest* (1929); C. Wittke, *Tambo and Bones* (1930), minstrelsy. See also Chap. 8.

NEWSPAPERS AND MAGAZINES. E. F. Brown, *Raymond of the Times* (1951); O. Carlson, *James Gordon Bennett* (1942); R. Cortissoz, *New York Tribune* (1923); R. E. Finley, *Lady of Godey's: Sarah Josepha Hale* (1931), interesting; C. L. Gohdes, *Periodicals of Transcendentalism* (1931), good monograph; W. H. Hale, *Horace Greeley* (1950); R. Hooker, *Independent Newspaper* (1924), Springfield *Republican*; M. A. D. Howe, *Atlantic Monthly* (1919); G. Johnson and others, *Sunpapers of Baltimore* (1937); N. N. Luxon,

Niles' Weekly Register (1947); A. Nevins, *Evening Post* (1922); F. M. O'Brien, *Story of the Sun* (1928); C. J. Rosebault, *When Dana Was the Sun* (1931); D. C. Seitz, *James Gordon Bennetts* (1928); A. H. Shaw, *"The Plain Dealer"* (1942), Cleveland; J. E. Smith, *Hartford's Courant* (1949), scholarly; K. Stewart and J. Tebbel, *Makers of Modern Journalism* (1952), biographical. See also Chap. 8.

LITERATURE. N. F. Adkins, *Fitz-Greene Halleck* (1930), definitive; N. Arvin, *Hawthorne* (1929), *Melville* (1950), *Whitman* (1938), excellent; E. D. Branch, *Sentimental Years* (1934), 1830 to 1860—flippant; V. W. Brooks, *Flowering of New England* (1936), 1815 to 1865, *Melville and Whitman* (1947), *Washington Irving* (1944); J. T. Flanagan, *James Hall* (1941), Westerner; M. E. Flower, *James Parton* (1951), biographer—good; J. Grossman, *James Fenimore Cooper* (1949); G. S. Haight, *Mrs. Sigourney* (1930), excellent; A. L. Herold, *James Kirke Paulding* (1926); M. Kiefer, *American Children through Their Books* (1948), to 1835; J. W. Krutch, *Henry David Thoreau* (1948); V. Loggins, *The Hawthornes* (1951); L. Lorenz, *Sidney Lanier* (1935); F. O. Mathiessen, *American Renaissance* (1941); R. B. Nye, *George Bancroft* (1944), historian; F. L. Pattee, *Feminine Fifties* (1940), women writers; J. A. Pollard, *John Greenleaf Whittier* (1949), leisurely; A. H. Quinn, *Edgar Allan Poe* (1941); L. Rhea, *Hugh Swinton Legaré* (1934); R. L. Rusk, *Ralph Waldo Emerson* (1949); E. Shanks, *Edgar Allan Poe* (1937); R. Thompson, *American Literary Annuals* (1936); E. M. Tilton, *Amiable Autocrat* (1947), excellent on Holmes; M. Wade, *Margaret Fuller* (1940); S. T. Williams, *Washington Irving* (2 vols., 1935). See also Chap. 8.

AMUSEMENTS. L. F. Brewster, *Summer Migrations* (1947), scholarly; R. W. Henderson, *Bell, Bat and Bishop* (1947), baseball; A. Johnston, *Ten—and Out* (1927), boxing; E. C. May, *The Circus* (1932); R. M. Smith, *Baseball* (1947); J. Williamson, *The American Hotel* (1930). See also Chap. 8.

CHAPTER 20. SEEKING PERFECTION

GENERAL. P. M. Bannon, *Arthur and Lewis Tappan* (1950), reformers; A. A. Ekirch, *Idea of Progress* (1944); C. A. Madison, *Critics and Crusaders* (1947), biographies; G. Seldes, *Stammering Century* (1928); A. F. Tyler, *Freedom's Ferment* (1944), social reform. See also Chap. 18.

RELIGION. E. D. Andrews, *People Called Shakers* (1953); R. A. Billington, *Protestant Crusade* (1938), anti-Catholic agitation; H. S. Commager, *Theodore Parker* (1936), excellent; C. M. Drury, *Presbyterian Panorama* (1952), missions; H. O. Dwight, *American Bible Society* (2 vols., 1916); C. R. Kellar,

Second Great Awakening in Connecticut (1942), 1795 to 1830; T. Maynard, *Orestes Brownson* (1943); S. E. Mead, *Nathaniel William Taylor* (1942), Connecticut liberal; J. N. Nelson, *Schism in Methodist Church* (1923), over slavery; F. D. Nichol, *Midnight Cry* (1944), favorable to Millerites; S. Persons, *Free Religion* (1947), Unitarian secession; A. Post, *Freethought in America* (1943), 1825 to 1850; A. M. Schlesinger, Jr., *Orestes Brownson* (1939); C. E. Sears, *Days of Delusion* (1924), critical of Millerites; C. C. Sellers, *Lorenzo Dow* (1928), revivalist; W. R. Whitney, *Burned-over District* (1950), revivalism. See also Chap. 8.

MORMONS. N. Anderson, *Desert Saints* (1942), fine monograph; P. Bailey, *Sam Brannon* (1943), entertaining; F. M. Brodie, *No Man Knows My History* (1945), excellent on Smith; L. H. Creer, *Founding of an Empire* (1947), *Utah and the Nation* (1929); J. H. Evans, *Joseph Smith* (1933); S. Y. Gates, *Brigham Young* (1930), by daughter; F. A. Golden, *March of Mormon Battalion* (1928); M. R. Hunter, *Brigham Young* (1940), as colonizer; G. O. Larson, *Prelude to the Kingdom* (1947), conquest of desert; E. E. McGavin, *U.S. Soldiers Invade Utah* (1937), sympathetic to Mormons; W. J. McNiff, *Heaven on Earth* (1940), Utah life; M. M. Quaife, *Kingdom of Saint James* (1930), Strang; O. W. Riegel, *Crown of Glory* (1935), Strang; M. R. Werner, *Brigham Young* (1925), entertaining.

REFORM MOVEMENTS. H. Asbury, *Great Illusion* (1950), prohibition; G. H. Barnes, *Anti-slavery Impulse* (1933); A. S. Blackwell, *Lucy Stone* (1930); G. W. Brown, *Black Communism* (1941), Liberia; H. Buckmaster, *Let My People Go* (1941), Underground Railroad; M. C. Curti, *American Peace Crusade* (1929), *The Learned Blacksmith* (1937), peace movement, *Peace or War* (1936); T. E. Drake, *Quakers and Slavery* (1950), good monograph; E. L. Fox,

American Colonization Society (1919), detailed; W. F. Galpin, *Pioneering for Peace* (1933), to 1846; A. Graham, *Ladies in Revolt* (1934); S. Graham, *There Once Was a Slave* (1947), Frederick Douglass; L. C. M. Hare, *Lucretia Mott* (1937), vivid; R. V. Harlow, *Gerrit Smith* (1939); W. S. Jenkins, *Proslavery Thought in Old South* (1935), excellent; J. A. Krout, *Origins of Prohibition* (1925), to 1851; A. Y. Lloyd, *Slavery Controversy* (1939), Southern view; A. Lutz, *Created Equal* (1940), Stanton; J. Macy, *Anti-slavery Crusade* (1919); H. E. Marshall, *Dorothea Dix* (1937); R. B. Nye, *Fettered Freedom* (1949), civil liberties and abolition, 1830 to 1860; A. J. G. Perkins and T. Wolfson, *Frances Wright* (1939); E. Sachs, *Terrible Siren* (1928), popularized on Victoria Woodhull; W. H. Siebert, *Underground Railroad* (1898), standard, *Ohio Underground Railroad* (1951); L. Swift, *William Lloyd Garrison* (1911); B. P. Thomas, *Theodore Weld* (1950); M. Thorp, *Female Persuasion* (1949), outstanding women; W. R. Waterman, *Frances Wright* (1924), scholarly; R. F. Wilson, *Crusader in Crinoline* (1941), Stowe; H. C. Wolf, *On Freedom's Altar* (1952), martyr complex.

UTOPIAN COMMUNITIES. A. E. Bestor, Jr., *Backwoods Utopia* (1950), New Harmony; F. E. Haynes, *Social Politics* (1924); W. A. Hinds, *American Communities* (1902), old but best; H. W. Laidler, *Socialist Thought* (1927); R. W. Leopold, *Robert Dale Owen* (1940), New Harmony; A. E. Lincoln, *Incorrigible Idealist* (1940), R. D. Owen; A. E. McBee, *From Utopia to Florence* (1947), transcendental community; M. F. Melcher, *Shaker Adventure* (1941); P. B. Noyes, *My Father's House* (1937), Oneida; R. A. Parker, *A Yankee Saint* (1935), Noyes; C. E. Sears, *Bronson Alcott's Fruitlands* (1915); L. Swift, *Brook Farm* (1900); G. G. Van Deusen, *Horace Greeley* (1953).

CHAPTER 21. WESTWARD EXPANSION

IMMIGRATION. W. F. Adams, *Ireland and Irish Immigration* (1932); K. C. Babcock, *Scandinavian Element* (1914); L. M. Bergmann, *Americans from Norway* (1950); T. C. Blegen, *Norwegian Immigration* (2 vols., 1931–1940); R. Ernst, *Immigrant Life in New York* (1949), 1825 to 1863; F. E. Gibson, *Attitude of New York Irish* (1951), from 1848; O. Handlin, *Boston's Immigrants* (1941), 1790 to 1865; C. C. Qualey, *Norwegian Settlement* (1938), 1825 to 1860; C. F. Wittke, *Refugees of Revolution* (1952), Revolution of 1848. See also Chap. 7.

GENERAL WESTERN HISTORIES. See Chap. 9.

OLD NORTHWEST. C. W. Alvord (ed.), *Centennial History of Illinois* (6 vols., 1918–1922); R. C. Buley, *Old Northwest* (2 vols., 1950); E. E. Calkins, *They Broke the Prairie* (1937), Galesburg, Ill.; L. Esarey, *Indiana* (3 vols., 1925); P. W. Gates, *Frontier Landlords* (1945), short study; H. C. Hubbard, *Older Middle West* (1936), heavily political from 1840; T. C. Pease, *Story of Illinois* (1949); B. L. Pierce, *Chicago* (2 vols., 1937–1940); M. N. Quaife and S. Glazer, *Michigan* (1948); W. F. Raney, *Wisconsin* (1940); J. Schafer, *Wisconsin Lead Region* (1932); H. J. Smith, *Chicago's Great Century* (1933); B. Still, *Milwaukee*

(1948), comprehensive; F. B. Woodford, *Lewis Cass* (1950), Michigan. See also Chap. 9.

OLD SOUTHWEST. T. P. Abernethy, *Formative Period in Alabama* (1922), 1815 to 1828; J. G. Baldwin, *Flush Times in Alabama and Mississippi* (1853), classic; M. C. Boyd, *Alabama in the Fifties* (1931), monograph; K. T. Hanna, *Florida* (1949); A. B. Longstreet, *Georgia Scenes* (1897), contemporary classic; S. W. Martin, *Florida during Territorial Days* (1944); S. C. Williams, *Beginnings of West Tennessee* (1930). See also Chap. 9.

TRANS-MISSISSIPPI. E. E. Dale and M. L. Wardell, *Oklahoma* (1948); J. G. Fletcher, *Arkansas* (1947); G. Foreman, *Oklahoma* (1942); I. Richman, *Ioway to Iowa* (1931); F. C. Shoemaker, *Missouri* (5 vols., 1943).

INDIANS. A. Bass, *Cherokee Messenger* (1936), good on Indian newspaper; C. Cole, *I Am a Man* (1938), Black Hawk; A. Debo, *And Still the Waters Run* (1940), Civilized Tribes in Oklahoma, *Rise and Fall of Choctaw Republic* (1934), *Road to Disappearance* (1941), Creek—excellent; G. Foreman, *Five Civilized Tribes* (1934), in Oklahoma before 1860, *Indian Removal* (1932), *Last Trek of Indians* (1946), minor tribes in Oklahoma, *Sequoyah* (1938), Cherokee genius; G. D. Harmon, *Sixty Years of Indian Affairs* (1941), detailed; A. Keiser, *Indian in American Literature* (1933); J. P. Kinney, *A Continent Lost—a Civilization Won* (1937); J. C. Malin, *Indian Policy and Westward Expansion* (1921), fine on permanent frontier; M. L. Starkey, *Cherokee Nation* (1946), fascinating; M. L. Wardell, *Cherokee Nation* (1938), political, 1838 to 1907. See also Chap. 1 (America of Red Man).

LAND DISPOSAL. G. M. Stephenson, *History of Public Lands* (1917), 1840 to 1862; R. G. Wellington, *Influence of Public Lands* (1914), 1828 to 1842. See also Chap. 5.

EXPLORATION. J. C. Bell, *Opening a Highway to Pacific* (1921), 1838 to 1846; R. P. Bieber and L. R. Hafen (eds.), *Southwest Historical Series* (12 vols., 1931–1943), travels; R. G. Cleland, *Pathfinders* (1929), travelers to California; W. E. Hollon, *Lost Pathfinder* (1949), good on Pike; J. Monaghan, *Overland Trail* (1947), history; D. L. Morgan, *Great Salt Lake* (1947); A. Nevins, *Frémont* (1939); G. L. Nute, *Lake Superior* (1944), excellent; P. H. Parish, *Before the Covered Wagon* (1931); C. E. Phillips, *Jessie Benton Frémont* (1935); M. M. Quaife, *Lake Michigan* (1944); R. G. Thwaites (ed.), *Early Western Travels* (32 vols., 1904–1907). See also Fur Trade, below.

FUR TRADE. R. G. Cleland, *Reckless Breed of Men* (1950), trappers; H. C. Dale, *Ashley-Smith Explora-* tions (1918); B. de Voto, *Across the Wide Missouri* (1947); E. Dick, *Vanguards of the Frontier* (1941); A. H. Favour, *Old Bill Williams* (1936); G. L. Nute, *The Voyageur* (1931), excellent; M. S. Sullivan, *Jedediah Smith* (1936); C. A. Vandiveer, *Fur Trade and Exploration* (1929); S. Vestal, *Jim Bridger* (1946), *Kit Carson* (1928), *Mountain Men* (1937). See also Oregon, below.

SANTA FE TRADE. C. Coan, *New Mexico* (3 vols., 1925); R. L. Duffus, *Santa Fe Trail* (1930); E. Fergusson, *New Mexico* (1951); H. Fergusson, *Rio Grande* (1933); J. Gregg, *Commerce of Prairies* (2 vols., 1844), various reprints; S. Vestal, *Old Santa Fe Trail* (1939).

TEXAS. E. C. Barker, *Stephen F. Austin* (1925); O. Morton, *Terán and Texas* (1948); R. N. Richardson, *Texas* (1943); J. F. Rippy, *United States and Mexico* (1926); L. Saxon, *Lafitte* (1930), pirate; R. W. Steen, *Texas Story* (1948); N. W. Stephenson, *Texas and Mexican War* (1921); H. G. Warren, *The Sword Was Their Passport* (1943), scholarly on filibustering; O. P. White, *Texas* (1945).

OREGON. C. J. Brosnan, *Jason Lee* (1932), scholarly; C. H. Carey, *Oregon* (2 vols., 1935–1936), detailed; J. C. Caughey, *History of Pacific Coast* (1933); C. M. Drury, *Spalding* (1936), *Whitman* (1937), detailed, *Elkanah and Mary Walker* (1940); G. W. Fuller, *Inland Empire* (3 vols., 1928), informative; W. J. Ghent, *Road to Oregon* (1929); A. B. Hulbert (ed.), *Call of Columbia* (1934), (ed.), *Oregon Crusade* (1935), (ed.), *Whitman* (3 vols., 1936–1941); R. G. Montgomery, *White-headed Eagle* (1934), McLoughlin; H. O'Connor, *The Astors* (1941); K. W. Porter, *John Jacob Astor* (2 vols., 1931); F. W. Powell, *Hall Jackson Kelley* (1917); C. L. Skinner, *Adventurers of Oregon* (1920); O. O. Winther, *Great Northwest* (1947), *Old Oregon Country* (1950).

CALIFORNIA. J. C. Caughey, *California* (1940), *Gold Is the Cornerstone* (1948), gold rushes, *Pacific Coast* (1933); C. E. Chapman, *California* (1921), Spanish period; R. G. Cleland, *California* (1922), American period, *Wilderness to Empire* (1944); O. C. Coy, *Gold Days* (1929), *Great Trek* (1931), routes; A. B. Hulbert, *Forty-niners* (1931), synthetic diary; R. D. Hunt, *John Bidwell* (1942); J. H. Jackson, *Anybody's Gold* (1941), mining towns; C. Kelly, *Salt Desert Trails* (1930); J. R. Korns, *West from Fort Bridger* (1951); O. Lewis, *Sea Routes to Gold Fields* (1949); I. D. Paden, *Wake of the Prairie Schooner* (1943); R. W. Paul, *Cailfornia Gold* (1947), excellent; G. C. Quiett, *Pay Dirt* (1936), gold rushes; G. R. Stewart, Jr., *Ordeal by Hunger* (1936), Donner party; R. L. Underhill, *Cowhides to Golden Fleece* (1946), Larkin; G. F. Willison, *Here They Dug the Gold* (1931); J. P. Zollinger, *Sutter* (1939), excellent.

MINING. P. S. Fritz, *Colorado* (1941); W. B. Gates, *Michigan Copper* (1951), scholarly; C. B. Glasscock, *Big Bonanza* (1931), Comstock; L. R. Hafen, *Colorado* (1933); O. Lewis, *Silver Kings* (1947), readable; G. D. Lyman, *Comstock Lode* (1934), episodical; E. M. Mack, *Nevada* (1936), scholarly; T. A. Rickard, *American Mining* (1932); W. J. Trimble, *Mining Advance* (1914), scholarly, 1855 to 1870; R. K. Wyllys, *Arizona* (1950).

CHAPTER 22. NATIONALISTIC POLITICS

GENERAL POLITICAL. J. T. Carpenter, *South as Conscious Minority* (1930); G. Dangerfield, *Era of Good Feelings* (1951), excellent. See also Chap. 10. MISSOURI COMPROMISE. F. H. Hodder, *Sidelights on Missouri Compromise* (1909); G. Moore, *Missouri Compromise* (1953); F. C. Shoemaker, *Missouri's Struggle for Statehood* (1916). See also Shoemaker, Chap. 21 (Trans-Mississippi). TARIFF. See economic histories, Chaps. 7 and 16. INTERNAL IMPROVEMENTS. See economic histories, Chaps. 7 and 17.

BIOGRAPHIES. J. Q. ADAMS. H. Agar (ed.), *Formative Years* (2 vols., 1947); S. F. Bemis, *Adams and Foreign Policy* (1949); B. C. Clark, *John Quincy Adams* (1932); W. C. Ford (ed.), *Writings* (7 vols., 1913–1917); A. Nevins (ed.), *Diary* (1928). CALHOUN. See Chap. 14. CLAY. See Chap. 14. JACKSON. See Chap. 23. MARSHALL. See Chap. 11; constitutional histories, Chap. 10. MONROE. W. P. Cresson, *James Monroe* (1946); S. M. Hamilton, *Writings* (7 vols., 1898–1903); A. Styron, *Last of Cocked Hats* (1945). RANDOLPH. See Chap. 11. WEBSTER. S. H. Adams, *Godlike Daniel* (1930); C. M. Fuess, *Daniel Webster* (2 vols., 1930).

CHAPTER 23. THE JACKSONIAN ERA

GENERAL POLITICAL. C. G. Bowers, *Party Battles of Jackson Period* (1922), animated; E. M. Carroll, *Origins of Whig Party* (1925); A. C. Cole, *Whig Party in South* (1913), 1830 to 1861; A. Craven, *Repressible Conflict* (1939); A. B. Darling, *Political Changes in Massachusetts, 1824–1848* (1925); D. G. Fowler, *Cabinet Politician* (1943), Postmaster General; S. R. Gammon, *Campaign of 1832* (1922); R. C. McGrane, *Foreign Bondholders and American State Debts* (1935), *Panic of 1837* (1924); H. R. Mueller, *Whig Party in Pennsylvania* (1922); F. A. Ogg, *Reign of Andrew Jackson* (1919); A. M. Schlesinger, Jr., *Age of Jackson* (1945); F. B. Simkins, *South Old and New* (1947); C. S. Sydnor, *Southern Sectionalism* (1948); F. J. Turner, *The United States, 1830–1850* (1935); J. G. van Deusen, *Disunion in South Carolina* (1928), 1830 to 1850. See also Chap. 10; Carpenter, Chap. 22.

BIOGRAPHIES. J. Q. ADAMS. See Chap. 22. BENTON. W. M. Meigs, *Thomas Hart Benton* (1904). BIDDLE. R. C. McGrane (ed.), *Correspondence* (1919). CALHOUN. See Chap. 14; F. Bancroft, *Calhoun and Nullification* (1928); J. P. Pritchett, *Calhoun: His Defense of South* (1937). CASS. F. B. Woodford, *Lewis Cass* (1950). EATON. P. Eaton, *Autobiography* (1932); Q. Pollack, *Peggy Eaton* (1931). GRUNDY. J. H. Parker, *Felix Grundy* (1940), War Hawk. JACKSON. J. S. Bassett (ed.), *Correspondence* (7 vols., 1926–1935); M. James, *Andrew Jackson* (2 vols., 1933–1937); D. Karsner, *Andrew Jackson* (1929); W. G. Sumner, *Andrew Jackson* (1924). TANEY. B. W. Palmer, *Marshall and Taney* (1939); C. W. Smith, Jr., *Roger B. Taney* (1936); C. B. Swisher, *Roger B. Taney* (1936), definitive. VAN BUREN. H. Alexander, *American Talleyrand* (1935); J. C. Fitzpatrick (ed.), *Autobiography* (1920); D. T. Lynch, *An Epoch and a Man* (1929). WEBSTER. See Chap. 22.

CHAPTER 24. WHIG VERSUS DEMOCRAT

GENERAL. O. D. Lambert, *Presidential Policies, 1841–44* (1936); J. C. N. Paul, *Rift in the Democracy* (1951), nomination of 1844; K. H. Porter, *National Party Platforms* (1924); R. R. Russell, *Economic Aspects of Southern Sectionalism* (1924). See also Cotterill, Eaton, Hesseltine, Chap. 2; Carpenter, Chap. 22; Cole, Craven, Simkins, Sydnor, Chap. 23.

SLAVERY. D. L. Dumond, *Antislavery Origins of Civil War* (1939). See also Chaps. 15 and 20.

BIOGRAPHIES. G. W. Johnson, *American Heroes* (1943), includes Van Buren and Harrison. CALHOUN. See Chaps. 14, 23. C. M. Wiltse, *John C. Calhoun, Sectionalist* (1951). CASS. See Chap. 23. CHASE. See Chap. 31. CLAY. See Chap. 14. C. R. Poage, *Henry Clay* (1936). DAVIS. See Chap. 34. DOUGLAS. See

Chap. 29. HARRISON. F. Cleaves, *Old Tippecanoe* (1939); D. B. Goebel, *William Henry Harrison* (1926); J. A. Green, *William Henry Harrison* (1941), eulogistic. POLK. E. I. McCormac, *James K. Polk* (1922); A. Nevins, *Polk: Diary* (1929). SEWARD. See Chap. 31. TYLER. O. P. Chitwood, *John Tyler* (1939). VAN BUREN. See Chap. 23. WEBSTER. See Chap. 22. WILMOT. C. C. Going, *David Wilmot* (1924).

CHAPTER 25. A MORE NATIONALISTIC DIPLOMACY

GENERAL DIPLOMATIC HISTORIES. See Chap. 4.

SPAIN AND FLORIDA TREATY. P. C. Brooks, *Diplomacy and the Borderlands* (1939), scholarly on treaty of 1819; C. C. Griffin, *United States and Disruption of Spanish Empire* (1937), 1810 to 1822; K. T. Hanna, *Florida* (1949); A. P. Whitaker, *United States and Independence of Latin America* (1941), lectures.

RUSSIA. T. A. Bailey, *America Faces Russia* (1950); F. R. Dulles, *Road to Teheran* (1944); F. A. Golder, *Russian Expansion in Pacific* (1914); B. P. Thomas, *Russo-American Relations* (1930), 1815 to 1867; W. A. Williams, *American Russian Relations* (1952).

BRITAIN AND MONROE DOCTRINE. J. R. Clark, *Memorandum on Monroe Doctrine* (1930), official; W. P. Cresson, *Holy Alliance* (1922); R. B. Mowat, *Diplomatic Relations of Great Britain and United States* (1925); D. Perkins, *Hands Off* (1941), best single volume, *Monroe Doctrine, 1823–1826* (1927), *Monroe Doctrine, 1826–1867* (1933), *Monroe Doctrine, 1867–1907* (1937); J. H. Powell, *Richard Rush* (1942), Minister to England; J. F. Rippy, *Rivalry of*

United States and Great Britain over Latin America (1929), 1808 to 1830; W. S. Robertson, *Hispanic-American Relations* (1923); E. H. Tatum, *United States and Europe, 1815–1823* (1936); H. W. V. Temperley, *Foreign Policy of Canning* (1925); C. K. Webster, *Foreign Policy of Castlereagh* (1925).

FRANCE. R. A. McLemore, *Franco-American Diplomatic Relations* (1941), *French Spoliation Claims* (1932).

CANADA. J. B. Brebner, *North Atlantic Triangle* (1945); J. M. Callahan, *Canadian Relations* (1937), factual; P. E. Corbett, *Canadian-American Disputes* (1937), monograph; A. B. Corey, *Crisis of 1830–1842* (1941); E. W. McInnis, *Unguarded Frontier* (1942); C. Wittke, *Canada* (1941).

BIOGRAPHIES. J. Q. ADAMS. See Chap. 22. CALHOUN. See Chaps. 14, 23. HARRISON. See Chap. 24. JACKSON. See Chap. 23. JEFFERSON. See Chap. 11. MADISON. See Chap. 14. MONROE. See Chap. 22. TYLER. See Chap. 24. VAN BUREN. See Chap. 23. WEBSTER. See Chap. 22.

CHAPTER 26. MANIFEST DESTINY

GENERAL. G. P. Garrison, *Westward Extension* (1906); L. Green, *The Filibuster* (1937), Walker; W. O. Scroggs, *Filibusters and Financiers* (1916), Walker; A. K. Weinberg, *Manifest Destiny* (1935), reasons advanced. POLK, TYLER. See Chap. 24.

OREGON. See Chap. 21.

TEXAS. W. C. Binkley, *Expansionist Movement in Texas* (1925), *Texas Revolution* (1952), excellent lectures; W. H. Calcott, *Santa Anna* (1936); J. M. Callahan, *Mexican Relations* (1932), detailed; F. Copeland, *Kendall of the Picayune* (1943), Santa Fe

expedition; F. S. Dunn, *Protection of Americans in Mexico* (1933); H. Gambrell, *Anson Jones* (1948), last president of Texas; J. D. Hill, *Texas Navy* (1937); W. R. Hogan, *Texan Republic* (1946); M. James, *The Raven* (1929), Houston; W. R. Manning, *United States and Mexico* (1916), before 1830; J. P. Rippy, *United States and Mexico* (1931); J. W. Schmitz, *Texas Statecraft* (1941); L. M. Sears, *John Slidell* (1925); J. H. Smith, *Annexation of Texas* (1911); W. P. Webb, *Texas Rangers* (1935). ADAMS. See Chap. 22. CALHOUN, CLAY. See Chap. 14. JACKSON. See Chap. 23. POLK, TYLER. See Chap. 24.

CHAPTER 27. **THE MEXICAN WAR**

A. H. Bill, *Rehearsal for Conflict* (1947); B. de Voto, *Year of Decision: 1846* (1943), interesting; B. Dyer, *Zachary Taylor* (1946), excellent; C. W. Elliott, *Winfield Scott* (1937), scholarly; J. D. P. Fuller, *Movement for Acquisition of All Mexico* (1930); P. N. Garber, *Gadsden Treaty* (1923); H. Hamilton, *Zachary Taylor* (2 vols., 1941–1951); R. S. Henry, *Mexican War* (1950), Smith point of view; A. D.

Howden-Smith, *Old Fuss and Feathers* (1937), popular on Scott; J. H. Smith, *War with Mexico* (2 vols., 1919). See also army histories under Chap. 4 (War on Land); Richardson, Rippy, Steen, Stephenson, Chap. 21; Callahan, Dunn, Smith, Chap. 26. MORMON BRIGADE. See Chap. 20. FRÉMONT. See Chap. 21. LEE AND GRANT. See Chap. 32. SANTA ANNA. See Chap. 26.

CHAPTER 28. **THE DIPLOMACY OF SECTIONALISM**

GENERAL. DIPLOMATIC HISTORIES. See Chap. 12. BRITAIN. See Chap. 26. A. C. Cole, *Irrepressible Conflict* (1934); A. Nevins, *Ordeal of the Union* (2 vols., 1947), very fine.

SPECIFIC. R. G. Caldwell, *Lopez Expedition* (1915); T. Dennett, *Americans in Eastern Asia* (1922), detailed; A. A. Ettinger, *Mission of Soule* (1932), 1853 to 1855; C. M. Fuess, *Caleb Cushing* (2 vols., 1923),

Chinese treaty; R. F. Nichols, *Franklin Pierce* (1931); B. Rauch, *American Interest in Cuba* (1948), 1845 to 1855; L. B. Shippee, *Canadian-American Diplomacy* (1939); P. J. Treat, *United States and Japan* (3 vols., 1932–1938); M. W. Williams, *Anglo-American Isthmian Diplomacy* (1916). BUCHANAN. See Chap. 30. WALKER. See Chap. 26. WEBSTER. See Chap. 22. MEXICO. See Chap. 26.

CHAPTER 29. **THE CLOUDS GATHER**

GENERAL POLITICAL. A. O. Craven, *Coming of the Civil War* (1942), *Growth of Southern Nationalism* (1953); F. Curtis, *Republican Party* (2 vols., 1904). See also Chap. 10; Carpenter, Chap. 22; Porter, Russell, Chap. 24; Cole, Nevins, Chap. 28.

SOUTHERN POSITION AND SLAVERY. C. S. Boucher, *Nullification in South Carolina* (1916); W. E. Dodd, *Expansion and Conflict* (1916); P. S. Foner, *Business and Slavery* (1941); P. M. Hamer, *Secession Movement in South Carolina* (1918), 1847 to 1852; T. D. Jervey, *Robert Y. Haynes* (1909); U. B. Phillips, *Robert Toombs* (1913); H. S. Schultz, *Nationalism and Sectionalism in South Carolina* (1950), 1852 to 1860, good; R. H. Shryock, *Georgia in 1850* (1926); H. H. Simms, *Decade of Sectional Controversy* (1942), monograph, *Robert M. T. Hunter* (1935). SLAVERY. See Chap. 15. ABOLITION. See Chap. 20.

SCOTT. See Chap. 27. JOHN BROWN. See Chap. 30.

DEMOCRATS AND KANSAS-NEBRASKA ACT. W. E. Connelley, *Kansas* (5 vols., 1928); W. E. Griffis, *Millard Fillmore* (1915); A. Johnson, *Stephen A. Douglas* (1908), still good; G. F. Milton, *Eve of Conflict* (1934), Douglas; R. F. Nichols, *Democratic Machine* (1923), 1850 to 1854; P. O. Ray, *Repeal of Missouri Compromise* (1909); H. M. Tinckom, *John White Geary* (1940), Kansas Governor. PIERCE. See Chap. 28.

REPUBLICANS. F. Bancroft, *Seward* (2 vols., 1900); R. J. Bartlett, *Frémont* (1930); A. W. Crandall, *Republican Party* (1930), 1854 to 1856; L. F. Crippen, *Cameron* (1942); G. H. Haynes, *Sumner* (1910); A. Nevins, *Frémont* (1939); G. G. van Deusen, *Weed* (1947).

CHAPTER 30. **APPROACHING DISSOLUTION**

GENERAL. P. G. Auchampaugh, *James Buchanan* (1926), defense; W. N. Brigance, *Jeremiah Sullivan Black* (1934), Buchanan administration; F. E. Chad-

wick, *Causes of Civil War* (1906), 1859 to 1861; V. C. Hopkins, *Dred Scott's Case* (1951); A. Nevins, *Emergence of Lincoln* (2 vols., 1950), excellent on

1857 to 1859; R. F. Nichols, *Disruption of American Democracy* (1948), good on Buchanan administration; P. L. Rainwater, *Mississippi* (1938), 1856 to 1861. See also Chap. 29. TANEY. See Chap. 23.

JOHN BROWN. W. E. B. du Bois, *John Brown* (1909), defense; J. C. Malin, *John Brown and Legend of Fifty-six* (1942), very scholarly; O. G. Villard, *John Brown* (1910), defense; R. P. Warren, *John Brown* (1929); H. P. Wilson, *John Brown* (1913), hostile.

LINCOLN. P. A. Angle (ed.), *Lincoln Reader* (1947), synthetic biography; W. E. Baringer, *Lincoln's Rise*

to Power (1937), *Lincoln as President Elect* (1945); R. P. Basler (ed.), *Collected Works* (9 vols., 1953); A. J. Beveridge, *Abraham Lincoln* (2 vols., 1928), good; Lord Charnwood, *Abraham Lincoln* (1916), delightful; H. H. Horner, *Lincoln and Greeley* (1953); R. H. Luthin, *First Lincoln Campaign* (1944); J. G. Randall, *Lincoln* (4 vols., 1945–1952), definitive; R. P. Randall, *Mary Lincoln* (1953); C. Sandburg, *Abraham Lincoln* (6 vols., 1926–1939), fictionalized; N. W. Stephenson, *Lincoln* (1922), *Abraham Lincoln* (1918).

CHAPTER 31. **THE UNION CRACKS**

GENERAL. H. J. Carman and R. H. Luthin, *Lincoln and the Patronage* (1943); O. Crenshaw, *Slave States in Presidential Election of 1860* (1945); D. L. Dumond, *Secession Movement* (1931), 1860 to 1861; C. Eaton, *Southern Confederacy* (1954), excellent; C. R. Fish, *American Civil War* (1937), reads well; E. D. Fite, *Presidential Campaign of 1860* (1911); A. B. Hart, *Salmon Portland Chase* (1899); R. S. Henry, *Story of Confederacy* (1931); D. M. Potter, *Lincoln and Secession Crisis* (1942); I. Ross, *Proud Kate* (1953), Kate Chase; M. Scrugham, *Peaceable Americans of 1860–1861* (1921); K. M. Stampp, *And the War Came* (1950), good from election of Lincoln to Sumter; J. S. Tilley, *Lincoln Takes Command* (1941),

Sumter—blames Lincoln. See also Chap. 29; Chadwick, Chap. 30.

SOUTHERN POSITION. W. M. Caskey, *Secession and Reconstruction in Louisiana* (1938); C. C. Cauthen, *South Carolina Goes to War* (1950); C. P. Denman, *Secession Movement in Alabama* (1933); G. R. Gaeddert, *Birth of Kansas* (1940); J. W. Patton, *Unionism and Reconstruction in Tennessee* (1934); W. W. Ryle, *Missouri* (1931); H. F. Shanks, *Secession in Virginia* (1934); J. C. Sitterson, *Secession Movement in North Carolina* (1939). See also Chap. 29.

CHAPTER 32. **BLUE VERSUS GRAY**

GENERAL. H. S. Commager (ed.), *The Blue and Gray* (2 vols., 1950), original accounts; F. R. Dulles, *Red Cross* (1950); O. Eisenschiml and R. Newman, *American Iliad* (1947), mostly in words of contemporaries; C. R. Fish, *Civil War* (1937); J. D. Horan, *Confederate Agent* (1954); R. S. Henry, *Story of Confederacy* (1931); R. Meredith, *Mr. Lincoln's Camera Man* (1946), pictures; G. F. Milton, *Conflict* (1941); B. Quarles, *Negro in Civil War* (1953); J. G. Randall, *Civil War and Reconstruction* (1937); J. C. Ropes and W. R. Livermore, *Story of Civil War* (4 vols., 1894–1913), good on military; G. E. Turner, *Victory Rode the Rails* (1953), part of railroads; B. I. Wiley, *Life of Billy Yank* (1952), *Life of Johnny Reb* (1943). See also Chaps. 4, 31.

CAMPAIGNS. A. H. Bill, *Beleaguered City* (1946), exciting on Richmond; A. H. Burne, *Lee, Grant, and Sherman* (1939), campaign of 1864–1865; B. Catton, *Glory Road* (1952), Fredericksburg to Gettysburg, *Stillness at Appomattox* (1953); B. Deaderick, *Strat-*

egy in the Civil War (1946); T. R. Hay, *Hood's Tennessee Campaign* (1929); S. Horn, *Army of Tennessee* (1952); A. Hunt, *Army of the Pacific* (1951); A. Kearsey, *Shenandoah Valley Campaign* (1930), 1861–1862; E. S. Miers and R. A. Brown (eds.), *Gettysburg* (1948), in words of participants.

BORDER AND SOUTHERN STATES. C. H. Ambler, *West Virginia* (1940); C. E. Cauthen, *South Carolina Goes to War* (1950); E. M. Coulter, *Civil War and Reconstruction in Kentucky* (1926); W. W. Davis, *Civil War and Reconstruction in Florida* (1913); W. L. Fleming, *Civil War and Reconstruction in Alabama* (1905); J. C. McGregor, *Disruption of Virginia* (1922); E. C. Smith, *Borderland in Civil War* (1927); D. Y. Thomas, *Arkansas in War and Reconstruction* (1926). See also state histories, Chaps. 37, 38.

LEADERS. G. Bradford, *Confederate Portraits* (1914), *Union Portraits* (1916); D. Wecter, *Hero in Amer-*

ica (1941). BANKS. F. H. Harrington, *Fighting Politician* (1948). BEAUREGARD. H. Basso, *Beauregard* (1933). BRAGG. D. C. Seitz, *Braxton Bragg* (1924). FORREST. R. S. Henry, *"First with the Most" Forrest* (1944). GORGAS. F. E. Vandiver, *Ploughshares into Swords* (1952). GRANT. W. E. Brooks, *Grant of Appomattox* (1942); A. L. Conger, *Rise of U. S. Grant* (1931); J. F. C. Fuller, *Generalship of Grant* (1929), *Grant and Lee* (1933); L. Lloyd, *Captain Sam Grant* (1950), excellent on early life; C. E. Macartney, *Grant and His Generals* (1953); H. Todd, *A Man Named Grant* (1940); W. E. Woodward, *Meet General Grant* (1928). HAMPTON. M. W. Wellman, *Giant in Gray* (1949). HOOD. J. P. Dyer, *The Gallant Hood* (1950); R. O'Connor, *Hood* (1949). HOOKER. J. P. Dyer, *"Fighting" Joe Hooker* (1941); W. H. Herbert, *Fighting Joe Hooker* (1944). JACKSON. G. F. R. Henderson, *Stonewall Jackson* (1936). LEE.

D. S. Freeman, *R. E. Lee* (4 vols., 1934–1935), definitive, *Lee's Lieutenants* (3 vols., 1942–1944), *Lee's Dispatches* (1915); B. J. Hendrick, *Lees of Virginia* (1935); F. B. Maurice, *Robert E. Lee* (1925); C. C. Rister, *Lee in Texas* (1946); R. W. Winston, *Robert E. Lee* (1934). LONGSTREET. H. J. Eckenrode and B. Conrad, *James Longstreet* (1936); D. B. Sanger and T. R. Hay, *James Longstreet* (1952). MCCLELLAN. H. J. Eckenrode and B. Conrad, *George B. McClellan* (1941); W. S. Myers, *Study in Personality* (1934). MEADE. G. G. Meade, *General George Gordon Meade* (2 vols., 1913), by son. MORGAN. C. F. Holland, *Morgan and His Raiders* (1942). PEMBERTON. J. C. Pemberton, *Pemberton* (1942). SHERIDAN. R. O. O'Connor, *Sheridan* (1953). SHERMAN. L. Lewis, *Sherman* (1932), reads well. STUART. J. W. Thomason, Jr., *Jeb Stuart* (1930). THOMAS. F. Cleaves, *Rock of Chickamauga* (1948).

CHAPTER 33. ON THE SEAS AND ACROSS THE SEAS

GENERAL. See Chaps. 31, 32.

NAVAL. J. P. Baxter III, *Introduction of Ironclad Warship* (1933); H. W. Briggs, *Doctrine of Continuous Voyage* (1926), monograph; J. D. Hill, *Sea Dogs of the Sixties* (1935), picturesque; S. F. Horn, *Gallant Rebel* (1947), blockade running; C. L. Lewis, *David Glasgow Farragut* (2 vols., 1941–1943); R. S. McCordock, *Yankee Cheese Box* (1938); W. A. Roberts, *Semmes of the* Alabama (1938); W. M. Robinson, Jr., *Confederate Privateers* (1928), good; H. A. Trexler, *Confederate Ironclad "Virginia"* (1938); G. Welles, *Diary* (3 vols., 1911), Secretary of Navy; R. S. West, Jr., *Gideon Welles* (1943), Second Ad-

miral (1937), Porter. See also naval histories, Chap. 4.

DIPLOMATIC. C. F. Adams, Jr., *Charles Francis Adams* (1900); E. D. Adams, *Great Britain and American Civil War* (2 vols., 1925); J. M. Callahan, *Diplomatic History of Southern Confederacy* (1901), factual; M. Clapp, *Forgotten First Citizen* (1947), Bigelow's French mission; D. Jordan and E. J. Pratt, *Europe and American Civil War* (1931); J. Monaghan, *Diplomat in Carpet Slippers* (1945), Lincoln; F. L. Owsley, *King Cotton Diplomacy* (1931); L. M. Sears, *John Slidell* (1925); W. R. West, *Contemporary French Opinion* (1924). See also general histories, Chap. 4.

CHAPTER 34. BEHIND THE GRAY LINES

LIFE IN CONFEDERACY. R. C. Black, *Railroads of Confederacy* (1952), excellent; T. C. Bryan, *Confederate Georgia* (1953), scholarly; L. Buchanan, *Pictorial History* (1951); R. S. Henry, *Story of Confederacy* (1931); E. Lonn, *Foreigners in Confederacy* (1940), *Salt in Confederacy* (1933), scholarly; M. E. Massey, *Ersatz in Confederacy* (1952), detailed; A. B. Moore, *Conscription in Confederacy* (1924); F. L. Owsley, *State Rights in Confederacy* (1925); C. W. Ramsdell, *Behind the Lines* (1944); W. M. Robinson, *Justice in Grey* (1941); F. B. Simkins and J. W. Patton, *Women in Confederacy* (1936); N. W. Stephenson, *Day of the Confederacy* (1919); G. L. Tatum, *Disloyalty in Confederacy* (1934); C. H. Wesley, *Collapse of Confederacy* (1937), morale problem; B. I.

Wiley, *Plain People of Confederacy* (1943), *Southern Negroes, 1861–1865* (1938). See also Chap. 31.

SOUTHERN LEADERS. B. J. Hendrick, *Statesmen of Lost Cause* (1939); R. W. Patrick, *Jefferson Davis and Cabinet* (1944). BENJAMIN. R. D. Meade, *Judah P. Benjamin* (1943). BROWN. L. B. Hill, *Joseph E. Brown* (1939), governor of Georgia. DAVIS. O. E. Cutting, *Jefferson Davis* (1930); C. Dowdey, *Experiment in Rebellion* (1946), delightful on Davis in Richmond; R. M. McElroy, *Jefferson Davis* (2 vols., 1937); A. Tate, *Jefferson Davis* (1929); R. W. Winston, *High Stakes and Hair Trigger* (1930). JOHNSON. P. S. Flippin, *Herschel V. Johnson* (1931). STEPHENS. R. van Abele, *Alexander H. Stephens* (1946), excellent.

CHAPTER 35. **BEHIND THE BLUE LINES**

LIFE IN NORTH. G. W. Adams, *Doctors in Blue* (1952), detailed; C. F. Dunham, *Attitude of Northern Clergy* (1942); W. Gray, *Hidden Civil War* (1942), Copperheads; W. B. Hesseltine, *Civil War Prisons* (1930); S. R. Kamm, *Thomas A. Scott* (1940); E. C. Kirkland, *Peacemakers of 1864* (1927), excellent; H. M. Larson, *Jay Cooke* (1936); J. F. Leach, *Conscription* (1952); M. Leech, *Reveille in Washington* (1941), readable; E. Lonn, *Desertion during Civil War* (1928); A. H. Meneely, *War Department, 1861* (1928); E. P. Oberholtzer, *Jay Cooke* (2 vols., 1907); R. S. Rankin, *When Civil Law Fails* (1939); F. A. Shannon, *Organization and Administration Union Army* (2 vols., 1928); L. Smith, *American Democracy and Military Power* (1951), civil control of the military; F. P. Summers, *Baltimore and Ohio in Civil War* (1939); T. Weber, *Northern Railroads in Civil War* (1952); N. Weyl, *Treason* (1950), includes Copperheads; B. C. Williams, *Clara Barton* (1941); E. N. Wright, *Conscientious Objectors in Civil War* (1931).

LEADERS. CAMERON. See Chap. 29. CHASE. See Chap. 31. D. V. Smith, *Chase and Civil War Politics* (1931). LINCOLN. See Chap. 30. B. J. Hendrick, *Lincoln's War Cabinet* (1946); W. B. Hesseltine, *Lincoln and War Governors* (1948); G. F. Milton, *Lincoln and Fifth Column* (1942), Copperheads; J. G. Randall, *Constitutional Problems under Lincoln* (1951); T. H. Williams, *Lincoln and His Generals* (1952), very good, *Lincoln and the Radicals* (1931). STANTON. G. C. Gorham, *Edwin M. Stanton* (2 vols., 1899). SUMNER, WEED. See Chap. 29. WELLES. See Chap. 33.

CHAPTER 36. **RECONSTRUCTION DIPLOMACY**

GENERAL. A. Nevins, *Emergence of Modern America* (1927), *Hamilton Fish* (1936); G. Smith, *Treaty of Washington* (1941). See also diplomatic histories under Chap. 4 (Foreign).

MEXICO AND CARIBBEAN. T. A. Bailey, *America Faces Russia* (1950); J. M. Callahan, *Mexican Relations* (1932); B. Harding, *Phantom Crown* (1934), Maximilian; M. M. Hyde, *Mexican Empire* (1946); J. F. Rippy, *United States and Mexico* (1931); R. Roeder, *Juarez and His Mexico* (2 vols., 1947); C. C. Tansill,

United States and Santo Domingo, 1798–1873 (1938); S. Welles, *Naboth's Vineyard* (1928), San Domingo from 1844.

PACIFIC. J. M. Callahan, *Alaska Purchase* (1908); H. W. Clark, *Alaska* (1930); F. R. Dulles, *America in Pacific* (1932); V. J. Farrar, *Annexation of Russian America* (1937); J. P. Nichols, *Alaska* (1924); S. R. Tompkins, *Alaska* (1945); P. A. Williams, *American Russian Relations* (1952).

CHAPTERS 37 AND 38. **EXECUTIVE RECONSTRUCTION AND THE RADICAL JUGGERNAUT**

GENERAL. C. G. Bowers, *Tragic Era* (1929), readable; P. H. Buck, *Road to Reunion* (1937), excellent; H. H. Donald, *Negro Freedman* (1952), critical of Negro in early years after war; W. E. B. du Bois, *Black Reconstruction* (1935), Negro view; W. L. Fleming, *Sequel to Appomattox* (1919); R. S. Henry, *Story of Reconstruction* (1938), detailed; G. F. Milton, *Age of Hate* (1930); A. Nevins, *Emergence of Modern America* (1927); J. G. Randall, *Civil War and Reconstruction* (1937); G. T. Stephenson, *Race Distinctions* (1910), includes Black Codes.

SOUTH. T. B. Alexander, *Reconstruction in Tennessee* (1950); W. M. Caskey, *Secession and Restoration in*

Louisiana (1938); D. T. Clark, *Kentucky* (1937); E. M. Coulter, *Civil War and Reconstruction in Kentucky* (1926), *South during Reconstruction* (1947); S. L. Davis, *Ku Klux Klan* (1924); J. W. du Bose, *Alabama's Tragic Decade* (1940); C. R. Fish, *Restoration of Southern Railroads* (1919); J. G. Fletcher, *Arkansas* (1947); J. W. Garner, *Reconstruction in Mississippi* (1901); J. G. de R. Hamilton, *Reconstruction in North Carolina* (1914); K. T. Hanna, *Florida* (1949); W. B. Hesseltine, *Confederate Leaders* (1950), careers after war; S. F. Horn, *Invisible Empire* (1939), Ku Klux Klan; H. M. Jarrell, *Wade Hampton and the Negro* (1950), South Carolina; G. W. McGinty, *Louisiana* (1949), *Louisi-*

ana Redeemed (1941); J. C. McGregor, *Disruption of Virginia* (1922); J. W. Patton, *Unionism and Reconstruction in Tennessee* (1934); C. W. Ramsdell, *Reconstruction in Texas* (1910); R. N. Richardson, *Texas* (1943); F. B. Simkins and R. H. Woody, *South Carolina during Reconstruction* (1932); R. W. Steen, *Texas Story* (1948); H. L. Swint, *Northern Teacher in South* (1941); A. A. Taylor, *Negro in Reconstruction in Virginia* (1926), *Negro in South Carolina during Reconstruction* (1924), *Negro in Tennessee* (1941); D. Y. Thomas, *Arkansas in War and Reconstruction* (1926); C. M. Thompson, *Reconstruction in Georgia* (1915); M. W. Wellman, *Giant in Gray* (1949), Wade Hampton; V. L. Wharton, *Negro in Mississippi* (1947); O. P. White, *Texas* (1945). See also Negro histories under Chap. 7 (Labor, Negro).

PRESIDENT AND CONGRESS. H. K. Beale, *Critical Year*

(1930), excellent on year 1866; C. H. Coleman, *Election of 1866* (1933), *Election of 1868* (1933); M. Josephson, *The Politicos* (1938); B. B. Kendrick, *Journal of Joint Committee of Fifteen* (1914); J. M. Mathews, *History of Fifteenth Amendment* (1909); P. S. Peirce, *Freedmen's Bureau* (1904); J. Ten Broek, *Antislavery Origins of Fourteenth Amendment* (1951).

PERSONALITIES. BLACK. W. N. Brigance, *Jeremiah Sullivan Black* (1939), advised Johnson. CONKLING. D. B. Chidsey, *Gentleman from New York* (1935). GRANT. See Chap. 32. JOHNSON. L. P. Stryker, *Andrew Johnson* (1929); R. W. Winston, *Andrew Johnson* (1928). SEYMOUR. R. S. Mitchell, *Horatio Seymour* (1938). STEVENS. R. N. Current, *Old Thad Stevens* (1942); A. B. Miller, *Thaddeus Stevens* (1939); T. F. Woodley, *Thaddeus Stevens* (1934). SUMNER, WEED. See Chap. 29.

CHAPTER 39. THE AGE OF GRANT

GENERAL. D. T. Lynch, *Wild Seventies* (1941); D. C. Seitz, *Dreadful Decade* (1926). See also Bowers, Nevins, Chaps. 37 and 38.

GRANT AND SCANDALS. R. H. Fuller, *Jubilee Jim* (1928), Fisk (for Vanderbilt and Drew, see Chap. 17); M. Gresham, *Walter Quintin Gresham* (2 vols., 1919); W. B. Hesseltine, *Ulysses S. Grant* (1931), politics after war (for biographies, see Chap. 32); F. C. Hicks (ed.), *High Finance of Sixties* (1929); D. T. Lynch, *"Boss" Tweed* (1927); D. S. Muzzey, *James G. Blaine* (1934); S. A. Pleasants, *Fernando Wood* (1948), Tammany; C. E. Russell, *Blaine of Maine* (1931); W. H. Smith, *Schuyler Colfax* (1952); C. C. Tansill, *Thomas Francis Bayard* (1946); R. I. Warshow, *Jay Gould* (1928); M. R. Werner, *Tammany Hall* (1928), full account.

ELECTIONS 1872 AND 1876. H. J. Eckenrode, *Rutherford B. Hayes* (1930); A. C. Flick, *Samuel Jones*

Tilden (1939); W. H. Hale, *Horace Greeley* (1950); P. L. Haworth, *Hayes-Tilden Election* (1906); E. D. Ross, *Liberal Republican Movement* (1919); H. L. Stoddard, *Horace Greeley* (1946); G. G. van Deusen, *Horace Greeley* (1953); C. R. Williams, *Rutherford Burchard Hayes* (2 vols., 1914); C. V. Woodward, *Reunion and Reaction* (1951), important on election of 1876.

MONEY AND GREENBACKS. D. C. Barrett, *Greenbacks and Resumption* (1931); S. J. Buck, *Agrarian Crusade* (1921); M. R. Dearing, *Veterans in Politics* (1952), GAR; D. R. Dewey, *Financial History* (1936); N. Fine, *Labor and Farmer Parties* (1928); E. R. McCartney, *Crisis of 1873* (1935); W. C. Mitchell, *History of Greenbacks* (1903); J. W. Oliver, *Civil War Military Pensions* (1917); M. S. Wildman, *Money Inflation* (1905). See also general economic histories, Chap. 7; for Jay Cooke, see Chap. 35 (Life in North).

The Declaration of Independence

In Congress, July 4, 1776

**THE UNANIMOUS DECLARATION
OF THE THIRTEEN UNITED STATES
OF AMERICA**

When in the Course of human events, it becomes necessary for one people to dissolve the political bands which have connected them with another, and to assume among the Powers of the earth, the separate and equal station to which the Laws of Nature and of Nature's God entitle them, a decent respect to the opinions of mankind requires that they should declare the causes which impel them to the separation.

We hold these truths to be self-evident, that all men are created equal, that they are endowed by their Creator with certain unalienable Rights, that among these are Life, Liberty and the pursuit of Happiness. That to secure these rights, Governments are instituted among Men, deriving their just powers from the consent of the governed, That whenever any Form of Government becomes destructive of these ends, it is the Right of the People to alter or to abolish it, and to institute new Government, laying its foundation on such principles and organizing its powers in such form, as to them shall seem most likely to effect their Safety and Happiness. Prudence, indeed, will dictate that Governments long established should not be changed for light and transient causes; and accordingly all experience hath shown, that mankind are more disposed to suffer, while evils are sufferable, than to right themselves by abolishing the forms to which they are accustomed. But when a long train of abuses and usurpations, pursuing invariably the same Object evinces a design to reduce them under absolute Despotism, it is their right, it is their duty, to throw off such Government, and to provide new Guards for their future security.— Such has been the patient sufferance of these Colonies; and such is now the necessity which constrains them to alter their former Systems of Government. The history of the present King of Great Britain is a history of repeated injuries and usurpations, all having in direct object the establishment of an absolute Tyranny over these States. To prove this, let Facts be submitted to a candid world.

He has refused his Assent to Laws, the most wholesome and necessary for the public good.

He has forbidden his Governors to pass Laws of immediate and pressing importance, unless suspended in their operation till his Assent should be obtained; and when so suspended, he has utterly neglected to attend to them.

He has refused to pass other Laws for the accommodation of large districts of people, unless those people would relinquish the right of Representation in the Legislature, a right inestimable to them and formidable to tyrants only.

He has called together legislative bodies at places unusual, uncomfortable, and distant from the depository of their Public Records, for the sole purpose of fatiguing them into compliance with his measures.

He has dissolved Representative Houses repeatedly, for opposing with manly firmness his invasions on the rights of the people.

He has refused for a long time, after such dissolutions, to cause others to be elected; whereby the Legislative Powers, incapable of Annihilation, have returned to the People at large for their exercise; the State remaining in the mean time exposed to all the dangers of invasion from without, and convulsions within.

He has endeavoured to prevent the population of these States; for that purpose obstructing the Laws of Naturalization of Foreigners; refusing to pass others to encourage their migration hither, and raising the conditions of new Appropriations of Lands.

He has obstructed the Administration of Justice, by refusing his Assent to Laws for establishing Judiciary Powers.

He has made Judges dependent on his Will alone, for the tenure of their offices, and the amount and payment of their salaries.

He has erected a multitude of New Offices, and sent hither swarms of Officers to harass our People, and eat out their substance.

He has kept among us, in times of peace, Standing Armies without the Consent of our legislature.

He has affected to render the Military independent of and superior to the Civil Power.

He has combined with others to subject us to a jurisdiction foreign to our constitution, and unacknowledged by our laws giving his Assent to their acts of pretended legislation:

For quartering large bodies of armed troops among us:

For protecting them, by a mock Trial, from Punishment for any Murders which they should commit on the Inhabitants of these States:

For cutting off our Trade with all parts of the world:

For imposing taxes on us without our Consent:

For depriving us in many cases, of the benefits of Trial by jury:

For transporting us beyond Seas to be tried for pretended offences:

For abolishing the free System of English Laws in a neighboring Province, establishing therein an Arbitrary government, and enlarging its Boundaries so as to render it at once an example and fit instrument for introducing the same absolute rule into these Colonies:

For taking away our Charters, abolishing our most valuable Laws, and altering fundamentally the Forms of our Governments:

For suspending our own Legislature, and declaring themselves invested with Power to legislate for us in all cases whatsoever.

He has abdicated Government here, by declaring us out of his Protection and waging War against us.

He has plundered our seas, ravaged our Coasts, burnt our towns, and destroyed the lives of our people.

He is at this time transporting large armies of foreign mercenaries to compleat the works of death, desolation and tyranny, already begun with circumstances of Cruelty & perfidy scarcely paralleled in the most barbarous ages, and totally unworthy the Head of a civilized nation.

He has constrained our fellow Citizens taken Captive on the high Seas to bear Arms against their Country, to become the executioners of their friends and Brethren, or to fall themselves by their Hands.

He has excited domestic insurrections amongst us, and has endeavoured to bring on the inhabitants of our frontiers, the merciless Indian Savages, whose known rule of warfare, is an undistinguished destruction of all ages, sexes and conditions.

In every stage of these Oppressions We have Petitioned for Redress in the most humble terms: Our repeated Petitions have been answered only by repeated injury. A Prince, whose character is thus marked by every act which may define a Tyrant, is unfit to be the ruler of a free People.

Nor have We been wanting in attention to our British brethren. We have warned them from time to time of attempts by their legislature to extend an unwarrantable jurisdiction over us. We have reminded them of the circumstances of our emigration and settlement here. We have appealed to their native justice and magnanimity, and we have conjured them by the ties of our common kindred to disavow these usurpations, which would inevitably interrupt our connections and correspondence. They too have been deaf to the voice of justice and of consanguinity. We must, therefore, acquiesce in the necessity, which denounces our Separation, and hold them, as we hold the rest of mankind, Enemies in War, in Peace Friends.

We, therefore, the Representatives of the United States of America, in General Congress, Assembled, appealing to the Supreme Judge of the world for the rectitude of our intentions, do, in the Name, and by Authority of the good People of these Colonies, solemnly publish and declare, That these United Colonies are, and of Right ought to be Free and Independent States; that they are Absolved from all Allegiance to the British Crown, and that all political connection between them and the State of Great Britain, is and ought to be totally dissolved; and that as Free and Independent States, they have full Power to levy War, conclude Peace, contract Alliances, establish Commerce, and to do all other Acts and Things which Independent States may of right do. And for the support of this Declaration, with a firm reliance on the Protection of Divine Providence, we mutually pledge to each other our Lives, our Fortunes and our sacred Honor. JOHN HANCOCK [1]

[1] The remaining signatures are omitted.

Constitution of the United States of America

We, the people of the United States, in order to form a more perfect union, establish justice, insure domestic tranquility, provide for the common defence, promote the general welfare, and secure the blessings of liberty to ourselves and our posterity, do ordain and establish this Constitution for the United States of America.

ARTICLE I

Section 1. All legislative powers herein granted shall be vested in a Congress of the United States, which shall consist of a Senate and House of Representatives.

Section 2. (1) The House of Representatives shall be composed of members chosen every second year by the people of the several States, and the electors in each State shall have the qualifications requisite for electors of the most numerous branch of the State legislature.

(2) No person shall be a Representative who shall not have attained to the age of twenty-five years, and been seven years a citizen of the United States, and who shall not, when elected, be an inhabitant of that State in which he shall be chosen.

(3) Representatives and direct taxes shall be apportioned among the several States which may be included within this Union, according to their respective numbers, [which shall be determined

by adding to the whole number of free persons,] [1] including those bound to service for a term of years, and excluding Indians not taxed, [three fifths for all other persons].[2] The actual enumeration shall be made within three years after the first meeting of the Congress of the United States, and within every subsequent term of ten years, in such manner as they shall by law direct. The number of Representatives shall not exceed one for every thirty thousand, but each State shall have at least one Representative; [and until such enumeration shall be made, the State of New Hampshire shall be entitled to choose three, Massachusetts eight, Rhode Island and Providence Plantations one, Connecticut five, New York six, New Jersey four, Pennsylvania eight, Delaware one, Maryland six, Virginia ten, North Carolina five, South Carolina five, and Georgia three.] [3]

(4) When vacancies happen in the representation from any State, the executive authority thereof shall issue writs of election to fill such vacancies.

(5) The House of Representatives shall choose their Speaker and other officers; and shall have the sole power of impeachment.

Section 3. [(1) The Senate of the United States shall be composed of two Senators from each State, chosen by the legislature thereof, for six years; and each Senator shall have one vote.] [4]

---

[1] Modified by Fourteenth Amendment.
[2] Superseded by Fourteenth Amendment.
[3] Temporary provision.
[4] Superseded by Seventeenth Amendment.

(2) Immediately after they shall be assembled in consequence of the first election, they shall be divided as equally as may be into three classes. The seats of the Senators of the first class shall be vacated at the expiration of the second year, of the second class at the expiration of the fourth year, and of the third class at the expiration of the sixth year, so that one third may be chosen every second year; [and if vacancies happen by resignation, or otherwise, during the recess of the legislature of any State, the executive thereof may make temporary appointments until the next meeting of the legislature, which shall then fill such vacancies.] [1]

(3) No person shall be a Senator who shall not have attained to the age of thirty years, and been nine years a citizen of the United States, and who shall not, when elected, be an inhabitant of that State for which he shall be chosen.

(4) The Vice President of the United States shall be president of the Senate, but shall have no vote, unless they be equally divided.

(5) The Senate shall choose their other officers, and also a president pro tempore, in the absence of the Vice President, or when he shall exercise the office of President of the United States.

(6) The Senate shall have the sole power to try all impeachments. When sitting for that purpose, they shall be on oath or affirmation. When the President of the United States is tried, the Chief Justice shall preside: and no person shall be convicted without the concurrence of two thirds of the members present.

(7) Judgment in cases of impeachment shall not extend further than to removal from office, and disqualification to hold and enjoy any office of honor, trust, or profit under the United States: but the party convicted shall nevertheless be liable and subject to indictment, trial, judgment, and punishment, according to law.

Section 4. (1) The times, places, and manner of holding elections for Senators and Representatives shall be prescribed in each State by the legislature thereof; but the Congress may at any time by law make or alter such regulations, except as to the places of choosing Senators.

[(2) The Congress shall assemble at least once in every year, and such meeting shall be on the first Monday in December, unless they shall by law appoint a different day.] [2]

[1] Modified by Seventeenth Amendment.
[2] Superseded by Twentieth Amendment.

Section 5. (1) Each House shall be the judge of the elections, returns, and qualifications of its own members, and a majority of each shall constitute a quorum to do business; but a smaller number may adjourn from day to day, and may be authorized to compel the attendance of absent members, in such manner, and under such penalties, as each House may provide.

(2) Each House may determine the rules of its proceedings, punish its members for disorderly behavior, and, with the concurrence of two thirds, expel a member.

(3) Each House shall keep a journal of its proceedings, and from time to time publish the same, excepting such parts as may in their judgment require secrecy; and the yeas and nays of the members of either House on any question shall, at the desire of one fifth of those present, be entered on the journal.

(4) Neither House, during the session of Congress, shall, without the consent of the other, adjourn for more than three days, nor to any other place than that in which the two Houses shall be sitting.

Section 6. (1) The Senators and Representatives shall receive a compensation for their services, to be ascertained by law, and paid out of the Treasury of the United States. They shall in all cases, except treason, felony, and breach of the peace, be privileged from arrest during their attendance at the session of their respective Houses, and in going to and returning from the same; and for any speech or debate in either House, they shall not be questioned in any other place.

(2) No Senator or Representative shall, during the time for which he was elected, be appointed to any civil office under the authority of the United States, which shall have been created, or the emoluments whereof shall have been increased, during such time; and no person holding any office under the United States shall be a member of either House during his continuance in office.

Section 7. (1) All bills for raising revenue shall originate in the House of Representatives; but the Senate may propose or concur with amendments as on other bills.

(2) Every bill which shall have passed the House of Representatives and the Senate, shall, before it become a law, be presented to the President of the United States; if he approve he shall

sign it, but if not he shall return it, with his objections, to that House in which it shall have originated, who shall enter the objections at large on their journal, and proceed to reconsider it. If after such reconsideration two thirds of that House shall agree to pass the bill, it shall be sent, together with the objections, to the other House, by which it shall likewise be reconsidered, and if approved by two thirds of that House, it shall become a law. But in all such cases the votes of both Houses shall be determined by yeas and nays, and the names of the persons voting for and against the bill shall be entered on the journal of each House respectively. If any bill shall not be returned by the President within ten days (Sundays excepted) after it shall have been presented to him, the same shall be a law, in like manner as if he had signed it, unless the Congress by their adjournment prevent its return, in which case it shall not be a law.

(3) Every order, resolution, or vote to which the concurrence of the Senate and House of Representatives may be necessary (except on a question of adjournment) shall be presented to the President of the United States; and before the same shall take effect, shall be approved by him, or being disapproved by him, shall be repassed by two thirds of the Senate and House of Representatives, according to the rules and limitations prescribed in the case of a bill.

Section 8. (1) The Congress shall have the power to lay and collect taxes, duties, imposts, and excises, to pay the debts and provide for the common defense and general welfare of the United States; but all duties, imposts, and excises shall be uniform throughout the United States;

(2) To borrow money on the credit of the United States;

(3) To regulate commerce with foreign nations, and among the several States, and with the Indian tribes;

(4) To establish a uniform rule of naturalization, and uniform laws on the subject of bankruptcies throughout the United States;

(5) To coin money, regulate the value thereof, and of foreign coin, and fix the standard of weights and measures;

(6) To provide for the punishment of counterfeiting the securities and current coin of the United States;

(7) To establish post offices and post roads;

(8) To promote the progress of science and useful arts, by securing for limited times to authors and inventors the exclusive right to their respective writings and discoveries;

(9) To constitute tribunals inferior to the Supreme Court;

(10) To define and punish piracies and felonies committed on the high seas, and offenses against the law of nations;

(11) To declare war, grant letters of marque and reprisal, and make rules concerning captures on land and water;

(12) To raise and support armies, but no appropriation of money to that use shall be for a longer term than two years;

(13) To provide and maintain a navy;

(14) To make rules for the government and regulation of the land and naval forces;

(15) To provide for calling forth the militia to execute the laws of the Union, suppress insurrections, and repel invasions;

(16) To provide for organizing, arming, and disciplining the militia, and for governing such part of them as may be employed in the service of the United States, reserving to the States respectively the appointment of the officers, and the authority of training the militia according to the discipline prescribed by Congress;

(17) To exercise exclusive legislation in all cases whatsoever, over such district (not exceeding ten miles square) as may, by cession of particular States, and the acceptance of Congress, become the seat of the government of the United States, and to exercise like authority over all places purchased by the consent of the legislature of the State in which the same shall be, for the erection of forts, magazines, arsenals, dockyards, and other needful buildings; and

(18) To make all laws which shall be necessary and proper for carrying into execution the foregoing powers, and all other powers vested by this Constitution in the government of the United States, or in any department or officer thereof.

Section 9. [(1) The migration or importation of such persons as any of the States now existing shall think proper to admit, shall not be prohibited by the Congress prior to the year one thousand eight hundred and eight, but a tax or duty may be imposed on such importation, not exceeding ten dollars for each person.] [1]

1 Temporary provision.

(2) The privilege of the writ of habeas corpus shall not be suspended, unless when in cases of rebellion or invasion the public safety may require it.

(3) No bill of attainder or ex post facto law shall be passed.

[(4) No capitation, or other direct, tax shall be laid, unless in proportion to the census or enumeration hereinbefore directed to be taken.] [1]

(5) No tax or duty shall be laid on articles exported from any State.

(6) No preference shall be given by any regulation of commerce or revenue to the ports of one State over those of another: nor shall vessels bound to, or from, one State, be obliged to enter, clear, or pay duties in another.

(7) No money shall be drawn from the Treasury, but in consequence of appropriations made by law; and a regular statement and account of the receipts and expenditures of all public money shall be published from time to time.

(8) No title of nobility shall be granted by the United States: and no person holding any office of profit or trust under them, shall, without the consent of the Congress, accept of any present, emolument, office, or title, of any kind whatever, from any king, prince, or foreign State.

Section 10. (1) No State shall enter into any treaty, alliance, or confederation; grant letters of marque and reprisal; coin money; emit bills of credit; make anything but gold and silver coin a tender in payment of debts; pass any bill of attainder, ex post facto law, or law impairing the obligation of contracts, or grant any title of nobility.

(2) No State shall, without the consent of the Congress, lay any imposts or duties on imports or exports, except what may be absolutely necessary for executing its inspection laws: and the net produce of all duties and imposts, laid by any State on imports or exports, shall be for the use of the treasury of the United States; and all such laws shall be subject to the revision and control of the Congress.

(3) No State shall, without the consent of Congress, lay any duty of tonnage, keep troops, or ships of war in time of peace, enter into any agreement or compact with another State, or with a foreign power, or engage in war, unless actually invaded, or in such imminent danger as will not admit of delay.

[1] Modified by Sixteenth Amendment.

ARTICLE II

Section 1. (1) The executive power shall be vested in a President of the United States of America. He shall hold his office during the term of four years, and, together with the Vice President, chosen for the same term, be elected, as follows:

(2) Each State shall appoint, in such manner as the legislature thereof may direct, a number of electors, equal to the whole number of Senators and Representatives to which the State may be entitled in the Congress: but no Senator or Representative, or person holding an office of trust or profit under the United States, shall be appointed an elector.

[The electors shall meet in their respective States, and vote by ballot for two persons, of whom one at least shall not be an inhabitant of the same State with themselves. And they shall make a list of all the persons voted for, and of the number of votes for each; which list they shall sign and certify, and transmit sealed to the seat of the government of the United States, directed to the president of the Senate. The president of the Senate shall, in the presence of the Senate and House of Representatives, open all the certificates, and the votes shall then be counted. The person having the greatest number of votes shall be the President, if such number be a majority of the whole number of electors appointed; and if there be more than one who have such majority, and have an equal number of votes, then the House of Representatives shall immediately choose by ballot one of them for President; and if no person have a majority, then from the five highest on the list the said House shall in like manner choose the President. But in choosing the President, the votes shall be taken by States, the representation from each State having one vote; a quorum for this purpose shall consist of a member or members from two thirds of the States, and a majority of all the States shall be necessary to a choice. In every case, after the choice of the President, the person having the greatest number of votes of the electors shall be the Vice President. But if there should remain two or more who have equal votes, the Senate shall choose from them by ballot the Vice President.] [2]

[2] This paragraph superseded by Twelfth Amendment, which, in turn, is modified by the Twentieth Amendment.

(3) The Congress may determine the time of choosing the electors, and the day on which they shall give their votes; which day shall be the same throughout the United States.

(4) No person except a natural-born citizen, or a citizen of the United States, at the time of the adoption of this Constitution, shall be eligible to the office of President; neither shall any person be eligible to that office who shall not have attained to the age of thirty-five years, and been fourteen years a resident within the United States.

(5) In case of the removal of the President from office, or of his death, resignation, or inability to discharge the powers and duties of the said office, the same shall devolve on the Vice President, and the Congress may by law provide for the case of removal, death, resignation, or inability, both of the President and Vice President, declaring what officer shall then act as President, and such officer shall act accordingly, until the disability be removed, or a President shall be elected.

(6) The President shall, at stated times, receive for his services a compensation, which shall neither be increased nor diminished during the period for which he shall have been elected, and he shall not receive within that period any other emolument from the United States, or any of them.

(7) Before he enter on the execution of his office, he shall take the following oath or affirmation: "I do solemnly swear (or affirm) that I will faithfully execute the office of President of the United States, and will, to the best of my ability, preserve, protect, and defend the Constitution of the United States."

Section 2. (1) The President shall be commander in chief of the army and navy of the United States, and of the militia of the several States, when called into the actual service of the United States; he may require the opinion, in writing, of the principal officer in each of the executive departments, upon any subject relating to the duties of their respective offices, and he shall have power to grant reprieves and pardons for offenses against the United States, except in cases of impeachment.

(2) He shall have power, by and with the advice and consent of the Senate, to make treaties, provided two thirds of the Senators present concur; and he shall nominate, and by and with the advice and consent of the Senate, shall appoint ambassadors, other public ministers and consuls, judges of the Supreme Court, and all other officers of the United States, whose appointments are not herein otherwise provided for, and which shall be established by law: but the Congress may by law vest the appointment of such inferior officers, as they think proper, in the President alone, in the courts of law, or in the heads of departments.

(3) The President shall have power to fill up all vacancies that may happen during the recess of the Senate, by granting commissions which shall expire at the end of their next session.

Section 3. He shall from time to time give to the Congress information of the state of the Union, and recommend to their consideration such measures as he shall judge necessary and expedient; he may, on extraordinary occasions, convene both Houses, or either of them, and in case of disagreement between them, with respect to the time of adjournment, he may adjourn them to such time as he shall think proper; he shall receive ambassadors and other public ministers; he shall take care that the laws be faithfully executed, and shall commission all the officers of the United States.

Section 4. The President, Vice President, and all civil officers of the United States, shall be removed from office on impeachment for, and conviction of, treason, bribery, or other high crimes and misdemeanors.

ARTICLE III

Section 1. The judicial power of the United States shall be vested in one Supreme Court, and in such inferior courts as the Congress may from time to time ordain and establish. The judges, both of the Supreme and inferior courts, shall hold their offices during good behavior, and shall, at stated times, receive for their services a compensation, which shall not be diminished during their continuance in office.

Section 2. (1) The judicial power shall extend to all cases, in law and equity, arising under this Constitution, the laws of the United States, and treaties made, or which shall be made, under their authority;—to all cases affecting ambassadors, other public ministers, and consuls;—to all cases of admiralty and maritime jurisdiction;—to controversies to which the United States shall be a party;—to controversies between two or more States; [—between a State and citizens of another State;] [1]—between citizens of different States;—between citizens of the same State claiming lands under grants of different States, and between a State, or the citizens thereof, and foreign States, citizens, or subjects.

(2) In all cases affecting ambassadors, other public ministers, and consuls, and those in which a State shall be party, the Supreme Court shall have original jurisdiction. In all the other cases before mentioned, the Supreme Court shall have appellate jurisdiction, both as to law and fact, with such exceptions, and under such regulations, as the Congress shall make.

(3) The trial of all crimes, except in cases of impeachment, shall be by jury; and such trial shall be held in the State where the said crimes shall have been committed; but when not committed within any State, the trial shall be at such place or places as the Congress may by law have directed.

Section 3. (1) Treason against the United States shall consist only in levying war against them, or in adhering to their enemies, giving them aid and comfort. No person shall be convicted of treason unless on the testimony of two witnesses to the same overt act, or on confession in open court.

(2) The Congress shall have power to declare the punishment of treason, but no attainder of treason shall work corruption of blood, or forfeiture except during the life of the person attainted.

ARTICLE IV

Section 1. Full faith and credit shall be given in each State to the public acts, records, and judicial proceedings of every other State. And the Congress may by general laws prescribe the manner in which such acts, records, and proceedings shall be proved, and the effect thereof.

Section 2. (1) The citizens of each State shall be entitled to all privileges and immunities of citizens in the several States.

(2) A person charged in any State with treason, felony, or other crime, who shall flee from justice, and be found in another State, shall, on demand of the executive authority of the State from which he fled, be delivered up, to be re-

[1] Limited by Eleventh Amendment.

moved to the State having jurisdiction of the crime.

[(3) No person held to service or labor in one State, under the laws thereof, escaping into another, shall, in consequence of any law or regulation therein, be discharged from such service or labor, but shall be delivered up on claim of the party to whom such service or labor may be due.] [2]

Section 3. (1) New States may be admitted by the Congress into this Union; but no new State shall be formed or erected within the jurisdiction of any other State; nor any State be formed by the junction of two or more States, or parts of States, without the consent of the legislatures of the States concerned as well as of the Congress.

(2) The Congress shall have power to dispose of and make all needful rules and regulations respecting the territory or other property belonging to the United States; and nothing in this Constitution shall be so construed as to prejudice any claims of the United States, or of any particular State.

Section 4. The United States shall guarantee to every State in this Union a republican form of government, and shall protect each of them against invasion; and, on application of the legislature, or of the executive (when the legislature cannot be convened), against domestic violence.

ARTICLE V

The Congress, whenever two thirds of both Houses shall deem it necessary, shall propose amendments to this Constitution, or, on the application of the legislatures of two thirds of the several States, shall call a convention for proposing amendments which, in either case, shall be valid to all intents and purposes, as part of this Constitution, when ratified by the legislatures of three fourths of the several States, or by conventions in three fourths thereof, as the one or the other mode of ratification may be proposed by the Congress; provided [that no amendment which may be made prior to the year one thousand eight hundred and eight shall in any manner affect the first and fourth clauses in the ninth section of the first article; and] [3] that no State,

[2] Superseded by Thirteenth Amendment so far as it relates to slaves.

[3] Temporary provision.

without its consent, shall be deprived of its equal suffrage in the Senate.

ARTICLE VI

(1) All debts contracted and engagements entered into, before the adoption of this Constitution, shall be as valid against the United States under this Constitution, as under the Confederation.

(2) This Constitution, and the laws of the United States which shall be made in pursuance thereof; and all treaties made, or which shall be made, under the authority of the United States, shall be the supreme law of the land; and the judges in every State shall be bound thereby, anything in the constitution or laws of any State to the contrary notwithstanding.

(3) The Senators and Representatives before mentioned, and the members of the several State legislatures, and all executive and judicial officers, both of the United States and of the several States, shall be bound by oath or affirmation to support this Constitution; but no religious test shall ever be required as a qualification to any office or public trust under the United States.

ARTICLE VII

The ratification of the conventions of nine States shall be sufficient for the establishment of this Constitution between the States so ratifying the same.

Done in convention by the unanimous consent of the States present the seventeenth day of September in the year of our Lord one thousand seven hundred and eighty-seven, and of the independence of the United States of America the twelfth. In witness whereof, we have hereunto subscribed our names.

AMENDMENTS

ARTICLE I

Congress shall make no law respecting an establishment of religion, or prohibiting the free exercise thereof; or abridging the freedom of speech, or of the press; or the right of the people peaceably to assemble, and to petition the government for a redress of grievances.

ARTICLE II

A well regulated militia, being necessary to the security of a free State, the right of the people to keep and bear arms shall not be infringed.

ARTICLE III

No soldier shall, in time of peace, be quartered in any house, without the consent of the owner, nor in time of war, but in a manner to be prescribed by law.

ARTICLE IV

The right of the people to be secure in their persons, houses, papers, and effects, against unreasonable searches and seizures, shall not be violated, and no warrants shall issue, but upon probable cause, supported by oath or affirmation, and particularly describing the place to be searched, and the persons or things to be seized.

ARTICLE V

No person shall be held to answer for a capital or otherwise infamous crime, unless on a presentment or indictment of a grand jury, except in cases arising in the land or naval forces, or in the militia, when in actual service in time of war or public danger; nor shall any person be subject for the same offence to be twice put in jeopardy of life or limb; nor shall be compelled in any criminal case to be a witness against himself, nor be deprived of life, liberty, or property, without due process of law; nor shall private property be taken for public use, without just compensation.

ARTICLE VI

In all criminal prosecutions the accused shall enjoy the right to a speedy and public trial, by an impartial jury of the State and district wherein the crime shall have been committed, which district shall have been previously ascertained by law, and to be informed of the nature and cause of the accusation; to be confronted with the witnesses against him; to have compulsory process for obtaining witnesses in his favor, and to have the assistance of counsel for his defense.

ARTICLE VII

In suits at common law, where the value in controversy shall exceed twenty dollars, the right of trial by jury shall be preserved, and no fact tried by a jury shall be otherwise re-examined in any court of the United States than according to the rules of the common law.

ARTICLE VIII

Excessive bail shall not be required, nor excessive fines imposed, nor cruel and unusual punishments inflicted.

ARTICLE IX

The enumeration in the Constitution of certain rights shall not be construed to deny or disparage others retained by the people.

ARTICLE X

The powers not delegated to the United States by the Constitution, nor prohibited by it to the States, are reserved to the States respectively, or to the people.[1]

ARTICLE XI [2]

The judicial power of the United States shall not be construed to extend to any suit in law or equity, commenced or prosecuted against one of the United States by citizens of another State, or by citizens or subjects of any foreign State.

ARTICLE XII [3]

The electors shall meet in their respective States, and vote by ballot for President and Vice President, one of whom, at least, shall not be an inhabitant of the same State with themselves; they shall name in their ballots the persons voted for as President, and in distinct ballots the persons voted for as Vice President, and they shall make distinct lists of all persons voted for as President, and of all persons voted for as Vice President, and of the number of votes for each, which lists they shall sign and certify, and transmit sealed to the seat of the government of the United States, directed to the president of the Senate;—the president of the Senate shall, in the presence of the Senate and House of Representatives, open all the certificates, and the votes shall then be counted;—the person having the greatest number of votes for President, shall be the President, if such number be a majority of the whole number of electors appointed; and if no person have such majority, then from the persons having the highest numbers not exceeding three on the list of those voted for as President, the House of Representatives shall choose immediately, by ballot, the President. But in choosing the President, the votes shall be taken by States, the representation from each State having one vote; a quorum for this purpose shall consist of a member or members from two thirds of the States, and a majority of all the States shall be necessary to a choice. And if the House of Representatives shall not choose a President whenever the right of choice shall devolve upon them, before the fourth day of March next following, then the Vice President shall act as President, as in the case of the death or other constitutional disability of the President.—The person having the greatest number of votes as Vice President, shall be the Vice President, if such number be a majority of the whole number of electors appointed, and if no person have a majority, then from the two highest numbers on the list, the Senate shall choose the Vice President; a quorum for the purpose shall consist of two thirds of the whole number of Senators, and a majority of the whole number shall be necessary to a choice. But no person constitutionally ineligible to the office of President shall be eligible to that of Vice President of the United States.[4]

ARTICLE XIII [5]

Section 1. Neither slavery nor involuntary servitude, except as a punishment for crime whereof the party shall have been duly convicted, shall exist within the United States, or any place subject to their jurisdiction.

Section 2. Congress shall have power to enforce this article by appropriate legislation.

ARTICLE XIV [6]

Section 1. All persons born or naturalized in the United States, and subject to the jurisdiction thereof, are citizens of the United States and of the State wherein they reside. No State shall make or enforce any law which shall abridge the privileges or immunities of citizens of the United States; nor shall any State deprive any person of

[1] The first ten amendments appear to have been in force from November 3, 1791.
[2] Proclaimed January 8, 1798.
[3] Proclaimed September 25, 1804.

[4] This amendment modified by the Twentieth.
[5] Proclaimed December 18, 1865.
[6] Proclaimed July 28, 1868.

life, liberty, or property, without due process of law; nor deny to any person within its jurisdiction the equal protection of the laws.

Section 2. Representatives shall be apportioned among the several States according to their respective numbers, counting the whole number of persons in each State, excluding Indians not taxed. But when the right to vote at any election for the choice of electors for President and Vice President of the United States, Representatives in Congress, the executive and judicial officers of a State, or the members of the legislature thereof, is denied to any of the male inhabitants of such State, being twenty-one years of age, and citizens of the United States, or in any way abridged, except for participation in rebellion, or other crime, the basis of representation therein shall be reduced in the proportion which the number of such male citizens shall bear to the whole number of male citizens twenty-one years of age in such State.

Section 3. No person shall be a Senator or Representative in Congress, or elector of President and Vice President, or hold any office, civil or military, under the United States, or under any State, who, having previously taken an oath, as a member of Congress, or as an officer of the United States, or as a member of any State legislature, or as an executive or judicial officer of any State, to support the Constitution of the United States, shall have engaged in insurrection or rebellion against the same, or given aid or comfort to the enemies thereof. But Congress may by a vote of two thirds of each House, remove such disability.

Section 4. The validity of the public debt of the United States, authorized by law, including debts incurred for payment of pensions and bounties for services in suppressing insurrection or rebellion, shall not be questioned. But neither the United States nor any State shall assume or pay any debt or obligation incurred in aid of insurrection or rebellion against the United States, or any claim for the loss or emancipation of any slave; but all such debts, obligations, and claims shall be held illegal and void.

Section 5. The Congress shall have power to enforce, by appropriate legislation, the provisions of this article.

ARTICLE XV [1]

Section 1. The right of citizens of the United States to vote shall not be denied or abridged by the United States or by any State on account of race, color, or previous condition of servitude.

Section 2. The Congress shall have power to enforce this article by appropriate legislation.

ARTICLE XVI [2]

The Congress shall have power to lay and collect taxes on incomes, from whatever source derived, without apportionment among the several States, and without regard to any census or enumeration.

ARTICLE XVII [3]

The Senate of the United States shall be composed of two Senators from each State, elected by the people thereof, for six years; and each Senator shall have one vote. The electors in each State shall have the qualifications requisite for electors of the most numerous branch of the State legislature.

When vacancies happen in the representation of any State in the Senate, the executive authority of such State shall issue writs of election to fill such vacancies:

Provided, That the legislature of any State may empower the executive thereof to make temporary appointments until the people fill the vacancies by election as the legislature may direct.

This amendment shall not be so construed as to affect the election or term of any Senator chosen before it becomes valid as part of the Constitution.

ARTICLE XVIII [4]

Section 1. After one year from the ratification of this article the manufacture, sale, or transportation of intoxicating liquors within, the importation thereof into, or the exportation thereof from the United States and all territory subject to the

[1] Proclaimed March 30, 1870.

[2] Passed July, 1909, proclaimed February 25, 1913.

[3] Passed May, 1912, in lieu of Article I, Section 3, Clause 1, of the Constitution and so much of Clause 2 of the same Section as relates to the filling of vacancies; proclaimed May 31, 1913.

[4] Passed December 3, 1917; proclaimed January 29, 1919. Repealed by the Twenty-first Amendment.

jurisdiction thereof for beverage purposes is hereby prohibited.

Section 2. The Congress and the several States shall have concurrent power to enforce this article by appropriate legislation.

Section 3. This article shall be inoperative unless it shall have been ratified as an amendment to the Constitution by the legislatures of the several States, as provided in the Constitution, within seven years from the date of the submission hereof to the States by the Congress.

ARTICLE XIX [1]

(1) The right of citizens of the United States to vote shall not be denied or abridged by the United States or by any State on account of sex.

(2) Congress shall have power, by appropriate legislation, to enforce the provisions of this article.

ARTICLE XX [2]

Section 1. The terms of the President and Vice President shall end at noon on the 20th day of January, and the terms of Senators and Representatives at noon on the 3rd day of January, of the years in which such terms would have ended if this article had not been ratified; and the terms of their successors shall then begin.

Section 2. The Congress shall assemble at least once in every year, and such meeting shall begin at noon on the 3rd day of January, unless they shall by law appoint a different day.

Section 3. If, at the time fixed for the beginning of the term of the President, the President elect shall have died, the Vice President elect shall become President. If a President shall not have been chosen before the time fixed for the beginning of his term, or if the President elect shall have failed to qualify, then the Vice President elect shall act as President until a President shall have qualified; and the Congress may by law provide for the case wherein neither a President elect nor a Vice President elect shall have qualified, declaring who shall then act as President, or the manner in which one who is to act shall be selected, and such person shall act accordingly until a President or Vice President shall have qualified.

[1] Proclaimed August 26, 1920.
[2] Proclaimed February 6, 1933.

Section 4. The Congress may by law provide for the case of the death of any of the persons from whom the House of Representatives may choose a President whenever the right of choice shall have devolved upon them, and for the case of the death of any of the persons from whom the Senate may choose a Vice President whenever the right of choice shall have devolved upon them.

Section 5. Sections 1 and 2 shall take effect on the 15th day of October following the ratification of this article.

Section 6. This article shall be inoperative unless it shall have been ratified as an amendment to the Constitution by the legislatures of three fourths of the several States within seven years from the date of its submission.

ARTICLE XXI [3]

Section 1. The eighteenth article of amendment to the Constitution of the United States is hereby repealed.

Section 2. The transportation or importation into any State, Territory, or possession of the United States for delivery or use therein of intoxicating liquors, in violation of the laws thereof, is hereby prohibited.

Section 3. This article shall be inoperative unless it shall have been ratified as an amendment to the Constitution by conventions in the several States, as provided in the Constitution, within seven years from the date of submission hereof to the States by the Congress.

ARTICLE XXII [4]

Section 1. No person shall be elected to the office of the President more than twice, and no person who has held the office of President, or acted as President, for more than two years of a term to which some other person was elected President shall be elected to the office of the President more than once. But this Article shall not apply to any person holding the office of President when this Article was proposed by the Congress, and shall not prevent any person who may be holding the office of President, or acting as President, during the term within which this

[3] Proclaimed December 5, 1933. This amendment was ratified by state conventions.
[4] Adopted February 27, 1951.

Article becomes operative from holding the office of President, or acting as President during the remainder of such term.

Section 2. This Article shall be inoperative unless it shall have been ratified as an amendment to the Constitution by the legislatures of three-fourths of the several States within seven years from the date of its submission to the States by the Congress.[1]

[1] Five amendments have been proposed but not ratified. The first and second were proposed on Sept. 25, 1789, along with ten others which became the Bill of Rights. The first of these dealt with the apportionment of members of the House of Representatives. It was ratified by ten states, eleven being the necessary three-fourths. The second provided that "No law, varying the compensation for the services of the Senators and Representatives, shall take effect, until an election of Representatives shall have intervened." It was ratified by six states, eleven being necessary. A third was proposed on May 1, 1810, which would have abrogated the citizenship of any persons accepting foreign titles or honors. It was ratified by twelve states, fourteen being necessary. A fourth was proposed on Mar. 4, 1861, which prohibited the adoption of any amendment "to abolish or interfere, within any state, with the domestic institutions thereof, including that of persons held to labor or service by the laws of that state." This was approved by three states. The fifth, the proposed child-labor amendment, was proposed on June 2, 1924. It provides:

Section 1—The Congress shall have power to limit, regulate, and prohibit the labor of persons under eighteen years of age.

Section 2—The power of the several States is unimpaired by this article except that the operation of State laws shall be suspended to the extent necessary to give effect to legislation enacted by Congress.

This has been ratified by twenty-eight states and rejected in eleven. The approval of thirty-six states is necessary to complete ratification.

States—Dates of Admission, Area, Population

State	Date of Admission	Area, square miles	Population, 1950
Alabama	1819	51,609	3,061,743
Arizona	1912	113,909	749,587
Arkansas	1836	53,104	1,909,511
California	1850	158,693	10,586,223
Colorado	1876	104,247	1,325,089
Connecticut	1788	5,009	2,007,280
Delaware	1787	2,057	318,085
District of Columbia	(1791)	69	802,178
Florida	1845	58,560	2,771,305
Georgia	1788	58,876	3,444,578
Idaho	1890	83,557	588,637
Illinois	1818	56,400	8,712,176
Indiana	1816	36,291	3,934,224
Iowa	1846	56,290	2,621,073
Kansas	1861	82,276	1,905,299
Kentucky	1792	40,395	2,944,806
Louisiana	1812	48,523	2,683,516
Maine	1820	33,215	913,774
Maryland	1788	10,577	2,343,001
Massachusetts	1788	8,257	4,690,514
Michigan	1837	58,216	6,371,766
Minnesota	1858	84,068	2,982,483
Mississippi	1817	47,716	2,178,914
Missouri	1821	69,674	3,954,653
Montana	1889	147,138	591,024
Nebraska	1867	77,227	1,325,510
Nevada	1864	110,540	160,083
New Hampshire	1788	9,304	533,242
New Jersey	1787	7,836	4,835,329
New Mexico	1912	121,666	681,187

493

State	Date of Admission	Area, square miles	Population, 1950
New York	1788	49,576	14,830,192
North Carolina	1789	52,712	4,061,929
North Dakota	1889	70,665	619,636
Ohio	1803	41,222	7,946,627
Oklahoma	1907	69,919	2,233,351
Oregon	1859	96,981	1,521,341
Pennsylvania	1787	45,333	10,498,012
Rhode Island	1790	1,214	791,896
South Carolina	1788	31,055	2,117,027
South Dakota	1889	77,047	652,740
Tennessee	1796	42,244	3,291,718
Texas	1845	267,339	7,711,194
Utah	1896	84,916	688,862
Vermont	1791	9,609	377,747
Virginia	1788	40,815	3,318,680
Washington	1889	68,192	2,378,963
West Virginia	1863	24,181	2,005,552
Wisconsin	1848	56,154	3,434,575
Wyoming	1890	97,914	290,529
Territories:			
Hawaii		6,423	499,794
Alaska		586,400	128,643
Commonwealth:			
Puerto Rico		3,435	2,210,703
Possessions:			
Guam		206	59,498
Virgin Islands		133	26,665
Samoa		76	18,937
Others		38	1,119
Canal Zone		553	52,822
Corn Islands		4	1,304
Trust Territory of the Pacific Islands (under UN)		8,475	54,843 (1940)
Other population abroad			481,545

Presidential Elections

Date	Candidates	Electoral Vote	Popular Vote	Secretary of State
1789	Washington	69 *		Jefferson, 1789
	Adams, J.	34		
	Scattering	35		
1792	Washington (FED.)	132 *		Randolph, 1794
	Adams, J. (FED.)	77		Pickering, 1795
	Clinton (ANTI-FED.)	50		
	Jefferson (ANTI-FED.)	4		
	Burr (ANTI-FED.)	1		
1796	Adams, J. (FED.)	71 *		
	Jefferson (DEM.-REP.)	68		Marshall, 1800
	Pinckney, T. (FED.)	59		
	Burr (DEM.-REP.)	30		
	Scattering	48		
1800	Jefferson (DEM.-REP.)	73 *		Madison, 1801
	Burr (DEM.-REP.)	73		
	Adams, J. (FED.)	65		
	Pinckney, C. C. (FED.)	64		
	Jay (FED.)	1		
1804	Jefferson (DEM.-REP.)	162		
	Pinckney, C. C. (FED.)	14		
1808	Madison (DEM.-REP.)	122		Smith, 1809
	Pinckney, C. C. (FED.)	47		Monroe, 1811
	Clinton (DEM.-REP.)	6		
1812	Madison (DEM.-REP.)	128		
	Clinton (FED.)	89		

* Each elector through 1800 voted for two men without specifying whether for President or Vice-President. Washington actually was the unanimous choice for the presidency in 1789 and 1792.

Date	Candidates	Electoral Vote	Popular Vote	Secretary of State
1816	Monroe (DEM.-REP.)	183		Adams, 1817
	King (FED.)	34		
1820	Monroe (DEM.-REP.)	231		
	Adams, J. Q. (DEM.-REP.)	1		
1824	Adams, J. Q. (NAT. REP.)	84	105,321	Clay, 1825
	Jackson (NAT. REP.)	99	155,872	
	Clay (NAT. REP.)	37	46,587	
	Crawford (NAT. REP.)	41	44,282	
1828	Jackson (DEM.) †	178	647,231	Van Buren, 1829
	Adams, J. Q. (NAT. REP.)	83	509,097	Livingston, 1831
1832	Jackson (DEM.)	219	687,502	McLane, 1833
	Clay (NAT. REP.)	49	530,209	Forsyth, 1834
	Floyd (IND.)	11 ⎫	33,108	
	Wirt (ANTI-MASON)	7 ⎭		
1836	Van Buren (DEM.)	170	762,678	
	Harrison, W. H. (WHIG)	73	548,007	
	Scattering	11	187,643	
1840	Harrison, W. H. (WHIG) and Tyler (1841)	234	1,275,017	Webster, 1841
	Van Buren (DEM.)	60	1,128,702	Legare, 1843
				Upshur, 1843
				Calhoun, 1844
1844	Polk (DEM.)	170	1,337,243	Buchanan, 1845
	Clay (WHIG)	105	1,299,068	
1848	Taylor (WHIG) and Fillmore (1850)	163	1,360,101	Clayton, 1849
	Cass (DEM.)	127	1,220,544	Webster, 1850
	Van Buren (FREE SOIL)	0	291,263	Everett, 1852
1852	Pierce (DEM.)	254	1,601,474	Marcy, 1853
	Scott (WHIG)	42	1,386,578	
	Hale (FREE DEM.)	0	156,149	
1856	Buchanan (DEM.)	174	1,838,169	Cass, 1857
	Frémont (REP.)	114	1,341,264	Black, 1860
	Fillmore (AMER.)	8	874,534	
1860	Lincoln (REP.)	180	1,866,352	Seward, 1861
	Breckenridge (DEM.)	72	847,514	
	Bell (CONST. UNION)	39	587,830	
	Douglas (IND. DEM.)	12	1,375,157	
1864	Lincoln (REP.-NAT. UNION) and Johnson (1865)	212	2,330,552	
	McClellan (DEM.)	21	1,835,985	
1868	Grant (REP.)	214	3,012,833	Washburne, 1869
	Seymour (DEM.)	80	2,703,249	Fish, 1869
1872	Grant (REP.)	286	3,579,070	
	Greeley (DEM., LIB. REP.)	66	2,834,079	

† The names of the political parties were not thoroughly stabilized in 1828 and 1832.

Date	Candidates	Electoral Vote	Popular Vote	Secretary of State
1876	Hayes (REP.)	185	4,033,950	Evarts, 1877
	Tilden (DEM.)	184	4,284,757	
1880	Garfield (REP.) and			
	Arthur (1881)	214	4,454,416	Blaine, 1881
	Hancock (DEM.)	155	4,444,952	Frelinghuysen, 1881
	Weaver (GREENBACK)	0	307,578	
1884	Cleveland (DEM.)	219	4,874,986	Bayard, 1885
	Blaine (REP.)	182	4,851,981	
	Butler (GREENBACK)	0	175,370	
1888	Harrison, B. (REP.)	233	5,439,853	Blaine, 1889
	Cleveland (DEM.)	168	5,540,329	Foster, 1892
1892	Cleveland (DEM.)	277	5,556,928	Gresham, 1893
	Harrison, B. (REP.)	145	5,176,100	Olney, 1895
	Weaver (PEOPLE'S)	22	1,041,021	
1896	McKinley (REP.)	271	7,107,304	Sherman, 1897
	Bryan (DEM., PEOPLE'S)	176	6,533,080	Day, 1898
				Hay, 1898
1900	McKinley (REP.) and			
	T. Roosevelt (1901)	292	7,218,491	
	Bryan (DEM., PEOPLE'S)	155	6,356,734	
1904	Roosevelt, T. (REP.)	336	7,624,489	Root, 1905
	Parker (DEM.)	140	5,082,754	
	Debs (SOC.)	0	402,280	
1908	Taft (REP.)	321	7,677,788	Bacon, 1909
	Bryan (DEM.)	162	6,407,982	Knox, 1909
	Debs (SOC.)	0	420,890	
1912	Wilson (DEM.)	435	6,293,019	Bryan, 1913
	Roosevelt, T. (PRO.)	88	4,119,507	Lansing, 1915
	Taft (REP.)	8	3,484,956	
	Debs (SOC.)	0	901,873	
1916	Wilson (DEM.)	277	9,129,606	
	Hughes (REP.)	254	8,538,221	Colby, 1920
	Benson (SOC.)	0	585,113	
1920	Harding (REP.) and			
	Coolidge (1923)	404	16,147,249	Hughes, 1921
	Cox (DEM.)	127	9,140,864	
	Debs (SOC.)	0	897,704	
	Christensen (FARM-LABOR)	0	265,305	
1924	Coolidge (REP.)	382	15,725,016	Kellogg, 1925
	Davis (DEM.)	136	8,386,503	
	La Follette (PRO., SOC.)	13	4,822,856	
1928	Hoover (REP.)	444	21,392,190	Stimson, 1929
	Smith (DEM.)	87	15,016,443	
	Thomas (SOC.)	0	267,420	

Date	Candidates	Electoral Vote	Popular Vote	Secretary of State
1932	Roosevelt, F. D. (DEM.)	472	22,821,857	Hull, 1933
	Hoover (REP.)	59	15,761,841	
	Thomas (SOC.)	0	884,781	
	Foster (COM.) ‡	0	102,991	
1936	Roosevelt, F. D. (DEM.)	523	27,751,597	
	Landon (REP.)	8	16,679,583	
	Lemke (UNION)	0	822,479	
	Thomas (SOC.)	0	187,720	
1940	Roosevelt, F. D. (DEM.)	449	27,243,466	
	Willkie (REP.)	82	22,304,755	Stettinius, 1944
	Thomas (SOC.)	0	99,557	
1944	Roosevelt, F. D. (DEM.) and Truman (1945)	432	25,602,646	Byrnes, 1945
	Dewey (REP.)	99	22,017,592	Marshall, 1947
	Thomas (SOC.)	0	79,010	
1948	Truman (DEM.)	303	24,179,623	Acheson, 1949
	Dewey (REP.)	189	21,991,290	
	Thurmond (STATES' RIGHTS DEM.)	39	1,176,154	
	Wallace (PRO.)	0	1,157,326	
	Thomas (SOC.)	0	139,588	
1952	Eisenhower (REP.)	442	33,824,351	Dulles, 1953
	Stevenson (DEM.)	89	27,314,987	

‡ Later Communist votes were negligible—80,159 in 1936 and 46,251 in 1940. In 1944, 1948, and 1952 the Communist party ran no candidate of its own.

Index

Abercrombie, James, in Great War for the Empire, 34

Abolition of Negro slavery (*see* Abolitionists; Negroes; Slavery)

Abolitionists, in colonial South, 91; early activities, 251–252; later activities, 296–298, 300, 301; and Anthony Burns, 349; support John Brown, 362; and Southern secession, 369 (*see also* Radical Republicans)

Acadia (Nova Scotia) taken by British, 1713, 32

Adams, Charles Francis, as diplomat, 395–396; as Liberal Republican, 448

Adams, John, defends British soldiers, 46n.; works on Declaration of Independence, 50; as peace commissioner in Paris, 62, 64; elected President, 1796, 137; described, 137; domestic policies of, 137–138; defeated for reelection, 1800, 139; and judiciary appointments, 142; rapprochement with Jefferson, 145; and France, 152–153

Adams, John Quincy, at Ghent, 173–175; and abolitionist petitions, 251; elected President, 1824, 276; described, 277; domestic policies of, 277; defeated for reelection, 1828, 278–279; fights gag resolution, 298; and Florida, 308–309; and Monroe Doctrine, 312; foreign policies under, 313; and Oregon, 320; and Texas, 323–324

Adams, Samuel, favors independence, 46; and Boston Tea Party, 47; escapes British, 48; in First Continental Congress, 66; opposes Constitution, 84

Adams, William, at Ghent, 174

Adams–de Onís Treaty (1819), and Florida, 308–309; and Oregon, 309, 320; and Texas, 323

Adet, Pierre, dismissed, 152

Africa, Portuguese in, 5; slave trade in, 90; Barbary wars with, 158–159; freed slaves exported to, 251, 297; naval blockade against slave trade, 316–317

Age of Metternich, in Europe, 305–307; and Latin America, 309–312

Age of Reason, The (Paine), deistic work, 49n., 110

Agricultural fairs started, 183

Agriculture, Department of, 185

Agriculture, Indian, 13, 15; to 1815, 68–69, 87–91; in early West, 117–118; 1815–1860, rural life, 177–178; crops, 178–179; in South, 179–182; livestock, 182–183; changes in, 183–184; discontent in, 184–186; in Confederacy, 403–404; in Union, 412–413; in postwar South, 428

Aix-la-Chapelle, Treaty of (1748), 33

Aix-la-Chapelle Dispatch, 1854 ("Ostend Manifesto") and Cuba, 342

Alabama, Confederate raider, 392; Civil War Anglo-Union crisis over, 395–396; postwar claims controversy, 425–426

Alabama, admitted, 257; secedes, 367

Alamo massacre of Texans, 325

Alaska, in Tsar's Ukase of 1821, 310; purchased, 422–423

Albany in American Revolution, 56

Albany Congress, Franklin's plan of union at, 47n.

Albert, British Prince Consort, and *Trent*, 395

Alcott, Bronson, as educator, 225–226; utopianism of, 253

Alexander I of Russia, and War of 1812, 173; and Holy Alliance, 305, 307; Ukase of 1821, 310

Alexander II of Russia sells Alaska, 423

Alexander VI, Papal Line of Demarcation of, 5n.

Alexandria, Confederate raider seized by British, 396

Algeria insults United States, 159

Alien Acts (1798) sponsored by Federalists, 137

Allen, Ethan, in American Revolution, 55n.; in Vermont, 73; as deistic author, 110

Allston, Washington, artist, 234

Amending process described, 82

Amendments to the Constitution listed, 82–83

American Academy of Arts and Sciences, 100, 108

American Antislavery Society, 251

American Bible Society, 248

American Board of Commissioners for Foreign Missions, 111, 248

American Colonization Society exports freed slaves to Africa, 251, 297

American Eclectic Medicine Society of Samuel Thomson, 232

American Fur Company of John Jacob Astor, 260–261, 320

American Home Missionary Society, 248

American Journal of Dental Science, 232

American Journal of Pharmacy, 232

American Journal of Science, 229

American Medical Association, 230

American Peace Society, difficulties of, 250

American Philosophical Society, 101, 108

American Revolution, causes, 41–48; outbreak, 48; in New England, 48, 54–56; rival powers, 51–54; finances, 52, 67, 97–98; as civil war, 52–53; and Canada, 55–56; in Middle States, 56–58, 61, 62; diplomacy, 58–60; naval war, 60–61; in West, 61; in South, 61–62; ended by Treaty of Paris (1783), 62–64; social effects of, 65; and politics, 65–67; and economics, 67–69

American Society for the Promotion of Temperance, 250–251

American Sunday School Union, 248

American System, of Henry Clay, tariff, 269–270; Second Bank of United States, 270–271; internal improvements, 271–272

American Tract Society, 248

American Watch Company, 193

Ames, Fisher, in Essex Junto, 140

Amherst, Jeffrey, in Great War for the Empire, 34

Amiens, Peace of (1802), ends Wars of French Revolution, 154, 156

Amusements, in West, 127; 1815–1860, 240–241

Anderson, Robert J., at Fort Sumter, 373

Andersonville, Ga., Confederate prison at, 419, 431n.

Andover Theological Seminary, 110, 228

André, John, executed, 62n.

Andros, Sir Edmund, governor of the Dominion of New England, 40–41

Anesthetics introduced, 231

Anglican Church (see Church of England)

Annapolis Convention, forerunner to Constitutional Convention, 76

Anne of England relaxes empire controls, 37

Anthony, Susan B., and women's rights, 252

Antietam (Sharpsburg), Md., Civil War battle, 383–384; diplomatic effects of, 395; and Emancipation Proclamation, 395, 417

Antifederalists oppose Constitution, 85–86

Antigua, British West Indies, settled, 29

Anti-Mason party and national conventions, 281

Antislavery movement (see Abolitionists)

Apache Canyon, Ariz., Civil War battle, 380n.

Appomattox Courthouse, Va., Lee surrenders, 389

Aranjuez, Treaty of (1779), Franco-Spanish, 59–60

Architecture, to 1815, 107; 1815–1860, 235–236

Aristocracy to 1815, 102

Arizona, Spanish control of, 8

Arkansas, admitted, 257; secedes, 368

Armed Neutrality against Great Britain, 1780s, 60; 1790s, 150

Armies, eighteenth-century British, 33; in American Revolution, 48–49, 51–52, 54–58, 61–62; in War of 1812, 168–173; in Mexican War, 330–333; in Civil War battles, 374–389; Confederate recruitment, 401–402; Union recruitment, 409–410

Arnold, Benedict, in American Revolution, 55, 56n.; treason of, 62n.

Aroostook War in Maine, 315

Art, to 1815, 107–108; 1815–1860, 234–235

Articles of Confederation, proposed, 67; described, 69–70; and the states, 69; Constitutional Convention to amend, 76–78

Ashburton, Lord, in Webster-Ashburton Treaty, 315–317

Asia, China, early trade with, 97; later relations with, 343–344; Japan, relations with, 344–345

Assembly in colonies, 41

Astor, John Jacob, in fur trade, 260–261, 320

Astor House, hotel, 221

Astor Theater riot, 241

Astoria, Ore., founded, 261

Atchison, David, and Kansas-Nebraska Act, 351

Atlanta captured by Union, 386

Atlantic cable, 201

"Auburn plan" of prison reform, 250

Audubon, John James, scientist, 229

Austerlitz, Napoleonic battle, 161–162

Austin, Moses, in Texas, 263, 324

Austin, Stephen F., in Texas, 263, 324

Austria insulted by Daniel Webster, 336

Azores discovered, 5

Aztec Indians conquered by Cortes, 6

Babcock, Orville E., and Whisky Ring, 449

Bacon, Nathaniel, leads Virginia rebellion, 40

Bagot, Sir Charles, in Rush-Bagot Agreement, 175

Bahama Islands settled, 29

Balboa, Vasco Núñez de, explorer, 6

Baldwin, Joseph G., author, 239

Ballou, Hosea, and Universalism, 110

Baltimore, to 1815, described, 101; in War of 1812, 171

Baltimore and Ohio Railroad, 212, 214

Bancroft, George, as Jacksonian Democrat, 282

Bank of United States, First, Hamilton founds, 132–133; charter expires, 167–168

Bank of United States, Second, chartered, 270–271; in *McCulloch v. Maryland*, 272–273; Jackson fights, 287–289

Bank of United States, proposed Third, Tyler vetoes, 293

Banking, in 1780s, 98; and industry, 188–189; First Bank of United States, 132–133, 167; Second, 270–271, 287, 288; in Union, 411

Banks, Nathaniel, in Civil War, Louisiana, 380; Shenandoah Valley, 383

Baptists, in early West, 127; splits among, 246

Baranov, Alexander, and Alaska, 422–423

Barbados settled, 29

Barbary States, wars against, 158–159

Barlow, Joel, poet, 106; in Scioto Company, 119

Barnard, Henry, educator, 224

Barnburners, Radical Democrats, 1840s, 205

Barnum, Phineas T., showman, 236, 242, 243

Barron, James, and *Chesapeake-Leopard*, kills Decatur, 162

Barton, Clara, in Civil War, 410

Bartram, William, scientist, 108

Bates, Edward, misses presidential nomination, 1860, 366; in Lincoln's Cabinet, 409

Bathurst, Lord, at Vienna, 173

"Battle in the Clouds" in Civil War, 385

Battle of the Saints, Anglo-French naval battle, 62n.

Baton Rouge seized, 1810, 159

Bayard, James, at Ghent, 173

Bayonne Decree of Napoleon, 163

Beaumarchais, Pierre Augustin Caron de, assists American Revolution, 58

Beaumont, William, doctor, 231–232

Beauregard, Pierre, in Civil War, bombards Fort Sumter, 373; at First Bull Run, 376; in Mississippi, 379

Beecher, Henry Ward, abolitionist minister, 356n.

Beecher, Lyman, as educator, 228; and temperance, 250

"Beecher's Bibles," rifles in Kansas, 356

Belize (British Honduras), British at, 338

Belknap, William W., Grant's Secretary of War, 444; corruption of, 449–450

Bell, John C., defeated for presidency, 1860, 367

Ben Sherrod, steamer, burns, 208

Benét, Stephen Vincent (*John Brown's Body*), quoted on blockade-running, 405

Benjamin, Judah P., Confederate Secretary of State, 399; flees abroad, 432n.

Bennett, James Gordon, and New York *Herald*, 237

Bennington, Vt., Revolutionary battle, 56

Benton, Thomas H., fights Jackson, 278, 280; and Foot Resolution, 284; quoted on Bank, 287; and Kansas-Nebraska Act, 351

Berkeley, John, proprietor of New Jersey, 27

Berkeley, Sir William, fights Bacon's Rebellion, 40

Berlin Decree of Napoleon, 162

Bermuda settled by British, 29

Bernadotte of Sweden crowned, 305

Bessemer-Kelly process in steel, 190

Biddle, Nicholas, president of Second Bank of United States, 271; against Jackson, 287–288

Bigelow, Erastus, and carpets, 191

Bill of Rights (United States), described, 82–83; adopted, 131

Bills of attainder prohibited by Constitution, 80

Bird, Robert Montgomery, author, 238

Birney, James G., Free Soiler, 252

Black Ball Line, first packets to Europe, 205

Black Codes, anti-Negro Southern legislation, 429–430

"Black Friday," gold corner on, 446

Black Hawk's War against Sac and Fox Indians, 258–259

Black Warrior seized by Spaniards, 342

Bladensburg, Md., War of 1812 battle, 171

Blaine, James G., misses presidential nomination, 1876, 451

Blair, Francis Preston, in Jackson's "kitchen cabinet," 283

Blair, Francis Preston, Jr., in Civil War, 378

Blair, Montgomery, in Lincoln's Cabinet, 409

Blenheim, Germany, War of the Spanish Succession battle, 32

Blockade, Union, in Civil War, 390, 405

Blockade-running, Confederate, 405

"Bloody Angle" at Spotsylvania Courthouse, 388

Blount, William, in early Tennessee, 119, 120, 122–123

Board of Trade Privy Council committee, 39

Bonds, sales of, in American Revolution, 52; in Confederacy, 402; in Union, 411

Bonhomme Richard defeats *Serapis*, 60

Booneville, Mo., Civil War battle, 378

Booth, John Wilkes, assassinates Lincoln, 418

Border slave states, mixed sentiments in, 1860–1861, 368, 370

Borie, Adolph E., Grant's Secretary of Navy, 444

Boston, founded, 23; crises with British in, 46–47; outbreak of American Revolution in, 48; during American Revolution, 54–55; to 1815, described, 100

Boston and Albany Railroad, 213

Boston Latin School, 103

"Boston Massacre," 46

Boston News-Letter, newspaper, 105

Boston Prison Discipline Society, 250

Boston Tea Party, 47

Bounties, Confederate, 401; Union, 409

Boutwell, George, as Radical Republican, 433; as Grant's Secretary of Treasury, 444, 449

Bowditch, Nathaniel, and navigation, 108

Bowdoin, James, opposes Shays' Rebellion, 69; and arts and sciences, 100

Bowdoin College, 104

Bowles, William A., invades Florida, 123

Braddock, Edward, in Great War for the Empire, 33

Bradford, William, governor of Plymouth Colony, 21

Bradley, Joseph P., and election of 1876, 452

Bragg, Braxton, in Mexican War, 331; in Civil War, 385

Brandywine Creek, Pa., American Revolutionary battle, 58

Brazil in Portuguese Empire, 5

Breckinridge, John C., defeated for presidency, 1860, 365, 367

Breed's Hill (Charlestown, Mass.), American Revolutionary battle, 55

Breton fishermen, voyages to America of, 2n.

Bridger, James, mountain man, 260

Bridgman, Laura, blind and deaf-mute educated, 249

Bristow, Benjamin H., Grant's Secretary of Interior, 444, 449

British East India Company, founded, 14; and Boston Tea Party, 47

Brock, Sir Isaac, in War of 1812, 168, 169

Brook Farm (Massachusetts) utopian community, 253

Brooks, Preston, canes Sumner, 358

Brown, Charles Brockden, author, 106, 112

Brown, Jacob, in War of 1812, 171

Brown, John, in Kansas, 357; raids Harpers Ferry, 362–363

Brown, Joseph E., Civil War governor of Georgia, 401

Brown University, 103

Bruinsburg, Miss., captured by Union, 379

Bryant, William Cullen, as poet and publisher, 106; as Jacksonian Democrat, 282

Buchanan, James, as Jacksonian Democrat, 282; in Great Britain, 336; and Aix-la-Chapelle Dispatch, 342; and Cuba, 343; elected President, 1856, 358; described, 358–359; domestic policies of, 359–360; and Southern secession, 370, 371

Buckner, Simon B., in Civil War, 379

Buena Vista, Mexican War battle, 331–332

Buffalo, N.Y., as terminus of Erie Canal, 209

Bulfinch, Charles, architect, 107, 235

Bull, Ole, violinist, 236

Bull Run (Manassas Junction), Va., Civil War battle, first, 376–377; second, 383

Bulwer, Sir Henry Lytton, and Clayton-Bulwer Treaty, 339–340

Bunker Hill (Breed's Hill), American Revolutionary battle, 55

Burgoyne, John, in American Revolution, 56–57

Burke, Edmund, supports American Revolution, 53; opposes French Revolution, 147

Burlingame, Anson, in China, 344

Burlingame Treaty (1868) with China, 344

Burns, Anthony, fugitive slave returned, 349–350

Burnside, Ambrose E., in Civil War, at Fredericksburg, 384; arrests Vallandigham, 415

Burr, Aaron, western intrigues of, 123, 144; in election of 1800, 139–140; New York intrigues of, 144; kills Hamilton, 144

Burritt, Elihu, reformer, 250

Business (see Industry)

Butler, Anthony, in Mexico, 324

Butler, Benjamin F., in Civil War, 379n.; as Radical Republican, 433; as political boss, 445, 449

Butler, Pierce, insulted by Sumner, 358

Butler, Walter, in American Revolution, 61

Butterfield Overland Stage Company in Far West, 214–215, 267

Byrd, William, as scientist, 108

Cabet, Etienne, utopian, 253

Cabeza de Vaca, Alvar Núñez, explorer, 6

Cabinet, British, succeeds Privy Council, 39n., 42

Cabinet, United States, and President, 81, 82; Washington's, 130–131; Jackson's, 282–283; Davis's, 399; Lincoln's, 408–409; Grant's, 130–131

Cable, Atlantic, of Cyrus Field, 201

Cabot, George, New England Federalist, 100; at Hartford Convention, 173

Cabot, John, explorer, 9

Cadore, Duc de, letter, 165

Cahokia, Ill., captured by Clark, 61

Caldwell, Charles, phrenologist, 233

Calhoun, John C., as War Hawk, 165; and Eastern Indians, 257;

and tariff, 270, 275–276; clashes with Jackson, 282–283, 285–287; described, 285; and nullification, 285–286; in election of 1832, 288; rejoins Democratic party, 293–294; opposes Compromise of 1850, 301, 349; and Florida, 308; and Texas, 327

California, under Spain, 8; first Americans, 264, 299; gold rush, 265; and slavery, 300–302; admitted as state, 301; in Mexican War, 332; in Treaty of Guadalupe Hidalgo, 332

California Trail described, 264

Calvert family founds Maryland, 18

Calvin, John, French religious leader, 21

Calvinism, in Great Britain, 1500s, 10; described, 21–22

Camden, S.C., American Revolutionary battle, 61

Cameron, Don, political boss, 445

Cameron, Simon, misses presidential nomination, 1860; as Lincoln's Secretary of War, 408, 413

Canada, French settle (New France), 30–31; in colonial wars with British, 31–35; becomes British, 35–36; Tories settle in, 53; in American Revolution, 55–56; United States hopes to annex, 166, 337–338; in War of 1812, 168–169, 170, 171; boundary settled, 1818, 175; and rebellion of 1837, 314; in Maine boundary dispute, 315–316; reciprocity with, 337–338; Fenians attack, 425n.; fishing controversy with, 425–426

Canals, to 1815, 96; 1815–1860, 209–211; hopes for Central American, 338–339 (see also specific canals)

Canning, George, and Monroe Doctrine, 311–312; and West Indian trade, 313

Canton, China, trade with, 97, 344

Cape Breton Island, French in, 32, 33

Cape Verde Islands discovered, 5

Carey, Matthew, magazine publisher, 106

Caribbean (see Cuba; West Indies)

Carleton, Sir Guy, in American Revolution, 55n.

Carlota, Mexican Empress, 421, 422

Caroline, Anglo-American crisis over, 315, 316

Carpetbaggers in Reconstruction South, 440–441

Carroll, Charles, and Baltimore and Ohio Railroad, 210

Carroll, John, first American Roman Catholic Bishop, 111

Carteret, Sir George, proprietor of New Jersey, 27

Cartier, Jacques, explorer, 30

Cass, Lewis, in Jackson's Cabinet, 283; loses presidency, 1848, 295

Castlereagh, Viscount, at Vienna, 173, 305

Catholics, Roman, in Europe, 2, 3; in Tudor England, 10; in colonial Maryland, 18; given rights in Canada, 47; early hostility toward, 66, 109–110; later hostility toward, 248, 256; Native American party against, 353–354; in Texas, 324

Central America, Anglo-American clashes in, 338–340

Central Pacific Railroad in transcontinental system, 216–217

Cerro Gordo, Mexican War battle, 333

Champlain, Samuel de, founds New France, 30

Chancellorsville, Va., Civil War battle, 384

Chandler, Zachariah, as Radical Republican, 433; as political boss, 445; in election of 1876, 451

Channing, William Ellery, Unitarian, 246

Chapultepec Heights, Mexican War battle, 333n.

Charles I of England, colonial charters granted by, 18, 23; defeated in English Civil War, 19; and Calvinists, 22–23

Charles II of England, becomes king, 19; colonial charters granted by, 19, 25, 27, 28; increased empire controls, 37; quoted on Bacon's Rebellion, 40

Charles III of Spain, and Nootka, 146; and Pinckney Treaty, 151

Charles IV of Spain cedes Louisiana to France, 155

Charles River Bridge v. Warren Bridge, and Taney, 273n., 359

Charleston, S.C., founded, 19; British capture, 61; to 1815, described, 100–101; Union captures, 387, 405; postwar ruin described, 428

Charlestown, Mass., in American Revolution, 55

Charter colony (see specific colonies)

Chase, Salmon P., in Compromise of 1850, 300; misses presidential nomination, 1860, 366; as

Lincoln's Secretary of Treasury, 408, 411; at Johnson's trial, 437; misses presidential nomination, 1868, 438; as Chief Justice, 442, 448; as Liberal Republican, 448

Chase, Samuel, enforces Sedition Act, 138; impeachment fails, 142

Chattanooga, Tenn., Civil War battle, 385

Checks and balances in Constitution, 84

Cherokee Indians, described, 125; removed to West, 259, 284

Cherokee Nation v. Georgia, 284

Cherry Valley, N.Y., American Revolutionary massacre, 61

Chesapeake, warship, fights *Leopard*, 162; in War of 1812, 170

Chesapeake and Ohio Canal, 210

Chicago and Northwestern Railroad and transcontinental system, 217

Chicago *Times*, Copperhead paper, 414

Chickamauga, Ga., Civil War battle, 385

Chickasaw Indians, described, 125; removed to West, 125

Child labor, 197–198

China, early trade with, 97; later relations with, 343–344

Chippawa, War of 1812 battle, 171

Choctaw Indians, described, 125; removed to West, 259

Christy, Edwin P., minstrels, 241

Church of England, founded by Henry VIII, 9; and dissenters, 20; in Massachusetts Bay, 23, 40

Churches (*see* Religion; specific denominations)

Churchill, John, Duke of Marlborough, in War of the Spanish Succession, 33

Churubusco, Mexican War battle, 333

Circus, rise of, 243

Cities, to 1815, 99–101; in West, 126; 1815–1860, 220–222

Civil Rights bill for Negroes, 434

Civil War, events leading toward, 346–373; outbreak, 373; tragedy of, 373; rival powers, 374–376; basic strategy, 376; military action, 376–389; naval action, 390–392; diplomacy of, 392–397; home-front conditions, Confederacy, 398–406; Union, 407–418; conclusions about, 418–419

Civil wars, English, 9, 19

Clark, George Rogers, in American Revolution, 61; western intrigues of, 121, 148

Clark, William, on Lewis and Clark expedition, 143, 157–158

Classical revival in architecture, 235

Clay, Henry, as War Hawk, 165, 166; at Ghent, 173–175; as farmer, 183; described, 269; American System of, 269–272; and Compromise of 1820, 274; loses presidential election, 1824, 276; and Compromise of 1833, 287; loses presidential election, 1832, 288; misses presidential nomination, 1840, 292; breaks with Tyler, 293; loses presidential election, 1844, 294, 327; and Compromise of 1850, 300–301

Clayton, John M., and Central America, 339–340

Clayton-Bulwer Treaty (1850) with Great Britain, 339–340

Clermont, Fulton's ship, 96, 206

Clinton, DeWitt, loses presidential election, 1812, 167; and Erie Canal, 209

Clinton, George, opposes Constitution, 84, 86

Clinton, Sir Henry, in American Revolution, 54, 61

Clipper ships, 343–344

Clive, Robert, in Great War for the Empire, 35

Coal in industry, 189

Cobb, Howell, as Speaker of House, 300; in Buchanan's Cabinet, 358

Cobbett, William, newspaper publisher, 135

Cohens v. Virginia and nationalism, 272

Cold Harbor, Va., Civil War battle, 388

Colden, Cadwallader, governor of colonial New York, 41

Cole, Thomas, artist, 234

Colfax, Schuyler, in Crédit Mobilier scandal, 447

Colleges, 226–228 (*see also* Education)

Collins Line steamships, 205–206

Colombia (New Granada), Treaty of 1846 with, 338

Colonies against Great Britain after 1763, 43–44 (*see also* specific colonies)

Colt, Samuel, and repeating pistol, 193

Columbia, S.C., in Civil War, 387; postwar ruins described, 428

Columbian Academy of Painting, 100

Columbus, Christopher, voyages to America, 6

Commerce (*see* Industry; Trade)

Committees of Correspondence formed by radicals, 46, 47

Common Sense (Paine) urges American independence, 49

Commonwealth v. Hunt and unions, 199

Communications, 1815–1860, 201; in Far West, 214–215; as unifying factor, 1850s, 347

Communities, religious, 246–247; utopian, 252–253

Compromise of 1820 (Missouri Compromise), adopted, 274–275; repealed by Kansas-Nebraska Act, 351; and Dred Scott case, 359

Compromise of 1833 on tariff, 287

Compromise of 1850, adopts omnibus bill, 300–303; solidified in election of 1852, 348; and railroads and territories, 350

Compromise of 1877 adopted, 453

Comstock Lode silver rush, 265–266

Concord, Mass., American Revolutionary battle, 48

Concord (N.H.) coaches, use of, 203–204

Confederacy (Confederate States of America), established, 369; constitution of, 369; advantages of, 374–375; military action of, 373, 376–389; sea power of, 391–392; diplomacy of, 393–394; and Davis administration, 398–399; domestic opposition in, 399–401; manpower in, 401–402; money in, 402; varied aspects, 403–406

Congregationalists, as Calvinists, 22; schisms among, 246

Congress, Articles of Confederation, described, 69–74; United States, constitutional powers of, 80–81 (*see also* Continental Congress)

Conkling, Roscoe W., as Radical Republican, 433; as political boss, 445

Connecticut, founded, 25; and Wyoming Valley dispute, 73

"Connecticut Compromise" at Constitutional Convention, 77, 78

Conscription, Confederate, 400, 401; Union, 409–410

Consolidated Calumet & Hecla Company and copper, 190

Constitution (United States), described, 79–83; conclusions about, 83–84; checks and balances in, 84; ratified, 84–86

Constitution, warship, defeats

L'Insurgente, 153; in War of 1812, 170

Constitutional Convention described, 76–79

Constitutional Union party in election of 1860, 366–367

Continental Association and anti-British embargo, 48

Continental Congress, First, convenes, 47–48; described, 66–67; Second, convenes, 48; and Declaration of Independence, 49–50; in American Revolution, 51–53, 67

Continental system of Napoleon, 162

Continuous voyage, *Essex* decision against, 160

Contract and Finance Company scandals, 217

Contreras, Mexican War battle, 333

Convention of 1800 with France, 153

Convention of 1818 with Great Britain, 175, 320

Convention of Miramar (1864), Franco-Mexican, 421

Conway Cabal, American revolutionary plot, 61*n.*

Cook, James, explorer, 320

Cooke, Jay, and Union bonds, 411; in depression of 1873, 450

Cooper, James Fenimore, as author, 238; antidemocracy of, 240

Copley, John Singleton, artist, 107

Copper production, 190

Copperheads ("Peace Democrats"), during 1860–1861, 369; in Civil War, 414–415, 418

Corn cultivation, 178

Corn Laws in Great Britain repealed, 337*n.*

Cornwallis, George, in American Revolution, 61–62

Coronado, Francisco Vasquez de, explorer, 6

Corporations, 191

"Corrupt bargain" of Clay and John Quincy Adams, 276

Corruption, post-Civil War, in carpetbag South, 440–441; city and state, 444–445; national, 445–447, 449–450

Cortes, Hernando, conquers Mexico, 6

Cotton, John, Massachusetts Bay cleric, 23

Cotton, cultivation of, to 1815, 91; 1815–1860, 179; Confederate misconceptions about, 393–394

Coureurs de bois, French fur trappers, 31

Courts (*see* Judiciary; Supreme Court)

Cox, Jacob B., as Grant's Secretary of Interior, 444

Craig v. Missouri and debts, 273–274

Crawford, William H., and election of 1824, 276

Crédit Mobilier Company scandals, 217, 446–447

Creek Indians, described, 125; in War of 1812, 172; removed to West, 259

Creole, slave mutiny on, 315, 316*n.*

Crime and criminals, reforms in, 250

Crisis, The (Paine), aids American Revolution, 49

Crittenden, John J., and secession crisis, 370

Crittenden Compromise fails, 370

Cromwell, Oliver, Lord Protector of English Commonwealth, 19

Croton, N.Y., water from, 221

Crusades, effects of, on Europe, 2–3

Cuba, retained by Spain, 1763, 35*n.*; Pierce's interest in, 340–343; Grant's interest in, 424–425

Cumberland River opened by Union, 379

Cumberland Road (National Road) constructed, 202, 271–272

Currency (*see* Money)

Curtis, Benjamin R., and Dred Scott case, 359

Curtis, George William, reformer, 447

Curtis, Samuel R., in Civil War, 378

Cushing, Caleb, and China, 344

Cutler, Manasseh, with Ohio Company, 119

Daguerreotypes invented, 193, 242–243

Dale, Sir Thomas, governor of colonial Virginia, 17

Danish West Indies, Seward fails to purchase, 422

Dartmouth College, 103, 227

Dartmouth College v. Woodward, and nationalism, 273; and property rights, 273

Davenport, John, founds New Haven colony, 25

Davenport, Thomas, and electric motor, 229

Davis, Andrew Jackson, hypnotist, 233

Davis, David, in election of 1876, 452

Davis, Jefferson, and Western transportation, 214, 350; in Compromise of 1850, 300; in Mexican War, 331; elected Confederate President, 369; described, 398–399; and domestic opposition, 399–401; postwar treatment of, 432*n.*

Day, Benjamin, founds New York *Sun,* 236

Deane, Silas, in France, 58

Dearborn, Henry, in War of 1812, 169, 171

Debtor relief, early movement for, 112

Decatur, Stephen, quoted on nationalism, 114; in Tripolitan War, 159; duels with Barron, 162*n.*; in War of 1812, 170

Declaration of Independence, Jefferson writes, 49–50

Declaration of the Rights of Man (France) approved by America, 147

Declaratory Act and Parliamentary control, 46

Deerfield, Mass., attacked by Indians, 32

Deism, strength of, 110

Delaware founded, 28

Democracy, and Calvinism, 22; in colonies, 23–24, 28, 41; in New France, 30–31; during 1780s, 66; to 1815, 102, 136; and Hamilton's financial program, 133–134; and Jefferson, 141; confidence in, 1815–1860, 219; Jacksonian, 280–282

Democratic party, develops from Democratic-Republican party, 278, 281–282; in election of 1832, 289; in election of 1836, 291; in election of 1840, 292–293; in election of 1844, 294; in election of 1848, 295; and Cuba, 343; in election of 1852, 348; and Kansas-Nebraska Act, 353; in election of 1856, 358; in congressional elections of 1858, 361; splits during election of 1860, 365–367; during Civil War, 414, 417–418; in congressional elections of 1866, 435; in election of 1868, 438; in election of 1872, 448; in congressional elections of 1874, 451; in election of 1876, 451–453; and Compromise of 1877, 453

Democratic-Republican party,

founded, 135; in election of 1796, 137; and Sedition Act, 138; and French Revolution, 147; and Jay Treaty, 150; and France, 1798–1800, 153; in election of 1800, 139–140; factions in, 144–145; in election of 1808, 164; War Hawks in, 165–166; in election of 1812, 167; in election of 1816, 173, 268; swings toward Federalism, 269; becomes one party, 274; in election of 1820, 274; factions in election of 1824, 276; splits into National Republican party and Democratic party, 278

Dennie, Joseph, newspaper publisher, 104

Dentistry, growth of, 232

Depression, of 1780s, 89; of 1819, 271; of 1837, 289, 290; of 1857, 360–361; of 1873, 450–451

Deseret, Mormon Utah, 247

Desertion, from Continental army, 51–52; from British navy, 160–161; from Confederate army, 401–402; from Union army, 410

de Soto, Hernando, explorer, 6

Detroit, resists Pontiac, 44; in War of 1812, 168–169

Dew, Thomas, slavery apologist, 251, 298

Dial, The, transcendentalist magazine, 239

Dias, Bartholomeu, explorer, 5

Dickens, Charles, American trip, 238

Dickinson, Charles, duels with Jackson, 278

Dickinson, John, and colonial taxation, 44; at Constitutional Convention, 77

Dinwiddie, Robert, governor of colonial Virginia, 33

Directory in France and John Adams, 152–153

Discovery, ship, to Virginia, 1

Disquisition on Government (Calhoun) and nullification, 285

Divisive forces in United States, 1850s, 348–350; triumph of, 363–364

Divorce, increase in, 223

Dix, Dorothea, reformer, 249

Dominion of New England and James II, 40–41

Doniphan, Alexander, in Mexican War, 332

Dorchester, Mass., in American Revolution, 55

Douglas, Stephen A., and Illinois Central Railroad, 216; against Wilmot Proviso, 296; in Compromise of 1850, 300; described,

350–351; and Kansas-Nebraska Act, 351–353; splits with Buchanan, 360; debates with Lincoln, 361–362; loses presidential election, 1860

Dover, N.H., founded, 25

Dow, Neal, prohibitionist, 251, 353

Downing, Andrew Jackson, architect, 235–236

Downing, Jack, humorist, 238

Draft in Civil War (*see* Conscription)

Draft riots, in New York City, 410, 414; and Horatio Seymour, 438

Drake, Sir Francis, attacks Spanish shipping, 10

Dred Scott v. Sandford and slavery in territories, 359

Drew, Daniel, and steamboats, 206; described, 446

"Dumping," British use of, 270

Durfee, Amos, killed on *Caroline,* 314

Dutch East India Company, seizes East Indies, 9; and Henry Hudson, 26n.

Dutch West India Company settles New Netherlands, 9, 26

Early, Jubal A., in Civil War, 388

East Florida acquired, 308

East Indies, Europeans in, 5, 9

Eaton, John H., in Jackson's Cabinet, 282–283

Eaton, Peggy, social troubles of, 282–283

Eaton, Theophilus, founds New Haven colony, 25

Eaton, William, in Tripolitan War, 159

Education, agricultural, 90, 185; to 1815, 102–105; in early West, 127; 1815–1860, described, 223–224; elementary, 224–226; secondary, 226; colleges, 226–228; graduate, 228; medical, 230, 231; of handicapped, 249

Edwards, Jonathan, colonial cleric, 109

"Elastic clause" in Constitution, 82

Election, of 1792, 135; of 1796, 137; of 1800, 139–140; of 1804, 144; of 1808, 164; of 1810, congressional, 165; of 1812, 167; of 1816, 173, 268; of 1820, 274; of 1824, 276; of 1828, 278–279; of 1832, 288; of 1836, 289; of 1840, 292; of 1844, 294, 327; of 1848, 295; of 1852, 348; of

1856, 354, 358; of 1858, congressional, 361; of 1860, 365–367; of 1862, congressional, 417; of 1864, 417–418, 430; of 1866, congressional, 435; of 1868, 438–439; of 1872, 448–449; of 1874, congressional, 451; of 1876, 451–453

Electoral College described, 81

Electricity developed, 229

Elementary school, 224–226 (*see also* Education)

Eleventh Amendment described, 82

Elgin, Earl of, and Reciprocity Treaty (1854), 337–338

Elizabeth I of England, and Spain, 10

Ellsworth, Oliver, at Constitutional Convention, 77, 78

Elmira, N.Y., Union prison at, 419

Elssler, Fanny, dancer, 241

Emancipation (*see* Abolitionists)

Emancipation Proclamation of Lincoln, 416–417

Emancipator, The, abolitionist journal, 251

Embargo described, 163

Emerson, Ralph Waldo, as transcendentalist, 239; quoted on Fugitive Slave Act, 350; supports John Brown, 362

Emigrant Aid Society and Kansas civil war, 356

Empress of China, first ship to China, 97

Enclosure system in Great Britain, 9–10

Encomienda, Spanish colonial economic system, 8

England (*see* Great Britain)

Entail abolished, 113

"Enumerated commodities" in Navigation Act (1660), 38

Episcopalians, splits among, 246

"Era of Good Feeling," Monroe's administrations, 274

Eric the Red, Viking explorer, 2n.

Ericsson, John, develops screw propeller, 205; builds *Monitor,* 391

Erie Canal, 209–211

Erie Railroad, 213–214

Erskine, John, negotiates with Madison, 164–165

Essex in War of 1812, 170

Essex decision and American trade, 160

Essex Junto, ultra Federalist group, 140; and Burr, 144; opposes Embargo, 163; in War of 1812, 173

Europe, before Columbus, 2–6; attitude toward early Republic,

146; post-1815 reaction of, 304–307, 309–312; revolutions of 1848, 336

Evangelicalism (see Revivalism)

Evans, George Henry, reformer, 200

Evans, Oliver, and steam engine, 190; and screw propeller, 205

Ex parte Merryman and habeas corpus, 415

Ex parte Milligan and military arrests, 415

Ex post facto laws prohibited by Constitution, 80

Executive branch, 80–81

Extraterritorialism, right of, in China, 344n.

Factories (see Industry)

Fallen Timbers, Ohio, Indians checked at, 125

Farmers and farming (see Agriculture)

Farragut, David G., in Civil War, New Orleans, 379; Mobile, 391

Federal Commission of Agriculture, 413

Federal Society of Journeymen Cordwainers, early union, 94

Federalism in Constitution, 79

Federalist, The (Hamilton, Madison, Jay), supports Constitution, 85

Federalist party, founded, 134–135; in election of 1796, 137; and Sedition Act, 137–138; and French Revolution, 147–148; and Jay Treaty, 150; and France, 153; in election of 1800, 139–140; assessed, 140–141; decline of, 140, 173; in election of 1808, 164; and War of 1812, 166, 173; in election of 1812, 167; in election of 1816, 174; collapse of, 268–269; beliefs continued, 269

Federalists support Constitution, 84–86

Fenians attack Canada, 425n.

Ferdinand VII of Spain, restored to throne, 306; and Latin America, 310

Feudalism, in colonies, 18, 19, 26; in New France, 30; American Revolutionary effect on, 65; vestiges of, 1780s, 113

Field, Cyrus W., and Atlantic cable, 201

Field, Marshall, store of, 193

Fifteenth Amendment described, 439

Fillmore, Millard, becomes President, 301; and Compromise of

1850, 354; in election of 1856, 354, 358

Finance (see Banking; Money)

Finney, Charles Grandison, revivalist, 245

Fish, Hamilton, Grant's Secretary of State, 424, 444; and Caribbean, 424–425; and Alabama claims, 425–426

Fishing in colonies, 92

Fishing rights, Anglo-American controversy over, in Treaty of Paris (1783), 64; Clay and John Quincy Adams dispute, 175; in Convention of 1818, 175; in 1850s, 337, 338; postwar, 426

Fisk, James, in gold corner, 446

Fitch, John, and steamboats, 96

Fitzhugh, George, slavery apologist, 298

Five Forks, Va., Civil War battle, 389

Five Nations (Iroquois Indians), 26, 31

Fletcher v. Peck, state act invalidated, 143

Flint, Timothy, author, 239

Florida, under Spain, 8; ceded to Britain, 1763, 35n.; ceded to Spain, 1783, 64; boundary disputes, to 1795, 115; and Pinckney Treaty, 151; and War Hawks, 165; admitted as state, 259; territory acquired from Spain, 307–309; East Florida acquired, 308; secedes, 367; in election of 1876, 451 (see also West Florida)

Florida, Confederate raider, 392

Floyd, John B., in Buchanan's Cabinet, 358–359

Foot, Samuel, and Western land sales, 284

Foote, Andrew H., in Civil War, 379

Forbes, John, in Great War for the Empire, 34

Force Act (1832) and Jackson, 286–287

Force Acts (1871) against Ku Klux Klan, 442, 447

Foreign debt paid by Hamilton, 132

Forrest, Edwin, actor, 240, 241

Forrest, Nathan Bedford, founds Ku Klux Klan, 441; dissolves Klan, 442

Fort Crown Point in American Revolution, 48

Fort Dearborn (Chicago) in War of 1812, 169

Fort Donelson, Tenn., captured by Union, 379, 390

Fort Duquesne, Pa., Braddock defeated near, 33

Fort Henry, Tenn., captured by Union, 379, 390

Fort Jefferson relieved by Union, 371

Fort McHenry in War of 1812, 171

Fort Massac, Ill., founded, 123

Fort Michilimackinac, Mich., in War of 1812, 169

Fort Mims, Ala., Creek massacre at, 125, 172

Fort Niagara, resists Pontiac, 44; in War of 1812, 169, 171

Fort Orange (Albany) founded, 26

Fort Oswego in Great War for the Empire, 34

Fort Pickens relieved by Union, 371, 373

Fort Pitt resists Pontiac, 44

Fort Sumter, S.C., Union attempts relief, 370, 371, 373

Fort Taylor relieved by Union, 371

Fort Ticonderoga in American Revolution, 48, 55n.

Fort William Henry in Great War for the Empire, 34

Forts, British-held in United States, 149, 150

Forty-niners in gold rush, 265

Foster, Augustus, British diplomat, 165

Foster, Stephen C., composer, 236

Fourier, François Marie Charles, French utopian, 253

Fourteenth Amendment, described, 434–435; and Reconstruction, 439

France, historical background, 9; in colonial wars with British, 30–36; in American Revolution, 58–60; Washington's troubles with, 147–149; Adams's troubles with, 152–153; undeclared naval war with, 153; Convention of 1800 with, 153; and Louisiana Purchase, 154–158; and Jefferson, 162, 163; and Madison, 164–165, 167; in Quadruple Alliance, 305, 307; and Jackson, 313–314; in Mexico, 1838, 331; and China, 344; during Civil War, 372, 392–393; and Mexico, 1860s, 420–422

France in America (see New France)

Franchise (see Democracy)

Franco-American Military Alliance, in American Revolution, 59, 62, 67; later troubles with, 147–148; abrogated, 153

Franco-American Pact of Amity and Commerce, 59

Franklin, Benjamin, and colonial union, 47n.; and Declaration of Independence, 50; in France, 59, 62–64, 67; at Constitutional Convention, 76, 78; supports Constitution, 85; expands postal service, 95; as publisher, 105–106

Franklin, James, newspaper publisher, 105

Franklin, state of (Tennessee), 120–121

Franklin, Tenn., Civil War battle, 387

Franklin and Marshall College founded, 104

Frederick II ("The Great") of Prussia in Great War for the Empire, 34–35

Fredericksburg, Va., Civil War battle, 384

Free Soil party, activities of, 293, 299, 353

Freedman's Bureau, Johnson opposes, 434; work of, 434; and Reconstruction, 439

Freedmen (see Negroes)

Freeman's Farm, N.Y., American Revolutionary battle, 56

Freeport, Ill., Lincoln-Douglas debate at, 361

Frémont, Jessie Benton, in election of 1856, 358

Frémont, John Charles, as explorer, 260; in Mexican War, 329, 332; loses presidential election, 1856, 358; in Civil War, 378; abolitionists support, 416

French and Indian War (Great War for the Empire), 33–36

French Revolution, reaction to, 147–148

Freneau, Philip, poet, 105

Friends of Universal Reform, 249

Frobisher, Sir Martin, attacks Spanish shipping, 10

Frontenac, Comte de, governor of New France, 31

Frontier, influence of, 113

Fruitlands, Mass., utopian community, 253

Fugitive Slave Act, in Compromise of 1850, 300, 301; described, 349–350

Fuller, Margaret, reformer, 239

Fulton, Robert, develops steamboating, 96; monopoly of, 206, 273

Fundamental Orders, colonial Connecticut constitution, 25

Fur trade, colonial, 19, 26; in New France, 31; to 1815, 92; 1815–1860, in West, 260–262, 320

Gadsden, James, and Mexico, 334

Gadsden Purchase with Mexico, 334, 338, 350

Gag resolution against abolitionists, 298

Gage, Thomas, in American Revolution, 48, 55

Gallatin, Albert, Jefferson's Secretary of Treasury, 143, 271; at Ghent, 173, 174

Gallaudet, Thomas H., reformer, 249

Gallipolis, Ohio, and Scioto Company, 120

Galloway, Joseph, in First Continental Congress, 47, 67

Galveston in Civil War, 405

Gama, Vasco da, explorer, 5

Gambier, Baron, at Ghent, 174

Garcia, Manuel, operatic impresario, 236

Gardiner, Me., Lyceum at, 183

Gardoqui, Diego, and John Jay, 70

Garfield, James, and Crédit Mobilier scandal, 447

Garrison, William Lloyd, as peace advocate, 205; as abolitionist, 252

Gates, Horatio, in American Revolution, 57, 61

General Trades' Union founded, 198

Genet, Edmond, western intrigues of, 122; and American neutrality, 148–149

Geneva, Switzerland, *Alabama* claims arbitration at, 426

George I of Great Britain, 42

George II of Great Britain and the Cabinet, 42

George III of Great Britain, described, 42–43; attacked by Paine, 49; assailed in Declaration of Independence, 50; opposed by British liberals, 53

George Washington, warship, and Algeria, 159

Georgetown University, 104

Georgia, settled, 19–20; in American Revolution, 61; University of, 104; cedes Western lands, 118–119; Yazoo frauds in, 143; and Cherokees, 284; secedes, 367; Sherman marches through, 387

Germain, Lord George, and American Revolution, 54

German immigration, 255

Germantown, Pa., American Revolutionary battle, 58

Gerry, Elbridge, opposes Constitution, 84; French mission of, 152, 153

Gettysburg, Pa., Civil War battle, 384–385

Ghent, Treaty of (1815), ends War of 1812, 173–175

Gibbons, Thomas, and steamboat monopoly, 273

Gibbons v. Ogden, steamboat monopoly crushed, 206; and nationalism, 273

Gibraltar, Spain loses, 32; tries to regain, 59–60, 64

Gift books and magazines, 237–238

Gilbert, Sir Humphrey, attacks Spanish shipping, 10; tries to colonize Newfoundland, 11

Girard, Stephen, as reformer, 249

Girondins in French Revolution, 148

Glorious Revolution of 1689, ousts James II, 37; Locke justifies, 50

Godey's Lady's Book, 237

Godkin, Edwin L., as Liberal Republican, 448

Gold, Gould and Fisk Corner, 446

Gold rushes in West, 265, 266

Goliad, Tex., massacre, 325

Goodrich, Samuel G., textbooks of, 225

Goodspeed, ship, to Virginia, 1

Goodyear, Charles, and rubber, 190

Gordon, John B., in Civil War, 383n.

Gorgas, Josiah, arms Confederacy, 403

Gorges, Sir Ferdinando, and Maine, 25

Gosnold, Sir Bartholomew, on Virginia expedition, 1

Goulburn, Henry, at Ghent, 174

Gould, Jay, described, 445–446; in gold corner, 446

Government, in medieval Europe, 4; in England, 1500s, 9, 11; in New France, 30–31; colonial, 18, 40–41; in Great Britain, 1700s, 42–43; American Revolutionary aspects of, 65–67; under Articles of Confederation, 69–74; under Constitution, 78–83; in early West, 120–121

Governor's Council in colonies, 41

Graham, Sylvester, and diet, 232

Grant, Ulysses S., in Mexican War, 333; described as general, 378; in Civil War, Tennessee, 378–379; takes Vicksburg, 379; at Chattanooga, 385; against Richmond, 388–389; Lee surrenders to, 389; attempted assassination of, 418; and Caribbean, 424–425; and *Alabama* claims, 425–426; as Radical Republican, 433, 436n., 437; elected President, 1868, 438–

439; against Ku Klux Klan, 442; described as President, 443–444; and corruption, 445, 446, 449–450; Reconstruction policy of, 447, 450; and greenbacks, 447–448; reelected President, 1872, 448–449

Grasse, Comte de, in American Revolution, 62

Gray, Asa, scientist, 229

Gray, Robert, explorer, 97, 263, 320

Great Awakening, colonial revival, 109

Great Britain, historical background, 9–11; colonizes America, 16–30; in colonial wars with French, 30–36; early empire controls of, 38–40; post-1763 attitude of, 44–47; in American Revolution, weaknesses of, 53–54; military action of, 48, 54–58, 61–62; Treaty of Paris (1783) with, 62–64; in Nootka controversy, 146–147; Washington's disputes with, 149–150; Jay Treaty with, 150; neutral controversies with, 160, 162; and impressment, 160–161; and Chesapeake-Leopard, 162; and Embargo, 163; Madison's difficulties with, 164–165; in War of 1812, 168–172; Treaty of Ghent with, 173–175; Rush-Bagot Agreement with, 175; Convention of 1818 with, 175; post-1815 trade war of, 270; emancipates slaves, 297, 316; and Quadruple Alliance, 306; and Latin America, 310–311; and Canadian Rebellion, 314–315; Webster-Ashburton Treaty with, 314–317; and Oregon, 320–323; internal conditions in, 1840s, 323; and Texas, 326–327; and Canadian reciprocity, 337–338; Central American conflicts with, 338–340; in China, 344; opinion of Civil War, 393; and Confederacy, 393–394; and Union, 394–397; postwar quarrels with, 425–426

Great Lakes, French on, 31; in Great War for the Empire, 34; in War of 1812, 168, 170; demilitarized, 175

"Great migration" to West, 1815–1819, 256–257

Great Plains of West, population halts at, 257

Great Revival in Kentucky, 110–111

Great War for the Empire, 1754–1763, described, 33–36; effects of, on British-colonial relations, 41, 43–44

Great Western, oceanic steamboat, 205

Greeley, Horace, founds New York Tribune, 237; and Dred Scott case, 359; and Confederacy, 369; "Prayer of Twenty Millions," 416; loses presidential election, 1872, 448–449

Green, Duff, in Jackson's kitchen cabinet, 283

Greenbacks, Union issues, 411; postwar problem of, 447–448

Greene, John, in China trade, 97

Greene, Nathanael, in American Revolution, 61–62

Greenough, Horatio, sculptor, 235

Greenville, Treaty of, with Indians, 125

Grenville, Lord George, and colonial taxation, 44–46

Greytown, Nicaragua, bombarded, 340

Grimké, Angelina, quoted, 220

Grundy, Felix, War Hawk, 166

Guadalupe Hidalgo, Treaty of, ends Mexican War, 333–334

Guadeloupe, French West Indies, colonial value of, 29; retained, 1763, 35

Guilford Courthouse, N.C., American Revolutionary battle, 61

Guiteau, Charles, at Oneida Community, 247

Guitterez-Magee expedition to Texas, 262

Gunboats of Jefferson, 143

Habeas corpus, in Constitution, 80; lifted in Confederacy, 400; lifted in Union, 415

Habeas Corpus Act (1863), 415

Hackett, James, actor, 241

Hahnemann, Samuel C. F., and homeopathic medicine, 232

Haiti, France retains, 1763, 35; slaves rebel in, 155; and Louisiana, 155–156

Hakluyt, Richard, supports English colonization, 11

Hale, Sarah J., magazine editor, 237

Hall, James, author, 239

Halleck, Henry W., in Civil War, 378

Hamilton, Alexander, at Annapolis Convention, 76; at Constitutional Convention, 77–79; supports Constitution, 85, 86; and Report on Manufactures, 93, 133; and education, 103; as newspaper publisher, 104; and western intrigues, 123; described, 130–131; financial program of, 131–133; and taxes, 134; opposes Whisky Rebels, 134; and land sales, 136; in election of 1796, 137; in election of 1800, 139, 140; killed by Burr, 144; and Jay Treaty, 150

Hamilton, Henry, in American Revolution, 61

Hammond, George, and Alexander Hamilton, 150

Hancock, John, escapes British at Lexington, 48

Hannibal and St. Joseph Railroad reaches Missouri River, 214

Hannigan, Edward A., opposes Oregon settlement, 323

Hanover, House of, comes to British throne, 37, 42

Hare, Robert, inventor, 108

Harmar, Josiah, defeated by Indians, 124

Harper, William, as slavery apologist, 298

Harpers Ferry, John Brown's raid on, 362

Harper's Magazine attacks Tweed, 445

Harris, Townsend, mission to Japan, 345

Harrison, William Henry, fights Tecumseh, 125; in War of 1812, 170–171; elected President, 1840, 292–293; dies, 293

Hartford founded, 25

Hartford Convention of New England Federalists, 173

"Hartford Wits," literary group, 106

Harvard University, founded, 103; in 1830s, 227

Hat Act and mercantilism, 39–40

Hattie, Confederate blockade-runner, 405

Haverhill, Mass., attacked by Indians, 32

Hawaiian Islands, Seward fails to annex, 422

Hawkins, Sir John, attacks Spanish shipping, 10

Hawthorne, Nathaniel, author, 239

Hayes, Rutherford B., elected President, 1876, 451–453; in Compromise of 1877, 453

Hayne, Robert Y., debates with Daniel Webster, 284, 285

Helper, Hinton R., antislavery author, 363

Henry, Prince of Portugal, and exploration, 5

Henry IV of France solidifies royal rule, 9, 30

Henry VII of England, finances of, 9

Henry VIII of England, changes brought about by, 9

Henry, Joseph, and electricity, 229

Henry, Patrick, against Stamp Act, 45; in American Revolution, 61; in First Continental Congress, 66; opposes Constitution, 84

Hepburn v. Griswold and greenbacks, 448

Herkimer, Nicholas, in American Revolution, 56

Herrera, José, Mexican President, 328–329

Hessians in American Revolution, 49, 54, 56

Hicks, Elias, Quaker rebel, 246

"Higher law" of Seward, 301

Hill, Isaac, in Jackson's kitchen cabinet, 283

Hoar, E. Rockwood, Grant's Attorney-General, 444

Hoar, George, quoted on Radical Republicans, 433

Holbrook, John E., scientist, 229

Holladay, Benjamin, stagecoach line of, 215

Holmes, Oliver Wendell, as doctor, 231, 232; as poet, 240

Holy Alliance of Alexander I, 307

Home, typical American, 1815–1860, 220–221

Homestead Act (1862), effects of, 185–186, 200, 413

Honduras, British interests in, 338

Hood, John B., in Civil War, 386–387

Hooker, Joseph, in Civil War, at Chancellorsville, 384; at Chattanooga, 385

Hooker, Thomas, founds Hartford, 25

Hopedale, Mass., utopian community, 253

Hornet, warship, in War of 1812, 170

Horseshoe Bend, Ala., Creeks defeated at, 125, 172

Hotels, 1815–1860, 221–222

House of Burgesses in colonial Virginia, 17

House of Representatives, Constitutional powers of, 80

Housing, 107, 220–221, 235–236

Houston, Samuel, and Texas, 325; opposes secession, 367–368

Howard, Oliver O., heads Freedman's Bureau, 439

Howe, Elias, and sewing machine, 190–191

Howe, Lord Richard, in American Revolution, 54, 56

Howe, Samuel Gridley, teaches the blind, 249

Howe, Sir William, in American Revolution, 54, 56–58

Hudson, Henry, explorer, 26*n.*

Hudson Bay to Britain, 1713, 32

Hudson River Railroad, 213

Hudson River school of art, 234–235

Hudson River steamboat travel, 206

Hudson's Bay Company (fur) in Oregon, 261, 263, 320

Huguenots, French Protestants, and Edict of Nantes, 9*n.*; in South Carolina, 19; denied entry to New France, 30

Hull, William, in War of 1812, 168–169

Humanitarianism, to 1815, 111–113; 1815–1860, varied movements, 249–250; temperance, 250–251; abolition, 251–252; women's rights, 252

"Hunkers," conservative Democrats, 1840s, 295*n.*

Hunter's Lodges, anti-British secret society, 314

Huntsley, Confederate submarine, 391

Hussey, Obed, and reaper, 184

Hutchinson, Ann, in colonial Rhode Island, 24

Hyer, Tom, prize fighter, 243

Hypnotism fad, 233

Illinois admitted, 257

Illinois Central Railroad, aid to, 216, 351

Immigration, to 1815, 86; 1815–1860, and labor, 195; described, 255–256; intolerance toward, 256, 354

Impeachment process, described, 80*n.*; and President, 81

Impending Crisis of the South . . . The (Helper), attacks slavery, 363

Impressment of American sailors, 162–163

"Impressment Act" and Confederate economics, 403

Inca Indians conquered by Pizarro, 6–7

Indentured servitude in colonies, 17, 91

Independence sets packet record, 205

Independence, Mo., gateway to Far West, 262

Independent Treasury, of Van Buren, 290; restored, 294

India, Portuguese reach, 5; in Great War for the Empire, 35

Indian Council allows Western travel, 266

Indiana admitted, 257

Indians, American, described, 13–

15; white colonial treatment of, 14–15; contributions of, 15; in colonial Virginia, 17; and Pontiac's uprising, 44; and Proclamation of 1763, 44; difficulties with, 1780s, 73; in early West, 123–126; and British-held forts, 149; in War of 1812, 168–169, 170, 172; removed to West, 257–259; and fur trade, 263–264; Andrew Jackson's treatment of, 284 (*see also* specific tribes)

Indigo, colonial cultivation of, 91

Industry, Calvinist influence on, 22; after American Revolution, 67; to 1815, described, 92–94; Hamilton's efforts to promote, 133; 1815–1860, tariffs, 187–188; money and banking, 188–189; raw materials, 189–190; power, 190; markets and management, 190–191; specific industries, 191–194; labor force, 194–200; as unifying force, 1850s, 347; in Confederacy, 402–403; in Union, 411–413; lack of, in postwar South, 428–429

Inflation, in American Revolution, 52, 67; under Jackson, 289; in Confederacy, 402, 403; in Union, 411

Ingersoll, Robert G., nominates Blaine, 1876, 451

Institutes of the Christian Religion (Calvin) as essence of Calvinism, 21

Internal improvements, in American System, 271–272; and John Quincy Adams, 277; and Andrew Jackson, 283–284; and Polk, 294

Intolerable Acts described, 47

"Invincible Armada" destroyed, 10

Iowa admitted, 256

Irish, 1815–1860, opinion of, 196; immigration of, 255

Iron, colonial production of, 92; in industry, 1815–1860, 189–190

Iron Act described, 40

Iroquois Indians, hostility to French, 31; in colonial fur trade, 26

Irving, Washington, author, 238

Island No. 10, Tenn., captured by Union, 379, 390

Isolationism, post-Civil War, 420, 426

Jackson, Andrew, against Creeks, 125, 172; in War of 1812,

172; loses presidential election, 1824, 276; elected President, 1828, 278–279; inaugurated, 279; described, 279–280, 290; and democracy, 280–282; Cabinet troubles of, 282–283; "kitchen cabinet," 283; and West, 283–284; and nullification, 286–287; fights Second Bank of United States, 287–289; reelected President, 1832, 288; and election of 1836, 289–290; Florida campaign of, 1818, 307–308; foreign policy of, 313–314; and Texas, 324, 325

Jackson, Claiborne, Civil War Governor of Missouri, 378

Jackson, Francis Charles, insults Madison, 165

Jackson, Rachel, smeared in election of 1828, 279, 280

Jackson, Thomas J. ("Stonewall"), in Civil War, at First Bull Run, 376–377; described, 382; in Shenandoah Valley, 382–383; at Second Bull Run, 383; killed at Chancellorsville, 384

Jackson, Mich., and Republican party, 354

Jackson, Miss., captured by Union, 379

Jacksonian Democracy, 280–282

Jacobin clubs of Democratic-Republicans, 135

Jacobins in French Revolution, 148

Jacobite tory uprisings in Britain, 42

Jamaica, conquered by British, 29; naval squadron at, 1850s, 338

James I of England, and Virginia, 17–18; and Separatists, 20

James II of England, and New York, 27; and Dominion of New England, 40–41; ousted, 41

Jamestown, Va., founded, 16

Japan, relations with, 344–345

Jay, John, in Spain, 59n.; at Paris, 62–64; in First Continental Congress, 67; and Gardoqui, 71; supports Constitution, 85; as first Chief Justice, 131; mission to Great Britain, 149–150

Jay Treaty (1794), with Great Britain, 150; and French reaction, 152

Jefferson, Thomas, writes Declaration of Independence, 49–50; and Western lands, 72; and education, 103; and classical architecture, 107, 235; quoted on slavery, 112; as Washington's Secretary of State, described, 130–131; opposes Hamilton,

132, 133; elected Vice-President, 1796, 137; writes Kentucky Resolution, 138; elected President, 1800, 139–140; and judiciary, 142–144; and Burr, 144; reelected President, 1804, 144; in retirement, 145; and Genet, 148; and Louisiana Purchase, 156–158; and Barbary War, 159; and West Florida, 159–160; neutral trade difficulties of, 160–162; applies Embargo, 163; and internal improvements, 271; supports Anglo-American joint action, 312

Jeffersonian Democracy, 141 (see also Jefferson, Thomas)

Jerome, Chauncey, and clocks, 192

Jesuit missionaries to Indians, 31

Jews, in colonies, 109; immigration of, 1815–1860, 255

John Brown's Body (Benét), quoted, 405

Johnson, Andrew, foreign policies of, Mexico, 420–422; Alaska, 422–423; as Vice President, 430, 435n.; becomes President, 1865, 430; described, 430–431; Reconstruction plans of, 431–432; fights Radical Republicans, 432–435; in congressional elections, 1868, 435; impeachment and trial of, 437–438; and greenbacks, 447

Johnson, Albert Sidney, in Civil War, 379

Johnston, Joseph E., in Civil War, at First Bull Run, 376; at Atlanta, 386; opposes Sherman, 387; surrenders, 389

Joint Committee on Conduct of War packed by Radical Republicans, 416, 434

Joint Committee on Reconstruction organized by Radicals, 434

Joint-stock companies in Europe, 4 (see also specific companies)

Joliet, Louis, explorer, 31n.

Jones, John Paul, in American Revolution, 60

Jones, Joseph S., playwright, 240–241

Jones, William, banker, 271

Jones, Willie, opposes Constitution, 84

Juárez, Benito, Mexican President, against France, 421–422

Judicial branch (see Supreme Court)

Judicial review, in Constitution, 82; in Judiciary Act (1789), 131

Judiciary, Jefferson moves against, 142

Judiciary Act (1789), Federal courts established, 131

Julian, George W., as Radical Republican, 433

Kalb, Baron de, in American Revolution, 33

Kanagawa, Treaty of (1854), with Japan, 345

Kansas, admitted as state, 259; civil war in, 1855, 356–357; Lecompton Constitution in, 360

Kansas-Nebraska Act (1854), described, 351–353; political effects of, 353, 354

Kaskaskia, Ill., captured by Clark, 61

Kearney, Stephen, in Mexican War, 332

Kearsage sinks Alabama, 392

Keitt, Lawrence M., in Confederacy, 399

Kelley, Hall J., and Oregon, 263

Kelly, William, in Bessemer-Kelly steel process, 190

Kemble, Fanny, actress, 241

Kendall, Amos, in Jackson's kitchen cabinet, 283

Kennedy, John Pendleton, author, 238, 239

Kentucky settled, 120

Kentucky Resolution opposes Alien and Sedition Acts, 138

Key, Francis Scott, writes "Star Spangled Banner," 171

King, Rufus, defeated for President, 1816

"King Cotton," Confederate misconceptions about, 393–394

King George's War (War of the Austrian Succession), 33

King William's War (War of the League of Augsburg), 31–32

Kings, national, effects on exploration, 4

Kings Mountain, N.C., American Revolutionary battle, 61

Kino, Eusebio, explorer, 8

Kirby-Smith, Edmund, in Civil War, Louisiana, 380; surrenders, 389

"Kitchen cabinet" of Jackson, 283

Knickerbocker Magazine, 237

Knights of the Golden Circle, and Southern expansion, 340–341; as Copperhead society, 414

Knights of White Camellia in Reconstruction South, 441

Know-Nothing party (see Native American party)

Knox, Henry, in Washington's Cabinet, 131

Kossuth, Louis, Hungarian patriot, 336–337

Ku Klux Klan in Reconstruction South, 441–442; reaction against, 442

Labor, in South, to 1815, 91–92; general, 94; 1815–1860, and wages, 194–197; classes of, 195–196; of women, 196–197; unions, 198–199; and politics, 200; in Confederacy, 405–406; in Union, 411, 412; in postwar South, 428, 429 (*see also* Negroes; Slavery)
Ladd, William, reformer, 250
Lafayette, Marquis de, in American Revolution, 62
Laffite, Jean, in War of 1812, 172
Laird rams, Anglo-Union controversy over, 396
Lake Champlain, War of 1812 battle, 171, 174; boundary adjusted at, 316
Lake Erie, War of 1812 battle, 170
Lake Shore Railroad, 213
Lamar, Mirabeau Buonaparte, Texan President, 325
Lancaster County, Pa., colonial Germans settle, 28
Lancaster Turnpike, 95
Lancastrian system in education, 104, 224
Land, description of American, 11–12; in colonies, 17, 26–28; state claims to Western, 67, 69; in 1780s, 71–72; to 1815, 113; in early West, 118–120; demand for free, 185–186, 200; in later West, 260; and Jackson, 284–285
Land Act, 1796, 120, 136; 1800, 120, 136, 257; 1804, 136
Lane Seminary, 228
Lansing, John, opposes Constitution, 84
Larkin, Thomas, in early California, 264
La Salle, Sieur de, explorer, 31n.
Latin America, new republics in, 309–310; British trade with, 1820s, 310
Latrobe, Benjamin H., inventor, 108
Latter-day Saints (Mormons), growth of, 247; in Mexican War, 332
Lawrence, Kansas, in Kansas civil war, 357
Laydon, John, on first Virginia expedition, 1–2
Lead production, 190, 257
Leclerc, Charles, in Haiti, 155–166

Lecompton Constitution in Kansas, 360
Lee, Ann, founds Shakers, 246
Lee, Arthur, in France, 58
Lee, Charles, in American Revolution, 58
Lee, Richard Henry, proposes resolution for independence, 49–50; adopted, 50; opposes Constitution, 84
Lee, Robert E., in Mexican War, 333; captures John Brown, 362; in Civil War, described, 382; defends Richmond, 1862, 382–383; first invasion of North, 383–384; defeats Burnside and Hooker, 384; second invasion of North, 384–385; defends Richmond, 1864–1865, 388–389; surrenders, 389; and New York *Herald*, 415
Leggett, William, "Locofoco," 282
Legislative branch (*see* Congress)
Leisler, Jacob, New York rebel, 41
L'Enfant, Pierre Charles, designer of Washington, D.C., 141
Leopard, warship, fights *Chesapeake*, 162
Letters from a Farmer . . . (Dickinson), and taxation, 44
Letters from a Federal Farmer . . . (Richard Henry Lee), opposes Constitution, 84
Levant Company, Mediterranean trade of, 10
Lewin, Henry, artist, 234
Lewis, Meriwether, on Lewis and Clark expedition, 143, 157–158
Lexington, steamer, burns, 208
Lexington, Ky., early cultural center, 127
Lexington, Mass., American Revolutionary battle, 48; first normal school at, 225
Leyden, Netherlands, Pilgrims settle in, 20
Libby Prison, Union prisoners of war at, 419
Liberal Republican party in election of 1872, 448–449
Liberia, freed slaves sent to, 297
Liberty party, antislavery, 252; in election of 1844, 294n., 299
Lincoln, Abraham, in Black Hawk War, 259; favors Wilmot Proviso, 296; "spot resolution" of, 330; debates with Douglas, 361–362; on slavery in territories, 361; elected President, 1860, 366–367; opposes Crittenden Compromise, 370; inaugurated, 371–372; and Seward's "thoughts," 372; and Civil War military action, 381–385; quoted

on Union navy, 391; foreign policies of, 394–395; described, 407–408; issues Emancipation Proclamation, 416–417; domestic policies of, 417–418; and Radical Republicans, 415, 416, 430, 432; reelected President, 1864, 417–418, 430; Second Inaugural Address quoted, 418; assassinated, 418; and Mexico, 421; Reconstruction policy of, 431
Lincoln, Benjamin, in American Revolution, 61
Lincoln, Mary Todd, and Abraham Lincoln, 408
Lind, Jenny, Swedish soprano, 236, 242
Literature, newspapers, to 1815, 105, 135; 1815–1860, 237, 414–415; magazines, to 1815, 105–106; 1815–1860, 237–238; books, to 1815, 106; 1815–1860, 238–240
Little Sarah (Little Democrat), French privateer, 148
Livestock, 1815–1860, 182–183
Livingston, Edward, in Jackson's Cabinet, 283, 288; French mission of, 313
Livingston, Robert R., steamboat monopoly of, 96, 206, 273; and Louisiana Purchase, 156, 157
Locke, David R. (Petroleum V. Nasby), humorist, 408
Locke, John, writes Carolina colonial constitution, 19; influence of, on Declaration of Independence, 50
"Locofocos," radical Democrats in New York, 282
Log cabin introduced by Swedes, 27n.
Logan, John A., as Radical Republican, 433; as political boss, 445
London Company founds Virginia, 10, 16
"Lone Star Republic" (Texas), 1836–1845, 325
Long, Crawford W., and anesthetics, 231
Long, James, invades Texas, 262
Long, Stephen H., explorer, 260
Long Island, N.Y., first settled, 25, 27; American Revolutionary battle, 56
Longfellow, Henry Wadsworth, poet, 240
Longstreet, Augustus B., author, 239
Longstreet, James, in Civil War, 385
Lookout Mountain, Ga., Civil War battle, 385

Lopez, Narciso, filibusters in Cuba, 341–342

Lords of Trade and Plantations, Privy Council committee, 39

Louis XIV of France, revokes Edict of Nantes, 9n.; wars of, 31–32

Louis XV of France, in Great War for the Empire, 35

Louis XVI of France, Franklin at court of, 59; guillotined, 147

Louis XVIII of France restored to throne, 305

Louis Philippe of France and Andrew Jackson, 313

Louisbourg, in War of the Austrian Succession, fall of, 33

Louisiana (territory), founded by French, 31n.; ceded to Spain, 1763, 35–36; Western plots against, 121–123; and Genet, 148; ceded to France, 154–155; sold to United States, 156–157; (state) secedes, 367; in Civil War, 379, 380; in election of 1876, 451

Louisiana Purchase, European phase, 154–155; Haitian phase, 155–156; American phase, 156–157

Lovejoy, Elijah, abolitionist, murdered, 251

Loyalists in American Revolution (see Tories)

Lumber in colonies, 92

Lundy's Lane, Canada, War of 1812 battle, 171

Lynn, Mass., early shoe industry in, 93

Lyon, Matthew, imprisoned, 138

Lyon, Nathaniel, in Civil War, 378

McAdam, John L., and roads, 95

McClellan, George B., in Mexican War, 333; in Civil War, described, 381; Peninsular campaign of, 382, 383; at Antietam, 383–384; loses presidential election, 1864, 418

McCormick, Cyrus H., and reaper, 184

McCulloch v. Maryland and nationalism, 272–273

McDonald, John, in Whisky Ring, 449

Macdonough, Thomas, in War of 1812, 171, 174

McDowell, Irvin, in Civil War, at First Bull Run, 376; in Shenandoah Valley, 382, 383

McGuffey, William Holmes, textbooks, 225

Mackenzie, Alexander, explorer, 158

McLean, John, in Dred Scott decision, 359

McLeod, Alexander, Anglo-American crisis over, 314–315

McLoughlin, John, in Oregon, 261, 263, 320

Macon, Nathaniel, and neutral trade, 165

"Macon's Bill No. 2," effects of, 165

Macready, William Charles, actor, 241

Madison, James, at Constitutional Convention, 77; supports Constitution, 85; writes Virginia Resolution, 138; as Jefferson's Secretary of State, 154; elected President, 1808, 164; described, 164; difficulties of neutral trade, 164–165; and War of 1812, 166, 167, 171; reelected President, 1812, 167; and American System, 269, 271; supports Anglo-American joint action, 312

Madras, India, retained by France, 1748, 33

Magazines, to 1815, 105–106; 1815–1860, 237–238

Magellan, Ferdinand, circumnavigates world, 6

Maine, first settlements in, 25; in War of 1812, 172; admitted in Compromise of 1820, 275; in Webster-Ashburton Treaty, 315–316 (see also Massachusetts)

Maine law and prohibition, 251, 353

Malden, Canada, War of 1812 battle, 168–169

Mallory, Stephen R., Confederate Secretary of Navy, 399

Mandan Indians, agriculture of, 13

Manifest Destiny, expansionistic policies of, 318–320; in action, 320–334; sectional clash ends, 334–335

Mann, Horace, educator, 224

Manny, John H., and reaper, 184

Marbury v. Madison, judicial review strengthened, 142–143

Marcy, William L., and Aix-la-Chapelle Dispatch, 342–343

Marion, Francis, in American Revolution, 62

Marlborough, Duke of (John Churchill), in War of the Spanish Succession, 33

Marquette, Jacques, explorer, 31n.

Marshall, John, supports Constitution, 85; mission to France, 152; first years as Chief Justice, 142–143; frees Burr, 144; and nationalism, 272–273; and property, 273–274; assessed, 274; and Cherokees, 284

Martin, Luther, at Constitutional Convention, 77; opposes Constitution, 84

Martin v. Hunter's Lessee and nationalism, 272

Martinique, French West Indies, colonial value of, 29

Mary (Stuart) of Scotland opposes Elizabeth I of England, 10

Mary (Tudor) of England, marries Philip II of Spain, 10

Maryland, founded, 18; and Western lands, 67, 69; Civil War in, 383–384

Mason, George, at Constitutional Convention, 77

Mason, James M., and Trent, 394

Mason, John, and Maine, 25

Mason, John Y., and Aix-la-Chapelle Dispatch, 342

Mason, Lowell, hymnologist, 236

Massachusetts, founded, 23; colonial government of, 23–24, 41; in American Revolution, 54–55; Shays' Rebellion in, 69; ratification fight in, 85; loses Maine, 1820, 275; in Webster-Ashburton Treaty, 316

Massachusetts Bay Company, charter of, 23

Massachusetts Medical Society founded, 100

Matthews, Robert ("Matthias"), religious charlatan, 246

Maury, Matthew Fontaine, scientist, 229

Maximilian, Hapsburg Mexican Emperor, 421–422

Mayflower, voyage of, 21

Mayflower Compact signed, 21

Maysville Road vetoed by Jackson, 284

Meade, George Gordon, in Civil War, 384–385

Medicine, to 1815, 107; 1815–1860, status of, 230–231; progress in, 231–232; retrogression in, 232–233

Melville, Herman, author, 239

Memminger, Christopher C., Confederate Secretary of Treasury, 399

Memphis, founded, 121; race riot in, 435

Mercantilism, economic philosophy of, and West Indies, 29; and Navigation Acts, 38–39; in colonial internal affairs, 39–40

Mercenaries in American Revolution, 49, 54, 56

Merchant marine (*see* Trade)

Merrimac (*Virginia*) fights *Monitor*, 391–392

Merryman, John, in *ex parte Merryman*, 415

Mesmer, Anton, French hypnotist, 233

Methodists, 110, 111; in early West, 127; disputes among, 246

Metternich, Prince von, policies of, 305–307

Mexican War, background to, 328–330; military action in, 330–333; ended by Treaty of Guadalupe Hidalgo, 333–334

Mexico, conquered by Cortes, 6; revolts from Spain, 323; and Texas, 323–327; in Mexican War, 328–334; and Gadsden Purchase, 334; France invades, 1860s, 420–422

Mexico City, Scott captures, 333; French capture, 1863, 421

Miami-Maumee Canal, 210

Michaux, André, and Genet, 122

Michigan admitted, 257

Michigan Central Railroad, 213

Middle class as allies with kings, 4

Middle colonies founded, 26–28

Middle States in American Revolution, 56–58, 61, 62

Middle West (*see* West)

Midway Islands annexed by Seward, 422

Migration to early West, 115–117

Milan Decree of Napoleon, 162

Miller, William, founds Millerites, 246

Milligan, Lambdin B., in *ex parte Milligan*, 415

Mills, Robert, architect, 235

Minerals in industry, 1815–1860, 189–190

Mining, in West, described, 264–266; changes caused by, 266–267

Minnesota admitted, 259

Minorca, Balearic Islands, Britain takes, 1713, 32; Spain receives, 64

Minute Men, American Revolutionary militia, 48

Miquelon retained by France, 1763, 36

Missionary Ridge, Ga., Civil War battle, 385

Mississippi, admitted, 257; secedes, 367; in Civil War, 379

Mississippi River, steamboats on, 207–208; opened by Union, 378–380

Missouri, admitted, 257; in Kansas civil war, 356–357; Union conquers, 378

Missouri Compromise (Compromise of 1820), described, 274–275; repealed by Kansas-Nebraska Act, 351; nullified by Dred Scott decision, 359

Missouri Pacific Railroad to West, 214

Mobile captured by Farragut, 391, 405

Molasses Act, 1733, described, 39; 1764, "Sugar Act," 44

Molino del Rey, Mexican War battle, 333

Monetary Act (1792), first coinage system, 188

Money, colonial, 40, 96–97; during American Revolution, 52, 67; during 1780s, 68–70, 97–98; and Hamilton, 132–133; in War of 1812, 167–168; 1815–1860, 188; and Second Bank of United States, 270–271, 287, 288; and Specie Circular, 289; in Confederacy, 402, 403; in Union, 410–411; in postwar South, 428–429; and greenbacks, 447–448

Monitor fights *Merrimac*, 391–392

Monk, Maria, and anti-Catholicism, 248

Monmouth, N.J., American Revolutionary battle, 58

Monroe, James, at Constitutional Convention, 77; France dismisses, 152; mission to London, 161; elected President, 1816, 268; and American System, 269, 271; described, 274; reelected President, 1820, 274; and Compromise of 1820, 274–275; and Florida, 307–308; and Latin America, 309–312; Doctrine of (*see* Monroe Doctrine)

Monroe Doctrine (1823), described, 312–313; Polk resurrects, 322; France violates in Mexico, 421–422

Montcalm, Marquis de, in Great War for the Empire, 34

Monterrey, Mexico, captured by Taylor, 330

Montesquieu, Baron de, and American state governments, 66

Montezuma, Cortes seizes, 6

Montgomery, Richard, in American Revolution, 55

Montreal, founded, 30; falls, 1760, 34; American Revolutionary capture of, 55

Moore's Creek, N.C., American Revolutionary battle, 61n.

Morals, nineteenth-century American viewpoints on, 219–220, 222–223

Morgan, John H., in Civil War, 385

Mormons (Latter-day Saints), 247, 332

Morrill, Justin S., aids agricultural education, 185, 413; and tariff, 411

Morrill Tariff (1861), 411

Morris, Gouverneur, at Constitutional Convention, 77; supports Constitution, 85; France dismisses, 149

Morris, Robert, and American Revolutionary finances, 52, 70; at Constitutional Convention, 77; as land speculator, 89

Morse, Jedidiah, textbooks, 104

Morse, Samuel F. B., develops telegraph, 201, 229; as artist, 234

Morton, Oliver P., as Radical Republican, 433

Morton, Sarah Wentworth, author, 106

Morton, William T. G., and anesthetics, 231

Moselle, steamboat, explodes, 208

Mosquito Coast, Nicaragua, and Britain, 339, 340

Motley, John Lothrop, dismissed by Grant, 425

Mott, Lucretia, and women's rights, 252

Mountain men, early Western fur trappers, 260

Murfreesboro, Tenn., Civil War battle, 385

Murray, Lindley, textbooks, 105, 225

Muscovy Company trades with Russia, 10

Music, to 1815, 107; 1815–1860, 236–237

Nagasaki, Japan, trade with, 344

Nantes, Edict of, and Huguenots, 9n.

Nantucket, Mass., decline of whaling in, 413

Napoleon I of France, supports Convention of 1800, 153; and Louisiana, 154–157; and Haiti, 155–156; wins at Austerlitz, 161–162; and neutral trade, 162, 163; hoodwinks Madison, 165–167; defeated in Europe, 168, 171; exiled, 305

Napoleon III of France, plans Mexican invasion, 408; during Civil War, 392–393; and Mexico, 1860s, 420–422

Nasby, Petroleum V. (David R. Locke), humorist, 408

Nashville, Southern secessionist conventions at, 302; Civil War battle, 387

Nassau, Bahamas, blockade-runners at, 405

Nast, Thomas, cartoonist, and Tweed, 445; and Greeley, 448

Natchez races *Robert E. Lee*, 208

Natchez-under-the-hill, Miss., criminals in, 207

Natchez Trace, road to Nashville, 126

National Academy of Design, 235

National Bank Act (1863), of Chase, 411

National debt amortized by Hamilton, 132

National Police Gazette, 237–238

National Republican party, develops from Democratic-Republican party, 278

National Road (Cumberland Road) and Federal internal improvements, 202, 271–272

National Union party, of Lincoln, founded, 414; in congressional elections, 1862, 417; in election of 1864, 417–418, 430 (*see also* Radical Republicans)

Nationalism, in Constitution, 79–80; beginnings of, 113–114; in early West, 121; and American System, 269–272; and John Marshall, 272–273; strength of, 1850s, 346–348

Native American party (Know-Nothing party), described, 256; rise and fall of, 353–354; in election of 1856, 358

Native Sons of the South during Reconstruction, 441

Nauvoo, Ill., and Latter-day Saints, 247

Naval stores, colonial production of, 91

Navigation Acts, British Empire controls, 38–39; Grenville tries to enforce, 44

Navy, in American Revolution, 60; British, early 1800s, 160–162; in War of 1812, 170; Union, 390–391; Confederate, 391–392

Nebraska, admitted, 266; slavery loses in, 356

Negroes, prewar freedmen, 297–298; and Emancipation Proclamation, 416–417; freed by Thirteenth Amendment, 417, 429, 432; postwar problems of, 429–430; and Radical Republicans, 434, 435; made citizens in Fourteenth Amendment, 435; in election of 1868, 438–439; given vote in Fifteenth Amendment, 439; in Reconstruction

politics, 439–441 (*see also* Abolitionists; Slavery)

Nelson, Horatio, wins battle of Trafalgar, 161

Netherlands, historical background, 8–9; Pilgrims in, 20–21; settle New York, 26; in American Revolution, 60–67; and colonial slave trade, 90

Nevada, silver rush to, 265; admitted, 410*n.*

New Amsterdam (*see* New York City)

New Bedford, Mass., decline of whaling in, 413

New Brunswick, Maine boundary dispute with, 315–316

New Christina, Del., captured by Dutch, 27

New England, settled, 20–26; and New France, 31–32; Dominion of, 40–41; in American Revolution, 48, 54–56; attitude on impressment, 161; in War of 1812, 172–173; and tariff, 270, 275, 277

New England Association of . . . Working Men, labor union, 198

New England Confederation against Indians, 25

New France, founded, 30; described, 30–31; in colonial wars with British, 31–35; taken by Great Britain, 1763, 35–36; after 1763 (*see* Canada)

New Granada (Colombia), Treaty of 1846 with, 338

New Hampshire, founded, 25; declares independent government, 48; ratification fight in, 85

"New Hampshire Grants" (*see* Vermont)

New Haven Colony, founded, 25 (*see also* Connecticut)

New Helvetia in early California, 264

New Jersey, founded, 27; in American Revolution, 56, 58

New Mexico, Spanish control of, 8

New Netherland (*see* New York)

New Orleans, first Western steamboat, 207

New Orleans, to 1815, described, 101; early trade with, 126, 208–209; and Pinckney Treaty, 151; and Jefferson, 156; War of 1812 battle, 172; Union captures, 379, 391, 405; race riot in, 435

New Sweden conquered by Dutch, 27

New York, founded, 26; Leisler's revolt in, 41; in American Revolution, 56–58, 62; cedes Western land claims, 69, 118; rati-

fication fight in, 85–86; builds Erie Canal, 209; and Canadian Rebellion, 1837, 314–315 (*see also* New York City)

New York Anti-Slavery Society, 251

New York Central Railroad, 213

New York City, founded, 26; in American Revolution, 56, 58; to 1815, described, 100; Washington inaugurated in, 131; free city sentiment in, 1861, 371; draft riots in, 410, 414; Tweed Ring in, 445

New York *Daily News* quoted on Civil War, 414

New York *Express* and Mexican War, 330

New York *Herald*, founded, 237; during Civil War, 415

New York House of Refuge, reformatory, 250

New York *News* introduces Sunday newspaper, 237

New York Philharmonic Orchestra, 236

New York *Sun* founded, 237

New York *Times*, attacked in draft riots, 410; assails Tweed Ring, 445; in election of 1876, 451

New York *Tribune*, founded, 237; attacked in draft riots, 410

New York *World* bought by Gould, 446

Newburgh, N.Y., army mutiny at, 70

Newfoundland, and Sir Humphrey Gilbert, 11; Britain takes, 1713, 32

Newport, Christopher, on first Virginia expedition, 1

Newport, R.I., founded, 25

Newspapers, to 1815, 105; in early West, 126–127; in 1790s, 135; 1815–1860, 237; Union, 414–415 (*see also* specific newspapers)

Niagara, War of 1812 battles, 169, 171

Niagara Falls as vacation resort, 242

Nicaragua, Anglo-American clash in, 338–340

Niles' Weekly Register, newspaper, 237

Nolan, Philip, filibusters in Texas, 123, 262

Non-Intercourse Act (1809) against France and Britain, 164–165

Nootka controversy, threatens United States, 146–147; and Oregon, 320

Norfolk, Va., captured by Union, 391

North, Lord Frederick, and taxation, 46; resigns, 62

North, opinion on slavery, 1840s, 295–296; and Mexican War, 330; and Cuba, 341, 343; opposes Fugitive Slave Act, 349–350; and Kansas-Nebraska Act, 353–355; opinion in, 1860–1861, 363, 369–370; in Civil War (*see* Union); postwar conditions in, 427; postwar opinion on South, 430, 432–434

North American Review, 237

North Carolina, founded, 18–19; in American Revolution, 61*n*.; delays ratification, 86; University of, 104; secedes, 368; Sherman invades, 387

Northwest Company and fur trade, 261

Northwest Ordinance of 1787 described, 72–73, 121

Nova Scotia taken by Britain, 1713, 32

Noyes, John Humphrey, founds Oneida Community, 246–247

Nueces River, disputed Texan boundary on, 328, 329

Nullification, in Kentucky Resolution, 138; Calhoun's theory of, 285–286; and South Carolina, 286–287

Oberlin College, first coeducational, 228

Ogden, Aaron, in *Gibbons v. Ogden*, 273

Oglethorpe, James, founds Georgia, 20

Ohio admitted, 121

Ohio Company land speculations, 119

Ohio Plan and greenbacks, 447

Ohio River Valley, British and French clash in, 33

Omnibus bill in Compromise of 1850, 301–302

Oñate, Juan de, in New Mexico, 13

Oneida, N.Y., religious community at, 246–247

Onís, Luis de, in Adams–de Onís Treaty, 308–309

Opium War, Anglo-Chinese war, 344

Order of American Knights, Copperhead society, 414

Orders in Council, against American trade, 1790s, 149; 1800s, 162; repealed, 166

Ordinance of 1784 described, 72

Ordinance of 1785 and Federal lands, 72

Oregon, in Convention of 1818, 175; admitted as state, 259; first settlements in, 263–264, 320–321; Spanish claim ceded, 309; compromise with Great Britain, 1846, 321–323; in election of 1876, 451

Oregon Trail, 264, 321

Oriskany, N.Y., American Revolutionary battle, 56

Orr, John S. ("Angel Gabriel"), anti-Catholicism of, 248

Ostend Manifesto (Aix-la-Chapelle Dispatch), and Cuba, 342

O'Sullivan, John L., and Manifest Destiny, 319

Otis, Harrison Gray, at Hartford Convention, 173

Our American Cousin (play), Lincoln killed at, 418

Owen, Robert, as utopian, 246, 252–253

Packets, oceanic ships, 205

Paine, Thomas, American Revolutionary writer, 49; as Deist, 110 (*see also* specific books)

Painting (*see* Art)

Pakenham, Lord, and Oregon, 321–322

Pakenham, Sir Edward, in War of 1812, 172

Palmerston, Viscount, and Webster-Ashburton Treaty, 315; and Civil War, 395

Panama, in gold rush, 265; American interest in, 338

Panama Railroad, 338

Panics (*see* Depression)

Paredes, Mariano, Mexican President, 329

Paris, Treaty of, 1763, ends Great War for the Empire, 35–36; 1783, ends American Revolution, 64

Parker, Theodore, Unitarian minister, 246

Parliament, and Caribbean lobby, 30, 39; late 1700s, described, 42–43; colonial laws of, 1763–1774, 44–47

Parsons, Samuel H., in Ohio Company, 119*n*.

Patch, Sam, stunts of, 243

Paterson, N.J., early industry in, 93

Paterson, William, at Constitutional Convention, 77, 78

Patriots in American Revolution, 52–53

Patroon system in New Netherlands, 26–27

Pattie, James Ohio, explorer, 260

Paulding, James K., playwright, 241

Payne, John Howard, playwright, 240

Pea Ridge, Ark., Civil War battle, 378

Peale, Charles Willson, artist, 100, 108

Peale, Rembrandt, artist, 234

Pemberton, John C., in Civil War, 379

Pendleton, George H., in election of 1868; and greenbacks, 447

Penn, William, founds Pennsylvania, 27–28

Pennsylvania, founded, 27–28; in American Revolution, 57–58; clashes with Connecticut, 73; ratification fight in, 85; Whisky Rebellion in, 134; and internal improvements, 210; University of, 228, 231; in Civil War, 384–385

Pennsylvania Academy of the Fine Arts, 100, 235

"Pennsylvania Dutch," colonial Germans, 28*n*.

Pennsylvania Hospital founded, 112

Pennsylvania Prison Society, 250

Pennsylvania Railroad, 212, 214

Pennsylvania Society for the Encouragement of Manufacture and Useful Arts, 93

"Pennsylvania system" of prisons, 250

Pepperell, Sir William, captures Louisbourg, 33

Percy, George, quoted on Virginia, 11

Perry, Matthew C., and Japan, 345

Perry, Oliver Hazard, in War of 1812, 170

Peru conquered by Pizarro, 6–7

Petersburg, Va., in Civil War, 389

Petigru, James, antisecessionist, 368

Petroleum in Union, 412

Pettigrew, James J., in Civil War, 385

Philadelphia, warship, and Tripoli, 159

Philadelphia, founded, 28; in American Revolution, 53, 57–58; Constitutional Convention at, 75–78; to 1815, described, 99–100; plague in, 108

Philadelphia *Aurora*, newspaper, 135

Philip, "King," Indian chief, 13

Philip II of Spain, rules Netherlands, 9; against England, 10

Philippine Islands retained by Spain, 1763, 35*n*.

Philips Andover Academy founded, 104

Philips Exeter Academy founded, 104
Phips, Sir William, governor of Massachusetts Bay, 41
Phrenology fad, 233
Phyfe, Duncan, and furniture, 236
Pickering, John, impeached, 142
Pickering, Timothy, in Essex Junto, 140, 173
Pickett, George, in Civil War, 385
Pierce, Franklin, and Gadsden Purchase, 334; and Cuba, 342; elected President, 1852, 348; and Kansas, 353, 357, 359
Pike, Albert, author, 239
Pike, Zebulon M., explorer, 260
Pikes Peak, Col., gold rush, 265
Pilgrims, 20–21
Pinckney, Charles, at Constitutional Convention, 77
Pinckney, Charles Cotesworth, at Constitutional Convention, 77; loses presidential election, 1804, 144; mission to France, 152, 153; loses presidential election, 1808, 164
Pinckney, Thomas, mission to Spain, 151
Pinckney Treaty (Treaty of San Lorenzo) with Spain, 151
Pine-tree shilling in Massachusetts Bay, 40
Pinkney, William, mission to Britain, 161
Pirates, in 1600s and 1700s, 39; in Battle of New Orleans, 172
Pitt, William, "the Elder," Prime Minister in Great War for the Empire, 34; and colonies, 46; sympathizes with American Revolution, 53
Pizarro, Francisco, conquers Peru, 6–7
Plassey, India, Great War for the Empire battle, 35
Playfair, William, with Scioto Company, 119
Plymouth Colony founded, 21
Plymouth Company, joint-stock, 10; and New England, 16
Pocahontas marries John Rolfe, 17
Poe, Edgar Allen, as editor, 237, 240; as author, 238, 240
Poinsett, Joel R., in Mexico, 324
Polignac, Duc de, memorandum of, 310
Political parties founded, 134–136 (see also specific political parties)
Polk, James K., elected President, 1844, 294; described, 294; domestic policies of, 294–295; and Oregon, 321–322; and Texas, 327; and Mexican War, 328–332; and Treaty of Guadalupe

Hidalgo, 333–334; and Cuba, 341
Ponce de León, Juan, explorer, 6
Pontiac leads Indian uprising, 13, 44
Pony Express mail to Far West, 215
Pope, John, in Civil War, 383
Popular sovereignty, of Douglas, 300; in Kansas-Nebraska Act, 351
Population, to 1815, 87; 1815–1860, 254–255
Port Hudson, La., captured by Union, 380
Port Royal, Acadia, captured by English, 31
Porter, Horace, quoted on Civil War fighting, 388
Portsmouth, N.H., founded, 25
Portugal, maritime explorations of, 4–5
Postal service, colonial, 94–95; improved, 201; in Far West, 214–215, 266–267; and abolitionists, 298
Powers, Hiram, sculptor, 235
Poyen, Charles, hypnotist, 233
Preemption Act (1841), and Western settlement, 260, 293
Presbyterians, as Calvinists, 22; in early West, 127; disputes among, 246
President, constitutional powers of, 81
President, warship, defeats Little Belt, 166
Prevost, Sir George, in War of 1812, 170
Priestley, Joseph, scientist, 100, 108
Primogeniture abolished, 113
Princeton, N.J., American Revolutionary battle, 56; temporary capital at, 70
Princeton University, 103, 227, 228
Prisons, reforms in, to 1815, 111–112; 1815–1860, 250
Privateers, in American Revolution, 60–61, 67–68; and Genet, 148; in War of 1812, 170; Confederate, 392
Privy Council committees, 39
Proclamation of 1783 closes British West Indies, 68
Proctor, Henry, in War of 1812, 170
Prohibition (see Temperance)
Promontory Point, Utah, transcontinental railroad joined at, 217
Proprietary colonies (see specific colonies)
Providence, R.I., founded, 25

Prussia in Great War for the Empire, 34–35
Pruyn, Robert, mission to Japan, 345
Public Occurrences, both Foreign and Domestick, newspaper, 105
Puebla, Mexican War battle, 333
Puritan Commonwealth, of Cromwell, 19; increases empire controls, 37
Puritanism, 10, 21–22
Puritans, in colonial Maryland, 18; in English civil wars, 19; and Church of England, 20; in Massachusetts Bay, 23–24

Quadruple Alliance, and Europe, 306–307; and Latin America, 310–312
Quakers, in colonies, 24, 27–28; splits among, 246
Quantrill, William C., in Civil War, 380n.
Quartering Act and British troops in Boston, 47
Quebec, founded, 30; captured, 1759, 34; in American Revolution, 55
Quebec Act, gives West to Canada, 47; and American Revolution, 55
Queen Anne's War (War of the Spanish Succession), 32
Quids, Democratic-Republican faction, 145
Quimby, Phineas Parkhurst, hypnotist, 233
Quitrents abolished, 113

Radical Republicans, in Civil War, 381, 415–416, 432; oppose Johnson, 432, 434; Reconstruction program of, 432–435; in congressional elections, 1866, 435; in control, 436–438; in election of 1868, 438–439; in postwar South, 439–441
Rafinesque, Constantine S., scientist, 229
Railroads, developed, 211–213; to West, 213–214; transcontinental, 215–218; and Kansas-Nebraska Act, 350, 351; in Confederacy, 404–405; in Union, 412; in postwar South, 428
Raisin River, Mich., War of 1812 massacre, 170
Raleigh, Sir Walter, American colonization of, 11
Randolph, Edmund, at Constitutional Convention, 77; and Constitution, 84, 85; in Washington's Cabinet, 131

Randolph, John, opposes Jefferson, 144–145; names War Hawks, 165; opposes nationalism, 269

Rapp, George, founds Rappite community, 246

Ratification of Constitution, fight for, 83–85

Rawlins, John A., Grant's Secretary of War, 444

Reciprocity Treaty of 1854 with Great Britain, 337–338

Reconstruction, of postwar South, Lincoln's and Johnson's plan of, 431–432; Radical Republican plan of, 432–437; in effect, 439–442, 447, 450; ends, 453

Reconstruction Act (1867), described, 436–437; as applied to South, 439, 440

Reed, Rebecca, anti-Catholicism of, 248

Reeve, Tapping, law school of, 228

Reform Bill (1832), in Great Britain, 42n.

Reform movements (see Humanitarianism; specific reforms)

Reformed Church (Dutch) as Calvinistic, 22, 27

Religion, medieval, 3; during 1500s, 9, 10; of American Indians, 14; in colonial South, 18; New England, 20, 23–25; Calvinism, 21–22; in Middle colonies, 27–28; in New France, 30, 31; in 1780s, 65; to 1815, 109–111; in early West, 127–128; 1815–1860, and science, 229; described, 244–249; in Oregon, 263–264; slavery schism in, 349

Religious Toleration Act in colonial Maryland, 18

Removal Law (1830), and Eastern Indians, 258

Renaissance, Italian, effects of, 3

Report on Manufactures (Hamilton), influence of, 93, 123

Republican party, founded, 354–355; in election of 1856, 358; in congressional elections, 1858, 361; in election of 1860, 365–367; in Civil War period (see National Union party); becomes National Union party, 414; in election of 1868, 438–439; in election of 1872, 448–449; in election of 1876, 451–453; in Compromise of 1877, 453

Revenue Act (1673) described, 38–39

Revivalism, to 1815, 110–111; in early West, 127–128; 1815–1860, 245

Revolution, American (see American Revolution)

"Revolution of 1800" as surface agitation, 141

Rhett, Robert Barnwell, in Confederacy, 399

Rhode Island, founded, 24–25; early monetary policies of, 68; opposes Constitution, 77, 86

Rice, Thomas D. ("Jim Crow"), actor, 241

Rice, in colonies, 89, 91; later cultivation, 179

Richardson, William A., and corruption, 449

Richelieu, Cardinal, against Huguenots, 9n.; and New France, 30

Richmond in Civil War, McClellan's campaign, 382, 383; Grant's campaign, 388–389

Rio Grande River, disputed Texan boundary on, 328, 329

Ripon, Wis., and Republican party, 354

Roads, to 1815, 94; 1815–1860, 202–203; and internal improvements, 271–272

Roanoke Island, N.C., colony fails at, 11; Union captures, 391

Robert E. Lee, steamboat, races *Natchez,* 208

Robespierre, Maximilien, and Genet, 148–149

Rochambeau, Comte de, in American Revolution, 62

Rock Island Railroad, 214

Rockingham, Marquis of, and American Revolution, 53; forms ministry, 62

Rocky Mountain Fur Company in Oregon, 320

Rodney, George, defeats French, 1782, 62n.

Rodrique Hortalez et Cie., and American Revolution, 58

Rolfe, John, cures Virginia tobacco, 17

Roman Catholic Church (see Catholics)

Rosecrans, William S., in Civil War, 385

Ross, Edmund G., in Johnson's trial, 438

"Rotten boroughs" in Parliament, late 1700s, 42

Rousseau, Jean Jacques, and Indians, 14; influence of, 59

Rowson, Susanna H., author, 106

Royal African Company in slave trade, 91

Royal colonies (see specific colonies)

Royal Proclamation (1763) closes West, 44

Ruffin, Edmund, as farming innovator, 184; as slavery enthusiast, 298; fired first shot at Fort Sumter, 373n.; commits suicide, 389

Rule of 1756 enforced by British, 1790s, 149

Rum, in triangular trade, 30n.; distilling of, 93

Rush, Benjamin, doctor, 108

Rush, Richard, in Rush-Bagot Agreement, 175

Rush-Bagot Agreement, and demilitarization, 175

Russell, James, at Ghent, 173

Russell, Lord John, during Civil War, 395, 396

Russell, Majors & Waddell and Western freight, 215

Russell, William H., and Pony Express, 215

Russia, in Great War for the Empire, 34–35; against Napoleon, 168; and War of 1812, 173; in Holy Alliance, 305, 307; issues Ukase of 1821, 310; cedes claim to Oregon, 320; during Civil War, 396n.; sells Alaska, 422–423

Rutgers University founded, 103

Rutledge, John, at Constitutional Convention, 77

Ryswick, Treaty of (1697), ends War of the League of Augsburg, 31, 32

Sac and Fox Indians, Black Hawk War against, 258–259, 284

St. Augustine, Fla., founded, 8

St. Clair, Arthur, and Northwest Territory, 121; defeated by Indians, 124

St. Eustatius, Dutch West Indies, in American Revolution, 60

St. Kitts, British West Indies, settled, 29

St. Leger, Barry, in American Revolution, 56, 61

St. Marys, Md., founded, 18

St. Pierre retained by France, 1763, 36

"Salary grab" of Benjamin Butler, 449

Salem, Mass., founded, 23; witchcraft trials in, 24

Salt Lake City settled by Latterday Saints, 247

Saltillo in Mexican War, 332

Samuel Read Hall (Concord, Vt.), teachers trained at, 225

San Ildefonso, Treaty of (1800), Franco-Spanish, 155

San Jacinto, Union warship, seizes *Trent,* 394

San Jacinto, Tex., Texas revolutionary battle, 325

San Juan Islands, Wash., Anglo-American controversy over, 426

Sanborn, John A., contracts of, 449

Sandwich, Earl of, in American Revolution, 54

Sanitary Commission assists Union troops, 410

Santa Anna, Antonio Lopez de, in Texas Revolution, 334–335; in Mexican War, 330–332, 335

Santa Fe, founded, 8; early trade with, 262; in Mexican War, 332

Santa Fe Trail from Missouri, 262

Santo Domingo, and Spain, 420; and Seward, 422; and Grant, 425

Sarah Constance, ship, to Virginia, 1

Saratoga, N.Y., American Revolutionary battle, 56–57

Saratoga Springs, summer resort, 102, 242

Savannah, founded, 20; in American Revolution, 61; Union captures, 387, 405

Say, Thomas, scientist, 229

"Scalawags" in Reconstruction South, 440

Schenck, Robert C., minister to Great Britain, 424

Schoolcraft, Henry R., explorer, 260

Schools (*see* Education)

Schurz, Carl, as Liberal Republican, 448

Science, to 1815, 108–109; 1815–1860, progress in, 228–229; inventions, 229; medicine, 230–233

Scioto Company, land speculations of, 119–120

Scioto-Muskingum Canal, 210

Scots-Irish in colonial Pennsylvania, 28n.

Scott, Winfield, in War of 1812, 171; as peacemaker, 314; in Mexican War, 332–333; loses presidential election, 1852, 348; as Union Chief of Staff, 376, 382

Seabury, Samuel, Episcopal bishop, 111

Secession, South threatens, 1850, 301, 302; of Lower South, 367; of Upper South, 368

Second Treatise on Government (Locke) and Declaration of Independence, 50

Secondary schools, 226 (*see also* Education)

Sedition Act (1798) sponsored by Federalists, 137–138

Selma, Ala., Confederate munitions center, 403

Seminole Indians, described, 125; removed to West, 259; war against, 284

Semmes, Raphael, Commands *Alabama*, 392

Senate, constitutional powers of, 80–81

Separatists and Plymouth Colony, 20

Seraphic Advocate, spiritualistic publication, 245

"Seven Cities of Cibola," search for, 6

Seven Days' Battle in Civil War, 383

Seven Years' War (Great War for the Empire), 33–36

Seventh-of-March speech of Daniel Webster, 301

Sevier, John, in early Tennessee, 120, 121

Seward, William H., and Zachary Taylor, 295; opposes Compromise of 1850, 300, 301; anti-slavery sentiments of, 347, 362n.; and election of 1852, 348–349; misses presidential nomination, 366; as Lincoln's Secretary of State, 372, 395; described, 408; attempted assassination of, 418; as Johnson's Secretary of State, and Mexico, 421–422; annexation hopes of, 422; and Alaska, 423

Seymour, Horatio, loses presidential election, 1868, 438

Shakers form religious community, 246

Shays, Daniel, leads Massachusetts rebellion, 69

Shelburne, Earl of, forms ministry, 62

Shenandoah, Confederate raider, 392

Shenandoah Valley, Va., in Civil War, Jackson raids, 382–383; Sheridan raids, 389

Shepherd, Alexander R. ("Boss"), of Washington, D.C., 445

Sheridan, Philip, in Civil War, 389; sent to Mexican border, 421

Sherman, Roger, at Constitutional Convention, 77

Sherman, William T., in Civil War, Tennessee, 385; described, 385–386; in Georgia and Carolinas, 386–387

Shiloh (Pittsburg Landing), Tenn., Civil War battle, 379

Ship building in colonies, 92

Shirley, William, governor of Massachusetts Bay, 41

Shoe making, 1815–1860, 192

Sibley, Henry H., in Civil War, 380

Sigorney, Lydia, and women's rights, 222; as author, 240

Silk production, 178–179

Silliman, Benjamin, scientist, 108, 229

Silver rushes to West, 265–266

Simms, William Gilmore, author, 238–239

Sirius, oceanic steamer, 205

Slater, Samuel, and industry, 93; as inventor, 107; and textiles, 269–270

Slave trade, Constitutional ban on, prohibited, 79; efforts to eliminate, 112; Anglo-American blockade against, 316–317; banned in Washington, D.C., 301

Slavery, Negro, in Spanish colonies, 7, 8; in colonial South, 17, 91–92; in West Indies, 29; and American Revolution, 65; in Northwest Ordinance, 73; Constitutional compromise on, 79; early opinion of, 112; in Haiti, 155; in South, 1815–1860, 179–182; moves West, 257; and Missouri Compromise, 274–275; controversy about, 1840s, 295–300; rebellions in, 298; in Compromise of 1850, 301–302; in Texas, 324, 325; and Fugitive Slave Act, 349–350; in Kansas, 356–357; and Dred Scott decision, 359–360; and Lincoln, 370; in Confederacy, 405–406; and Emancipation Proclamation, 416–417; and Thirteenth Amendment, 417

Slavery of whites, colonial, 17

Slidell, John C., in Mexico, 328–329; taken off *Trent*, 394

"Small-state plan" at Constitutional Convention, 78, 79

Smith, Caleb B., in Lincoln's Cabinet, 409

Smith, Jedediah, explorer, 260

Smith, John, in Virginia, 1, 17

Smith, Joseph, Latter-day Saint prophet, 247

Smugglers in colonies, 39, 47

Society for Alleviating the Miseries of Public Prisons, 111–112

Society for Establishing Useful Manufactures and Hamilton, 93

Society for the Promotion of Agriculture founded, 90

Sons of Liberty, Copperhead society, 414

Soulé, Pierre, in Spain, 342; and Aix-la-Chapelle Dispatch, 342–343

South, first settled, 16–20; in American Revolution, 61–62; in Constitutional Convention, 79; agriculture in, to 1815, 90–92; 1815–1860, 179; Negro slavery in, 179–182; and tariff, 270, 275–276; and internal improvements, 277; defends slavery, 296–299; and Nashville Conventions, 302; and Cuba, 340–341, 343; and transcontinental railroad, 350; and Kansas-Nebraska Act, 351–353; escapes depression of 1857, 361; and John Brown, 362; opinion in, 1860, 363–364; secession of Lower, 367; unionist sentiment in, 367–368; secession of Upper, 368; prosecessionist sentiments in, 369–370; in Civil War (*see* Confederacy); postwar ruin in, 406, 427–429; and freedmen, 429–430; whites disfranchised in, 431, 435, 437; under military rule, 439–440; under carpetbag rule, 440–441; counterattacks of, 441–442; and Grant, 447, 450, 451; home rule returns to, 453

South Carolina, founded, 19; in American Revolution, 61; and tariffs, 270, 275–277; and nullification, 286–287; secedes, 367; in Civil War, 387; and election of 1876, 451

South Carolina Exposition, The (Calhoun), and nullification, 285–286

South Carolina Railroad, 212

Southern Literary Messenger, magazine, 237

Spain, historical background, 5–6; in America, 6–8, 14–15; and England, 10; in colonial wars, 32, 33*n*., 34; in American Revolution, 59–60, 64, 67; in Jay-Gardoqui discussions, 70–71; and Florida boundary, 115; western intrigues against, 121–123; in Nootka controversy, 146–147; Pinckney Treaty with, 151; cedes Louisiana to France, 154–155; cedes Florida, 307–309; Latin American revolts against, 309–310; cedes Oregon claim, 309, 320; keeps Cuba, 340–343; and Seward, 372; and Santo Domingo, 420; and Mexico, 421; Cuban revolt against, 424–425

Sparks, Jared, archivist, 316

Specie Circular of Jackson and money, 289

Speculation, in land, to 1815, 87–88; in early West, 117–120; in

finance, 98; and Hamilton, 132–133; in 1830s, 289

Spiritualism fad, 245

"Spoils system" of Jackson, 281

Sports (*see* Amusements)

"Spot Resolution" of Lincoln, 330

Spotsylvania Courthouse, Va., Civil War battle, 388

Springfield, Mass., in Shays' Rebellion, 69

Squatter sovereignty, 300, 351

Stamp Act described, 44–46

Stamp Act Congress convenes, 45–46

Stanford, Leland, and transcontinental railroad, 217

Stanton, Edwin M., as Lincoln's Secretary of War, 408–409; as Radical Republican, 433; and Johnson, 437

Stanton, Elizabeth Cady, and women's rights, 252

Staple Act described, 38

Star of the West and Fort Sumter, 370, 371

State debts assumed by Hamilton, 132

States, American Revolutionary changes in, 65–66; clashes among, 1780s, 73–74; constitutional prohibitions against, 79–80; powers retained by, 80; cede Western lands, 118–119

States' rights, philosophy of, in Virginia and Kentucky Resolutions, 138; and John Marshall, 142–143, 272–273; and Calhoun's nullification theory, 285–286; as contributing factor in Civil War, 369

Status quo ante bellum claimed at Ghent, 174

Steamships, to 1815, 96; 1815–1860, oceanic, 205–206; on Eastern rivers, 206; on Western rivers, 207–208; disasters, 208 (*see also* specific steamships)

Steel and Bessemer-Kelly process, 190

Stephens, Alexander H., as anti-secessionist, 367; elected Confederate Vice-President, 369; described, 399; as postwar senator, 432

Steuben, Baron von, in American Revolution, 33

Stevens, Thaddeus, described, 432; quoted on Negro suffrage, 434; and Johnson's impeachment, 437

Stewart, Alexander, in retail sales, 193–194; Grant tries to appoint, 444

Stoeckl, Edouard de, and Alaska Purchase, 423

Stone, Augustus, playwright, 240

Stowe, Harriet Beecher, writes *Uncle Tom's Cabin,* 349

Strikes (*see* Labor)

Stuart, Gilbert, artist, 107–108

Stuart, James Ewell Brown (Jeb), in Civil War, 382

Stuarts, British royal family, and empire trade restrictions, 37

Studebaker wagons, success of, 193

Stuyvesant, Peter, governor of New Netherlands, 27

Submarines, Confederate, 391

Suffolk Resolutions of colonial resistance, 47

Suffolk system in banking, 188

Suffrage (*see* Democracy)

Sugar cultivation, to 1815, 91; 1815–1860, 179

Sugar Act (1764) passed by Grenville, 44

Sully, Thomas, artist, 234

Sultana, steamship, disaster, 208

Sumner, Charles, caned by Brooks, 357–358; and Alaska, 423; and Santo Domingo, 425; and *Alabama* claims, 425–426; as Radical Republican, 432–433

Sumter, Confederate raider, 392

Supreme Court, Constitutional powers of, 81–82; established, 131; and Jefferson, 142; under John Marshall, 142–143, 272–274; and Jackson, 284; and slavery, 359; during Civil War, 415; during Reconstruction, 442, 448

Sutter, John A., in California, 264, 265

Sweden, American colony of, 27

Symmes, John Cleves, land speculator, 119

Taiping Rebellion in China, 344

Talleyrand-Périgord, Charles Maurice de, in French Directory, 152, 153; and Louisiana, 156

Tammany Hall, "Locofocos" in, 282; under Tweed, 445

Taney, Roger B., as Chief Justice, Charles River Bridge case, 273*n*.; Dred Scott case, 358; *ex parte Merryman,* 415; in Jackson's Cabinet, 283, 288

Tappan, Arthur, abolitionist, 251

Tappan, Lewis, abolitionist, 251

Tariff, in 1780s, 73–74; and Hamilton, 134; generally described, 187–188; in American System, 269–270; of 1816, 270; of 1824, 275–276; of 1828 ("Abominations"), 277; of 1832, 286; and nullification, 286–287; of 1833, 287; of 1846 (Walker), 294;

reciprocity, 1854, 337–338; of 1861 (Morrill), 411

Taxation, opposition to British, 44–47; in American Revolution, 52; in Confederacy, 402; in Union, 411

Taylor, John, opposes Jefferson, 144; opposes nationalism, 269

Taylor, Zachary, elected President, 1848, 295; opposes Compromise of 1850, 301; dies, 301; in Mexican War, 329, 330–332

Tea Act (1773) resisted, 47

Tecumseh, forms Indian Confederation, 125; killed, 170

Tehuantepec, Isthmus of, in Gadsden Purchase, 334n., 338

Telegraph, developed, 201; in Far West, 215

Telford, Thomas, and roads, 95

Temperance, to 1815, 112; 1815–1860, 250–251

"10 per cent plan," of Lincoln, 431

Tennent, Gilbert, colonial cleric, 109

Tennessee, settled, 120–121; secedes, 368; in Civil War, 378–380, 385, 387

Tennessee River opened by Union, 379

Tenure of Office Act against Johnson, 436, 437

Territories, and Northwest Ordinance, 72; slavery in, 299–300; New Mexico and Utah become, 302; and Kansas-Nebraska Act, 350–351; in Dred Scott case, 359; and Crittenden Compromise, 370

Texas, Spanish control of, 8; filibusterers in, 123; first American settlements in, 262–263, 323–324; size reduced in omnibus bill, 302; claim to, renounced, 1819, 309; Revolution of 1836 in, 324–325, 329–330; Republic of, 325–327; annexed, 327; secedes, 367

Texas v. White and Radical Republicans, 442

Texas and Pacific Railroad in Compromise of 1877, 453

Textiles, 1815–1860, 191–192, 196–197; and tariffs, 269–270

Thames, Canada, War of 1812 battle, 170

Theater, to 1815, 106–107; 1815–1860, 240–241

Thirteenth Amendment frees slaves, 417, 429, 432

Thomas, George H., in Mexican War, 331; in Civil War, Chattanooga, 385; Nashville, 386

Thomas, Lorenzo, Johnson tries to appoint, 437

Thomas, Seth, and clocks, 192

Thompson, Jacob, in Buchanan's Cabinet, 359

Thompson, J. Edgar, and Pennsylvania Railroad, 214

Thomson, Samuel, medical theories of, 232

Thoreau, Henry, author, 239

Tiffany, Charles L., store of, 193

Tilden, Samuel J., attacks Tweed Ring, 445; defeated for President, 1876, 451–453; in Compromise of 1877, 453

Tippecanoe, Ind., Indian battle, 125

Titusville, Pa., and petroleum, 412

Tobacco cultivation, colonial, 17, 89, 91; 1815–1860, 179

Toombs, Robert A., in Compromise of 1850, 349; in Confederacy, 399

Tories, in American Revolution, difficulties of, 52–53; in battle, 53, 61; compensation for, 53, 64, 149, 150n.

Tory party in Britain, 1700s, 42

Toussaint L'Ouverture, Pierre, in Haiti, 155, 156

Townshend, Charles, taxation policy of, 46

Townshend Acts repealed, 46

Trade, colonial, with West Indies, 29–30, 39, 68; during American Revolution, 68; in 1780s, 70; to 1815, 96–97; in early West, 126; and Jay Treaty, 150; and Pinckney Treaty, 151; 1815–1860, 204–205; with Santa Fe, 262; and Britain, 270; with China, 343–344; with Japan, 344–345

Trafalgar, Anglo-French naval battle, 161

Trails to West, 262, 264

Transcendentalism, beliefs of, 239

Trans-Mississippi Department in Confederacy, 379, 380

Transportation, to 1815, roads, 94–96; water, 96; in early West, 126; 1815–1860, need for, 201–202; roads, 202–204; oceanic, 204–205; steamships, 205–209; railroads, 211–218; to Far West, 266–277; and internal improvements, 271–272, 277; as unifying factor, 346–347

Transylvania University, founded, 104, 127

Treason, constitutional definition of, 82

Treaty of 1846 with New Granada (Colombia), 338

Treaty-making powers in Constitution, 81

Tredegar Iron Works, Confederate munitions center, 402, 403

Tremont House, hotel, 221

Trent, Anglo-Union crisis over, 394–395

Trenton, N.J., American Revolutionary battle, 56

Trevett v. Weeden and debtors, 68–69n.

"Triangular trade" of New England, 30n.

Tripoli, war against, 159

Trist, Nicholas P., writes Treaty of Guadalupe Hidalgo, 333–334

Trumbull, John, artist, 108, 234

Trumbull, Lyman, as Liberal Republican, 448

Tudor, House of, in England, 9

Turner, Nat, leads slave rebellion, 298

Tuscany ceded to Spain, 155

Tweed, William M., corrupt ring of, 445

Twelfth Amendment adopted, 140n.

Tyler, John, elected Vice-President, 1840, 292–293; becomes President, 293; opposes Whig program, 293–294; and Webster-Ashburton Treaty, 315–317; and Texas, 327; attempts compromise, 1861, 371

Tyler, Royall, playwright, 107

Typographical Society of New York, early union, 94

Ukase of 1821 of Alexander I, 310

Uncle Tom's Cabin (Stowe), reaction to, 349

Underground Railroad aids slaves escape, 350

Unifying forces in 1850s, 346–348

Union, in Civil War, advantages, 374; strategy, 376; military action, 373, 376–389; sea power, 390–391; diplomacy, 394–397; Lincoln administration, 407–409; manpower, 409–410; money, 410–411; industry, 411–412, 413; agriculture, 412–413; domestic opposition, 413–418

Union College, 227

Union League in Reconstruction South, 439–440

Union Pacific Railroad, and transcontinental system, 216–217; and Crédit Mobilier, 446

Union Theological Seminary, 246

Unions (see Labor)

Unitarians, revolt against Calvinism, 110; and transcendentalism,

239; split from Congregationists, 246

United States, warship, in War of 1812, 170

United States Agricultural Society founded, 185

United States Pharmacopoeia, 232

Universalists revolt against Calvinism, 110

Upshur, Abel P., dies, 293; and Texas, 327

Utah settled by Latter-day Saints, 247

Uti possidetis claimed at Ghent, 174

Utopian communities, 252–253

Utrecht, Treaty of (1713), ends War of the Spanish Succession, 32

Valcour Island, N.Y., American Revolutionary battle, 56n.

Vallandigham, Clement L., Copperhead, 415

Valley Forge, Pa., in American Revolution, 58

Van Buren, Martin, in Jackson's Cabinet, 282–283; elected President, 1836, 289; domestic policies of, 290–291; loses presidential election, 1840, 292–293; misses presidential nomination, 1844, 294; as Free Soil candidate, 1848, 295; and Canadian revolt, 314–315; and Texas, 325

Vance, Zebulon B., in Civil War North Carolina, 400–401

Vancouver, George, explorer, 320

Vancouver Island in Oregon Compromise, 321, 323

Vandalia and screw propeller, 205

Vanderbilt, "Commodore" Cornelius, and steamship, 206

Van Rensselaer, Stephen, in War of 1812, 169

Vans Murray, William, mission to France, 153

Vera Cruz, French bombard, 330; Scott captures, 332; French capture, 421

Vergennes, Comte de, forecasts American Revolution, 43; urges independence, 49; American policy of, 58–59; Spanish policy of, 59–60; and Treaty of Paris (1783), 64

Vermont, suffrage in, 66; settled, 74; University of, founded, 104

Verrazano, Giovanni da, explorer, 30

Vespucci, Amerigo, explorer, 6

Vicksburg, Miss., captured by Union, 379, 380, 390

Vienna, Congress of, and reaction, 305–307

Vincennes, Ind., captured by Clark, 61

Virginia, founded, 17–18; in Great War for the Empire, 33; Bacon's Rebellion, 40; proclaims independence, 50n.; in American Revolution, 62; ratification fight in, 85; and religious toleration, 111; University of, 145, 227; secedes, 368; attempts compromise, 1861, 371; in Civil War, 376–377, 380–384, 388–389

Virginia Company, charter of, 16–18

Virginia plan at Constitutional Convention, 78, 79

Virginia Resolution opposes Alien and Sedition Acts, 138

Virginius seized by Spaniards, 425n.

Voting (*see* Democracy)

Voyageurs, French fur trappers, 31

Wabash-Maumee Canal, 210

Wade, Benjamin F., quoted on slavery, 343; as Radical Republican, 430, 433; and Johnson's trial, 437

Wade-Davis bill opposed by Lincoln, 416

Wade-Davis Manifesto against Lincoln, 416

Walk-in-the-Water, Great Lakes steamboat, 207

Walker, Robert J., in Democratic convention, 1844, 294; tariff of, 294; in Kansas, 359–360

Walker, William, in Nicaragua, 340

Walker Tariff, lower rates, 205

Walpole, Sir Robert, and Spain, 33n.

Wanghia, Treaty of, with China, 344

War of the Austrian Succession (King George's War), 33

War of 1812, outbreak of, 166–167; rival powers in, 167–168; military campaigns of, 168–172; naval action in, 170; New England in, 172–173; peace negotiations of, 173–175; assessed, 175–176

War of Jenkins' Ear and War of the Austrian Succession, 33n.

War of the League of Augsburg (King William's War), 31–32

War of the Spanish Succession (Queen Anne's War), 32

War between the States (*see* Civil War)

War Democrats in National Union party, 414

War Hawks and War of 1812, 165–166

Ward, Artemus, humorist, 408

Warren, John C., and anesthetics, 231

Warren, Josiah, anarchist, 199

Warren, Mercy Otis, playwright, 107

Wars of the French Revolution, United States neutral in, 147–148; Peace of Amiens ends, 154, 156

Wars of the Roses in England, 9

Washburn, Elihu B., as Secretary of State, 424, 444

Washington, George, in Great War for the Empire, 33; appointed Revolutionary Commander in Chief, 48; difficulties of, 51–52; in New England campaign, 54–55; in Middle States campaign, 56–58, 62; at Yorktown, 62; at Constitutional Convention, 76, 77; supports Constitution, 85; as farmer, 89; and western intrigues, 123; described, 129–130; inaugurated President, 131; and Hamilton's financial program, 131–134; other domestic policies, 134–136; reelected President, 1792, 135; and West, 136; in retirement, 136; and Great Britain, 146–147, 149–150; and France, 147–149; and Spain, 151; Farewell Address, 151–152

Washington, D.C., as capital, 141; in War of 1812, 171; corruption in, 1870s, 445

Washington, Treaty of, Anglo-American, 426

Wasp, warship, in War of 1812, 170

Watson, Elkanah, and agricultural fairs, 183

Wayne, Anthony, against Indians, 122, 124

Webster, Daniel, quoted on Hamilton, 133; and tariffs, 270; in Dartmouth College case, 273; described, 284–285; debates with Hayne, 285; in election of 1832, 288; and Second Bank of United States, 288; in Tyler's Cabinet, 293n.; supports Compromise of 1850, 301; negotiates with Ashburton, 315–317; insults Austria, 336

Webster, Noah, quoted on patriotism, 103; and textbooks, 104, 225; as magazine publisher, 106

Webster-Ashburton Treaty with Britain, 315–317

Weld, Theodore, abolitionist, 251

Welles, Gideon, Lincoln's Secretary of Navy, 409

Wellington, Duke of, at Vienna, 173, 305, 310; and War of 1812, 174

Wells, Horace, and anesthetics, 231

West, Benjamin, artist, 107, 108, 234

West, and Royal Proclamation, 1763, 44; and Quebec Act, 47; in American Revolution, 61; and Spain, 1780s, 70–71; and state claims, 71–73; and Constitution, 79; frontier influence on, 113; early migration to, 115–117; and public lands, 117–120; domestic and foreign intrigues in, 120–123, 148; and Indians, 123–126; dream and reality, 126–128; and Whisky Rebellion, 136; and British-held forts, 149; and Spain, 151; and War Hawks, 165–166; later communications with, 214–215; and transcontinental railroad, 215–218; migration to, 256–257; Indians removed to, 257–259; boom in, 259–260; opening of Far West, 260–267; and Andrew Jackson, 281–282; Far West in Civil War, 380

West Florida, and Jefferson, 156, 159; portion seized, 1810, 159–160; 1813, 172; 1819, 308

West Indies, Columbus lands in, 6; and South Carolina, 19; British settle, 28–29; value of, 1700s, 29–30; and Molasses Act, 39; and French trade, 68, 149, 160; and British trade, 150; and Jackson, 313; and Civil War, 405 (see also Cuba; Haiti; Santo Domingo)

West Point, N.Y., Arnold's treason at, 62

Western and Atlantic Railroad, 214

Westward migration, 1815–1860, 256–257

Whaling, in colonies, 92; and Shenandoah, 392; decline of, 413

Wheat cultivation, 178

Whig party, in Britain, 1700s, 42; in United States, founded, 289; in election of 1840, 292–293; in election of 1844, 294; in election of 1848, 295; in election of 1852, 348; wrecked by Kansas-Nebraska Act, 353

Whisky Rebellion in Pennsylvania, 134

Whisky Ring scandal, 449

White Brotherhood in postwar South, 441

White Plains, N.Y., in American Revolution, 56

White Sulphur Springs, Va., summer resort, 242

Whitefield, George, colonial revivalist, 109

Whitman, Marcus, in Oregon, 321

Whitman, Walt, poet, 240

Whitney, Eli, invents cotton gin, 91; and interchangeable parts, 94

Whittier, John Greenleaf, as abolitionist, 239, 251, 301; as poet, 240

Wilderness, The, Va., Civil War battle, 388

Wilderness Road to Kentucky, 117

Wilkes, Charles, seizes Trent, 394–395

Wilkinson, James, western intrigues of, 122–123, 262; in War of 1812, 172

Willamette Valley, Ore., settled by Americans, 321

William and Mary of England, in War of the League of Augsburg, 31; relax empire controls, 37

William and Mary College founded, 103

Williams, Roger, founds Rhode Island, 24–25

Wilmington, N.C., captured by Union, 391, 405

Wilmot, David C., Proviso of, against slavery, 296

Wilson, Alexander, scientist, 108

Wilson, James, at Constitutional Convention, 77; supports Constitution, 85

Wilson's Creek, Mo., Civil War battle, 378

Winthrop, John, governor of Massachusetts Bay, 23

Winthrop, Robert, defeated for Speaker, 1850, 300

Wirz, Henry, executed, 431n.

Wisconsin admitted, 259

Witchcraft, in Salem, Mass., 23; in Europe, 24

Wolfe, James, captures Quebec, 34

Wollstonecraft, Mary, and women's rights, 111

Women's rights, to 1815, 112–113; 1815–1860, 252

Wood, Fernando E., Mayor of New York, 1860, 371

Wood, Jethro, and iron plow, 184

Woolens Act described, 39

Worcester v. Georgia and Cherokees, 284

Wright, Frances ("Fanny"), utopianism of, 253; as Locofoco, 282

Wyoming Valley, Pa., in American Revolution, 61; Pennsylvania and Connecticut dispute in, 73

Wythe, George, at Constitutional Convention, 77; supports Constitution, 85

"XYZ affair," French corruption in, 153

Yale University, 103, 227, 228

Yancey, William L., opposes Douglas, 365; in Confederacy, 399

Yates, Robert, opposes Constitution, 84

Yazoo, Georgia land frauds, 143

Yorktown, Va., American Revolutionary battle, 62; Union captures, 382

Young, Brigham, Latter-day Saints' leader, 247

Zenger, John Peter, and freedom of press, 105